Le Huu Phuoc

With architectural drawings
by the author

BUDDHIST ARCHITECTURE

Grafikol

First published in April 2010 by Grafikol

Copyright © Le Huu Phuoc

All rights reserved. No part of this publication shall be reproduced, transmitted in any forms or by any means, electronic or mechanical, or stored in a retrieval system without the written permission from the publishers.

ISBN 978-0-9844043-0-8

Library of Congress Control Number: 2010900935

Printed in the United States of America

Designed by Le Huu Phuoc

CONTENTS

Preface ... 4

Part I. Background
Chapter 1. Indus Civilization ... 6
Urban Planning, 9 . Architecture, 11
Chapter 2. Foundation of Buddhism ... 14
Buddha and Early Buddhism, 15 . Theravada School, 18 . Mahayana School, 21 . Vajrayana School, 22

Part II. Architecture
Chapter 3. Asoka Pillar ... 30
Emperor Asoka and Buddhism, 30 . Emperor Asoka's Edicts, 34 . Asoka Pillars, 36
Chapter 4. Monastery ... 46
Jivakavanarama, 46 . Takht-i-Bahi, 50 . Nalanda, 58 . Horyuji, 66 . Somapura, 70 . Vijayarama, 74 . Indrapura, 81 . Alchi, 87
Chapter 5. Rock-hewn Cave ... 97
India, 97 . Afghanistan, Central Asia, and Turkistan, 115 . China, 128 . Korea, 135
Chapter 6. Stupa ... 140
Indian *stupa*, 141 . *stupa* in Pakistan, Afghanistan, Central Asia, and Turkistan, 171 . *t'a, t'ap, tháp, to* in China, Korea, Vietnam, and Japan, 181 . *dagaba* in Sri Lanka, 189 . *candi* in Indonesia, 192 . *zedi, chedi, chedei, that* in Myanmar, Thailand, Kampuchea, and Laos, 205 . *caitya* in Nepal, 213 . *chorten* in Tibet, Indian Himalaya, Bhutan, and Mongolia, 224
Chapter 7. Temple ... 233
Early Indian Buddhist Temples, 233 . Mahabodhi Temple, 238 . Candi Sewu, 248 . Ananda Temple, 251 . Bayon Temple of Angkor Thom, 255
Chapter 8. Four Holiest Sites ... 267
Lumbini, 267 . Bodhgaya, 271 . Sarnath, 275 . Kushinagar, 281

Glossary ... 287
Chronology ... 293
Maps ... 296
Illustrations and Credits ... 301
Bibliography ... 302
Index ... 325

Preface

In exploring Asian arts and architecture, perhaps none can play the prominent and pan-Asian role as 'the heart of Asia' than Buddhism. From the time when Prince Siddhartha Gautama preached his first sermon to his first five disciples at Sarnath in India in the sixth century BCE and became known to the world as Buddha, Buddhism has spread beyond the Indian border and become one of the world's greatest religions with more than 500 million followers. By the first century CE, it already reached Central Asia and China; the eleventh century CE Muslim historian Al-Biruni also reported that Buddhism and its monasteries had been present as far as Syria centuries before the rise of Islam. Buddhism is essentially a pan-Asian religion and it has played a significant spiritual and cultural role in India and Asia since its commencement. Its contributions to the development of the civilized world are immense as it not only provides solace and comfort to countless followers throughout Asia but it also inspires centuries of magnificent creations in arts and architecture. Early distinguished pioneers of Indian and Buddhist scholarships who had written exclusively on architecture were James Fergusson and Percy Brown; later scholars like Benjamin Rowland, Susan Huntington, and James Harle generally combined Indian arts and architecture in a single volume. The works of all these scholars mostly focused on India and lesser on Asia which encompassed Buddhist, Hindu, and Jain architecture and they also covered Indo-Islamic architecture; above all, their studies did not specifically concentrate on Buddhist subjects. Thus in the process of lumping Buddhist and non-Buddhist works they have unfortunately minimized, to the point of distorting, the historical and pioneering role of Buddhism in India and Asia. Furthermore, the general public is seemingly unaware that Central Asia, Pakistan, Bangladesh, and Indonesia once had great Buddhist civilizations long before their conversions to Islam. A few recent scholars who have written exclusively on Buddhist arts and architecture in Asia are Dietrich Seckel, Chikyo Yamamoto, and Robert E. Fisher. However, the information presented by these scholars is generally old and lacks sufficiently in-depth analyses; their works also contain many inaccurate and incomplete architectural drawings and they have not endeavored to restore the original appearances of many Buddhist monuments. Moreover works like 'Buddhist Monuments' by Debala Mitra only deal with Buddhist architecture in the Indian subcontinent in India, Pakistan, Bangladesh, and the Nepalese Terai; her classification of the architectural types, which are essentially based on Fergusson's, are brief, imprecise, and lacking in a detailed developmental perspective. For examples, some of the monuments have been interchangeably presented as a monastery, *caityagriha*, and temple; and there should be two additional types, namely the Asoka pillar and rock-hewn cave. Therefore in writing this book I have attempted, where deems appropriate and necessary, to correct possible misrepresentations and inaccuracies of past scholarships and rightly restore Buddhism as the chief contributor to the artistic and architectural heritage of India and Asia. My study presents the latest and exhaustive information that also include the architectural restorations of the original forms of many Buddhist monuments. Earlier and lingering controversial issues will also be addressed whilst new topics that were absent in the previous works will also be covered in this book such as the Aniconic and Iconic temples and Tantric (Vajrayana) architecture alongwith the Indus Civilization as the forerunner of the subsequent Indian and Buddhist architecture. Many past Western and Asian writers have also developed strong biased views toward Asian architecture and naturally favored a Western-centric model; they unreservedly endorsed the premise that arts and architecture flowed from west to east. However, my research has categorically refuted these false assumptions and uncovered many significant and unique features about Buddhist arts and architecture that have been virtually overlooked by past scholars. In particular I propose that the pointed and ogee arches originated in India which have permeated Islamic and Gothic architecture. The classic quincunxial design of Islamic mosques, with four tall minarets in the corners flanking a central edifice, is most likely derived from Gandhara (Pakistan) and Indian Buddhist *stupa*s after the protracted engagement between Islamic and Buddhist architecture. The Roman and early Christian apsidal basilicas also dated much later than a similar design of Indian Buddhist cave temples or the *caityagriha*; Indian Buddhist architecture also produces among the oldest and biggest domed and vaulted structures as well as the tallest monuments in the ancient world.

The scope of this book concentrates on Buddhist architecture and the analyses aim to build a comprehensive account of themes, styles, and chronologies of the Buddhist monuments throughout Asia with a special focus on India. The emphasis is to describe the visual presentations and processes in Buddhist architecture without dwelling inordinately on its structural or technical aspects; the examples considered for discussions are preferably of historical, unique, and influential values. The goals are to clarify the sources and similarities in all of these works and discover the common threads that bind them together; hence this study is above all not a list of all Buddhist monuments. The results are classified thematically, stylistically, and chronologically in accordance to their proper epochs and geographical locations for expedient recognition while facilitating a better understanding the intricate relationships between them. The volume is organized into two parts in which Part I traces the background and sources for the Indian and Buddhist architectural tradition while Part II studies in details the architectural types. Each chapter and the individual sites typically begin with the introduction into the historical and artistic contexts alongwith the secular and non-Buddhist architecture of the country in which the sites are located before proceeding into the description of the actual sites themselves. Buddhist architecture is a vast subject to study and comprehend in a single volume as there are countless minor variations in the styles and forms as well as diverse sources of influences; naturally some insignificant and late works, especially those after c. 1200 CE, alongwith modern and recent ones will be beyond the scope of this book.

Le Huu Phuoc
December 2009

Part I. Background

Chapter 1. Indus Civilization

More than two millennia before the ascendancy of Buddhism in India, there appeared along the lower valleys and tributaries of the Indus River an oldest civilization in South Asia with a culture as ancient as other great civilizations like Egypt and Mesopotamia. The majority of its sites are concentrated in the southern end of the Indus River and its tributaries comprising much of the southern two-thirds of Pakistan as well as the regions along the Indo-Pakistani border on the Indian side including Punjab, Rajasthan, Haryana, and Gujarat. The Indus or Harappa Civilization produced the earliest forms of arts, religion, and culture in the Indian subcontinent as revealed in the recovered artifacts and numerous archaeological sites scattered throughout the region. Its two most important cities were Mohenjo-daro and Harappa known for their advanced town planning and architecture, sculptures, and miniature stamp seals with an undeciphered language engraved on them; these are the most representative of the Indus Civilization.

The prehistoric people along the Indus River valley were likely nomadic hunters-gathers without engaging in agriculture; eventually they began to establish the first permanent homelands in the foothills of Baluchistan in Pakistan. They practiced a subsistent economy based on a mixture of agriculture and pastoralism by relying on domesticated animals such as cattle, sheep, and goats with partial field cultivation of cereal crops. Among the earliest sites was Mehrgarh in Baluchistan dated as early as the seventh millennium BCE {Posssehl 1993: 79-84, 295-320}. Overtime settlements became permanent, the population grew, and newly primitive industries sprang up to accommodate the settled lifestyles while basic crafts would be created such as clay potteries and stone tools. Limited construction of mud brick houses also began in which many had square plans and attached to one another and some were arranged around courtyards with fire pits inside; these were the forerunners of mature Indus houses. Numerous settlements like Mehrgarh would be built throughout Baluchistan and these gradually became regionalized while still maintained economic and cultural contacts between them. With the growing population and limited resources in these areas, people began to move down to the alluvial lowlands along the Indus River where a more tolerable climate, proximity to resources (water, games, etc.), and fertile lands would be available to sustain them and allow long-term expansion. In this stage, agricultural technologies such as brick retaining walls were employed to keep the water out (flood control) and in (reservoirs for agricultural uses). Time would prove the crucial role of the Indus River in the flowering of the Indus Civilization as the principal commercial and cultural artery between different regions along its banks. It facilitated faster transportation and communication and as a result a higher degree of economic and cultural integration has been observed throughout the Indus Civilization. Between c. 3500-2500 BCE, increasing specialization in the manufacturing process led to further advancement in the fields of the arts and architecture. A former village would grow into a small town pushing cultivable lands further and the newly urbanites were free to pursue their specialized professions and invent new crafts and technologies to better their lives and those of the village folks. Stone tools were replaced by copper and bronze ones while ceramic items were molded by hands or wheels into various shapes and sizes to be decorated with different decorative motifs. Clay figurines, seals, and personal ornaments such as jewelries also appeared for the first time. The Indus people also produced the first known writing as graffiti marks on their vessels {Wheeler 1968: 9-24}{Posssehl 1979: 66-89}; possibly there were networks of trade and cultural exchanges throughout the Indus region. This transitional stage of the Indus Civilization from a rural economy into an urban one can be observed in the towns of Quetta, Kulli, Amri, and Kot Diji. The mature phase of the Indus Civilization was an intense period of urbanization in conjunction with the commercial and cultural spread throughout the lower Indus River valley that lasted between c. 2500-1700 BCE. The rise of urban settlements with distinct cultures and economies can be seen at large cities like Mohenjo-daro [1.1] and Harappa; Mohenjo-daro, the biggest city in the Indus Civilization at the time, had a complex planning where habitation was grouped into zones with the residential zones on the lower ground whilst the public and administrative zones would occupy the higher ground called mounds or citadels. Gridded streets intersected each other while intricate systems of residential and public sewage and drainage were also installed to improve sanitation; buildings of typically kiln-dried and mud bricks would then be constructed along these streets as the designs of the houses were also standardized. These suggest the existence of a well-organized political body within these cities and it is estimated that the population of Mohenjo-daro and Harappa in its heyday was around 41,000 and 24,000 respectively; no doubt many were urban dwellers devoting a bulk of their times in the arts and architecture while engaging in trade with the neighboring regions and countries. The main dietary consumption of the Indus people was wheat and barley in the Indus valley and peas and rice in Gujarat, India while meat sources came from cattle, goat, and sheep; the bull was evidently among the most prized item in the Indus realm for its agricultural value and many had been depicted on seals. Artistic creations also reached their apogee as they not only displayed excellent craftsmanship and realism but also revealed for the first time the cultural aspects and religious beliefs of the Indus people. Among the finest artistic achievements included numerous figurines, statuettes depicted with a remarkable degree of realism, black-on-red wares, and steatite seals of carved animals and human figures that were engraved with an unknown script on them.

The foremost controversial issue in the Indus studies is the purported relationship between Mesopotamia and the Indus Civilization. There were evidences suggesting limited international trade at the site of Lothal in Gujarat and the presence of the Indus people at the trade colony of Shortugai in the vicinity of the Oxus River in northern Afghanistan {Posssehl 1993: 65}{Posssehl 1979: 212-218}. The discovery of seals, potteries, Indus-styled figurines, carnelian beads from Indus Civilization in Mesopotamia and the Arabian Peninsula alongwith a Persian Gulf seal at Lothal, though very meager in numbers, has led archaeologists to speculate that there could be a maritime trade between the Indus Civilization and western Asia {Posssehl 1979: 115-150, 174-175}{Posssehl 1993: 323-378}. However, there were no Mesopotamia artifacts ever found in the Indus valley while conversely many Indus-styled items have been found in Mesopotamia and northern Afghanistan (Shortugai) suggesting the Harappans had traveled far from their homelands and were probably in contact with people from the distant lands. Archaeologists have long suspected Meluhha as the land of the Indus Civilization and its ships might have once anchored at Agade, the capital of King Sargon (r. 2334-2279 BCE) in Mesopotamia. Meluhha trading ships reportedly brought with them ivory, carnelian, woods, etc., the very items that were abundant in the Indus Civilization; hence there could be trade relations between the two regions {Posssehl 1993: 365-78}. Moreover, the Indus script has been found to be related to the Elamite language while Indus seals and inscriptions have also been discovered at Altin-tepe in eastern Turkey and Yahya-tepe in Iran {Posssehl 1993: 65}; since Elam (Iran) was situated between Sumer and the Indus Civilization and so the Harappans could have contacted with Mesopotamia vis-à-vis Elam. There were similarities between Mesopotamia and the Indus Civilization in their city infrastructure, the use of bricks in construction, and the prevalence of the seals; since Sumer is an older civilization than the Indus Civilization, one may postulate that the latter has been influenced by the former as proposed by Mortimer Wheeler {Wheeler 1968: 135}:

> But it can at least be averred that, however translated, the *idea* of civilization came to the Indus from the Euphrates and Tigris, and gave the Harappans their initial direction, or at least informed their purpose.

Others like Walter Fairservis have since challenged the view that Mesopotamia was the forerunner for the Indus Civilization {Posssehl 1979: 76}:

> The evidence indicates that the urban situation in the Indus River Valley was a logical development from advanced village farming in an optimum situation. In a complex of traits for which we have good evidence, India is prominent: multi-faced deities, the "yoga" position, sacred cobras, phallic worship, cattle cults, ritual bathing, numerous bangles as female ornaments, cattle painting, motifs based on local fauna and flora, and horned headdresses all can be said to be subcontinental traits of the Harappan civilization.

Archaeological evidence also suggests definite differences in the formation and organization of governmental and religious institutions between Mesopotamia and the Indus Civilization. If there was a centralized and powerful government in the Indus realm there would be special zones reserved for kings and nobilities such as palaces and sumptuous jewelries and ornaments would have already been discovered as in the case of Mesopotamia; so far these features have been detected in any Indus sites and thus the political structure of the Harappans might not have been concentrated in the hands of a privileged and powerful class as in contemporary Mesopatamia and Egypt. Possibly there existed a 'democratic' government with the authorities delegated to those selected with the approval of the qualified individuals or an electorate; Walter Fairservis suggested 'chiefdom' as the form of the Indus governance {Posssehl 1996: 12}. This is clearly different from the dynastic rules of Mesopotamia and powerful pharaohs of Egypt; moreover there were no monumental religious architecture within the Indus domains that dedicated to the powerful gods or god-kings as the ziggurats of Mesopotamia or the immense pyramids and temples of Egypt. For the most parts, the religious affairs of the Indus people probably resembled simple individual cults rather than organized religions as understood today. The Great Bath of Mohenjo-daro [1.2-1.3] is believed to have been used for ritual bathing while the 'fire altars' at Lothal and Kalibangan and the 'religious' buildings at Harappa alongwith many Mother Goddess figurines also testify that the Indus religion was probably a private matter and not mass religions like later Hinduism and Buddhism. In summary, from the analyses of archaeological remains some general observations can be made:

- The rise of the Indus Civilization was a natural indigenous development over an extended period of time due to many contributory factors such as internal pressures (population and economic growth), environmental advantage (water, land, resources), and a limited external trade (with Central and West Asia, Near East). The expansion of later cities throughout the Indus domains were likely a result of internal migration rather than trade as the Indus economy was likely self-sufficient. Advances in technology, from simple to complex, enabled urbanization and cultural integration between different regions throughout the Indus valley.
- Influences from Mesopotamia, if any, were limited. Indirect diffusion of ideas and culture (Mother Goddess figurines, seals, writing) might have been emanated from Mesopotamia but the expression of these ideas was uniquely Harappa.
- Decentralized forms of governmental and religious institutions. The enforcement of authorities might have been relied upon mass consensus and demanded cooperative efforts between different groups through 'democratic' means. Hence the regionalization of power was likely prominent during the Indus time though there seems to be a common cultural thread between the regions as observed in similar seals, potteries, figurines, systems of weights, walled citadels, etc. throughout the Indus cities. Among the large and prosperous cities at the height of the Indus Civilization were Mohenjo-daro, Harappa, Judeirjo-daro, Chanhu-daro, Kalibangan, and Lothal.

After a sustained period of prosperity, the Indus Civilization would experience a gradual decline between c. 1700-1200 BCE and not a sudden collapse as some believed; a few cities continued to function while others like the once mighty Mohenjo-daro and Harappa were totally abandoned. The Indus people probably began migrating to different regions mainly southeastward and northeastward toward India and possibly gradually assimilated into the local population. There are considerable debates among scholars on the causes of the collapse and disappearance of the once vibrant Indus Civilization; foremost among these is the theory of the environmental and climate changes, specifically from abundance of water to desiccation. John Marshall was among eminent archaeologists to have articulated it and he believed the climate had been wetter then since the animals depicted on the Indus seals like rhinoceros, tigers, elephants, etc. should have predominantly populated moist jungles {Marshall 1931: 2}; however, the majority of the depicted animals on the seals is the mythical unicorn. The choice of baked bricks in the Indus architecture has also been suggested as the evidence of the abundance of trees in the region for the repeating use in burning bricks. Other scholars have since challenged the view that burning bricks, hence the implication of the abundance of trees, denuded the surrounding forests and in turn destroyed the life supports that the Indus people relied on. Based on various calculations, it probably took 400 acres of forest for the reconstruction of Mohenjo-daro every 140 years; keep in mind that this city lasted for centuries so that the amount of the consumed forests seems minimal to have really caused the fall of Mohenjo-daro. Moreover, the type of trees used in burning these bricks might be the fast-growing type so that there could be plenty of burning fuels; other waste items could also be used as fuels such as cattle dungs {Possehl 1979: 87, 231}. Burnt bricks also had higher structural strength and low water absorption property and it made sense to use them in flood-prone areas; they also allowed the built-up of many construction layers as observed at Mohenjo-daro. Had mud bricks been used, the excessive water absorption from repeated floods, rains, and heavy loads from many periods of rebuilding would have destroyed the remains. Numerous dams called garbabands might have been built to store water for agricultural and personal uses; the implicit suggestion here was the presence of abundant rain water to justify the construction of these dams {Marshall 1931: 7}. However, most likely these dams might have been constructed to hold flood water for agricultural use while the silt deposited by floods also provided great nutrition for field cultivation {Possehl 1979: 223-224}. The periodic and catastrophic floods of the Indus River that had plagued these sites are also well attested as there are seven strata of construction at Mohenjo-daro with the lowest one buried some 30' below the present ground level {Marshall 1931:

1-7, 9-10}. Other possible causes for the abandonment of Indus cities were the desiccation and possible changes in the courses of the Indus River and its tributaries which deprived the Indus population of its life support {Possehl 1993: 223-231}. Another common belief is that the Aryans, who were presumably the nomadic people from the northern steppes of Central Asia, obliterated Indus settlements and their population before entering India. Most scholars agreed that they entered India around c. 1200 BCE when the Indus Civilization had already been in decline for over half a millennium; thus they could not have caused the disappearance of this civilization {Possehl 1979: 287}. The Rig-veda also described instances wherein the proud Aryans and their gods destroyed their enemy cities and some have suggested these as evidences of the Aryans' massacres of the Mohenjo-daro population {Wheeler 1968: 131-133}{Possehl 1979: 291}. However, the Aryans had already been through long periods of wandering and probably fighting their ways through vast territories before entering the subcontinent and therefore the descriptions of their epic battles might have been taken place elsewhere; besides, the Rig-veda was essentially a religious text which certainly included scenes out of pure fantasy intended for the glorification of its Aryan gods. Regarding the supposed destruction of the Harappans in the hands of the invading Aryans and specifically Mohenjo-daro, George Dales had this to say {Possehl 1979: 293-296}:

> Despite the extensive excavations at the largest Harappan sites, there is not single bit of evidence that can be brought forth as unconditional proof of an armed conquest and the destruction on the supposed scale of the Aryan invasion.

Moreover, had the Aryans come into contact with the Harappans then they should have at least inherited features from the Indus Civilization such as urban planning, architecture, etc. However virtually no traces of the Indus culture in India that can be dated in the period between the Aryan invasions and the rise of the Maurya Empire; thus, the Indus Civilization likely ceased to exist long before the arrivals of the Aryans. Moreover, no Aryan sites have been discovered in either Pakistan or India which makes it impossible to draw any conclusions on the relationships between the Harappans and the Aryans. Some prefer to categorize this late phase of the Indus Civilization as 'deurbanization' rather than a sudden collapse due to the dwindling population and decline in trade and possibly people began to move back to villages or to the northeast and southeast toward India {Possehl 1993: 381-384, 445-54}. In conclusions, the fall of the Indus Civilization could be caused by a combination of different factors:

- Environmental factors such as deforestation, climate, catastrophic floods, reduction of the land productiveness, etc. and natural resources ceased to be able to sustain the population. The flight of people into cities, which mainly relied on farmers for food, could have deprived agriculture of much needed labor and the problem could also be exacerbated by migrations to new territories.
- It is unlikely that the Aryans could have destroyed the Indus Civilization.
- Possible establishments of new settlements, generally northeastward and southeastward of the Indus territories in India where the Indus people and culture eventually merged with the local population; the arrival of the Aryans might have further erased any remaining traces of the Indus Civilization.

A. Urban Planning

Urban planning in many Indus cities was as sophisticated as any other cities in the ancient world with technological advances reminiscent of modern cities. The most important and biggest of all Indus cities was Mohenjo-daro followed by Harappa; an overwhelming majority of the Indus artifacts have been discovered at Mohenjo-daro and Harappa that strongly confirm these as the political and cultural centers in the Indus Civilization. Mohenjo-daro is about three miles in circuit of about 5 1/2 million square feet, 10,428 houses excluding other administrative and religious buildings, and a large population of about 41,250 people {Possehl 1979: 83}. The buildings at Mohenjo-daro were constructed of burnt bricks which are now buried under a thick layer of alluvium with the lowest of the seven occupational strata some 30' below the current ground level. There are two distinct zones in the city with one to the east and the other to the west and both are situated on high mounds separated by a gully. The eastern sector is a vast array of residential houses with major and minor streets intersecting each other; the houses and their entrances are generally aligned along these streets. The higher western sector or the Citadel [1.1] is about 300 x 500 yards and probably functioned as the public zone in the city; the Citadel, Assembly Area, and Great Bath were possibly administrative, civic, and religious buildings. Though there are fortifications in the southern end of the Citadel, there are no signs that Mohenjo-daro was a fortified city; the apparent absence of an enclosed city wall suggests the city might have

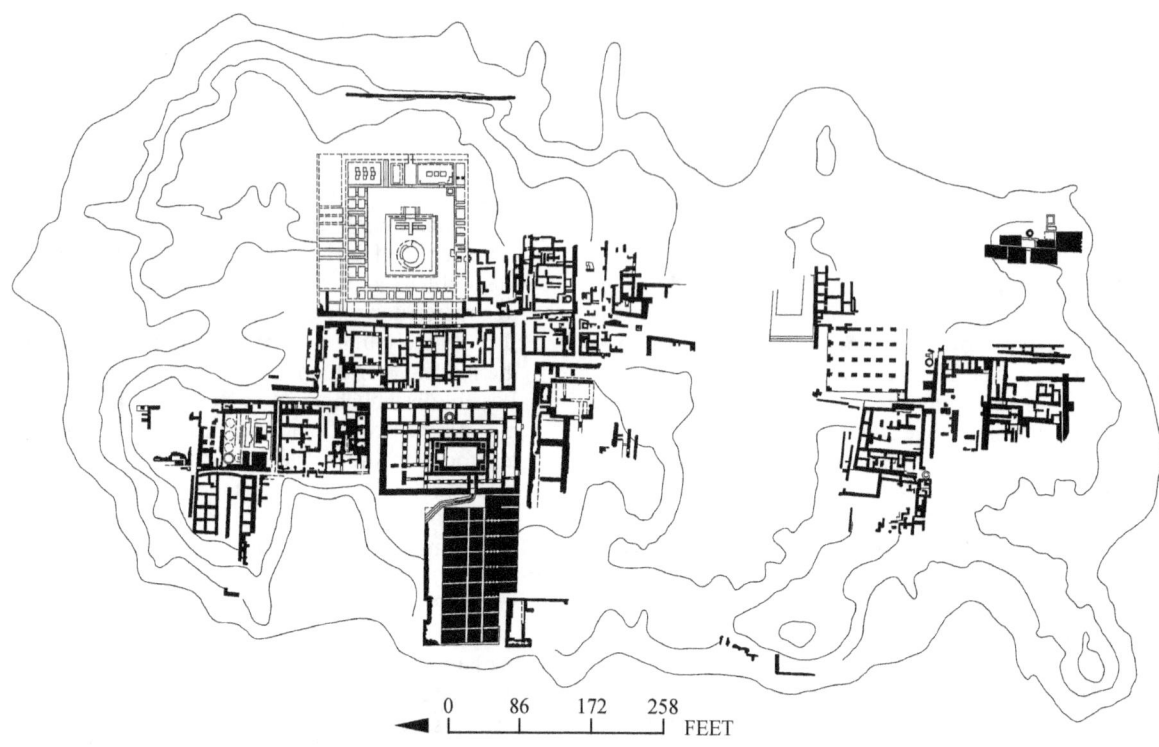

1.1. Site plan of the Citadel. c. 2500-2000 BCE. Mohenjo-daro, Larkana- Pakistan

been a relatively peaceful place and wars were probably rare during its lifetime. Many other buildings might have secular and religious functions as houses for members of the elites or storage facilities like the Granary to store harvested crops. The massive Granary in the west was evidently a measure of wealth of Mohenjo-daro and it testified that the Harappa economy, though largely an urbanized one, was basically agrarian {Wheeler 1968: 34-35, 84}. The Pillar Hall in the south, with its twenty rectangular 3' x 5' pillars and built-in benches, was probably used as an assembly area or public gatherings; the Citadel, which occupies the most prominent place in the city, was the most representative feature of many Indus cities. During the Kushan Dynasty, a Buddhist *stupa* and *vihara* were constructed on top of it and below them is a huge mud platform with brick retaining walls enclosing its perimeter and an elaborate drainage system {Marshall 1931: 113-130}. No clues to the real functions of the Citadel really were; however due to its lofty location and proximity to the Great Bath and other important structures at Mohenjo-daro and its commanding view of the eastern residential sector; it could certainly have been the administrative center of the city.

Mohenjo-daro reflected the ingenious mastery of the Harappans in urban planning, civil engineering, and architecture. The division of the city into distinct zones according to their public and private functions, the organized street layout, and the locations on high mounds to avoid floods are indicative of a highly rational planning. The placement of structures along gridded streets facilitated accessibility and allowed future growth of the city by simply adding new constructions along these routes. These streets ranged from over 30' wide for main arteries to 5'-10' for smaller roads and they were once paved with compacted mud while burnt bricks were exclusively reserved for buildings. Another important technology was an elaborate system of drains embedded along the streets throughout Mohenjo-daro, which John Marshall observed that {Marshall 1931: 278-282}:

A remarkable feature of the city of Mohenjo-daro is the very elaborate drainage system that exists even in the poorest quarters of the city. Every street and lane had one or two water-channels with brick or stone covers that could readily be lifted to remove obstructions. These drains, as a rule, were situated from 18 inches to 2 feet below the surface of the street, but some were certainly not set so low… Practically every house had one or more apertures in its walls through which waste water ran out into the street drain.

At the street intersections, there were rectangular soak-pits of about 3' wide x 5' long x 5' deep buried below ground to collect water from the drains that would be freely absorbed into the ground. John Marshall also believed that this system of drains and soak-pits was probably not used as a municipal sewage system since the drain sizes were small to be able to carry large waste matters that could potentially choke the drains, pollute the ground water, and spread diseases. Alternatively, these drains could have been used to channel little amount of rainfalls or discharge residential waste water from bathing and dishwashing. Though the drainage system at Mohenjo-daro was far from perfect compared to modern sewage systems, their similarities in functions and designs are striking even more than four millennia ago.

B. Architecture

Another conspicuous feature at Mohenjo-daro is its architecture, especially its plain houses. Burned clay bricks with an average size of 11" x 5 1/2" x 2 1/2" were exclusively used in buildings and they typically had rectangular shapes although wedge shapes have also been found in the constructions of wells; mud was used as mortar to join bricks. Some of these houses were as large as 80' wide x 100' deep and many had two levels. In a typical house, there were entrances facing streets while interior rooms were generally arranged around a centrally open courtyard or series of interconnected courtyards depending on the size of the house in order to maximize natural ventilation and light; porters' closets were also present alongwith other common architectural features such as bathrooms, stairs, kitchens, storage, etc. Interior stairs were generally narrow and steep to conserve space with 11" treads x 5 1/4"-8 1/2" risers while some stairs also connected to the rooftops, which were most likely outdoor terraces; the stairs of the Great Bath, on the other hand, had wider treads and lower risers due to its public function. There were niches in the interior walls of the houses about half of the wall depth that might have been used as shelves to display important items like cult images {Marshall 1931: 276}. Usually there were several entry doors with door panels likely made of wood while windows, probably latticed, were generally absent from the exterior as they mainly occurred in the interior walls

around an open courtyard to preserve the occupants' privacy while maximizing ventilation and sunlight; according to John Marshall, the lintels of these doors were timber in combination with corbelled brick arches {Marshall 1931: 275}. The entry doors had thresholds and were several feet above the street level to be connected with flights of stairs; John Marshall inferred that this was a precautionary design to protect the house from flooding {Marshall 1931: 266}. Periodic floods had deposited a great amount of silt in these houses so a simple solution for the Harappans was to build new constructions over existing foundations. Walls, whether exterior or interior, have been found to be devoid of decorative treatments; many interior walls had a 3/4" layer of grass-and-mud plaster and coated with a final layer of fine plaster. Many exterior walls slightly sloped outward while the interior walls remained straight and they might also have beam pockets to carry timber members to support the roof. The roofs of these houses were generally flat and probably constructed of wooden planks to be covered with several layers of grass-and-mud plaster to prevent water penetration; scuppers would be placed throughout the roof to properly discharge water to the ground below {Marshall 1931: 277}. It seems contradictory to suggest a wetter climate during the Harappa time, as John Marshall did, since these flat mud roofs apparently do not disperse or repel water well like the pitched roof. The design of the stairwell puncturing through the flat roof in a wet climate clearly does not make any architectural sense. In fact the courtyard-and-flat roof houses are often found in a semi-arid or arid climate rather than in a wet one, as in Afghanistan and Tibet. Numerous wells were built at Mohenjo-daro to collect the ground water and this was indicative of a semi-arid region. The floors of these houses were paved in bricks throughout with a meticulous care in laying the brick layers, which were four or five courses thick in some instances; bathroom drains also connected directly to the street drains to discharge used water while covered drains were also buried below the courtyard floors. Some clay drains were embedded inside the interior walls most likely as plumbing pipes; these average about 22 3/10" per section with a 6 3/10" top diameter and an 8 1/10" base diameter which were tied together with 2" flanges. They connected the top floor with the one below and were probably used to channel waste water down from the floor above; in other houses they might have been used as trash chutes where trash would be collected by a bin placed at the bottom of the shaft in the bottom floor {Marshall 1931: 16, 280}. This could be among the most advanced prototypes of indoor plumbing and sanitary system in the ancient world. The facts that

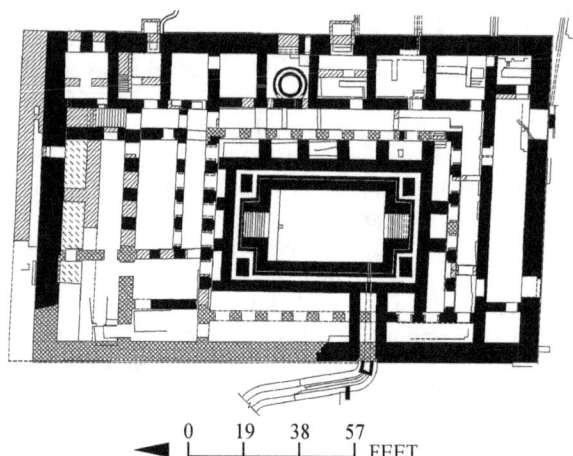

1.2. Great Bath plan
c. 2500-2000 BCE
Mohenjo-daro, Larkana- Pakistan

1.3. Great Bath view
c. 2500-2000 BCE
Mohenjo-daro, Larkana- Pakistan

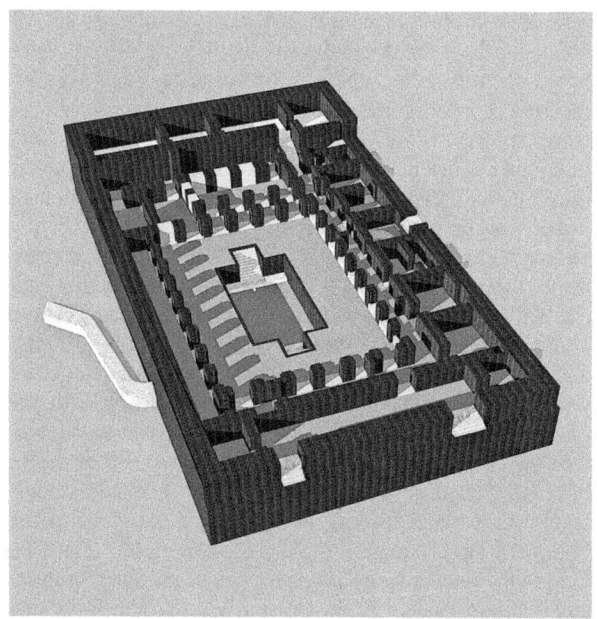

the Harappans devoted inordinate attention to elaborate systems of sanitation and drainage, natural ventilation and lighting while their houses, public buildings, and streets were deemed to be exceptionally clean, well-maintained, and carefully designed throughout, all clearly suggest that the Harappans were highly civilized, clean, healthy, and probably a very happy people.

Among the most meticulously constructed and frequently mentioned structure at Mohenjo-daro is the so-called Great Bath [1.2-1.3]; in fact, its large-sized and prominent location demonstrated its important and intimate connections to the daily lives of Mohenjo-daro citizens. The 108' x 180' structure was built entirely of burnt bricks having an 8' thick exterior wall, which was battered at six degrees to the vertical. In the center is a 23' x 39' x 8' deep rectangular pool with two staircases, which were originally fastened with wooden treads, at both ends descending to the bottom of the pool; platforms of 3'4" wide x 1'4" high above the base of the tank were built probably for the convenience of bathers standing in the shallow water. Based on the size of the tank, approximately 224 people could bathe in the tank at one time. Surrounding the pool is a continuous piered verandah on all sides with a row of large cells having a well and a bathroom on the eastern side; these cells might have been used for changing clothes and cleansing oneself after bathing in the pool. The two main entries are located at the southern end having two cubicles on both sides of the entry hall which might have been used to store personal items such as shoes, clothes, etc. The Great Bath apparently has two levels with the northern end higher than the rest of the building from the presence of the two flights of stairs; the northeastern corner of this area was probably reserved for privileged individuals such as priests or administrators to observe the spectacle or festive atmosphere below. The northern stair is about 8' wide with 10" tread x 8" riser; both stairs were obviously connected to the roofs or roof terraces, which were likely flat and not unlike those in residential houses. The bathing tank itself probably did not have a roof or awning in order to collect rain water and allow sunlight into the interior. There was evidently great technological advance in the construction of the Great Bath; an average size of its burnt bricks is around 10 1/2" x 5 1/10" x 2 1/5" with a total thickness of the brick lining around the pool of about 4'6" thick. The cement used in the mortar to join the bricks is a mixture of gypsum (43 3/4 percent), lime (13 39/50 percent), sand (forty percent), and salt (2 47/100 percent), a property similar to modern cement. The brick linings on all four sides of the pool were spread on the back with 1" bitumen, another layer of bricks behind it, and then clay would be filled in between this brick layer and another one behind it. Apparently the builder took great care in sealing the tank to prevent water from seeping into the surrounding ground to prevent subsidence; this has clearly ensured the remarkable longevity of the Great Bath for over four millennia. In the southwestern corner is a large brick drain of 4'7" wide x 6'6" high of a corbelled construction which was obviously meant to channel the used waste water from the pool away from the structure. A group of buildings on the western side of the Great Bath were earlier believed to be hot-air baths of a hypocaust system with ducts delivering warm air to dry the bathers {Marshall 1931: 26, 143}; however, these have later been identified as possible platforms of the Granary {Wheeler 1968: 43}. For what purposes that have motivated the Harappans to devote so much effort into the construction of this Great Bath? Ever since Mohenjo-daro was first discovered, the most popular theory for the construction of such a well-designed structure was for religious reasons, particularly ritual bathing. Religious bathing in later Indian religions like Hinduism was a paramount ritual to cleanse oneself of past sins and one could attribute this subcontinental practice to the Indus people as exemplified in this Great Bath. However the Harappans' apparent obsession with bathing and cleanliness could be due to their healthy habits as seen in the numerous bathrooms in both public buildings and private houses and not necessarily ritual bathing. Moreover, if ritual bathing was prevalent in the Indus Civilization then why were there no public baths in other Indus cities? And there were no definite proofs that the Harappans were an extremely religious people. Small figurines of Mother Goddesses and 'religious' scenes on their little seals are not sufficient evidences proving their devoutness; on the other hand, their rationalism has been well attested in urban planning, architecture, arts, etc. Taken together one might conclude that the Great Bath could have been built for public leisure, just like the Roman baths, as the prosperity of Mohenjo-daro's citizens could well afford it. Ritual bathing in the Indus Civilization, if it ever existed, is probably not to be understood as in Hinduism in which the act of bathing is to cleanse oneself spiritually, erase past sins, and unite with the gods. One thing is certain that bathing and cleansing indeed played a very important role in the daily life of the Harappans and ritual cleansing via the medium of water was probably not a rarity at the time. Moreover if later Indian arts had their roots in the Indus Civilization, as many have noticed, then one could as well conclude that some religious practices of the Harappans, such as the purported ritual bathing, might have also survived in the later Indian tradition.

In conclusion, the evidences clearly suggest the profound influence or cultural continuity that the Indus Civilization might have had upon the subsequent Ganga civilization in North India through its arts and architecture, religion, government, and social structures. These indigenous features of the Indian subcontinent would probably subsequently be fused with those brought to India by the Aryans to form a newly synthesized culture that was to be the imprint for the Indian tradition. Some distinct features of the Indus Civilization can be summarized in the followings:

- The well-planned layouts of its cities and remarkable achievements in civil engineering and architecture such as elaborate systems of street drains and sanitation as well as indoor plumbing; these could be the precursors of later Indian cities.
- Brick construction, corbelled arches, and the use of plaster in architecture; these were also prevalent in Indian and Buddhist architecture.
- A pillared hall and its use of built-in benches; these were also common in Indian and Buddhist architecture, particularly Buddhist caves.
- Architecture with cellar compartments surrounding a centrally open and piered courtyard; this is also the classic plan of many Buddhist caves and monasteries.

Chapter 2. Foundation of Buddhism

While the Indus Civilization was the forerunner of later Indian urbanism, North India was the birthplace of the spiritual heritage for the majority of Indians and millions of Asians in general as this region was the holyland of great world religions like Hinduism and Buddhism. Some of the ideas and concepts in all Indian religious systems including Buddhism were deeply rooted in Vedic Hinduism which first appeared after the arrival of the Aryans around c. 1200 BCE. These foreign Aryans probably compiled the Vedas, the sacred religious texts of the Hindus, with the assistance of native Indian theologians after they had settled in India {Radhakrishnan 1989 Volume I: 75}; this formative period in Indian history is known as the Vedic Period (c. 1200-600 BCE) as distinguished from the subsequent Epic Period (c. 600 BCE-200 CE). The Vedas consist of four separate texts, namely Rig-veda, Yajur-veda, Sama-veda, and Atharva-veda; each is further divided into three main parts, namely *Mantra*s (hymns), Bhahmanas (religious rituals and duties), and Upanisads (philosophy). Some fundamental features of Vedic Hinduism, as distinguished from later Hinduism and Buddhism, are:

a. Natural Polytheism

Numerous religious hymns in the Rig-veda are devoted to the gods deified from natural phenomena; many of these gods would subsequently be incorporated into the Buddhist pantheon though in subordinate ranks. Some well-known gods in the Vedas are Varuna (Sky God), Surya (Sun God), Visnu (God of Three Strides), Agni (Fire God), Yama (Lord of the Dead), Brahma (Creation God), and Indra or Sakra (Atmosphere and War God) {Radhakrishnan 1989 Volume I: 72-89}. Among these Brahma, Surya, and Indra frequently appear in Buddhist literature as Buddha's attendants and have also been depicted in early Buddhist arts. By the time Buddha preached his first sermon and founded Buddhism in c. 532 BCE, Vedic Hinduism had already become an integral part of the Indian society so that Buddhism had to incorporate some of these Vedic gods and religious beliefs into its system to be accepted among the local population and facilitate new conversions.

b. Formal Ritualism

Eventually the foreign beliefs of the Aryans, who were likely the minority among the locals, as exemplified in the Rig-veda, would merge with those of the indigenous. The Arthava-veda reflects this new and harmonizing spirit with the introduction of 'superstitious' and tribal elements like magic, exorcism, sacrificial rituals, etc. to appease evil and terrifying spirits. And who else could perform these sacred sacrificial ceremonies and communicate with the spirits and gods than the *brahmin*s or priests who specialize in religious rites and the sole authorities on the Vedas. According to the *brahmin*s, only they can perform these religious rituals and properly propitiate the gods since they know how to utter the correct prayers and spells for the successful completion of the rites. The Yajur and Sama-vedas are liturgical books that give ritual instructions to priests to be performed at the ceremonies to maximize the religious efficacy of the rituals {Radhakrishnan 1989 Volume I: 117-123}.

c. Caste

Though socio-economic castes, which are largely based on wealth and profession, might have had their roots in the Indus Civilization, religious castes, which are hereditary and survive until this day among the Hindus in India though abolished by the Indian government, first appeared in the Vedic Period. The Hindu society was then divided into four castes in descending order, namely *brahmin* (priests), *ksatriya* (warriors, rulers, administrators, aristocrats), *vaisya* (merchants, bankers), *sudra* (workers, servants); the *brahmin*s, due to their special knowledge of Sanskrit and the Vedas, hold exclusive rights in religious functions. Gradually the priest class or the *brahmin*s became hereditary alongwith the other three castes and the caste system would effectively be transformed into a social and religious institution; those who did not belong to any of these four castes were outcaste or untouchables and had to do the most demeaning works of all. The caste system, though essentially rooted in religious beliefs, was clearly a socio-economic institution that was meant to preserve the social order and an instrument for the powerful elites to safeguard and maintain their own self-interests {Radhakrishnan 1989 Volume I: 111-113, 132-133}. It was this rigid caste system that eventually set the stage for the continuing power struggle among the different castes and many, especially those of the lower castes, rebelled against it. Buddha, who was a *ksatriya*, clearly did not favor the *brahmin*s and he became one of the staunchest critics of the caste system.

d. Monism

The natural polytheism and formal ritualism of the earlier period would lastly give way to the Upanisads, the concluding portions of the Vedas, which are full of metaphysical speculations; these are intellectual reactions to the polytheism and artificial rituals in the earlier Vedas through lofty philosophy and rigorous metaphysical inquiries. The Upanisads created the oldest philosophical system in India in which aim was not to demolish the old religious order but to reform it in order to preserve its purity. They posited the idea of an *atman* (essence, being, soul, self, ego, or personality) in all individuals which is permanent, eternal, and not subject to decay or death; after death this *atman* would merge with *Brahman*, the cosmic counterpart of the *atman*. The *Brahman* is essentially a metaphysical absolute and a Supreme or Universal Being behind all world phenomena whilst the *atman* is the absolute reality within a person; even great gods like Indra, Surya, Visnu, etc. are also manifestations of this cosmic *Brahman*. But one must see the non-dual reality or oneness between the *atman* and *Brahman* as they are identical in the absolute sense and whoever realizes this is *Brahman*; in this sense, the Upanisads did not recognize the first and all-powerful Creator or God. One must understand that the *Brahman* is not a theistic God but an Absolute Being or Existence, or a metaphysical God if you will {Radhakrishnan 1989 Volume I: 151-173, 181-198}.

According to the Upanisads, one's life is determined by his *karma* (action, deed) or the moral effect as a result of his actions upon the surrounding environment; a good deed will bring a good return and an evil deed will bring suffering and a bad return. It is this accumulative effect of one's own deeds during his lifetime and the previous life that ultimately binds him to the cycles of birth and rebirth or *Samsara*; his *karma* in the past lives will determine whether the outcome of his birth in the next life is good (a reward) or bad (a punishment). Thus theoretically a man of a high caste could be born into a lower caste, or even animals, if he committed evils and accumulated bad *karma*s in his previous life and vice versa. Thus *karma* determines the outcome or status of one's reincarnation in the next life and due to the perpetual effect of *karma* he continues to drown in *Samsara* as long as he is still accumulating his *karma*s {Radhakrishnan 1989 Volume I: 245-256}. The ultimate religious goal is *Moksa* or spiritual release from one's *karma*s and *Samsara* as one's earthly body would be dissolved and the *atman* would merge to become one with *Brahman*; one's union and existence with *Brahman* is pure and eternal {Radhakrishnan 1989 Volume I: 236-242}. To seek the everlasting union with *Brahman* one has to fulfill his religious and social duties (*dharma*s) and live according to a devout Hindu way of life by conforming to the four stages in life, namely student, householder, hermit, and ascetic. Once his worldly duties have been fulfilled, a religious man becomes a homeless mendicant leading a holy life and performing various kinds of austerities to seek penance with the gods. In the final stage he becomes a holy ascetic or a *yogin* practicing yoga, a method of physical discipline and controlling breathing to purify one's mind, and meditates upon his eternal union with *Brahman*; these will enable him to break free of the cycles of *Samsara*, attain *Moksa*, and finally unite with *Brahman* {Radhakrishnan 1989 Volume I: 132, 219-222, 260-263}.

A. Buddha and Early Buddhism (c. 567-387 BCE)

The epoch that Buddha lived was in the beginning of the Epic Period during which different regional clans, which rules were governed by their representative leaders or kings called *raja*s, gradually began to form small republics with a few larger ones dominated smaller ones; among these Kosala and Magadha were the most powerful. During this period the small Sakya Republic, with Kapilavastu as its capital, was ruled by Suddhodana, Buddha's father; it was a vassal of the powerful Kosala where the ancestors of the Sakyas were believed to have immigrated from; Sakya was eventually conquered by Kosala shortly before Buddha's death in c. 487 BCE. Within this relatively peaceful time a newly religious movement called *Sramana*, which was led by well-known heterodox leaders like Buddha, was flowering all over North India with its key messages of religious freedom and in opposition to the authority of the Vedas and the *brahmin*s who comprised the orthodox and opposing *Brahmana* camp. The results were the full blossom of fresh religious and philosophical ideas and practices as well as the competition among the *sramana*s themselves and the *brahmana*s; all later schools of Indian philosophy, including Buddhism, could trace their roots during this period {Schumann 1989: 1-5, 34-43}. The majority of the *sramana*s were homeless wanderers seeking religious truths and salvation from different teachers and sects or through their own heroic efforts; many engaged in severe asceticism while others spent endless hours in philosophical disputes. Some became eminent leaders and founded great religions that last to this day like Buddhism and Jainism; it was during this unfettered and lively religious atmosphere that Buddha entered the scene.

1. Biography of Buddha {Schumann 1989: 6-263}

Prince Siddhartha Gautama (c. 567-487 BCE), Buddha's clan name before Enlightenment, was born on c. May 567 BCE, or c. 563 BCE according to some scholars depending whether Emperor Asoka's date of ascension to the throne in c. 269 BCE or c. 273 BCE, in Lumbini [8.1-8.2] in the Sakya Republic, which was then in North India but now a part of Nepal. King Suddhodana and Queen

Maya were his parents belonging to the Sakya and Koliya clans respectively; Prince Siddhartha had a privileged upbringing and his parents showered him with all the affection and riches as expected of being the only son and a scion of the Sakya kingdom. The prince was married at sixteen to Princess Yosadhara, also sixteen, and the couple had a son named Rahula. According to scriptural sources, one day Prince Siddhartha and his attendant took a chariot ride outside the palace compound and encountered the Four Signs, namely a sick man, an old man, a dead man, and a wandering mendicant. The signs stirred up the growing discontent inside Prince Siddhartha that he had been feeling for some times, perhaps the dissatisfaction about living an empty and meaningless life of luxury confined within the palace walls. Prince Siddhartha began yearning for the life outside the palace as an ascetic searching for spiritual freedom from the daily fetters of the material world; the sight of the peaceful monk in the last ride, in contrast to the suffering of the others, became the spiritual model that he was seeking for. One night, at the age of twenty-nine (c. 538 BCE), he left his luxurious palace at Kapilavastu and his kingdom alongwith his wife and son and headed south toward the region along the Ganga River in modern Uttar Pradesh and Bihar in search for spiritual enlightenment. This area in the sixth century BCE was the commercial and spiritual heart of North India; the Ganga was also a holy river for the Hindus where they came to bathe, cremate their relatives, and scatter their ashes into the holy water to cleanse their sins and seek for a higher rebirth in the next life and eternal union with the gods. Prince Siddhartha sought for spiritual guidance from different famous teachers of the days and after spending an extended period learning from them he was still not satisfied with his spiritual progress and decided to go his separate way in search for enlightenment on his own. The path to enlightenment was not an easy one for Prince Siddhartha and it took him six years of severe asceticism and extreme self-discipline with his five companions before he could achieve his ultimate aim. He finally attained Enlightenment or *Bodhi* in Bodhgaya **[7.6-7.11, 8.3-8.4]** at the age of thirty-five (c. 532 BCE) after a sustained period of intense spiritual introspection and meditation under the *bodhi*-tree, which subsequently became the holy tree to the Buddhists; from then on Prince Siddhartha became known to the world as Buddha or the Enlightened One. Soon afterward he proceeded to Isipatana or Sarnath **[8.5-8.6]** near modern day Varanasi where he preached his first sermon in the same year (c. 532 BCE) to his former five ascetic-companions (Ajnata-Kaundinya, Bhaddiya, Vappa, Mahanama, Assaji); they became his first monk-disciples (*bhiksu*) and together they formed the *Sangha* or the Community of Buddhist Monks and later including Nuns. For the next forty-five years Buddha and his disciples traveled throughout North India to spread his teachings, known as *Dharma*, and won many converts including kings, commoners, violent criminals, and even women who were also ordained into his *Sangha* in c. 527 BCE as nuns (*bhiksuni*). Buddha finally passed away in Kushinagar **[8.7-8.10]** in c. 487 BCE at the age of eighty; Subhadha was the last monk to be admitted into the *Sangha*. The last words he uttered to his disciples were, "All compound things are inherently impermanent; strive diligently for your own salvations." There are a few important epithets for which he has been universally known, including Buddha (Enlightened One), Sakyamuni (Sage of the Sakya Clan), Sakyasimha (Lion of the Sakyas), Tathagata (One Who Has Come and Gone Thus), and Bhagavan (Blessed One).

2. Core Teachings of Buddha

By the time of Buddha, the Vedic religion had already entrenched in the Indian society; ideas like *atman*, *Brahman*, yoga practices and asceticism, *Samsara*, *karma*, rebirth and reincarnation, etc. were the commonplace. Buddha's teachings and other *Sramana* religions, while not denying these, gave fresh interpretations with fundamental differences primarily centered on doctrinal issues regarding the nature of *atman*, *Brahman*, and other 'superstitious' practices such as ritual bathing and animal sacrifices. The followings summarize the main points of Buddha's original teachings which all schools of Buddhism agree to:

a. Suffering (*Dukkha*) {Rahula 1974: 16-50, 92-94}

Buddha expounded the Four Noble Truths in life, namely Suffering, Causes of Suffering, Cessation of Suffering, and Paths to the Cessation of Suffering, in his first sermon called Dharmacakrapravartana-sutra (Setting in Motion the Wheel of Truths Sermon) at Sarnath in c. 532 BCE; this very first sermon marked the beginning of Buddhism in India.

- First Noble Truth: Suffering
  Suffering is the life experience of every sentient being, including the gods and animals, and Buddha had experienced it himself during his princely life. Birth, old age, sickness, and death are suffering, associating with the painful and separating from the pleasant are suffering, not able to achieve one's aim is also suffering, and so are despair, sorrow, etc. In short the Five Aggregates (*skandha*) that make up a composite individual, namely Form, Sensation, Perception, Mental Formations, and Consciousness, are suffering because of their impermanent nature.
- Second Noble Truth: Cause of Suffering

The cause of suffering is the craving including attachment or holding on to people, animals, things, ideas, etc. It is the craving for sensual pleasures, for existence and becoming (rebirth), and for non-existence (self-extinguishing); it is this craving that gives rise to the delusion of *atman* and leads to the continuation of *Samsara*.
- Third Noble Truth: Cessation of Suffering
The cessation of craving will end suffering; one must detach, abandon, and renounce this craving along-with the sources of this craving; one must also follow the Noble Eightfold Path, as stated below, to completely eradicate the sources of suffering from one's life. The end of suffering is also the end of *Samsara* and the beginning of *Nirvana* in this very life.
- Fourth Noble Truth: The Paths to the Cessation of Suffering
The paths are the Middle Path and the Noble Eightfold Path. The Middle Path avoids two extremes of sensual pleasures and self-mortification as both are vulgar, low, painful, unfruitful, and the way of the commoners. It is imperative that this Middle Path is the path of moderation and non-commitment not an attachment to the centrist position since attachment, even to the middle position, is also one of the causes of suffering. The Noble Eightfold Path is Right Speech, Right Action, Right Livelihood, Right Thought, Right Understanding, Right Effort, Right Mindfulness, and Right Concentration. The first threes cultivate Ethics (*sila*), the next two develop Wisdom (*prajna*), and the last three build Mental Discipline (*samadhi*); *sila* and *prajna* are moral instructions for Buddhists on how to properly relate to the wider world while *samadhi* is for self-cultivation and self-discipline on the personal level. The 'Right' in *sila* and *prajna* generally means one shall embrace the Middle Path and refrain from causing suffering to others while bringing joy and benefits to fellow beings. The 'Right' in Buddhist views essentially requires the rejection of 'superstitious' and Hindu rituals such as animal sacrifices, ritual bathing, etc. and the refrainment of engaging in fruitless metaphysical discussions about the natures of the universe, *Brahman, atman, Nirvana,* etc. The 'Right' in *samadhi* is meant to purify the mind through meditation, refrain from thoughts causing suffering to others, and cultivate positive thoughts of bringing about happiness and benefits to fellow beings.
b. Impermanence (*Anicca*) {Rahula 1974: 25-26} {Radhakrishnan 1989 Volume I: 366-370, 372-380}
All elements in the universe are in a state of constant flux without any permanent or unchanging entity and likewise birth, decay, and death also belong to an ever-changing reality and therefore impermanent. All phenomena are conditioned and hence their impermanent nature and whatever impermanent is non-*atman* and hence attachment to the impermanent will cause suffering; thus the concept of a permanent and unchanging *atman* or *Brahman* behind all phenomena in the Upanisads was categorically rejected or implicitly denied by Buddha.
c. Non-*atman* (Non-Soul or Non-Self) {Rahula 1974: 20-26, 51-66}
According to the Hindu tradition, there is a permanent, absolute, everlasting, independent, unconditioned entity existing within oneself called an *atman* (Pali *atta*), a Sanskit word equivalent of a soul, self, personality, I, free will, ego, or being. This *atman* experiences, accumulates, and inherits *karma*s in the past and present while it transforms and transmigrates (rebirth and reincarnation) into the next life as pre-determined by its past *karma*s. Buddha and all schools of Buddhism deny the existence of *atman* since one shall see himself as a composite person defined by the five *skandha*s which are impermanent, conditioned, and dependent on other elements for their existence and hence none of them is *atman*. The analysis of Dependent Origination, as described below, that all elements are impermanent, relative, conditioned, and interdependent also leads to the conclusion of non-*atman*. An individual relates to the inner and outer world through the Six Organs (eye, ear, tongue, nose, body, and mind) and the Six Faculties corresponding to the Six Senses (sight, sound, taste, smell, touch, and thoughts); all these organs and senses are interdependent, impermanent, and conditioned and hence none of them is considered *atman*.
d. Dependent Origination (*Paticca Samuppada*) {Rahula 1974: 53-55}
According to Buddha there are twelve factors in the causal chain that are the main causes for the continuation of *Samsara* and the delusion of *atman*; these are:
- Ignorance is conditioned by
- Volitional Actions are conditioned by
- Consciousness is conditioned by
- Mental and Physical Phenomena is conditioned by
- Six Faculties are conditioned by
- Sensory and Mental Contact is conditioned by
- Sensation is conditioned by
- Craving is conditioned by
- Clinging is conditioned by
- Becoming is conditioned by
- Birth is conditioned by
- Death, decay, suffering, etc.

It is important to remember this is a circular chain with no beginning or end and these twelve factors are conditioned, relative, interdependent, interconnected, and impermanent; hence no first or last cause is possible. Ignorance generally means the delusion of an *atman* and permanence; if one cut off Ignorance, the most important factor, the chain is ceased and there is no more *Samsara* and *Nirvana* then appears. This Causality Law can also be summarized as this:

> When this is, that is; when this is not, that is not.
> When this arises, that arises; when this ceases, that ceases.

All elements are interdependent and none can be independent, separate, or uncaused; hence the ideas of *atman*, *Brahman*, Creator, or God are unacceptable to Buddhists from the philosophical point of view.

e. *Nirvana* {Rahula 1974: 35-44} {Radhakrishnan 1989 Volume I: 446-453}

The teachings of Buddha are ultimately for the realization of *Nirnava*, the most important religious goal for all Buddhists and it is the same as Enlightenment. On the intellectual level one grasps the essential doctrines the Four Noble Truths, Impermanence, Non-*atman*, and Dependent Origination while on the physical level one acknowledges and experiences equanimity, dispassion, and the cessation of craving. *Nirvana* can be realized in this very life while *Parinirvana* is the *Nirvana* after the physical dissolution of the five *skandha*s, or death; Buddhists refer to the great decease of Buddha as *Parinirvana*. The Buddhist *Nirvana* is fundamentally different from the Hindu *Moksa* of the Upanisads; the latter is the eternal union of man, *atman*, and *Brahman* while Buddha's *Nirvana* is the dissolve of all elements and concepts and hence it is not the merge with any eternal Being. *Nirvana* is also the final release from *Samsara* and suffering and hence it is the ultimate liberation for all sentient beings.

3. Other Religious Views and Practices
a. Karma {Rahula 1974: 32}

In the Indian religious systems, *karma* generally means rewards-punishments that the *atman* experiences, accumulates, and inherits in the past, present, and future; the idea of *karma* as a rewarding or punishing system is a popular religious belief in India and Buddhist Asia. *Karma* in the Buddhist tradition refers to one's actions-reactions and actions-consequences as good actions result in good effects and bad actions will produce bad consequences; having the delusion of *atman* one acts and therefore continues to accumulate *karma*s, which perpetuate *Samsara*. So one must cultivate good *karma*s when leading a holy life; once *Nirvana* has been attained one's past *karma*s, good or bad, will effectively be dissolved since an enlightened being, like a Buddha or *arhat*, no longer has the delusion of *atman*, or literally speaking his act is not self-ish or *atman*-ish as he is non-*atman* in essence.

b. *Samsara*, Rebirth, Reincarnation {Rahula 1974: 33-34}

Like *karma*, Buddha also accepted the pan-Indian Vedic concept of rebirth and *Samsara*. A new rebirth in the next life is evidently dependent upon one's past *karma*s; good *karma*s produce high reincarnations while bad *karma*s will result in low reincarnations. Hence the concepts of *karma* and rebirth are popular religious conventions that encourage people to strive for a higher moral ground and hopefully a better reward or a more advantageous reincarnation in the next life.

c. Meditation {Rahula 1974: 67-75, 109-119} {Walshe 1995: 335-350}

Though Buddhist meditation had its root in the Vedic yoga but the fundamental difference is that in Hindu yoga practitioners contemplate on realizing *atman* and union with *Brahman*, the very metaphysical concepts that Buddha denied. Instead Buddhist meditation emphasizes on the body and mind; body meditation cultivates physical mindfulness such as the control and concentration on breathing while mind meditation contemplates Buddha's teachings such as Suffering, Non-*atman*, Dependent Origination, etc. Practitioners contemplate on the signs and sources of suffering like old age, sickness, death, etc. in order to detach from painful attachments; long periods of mindfulness would lead to calming one's mind, expelling unwholesome thoughts, and ultimately leading to *Nirvana*. Thus the practice of extreme asceticism, as often found in Hindu yoga to seek penance with the gods, had categorically been rejected by Buddha in his first sermon at Sarnath; so too is the rejection of sexual yoga, which certainly would not have been accepted by Buddha but it percolated the Vajrayana School in the late phase of Buddhism.

B. Theravada School (c. 387 BCE)

1. Introduction

Shortly before Buddha's impending death he instructed his disciples that after his death his Teachings (*Dharma*) and Monastic Rules (*Vinaya*) should become their guides. In the subsequent centuries his disciples would periodically gather in great councils to consolidate their master's *Dharma* and strengthen the *Sangha* and its influence in the Indian society; these councils also settled and resolved disputes among the monks and where schisms within the *Sangha* also became official. The successful internationalization of Buddhism in the subsequent centuries could also be credited to the zealous missionaries of Buddhist monks and the generous patronage from the wealthy laity such as kings and merchants; these councils, as a rule, would disseminate new missionaries to the foreign lands to propagate Buddhism after the conclusion of each council. There were four important councils, the latest held in 1956 CE in Myanmar, held by the *Sangha* within the first six centuries after Buddha's death; three councils were in India and one in Kashmir.

a. First Council (c. 487 BCE) {Barua 1997: 21-39}

This council was held in Rajagriha, Bihar about four months after Buddha's death to consolidate Buddha's *Dharma* and *Vinaya*, strengthen, and prevent the disintegration of the *Sangha* after the lost of its master. A total of 500 *arhat*s (Buddha's disciples and later Theravada saints) gathered at the council with Mahakassapa, one of Buddha's most distinguished disciples, as its presiding president; Ananda, Buddha's cousin and constant attendant, recited the *Sutra* (Buddha's *Dharma* compiled in sermons) while Upali, another of Buddha's important disciples, recited the *Vinaya*; these comprised the two Baskets (*Pitaka*) containing Buddha's original words. The Third Basket or *Abhidharma* (Scholastic Commentaries) would be compiled in the Third Council (c. 249 BCE) and together they made up the Three Baskets (*Tripitaka*) in the Pali canons, the core literature of the Theravada.

b. Second Council (c. 387 BCE) {Barua 1997: 47-79}

This council was held in Vaishali, Bihar in c. 387 BCE or a century after Buddha's *Parinirvana* during Kalasoka's reign; it was attended by 700 *thera*s (Theravada monk-elders) to settle disputes about a group of Vaishali monks who had committed ten indulgences contrary to the *Vinaya*. To decide on the matter, the council was convened and presided over by a president, Thera Reveta, and a jury of eight senior monks including Sabbakami, Khujjasobhita, Salha, Sambhuta, Sanavasi, Yasa, Vasabhagamika, and Sumana. These ten indulgences or offenses were:

- Storing salt in a horn vessel.
- Taking a meal slightly after mid-day.
- Taking a second meal in the same day while visiting the laity away from the monastery.
- Holding different in-house ceremonies within the same monastery ground.
- An ecclesiastical act might be performed first then got approvals at a later time.
- The practice of using precedents as authority.
- Taking milk, whey, or liquid food after a mid-day meal.
- Taking a strong drink that might contain intoxicating drink like palm-juice or wine.
- Sitting on a borderless mat.
- Accepting gold and silver.

The council found the Vaishali monks guilty and they were expelled from the *Sangha*. The Vaishali monks, who considered themselves more liberal and progressive, did not abide by the decision and subsequently formed a separate council of their own; their council would be named 'Great Assembly' and they the 'Great Assemblyers' or Mahasanghikas. Despite the schism, the Mahasanghikas continued to follow Buddha's *Dharma* while living alongside with the *thera*s but they followed a less stringent *Vinaya* of their own. Another separate council was held later in Pataliputra in c. 350 BCE and this time the attack was not directed at the *Vinaya* but about the status of an *arhat*; it was lead by Mahadeva who proposed five points about an *arhat*:

- An *arhat* might subject to temptation.
- An *arhat* might have ignorance.
- An *arhat* might have doubts.
- Arhatship can not be attained without the help of a teacher.
- The path (of becoming an *arhat*) is attained with an exclamation 'Aho!'

The Theravadins could not agree with these propositions which were clearly directed against them; it also became clear from these councils that the some monks within the *Sangha* opposed the authority of the *thera*s and power struggle was inevitable. These councils made it official the split of *Sangha* into two sub-schools, namely the Theravada consisting of orthodox monks who upheld Buddha's tradition and the Mahasanghika who considered more progressive and worldlier.

c. Third Council (c. 249 BCE) {Barua 1997: 85-99}

Between the Vaishali council in c. 387 BCE and the Third Council held in Pataliputra in c. 249 BCE, the *Sangha* further split into eighteen different sects, eleven by the Theravada and seven by the Mahasanghika; besides Buddha's original teachings, each sect also developed additional doctrines and monastic rules of their own. By this time, the prestige of the *Sangha* would be greatly boosted with the conversion of Emperor Asoka (r. 269-233 BCE), the third emperor of the Maurya Dynasty, who not only patronized the *Sangha* generously but also disseminated Buddhist missionaries throughout the known world. The zealous emperor built many great monuments dedicated to Buddhism such as the stone pillars bearing his name (Chapter 3) as well as countless *stupa*s and *caitya*s throughout his empire; he was also the official sponsor of the Third Council. Under such favorable conditions, there were a large number of newcomers joining the *Sangha* to gain prestige and benefits from the immense wealth donated by the laity and Asoka. Many of them were corrupt elements and heretics who continued practicing their old faiths or had limited comprehension of Buddha's teachings while some unknowingly or deliberately distorted Buddha's messages. Furthermore, the split within the *Sangha* also worsened the situation as there were a wide range of doctrines and practices by different sects that threatened to relegate Buddha's original teachings into oblivion. Under this bewildering environment, the Third Council was convened to purge non-Buddhist elements from the *Sangha* and purify Buddha's *Dharma* from heresies; it has been said that 80,000 heretics were expelled from the *Sangha* after the conclusion of the council and many were no doubt opponents of the orthodox Theravadins. A total of 1,000 *thera*s attended this council under the prestigious leadership of Moggaliputa Tissa; however the effort to unify the *Sangha* was futile as other Buddhist sects refused to recognize the Theravadins, whom in the end received personal approval from Asoka. Moggaliputa Tissa was a renowned Theravada monk and believed to be Asoka's younger brother or Tissakumara according to some scholars {Chaudhury 1969: 21}. The ultimate outcomes of this council were the compilation of the third *Pitaka*, or *Abhidharma*, to complete the *Tripitaka*. The missionary sent to Sri Lanka immediately after this council, which was headed by Mahendra and Sanghamitra or Asoka's son and daughter, also brought with them the *Tripitaka* that would finally be committed into writings in c. 88 BCE. Perhaps the greatest contribution to the expansion of Buddhism as a world religion was the missionaries sent throughout India and the world after the conclusion of this council:

- Diplomatic and Buddhist missionaries were sent by Asoka to the Greek country and colonies in Macedonia, Epirus, Syria, Egypt, and Cyrene (Libya) as stated in Asoka's edicts (Major Rock Edicts II, V, XIII) {Hultzsch 1969: 3-4, 10, 24-25}.
- Nine Buddhist missionaries were also sent by Moggaliputa Tissa to India's neighbors as recorded in the Sri Lankan annals, the Dipavamsa and Mahavamsa: (1) Kashmir and Gandhara headed by Majjhantika, (2) Aparantaka (probably southeastern Afghanistan, southeastern Pakistan or Sindh, and western India or Gujarat) headed by the a *Yona* (Greek) monk Dhammarakkhita, (3) Himavanta (Himalaya countries) headed by Majjima, (4) *Yona* countries (probably Bactria, northern Afghanistan) headed by Maharakkhita, (5) Maharattha (Maharashtra) headed by Mahadhammarakkhita, (6) Vanavasi (north Kanara, Karnataka) headed by Rakkhita, (7) Mahisamandala (Mysore, Karnataka) headed by Mahadeva, (8) Suvarnabhumi (probably Myanmar) headed by Sona and Uttara, (9) Tambapanna (Sri Lanka) headed by Mahendra, Asoka's son, and Moggaliputa Tissa's disciples, including Itthiya, Uttiya, Sambala, and Bhaddasala {Dutt 1962: 115}{Chaudhury 1969: 21-22}. The relics of some of these monks have been discovered in Sanchi Stupa II, Sonari Stupa II, and Andher Stupa II-III thus confirmed the historical authenticity of these missionaries (Chapter 6).

d. Fourth Council (second century CE) {Barua 1997: 106-117}

This last important council was held in Kashmir during the reign of King Kanishka (r. 128-151 CE) who was the sponsor of the council; like Asoka, Kanishka was also a great patron of Buddhism. He was a ruler of the Yuehchi (Kushan) tribe that had migrated across Central Asia from western China between the second-first centuries BCE; the Kushans finally managed to rule a vast territory in the second century CE encompassing northwestern India, Kashmir, Gandhara, Afghanistan, Central Asia, and Turkistan. This council was an attempt to harmonize Buddha's teachings and compile the *sutra*s; in reality, as in the previous councils, it was more about the dominance and recognition of one school or sect over the others. This council was held by the Sarvastivada, one of the preeminent and progressive sects of the orthodox Theravada School that had risen to prominence after the Third Council and became predominant within Kanishka's empire. About 500 *arhat*s reportedly attended this council but there was not a presiding chairman at this time; it concluded with the compilation of the Sarvastivadins' own edition of the *Tripitaka* and missionaries would also be launched throughout Asia. As expected, the orthodox Theravadins neither recognized this council nor the literature compiled by the Sarvastivadins. The Sarvastivada, together with the Mahasanghika, became the precursors of the Mahayana as many of the tenets of the latter had been extracted from these two influential sects; most importantly, the Sarvastivada was presumably the sect that authorized the creation of the first Buddha image.

2. Religious Foundations {Dutt 1970: 266-268}{Dutt 1973: 82-85}{Radhakrishnan 1989 Volume I: 586-589}

It is important not to confuse between the Theravada School and the Theravada Sect. The former generally refers to the orthodox school that split with the Mahasanghika after the Second Council; those who follow this school call themselves *thera*, hence the name Theravada. The Theravada Sect, on the other hand, was founded in c. 150 BCE as an offshoot of the Vibhajjavada (another Theravada sect); the latter survived in Sri Lanka and Southeast Asia thanks to the missionaries after the Third Council {Barua 1997: 145}. The Theravada School was historically the oldest Buddhist school with its orthodox teachings and practices closer to Buddha than any other schools; its religious ideal is that of an *arhat*, or one who has already achieved *Nirvana* and release from *Samsara*. Some basic tenets of this school are:

- It is historical and ethical; its literature is mostly written in Pali. In its *Tripitaka*, the *Sutra* and *Vinaya* are considered Buddha's original words while the *Abhidharma* has been a later addition by the Theravadins in the Third Council. The popular *jataka*s (Buddhist moral folklores) are also the Theravadins' well-known creation; however, many might have been told by Buddha himself.
- The Theravadins recognize Buddha not as a deity or God but as a superhuman, a historical teacher, and an *arhat* who has led sentient beings out of their sufferings through his exemplary deeds. The Theravadins also permit a few non-Buddhist deities into their literature but their ranks are decidedly inferior to Buddha and the *arhat*s; Maitreya, whose origin is in the Theravada, is the only *bodhisattva* and Future Buddha popularly accepted by all Buddhist schools.
- Its religious goals are for the attainment of arhathood and the cessation of all suffering and craving.
- Philosophically, all phenomena exist only as designates; however, the elements and components of these phenomena do exist but their existence is only momentary.
- *Nirvana* is recognized as separate from *Samsara* and an *arhat* progresses spiritually from *Samsara* to *Nirvana*; once an *arhat* has attained *Nirvana* his existence in *Samsara* ceases.
- The Theravada does not have a complicated pantheon as the Mahayana or Vajrayana; their main object of devotion is Sakyamuni and his disciples, all are considered historical *arhat*s and human beings.

C. Mahayana School (first century CE)

1. Introduction

Historically it has not been possible to trace a direct development of the Mahayana School from any Buddhist sects. The Mahayana had initially been a disparate movement that converged some times in the first century CE and it was no doubt a reaction against the Theravada; in doctrines and practices, however, it has borrowed a great deal from the latter and particularly those works of the Sarvastivada and Mahasanghika. In the past the Mahayana (Great Vehicle) derogatorily called the Theravada as the Hinayana (Little Vehicle) School; the former maintained that their way was superior, adaptable, and open to all while the latter's way was for pragmatic individualists whose 'selfish' concerns were only for their own liberation. However, some Mahayana ideas have been deemed more radical and liberal than the conservative Theravada and Buddha's teachings. The Mahayana probably originated in South India in the first century BCE and gradually grew to a newly distinct school of Buddhism around the first century CE {Dutt 1970: 274-278}. Contrary to popular beliefs, the Mahayana was not a direct descendent of the Mahasanghika as the latter was essentially a Theravada sect with a few 'rebellious' ideas and practices. Upon further reflection the Theravada, especially the Sarvastivada and Mahasanghika sects, have contributed many important concepts and practices to the Mahayana {Dutt 1970: 260-266}. The Mahayanists often pride themselves on their intellectual superiority and these can be credited a few pioneering Mahayana philosophers like Nagarjuna (second century CE), Vasubhanhu and Asanga (fourth century CE). The works of these brilliant monks still essentially lie within the framework of Buddhist philosophy as they have been built upon earlier foundations of the Theravada and Buddha himself. The Mahayana works, however, are fresh and often radical interpretations which form a coherent and logical system that has profoundly influenced other philosophical systems in India and abroad including the Buddhist, Hindu, Daoist, and even Confucianist. The Mahayana intellectual success, however, had been compromised in practice as its progressive outlook practically allowed many foreign elements to seep into Buddhism. First, Buddha had been elevated to the status of a supreme and god-like being and there also appeared a myriad of non-historical and divine beings called *bodhisattva*s; next, the historical Sakyamuni Buddha would gradually be relegated into the background until he became virtually indistinguishable or could not compete with countless other celestial Buddhas. 'Superstitions' and complex rituals also appeared in monasteries while spiritual salvation could be instantly attained simply by worshipping images and reciting the names of the various Buddhas. Extreme cases of Mahayana practices can be found in the Pure Land Sect in which salvation can be attained by simply reciting the name of Amitabha or one would instantly be transported to his Western Paradise if calling his name in one's deathbed.

2. Religious Foundations {Dutt 1970: 269-280}{Dutt

1973: 82-85}{Radhakrishnan 1989 Volume I: 589-605}{Klimburg-Salter 1989: 61-63}

The Mahayana also inherited many concepts from the Theravada; the difference between them is essentially in a matter of emphasis since both ultimately aim to achieve liberation and *Nirvana*. Hallmark concepts of the Mahayana such as *bodhisattva*, the practice of six *paramita*s (perfections), the aspiration of reaching Buddhahood through the ten *bhumi*s (spiritual stages), *trikaya*s (triple-Buddha bodies), etc. can disparately be found in the earlier Theravada works, particularly those of the Sarvastivada and Mahasanghika; the Mahayana, however, has systematized and put them into practice with a renewed vigor. Some fundamental features of the Mahayana are:

- It combines religious, often with a great deal of devotionalism, and metaphysical speculations; its literature is written in Sanskrit. Besides the *sutra*s, or discourses originally spoken by Buddha that are recognized by all Buddhist schools, Mahayana literature also contains a vast amount of *sastra*s, or philosophical treatises and commentaries by Buddhist philosophers and the cornerstones of Mahayana philosophy.
- Its progressive outlook allows Buddha to be deified as a supreme Buddha who functions like a supreme God while the *bodhisattva*s become celestial saints; together with myriads of other Buddhas in countless world systems they labor tirelessly for the liberation of the suffering world.
- The Mahayana religious ideal is a *bodhisattva*, or one whose essence is enlightenment and equivalent to a Theravada *arhat*; he practices high virtues, endures countless sacrifices in the past and present lives, and vows to lead sentient beings to enlightenment before ultimately becoming a Buddha. The *arhat* of the Theravada, as the Mahayanists have contended, is a selfish individualist whose only concern is for his own liberation while ignoring the cries of suffering beings.
- On the philosophical ground, the Mahayana holds that the real essence of all phenomena is *Sunya* (Empty) and hence all concepts of existence and non-existence are no longer valid (Madhyamika sect's view). Or the real essence of all phenomena is *Alayavijnana* (Pure or Store Consciousness) as all concepts exist only in the mind and thoughts, that are constantly changing and therefore unreal (Yogacara sect's view).
- *Nirvana* and *Samsara* is philosophically identical in the absolute reality since their essence is *Sunya*; hence an enlightened being does not progress spiritually from *Samsara* to *Nirvana* as in the Theravada view.
- The Mahayana pantheon allows the worship of many Buddhas and *bodhisattva*s who might have been deified from historical and non-historical individuals or purely divine beings and they generally appear to have more magical powers than the *arhat*s. Among the most popular deities in the Mahayana pantheon are Amitabha, Buddha of the Western Paradise, and Avalokitesvara, the Bodhisattva of Compassion; moreover Buddhas and *bodhisattva*s, like the *arhat*s, are in essence enlightened beings and therefore considered superior to all other non-Buddhist gods.

D. Vajrayana School (sixth century CE)

1. Introduction

While the Theravada and Mahayana were the first and second phase of Buddhism, the Vajrayana School, also known as Esoteric or Tantric Buddhism, was the third and last phase of Indian Buddhism. This school appeared as early as the sixth century CE about the same time when the strength of Buddhism in India gradually declined and finally disappeared altogether after c. 1200 CE. In this final phase of Indian Buddhism there were many non-Buddhist elements infiltrating Buddhism, particularly from the Tantric branches of Hinduism. The Vajrayana was formerly considered as an offshoot of the Mahayana as many of its philosophical concepts and practices had been adopted from the latter; however, the fusion of Tantricism and Buddhism has led to the recognition of the Vajrayana as a new and distinct Buddhist school. To Buddha and the Theravadins individual self-mastery is the way to *Nirvana* while the Mahayanists insist on intellectual enlightenment through rigorous metaphysical inquiries; the Vajrayana believes in enlightenment that can be attained in the practitioner's lifetime through symbolic rituals, complex rites and imageries. It is important not to confuse between the Vajrayana and Tibetan Buddhism, or Lamaism, as the former was the latter's Indian predecessor when Tibet became a Vajrayana stronghold after the demise of Indian Buddhism; the fusion of the Vajrayana and native Bon religion of Tibet gave rise to Tibetan Buddhism around the eighth century CE {Snellgrove 1987: 388-393, 396-407}.

2. Religious Foundations {Snellgrove 1987: 117-304}

The Vajrayana generally accepts basic premises of the Mahayana including *Sutra*, *Vinaya*, and *sastra*s; however, its religion is a combination of Buddhist and Tantric practices and so it has also developed its own canons over times. The Vajrayanists, like other sectarian Buddhists before them, also believe their special branch of Buddhism even superior to either the Mahayana or Theravada; they adopt most Mahayana tenets such as the *bodhisattva* concept, the pantheon of Buddhas and *bodhisattva*s, the doctrines of the Madhyamikas and the Yogacaras, etc. They further supplement the ideal of a *siddha* (the Perfected) or a Tantric Buddhist spiritual adept and guru who has already attained enlightenment and spiritual power and ready to guide unenlightened beings to achieve their religious goals even in their lifetime. The essential difference between the Mahayana and Vajrayana lies in the latter's transformation of Mahayana doctrines into symbolic terms, in both literature and religious imageries, with the infusion of numerous Tantric elements. These esoteric elements have occasionally surfaced throughout the Vedas, especially the Atharva-veda {Radhakrishnan 1989 Volume I: 117-123}; however, their reappearance in later Tantric Hinduism and the Vajrayana was advanced versions. In this latest phase of Buddhism, one can clearly discern vast differences in doctrines and practices between the Vajrayana and those of the Theravada and Buddha's *Dharma*. Some fundamental characteristics of the Vajrayana are:

a. *Tantra*

*Tantra*s are the foremost canonical literature of the Vajrayana centering on yoga practices, ritualism, iconography, etc.; they are divided into four categories: *kriya-tantra* (Action *Tantra*s), *carya-tantra* (Performance *Tantra*s), *yoga-tantra* (Yoga *Tantra*s), and *anuttarayoga-tantra* (Supreme Yoga *Tantra*s). *Kriya-tantra*s and *carya-tantra*s emphasize magical incantations or spells to achieve personal benefits and gain merits while the *yoga-tantra*s are instructions on attaining Buddhahood through a series of consecratory rites; the *anuttarayoga-tantra*s, the highest class, prescribe ritualized consecrations involving symbolic sexual union (*yuganaddha*) with members of the opposite sex. The first three categories of *tantra*s are scattered throughout late Mahayana *sutra*s and some deities in these *tantra*s also belong to the Mahayana. The *anuttarayoga-tantra*s, and particularly the *yogini-tantra*s since these emphasize females and involve sexual union with the female *yogini*s, were mainly the products of the wandering *yogin*s, *yogini*s, and non-celibate monks loosely associated with Buddhism. These Tantric Buddhist saints are collectively known as the *siddha*s; they were a class of highly unconventional individuals who were obviously not bounded by established religious conducts of a traditional Buddhist monastery or moral sanctions of the society.

b. *Mantra, Dharani, Mudra*

In sacred Vajrayana ceremonies, Tantricists often employ the *mantra* (an incantation invoking a particular deity) and *mudra* (a hand gesture often associated with the *mantra*) calling upon the presiding deities for protection and services; *dharani*s are also *mantra*s but they are generally longer from a sentence to several pages. The most well-known of all *mantra*s is 'Om Mani Padme Hum' calling upon Avalokitesvara for blessings and protection. It is important to distinguish between the Tantric *mudra*s and simple hand gestures in early Buddhist sculptures; the latter were the sculptors' inventions to associate the depicted images with the particular events in Buddha's life and they did not appear to have any supposedly magical powers as in the Vajrayana *mudra*s. The employment of *mantra*s and *mudra*s in religious rites could be traced back to the Vedic Hinduism; however, many *mudra*s in Vajrayana sculptures were iconographically derived from early Indian Buddhist sculptures.

c. Symbolism

Symbolism is a very important component of the Vajrayana and in the process of spiritual enlightenment; the manifestations of divinity and religious states would often be transformed into symbolic objects in Vajrayana practices and imageries. Thus the *vajra* (thunderbolt, diamond, unbreakable) symbolically represents *upaya* (Skillful Means), male, and the sun while the *ghanta* (bell) or *padma* (lotus) symbolizes *prajna* (Wisdom), female, and the moon. The symbolic sexual union (*yuganaddha*) between these two opposite elements in the *anuttarayoga-tantra*s personifies the ultimate state of Enlightenment (*Vajra*) and this concept is literally and graphically depicted in Vajrayana religious imageries. Scholars have also noticed the highly symbolic, deliberately incomprehensible, and even offensive language in many Vajrayana *tantra*s, especially those in the *anuttarayoga-tantra*s; the beginning of the Guhyasamaja-tantra states {Davidson 2002: 236, 248}:

> Thus have I heard. At one time, the Lord was residing in the vaginas of the women who are the adamantine body, speech, mind, and heart of all the Tathagatas [possibly denoting sexual yoga ritual].

And the Buddhadkapala-yogini-tantra-raja says:

> The Bhagavan - having correctly explained the mantras and all the tantras by means of adamantine words in the great adamantine site - this lord of all the Tathagatas placed his vajra [phallus] in his consort's lotus [vulva], and promptly entered final nirvana in the lady's vagina [possibly denoting sexual copulation ritual and enlightenment].

The seminal fluid might therefore symbolically be described in a fabulously allegorical term as *Bodhicitta* (Seed of Enlightenment) while the orgasmic experience could be expressed as *Mahasukha* (Great Bliss). Enlightenment, which is ultimately equated with Buddhahood, is achieved in this very moment of non-duality when all conceptual thoughts cease; it also represents the union of the male and female principle, or *upaya* and *prajna* respectively, in a non-dual, empty, and enlightened state called *Sunya* or *Vajra*. Another important icon in Vajrayana religious symbolisms is the *mandala* (circle); in the Vajrayana context, the *mandala* represents the sphere or field of an individual or a group of divinities like Buddhas, *bodhisattva*s, and other Tantric deities. A *mandala*, which is typically presided over by a demiurgic deity in the center, can therefore theoretically interact with one or countless other *mandala*s. In religious imageries, a *mandala* is often depicted as a circle or a set of circles circumscribed inside a square having four gates on the four sides; the main gate faces east which is also the direction Sakyamuni gazed when he attained Enlightenment. Other interpretations suggest the realm within the inner circle of a *mandala* represents *Nirvana* and the world of enlightened Buddhas and *bodhisattva*s while the outer square and periphery symbolize *Samsara* and the world of unenlightened beings. A *mandala* is essentially a ritual device for meditational practitioners to visualize and identify with the deities residing in it who would be manifested during the ritualized consecration; thus it is an important component in the process of enlightenment. There are two important types of *mandala*s, namely the *yoga-tantra mandala* and *anuttarayoga-tantra mandala*; the former is usually administered by a single male deity like Vairocana who is accompanied by male or female *prajna*s or *sakti*s whereas the latter typically involves a purely Tantric pair of male and female deities like Hevajra and Nairatmya in *yuganaddha* and their attendants can be all females in many cases.

d. Rites and Rituals

The Vajrayanists' emphasis on rituals and ceremonies means that a spiritual preceptor or teacher is crucial for a student in the realization of *Vajra*. Besides this requirement, a novice also has to go through a series of highly elaborate consecrations (*abhiseka*) full of symbolic and complex rites under the strict guidance of his guru to be initiated into the Vajrayana inner circles; the ultimate outcome of these consecratory rituals is the promise of a speedy enlightenment in one's lifetime.

e. *Vajra*

The Vajrayana derives its name from *Vajra*, the highest state of Enlightenment when the practitioner attains *Mahasukha*; once one realizes this non-dual *Vajra* state, which is also equated with *Sunya*, one attains Buddhahood. The practitioner can realize *Vajra* through a series of ritualized *abhiseka* involving esoteric symbolisms, complex imageries, and magical incantations. During such ceremonies, a religious belief is that a chosen Tantric deity, Buddha, or *bodhisattva* would descend, manifest, and merge with the practitioner to accelerate in his advancement toward enlightenment; once the *Boddhicitta* has been manifested during the consecration, the practitioner attains the state of *Mahasukha*. David Snellgrove lucidly summed up the complex Vajrayana philosophy pertaining to the attainment of enlightenment, which radically differs from the rigorous self-discipline of the Theravada and the compassionate selfless sacrifice of the Mahayana {Klimburg-Salter and Others 1982: 70}:

> The essence of Tantric practice may be described as the visualization of a certain "chosen divinity," [often identified with a certain *mandala*] believed to be the very essence of Buddhahood, and the deliberate identification of oneself with this divinity. Once this state of self-identification is realized, one achieves the state of enlightenment which the chosen divinity embodies.

Thus during an *abhiseka*, the Vajrayana practitioner would summon the chosen Tantric deity, *bodhisattva*, or even Buddha by performing precise rites in conjunction with the *mantra*s, *mudra*s, *mandala*s, etc. These will greatly amplify the potency of the rituals and facilitate the merger of the deity's 'enlightened essence' with that of the practitioner who subsequently also becomes enlightened or embodies enlightenment. The ultimate outcome is the realization of a transcendental and non-dual state between the practitioner and the 'other' power, the inner and outer, etc. since all are in essence *Sunya*; ordinary humans, however, still differentiate because of their unenlightened nature. Thus the Vajrayana radically differs from other Buddhist schools in that it employs a highly convoluted ritualized method to achieve rapid enlightenment even in one's lifetime. The orthodox Theravada, on the other hand, relies on a lifetime of self-discipline, as Buddha did, to attain their perfect state of *Nirvana* while the Mahayana emphasizes compassion and selfless sacrifice alongwith rigorous metaphysical and intellectual inquiries to attain Buddhahood. Despite their different methodologies, they all share similar traits that (a) they recognize gods, *bodhisattva*s, and Buddhas as medium or guidance to their enlightenment and not to be passively worshipped, (b) all living beings are capable of attaining the highest enlightened state and exalting status just like Buddhas, *arhat*s, and *bodhisattva*s, and (c) *Nirvana* and all phenomena in the absolute sense is of a non-dual and insubstantial nature. Thus to Buddha's view and the Theravada's "All *dharma*s are without self" and the Mahayana "All is *Sunya*;" the Vajrayana essentially affirms an identical view that "The absolute essence is *Vajra* and *Sunya*," which is indestructible but they use an object, the *vajra*, to symbolically represent this state.

f. Vajrayana Pantheon

Important Mahayana *bodhisattva*s like Avalokitesvara, Maitreya, Manjusri, etc. are also found in the Vajrayana pantheon but they are significantly marginalized. Vajrapani, a preeminent *bodhisattva* of the Vajrayana who previously appeared in Mahayana *sutra*s and Gandhara arts as a *yaksa* chief and Buddha's constant attendant, became the ultimate symbol of enlightenment wielding the *vajra* in his hand. His powerful and rising career evolved since the first century CE chronologically from a simple *yaksa* attending Buddha (Gandhara), one of Buddha's chief acolytes (Mathura), to a powerful *bodhisattva* in Buddha's *mandala* (Deccan caves), as a separate deity (Orissa and Pala arts), and finally attaining his fully independent and demiurgic status equal that of a Buddha in the final phase of Vajrayana arts as Trilokavijaya and Samvara. Vajrayana deities appear both in peaceful and wrathful miens and are generally divided into two categories: the *dharmapala* (Tibetan *chos-skyong* or protecting deities) and *istadevata* (Tibetan *yi-dam* or deities associated with Tantric initiation and consecration). The *dharmapala* includes Mahakala, Yamantaka, Acala, etc. while the *istadevata*, who often appears in the symbolic sexual posture *yuganaddha* (Tibetan *yab-yum*) with his female *prajna* or alternatively represents aniconically as the *ghanta* and *vajra*, includes important deities like Mahavairocana, Heruka, Hevajra, Kalacakra, Samvara/Cakrasamvara, and Vajrabhaivara; these purely Tantric deities belong to the *anuttarayoga-tantra* class. Many Vajrayana practitioners probably would not engage in sexual yoga literally but the practice was widely reported since King Yeshe-O (r. 967-1040 CE) of Guge once issued an edict banning such unBuddhist ritual. The deities of the *yoga-tantra* class, as listed in the Vajradhatu Mandala below, are also the *istadevata* type but they do not involve *yuganaddha*; the principal deity is Vairocana Buddha seated in the center of the *mandala* and surrounded by thirty-six other lesser deities, each occupying their proper directional positions {Klimburg-Salter and Others 1982: 70-74}:

(1) Jina Buddha: Vairocana (center).
(4) Jina Buddhas: Aksobhya (east), Amitabha/Amitayus (west), Amoghasiddhi (north), Ratnasambhava (south).
(4) Buddha *Prajna*s: Locana (southeast), Mamaki (southwest), Pandaravasini/Pandara (northwest), Tara (northeast)
(16) Vajra *Bodhisattva*s surrounding the four Jina Buddhas: Aksobhya (Vajradhara/Vajrapani/Vajrasattva, Vajrakarsa, Vajradhanu, Vajraharsa), Amitabha/Amitayus (Vajranetra/Avalokitesvara, Vajrabuddhi/Manjusri, Vajramanda, Vajravaca), Amoghasiddhi (Vajravisva, Vajramitra, Vajracanda, Vajramusti), Ratnasambhava (Vajragarbha/Vajraratna/Ratnapani, Vajraprabha, Vajrayasti, Vajrapriti).
(4) *Devi*s (Goddesses of Offering) in the inner circle: Vajralasya (Love), Vajramala (Garland), Vajragiti (Song), Vajranrtya (Dance).
(4) *Devi*s (Goddesses of Offering) in the outer circle: Vajradhupa (Incense), Vajrapuspa (Flower), Vajraloka (Lamp), Vajragandha (Scent).
(4) *Dvarapala*s (Door Guardians) on the outermost square: Vajrankusa (east), Vajrasphota (west), Vajravesa/Vajraghanta (north), Vajrapasa (south).

Theravada and Mahayana iconographies consist exclusively of male Buddhas and *bodhisattva*s that are depicted independently; however in the Vajrayana they are frequently accompanied by female *prajna*s or *sakti*s and have *bodhisattva* emanations. For examples, Vairocana has Prajnaparamita as his female *prajna* and Samantabhadra as his *bodhisattva* emanation, Aksobhya (Locana, Vajrapani), Amitabha (Pandaravasini, Avalokitesvara), Amoghasiddhi (Tara, Vajravisva), and Ratnasambhava (Mamaki, Ratnapani); these are known as the Five Jina/Dhyani Buddhas, each administering his own *mandala*. Each Jina Buddha is also assigned with a color and a distinct *mudra*: Vairocana (white, *dharmacakrapravatana-mudra*), Aksobhya (blue, *bhumisparsa-mudra*), Amitabha (red, *dhyana-mudra*), Amoghasiddhi (green, *abhaya-mudra*), and Ratnasambhava (yellow, *varada-mudra*). The pantheon of early *anuttarayoga-tantra* deities encompassed those listed above but it also added a sixth Buddha, namely Vajrasattva, Vajradhara, or Adi-Buddha, with Aksobhya now occupying the center of the *mandala* instead of his usual eastern position in the *yoga-tantra*s. With the appearance of the sixth Buddha, Vairocana seems to have been demoted and also given a *prajna* Vajradhatvisvari or Prajnaparamita like the other Jina Buddhas {Klimburg-Salter and Others 1982: 74-78}{Ghosh 1985: 91-95}{Sharma 2004: 108-121}. This sixth Buddha is theoretically identical with great *anuttarayoga-tantra* deities like Mahavairocana (not to be confused with the fifth Jina Buddha Vairocana), Heruka,

Hevajra, Kalacakra, Samvara/Cakrasamvara, and Vajrabhaivara. In the early years, as in Orissa sculptures (ninth century CE), he was depicted alone holding the *vajra* and *ghanta* in his hands; however subsequently in the sculptures of Bihar and Bengal (eleventh-twelfth centuries CE), he too would be accompanied by a *prajna* in *yuganaddha* with him. In the latest phase of Vajrayana iconography, all deities including minor ones would be depicted in *yuganaddha* symbolizing the non-dual reality or *Vajra*. In the *anuttarayoga-tantra*s, the Five Jina Buddhas are also the personification of the five *skandha*s while the supreme sixth Buddha symbolizes *Vajra* and/or *Sunya*. Thus on the philosophical level, the Vajrayana seems to have embraced the pan-Buddhist idea that all manifested phenomena in the absolute reality are Non-*atman* and *Sunya*. In the *anuttarayoga-tantra* class Aksobhya, whose emanations are the Five Jina Buddhas and manifestations identified with the sixth Buddha, Mahavairocana, Heruka, Hevajra, etc., occupies the center of the *mandala*; this Buddha is synonymous with Sakyamuni with his *bhumisparsa-mudra* which further demonstrates the Vajrayanists' implicit homage to the historical Buddha. In architecture, the Sumtsek of Alchi in Ladakh [4.13-4.15] and Tabo in Spiti are the quintessential examples of the *yoga-tantra* class while the Kumbum in Tibet [6.40-6.41] is the ideal model of the *anuttarayoga-tantra* class. Other hallmark features of the Vajrayana are the heavy emphasis on *prajna* and *sakti* (female energy, consort of the male deity) that have previously been absent from the male-dominated world of the Theravada and Mahayana. In Tantric Buddhism, *prajna* is a preferred term over *sakti*, a Hindu concept, as the latter generally applies to the female side of the lower-ranked deities below Buddha, that is the *bodhisattva*s and below, whereas the former typically represents the enlightened aspect of the female side of Buddhas; the male side of Buddhas is *upaya* and opposite of *prajna*. Thus every enlightened Buddha, according to the Vajrayana, embodies both *prajna* and *upaya*; this is seemingly analogous to the modern psychological concept of the feminine and masculine aspects of the human personality. Buddhist Tantricism also embraces the pan-Indian ideas of spiritual manifestations and emanations. Thus a Buddha, *bodhisattva*, or *prajna* can be manifested in many different forms, each having similar attributes and equal magical power as the original one, and who display peaceful or wrathful miens, has single or multiple limbs, and appears alone or in *yuganaddha*; a male can theoretically be manifested in a female form but this is rare or non-existent. Avalokitesvara, the most popular Mahayana *bodhisattva*, in his Tantric form has as many as 108 different manifestations and the most celebrated of these are Padmapani and Lokesvara. An emanation, on the other hand, is often in the form of a divinity of a lower rank than the original one while a male emanation from a female is undocumented but the reverse is common; thus the Five Jina Buddhas, who are emanated from the sixth Adi-Buddha, have five *bodhisattva* and five *prajna* emanations. Vajrayana iconography is further complicated with the deification of virtually all Buddhist concepts; thus Prajnaparamita, a well-known Mahayana *sutra*, was deified as the goddess Prajnaparamita while Buddha's *usnisa* became Usnisavijaya; this also does not take into account numerous Hindu deities that have been absorbed into the Vajrayana pantheon.

The Vedic religion, which might have been brought to the Indian soil by the nomadic Aryans, was simple in the beginning consisting of worshipping the gods of nature; with the nurture of the native Indians it gradually began to incorporate indigenous religious features such as tribal magics, castes, ritualism, and later in the philosophical speculations of the Upanisads. This was the religious background that Buddha inherited from Vedic Hinduism. However the Buddhism as propounded by Buddha, which was clearly anti-Brahmanism and opposition to castes, vastly differed from Vedic Hinduism in its anti-dogmatism, rationalism, and social ethics that greatly appealed to the underprivileged masses. The Theravada, while upholding Buddha's religion, fell into the traps of religious dogmatism, strict monasticism, and unresponsiveness to reforms which seemingly disregarded the voices of growing dissension within the *Sangha* as observed in the Second and Third Council. On the other hand the Mahayana, in its enthusiasm to accommodate change and overindulgence in the metaphysics, ultimately changed the original Buddhism itself as they practically allowed many features like idolatry and devotionalism to take over Buddhism. The Vajrayana took more radical steps by incorporating many non-Buddhist and seemingly offensive Tantric elements as well as local shamanistic beliefs that it diverged greatly from the original religion as preached by Buddha. Ironically the serene, contemplative, and tolerant religion that Buddha founded would in the end be replaced with the hypersexual and wrathful Tantric deities in the *anuttarayoga-tantra*s trampling on Hindu deities as symptomatic of a religion at the moment of its demise. The final blow to Indian Buddhism was the gradual triumph of Hinduism over Buddhism from the seventh century CE on while the expansion of Islam from the west with its destructions of Buddhist establishments and conversions of many Buddhist countries between the seventh-twelfth centuries CE ultimately annihilated Buddhism in Central Asia. Whatever left of the memories of Buddhism in India, the land of its birth, slowly disappeared through time; but due to its zealous missionaries, Buddhism has not only survived but also prospered beyond the Indian subcontinent. It might have been extinguished in India but the splendors of its arts, architecture, and profound philosophy remain an integral part of the Indian life long after its demise. Recent Buddhist activities from the nineteenth century CE on have greatly contributed to the resurrection of this ancient Indian religion all over India. At the present time the orthodox Theravada School can be found in the Indianized countries of Sri Lanka and Southeast Asia while the progressive Mahayana predominates the Sinicized countries in East Asia and the Vajrayana prevails in Tibet, the Tibetanized states in the Himalaya, and Mongolia. Since the Theravada prevails in southern Asia and the Mahayana predominates in northern Asia, they are also known as Southern and Northern Buddhism respectively.

Part II. Architecture

Buddhist architecture experienced a lengthy evolution since its commencement in the sixth century BCE; from India it would subsequently be propagated in foreign lands during Emperor Asoka's zealous missionaries in the third century BCE. True to the spirit of Buddhism, the development of Buddhist architecture had been an open-ended process during which it absorbed a great deal of foreign elements along its course of travel and modified its forms to acclimatize to the local conditions. Buddhist architecture, alongwith its arts, is above all an extension of its religious philosophy reflecting its numerous sects and diverse schools of thoughts; its forms are therefore a function of its flexible and expansive programs that have been translated into diverse architectural forms as observed throughout Buddhist Asia. Thus the interment of Buddhist relics and its ensuing cult necessitated the construction of the Buddhist *stupa* and the creation of Buddhist images also led to the erection of the temple while the Vajrayana *mandala* theory transformed architectural forms into *mandala*s. Despite its diverse forms manifested throughout Asia, Buddhist architecture can be classified into several distinct categories as determined by their architectural programs, namely the monastery, rock-hewn cave, *stupa*, and temple. Generally these types are not strictly isolated constructions since, as a rule, they are often found congregating in zones or groups of similar structures within the same site [4.4]. Many examples can also be classified as hybrid types; the East Asian pagoda [6.20-6.21], though considered as a Relic *stupa*, also houses Buddhist images for worship and therefore functionally it is also a temple. The Asoka pillars [3.1-3.6], which are among the oldest and most well-known extant Buddhist monuments, are isolated constructions that have exclusively been erected in the Asoka period. Though the holiest sites associated with Buddha's life (Chapter 8) are typologically not parts of this architectural categorization, some of Buddhism's most influential edifices like the Mahabodhi Temple [7.6-7.11] have been erected at these sites and they have contributed greatly to the evolution of Buddhist architecture.

It is crucial to establish the architectural criteria for the proper classification of Buddhist monuments. In general, the presence of Buddhist images or inscriptions is alone sufficient for the attribution to Buddhist origins; however there are many instances where identifications are not as clear-cut. In order to be qualified as a Buddhist structure, it should meet one of the following key requirements:

(1) The commencement was initiated by the Buddhists. Many Asoka pillars have stylistically been a-religious in the beginning and referred in a vaguely neutral term as '*dharma* pillars' ('morality pillars' or 'pillars of Buddha's *Dharma*'). Since Asoka was a well-known Buddhist emperor and his morality edicts were carved on these pillars after his conversion to Buddhism with overwhelming Buddhist tones, these pillars shall justly be classified as Buddhist.

(2) The work was associated with a Buddhist establishment and either occupied or utilized by the Buddhists after its completion. The Asoka pillar at Vaishali [3.1, 3.4] is considered Buddhist since it has been erected near an ancient Buddhist *stupa*. The Nalanda *vihara*s [4.4] had been commenced and patronized by Hindu kings but these were built for and occupied by Buddhist monks for many centuries; hence they are also Buddhist structures regardless whether they have been patronized or erected by Hindu builders. The superstructures of many Bagan temples and *stupa*s like Ananda Temple [7.14-7.15] are crowned with the Indian Hindu *sikhara* but since they have been built for the Buddhist usage they shall also be classified as Buddhist. Moreover after the demise of Buddhism in India, many of its monuments have been taken over, occupied, and reused by other faiths; however, if their original designs have not been modified considerably, they would still be considered as Buddhist as in the case of the Ter Temple [7.2-7.3].

(3) The completed design reflected past and contemporary Buddhist artistic and architectural lineage. When Buddhism rose to prominence in the regions patronized by Buddhist kings, as during the Pala Dynasty (c. 750-1199 CE) in Bihar and Bengal, some non-Buddhist sites might have been built over or converted to the Buddhist usage. Somapura [4.8], for example, might have been constructed over an original Jain site but its design was obviously modeled after the Buddhist monastic architectural tradition of the *vihara*; therefore it shall also be considered as Buddhist.

(4) Wherein factors (1), (2), and (3) are undetermined, inscriptions containing phases or terminologies associated with Buddhism and/or design features showing strong affinities to other Buddhist works will be served as determinative factors. Probably

all early Indian religious architecture, including the Buddhist, had been adopted from secular timber architecture and it was sometimes impossible to determine its exact religious affiliation; hence the method of educated attribution will be implemented for these problematic cases. Lomas Risi cave [5.1-5.2], for instance, has no inscriptions but its classic *caitya*-arched facade shows striking similarities with the Bharhut *torana* [6.7] and the *caityagriha* facades in the Buddhist Deccan caves [5.8]; it therefore shall duly be credited to the Buddhists. The Karna Chopar cave has a swastika, also a common symbol for the Buddhists, and an Asoka inscription mentioning its construction as a shelter during the rainy season. Now the Buddhists also had a well-established annual tradition of congregating and settling down during the rainy season known as the rain retreat (*vassavasa*) and so this cave might have been built as a shelter for the Buddhist monks; hence it shall also be qualified as the work of the Buddhists.

The survey of Buddhist architecture in the following chapters traces the evolution of its multiplicate forms and functions which are organized in according to their proper chronological and stylistical sequences. The monuments will be analyzed from the holistic standpoint so readers can perceive the subtle developmental relationships between those of India and other Asian countries.

Chapter 3. Asoka Pillar

Before the founding of the Maurya Empire, Indian architecture was mostly constructed of timber, at least for the superstructure, and so none survives the ravages of time. Buddhist literature also mentioned many of such buildings throughout northern India and these can still be studied from the sculptural reliefs on early Buddhist *stupa*s [6.5, 7.4-7.6]. The basic designs of the Asoka caves on the Barabar hills [5.1-5.2] and later Buddhist caves in the Deccan were definitely faithful stone translations of freestanding timber prototypes that were undoubtedly prevalent throughout contemporary India. It was not until Emperor Asoka's reign (r. 269-233 BCE) that the first large-scale and permanent stone monuments, in particular the rock-hewn caves [5.1-5.2] and stone pillars named after him [3.1-3.6], were constructed with full imperial finance. The majority was dedicated to Buddhism as Asoka himself was not only the third and most powerful emperor of the Maurya Dynasty (323-184 BCE) but also the greatest Buddhist monarch ever. Due to his generous patronage of Buddhism, Buddhist arts and architecture flourished throughout India and gradually began to spread throughout Asia and they remained the dominant and influential force in India for more than a millennium. Asoka's father and grandfather, Bindusara and Chandragupta respectively, left no permanent historical monuments that could be positively attributed to them; on the other hand Asoka, with his larger-than-life personality, left many monuments that could be identified with certainty as his own creations. These are the stone pillars (*stambha*) bearing his name, his imperial edicts engraved on these pillars and rocky outcroppings, and several rock-hewn caves on the Barabar hills donated to the Ajivika sect (Chapter 5). The following analyses on the subjects of Asoka arts and architecture will attempt to answer some fundamental questions: Was Asoka a Buddhist and his edicts Buddhistic? Were his arts and architecture, particularly the stone pillars and rock-hewn caves, Buddhistic? Could some of the Asoka arts and architecture, specifically the pillars, have been the works of previous emperors? Could foreign sources have inspired Asoka arts and architecture? Let's first have the discussion on Asoka's biography and his relation to the Buddhists.

A. Emperor Asoka and Buddhism

Between c. 1500-600 BCE the territories along the Ganga and Yamuna rivers in North India underwent a period of gradual urbanization and also witnessed the arrivals of the Aryans and later the formation of oligarchic republics during the Vedic Period. Magadha finally defeated all other republics and brought North India under its paramount control; Pataliputra (Patna) became its capital and also of the subsequent Maurya Dynasty. Successive rules of Magadha kings under the Sisunaga (684-424 BCE) and Nanda (424-323 BCE) dynasties would eventually be overthrown by the establishment of the first and most powerful dynasty and empire in India, the Maurya Dynasty (323-184 BCE); its founder was Chandragupta (r. 323-299 BCE), the grandfather of Asoka. He also defeated Seluecus Nikator, a strong Greek commander under Alexander the Great (r. 356-323 BCE) and the ruler of Persia and Near East after the latter's sudden death in 323 BCE; subsequent treaties between Seleucus and Chandragupta in c. 304 BCE increased the size of the Indian empire to encompass the eastern half of Afghanistan. Bindusara (r. 298-270 BCE) was Chandragupta's successor and also the father of Asoka; the latter, who assumed power in c. 273 BCE but actual consecration and ascension happened in c. 269 BCE, inherited a vast empire and brought the Maurya Dynasty to its zenith under his rule. Asoka continued his expansionist policy by conquering more territories; the most famous subjugation involved the annexation of Kalinga (Orissa) in c. 262 BCE. At the height of Asoka's rule his vast empire encompassed eastern Afghanistan (west), the foothills of the Himalaya, Kashmir, the Nepalese Terai (north), Bengal (east), and the Krishna River (south). The rules of Chandragupta, Bindusara, and Asoka also brought their empire into contact with Persia, Near East, and North Africa, which were then under the colonial rules of the Greek kings. Diplomatic emissaries, possibly accompanied with cultural and artistic exchanges, between India and its western neighbors were well-documented by contemporary Indian and Greek historians. Megasthenes, Seleucus's Greek ambassador to Chandragupta's court at Pataliputra, described in details in his book 'Indika' about Chandragupta's opulent court life and his vast empire. Some of Asoka's edicts (Major Rock Edict II, V, XIII) also recorded Buddhist missionaries and cultural contacts with the Greek colonies in Persia, Near East, and North Africa {Hultzsch 1969: 3-4, 10, 24-25}; it is clear that the first three monarchs of the Maurya Dynasty were very cosmopolitan, though not necessarily outward looking. This new epoch in the early Maurya Dynasty was undoubtedly full of imperial grandeur, national identity and pride, and international rivalry which, in my opinions, gave the impetus for the creations of the permanent monumental arts and architecture in India. Asoka's forty-year long reign at the pinnacle of the Maurya Dynasty had all the qualities of an enlightened rule including a centralized government based on the rule of laws as revealed in rock (RE) and pillar edicts (PE), the arts and architecture like the stone pillars and rock-hewn caves that were representative of the imperial house, and a universal religion (Buddhism) that deemed acceptable and practiced by all Indians and the world beyond.

Up to the present, over forty-two sites throughout the Indian subcontinent have been found with the Asoka stone pillars and rock surfaces containing his edicts in India (36), Nepal (2), Pakistan (2), and Afghanistan (2); the earliest discovery of these sites was in 1750 CE and the latest 1989 CE {Chowdhury 1997: 59-61}. The first scholar who successfully deciphered the Brahmi script, in which most of the Asoka edicts had been written, was James Princep in 1837 CE; the first translated edict was the one on the Delhi-Topra pillar. It was from the translations of these edicts in conjunction with cross-referencing Buddhist literature that their author was firmly identified as Emperor Asoka; in fact his name and legends had already been preserved in the Buddhist Pali chronicles of Sri Lanka for nearly two millennia. Asoka called himself 'Devanampriya Priyadarsin' in his edicts and this name also appeared in the Dipavamsa and Mahavamsa, the Sri Lankan chronicles {Hultzsch 1969: xvi-xvii, xxvii-xxxvi}. There were two versions of Asoka's life: one was a mixture of myths, legends, and facts, which were understandably written by the Buddhists and hence not entirely reliable sources, while the other was historical records in stone in the forms of pillar and rock edicts issued by the emperor himself. The Buddhist texts filled additional background details about his life whereas the edicts were valuable in evaluating the historicity of these stories. Prior to his conversion to Buddhism in c. 260 BCE, Asoka was nicknamed by the Buddhists as 'Asoka the Wicked' for his cruel and evil deeds. Theravada Buddhists maintained that Asoka killed all ninety-nine of his half-brothers, except his uterine brother Tissa, in the contest for the imperial throne. But this story can not be verified as Asoka's own edicts (Major RE V) revealed that his brothers, sisters, and relatives were still living thirteen years after the alleged murders of his brothers. The Theravadins also stated that Asoka's uterine brother Tissa was the famous monk Moggaliputa Tissa who was the presiding head of Third Buddhist Council; Mahendra and Sanghamitra, Asoka's son and daughter, reportedly traveled to Sri Lanka after this council to convert that island to Buddhism. Though the edicts did not specifically confirm these missionaries to Sri Lanka, Buddhist missionaries, which were primarily administered by the Dharma Mahamatras (Ministers of Moralities) appointed by Asoka, had actually been sent throughout the world as recorded in his edicts. Mahayana Buddhists, like the Theravadins, also presented the same evil image about Asoka in the Asokavadana in which Asoka allegedly cut off the heads of 500 ministers, burnt 500 women alive, and built hellish prisons to torture the inmates {Strong 1983: 210-219}. The image of Asoka as an evil emperor in Buddhist literature could not be historically confirmed since it was customary for the Buddhists to dramatize the moral story between evil (the wicked Asoka before his conversion to Buddhism) and good (the benevolent Asoka after his conversion to Buddhism) to inculcate morality in the devotees, as also popularized in the *jataka*s. Asoka was certainly not a benevolent emperor before his Buddhist conversion as told in his own words from the edicts; he ordered, with much remorse later, the famous conquest of Kalinga in c. 262 BCE that cost hundreds of thousand lives and 150,000 deported (Major RE XIII) {Hultzsch 1969: 47-49}. Curiously, for whatever reasons, the Pali scriptures were notably silent about this infamous war by Asoka as if it never existed to them. Historical evidence makes clear that Asoka, prior to his conversion to Buddhism, was a powerful ruler with aggressive policies toward his neighbors and people had much to fear and obey to his authority.

Asoka's wicked image began to change after his conversion to Buddhism in c. 260 BCE when he made a pilgrimage to the Mahabodhi Temple in Bodhgaya [7.6-7.11, 8.3-8.4] to pay homage to the spot where Buddha attained Enlightenment (Major RE VIII) {Hultzsch 1969: 15}. He also made numerous pilgrimages to other sites associated with Buddha's life in Nepal [8.1-8.2] and India [8.5-8.10]. This turning point in Asoka's life happened two years after the Kalinga war; the mass slaughter and destruction of the Kalingas, according to the emperor's own confessions, led to his decision to renounce violence and converted to Buddhism and he swore to permanently replace armed conquest with the conquest of morality (*dharmavijaya*) (Major RE XIII) {Hultzsch 1969: 47-49}. In the remaining years of his life, Asoka actively involved in the affairs of the *Sangha* (Sanchi, Sarnath, and Kausambi PEs), erected numerous stone pillars, and enlarged a few existing Buddhist *stupa*s (Rummindei and Nigali Sagar PEs) {Hultzsch 1969: 159-165}. Asoka's concern with moral ethics had induced him to issue imperial edicts to be engraved in stone; these were his rescripts on proper moral conducts to be addressed to his subjects throughout the empire. The emperor also established the Dharma Mahamatra (Ministry of Morality) to oversee religious and moral affairs of his people as well as disseminate missionaries throughout the world (Major RE V) {Hultzsch 1969: 10}. The key issue remains whether Asoka's edicts on morality or *dharma* were actually inspired by Buddha's *Dharma*; some scholars have alleged that the *dharma* on Asoka's edicts was too general and could have belonged to any of the contemporary religions. As one scholar observed {Chowdhury 1997: 78}:

> The general code of ethics and rules of behaviour as defined by Asoka are certainly familiar to Buddhist teaching and occur in Buddhist scripture. However, it needs to be kept in mind that such ideas are not unknown to Jaina teaching nor to various other sramanic sects which were popular during that period...The Asoka *dhamma* not only addressed itself to a large spectrum of opinion but drew its inspiration from an equally large body of ethical doctrine.

It has been well established that Asoka was an impartial ruler and, though as an ardent Buddhist, he also valued and respected all religions by showering them with gifts (Major RE VIII, XII / Major PE VII) {Hultzsch 1969: 15, 21-22, 133-137}; these would be expected of an enlightened and secular ruler and a devout Buddhist, a tradition which continued in later Indian emperors. However, many of his edicts on morality are definitely Buddhistic in tone such as the ban of animal sacrifice (Major RE I), the protection of animals from being hunted or killed (Major PE V), the prohibition of festivals involving the slaughter of animals (Major RE I), medical treatments for humans and animals (Major RE II), the conquest by morality rather than armed conquest (Major RE XIII), etc. A few remaining edicts on morality were on proper behaviors toward fellow humans which also had Buddhist overtones; the implicit endorsement of vegetarianism was also bordering on an imperial policy (Major RE I). Hindu Brahmanism was undoubtedly the most to suffer from such extreme measures by Asoka while the Buddhists were obviously the most benefited. Thus there is no evidence suggesting a Buddhist emperor like Asoka to have derived inspirations from non-Buddhist sources for his moral proclamations since these could also be found in Buddha's *Dharma* and Asoka was certainly very knowledgeable on Buddhist scriptures (Major RE III).

How did the traditional Buddhist accounts on Asoka's life after his conversion differ from those on the edicts? The Theravadins told the story of Asoka being converted by a novice Buddhist monk named Nigrodha after hearing the latter's sermon and Moggaliputa Tissa was his preceptor. After the conversion, the story went on to say that the pious emperor immediately withdrew his patronage to other non-Buddhist sects and transferred his benefactions (donations, construction projects, etc.) exclusively to the Buddhists {Chowdhury 1997: 44}. The Mahayanists maintained a similar position on Asoka's service to Buddhism with minor differences; in the Asokavadana, Samudra was the monk who converted Asoka and Upagupta was his senior teacher and it too credited the emperor for building 84,000 *stupa*s and *caitya*s for the Buddhists throughout his empire. Asoka was also described as a strong protector of the *Sangha* who showed no mercy to those who offended the Buddhists; it has been said that Asoka killed 18,000 Ajivikas and burnt the whole family of the offenders inside their houses for ridiculing Buddha {Strong 1983: 214-221, 232}. The stories about Nigrodha and Moggaliputa Tissa in the Theravada and their equivalents Samudra and Upagupta in the Mahayana are certainly sectarian in nature; these monks might have actually existed but their specific names are irrelevant in this context. The stories about Asoka's constructions of *stupa*s, *caitya*s, and *sangharama*s are certainly true as recorded in his edicts but the 84,000 number given by the Buddhists could be an exaggeration. What about Asoka's killings of non-Buddhist offenders to defend his religion? This might be factual but from his edicts and his generosity toward the Ajivikas (the Sudama and Visvakarma caves on the Barabar hills in Bihar were his donations to this non-Buddhist sect) rendered these wicked stories as pure fabrication and sectarian in nature.

There are several important issues that need clarifications: Why did Asoka choose Buddhism? To what extend was he devoted to the Buddhist cause? One might easily be misled to the conclusion that Asoka converted to Buddhism because of his remorse after the Kalinga conquest but this is just a part of the whole picture as a mighty emperor like Asoka would not have blindly professed his faith to a religion simply because he was feeling guilty. The Jains and Ajivikas, the latter's founder was Makkhali Gosala and a pupil of the Jain founder Nigantha Nataputtra, were naked ascetics and their religious observances of non-injury to living things were often taken to the extreme; the Jain founder fasted to death as a gesture of complete detachment from materialism. Moreover Hindu Brahmanism was certainly an exclusive belief where most social and religious powers were hereditary vested in the privileged *brahmin*s who considered themselves superior even to the *ksatrya*s; Asoka, and Buddha, was a *ksatrya* and certainly would not find the *brahmin*s favorable. Brahmanism emphasized purified cleansing, external rituals, and animal sacrifices while the caste system remained inflexible and served only the powerful elites, particularly the *brahmin*s; these clearly stood in contrast with Buddha's teachings and Asoka's equality and secularism as reflected in his edicts. B. M. Barua made this perceptive comparison between Brahmanism and Buddhism {Barua 1968: 323}:

> The main points of difference between secular Brahminism on the one hand and Buddhism on the other were that one was sacerdotal, the other rational in form; one clannish, the other universal in spirit; the commitment of one was to forms and procedures, that of the other to the inner essence of the thing; that one sought to base domestic and social relations on caste basis, the other on that of morality and piety. Thus no other form of government than monarchical found favor in Brahmanical rajadharma, while in Buddha's view the form, whether monarchical, oligarchical or democratic, was immaterial, if the state in any form had fulfilled all its main obligations.

Buddhism is a rational, non-violent, tolerant, ethical, egalitarian, non-ascetic, and certainly non-exclusive religion; therefore Asoka might have found it to be worthy of conversion by him, his people, and the world beyond; it is a religion seemingly imbued with universal humanistic principles which would deem acceptable anywhere compared to other Indian religions. Although Buddhism was Asoka's personal religion, nowhere in his edicts that he desired his subjects to be converted to Buddhism; in fact he maintained his generosity toward all religions and this made him a remarkably impartial and secular leader. And nowhere did he admit that his edicts on morality had been inspired or instructed by the Buddhists; the Buddhists' inflated claims about Asoka's selfless generosity toward them have evidently been discredited in his edicts. The Rummindei Edict reveals that even Lumbini, the place of Buddha's nativity, was still required to pay 'an eighth share of the produce;' this edict clearly contradicts the Buddhists' claim in the Divyavadana that Asoka spent 100,000 gold pieces on the Lumbini visit {Hultzsch 1969: 164-165}. It is obvious that Asoka was not an emperor who would foolishly squander his treasury for the cause of any religion, including his own Buddhism. While many Asoka pillars have also been erected within Buddhist localities, this does not conclusively prove Asoka's submission to Buddhism and Asoka's morality edicts, though clearly inspired by Buddhist ethics, mention no such Buddhist affiliation. There might be other ulterior motives for Asoka's erections of these pillars and edicts in Buddhist establishments as suggested by Niharranjan Ray that "the Sarnath quadripartite is on the other hand an exhibition of imperial pomp, power, and authority before the Buddhist monks of Sarnath…" {Ray 1975: 28}. The ban of certain festivals, the rescripts of morality, and the establishment of the Dharma Mahamatra to oversee proper behaviors of his subjects all over the empire, though appearing for the good of his people on the surface, can be likened to censorships and spies to silence his critics in order to ensure the stability of his throne and extend the lifespan of the Maurya Dynasty. In addition to the incessant inspection tours on morality throughout his empire, the emperor also required his edicts to be read in public three times a year, not to mention they had already been carved on pillars and boulders in every corner of his empire. This kind of benevolent control was necessary after repeated revolts in the northwestern frontier city of Taxila in Gandhara (Pakistan) and the devastating war with the Kalingas; the emperor's real intentions could have been to assimilate the peoples in the conquered territories into the Indian schemes. Asoka also had this message to the people in the conquered and vassal territories (Dhauli RE II):

> My only intention is that they live without fear of me, that they may trust me and that they I may give them happiness, not sorrow. Furthermore, they should understand that the king will forgive those who can be forgiven, and that he wishes to encourage them to practice Dhamma so that they may attain happiness in this world and the next.

Who and what could be forgiven were up to the emperor's will as his gentle message was accompanied with an implicit threat of punishment to those who disobeyed him; the edicts also openly endorsed Buddha's *Dharma* but they apparently did not enforce a full conversion on his subjects. It is clear that the emperor did not completely abandon his imperial ambitions and duties even after he became a Buddhist. Those who violated his moral decrees would be punished as recorded in one of his Aramaic edicts (Laghman RE I-II) {Mukherjee 1984: 12, 14}:

> In the year 16, King Priyadarsi dispersed and pushed out of the prosperous population the lovers of what is hunting of creatures and fishes and that which is worthless work.

This edict in Afghanistan published in Asoka's sixteenth regnal year (c. 253 BCE) also found similar echoes in the Delhi-Topra PE V about ten years later (c. 243 BCE); it showed how extreme measures had been taken to punish those who violated Asoka's rules on morality. It is unclear if these edicts, such as animal hunting and morality rescripts in general, might have been exploited as an excuse to punish non-Indian people in the northwestern frontier whose repeated revolts were documented in Buddhist literature; the edict also reveals that Asoka's religious zeal was bordered on fanaticism.

From the analyses above a clear image of Asoka begins to emerge that Asoka had been an ambitious and aggressive ruler prior to his conversion to Buddhism; after the conversion, the destructive side of his personality would be channeled into more positive endeavors and Buddhism was no doubt a big factor in this change. His aspirations were effectively dedicated to higher purposes; his eternal words in the edicts, his monumental pillars and extensive construction programs, and his generous donations to the various religions are tangible testaments to the constructive side of his personality. He was indeed the first secular ruler and a model for later Indian monarchs who were generally impartial toward all religions like Asoka before them. On the other hand, his overbearing and powerful personality remained strong long after his conversion to Buddhism; indeed he was the man in control of his religion and all religions rather than the other way around. Asoka's replacement of military conquests with cultural assimilation of his subjects throughout the empire has proven to be the least costly and most glorious of all his conquests. His administration was certainly secular but many of his morality edicts revealed a passionately religious side of his personality which might not be pragmatic at times; without a doubt religion, particularly Buddhism, played an important role behind many of his imperial policies.

B. Emperor Asoka's Edicts

The following discussions will delve into the classification, chronology, and circumstances in which these edicts were originally issued as well as their relations to the pillars and rock surfaces upon which they were engraved. Asoka's edicts were disseminated throughout his vast empire and hence several languages had been employed in the inscriptions so that the local population could read and understand his imperial policies. All Asoka's known rock and pillar edicts and cave inscriptions were issued after his conversion to Buddhism in c. 260 BCE. The majority of the edicts were written in Brahmi (India, Nepal) with a few in Kharosthi (Pakistan), Aramaic and Greek (Afghanistan, Pakistan); the Brahmi script is apparently not related to the Harappan script since there was over a millennium time lapse between them. These Asoka edicts have been carved on stone pillars, rock surfaces, and a rare stone tablet so that, in Asoka's own words, they might be of 'long duration' and endured 'as long as the moon and the sun shall shine.' Asoka also desired his words to last like Buddha's *Dharma* (Rupnath, Calcutta-Bairat, Delhi-Topra Edict VII) and hence his choice of stone was perfect for this purpose. Finally, the Maski RE makes it clear that these edicts have been issued by him since he identified himself in the inscription as 'Devanampriya Asoka' (the Beloved of the Gods Asoka). The Asoka edicts can be classified into three categories {Hultzsch 1969: liv-lv}{Chowdhury 1997: 49-61}:

1. Morality Edicts

These are rescripts issued to his subjects on proper moral and religious conducts.

(a) Rupnath, Sahasram, Bairat, Calcutta-Bairat, Maski, Erragudi, Gavimath, Palkigundu, Rajula-Mandagiri, Gujarra, Ahraura, Bahapur, Panguraria, Nittur, and Udegolam Minor REs (c. 255 BCE / four edicts / Brahmi): Asoka's initial reflections on his religious progress and involvement with Buddhism prior to the issue of the morality edicts.

(b) Brahmagiri, Siddapura, Jatinga-Ramesvara, Erragudi, Sannati Minor REs (c. 255 BCE / one edict / Brahmi): Asoka's first edicts on basic moral conducts.

(c) Girnar, Kalsi, Shahbazgarhi, Mansehra, Dhauli, Jaugada, Bombay-Sopara, Erragudi, Sannati, and Rajula-Mandagiri Major REs (c. 255-243 BCE / sixteen edicts / Brahmi, Kharosthi): Elaborations on moralilty already issued in (1b); Shahbazgarhi and Mansehra (Gandhara) were written in Kharosthi.

(d) Laghman, Pul-i-Darunta, Shar-i-Kuna, and Kandahar Minor REs (c. 253 BCE / six edicts / Aramaic, Greek): Morality edicts like (1b-1c) with special rescripts on the ban of animal hunting.

(e) Taxila Minor PE (c. 253 BCE / one edict / Aramaic): Morality edict like (1d).

(f) Delhi-Topra, Delhi-Mirath, Lauriya Araraj, Lauriya Nandangarh **[3.2]**, Rampurva 1, and Allahabad-Kausambi Major PEs (c. 243-242 BCE / seven edicts / Brahmi): Asoka's reflections on the edicts in (1b-1c) in the early years with further elaborations on the contents and definitions of morality.

2. Buddhist Edicts

These confirm Asoka's conversion and patronage of Buddhism.

(a) Rummindei PE (c. 249 BCE / one edict / Brahmi): Asoka's visit to the historical Sakyamuni Buddha's nativity in Lumbini **[8.1-8.2]** in his twentieth regnal

year; the town is now in Nepal but certainly within Asoka's empire then.
(b) Nigali Sagar PE (c. 249 BCE / one edict / Brahmi): Asoka's visit and enlargement of the *stupa* of Konakamuni Buddha also in his twentieth regnal year; the location, like Lumbini, is also in Nepal.
(c) Allahabad-Kausambi, Sanchi [6.3], and Sarnath [3.3, 3.6] PEs (c. 247-242 BCE / three edicts / Brahmi): Asoka's threat of expelling Buddhist monks who disrupted or caused schism in the *Sangha*.
3. Donative Edicts and Inscriptions

These confirmed Asoka's generous donations to non-Buddhist sects despite his conversion to Buddhism and they evidently demonstrated his impartiality, hence his secularism, toward all Indian religions.
(a) Barabar caves inscriptions (c. 257 BCE, c. 250 BCE / three inscriptions / Brahmi): Asoka's donations of the Sudama and Visvakarma caves to the Ajivika sect.
(b) Allahabad-Kausambi PE (c. 247-242 BCE / one edict / Brahmi): Under Asoka's order all donations made by Queen Kaluvati (Queen Edict), obviously his queen, to be credited to her name.

Close scrutiny of Asoka's edicts has shed some light on the chronology and progress of their contents; in all Asoka had issued a total of forty-one different edicts and three distinct inscriptions throughout his empire. In many cases one edict has been found in several locations and these are proofs that some surfaces were immediately carved after the edicts had been issued while the others might have been carved at a later time on previously blank surfaces; all rock edicts in (1a-1b) were apparently the first to be engraved in c. 255 BCE with (1a Rupnath) was the earliest of them all. The contents of the edicts were the amalgamation of previous paper and verbal rescripts first ordered by Asoka in c. 258 BCE and contemporary edicts; (1c-1e) were next to be issued and engraved while the PEs (1f) were the last to be engraved. The combined contents of (1a-1b) suggest that Asoka's morality edicts could have certainly been inspired by Buddhism; they also share similar contents, circumstances, and timelines and appear to have been issued in an uncoordinated and spontaneous manner. They show Asoka's initial inexperience on how to proceed and execute the transition from paper and verbal rescripts to actually engrave them on permanent stone surfaces as edicts; he seemed to be recalling from his past memories and then ordered his men to engrave them on stone as edicts. (1a Rupnath) also reveals Asoka's first order to engrave his edicts on rocks and stone pillars (c. 255 BCE) "wherever there are stone pillars" in his realm. This might imply, as many scholars

have argued, that some of Asoka pillars could have actually existed before this edict but without the engravings on them and therefore these pillars might or might not be of Asoka's own creations. However Asoka clearly stated in later edicts (Delhi-Topra PE VII in c. 242 BCE) that the '*dharma* pillars,' as he called these stone monuments, had been erected by him; this issue will be discussed later. (1d Pul-i-Darunta) is a rare edict engraved on a stone tablet which also satisfied Asoka's original requirements (Delhi-Topra PE VII) that the edicts should be carved on permanent materials. While the Asoka pillars serve as the ultimate imperial symbol the edicts themselves, most of which bear no relationship to the pillars upon which they have been engraved, carry important imperial sanctions to the emperor's subjects; apparently his aspirations for authority and enduring fame in history were the primary motives behind the creation of these monumental pillars. The subjects of Asoka's edicts, like the pillars themselves, are not without controversies as many scholars would like to connect them with Achaemenid Persia, which they believed to be the inspiration behind the Asoka edicts. Niharranjan Ray stated his view that {Ray 1975: 15-16}:

> The fact remains that the inscription themselves indicate the extent to which Asoka was indebted to his great Achaemenian predecessor Darius, not only for the idea of making his royal edicts known throughout his empire but also for the form and style of the inscriptions themselves.

In fact there are substantial parallels between earlier Achaemenid Persia and Maurya India as they once shared a common border; indeed communications and exchanges have been recorded between the two countries from the earliest times. Both had highly centralized governments and religions also played an important role in their empires while imperial arts and architecture were also very prominent in both countries; both governed vast empires and recognized many official languages {Ghirshman 1964: 128-241}. However, these are only superficial similarities as one might as well argue that a strong centralized government would be vital for India's survival after the Greek invasions by Alexander the Great between c. 327-325 BCE. It was also absolutely necessary to have multiple languages to ensure proper and uniformed understanding of the imperial policies throughout the vast empire. The decision to publicize Asoka's edicts was also due to his own ambitions and intimate associations with the Buddhists after his conversion to Buddhism; there were absolutely no equivalence between the forms and contents of Asoka's edicts, particularly his famous *dhar-*

mavijaya, with Darius's inscriptions. It is also significant that inscriptions on permanent surfaces have also been found in abundance throughout the Indus Civilization but it was Asoka who carried this deep-rooted Indian tradition to the monumental scale. Following Asoka's lead, later kings, artisans, artists, and sculptors have also left inscriptive marks on their monuments as testaments to their existence and ambition in Indian history. On the other hand, there are minor elements in Indian arts and architecture that may be qualified as Persian and Near Eastern origins such as the lion, honeysuckle motif, winged animals, etc.; however, these were easily recognized as foreign in the Indian context and would subsequently be assimilated or replaced with indigenous elements. It is appropriate at this point to begin the discussions on the monumental stone pillars which were the most representative of Maurya imperial arts and architecture and undoubtedly of Asoka's creations.

C. Asoka Pillars

Since first reported by the British in the eighteenth century CE and subsequent decipherment of the Brahmi script, these pillars have attracted much scholarly debates about them; these Brits, however, were not the first to notice these monumental pillars. Other prominent Buddhist pilgrims visited India in the past, most famously the Chinese monks Fa-hsien (in India between 399-414 CE) and Hsuan-tsang (in India between 629-645 CE), also wrote extensively in their travelogues on these massive stone monuments. The pillars, like the rocky outcrops, served as surfaces on which the edicts would ultimately be engraved; unlike the rock edicts, which have been found as far as Afghanistan, all pillars and their edicts can only be found in North India in Bihar, Uttar Pradesh, and Madhya Pradesh in the heart of the Maurya Empire. Besides carrying Asoka's rescripts, these inscribed boulders and conspicuous pillars could also serve to demarcate the cultural and political borders between India and its immediate neighbors. These massive monolithic pillars, the heaviest weighting over fifty tons, are in fine-grained sandstone sunk deep into the ground with the heights of their exposed portions between 20'-70' above the ground. All pillars have the characteristic glistening polish that is the hallmark of Asoka and Maurya arts; these freestanding and imposing pillars no doubt left deep impressions on the minds of those who saw them in the past. At the present, only two pillars are intact at Vaishali **[3.1, 3.4]** and Lauriya Nandangarh while the majority is either broken or missing capitals; another three pillars at Allahabad-Kausambi, Delhi-Topra, and Delhi-Mirath have been relocated to different locations in the past.

A typical pillar is divided into three components: the footing, the shaft, and the capital **[3.3]**; most pillars have a consistent and slight taper of one degree with an estimated proportion of the individual parts to the whole pillar is one (capital), one (below ground shaft), and four (above ground shaft). The exposed segment of the shaft above ground typically has a glistening polish and serves as the surface for engraving the edicts while the one below ground is dressed roughly, except for the pillars of Kumrahar Hall and Gotihawa which were smoothened, for enhanced friction and better anchoring with the surrounding ground. Depending on the strength of the soil and the weight of the pillar, it might rest directly on bedrock or compacted soil without the need for a footing slab (Sanchi, Allahabad-Kausambi, Kausambi, Rampurva 2, and Sankisa); other pillars were provided with thick stone slab footings to prevent sinking (Lauriya Nandangargh, Sarnath, Delhi-Topra, Rampurva 1, Gotihawa, etc.). If the underground soil had been deemed unstable, the footing slab would be reinforced around its perimeter with deep wood pilings for further stability (Lauriya Nandangargh). In the case of the heavy Vaishali pillar, a stepped footing carved out of a single stone slab would be employed to effectively dissipate the load of the shaft, provide better anchoring, and stabilize the surrounding soil; high compressive strength bricks and clay slabs had also been used as footings for the stone pillars of Kumrahar Hall. After the erection of the pillar, the excavation pit would be filled with compacted soil while brick and clay foundation walls were sometimes built around them for further reinforcement (Sarnath, Sanchi); the ground surface were usually paved with bricks or stone. The capital has three main components: the lotiform bell, the abacus, and the crowned animal; there are several echinus rings between the bell and the abacus and between the abacus and the shaft. The capital and the shaft were typically mortised and joined together at the center by a metal dowel as found in the Rampurva 1 pillar. Sculpting the shaft and the capital separately and erecting them jointly at the construction site would obviously reduce the added weight, length, and possible damage to the pillar during its transportation. Moreover, it is evidently more feasible and economical to work on individual sections separately and join them together than sculpting and erecting a giant monolithic pillar in one piece since a damaged section could be speedily replaced without having to recarve an entirely new pillar.

The following survey documents the extant pillars and their capitals that have been discovered up to the present time and there may be more to be uncovered in

Asoka Pillar

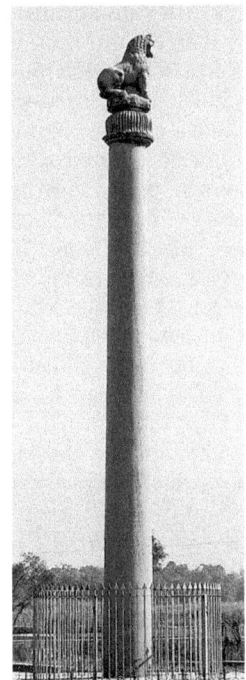

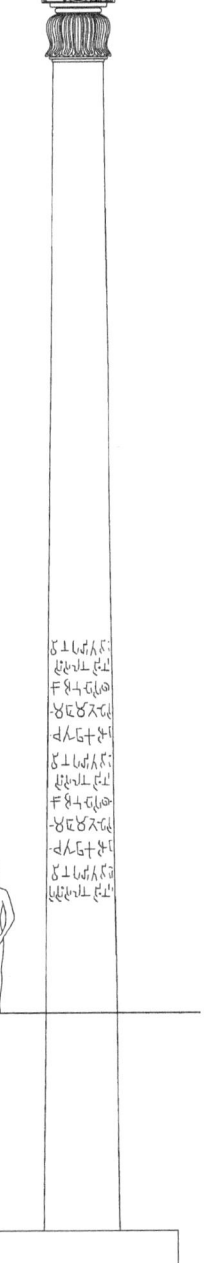

3.1. Vaishali pillar (*far above*)
c. 258 BCE
Basarh Bakhira- India

3.2. Lauriya Nandangargh pillar (*far below*)
c. 245 BCE
Lauriya Nandangargh- India

3.3. Sarnath pillar (restored) (*left*)
c. 241-233 BCE
Sarnath- India

3.4. Vaishali capital (*above left*)
c. 258 BCE
Basarh Bakhira- India

3.5. Rampurva 2 capital (*above right*)
c. 250 BCE
Rampurva- India
National Museum, Delhi- India

3.6. Sarnath capital (restored)
c. 241-233 BCE
Sarnath- India
Sarnath Museum, Sarnath- India

the future; the edicts engraved on some of these pillars have already been discussed in the previous section {Nagar 1992: 19-55}{Pandey 1982: 47-62}{Ray 1975: 19-26}{Gupta 1980: 19-51, 79-136, 237-246}{Singh 2003: 246-247}:

- Delhi-Topra (pillar missing capital, seven Asoka edicts): Most Asoka pillars have six PEs but only this one has an additional PE VII. The pillar originally stood in Topra but was removed to Delhi by Sultan Feroz Shah in the fourteenth century CE using a '42-wheel cart' on land and 'a number of large boats tied together' to float the pillar down the river; this method might have also been employed in Asoka's time to transport these enormous pillars from the quarry at Chunar to their erection sites.
- Delhi-Mirath (pillar missing capital, six Asoka edicts): This pillar was also removed from its original location at Mirath (Meerut) to Delhi by Sultan Feroz Shah.
- Lauriya Araraj (pillar missing capital, six Asoka edicts): The missing capital of this pillar was believed by some scholars to have been crowned with a *garuda*, a winged bird-human and vehicle of the Hindu god Visnu; but others speculated that the original crown had been replaced by a *garuda* during the Gupta Dynasty (320-647 CE). Could the crown animal be a winged lion or griffin, as also appeared on the abacus of the Udaigiri-Vidisa capital, instead of a *garuda*? Even the winged bird-human in Asoka's time certainly did not have the same religious meanings as the *garuda* in later Hinduism; in the same token the bull, which also crowned many Asoka pillars, certainly could not be equated with the bull Nandi of Siva. The animals on the crowns of the Asoka pillars did not appear to have religious symbolisms since even a camel, which is scarcely considered as a religious symbol, had also been depicted on the Udaigiri-Vidisa abacus. Moreover why would Asoka, a known secular Buddhist king, want to crown a well-known Hindu symbol on his pillars? My conclusion is that the *garuda* could not have crowned this particular pillar.
- Nigali Sagar (pillar missing capital, one Asoka edict): This pillar carries an Asoka edict recorded his visit and enlargement of the *stupa* of Konakamuni Buddha in his twentieth regnal year (c. 249 BCE), which was also the same erection date for the Rummindei (Lumbini) pillar; the location of the *stupa* and the capital of this pillar have not been found. This pillar, together with the Rummindei and Gotihawa pillars, were discovered in the Nepalese Terai appar-

ently within the former territory of the ancient Sakya Republic and Buddha's homeland. The Gotihawa pillar, which has no edicts and presumably commemorated the birthplace of Krakucchanda Buddha, is also similar in material and design as the pillars at the ruined Kumrahar Hall; hence these alongwith the Nigali Sagar and Lumbini pillars were likely erected by Asoka around c. 249 BCE.

- Rummindei (pillar missing capital, one Asoka edict) [8.2]: This pillar was also erected in the same year as Nigali Sagar, and possibly also Gotihawa, in c. 249 BCE to commemorate Asoka's pilgrimage to Lumbini, the nativity of Sakyamuni Buddha and the historical founder of Buddhism. The usual bell-shaped capital has been recovered showing 'the usual festoons in the face of the big cyma' {Rijal 1996: 117} but the horse, which Hsuan-tsang mentioned to have once crowned its capital, can not be traced.

- Allahabad-Kausambi (pillar and an abacus, eight Asoka edicts): This pillar contains six Major PEs, one Queen Edict, and a Schism Edict; it might have been moved from its original location in Kausambi to Allahabad by Emperor Akbar in the sixteenth century CE to commemorate the founding of this city. Another broken pillar without a capital still stands in its original location at Kausambi but it contains no edicts; thus the Kausambi and relocated Allahabad-Kausambi pillar could have originally been a pair like the Rampurva pillars. The capital of the Allahabad-Kausambi pillar, as one may expect its usual lotiform bell shape like all other Asoka capitals, is missing but it might have been mounted by a lion. Only its round abacus has been found which is decorated with honeysuckles alternating with stylized lotuses and small rosettes with the bead-and-reel patterns below; this abacus is almost identical with that of the Sankisa capital and hence they appear to be close in erection date.

- Rampurva 1 (pillar and a capital, six Asoka edicts): This pillar and Rampurva 2 were discovered together and they could have been a pair but only this one has Asoka edicts. The top segment of the shaft has a protruding tenon with a mortised hole in the center to receive a 4"-diameter copper dowel of about 2' long in order to secure the capital to the shaft below. The capital is the usual bell-shaped lotiform having plump bulging and crowned with a sejant lion; the round abacus is decorated with pairs of pecking geese facing each other and alternated with single geese. The double echinus rings between the abacus and the bell lotiform alongwith the bottom two astra-

gals joining the shaft are all plain.

- Sanchi (pillar and a capital, one Asoka edict) [6.3]: Only the stump of this 42' high pillar in front of Sanchi Stupa I remains and it also bears a Schism Edict on its shaft; the capital is of the usual bell-shaped lotiform of graceful bulging which is crowned with quadruple addorsed lions while its round abacus is decorated with pairs pecking geese facing each other and alternated with honeysuckle motifs. One of the double echinus rings between the abacus and the bell lotiform is plain while the other has a rope motif; the bottom two astragals joining the shaft are plain. According to John Marshall, it was originally not mounted with a *dharmacakra* (wheel of *dharma* or *Dharma*) like the Sarnath capital and hence stylistically it is of a transitional design {Marshall 1983: 25-26}; however, in my opinion the *dharmacakra* likely surmounted this capital.

- Sarnath (pillar and a capital, one Asoka edict) [3.3, 3.6]: This pillar only has an Asoka Schism Edict like the Sanchi pillar; it is considered the highest artistic achievement of all Asoka pillars. Its glistening capital is of the usual bell-shaped lotiform with graceful bulging; it is crowned with quadruple addorsed lions and likely surmounted with a *dharmacakra* since Hsuan-tsang once saw similar *dharmacakra* mounts at the eastern gate of the Jetavana Monastery in Sravasti. The round abacus is decorated with four popular and probably sacred animals, namely the lion, elephant, horse, and bull that are alternated with four *dharmacakra*s in between; the animals are depicted in clockwise movement as in the direction of the *pradaksina* path. The double echinus rings between the abacus and the bell lotiform alongwith the bottom two astragals joining the shaft are all plain.

- Lauriya Nandangarh (pillar intact, six Asoka edicts) [3.2]: This pillar and the Vaishali pillar are the only two pillars remaining virtually intact to this day but only this one has Asoka edicts. The capital also has the usual bell-shaped lotiform with plump bulging and it is crowned with a sejant lion with its rear end projecting beyond the edge of the round abacus; the latter is decorated with pecking geese walking gracefully in clockwise procession. A single echinus ring between the abacus and the bell lotiform is decorated with the rope motif; one of the bottom two astragals joining the shaft has a bead-and-reel pattern while the other is of the rope design.

- Rampurva 2 (pillar and a capital, no edicts) [3.5]: This pillar and Rampurva 1 were originally a pair but this one has no Asoka edicts and one may postulate that only a set of engraved edicts on Rampurva 1 would have been enough for the purpose; in the top center of the shaft is a socket to receive the copper dowel to join the capital with the shaft below as in the Rampurva 1 pillar. The capital is of the usual bell-shaped lotiform with plump bulging that is crowned with a standing bull; this pillar is similar to the one at the eastern gate of the Jetavana Monastery as described by Hsuan-tsang. The design motifs on its round abacus are honeysuckles alternated with stylized palmettes and small rosettes derived from the Greek anthemion and palmette, which ultimately originated in Assyrian arts {Frankfort 1970: fg. 152} {Curl 2005: 24}. A single echinus ring between the abacus and the bell lotiform is decorated with the rope motif; the bottom two astragals joining the shaft are all plain. The naturalistic carving style of the bull reveals a strong continuity with the Indus tradition nearly two millennia earlier.

- Vaishali (pillar intact and a capital, no edicts) [3.1, 3.4]: This pillar bears no Asoka edicts but it is certainly the most complete of all pillars besides the Lauriya Nandangarh pillar; it is also the most bulky, short, and least decorated compared to the other pillars which are generally slender, tall, and lavishly decorated. The capital is of the usual bell-shaped lotiform with plump bulging and crowned with a sejant lion; this pillar is stylistically unique and also the most controversial among the pillars as its abacus is uncharacteristically rectangular and plain. The bulging of the lotiform bell is more pronounced at the bottom in contrast to the graceful 'S' bulging in the other capitals. A single echinus ring between the abacus and the bell lotiform is decorated with the rope motif; one of the bottom two astragals joining the shaft has a bead-and-reel pattern while the other is of the rope pattern.
- Sankisa (capital): The round abacus of this capital is nearly identical to the Allahabad-Kausambi abacus. The decorative motifs in both cases are honeysuckles alternated with stylized lotuses and small rosettes alongwith the bead-and-reel patterns below; however, the rosettes on this capital are bigger. The capital is crowned with an elephant with stylized carvings of lotus leaves below its belly; a single echinus ring between the abacus and the bell lotiform is decorated with the rope motif and one of the bottom two astragals joining the shaft has a bead-and-reel motif while the other has a rope pattern.
- Kesariya (capital): This capital was found by Captain Markham Kittoe in 1862 CE at Kesariya Stupa [6.12] reportedly having a design identical with the Lauriya Nandangarh pillar except for the hind legs of its sejant lion, which did not protrude beyond the abacus.
- Udaigiri-Vidisa (capital): The capital is of the usual bell-shaped lotiform having graceful bulging and crowned with a sejant lion swinging the tail around its thigh; like the Sarnath capital, its round abacus is also decorated with four different animals, including the winged lion, elephant, horse, and camel all moving in the clockwise direction. One of the double echinus rings between the abacus and the bell lotiform is plain while the other has a rope motif; the bottom two astragals joining the shaft are plain.
- Patna (capital): This capital is crowned with four addorsed bulls having a socket in the center which serves the receptacle for a metal dowel to secure the *dharmacakra* to the shaft as in the Sarnath pillar.

There are other fragmentary pieces of pillars and capitals found at Gotihawa, Kausambi, Gaya (now moved to Bodhgaya), Prahladpur, Fatehabad, Bhopal, Sadargali, Udaigiri-Vidisa, Kushinagar, Masadh, Basti, Bhikana Pahari, Bulandibagh, Sandalpu, and five others while another broken pillar at Bhairon have been destroyed in 1908 CE during a riot; all these fragments reportedly did not contain any Asoka edicts on them. Fa-hsien and Hsuan-tsang also wrote in their journals as having seen numerous Asoka pillars in India and some have subsequently been identified by archaeologists; however many no longer exist today as in the cases of Kushinagar, the two pillars at the Jetavana Monastery in Sravasti, Rajagriha, and Mahasala. It is important to keep in mind that these celebrated monks were Buddhist pilgrims not art historians so their impressionistic observations have now and then been proven to be unreliable; thus they might have mistaken the imitative Gupta pillars for the Asoka ones. Overall there are over forty-one pillars, if counting the individual capitals as pillars, including those mentioned in historical literature. The *dharmacakra*s and animals are the most popular types to have crowned the capitals of the Asoka pillars; among the extant animal capitals are the lion (6), bull (2), elephant (1), horse (1), and the *dharmacakra* (2). Depictions on the abaci also include other animals, in addition to the ones already mentioned, such as geese, a camel, and a winged lion; floral and foliate motifs are also very popular particularly in the early pillars. Of all the monuments erected during the Maurya Dynasty, only the Nigali Sagar and Rummindei pillars alongwith several Barabar caves are definitely of Asoka's creations as clearly stated in the inscriptions on them. As already mentioned, all pillars are situated in the Indian heartland and generally around Pataliputra, the capital of the Maurya Dynasty. From their locations, it is clear that these pillars and their edicts were primarily meant for the Indian audience as also corroborated by the use of Brahmi in the majority of the inscriptions.

Available evidence overwhelmingly suggests that Asoka was the ultimate author of all these soaring stone monuments; the majority of the pillars are found near Buddhist *stupa*s, Buddhist settlements, or places associated with Buddha's life like Nigali Sagar, Rummindei, Gotihawa, Kausambi, Sarnath, Vaishali, Sankisa, Bodhgaya, Kushinagar, Sravasti, Sanchi, etc. These are definite proofs that Asoka, who was a Buddhist emperor, erected these pillars to demonstrate his Buddhist affiliation on the personal level and his imperial authority on the public level. As already stated, the REs were the first to be engraved in c. 255 BCE, the Nigali Sagar and Lumbini pillars were definitely erected in c. 249 BCE from their inscriptions, and finally the PEs were issued between c. 243-242 BCE. The Rupnath RE (c. 255 BCE), the earliest edict which inaugurated the practice of engraving imperial rescripts on permanent stone surfaces, revealed Asoka's specific instructions {Hultzsch 1969: 169}:

> And cause ye this matter to be engraved on rocks where an occasion presents itself. And (wherever) there are stone pillars here, it must be caused to be engraved on stone pillars.

The Delhi-Topra PE VII (c. 242 BCE), the very last of all Asoka and pillar edicts, revealed essentially the same message {Hultzsch 1969: 137}:

> This rescript morality must be engraved there, where either stone pillars or stone slabs are (available), in order that this may be of long duration.

Based on these edicts, many scholars have interpreted that the pillars might have already existed long before the emperor ordered the edicts to be engraved on them and Asoka might not be their author; and so the theory of pre-Asoka and Asoka pillars has been born. Benjamin Rowland, a proponent of the pre-Asoka theory, had this to say on the matter {Rowland 1977: 67}:

> It may well be, as is suggested by the words of Asoka's first and last edicts enjoining the carving of such inscriptions on rock or on pillars *already standing*, that many of the so-called Asokan columns, originally set up be an earlier Maurya emperor, were taken over and their symbolism, Brahmanical or zodiacal, syncretically reinterpreted for Buddhist usage.

Indeed the edicts engraved on existing pillars belonged to Asoka but to postulate that they were originally set up by an earlier Maurya emperor would be hasty. If there were existing pillars *at the time* of the issuance of the Rupnath RE they would have already been engraved as per Asoka's specific instructions; but none of the rock edicts have been found on the pillars and this clearly means that the pillars were erected after the rock edicts. Moreover the Arthasastra, a political treatise written by Kautilya Vishnugupta the political adviser and minister under Chandragupta, mentioned no such conspicuous and massive stone pillars within the Maurya domain. Megasthenes, the Greek ambassador to Chandragupta's court who had written extensively in his book 'Indika' about the contemporary Indian life, also did not report these conspicuous stone pillars {Gupta 1980: 289}. With such a powerful charisma and ambition like Asoka, who else could have had the wealth and religious devotion to undertake such enormous construction projects? Benjamin Rowland's assertions that the symbolisms of the Asoka pillars were 'Brahmanical or zodiacal' and that they were 'syncretically reinterpreted for Buddhist usage' are also far-fetched conclusions since these pillars and their crown animals did not yet acquire sectarian affiliation and religious symbolisms in this early stage of Indian arts and architecture. Ultimately in the Delhi-Topra PE VII, Asoka proudly declared that the stone pillars were his creations and he called them 'Morality Pillars' (*dharma stambha*) {Hultzsch 1969: 134}:

> Devanampriya Priyadarsin speaks thus. Having in view this very (matter), I have set up pillars of morality, appointed Mahamatras of morality, (and) issued [proclamations] on morality.

From the passage the emperor apparently initiated three tasks simultaneously in the earlier years: erected the pillars, created the Dharma Mahamatra, and published the morality rescripts; engraving the edicts on these pillars at a later time seemed to be his afterthoughts. One may also question as why some Asoka pillars (Kausambi, Rampurva 2, and Vaishali) do not have edicts if they belonged to Asoka; S. P. Gupta might have some answers for this matter {Gupta 1980: 39, 42}:

> The pillars of Asoka went side by side with the holy structures erected by him and they together formed an architectural scheme…If that is so, it is easily understandable that to fulfill their function the pil-

lars need not necessarily have to be inscribed...As at Rumpurva, it may be elsewhere also, for some reason or other two pillars had been set up near each other, and therefore it was thought proper to have only one inscribed.

Since the Kausambi and Rampurva pillars were originally erected as pairs close to each other so that only one set of edicts engraved on one pillar would be enough to convey the messages; it is also possible that the early pillars had been left unengraved as the practice was still in its infancy and it might initially deem unaesthetic to engrave texts on these pillars. Moreover, only edicts containing new morality rescripts would be chosen for engraving on several pillars; this is why the Rupnath RE and the Delhi-Topra PE VII are not found elsewhere. The ravages of time, human vandalism, and redecoration have also erased some of the edicts as, for instance, parts of the Sarnath edict have been obliterated by new Buddhist inscriptions at a later time; the unengraved Vaishali pillar may also be explained according to the reasons given above.

The evaluation of architectural and artistic evidences also supports the view that Asoka was the sole creator of all these pillars. The Rummindei and Nigali Sagar pillars alongwith some Barabar caves are confirmed donations by Asoka as they all display the characteristic glistening polish and carved in sandstone like the other Asoka pillars. The pillars share a stylistic consistency and identical configurations suggesting that they were all erected during Asoka's forty-year long reign. Moreover if the Barabar caves were rendered into stone from timber prototypes within a short timeframe and so why it should not be the case for the Asoka pillars; Asoka and his empire certainly had the wealth, manpower, and technical expertise to complete the tasks relatively quickly. Stylistic analyses of the pillars also suggest their construction dates within Asoka's reign with the Lumbini pillar, which was erected in the twentieth regnal year of Asoka's reign in c. 249 BCE, serving as the stylistic reference point. From a stylistic and technological viewpoint, the definite starting point must be the Vaishali pillar, then Sankisa, Allahabad-Kausambi, Rampurva 2, Rummindei, Lauriya Nandangarh, Kesariya, Rampurva 1, Sanchi, Udaigiri-Vidisa, Patna, and Sarnath. The starting Vaishali pillar is short, heavy, and static with an incongruous square abacus that visually does not appear to harmonize or smoothly integrate with the round shaft below; the latest Sarnath pillar, on the other hand, is tall, elegant, and dynamic with a seemingly self-rotating circular abacus. The capitals have also been subjected to simplification, particularly the decorative motifs on the echinus rings, by gradually eliminating distracting elements such as the rope and bead-and-reel patterns altogether. The profuse carvings of the foliate and floral motifs on the abaci in the earlier period would be completely replaced with animals in the later capitals, a design modification which is unquestionably complementary to the crowning animals above them. The animals in the earlier crowns are stiff, artificial, and hieratic while the animals in the later crowns are more graceful and natural with the lion as the leading crowning animal. The lion was no doubt a paramount symbol of Asoka's reign and imperial confidence as the sculptor's technical proficiency and realistic depiction certainly played a big part in this achievement. Artistic and technological advancement in the later pillars is apparent from the four addorsed animals crowning their capitals with the *dharmacakra* superimposed on top as the testament to the increasing fusion of secular and religious symbolisms. The most complicated capitals have four addorsed animals surmounted by the *dharmacakra* which were definitely reserved for special places, secular or religious, like Patna (the capital of the Maurya Dynasty), Sanchi (where *stupa*s containing relics of Buddha's chief disciples Maudgalyayana and Sariputra were interred), and Sarnath (the place where Buddha preached the first sermon).

While myths, legends, and symbolisms are important in arts and architecture, they might not be the sole reasons for its creations; functional requirements and patron's personal aspirations ultimately played the most decisive roles in the process. Thus the Asoka pillars reflected the emperor's ambitions to impose his own ideology and morality throughout his empire to regulate his subjects' daily behaviors; the intention was to instill deference and obeisance to his imperial authority. It appears that the pillars, though many had been erected at Buddhist *stupa*s and main thoroughfares, were not originally erected specifically to be worshiped as religious monuments like the *stupa*s. These were 'morality pillars' erected to sanctify and spread Asoka's moral ideals and bore witness to his Buddhist conversion; they were therefore authoritative and commemorative edifices; however, their imposing scales and Buddhist associations were captivating enough to stir up the religious devotions even in Asoka's days. The animals on these pillars did not appear to have any religious connotations and they might not be considered as sacred animals in the contemporary religious milieu; the camel was certainly not a sacred animal but it appeared on the Udaigiri-Vidisa capital. So only popular decorative motifs and important animals had been depicted by the sculptors and probably personally authorized by Asoka.

Horse-drawn chariots were vital components of the Maurya army and daily transportation and this could be why the horse and wheel are found on many pillars; the religious significance of the wheel, or precisely the *dharmacakra*, will be discussed later. Animals like the lion, bull, and elephant can also be found in India and it comes to no surprise that they have crowned many Asoka capitals. Still there are scholars who relied upon unfounded speculations to explain the symbolisms of these pillars and the Sarnath pillar will serve as an illustration. Afred Foucher believed the four animals on its abacus representing the Four Events in Buddha's life, with the elephant (Mayadevi's conception of Buddha), horse (Buddha's Great Renunciation), lion (Buddha as Lion of the Sakyas), and bull (the vigorous power of Buddhism) {Pandey 1982: 74}. First of all, the correct Four Events of Buddha's life should be Nativity, Enlightenment, First Sermon, and Decease and these might or might not correspond to the four animals on the abacus. Stylistically, the manner of depicting animals alternated with four wheels in between also perpetuate an earlier artistic convention as seen in the Rampurva 2 and Sanchi capitals, which also display similar alternated motifs. The latest capitals (Sanchi, Sarnath, and Patna) are crowned with four addorsed animals surmounted by a wheel in the center; the four addorsed animals have clearly been designed to secure the wheel and this was certainly a latest artistic and technical innovation. In any case, the wheel was certainly an imperial and religious emblem since it exclusively surmounted the four addorsed animal capitals. Vincent Smith held the view that the four animals representing guardians of the four quarters, namely the elephant (East), horse (South), bull (West), and Lion (North) {Pandey 1982: 74-75}. Now if the horse was the guardian of the South, why was it erected in the western quarter at Lumbini? Similarly, the lion pillar at Sarnath should have been erected in the northern quarter but instead it is located in the western side. Now had the four animals been the guardians of the four quarters, it should make more sense symbolically to erect the pillars with their animal crowns at the four proper quarters of the shrine; instead typically only one pillar had been erected per site. My view is that the pillars and their animal crowns were Asoka's personal preference and they primarily carried artistic and architectural convention and probably less on the religious symbolisms. The alleged connection between the Asoka pillars and the Vedic *yupa* (sacrificial post) also deserves a more careful review. The latter had typically been carved from a single sacred tree and finally shaped into an octagonal (top portion) and square shape (below) to which sacrificial items like animals would be fastened as offerings to the gods; the *yupa* was thus a religious medium facilitating the communication between the human and divine world in Vedic Hinduism {Dallapiccola 1980: 13-15, 260-61}. However, its material (wood) and shape (octagon and square) apparently have nothing in common with the round monumental stone Asoka pillars with their unique animal crowns; the oldest stone *yupa* dated in the second century BCE, a century and half after the first Asoka pillars. Moreover the idea of erecting a *yupa*, which involved sacrificial rites to the gods, would be clearly unacceptable to Buddha and he certainly would not endorse any Buddhists, including Asoka, to construct such *yupa*s and conduct sacrifices anywhere near Buddhist establishments. On the other hand, the majority of the Indians could have already exposed to such religious *yupa*s in the past and Asoka simply transformed the *idea* of a religious pillar into his pillars for the purpose of spreading his *dharma* or *Dharma* as well as commemorating his visits to the holy Buddhist sites. There are two important accounts that further facilitate the comprehension of the symbolisms of the wheel on the Asoka pillars. First, Sarnath was the place where Buddha first turned the Wheel of *Dharma*, that is preaching the first sermon, and *Dharma* collectively referred to his teachings, which were also metaphorically denoted as 'Lion's Roar.' Second, the Cakkavatti-sihanada-sutta in the Digha-nikaya, a canonical Buddhist literature likely dated before Asoka's time, told the story of a righteous king named Dalhanemi ruling a golden age in India. The wheel was the emblem of his righteousness and sovereignty which had guided him to the peaceful conquests in all directions, East, West, North, and South. Due to his righteousness, all kings submitted to him and after the victories the wheel remained suspended in the sky above his palace until the end of his life as a symbol of his shining and everlasting virtue; this righteous monarch was accordingly named a wheel-turning king (*cakravartin*) {Strong 1983: 44-56} {Walshe 1995: 395-405}. Thus according to these two versions, the symbolisms of the wheel can both be applied to Buddha and Emperor Asoka with the former as the 'emperor' of the religious and the latter of the secular world. In the case of Buddha, the symbolism of the wheel surmounted the four addorsed lions probably represents the propagation of his *Dharma*, his 'Lion's Roar,' to the four corners of the world; historically Buddhist missionaries had also been sent throughout the known world as recorded in the Asoka edicts. The association of the wheel with Buddha is palpable from the fact that pillars of this type are mostly found in Buddhist sites; thus the wheel, which represents Buddha's *Dharma*, is a symbolic religious vehicle that transports Buddhist practitioners to *Nirvana*. In the case of Asoka, his life also precisely matched the second description; his pre-Buddhist aggressions, his subsequent Buddhist conversion and replacement with *dharmavijaya*, alongwith his pillars and edicts all evidently support the view that he emulated or aspired to be a *cakravartin*. Accordingly the wheel was his royal insignia while the four addorsed lions symbolized the emanation of his imperial power and righteousness in the four directions. The exemplary Asoka wheel on the Sarnath capital would subsequently be adopted by the Indian government on its national flag and the four addorsed lions as the official emblem of India in 22nd July 1947 CE.

Among Maurya arts and architecture, the Asoka pillars have been a controversial topic for scholars since the day of their discovery as they seem to have suddenly appeared without historical antecedents. There are three main theories regarding the sources and origins of these pillars.

a. Near Eastern Origin

The Near East historically and culturally was the region encompassing Persia, Mesopotamia, Egypt, Asia Minor, and to a lesser extent Greece due to the heavy commercial, cultural, and political interactions between them; it is not surprising to see the arts and architecture of one country occurring in the others and tracing their sources is beyond the scope of this book. India was historically in contact with the Near East mostly via Persia and Greece; the latter country, led by Alexander the Great of Macedonia, completed the conquest of Persia and subsequently invaded northwestern India. The colonial Greeks later founded their kingdom in Bactria in northern Afghanistan and some scholars suggested that the pillars had been executed with the help of these Bactrian Greeks {Marshall 1983 Volume I: 89-92}. In fact, their kingdom in Bactria and its capital at Ai-khanum have been excavated with unmistakably Hellenized arts and architecture {Tissot 2006: 23-48}; thus the theory of the Bactrian Greeks' involvement in the carvings of these pillars, particularly their superb realism, certainly has its merits. Moreover, one can also notice the striking similarities between the architectural forms of the Asoka pillars and the Persian columns at Persepolis and the royal tombs of the Persian kings Artaxerxes and Darius, for examples the bell-shaped lotiform capitals with crowning animals, the tapering and smooth shaft of the Persian columns, etc. The fundamental difference is that these Persian columns are structural while the Asokas' pillars are freestanding and independent monuments. The crowning lions on the Asoka pillars are also similar to the Persian lions with its tongue protruding out of the open mouth between large canine teeth. Moreover, the Kumrahar palace capital dated in the Maurya Dynasty in the Patna Museum also shows definite Near Eastern influences such as its row of repeating rosettes on the abacus, the stylized ovolo, the bead-and-reel pattern, the wave-like scrolls, and the rosette-inscribed volutes. A bulk of the floral and foliate motifs on the abaci of early Asoka pillars (Allahabad-Kausambi, Sankisa, Rampurva 2) such as the honeysuckles, palmettes, and stylized lotuses likely originated in the Greek anthemion and Near Eastern arts. The Vaishali pillar, which is bulky and short with a large rectangular abacus slab, strongly resembles the Greek Doric order while later Asoka pillars, which are generally graceful and tall, are comparable to the Greek Ionic and Corinthian orders. The manner of depicting animals parading clockwise around the abaci also has antecedents in the Near East; the hieratic realism of the lions, with their visible veins and muscles, also suggests the Greek sculptural technique. Depiction of the addorsed animals on the pillars already occurred in Egyptian architecture while the Asoka pillars can also be thought of as the Indian version of the Egyptian obelisk.

b. Indian Origin

While some of the architectural features and decorative motifs might have originated in the Near East, other elements however are definitely Indian. The idea of erecting massive pillars engraved with edicts for secular and religious purposes was entirely an Indian conception; it had been a natural evolution from inscribing the edicts on rock surfaces in the earlier years to actually engrave them on pillars in the later years and this might have been inspired by the idea of the Vedic *yupa*. All crowning animals on the Asoka pillars, including the lion, can also be found in India; the lion is the most common animal which could reflect Asoka's own preference and might not have been influenced by the Near Eastern convention. Many scholars have pondered if wooden prototypes for the pillars might have once existed, as in the case for the Barabar caves; however no one has proven this since none of the timber examples from early Indian architecture survive. The Indian sculptors' mastery of naturalistic modeling is clearly evident in the depiction of the crowning animals; though separated nearly two millennia apart, the Asoka bull is strikingly reminiscent of the Harappa bull. Realism in sculptural modeling was not the sole domain of the Greeks as the Harappans had already displayed such technique thousands of years before. The Indian sculptors seemed to prefer naturalism, which imparts inner spirituality in the form, over the Greeks' penchant for realism and formality. Together the terracotta sculptures of the dancing girls from Bulandibagh (third-second centuries BCE) and the Barabar caves clearly demonstrate that Indian sculptors were entirely capable of naturalistic modeling {Gupta 1980: 157-171, pl. 73-81}. Even the mirror-like polish of the Asoka pillars, which was once believed to be an import from Near East, might also be traced back to the Son Bhandar caves; the superb Didarganj Yaksi (first century CE) also had an identical glistening polish. Another common misconception is that Indian arts and architecture only took off after the Greeks' contacts with India during the Maurya Dynasty or more precisely in Asoka's reign. The fallacy of this view is that Indian architecture, with surviving monuments like Piprahwa Stupa **[6.1-6.2]**, certainly had a deep-rooted tradition long before the Maurya Dynasty. Finally, the Indus Civilization is the testament that South Asia already had a lengthy and independent artistic tradition of its own long before its blossoming contacts with the Near East in the fourth century BCE.

c. A Combination of Near Eastern and Indian Origin

From the previous analyses, my proposition about the Asoka pillars is that they contain and fuse elements from both Indian and Near Eastern traditions. Their conception and workmanship are principally Indian with a few formal features and decorative patterns borrowed from the Near East; however, these foreign elements would immediately be subjected to Indianization to suit the Indian tradition. The freestanding Asoka pillars became a religious and imperial symbol in India while their Near Eastern counterparts remained as structural columns, with the exception of the Egyptian obelisk. In India, the bell-shaped lotiform had been modified into an elegant bulge resembling a graceful 'S' shape and the square abacus transformed into a circular form which perfectly blended to round shaft below. The four addorsed animals surmounted with crowning wheels of these Asoka pillars were fully imbued with native Indian symbolisms and pregnant with religious and imperial glory which had no equivalents in the Near East.

Emperor Asoka, as the greatest monarch of the Maurya Dynasty, was able to consolidate his empire and took it to the highest pinnacle of administrative and artistic successes; his majestic pillars not only reflected his brilliant imperial achievements and ambitions but it was also the emblem and embodiment of his imperial and religious ideals and the ultimate symbol of his people. Though no previous precursors of these stone pillars could be traced to with certainty, they had undeniably been created by the indigenous and experienced hands of the Indian sculptors and engineers with the incorporation of a few elements from the Near East. In spite of foreign borrowings, there was a strong artistic tradition in India to be able to absorb the artistic infiltration from the west; in the hands of the Indian sculptors, the Asoka pillars were uniquely Indian and had no contemporary equivalents anywhere else. Surprising enough, one might expect the extraordinary refinement of these pillars would ensure their survival in the subsequent periods; however, they seemed to have mysteriously disappeared with the fall of the Maurya Dynasty. Above all Maurya arts and architecture, especially the polished Asoka pillars, had been created and sanctioned by the imperial court and without the imperial patronage they would naturally wither away. On the other hand, the *stupa* arts and architecture in the subsequent periods were mainly the product of the common people reflecting the rise of popular religions like Buddhism, that was primarily financed by the wealthy merchant class. Without the imperial power to enforce its own artistic parameters, the folkish arts of the commoners began to flourish. Furthermore without sufficient imperial patronage the arts and architecture of the imperial family, as exemplified in the glistening Asoka pillars, could not survive due to the high labor costs and longer time to complete the projects whilst the ostentatious mirror polish was too costly duplicate and probably inappropriate for common religious purposes. The pillars, with their characteristic animal crowns, subsequently metamorphosed architecturally as the *torana* columns in Buddhist *stupa*s **[6.4, 6.7]** or as freestanding and structural pillars in many Buddhist caves **[5.9]**. The Barabar caves, foremost among these is the Lomas Risi cave **[5.1-5.2]** attributed to Asoka, subsequently become the model for later Buddhist *caityagriha*s in the Deccan **[5.3]** (Chapter 5). The gleaming polish of the Asoka pillars also appeared sporadically in later times, for instance in the celebrated Didarganj Yaksi sculpture. Distant reminiscence of the Asoka pillars could also be found as far as China in the Xiao Jing tomb of Southern Liang Dynasty (502-557 CE); its freestanding fluted stone pillar with a lotus-pedaled capital are also crowned with a lion and accompanied by a royal inscription on the placard on the pillar shaft in the manner of its Indian counterpart {Steinhardt 2002: fg. 3.11-3.12}.

Chapter 4. Monastery

Monasticism began from the earliest days of Buddhism as monasteries were constructed for the congregation of monks and nuns and for the causes and services of the religion. From the time of its commencement, the architectural program of a monastic establishment specified that its location ought not to be too far or too near a town and might be high above ground or in a park-like setting; generally it needed to be close to water and human resources, which were key requirements for the survival and spiritual advancement of the inmates. Almost all Buddhist monasteries had been designed with an inward orientation and enclosed within a high boundary wall to demarcate from the outside world; individual buildings could be single or multi-storied having different forms of roofs and walls as determined by its context and program. A continuous gallery often surrounded a centrally hypaethral courtyard and there might be chapels, temples, or *stupa*s to fulfill the various religious needs of the occupants. Architectural forms, materials, and construction systems in a Buddhist monastery primarily falls into three distinct groups. The Indian group generally employs permanent materials such as brick and stone, the Chinese group often selects perishable materials like timber, and the Tibetan group typically prefers adobe construction in combination with rubble and wood where feasible; these are of course a function of cultural and environmental factors. The quadrangular monastery has undoubtedly been the most common of all Buddhist monastic plans in Asia; the reason was primarily due to Buddhist monasticism which emphasized on meditation and self-discipline in the Theravada and scholasticism in the Mahayana; it demanded designs that could shelter the inmates from the outside world and secure a contemplative lifestyle. In the subsequent centuries after the commencement of Buddhist monasticism, the focus of the monastic life within a monastery would shift from the emphases on withdrawn meditation of the Theravada to scholasticism, image worship, and devotionalism of the Mahayana, and lastly the complex Tantric rituals of the Vajrayana; as a result of these changes the Buddhist monastery also incorporated *stupa*s and image chapels into its plan in response to the diverse religious needs. The development of the Buddhist monastery can chronologically be divided into several stages and types:

(a) Communal monastery without the *stupa*, as in Jivakavanarama [4.1].
(b) Organic or unplanned monastery centering on a major *stupa*, such as Sanchi [6.3] in India, Dharmarajika [6.13] in Gandhara, and Ruvenvali in Sri Lanka.
(c) Rock-hewn cave monastery (Chapter 5), for examples Bhaja [5.4, 5.6] in India, Bamiyan [5.14-5.16] in Afghanistan, Kizil [5.18] in Turkistan, and Mogao [5.20, 5.22] in China.
(d) Planned quadrangular monastery with *vihara*s, *stupa*s, and image chapels located in the same site, for examples Takht-i-bahi [4.2] in Gandhara, Nalanda [4.4] in India, and Somapura [4.8] in Bangladesh.
(e) Monastic university or *mahavihara* devoted to the religious and scholastic pursuits of Theravada, Mahayana, and Vajrayana subjects, for examples Nalanda [4.4] in India and Somapura [4.8] in Bangladesh.
(f) Monastery with separate precincts for the *vihara*s and worship areas, such as Horyuji [4.5] in Japan, Indrapura [4.11] in Champa, and Alchi [4.13] in Ladakh.
(g) Monastery with a centrally sacred precinct consisting of several functionally different structures, a central temple, *stupa*, or *stupa*-temple, for examples Somapura [4.8] in Bangladesh and Vijayarama [4.9] Sri Lanka.
(h) Fortress and/or hiltop monastery, for examples Drepung in Tibet and Tikse in Ladakh.

1. Jivakavanarama (c. 530-400 BCE) - India

Buddhism historically began in c. 532 BCE when Buddha preached the first sermon in Isipatana near Varanasi and founded the *Sangha*; the first five monk-disciples (*bhiksu*) were converted during this momentous occasion while the order of nuns (*bhiksuni*) would later be founded in c. 527 BCE in Vaishali. The life of a *bhiksu* or *bhiksuni* since the earliest days of Buddhism, as epitomized in Buddha's life, was that of a wandering mendicant which strictly adhered to the vows of poverty and renunciation as apt for spiritual emancipation and the pursuit of higher knowledge of reality. The itinerant *bhiksu*s often traveled from place to place without a permanent abode and they would rest or spend the night at suitable shelters away from dangers and annoyances like rain, wild beasts, insects, noise, etc. A well-known passage in the Cullavagga described vividly the wandering life of a Buddhist mendicant before the advent of permanent monasteries {Sarkar 1966: 8}:

So the *bhiksu*s dwelt now here, now there - in the woods, at the foot of trees, on hill-sides, in grottos, in mountain caves, in cemeteries, in forests, in open plains, and in heaps of straw.

One of the most favorite spots frequented by Buddha was the natural caves on the Gijjhakuta (Vulture Peak) in Rajagriha, Bihar {Fergusson and Burgess 1969: 51-52}. The *bhiksu*s' annual calendar also involved spending nine months of the dry season wandering about and settled down during the remaining three months of the monsoon called a *vassavasa* (rain retreat) when traveling was especially treacherous; this practice gradually led to the cessation of the wandering life and the beginning of Buddhist monasticism. The *vassavasa* witnessed important activities and ceremonies such as the *uposatha* (recital of the monastic rules or *pattimokkha*), *upasampada* (*bhiksu* ordinations), *pavarana* (confessional observances), *kathina* (distribution or offering of robes), discussion of Buddha's teachings, etc. It was also a special occasion to see *bhiksu*s from the four corners of the country congregating in one place for a common religious purpose which consequently resulted in the heightening the spirit and cohesion of the *Sangha* and the communal consciousness of the noble monkish fraternity {Schumann 1989: 170}; the observance of the *vassavasa* continues to this day in Buddhist Asia. The places in which the monks spent their *vassavasa*s soon became the first permanent Buddhist monasteries in India while these monastic retreats also provided a golden opportunity for the interactions among the members of the *Sangha* and between the monks and the laity; expectedly these would gradually develop into important centers of Buddhist learning. On the other hand, settling down in different monasteries and hosting the rain retreats in different regions also led to the regionalization of Buddhism and sectarianism that could cause schismatic tendency in the *Sangha*.

The shelters for the inmates during the *vassavasa* had been stipulated as either: (a) Temporary (*avasa*) erected by the *bhiksu*s themselves and to be taken down at the conclusion of the *vassavasa* and these were generally rudimentary structures like simple huts or (b) permanent (*arama*) as donated and maintained by wealthy lay patrons with the property vested to the *Sangha* for the '*bhiksu*s of four quarters now and in the future,' hence the word *sangharama* or monastery. At the height of Buddhist influences in India in the seventh century CE, 200 villages were donated to the great Nalanda monastery for its upkeep {Dutt 1962: 331}; the transference of wealth to the *Sangha* also led to the increasing clout of the monasteries over the local population and worldly affairs and politics. The account of the founding of the first Indian Buddhist monastery Veluvanarama in c. 531 BCE is well-known in Buddhist scriptures; it was originally a royal park or garden (*avana*) in Rajagriha belonging to the Magadha King Bimbisara which was donated to the *Sangha*. When inquired by Bimbisara about a suitable location for constructing a residence for Buddha, he replied {Chaudhury 1969: 100}:

> Not too far from the town, not too near, suitable for coming and going, easily accessible to all people, by day not too crowded, by night not exposed to noise and clamour, clean of the smell of the people, and hidden from men.

Such ideal places might be located in the suburb, near streams, or on the hills overlooking the city as in the case of many Gandhara monasteries; a monastery should obviously be within the walking distant to the city center where alms could easily obtained but far enough from the bustle and hustle where monks could retire peacefully at night. In addition to Veluvanarama, other important *sangharama*s founded during Buddha's time were Ghositarama (c. 531 BCE) in Kausambi donated by Ghosita the merchant and banker, Jetavanarama (c. 530 BCE) in Sravasti donated for the usage of Buddha and the *Sangha* by the generous banker Anathapindika, and Jivakavanarama (c. 530 BCE) **[4.1]** in Rajagriha donated by the royal physician Jivaka. Besides the elliptical plan of Jivakavanarama, the foundational remains of the contemporary Ghositarama and Jetavanarama also have a similar plan. Ghositarama probably survived until the fifth century CE and Jetavanarama lasted the longest to the very end of Buddhism in India in c. 1200 CE as probably also Veluvanarama. In all, there were eight important *sangharama*s reportedly donated to Buddha's *Sangha* not counting many insignificant ones {Dutt 1962: 60-65} {Sarkar 1966: 19-21}. Buddha's forty-five-year itinerant missionaries had been confined within the boundary of northern India (Bihar and eastern Uttar Pradesh) and the Nepalese Terai and expectedly the earliest monasteries were also located in these regions. Overall he spent six *vassavasa*s in Rajagriha (c. 531-528 BCE, c. 516 BCE, c. 513 BCE in Veluvanarama and probably also Jivakavanarama) and twenty-five *vassavasa*s in Sravasti (c. 519 BCE, c. 512-489 BCE with nineteen in Jetavanarama and six in Pubbarama); these were no doubt the celebrated monasteries in those days {Schumann 1989: 172}. It is also apparent that later in Buddha's life, the Jetavanarama became his permanent home and this undoubtedly set a precedent for the eventual cessation of the wandering mendicant lifestyle and further endorsed the establishment of permanent monasteries.

Ancient Buddhist scriptures contained a wealth of information about the designs and constructions of these earliest monasteries, in particular Veluvanarama and Jetavanarama {Chaudhury 1969: 72-75, 100-102}{Barua 1969: 17-18}. Veluvanarama was a bamboo (*velu*) grove enclosed by a high wall with a main gateway and towers that ensured the seclusion for the monks from city dwellers; inside there was a large reservoir as the main water source of the monastery for service and hygiene. A structure on the side of the main building in the monastery, the Ambalatthika, was a hall for Buddha's disciples who practiced austerities and possibly also for meditation; there were reportedly two *stupa*s, one containing the relics of Sariputra and Maudgalyayana and the other of Ajnata-Kaundinya, at the gate of this monastery. Jetavanarama also had similar features of a garden-setting monastery like Veluvanarama though on a grander scale since Buddha spent nineteen *vassavasa*s here; it was enclosed within a boundary wall, a gateway with a chamber or a pavilion over it alongwith wells and ponds. Within its walls there were dwelling rooms (*vihara*) and cells (*parivena*) for monks, store rooms and closets (*kotthana*), service halls such as refectory and kitchen (*agnisala*), gated chambers, fireplace halls, cloisters for walking meditation (*cankamanasala*), meditation halls, bathrooms including hot baths (*jantagriha*), sheds, pavilions, well-house (*udapanasala*), drug store (*kappiyakuti*), etc. The description also included detached buildings of various functions like privies, conference rooms, and possibly guest halls for the laity; there were also specialized structures like the *uposathagriha* and *upatthanasala* or meeting halls for performing important ceremonies like the *uposatha*, *upasampada*, *pavarana*, and *kathina*. Together these early freestanding dwellings comprised the five types of structures permitted by Buddha: (a) *Vihara* (private residence), (b) *addhyayoga* (house with turned-up eaves like a *garuda* bird), (c) *pasada* (mansion of more than two stories), (d) *hammiya* (pillared first story with a loft on top or a pillared pavilion), and (e) *guha* (rock-hewn cave) {Dutt 1962: 92-97}{Sarkar 1966: 8-14}; with the exception of the *guha* all others were freestanding types. These early buildings have all been destroyed over the centuries but their forms are better preserved among the surviving *stupa* reliefs [6.5, 7.4-7.6]. The development of the *guha*, which subsequently evolved into the rock-hewn cave monasteries that were chronologically positioned between the earliest monasteries and later Gandhara monasteries, will be explored in Chapter 5. Since the *vihara* was a private dwelling for monks, it was popularly and interchangeably synonymous with the *sangharama*; it and the *guha* became the most common types of dwellings for monks and nuns. What were the forms and materials for these early Buddhist monasteries? Architecturally, they were likely simple elongated and vaulted elliptical huts of bent bamboos or wooden members forming a ribbed structure having a roof covered in leaves or mats [4.1]; these were evidently more suited as the *avasa*s. Bhiksu Dhaniya, who had previous experience as a potter, attempted to build a solid adobe hut for himself by firing and harden the clay in the interior but Buddha ordered such permanent edifice to be destroyed since a durable structure might violate the monastic rules for an *avasa*, which should not be permanent {Schumann 1989: 173-174}. The situation would certainly be different for a *sangharama* since permanent materials could be used and this was likely the case for Veluvanarama and Jetavanarama. As recorded in scriptures, Buddha permitted five types of material to be used in the construction of the roof including brick, stone, stucco, grass, and leaves {Sarkar 1966: 13}; these or their combinations and timber could also be used for foundations and walls, the latter of which could be of reinforced mud or wattle-and-daub construction. The aforesaid adobe structure built by Bhiksu Dhaniya was an example of the wattle-and-daub construction which was certainly very common in contemporary architecture; moreover the citizens of Nadika, a town near Vaishali, also reportedly constructed a brick hall for Buddha {Chaudhury 1969: 60}. Furthermore, Buddha also reportedly permitted interior decorations such as murals painted on plaster surfaces; the themes would be limited to the floral and foliate designs {Sarkar 1966: 13}. Clearly early Buddhist builders borrowed and transformed a great deal of contemporary secular architecture into the designs and constructions of their *sangharama*s; however, their plans were functions of the monastic programs that reflected contemporary social, economic, and religious conditions. Also there were monks who functioned like architects to assist and instruct builders and craftsmen in the process of visualization and completion of the *sangharama*s {Misra 1998 Volume I: 39}.

The ruin of Jivakavanarama [4.1] is among the most ancient of Indian Buddhist monasteries associated with Buddha and early Buddhism. Originally as a mango orchard outside the eastern gate of the inner city wall of Rajagriha near the foot of the Gijjhakuta hill, it was donated to Buddha's *Sangha* by the royal physician Jivaka under King Bimbisara of Magadha. Jivaka was a well-known figure in his time who studied medicine at the prestigious Taxila University in Gandhara; he reportedly cured many including Buddha who was once treated inside this monastery when he was injured by Devadatta, Buddha's jeal-

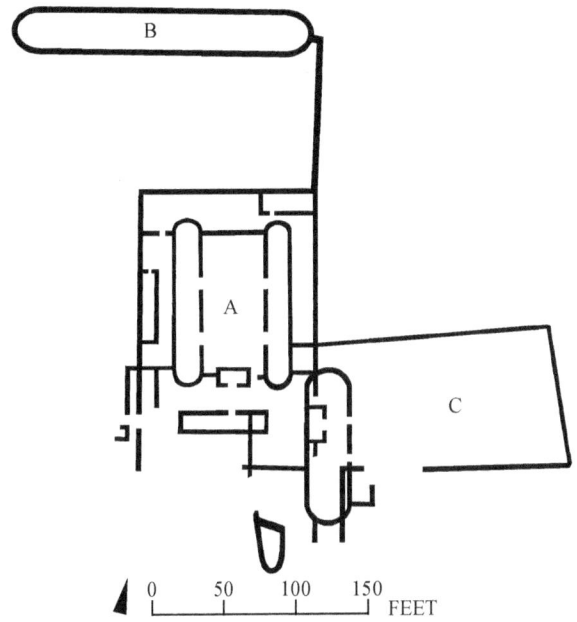

4.1. Plan. c. 530-400 BCE. Rajir- India

ous cousin and rival. The monastery seems to have been completed in two or three phases:

- Phase I (Area A) was probably the construction of the central precinct having two long and parallel elliptical halls that form an enclosed courtyard, each about 20' x 113' with two entrances. These were likely the communal *vihara*s where monks ate and slept all within the same space as common in early Buddhism; the area was obviously off-limit for the laity in those days. The communal characteristic of early *sangharama*s is also evident from the conspicuous absence of monks' private cells in these *vihara*s which were common in later cave monasteries [5.6] and quadrangular monasteries of Gandhara [4.2]. The area is enclosed by walls with the main entry in the south; there are several smaller buildings which might be entry pavilion, storage, service rooms, or some other functions. All buildings were once equipped with wooden doors and latches that have long perished or lost {Barua 1969: 17-18}. The apparent absence of access between the *vihara*s and the surrounding buildings might have been due to changes in elevation and stairs might have been provided to connect the different levels.
- Phase II (Area B) might constitute the construction of a rather extremely elongated elliptical hall 32' x 210' about 90' behind Area A. It might be a meditation hall or for monks who practiced austerities like the Ambalatthika in Veluvanarama; or it could also be used for congregational and ceremonial purposes involving a large number of people such as an assembly, meeting, and conference hall or for lecturing, preaching, or performing important rites like the *uposatha*, *upasampada*, *pavarana*, and *kathina*. This elliptical hall is different than the others as it does not have an entry doorway; probably the floor was originally at a higher level than the rest of the monastery and wooden or earthen staircases would be provided at the entrances which are no longer extant.
- Phase III (Area C) could be the new construction and enlargement of the monastery in its southeastern area including a large walled-in courtyard, which could be used for walking meditation exercises, and the huge elliptical hall nearly 33' x 106' with a small rectangular room inside that could be a private chapel, storage, or as the head monk's private cell. This hall could also be a reception hall where interactions between the *Sangha* and the laity took place or a service area.

Only the outlined rubble foundation of this monastery remains today and its floors were likely once paved with compacted earth and/or bricks; the walls might be of rubble-and-mud or wattle-and-daub construction while the roof might be covered in thatch {Dutt 1962: 62}. One can infer that these elliptical halls had semicircular barrel-vaulted ceilings with quadrantal vaults at both apsidal ends while the roofs certainly had dormers as shown in a similar example in the Bharhut relief [7.6]; the roofs of the rectangular buildings would likely be gable. Elliptical and apsidal designs were no doubt common in early Indian secular and religious architecture and extant examples can be found in the caves on the Barabar and Nagarjuni hills like Gopika and Lomas Risi [5.1-5.2].

There are evidences supporting the construction of Jivakavanarama between c. 530-400 BCE {Sarkar 1966: 16}:

- All later freestanding monasteries were quadrangular-and-celled type like Gandhara monasteries [4.2] dated no earlier than the first century CE.
- Elliptical apsidal and vaulted structures with side entries without interior columns were the hallmarks of the Maurya caves dated in the late third century BCE at the latest [5.1]; existing foundations of the Jetavanarama and Ghositarama also have similar plans {Sarkar 1966: 19}. This type also popularly occurred in the subsequent architecture of Gandhara, Kashmir, and India as in the Ter Temple [7.2-7.3] and late Hindu sites like Mamallapuram.

- The conspicuous absence of *stupa*s in or near the monastery. This feature is typically present in later and *stupa*-based monasteries generally from Asoka's reign onward like Sanchi [6.3] and before the quadrangular monasteries of Gandhara; this pushes Jivakavanarama to a pre-Mauyra and positively pre-Asoka date.
- The rubble foundation of Jivakavanarama is another evidence of its early date.
- Archaeological artifacts like iron nails, terracotta balls, animal figurines, and pottery have also been recovered from the site; the find of coarse red potteries have been dated not later than the fifth century BCE {Dutt 1962: 62}{Sarkar 1966: 16}.

2. Takht-i-bahi (first-fifth centuries CE) - Pakistan

Today the name Gandhara, once the second greatest Buddhist holy land after India, no longer remains on the Asian map and only Kandahar in Afghanistan distantly retains the name of this famous region. At its height between the second-third centuries CE, the core center of Gandhara encompassed the territory of Pakistan and eastern Afghanistan and bounded by the Hindu Kush in the west and Karakorum Mountains in the north with its most important urban centers in Taxila (ancient Takshasila) and Peshawar in Pakistan. The early history of Gandhara lies buried below the extensive remains of Taxila where archaeologists have uncovered successive periods of occupation since the sixth century BCE but apparently no earlier. Whether Taxila had any connections with the Indus Civilization over 300 miles to the south remains an open question but Bhir Mound, the earliest settlement in Taxila, certainly shares many similarities with the latter. The layout of its streets, soak-wells, and a pillared hall recall similar features in the Indus city of Mohenjo-daro {Marshall 1951: 11, 87-112}; the Taxilans and Gandharans were obviously aware of these Indus cities since they constructed a monastery and *stupa* on the top stratum of the Citadel at Mohenjo-daro [1.1]. Gandhara, like Kashmir, had repeatedly been subjected to foreign rules and remained a contested territory for much of its existence; yet during this time it continued to function as an important cosmopolitan center that facilitated the exchanges of goods, services, and ideas between India and other Asian countries as well as western Asia and Rome. Many famous foreigners and invaders of India traversed this well-known region from the Aryans, Alexander the Great, to celebrated Buddhist pilgrims like Fa-hsien and Hsuan-tsang, and latest the Muslims; some have left vivid accounts of the splendor during its heyday and utter ruins in the wake of foreign invasions.

The first foreign rule to have subjugated Gandhara was the Achaemenid Persians in the mid sixth century BCE when it became one of Persia's eastern satrapies; during the Persian rule (558-326 BCE), Taxila boasted one of the best universities in Asia. Jivaka, the famous royal physician and Buddha's disciple under King Bimbisara of Magadha, spent seven years studying medicine at Taxila University while King Prasenajit of Kosala, another supporter of Buddha, was also a student at this famous university; Angulimala, the fearsome bandit who was converted by Buddha, had reportedly studied here {Schumann 1989: 102, 108-109, 126}. The university taught many academic disciplines including laws, politics, government, medicine, philosophy, religion, combat skills, etc. and these were proofs of the cosmopolitan nature of Gandhara; Perian customs, arts, architecture, and religions, particularly Zoroastrianism, were undoubtedly familiar to the Taxilans during this time. Between c. 326-317 BCE, the possession of Gandhara was transferred to the Greek military rule under Alexander the Great who brought the region into direct contacts with western Asia and the Western World. Alexander's army eventually withdrew but a few contingents of its troops and no doubt civilian Greeks stayed behind and many scholars believe that these isolated pockets of Asian Greeks and their particular branch of Western arts were the sources for later Gandhara arts. After the Greeks' rule, Gandhara was in the hands of the Indian Maurya Dynasty (317-189 BCE) where Asoka and his son Kunala were its territorial governors; the Taxilans were known to have revolted numerous times under their rules. As already noted, Asoka was mainly responsible for the introduction and expansion of Buddhism in Gandhara in the third century BCE and several of his edicts were engraved on the boulders in Afghanistan and Gandhara at Shahbazgarhi, Mansehra, Laghman, Pul-i-Darunta, Shar-i-Kuna, and Kandahar; an Asoka edict has also been found on a pillar in Taxila. These Asoka edicts had been written in many languages mainly Aramaic, Greek, and Kharosthi reflecting the cosmopolitan and multi-ethnic nature of the Gandharans; the latter was the official language of Gandhara between the fourth century BCE-fifth centuries CE {Marshall 1951: 375-376}. Without a doubt Buddhism was on the rise in Gandhara under Asoka's reign.

In the early second century BCE the remaining Asian Greeks, popularly known as Bactrian Greeks for their kingdom in northern Afghanistan grappled Gandhara from the Indians after the collapse of the Maurya Dynasty. The Bactrian Greeks ruled Gandhara between c. 189-90 BCE though the final end of all Greek rules in Asia happened in c. 30 BCE with the death of Hermaeus; between c. 90-30 BCE the Bactrian Greeks were in constant struggles with the Sakas, also known as the Scythians or an Iranian-speaking nomadic tribe originated in Central Asia. The Bactrian Greeks meanwhile maintained cordial relations with the Indians under the Shunga Dynasty (184-72 BCE) and in all likelihood continued to adopt a secular policy toward all religions in the multi-cultural and multi-ethnic atmosphere of Gandhara; Buddhism, Zoroastrianism, Hinduism, and Jainism likely flourished side by side. The powerful Asian Greek king Menander (r. 163-150 BCE), known in Buddhist literature as Milinda, was reputedly converted by Thera Nagasena after hearing a convincing sermon by the latter on the Theravada theory of Non-*atman* {Radhakrishnan 1989: 345-346, 390-399}{Marshall 1951: 33}. Perhaps the greatest legacy of the Bactrian Greeks in Gandhara was the founding of Sirkap in Taxila which continued to be occupied and expanded by the succeeding Sakas and Parthians until c. 50 CE when the Kushans relocated their new capital to Sirsukh, also within the vicinity of Taxila. The Sakas, who ruled Gandhara intermittently between c. 90-30 BCE, finally extinguished the last of the Greek pockets in c. 30 BCE and their reign after this victory, dubbed Later Sakas, continued until c. 25 CE; it was during the Later Sakas that Gandhara arts and architecture, though still in its infancy, gradually began to emerge. The Sakas, whose official religion was probably Zoroastrianism from their Iraninan-related origin also tolerated all religions in their domain much like their predecessors. Another important group of Iranian-speaking peoples, who replaced the Sakas and ruled Gandhara between c. 25-50 CE, was the Parthians (c. 250 BCE-226 CE); their rule opened Gandhara into direct communications with western Asia and the Western World which further enabled the region to freely and directly borrow the arts and architecture from the latter. Conspicuous symbols of Western arts and architecture such as Corinthian and Ionic pilasters and columns alongwith Western-styled sculptures would become widespread in Gandhara from this time on. The zenith of Gandhara must be under the Kushans, or the Yueh-chis of the Chinese who migrated from Turkistan or western China, after they ousted the Parthians. The Kushan Dynasty (c. 50-454 CE) founded its new capital at Sirsukh, a little further north of Sirkap; their long rule was wrecked by several invasions and subjugations from the Sassanid Dynasty (c. 226-651 CE) of Iran, the first in c. 241 CE by Shapur I and the second in c. 350 CE by Shapur II. At its zenith, the vast Kushan Empire stretched all the way to the Aral Sea (west) and parts of Turkistan (north) to the Indian Ocean in Pakistan (south) and northwestern India (east). The territories included the Central Asian republics, eastern Afghanistan, much of Pakistan, Kashmir, northwestern India in Gujarat, Rajasthan, and Uttar Pradesh, and the western half of Turkistan {Frunkin 1970: 49-53}; Kushan influences certainly extended all the way to the Chinese frontier in Dunhuang as numerous Gandhara-styled murals, temples, and *stupa*s alongwith Kharosthi inscriptions have been discovered in Miran and Lou-lan. The main capital of the Kushans was in Peshawar in northwestern Pakistan with a second capital at Kapisa (Begram) in Afghanistan. The religious cosmopolitanism of the Kushans has well attested as Greek, Iranian, Hindu, and Buddhist deities were found on many Kushan coins but the prevailing religion was undoubtedly Buddhism {Rowland 1974: 80}. In the earlier years of the Kushans, Buddhism, which had remained stagnant in the previous centuries, received a tremendous boost under the patronage of the greatest Kushan King Kanishka (r. 128-151 CE). He sponsored the Fourth Buddhist Council in Kashmir, disseminated missionaries to Central Asia and China, and founded numerous new monasteries and *stupa*s during his illustrious reign; he was clearly following the footsteps of Asoka before him and undeniably the second greatest Buddhist king after Asoka thanks to his generous patronage of Buddhism. Under the Kushans' rule, the furthest western expansion of Buddhism reached as far as Merv in Turmenistan in the fifth century CE where foundations of monasteries and *stupa*s have been uncovered by archaeologists. This was decidedly the most glorious period of Gandhara and in particular Buddhist arts and architecture which radiated its influential reverberation throughout India, Central and East Asia. The numerous monasteries and imposing *stupa*s perched on the hillsides of Swat (probably ancient Uddiyana) with snow-capped mountains in the background must have dazzled the eyes of past pilgrims and visitors; the monks could not have chosen an ideal location for their monastic life. In Swat alone Fa-hsien, the Chinese monk-pilgrim, reported more than 600 monasteries and numerous *stupa*s while for the whole Gandhara the number must be in the thousands; even today their ruins still dot the Swat landscape. The soaring Kanishka Stupa [6.18] in Peshawar rising over 500' in height must have mesmerized Buddhist devotees all over Asia. After the eclipse of the Kushans, who had briefly managed to reestablish their rule in Gandhara as the Later or Kidara Kushans (c. 390-454 CE) after the Sassanian rule, Buddhism gradually declined in the region. The invasion and occupation of Gandhara by the White Huns (Hephthalites or Ephtalites) seriously weakened the Buddhist clout in the region; their anti-

Buddhist rule and persecutions, which lasted between c. 454-552 CE, destroyed many monasteries and *stupa*s and even so Buddhism continued to thrive. After the seventh century CE, Gandhara was variously ruled by Kashmir and Hindu dynasties until finally converted to Islam in 1013 CE.

The Buddhist ruins of Gandhara lied dormant for centuries but its former glories had vividly been preserved in the passages of Buddhist literature until reawaken in the early nineteenth century CE by the British. Driven by the hunger for antiquities, these colonial Brits roamed incessantly throughout the region searching for treasures; they opened and destroyed many *stupa*s, looted their precious contents, and brought many valuable pieces to Britain. The most notorious looter was Horace H. Wilson as openly retold in his book 'Ariana Antiqua;' even famous scholars like Alfred Foucher also carried off some priceless Buddhist statues from Gandhara back to France. Serious archaeological missions in the region began with Alexander Cunningham who surveyed many Gandhara ruins; unfortunately many monuments once described by him are no longer extant today and they continue to be destroyed by wars, lootings, and Muslim anti-idolatrous sentiments. The next great effort was carried out under John Marshall's tutelage which greatly accelerated the understanding Gandhara contribution to Buddhist arts and architecture; his surveys of Taxila and the surrounding monasteries have proven extremely valuable in resurrecting the splendid heyday of Buddhism in Gandhara. Spurious archaeological operations were also carried out by Aurel Stein in the 1930s CE but these were not systematic and lacking in depth. After the independence of Afghanistan and Pakistan, the French was once again active in Afghanistan while the Italians were meticulously digging and documenting the grounds of Swat under great leaderships like Domenico Faccenna. The Great Buddhas of Bamiyan, the only biggest and oldest extant Gandhara-Styled statues in the world, have been completely destroyed in March 2001 CE by the Muslim Talibans for religious (Islam is an iconoclastic religion) and ethno-political reasons (the Greco-Roman-styled Buddhas are the constant reminder of Western and Indian hegemony). Buddhism once again became the casualty in the struggle for the cultural and ethnic identity that had been going on in this region since its beginning history.

The ruins and recovered artifacts from Gandhara are vast to be adequately covered in a volume and readers shall also see Chapter 6 for further discussions on Gandhara architecture; here I will focus on the monastic remains. The architecture of Gandhara can be divided into two categories and periods: (a) The early period up to the Parthians had many non-Buddhist and secular remains though a few Buddhist structures were also constructed and (b) the Buddhist period was generally inaugurated by the Kushans. Great urban centers of Gandhara like Taxila comprise the first category of remains starting with Bhir Mound (sixth-early second centuries BCE), then Sirkap (early second century BCE-mid first centuries CE), and lastly Sirsukh (mid first-late fifth centuries CE). At Bhir Mound the streets were irregularly planned with rubble-walled houses, many having a second story, organized around central courtyards; their walls and roofs, the latter of which consisted of timber planks and beams, were coated with several layers of mud plaster. Sirkap, which was initially planned by the Bactrian Greeks, was laid out in grids with building blocks bounded by streets intersected at ninety-degree angles; for defensive purposes the city had a main gateway. The construction material was primarily rubble laid in mud; though the houses at Sirkap appeared more organized and symmetrical in plans than those at Bhir Mound, they were nevertheless very similar in forms. Some times during the Parthian Period, the rubble masonry would be replaced with the diaper masonry as a new method of construction; in the latter type, the spaces between large dressed stones were filled with rows of smaller and neatly cut stone pieces. John Marshall theorized that the introduction of this new construction technology, in particular its employment of heavy stone blocks, provided better reinforcement and protection than rubbles against the violent shaking of earthquakes {Marshall 1951 Volume I: 137}; moreover, the introduction of large stones in buildings were also vital in defensive purposes. At Sirkap there were numerous imposing religious edifices constructed within civic and residential blocks, most of which had probably been rebuilt in the newly diaper masonry after the allegedly great earthquake in c. 25 CE. In c. 50 CE, the Kushans built their new city at Sirsukh which was smaller than Sirkap though both shared many similarities in the architecture; the new features at Sirsukh were the uses of larger stones in the diaper masonry while its city walls would be fortified with circular and semicircular bastions.

There were numerous religious and secular structures, including Buddhist and non-Buddhist ones, throughout ancient Gandhara but virtually all have perished over the centuries save for their ruins. Ever since Asoka patronized Buddhism in the third century BCE, it probably eclipsed all other faiths in Gandhara from then on; however a surviving temple, the Jandial Temple, suggested that other religions also thrived alongside Buddhism. Its plan obviously imitated a Greek Ionic temple similar to the Temple of Apollo Epicurius at Bassae {Fletcher 1975: 220} though it was essentially an Asian Greek design; John Marshall thought that it had been built for the Zoroastrian religion but its true sectarian affiliation remains unknown. This temple had solid rubble walls punctured with rows of windows on the exterior with a flat roof covering the nave; possibly there was a *sikhara* towering above the inner sanctum at the back from its massive core and it could be among the earliest known *sikhara*s in the Indian subcontinent. Its Ionic columns were also Asian in conception in which the volutes of their capitals were without the hanging floral motif as in the Greek Ionic order; their Attic bases and unfluted shafts were clearly favored by the Romans and not Greeks as Marshall believed. Initially Marshall dated this temple in the early Sakas (c. 58 BCE) but he later credited it to the Bactrian Greeks (second century BCE) based on its Greek plan and coursed rubble masonry resembling the walls of Sirkap {Marshall 1951: 222-229}. However overwhelming evidences pointed to a late Saka date (c. 5 CE) based on: (a) The coins of likely Azes II discovered in a similar Ionic temple at Mohra Maliaran, (b) the Ionic columns were definitely more Roman than Greek, and (c) its course rubble walls appear neater and sturdier of a later type.

There are several Buddhist remains before the Kushans; the oldest is a fragment of an octagonal marble pillar at Block F in Sirkap containing an Aramaic inscription attributed to Asoka (third century BCE). Other Buddhist structures at Sirkap are the imposing Apsidal Temple (Later Sakas-Parthians or c. 30 BCE-50 CE), Block F Stupa (Later Sakas or c. 0 CE), Block G Stupa (Later Sakas or c. 25 CE), Block E' Stupa (Later Sakas-Kushans or c. 30 BCE-150 CE); the huge Apsidal Temple was probably the oldest of its kind in Gandhara which certainly originated in earlier Indian apsidal designs [4.1, 7.2-7.3]. Block F Stupa, also known as 'Stupa of Doubleheaded Eagle' and like Block G Stupa, was faced with precisely cut ashlars, which is a type of masonry earlier than the diaper type. The former *stupa* was of an earlier date which combined Greco-Roman and Indian elements and likely dated in the beginning of the Common Era; each *stupa* had a *vedika*, *anda*, and *harmika* on their plinths but the latter also had four tall freestanding columns in the four corners like Saidu Sharif Stupa I [6.14]. The core of Block E' Stupa is unique in having four intersecting walls likely to support the weight of the dome; similar examples can also be found in the Nagarjunakonda and Dhamarajika *stupa*s [6.13]. Dharmarajika is another preeminent Taxila *stupa* with a form similar to other *stupa*s outside Taxila like Manikyala and Butkara I; the biggest and tallest of all Gandhara *stupa*s was Kanishka Stupa [6.18]. During the Kushan Dynasty constructions of new Buddhist monasteries mushroomed all over Gandhara thanks to the generous patronage of King Kanishka; the scales of Gandhara monasteries grew tremendously, each usually having a main *stupa* enclosed by an image chapel area, a votive *stupa* area, and monks' residential quarter. Gandhara monasteries generally congregated around Taxila, the Peshawar Valley, and Swat which numbered in the thousands at the height of the Buddhist ascendancy in the region. Moreover, the extension of Gandhara cultural sphere also encompassed eastern Afghanistan, Central Asia, and Turkistan; unfortunately the monuments in these areas have been thoroughly destroyed beyond recognition over centuries of neglect, demolition, and constant warfare but visible outlines of their plans and recovered fragments still permit reliable reconstructions. Between the founding of earliest Indian *sangharamas*, as exemplified in Jivakavanarama [4.1], and the rise of the Gandhara quadrangular monasteries was the development of Indian rock-hewn cave monasteries, which had been mainly constructed in the Deccan between the second century BCE-first centuries CE (Chapter 5). With the rising popularity of the *stupa* cult first fomented by Emperor Asoka, isolated structures would begin to congregate randomly around a principal *stupa* and the site gradually grew into a monastic settlement as in Sanchi [6.3] in India and Dharmarajika and Butkara I in Gandhara. These were the unplanned or organic *stupa*-based monasteries that arose as a direct result of the *stupa* cult and contemporary Buddhist practices since monks still favored an itinerant lifestyle and had not yet been receptive to the prospect of settling down a comfortable life in well-built monasteries with all the amenities provided by wealthy donors. The situation began to change in the first century CE, which was induced by a new social and religious atmosphere, especially in Gandhara where it had been under the successive rules of non-Indians since the second century BCE. The Gandharans, with the Kushans foremost among them, were apparently not bounded by the strict orthodox Buddhist tradition as in India and willing to experiment and adopt new ideas that deemed suitable for their region. The rise of the influential and progressive Mahayana School could have also contributed to the liberalization of Buddhism in Gandhara. It was in Kashmir where the Fourth Buddhist Council, which was sponsored by King Kanishka, was held and attended by many Mahayana pioneers; the Sarvastivada, a Theravada sect with a Mahayana leaning, dominated this council and also predominant in Gandhara at the time. Such conditions were ripe for a new epoch in the history of Gandhara Buddhism in which it made two significant contributions to Buddhist architecture, namely the image temple (*pratimagriha*) and the planned quadrangular monastery. As we shall see later that even these creations already had antecedents in India but it was in Gandhara where they would be crystallized in their final forms and subsequently reintroduced back to India and Asia. The *pratimagriha* was a product of Mahayana devotionalism with its cult of tangible images of Buddhas and *bodhisattva*s that ultimately supplanted the relics as the principal emblem of Buddhism in the subsequent centuries. Regarding the origin of the quadrangular monastery, John Marshall clearly stated his position {Marshall 1951 Volume I: 233}:

> The quadrangular, high-walled monastery or vihara was of still later date than the stupa; for it seems to have made its first appearance in the sangharamas of the North-West during the first century A.D., and thence to have found its way southward and eastward to the rest of India.

Before going into its evolution, it is first necessary to give a general survey of some of the most important monasteries in Gandhara that have been discovered by archaeologists over the centuries; earlier foreign pilgrims also gave vivid accounts of contemporary Buddhist monasteries in Gandhara during their visits. In Swat alone Fa-hsien, the Chinese monk-pilgrim who passed through Gandhara in the early fifth century CE, reported more than 600 monasteries while Hsuan-tsang, another famous Chinese monk-pilgrim traveling in India in the early seventh century CE, reported over 1,400 monasteries in Swat and about 1,000 monasteries in Gandhara but only fifteen were active while the rest were in ruins. The great persecution of the Hephthalite King Miharakula in the early sixth century CE already destroyed 1,600 *stupa*s and monasteries in Gandhara {Sehrai 1982: 52}; the statistics no doubt reflected the strength of Buddhism in the region before its decline. Gandhara Buddhists literally embraced Buddha's recommendation 'not too far, not too near from town' for the establishment of their monasteries, which were often constructed on low-lying knolls overlooking towns, secluded hillocks near streams where water could be obtained, or around man-made wells; the three principal centers for Buddhist monasteries in Gandhara were in Taxila, the Peshawar Valley, and Swat. There were other great monastic centers in the outlying extensions of Gandhara in Afghanistan, Central Asia, and Turkistan; these were generally constructed later and heavily influenced by Gandhara models and will not be included in this section. The great monasteries on the hills surrounding Taxila have been thoroughly excavated by John Marshall between 1913-1934 CE and greatly contributed to the fundamental understanding of Gandhara monastic architecture {Marshall 1951 Volume I: 230-397}. These include Dharmarajika (third century BCE-seventh centuries CE) **[6.13]**, Khader Mohra-Akhauri or Chir Tope A-C, D1-D2 (first-second centuries CE), Jandial A-B (first-third centuries CE), Kalawan (first-fifth centuries CE), Giri (first-fifth cenrury CE), Kunala-Ghai (first-fifth centuries CE), Pippala (first-fifth centuries CE), Mohra Moradu (second-fifth centuries CE), Jaulian (second-fifth centuries CE), Lalchak (third-fifth centuries CE), and Bhamala (fourth-fifth centuries CE) **[6.17]**. In the Peshawar Valley, some of the biggest monasteries in the area include Takht-i-bahi (first-fifth centuries CE) **[4.2-4.3]**, Jamalgarhi (first-fifth centuries CE), and Sahri Bahlol (first-fifth centuries CE). A few important monasteries in Swat that have been thoroughly studied by Italian archaeologists include Butkara (third century BCE-fifth centuries CE) and Saidu Sharif (first-fifth cenrury CE) **[6.14]**. Gandhara monasteries generally flourished between the first-fifth centuries CE and most had been constructed in the prosperous period between Kanishka (r. 128-151 CE) to Vasudeva I (r. 202-230 CE). Between c. 241-390 CE Gandhara was under the Iranian control of the Sassanid Dynasty and Buddhist monasteries were probably relegated into the background or remained stagnant. The resurgence of monastery constructions between c. 390-454 CE, as documented by John Marshall, could be due to the rise of the Later/Kidara Kushans and fresh religious impetus from Gupta India. The analyses of Gandhara monasteries have also shed light on their development over the centuries:

- Early organic monasteries in Gandhara (c. 250 BCE-50 CE) are *stupa*-based monastic settlements centering on dominant *stupa*s as exemplified in Dharmarajika **[6.13]** and Butkara I. In Dharmarajika, initially a few *vihara* cells for monks were haphazardly constructed to the west and north of the main *stupa*; the next development was the construction of a ring of image chapels enclosing the main *stupa* similar to Jamalgarhi. These phases dated between c. 0-150 CE though the core of the *stupa* itself dated in the second century BCE; the *stupa*-based plan already had precursors in India like Sanchi **[6.3]**.
- At a slightly later date (c. 50-150 CE), the *stupa*-based monastery would be replaced with the characteristic quadrangular plan of Gandhara. Initially the main Gandhara-Styled *stupa* of a medium size like **[6.15]** was placed outside the quadrangular *vihara* with monks' cells on the three sides and a principal entrance in the remaining side (Chir Tope

A, C). Next, an assembly room and *caityagriha* chapels would be incorporated into the *vihara* and a few *pratimagriha*s added outside the *vihara* next to the main *stupa*; the latter was also surrounded with smaller votive *stupa*s (Chir Tope B). Eventually the *stupa* would be enclosed within a wall (Chir Tope D1) and finally placed inside a quadrangular *vihara* (Chir Tope D2); all the *vihara*s in these cases still had no verandahs. The Gandhara monastery at Mohenjo-daro [1.1] with a *stupa* in the center of the celled quadrangle might be constructed in this phase.

- In the next stage (c. 150-300 CE), all elements in the plan like the *vihara*, the main *stupa*, votive *stupa*s, and *pratimagriha*s would be typologically organized into zones to form a cohesive plan; the monastery also increased in size and height. An important step in this phase was the replacement of the *caityagriha* chapel inside the *vihara* with a *pratimagriha* concurrent with the rise of image worship over *stupa*. In rare instances independent Relic or Commemorative *stupa*s, not to be confused with the *caityagriha* chapels, would also be erected inside the cells in memory of deceased eminent monks. The *vihara* height had also been raised to two stories with colonnaded verandahs on both stories and a flat roof; the monastery also contained a drainage system buried underneath the floor to discharge excess water and wastes away from the building. The hypaethral and depressed courtyard in the center of the quadrangle now had a facility for bathing which might be constructed of timber initially but later replaced with brick; Kalawan was a typical example of this phase.

- Around the third-fourth centuries CE, further elaboration of the architectural details would be particularly emphasized such as the addition of image niches in the *vihara* and monks' cells were also provided with private windows and alcoves; the woodworks were meticulously carved with reliefs on the verandah walls; the final surfaces would likely be lavishly painted or gilded. Another important development in the fourth-fifth centuries CE was the incorporation of the service quarter (kitchen, refectory, scullery, etc.) into the quadrangular plan; among the earliest presence of a refectory in a Gandhara monastery came from a Kanishka inscription (c. 128-151 CE) mentioning its construction in the Kanishka (Shahji-ki-dheri) *vihara* {Yaldiz and Others 1987: 79}. Gandhara monasteries during this period accumulated enough wealth so that monks practically gave up the ancient orthodox tradition of begging for food as it was now essentially an obsolete custom; Mohra Moradu was an exemplary model of this phase.

- The final perfection of the Gandhara quadrangular plan was between the fourth-fifth centuries CE in which all previous elements would be organized and standardized into well-conceived and symmetrical plans; the configuration of the worship area with the main *stupa* surrounded by image chapels became the typical feature in the plan. There were also distinct zones within Gandhara monasteries for specialized activities such as the promenade for monks' walking exercises and relaxation as well meditational cells for monks' solitude or austerity practice. Jaulian and Takht-i-bahi [4.2-4.3] reflected these latest trends in the monastic design and were among the finest and archetypical of all Gandhara monasteries.

Being at the crossroads of Asia, Gandhara arts and architecture absorbed repeated waves of influences from western Asia and the West as much as India. The arch (ogee, pointed, semicircular, and corbelled) and vaulted constructions were not Gandhara inventions but they were frequently employed in monastic architecture; with the exception of the semicircular arch, which originated in Roman and Assyrian architecture, the other arches were of Indian origins. Vaulted and domed construction already occurred in Indian architecture at a very early stage as in Jivakavanarama [4.1] and Bairat Temple [7.1]. The pointed arch and vault can be found in the Indian Sitamarhi cave (c. 214-206 BCE) in Bihar {Fergusson 1910: 133, fg. 57} while the corbelled arch has already occurred in Harappa architecture; the pointed was employed in Takht-i-bahi at least in the second century CE and Indian architecture from the fifth century CE on {ASIAR 1910-1911: pl. XVII, XX}{Marshall 1960: fg. 80}. It would not be employed in Islamic architecture until the eighth century CE and Gothic architecture in the West until the eleventh century CE. Stucco, an exquisite material employed in high-end projects, might have been an import from the West which was common in Gandhara sculptures and architecture; Gandhara architecture principally employed, in chronological order, the rubble, diaper, and semi-ashlar masonries using mud or lime as mortar. According to the artifacts recovered from John Marshall's excavations, the structure of Gandhara monasteries consisted of timber members secured by iron bolts and nails; he further opined that the roofs could be "covered with a thick layer of mud," that is a flat roof. This may explain the reason for the massive foundations in these monasteries, besides supporting several floors {Marshall 1951 Volume I: 260-261, 369-371, 378, 382, pl. 55}; however, this does not rule out the possibilities of pitched or even curved (vaulted) roofs in Gandhara monasteries.

Takht-i-bahi **[4.2-4.3]** was not mentioned by Chinese pilgrims like Fa-hsien, Sung-yun, and Hsuan-tsang between the fifth-seventh centuries CE; this could be due to its seclusion or lesser prominence as a Buddhist center compared to those in Taxila; moreover, it might have sunk into obscurity after the ferocious Hephthalite persecutions in the early sixth century CE. Its name was probably derived from the word 'Takht' (seat) and 'Bahi' (reservoir) on the account of the two large reservoirs on the hill for the monastery usage {Sehrai 1982: 55-56}. The site has been known to Europeans as early as 1836 CE when it was mentioned by a French officer working under Ranjit Singh; from then on it was frequently visited by treasure collectors gathering ancient artifacts from the ruins. General Maclagan sent men here in 1869-1870 CE to collect sculptures for the Lahore Museum; more items would be removed from the site by Dr. Leitner in 1870 CE and Lieutenant Crompton in 1872 CE. Archaeological surveys of the site began in 1852 CE when it was briefly explored by Lieutenants Lumsden and Stokes and also described in details by H. W. Bellew in 1864 CE; the first preliminary excavation was conducted by Sergeant Wilcher in 1871 CE. Alexander Cunningham again excavated and made surveyed drawings of the site in 1872-

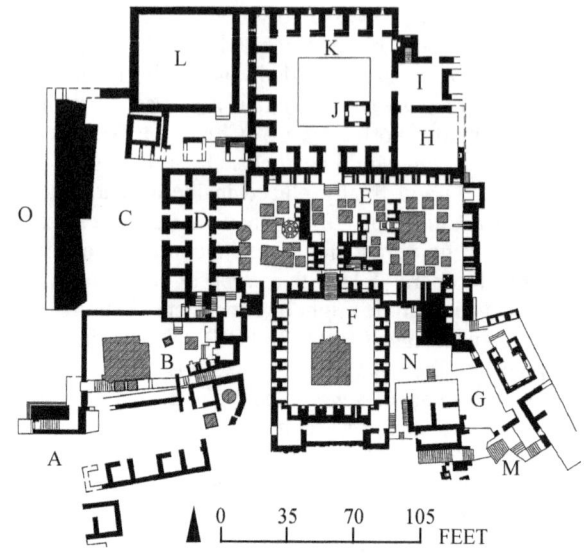

4.2. Plan
First-fifth centuries CE
Mardan- Pakistan

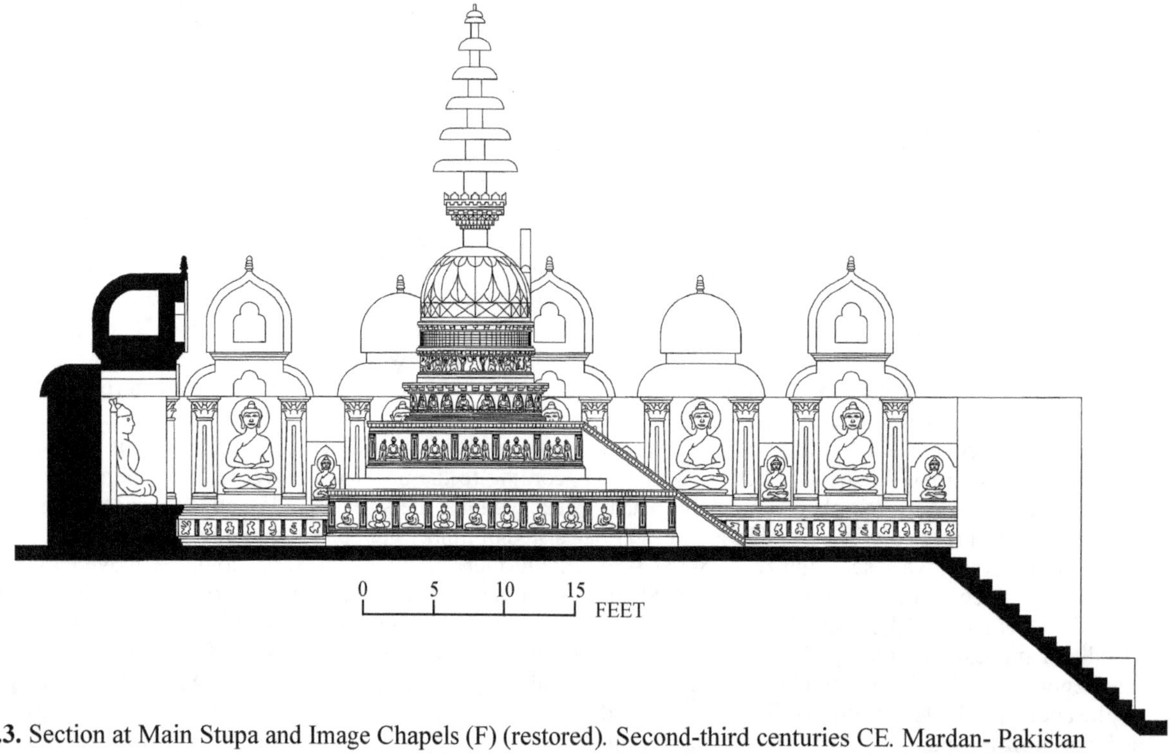

4.3. Section at Main Stupa and Image Chapels (F) (restored). Second-third centuries CE. Mardan- Pakistan

1873 CE followed by David B. Spooner's excavations between 1907-1911 CE and H. Hargreaves' between 1910-1913 CE; conservation works on the site began between 1907-1929 CE to secure the site from further decay {Sehrai 1982: 52-57}.

The site is situated fifty-two miles northeast of Peshawar perching on a hill overlooking the Peshawar Valley; its highly structured plan and an acme among Gandhara monasteries covers an area of 227' east-west x 230' north-south. There are two main approaches to the site from the southwest (A) and southeast (M); area (B) once contained six colossal standing stucco Buddhas of about 20' high each {ASIAR 1910-1911: 38, pl. XXI} while (G) consists of image chapels and *stupa*s outside the central zone that could be reserved for pilgrims or related facilities. Distinct zones can clearly be perceived from the plan with the quadrangular *vihara* (K) in the north that includes Assembly (L), Kitchen (I), Refectory (H), and an outdoor Bath (J). The meditational areas (C-D) in the west include monks' meditational cells (D) and a promenade for relaxation or walking meditation exercises (C); the court of small votive *stupa*s (E) lies between the *vihara* and the main *stupa* and image chapels (F). The *vihara*, which was likely two-storied high of an undetermined roof from the presence of a staircase north of (I), and the main *stupa*-chapels (F) are higher than the votive *stupa* court (E); the ground level of the latter continues in a flat roof spanning over the meditation cells (D). The ground level of the promenade (C) and meditation cells (D) is nearly two-storied below the upper main level which is demarcated and buttressed by a massive retaining wall (O) {ASIAR 1910-1911: 33-39}. The massive solid pier (N) in the southeast with a stair in the west side might once serve as an observation tower like similar cases in the monasteries of Dharmarajika Court G and Bhamala. Warnings would be issued to the monks to flee, or defend their abodes if such scenario really existed in Buddhism, in the case of impending dangers from approaching bandits or hostile forces {Marshall 1951 Volume I: 281}; the wealth and opulence of Gandhara monasteries during this time could certainly be very tempting and easy targets for those with power and weapons. This supposed observation tower could also be used as a bell tower to inform the inmates the transition to different activities, say from meditation to lunch time, in accordance to the daily schedule and monastic regulation. A similar procedure was also observed at Nalanda in the seventh century CE by the Chinese pilgrim I-tsing (683-727 CE) though a clepsydra or water-clock, drum, conch-shell, and bell were used instead {Dutt 1962: 335-336}. The *vihara* (K) of about 79' x 85' has cells on four sides, each with its own clerestory windows, and possibly preceded by timber pillared verandahs enclosing the hypaethral courtyard; there is an image chapel on the side of its stair in the eastern wall and a large cell in its northwestern corner which might be reserved for the abbot's room as in Nalanda {Misra 1998 Volume III: 196}. According to the estimate given by Alexander Cunningham, the total number of the inmates in Takht-i-bahi would amount to thirty-four if counting all the cells on the two floors of the *vihara* {ASIAR 1872-1873: 31-32}. The 62' x 72'6" worship court or chapel containing a main *stupa* in the center and image chapels (F) **[4.3]** is situated on the highest ground and certainly the centerpiece of the monastery. Its design evolved from earlier precursors in monasteries like Dharmarajika, Jamalgarhi, Kalawan, and Jaulian which consisted of a principal Gandhara-Styled *stupa* in the center having two diminishing terraces of a 20'3" x 29'7" base and probably in the range of 30s' high. The original form of this *stupa* was likely very similar to the one in the Indian Museum Kolkata **[6.15]**, Devnimori Stupa (fourth-seventh centuries CE) in Gujarat (India), and Mirpurkhas (fifth-tenth centuries CE) in Sindh (Pakistan) {Deva 1995: 9, 28}. Note that its receding terraces had clearly been described by Alexander Cunningham {ASIAR 1872-1873: 26} but Percy Brown did not show this in his conjectured restoration drawing {Brown 1965: Pl. XXXIII}. The *stupa* in the center is surrounded on three sides by image chapels of 4'8" x 6' plans of about 15'6"-17' high and alternated with smaller ones of 2'3"-2'10" x 2'11" of about about 7'5" high. These chapels are elevated on a continuous 2'9" high platform and which forms evolved from the earlier Indian apsidal design **[4.1, 7.2-7.3]**; the remaining side is a high retaining wall punctuated by a main staircase in the center with chapels facing Court (E). This *stupa*-chapel court, like other structures in the monastery, was constructed of the diaper and semi-ashlar masonry, finished with plaster, and decorated with pseudo-Corinthian pilasters, dentils, and polychrome or gilded stucco sculptures. The pointed arch in the vaulted passages in areas (B) and (D), as already stated above, was among the earliest instance of its structural employment in Gandhara architecture. Besides the architecture, hundreds of sculptural specimens have also been recovered from Takht-i-bahi which can be categorized into three types {Sehrai 1982: 79-81}: (a) Pre-Classic Gandhara (first century CE) shows mainly Indian influences including animal and floral designs and carved in stone, (b) Classic Gandhara (second-third centuries CE) contain Indian, west Asian, and Greco-Roman elements; the sculptures are generally based on Theravada themes with Buddha's Life Scenes and the *jataka*s; schist is the material of choice but stucco has also been used in modeling, (c) Late Gandhara (fourth-fifth centuries CE) favors Mahayana images of Buddhas and *bodhisattva*s like Maitreya and Avalokitesvara; stucco would supplant schist as the primary material. John Marshall clearly pointed out the differences between the Classic and late Gandhara schools of sculptures {Marshall 1951 Volume I: 254}:

> This is not the place to discuss the differences between these Gandhara reliefs and the later stucco reliefs of the Indo-Afghan School, but it may be noted in passing that scenes such as these, which are taken from the life of the Buddha or from the *Jataka* stories, are never illustrated among the sculptures of the later school, their place being taken by endless repetitions of Buddha and Bodhisattva figures with their attendant *deva*s and human devotees.

There are two fragments of Kharosthi inscriptions rediscovered at Takht-i-bahi that could help in determining the construction date of the monastery {ASIAR 1910-1911: 34}{Marshall 1951 Volume I: 58}. The first was written in the twenty-sixth year of the Parthian King Gondophares' reign and in the year 103 of Azes Era or c. 45 CE; another inscription found in (D) is undated and addressed 'to the Buddhist (monks) Community of the four quarters;' it is also possible to perceive the construction phases of the monastery from studying its plan. The earliest constructions (first century CE) were likely around the entrances, or (A), (B), (G), and (M), where isolated *vihara* cells, a *caityagriha* chapel, and various *pratimagriha*s are located; the remaining structures in the upper areas were constructed from the second century CE on from their well-organized plans. Like other Gandhara monasteries, Takht-i-bahi appeared to undergo major restorations and expansions between the fourth-fifth centuries CE with the installations of new stucco decorations and images.

Takht-i-bahi, like other Gandhara monasteries and Indian cave monasteries, was functionally not a communal monastery like Jivakavanarama [4.1] as a new spirit of individualism had clearly resonated in its celled quadrangular plan wherein the cells would be provided for individual monks. This plan certainly evolved from earlier Indian cave monasteries like Bhaja [5.6] which ultimately originated in the Indus Civilization like the Great Bath of Mohenjo-daro [1.2-1.3] from the presence of the cells, verandah, and hypaethral courtyard. Furthermore, Greco-Roman elements, which were mostly employed in the architectural decorations, permeated Gandhara and profoundly influenced its arts and architecture between the first-third centuries CE. Having been crystallized in Gandhara for several centuries, the quadrangular plan would subsequently be reintroduced back to India in celebrated monasteries like Nalanda [4.4] and Somapura [4.8]. From Gandhara it was disseminated to Central Asia, Turkistan, and to a lesser extent East Asia [4.5]; Gandhara monasteries with their mud flat roofs perching on the hills might have also inspired the Tibetan hilltop/fortress monasteries.

3. Nalanda (fifth-thirteenth centuries CE) - India

The quadrangular monastery, which was a natural progression from the Indian cave monasteries, evolved into its highly structured plan in Gandhara that would later be embraced wholeheartedly by the Indian Buddhists during the Gupta Dynasty (320-647 CE). On the Indian proper, thanks to the increases in wealth, influence, and fundamental changes in Indian Buddhism itself Indian Buddhists also developed an entirely new concept for the Buddhist monastery, a monastic university, with the Gandhara plan as its architectural model. With the emergence of the Mahayana in the early centuries of the Common Era, a newly liberal outlook was permeating the Buddhist *Sangha*. There were increasing interactions between members of the *Sangha* and between the *Sangha* with the laity as monks were burdened with the responsibility of inculcating the Buddhist doctrines in their followers and fellow monks. Consequently monasteries gradually became the focal point of Buddhist learning and some, like Nalanda, grew into major centers of Buddhist education and great monastic universities specializing in higher learning by training and teaching the new generations of Buddhist monks as well as non-Buddhists and seculars. The increasingly settled lifestyle of the monks in conjunction with the religious antagonism and competition among fellow Buddhists, particularly between the Mahayana and Theravada, and the competition from non-Buddhist faiths like Hinduism, which challenged the long-lived preeminent status enjoyed by Buddhism, all have contributed to the rise of the Buddhist monastic university. As Dutt rightly put it {Dutt 1962: 323}:

> It must have been felt at a certain stage that the mere 'study for faith' fell short of the standard set by the Lord himself for the perfect or accomplished monk - one who, having mastered the doctrine, is able also to spread it abroad and confute the doctrines of other faiths. It demanded the knowledge of 'other faiths' and also intellectual equipments to be gained from other and non-canonical sources.

These monastic universities were no typical monasteries as each composed of a conglomerate of huge *vihara*s or monasteries within a gigantic monastery as in Nalanda [4.4] much like great colleges within a university; the size of each *vihara* could comparatively fit a Gandhara monastery like Takht-i-bahi inside its walls and hence these monastic universities were aptly termed *mahavihara* (great monastery). It is undeniable that these *mahavihara*s have contributed greatly to the overall development of Buddhism and Buddhist schools, both in India and abroad. Numerous eminent Buddhist monks and philosophers as well as secular intellectuals and personalities, Indians and foreigners alike, had spent their most illustrious careers in these great monastic centers where missionaries and doctrines would be disseminated abroad upon their graduation. Valabhi Mahavihara (sixth-eighth centuries CE) in Sourashtra, Gujarat was a great Theravada center with about 6,000 monks belonging to the Sammitya sect, according to Hsuan-tsang who visited it in c. 640 CE {Dutt 1962: 224-232}. Perhaps the most renowned and well-documented Indian *mahavihara* was Nalanda (fifth-thirteenth centuries CE), a Mahayana monastic university in Bihar devoted exclusively to the religious and intellectual quests that primarily focused on the studies of Buddhism and its various schools of thoughts. In fact, Buddhist monasteries were so common in those days in Bihar so that its name, a Bengali word, originated from '*vihara.*' The Theravada School was virtually eclipsed by the Mahayana, at least in northern India, from the sixth century CE on and the latter would in turn be supplanted by the Vajrayana after the tenth century CE. Vajrayana *mahavihara*s, which will be discussed later, were architecturally modeled after their Mahayana predecessors like Nalanda but the curricula naturally concentrated on Vajrayana subjects. Famous Vajrayana centers in Bihar included Odantapura, Vikramasila, Somapura [4.8], and Jagaddala, all founded and flourished during the Pala Dynasty (c. 750-1199 CE); other important Vajrayana centers like Lalitagiri, Ratnagiri, and Udayagiri in Orissa thrived between the fifth-thirteenth centuries CE.

The fame of Nalanda has long been buried below the earth oblivious to the passage of time; the descriptions of its glorious past could only be illuminated through the historical records preserved in the numerous travelogues and accounts of past celebrated foreign monk-pilgrims studied at Nalanda like Hsuan-tsang, I-tsing, and Dharmasvamin. The site is about 7 1/2 miles north of Rajir and had been hidden under mounds of debris for centuries until discovered by the British in the early nineteenth century CE; the archaeological history of Nalanda has already been covered in great details by Mary Stewart {Stewart 1989} and here I will only give a brief summary. The first European to have discovered and made preliminary reports on Nalanda in 1811-1812 CE was the British Francis Buchanan Hamilton, a physician and surveyor working for the British East India Company. Major Markham Kittoe was the first to identify the extensive ruins as Nalanda in the 1847 CE JASB issue. Alexander Cunningham carried out the first official surveys of the site on the behalf of the ASI in 1861-1862 CE; he also made an attempt to connect the individual ruins at the site with those mentioned by Hsuan-tsang. Further archaeological excavations were also carried out by Captain Marshall (1863-1865 CE) and A. M. Broadley (1871-1872 CE); the latter made the first conjectural reconstruction of Caitya 12 in the 1872 CE JASB issue. Nalanda was placed under the protection of the Indian government in 1904 CE which prevented further vandalisms of the site by villagers who had been removing bricks for their personal use. The ASI finally acquired about forty-eight acres of land for the site and began the excavations under David B. Spooner (1915-1919 CE), Hiranand Sastri (1919-1921 CE), J. A. Page (1921-1929 CE), M. Kuraishi (1929-1932 CE), G. C. Chandra (1932-1936 CE), N. Nazim (1936-1937 CE), and finally Amalananda Ghosh (1937-1938 CE); about nine successive levels of occupation had been identified and the conservation of site was initiated. Numerous seal insignias of Nalanda have been recovered from the site bearing the typical legend 'Sri Nalanda Mahavihariyarya Bhikshusanghasya' (Vernerable Community of Monks at Nalanda Mahavihara). The antiquity and name of Nalanda apparently dated back to Buddha's time; his two chief disciples Sariputra and Maudgalyayana were born in Nalaka (Nala) and Kolitagama respectively, all within the walking distance of Nalanda. Buddha also converted Upali, who was the reciter of the *Vinaya* in the First Buddhist Council, at Nalanda while the banker Pavarika also built Pavarikambavanarama Monastery for Buddha in Nalanda. However, the latter monastery was certainly not connected with the Nalanda Mahavihara of the later Gupta Dynasty as none of Buddha's *vassavasa*s had been spent in this obscure monastery; Nalanda was then a Jain stronghold and this could be the reason why it remained relatively unknown compared with other Buddhist sites until the Gupta Dynasty. Fa-hsien (in India between 399-414 CE) stopped by Nala within the vicinity of Nalanda but did not mention any great Buddhist centers here. However by the time of Hsuan-tsang (in India between 629-645 CE), who studied at the great Nalanda Mahavihara for several years, Nalanda was then at its peak as a major international Buddhist center in India; thus its rise to fame happened some times after Fa-hsien's sojourn.

Hsuan-tsang specifically mentioned in his travelogue that the Nalanda *vihara*s had been constructed by successive Gupta kings beginning with Sakraditya, Buddhagupta, Tathagatagupta, Baladitya, and Vajra; Sakraditya has been identified with Kumaragupta I (r. 415-455 CE) and whose coins, and those of Baladitya, have been found among the ruins. Several inscribed bricks belonging to Phase V of Caitya 3, probably the oldest edifice at Nalanda, have also been dated in the early sixth century CE; however its core certainly dated earlier than Phase V. The Vajrayana likely began to make its first appearance at Nalanda around the mid seventh century CE but was probably not accepted as a mainstream school until the ninth century CE; there were reports of orthodox Sri Lankan monks destroying Vajrayana scriptures and images in Buddhist establishments {Misra 1998 Volume I: 185-191, 369}. By the Pala Dynasty, only eastern India (Bihar, Bengal, Orissa) and Bangladesh remained the Buddhist strongholds. Mahayana devotionalism and Vajrayana Tantricism might have reduced the lifespan of Buddhism by blurring the demarcation line between Buddhism and Hinduism; Buddha had already been deified as the ninth avatar of Visnu while secular and Hindu courses were also taught alongside with Buddhist ones at Nalanda. The final blow to Indian Buddhism was around c. 1200 CE when Nalanda and other famed monasteries in Bihar like Odantapura and Vikramasila were completely destroyed or badly damaged by the Afghan Muslim invaders led by Bakhtiyar Khalji. Remnants of the debilitated Buddhist community at Nalanda continued to struggle on under scarce resources and supports until c. 1400 CE when Chagalaraja was reportedly the last king to have patronized Nalanda {Misra 1998 Volume I: 206-213}.

The sublime concept of a monastic university had undoubtedly been the creation of the Buddhists; it was envisioned as a religious institution for advanced learning that devoted exclusively to religious and secular curricula for the intellectual development and benefits of Buddhism and the larger Indian society. Such lofty principles, probably born out of Mahayana idealism, also reflected the prosperous and tolerant religious atmosphere in contemporary India, which had historically been the spirit of the Indian heritage since the earliest days. Nalanda certainly contributed a great deal to the development and propagation of Buddhism in India and abroad, particularly the Mahayana with Nalanda as its preeminent Indian and international center. During its long and memorable lifespan Nalanda, though functioned primarily as a Buddhist university, also accommodated and trained countless individuals from diverse backgrounds including Buddhist and non-Buddhist, the novice and wise, the young and aged, the religious and secular, Indians and foreigners alike. Its acclaim peaked in the seventh century CE when Hsuan-tsang, who studied here between 637-642 CE, reported several thousand inmates, or about 10,000 students and 1,511 teachers according to his biographer, studying at Nalanda. I-tsing, who traveled to India between 671-695 CE and stayed at Nalanda between 675-685 CE, also reported about 3,500 students; he further stated that the revenues of 200 villages had been allocated to Nalanda for its maintenance {Misra 1998 Volume I: 235-236, 241}. Every student apparently must pass a severe admission test to be screened by knowledgeable gatekeepers while foreign students were probably exempt due their initial lack of the comprehension of the Indian language. According to Hsuan-tsang {Dutt 1962: 332}:

> If men of other quarter desire to enter and take part in the discussions, the keeper of the gate proposes some hard questions; many are unable to answer, and retire. One must have studied deeply both old and new (books) before getting admission.

These gatekeepers were no ordinary door guardians as they were extremely knowledgeable pandits, experts, and specialists in many fields, including religious and secular subjects, to be able to proficiently screen the candidates; the admission seekers obviously had to be well-educated as in the case of Hsuan-tsang who studied Buddhism in Kashmir and Gandhara for years before attending Nalanda. Naropa was the northern gatekeeper between 1049-1057 CE who taught Atisa for seven years at Nalanda; the latter was a well-known figure that was responsible for the second transmission of the Vajrayana into Tibet. Silabhadra, a Nalanda abbot and teacher of Hsuan-tsang, had mastered virtually all collections of Buddhist scriptures apparently from memory. The teacher-pupil pair Vajrabodhi (671-741 CE) and Amoghavajra (705-774 CE), who brought the Vajrayana to China in the eighth century CE, also spent several years at Nalanda. The duo eminent monks Santaraksita and Padmasambhava, who were especially eminent figures in Tibet for introducing the Vajrayana into that country in the eighth century CE, were also educated for some times at Nalanda. The most poignant moment in Nalanda history was during its final destruction around c. 1200 CE when only five teachers and seventy students left at the charred ruins of the once teeming *mahavihara*. To escape the Muslim slaughters Rahulasribhadra, then a ninety-year old abbot, had to be carried away on the shoulders of his devoted Tibetan student Dharmasvamin who studied at Nalanda between 1234-1236 CE and from whom we came to know about its final fate {Misra 1998 Volume I: 77-78, 209-211, 282-310}. Returning to its academic life, Nalanda was a pre-eminent Mahayana monastic university with the majority of its students and teachers predictably Buddhists and all its abbots were also Buddhist; the curricula naturally primarily concentrated on Buddhist studies. However non-Buddhist courses, including religious and secular subjects, had also been offered to students as clearly stated by I-tsing {Dutt 1962: 332-333}:

> The priests, belonging to the convent, or strangers (residing therein)...All study the Great Vehicle (Mahayana), and also the works belonging to the eighteen sects (Theravada), and not only so, but even ordinary [non-Buddhist and secular] works, such as the Vedas [Hindu] and other books, the Hetuvidya (Logic), Sabdavidya ([Sanskrit] Grammar and Philology), Cikitsavidya (Medicine), the works on Magic (Atharva Veda), Sankhya (system of philosophy); besides these, they thoroughly investigate the miscellaneous works [probably literature and general knowledge].

Fierce academic competition if not antagonism certainly existed at Nalanda and indeed in the wider Indian society between the Buddhist schools, especially between the Theravada and Mahayana, as well as between the Buddhists and Hindus as vividly told by Hsuan-tsang. The winner in an intellectual challenge would expectedly have to refute his opponent's theory with his intelligent logic while the loser suffered in humiliation and possible conversion to the winner's faith; such open intellectual rivalries already existed in Buddha's time when he confuted and converted many heretics though he did not condone such fruitless behaviors. Dinnaga, a famous Buddhist philosopher and founder of medieval Indian logic, defeated the Hindu philosopher Supurjaya and converted him to Buddhism; Hsuan-tsang also reputedly defeated and converted Simharasmi, a fellow monk, to the Yogacara philosophy; he also composed the 'Destruction of Heresy' and defeated his Theravada opponents in a grand assembly lasted for eighteen days {Misra 1998 Volume I: 258-260, 361-362}. The title pandit (*acarya*), or a scholar equivalent to the modern Doctorate degree, would be conferred upon those of outstanding academic achievements and who had mastered the five sciences (*vidya*), namely Sabdavidya (Grammar and Philology), Cikitsavidya (Medicine), Hetuvidya (Logic), Adhyatmavidya (Metaphysics), and Silpasthanavidya (Fine Arts) {Dutt 1962: 323}; Hsuan-tsang was the only Chinese ever at Nalanda granted the title *acarya*. Secular individuals, upon graduation and with proper recommendations from Nalanda, would be employed in the government or in service of the king {Misra 1998 Volume I: 261}; as one could imagine that earning such a prestigious degree from Nalanda would be an immense honor in contemporary Indian society.

In the foregoing passages I have briefly discussed the historical and religious backgrounds as well as the nature of the academic life at Nalanda, it is now appropriate to explore the remains at the site in order to shed light on its arts and architecture that have been created and left behind during its long existence; but first I want to clarify on the boundary of Nalanda. It is crucial not to confuse between Nalanda the town versus Nalanda the Buddhist university **[4.4]**; it has been a well-established fact that the latter was commenced, occupied, and administered by the Buddhists and where Buddhist curricula were mainly taught. Its immense size and influential stature, from its beginning (Gupta Dynasty) to its end (Pala Dynasty), as the center of activities in the Nalanda township were well attested historically; thus the Nalanda Mahavihara will be the focus of the discussions in this section. Bhaskaranatha Misra, in his great volume 'Nalanda,' has made some controversial claims in a seemingly deliberate attempt to minimize the importance of Nalanda as a Buddhist site by blurring the distinction between Nalanda the Buddhist university and its surrounding non-Buddhist sites, which include Hindu and Jain remains:

- The plan of the alleged Hindu Temple 2 (not shown on the plan) has always been included on the Nalanda plan in virtually every scholarly book in the past; however its location is behind Monastery 7-8, outside of the main Buddhist ground, and faces away from the site and thus it was obviously not a part of the original Buddhist plan and therefore I aptly exclude it on the site plan. Moreover, Misra's assertion that Temple 2 was Hindu having a curvilinear *sikhara* tower might also be an overstatement; the central temple of Somapura, for example, also had numerous Hindu images but it was as Buddhist monastery. From the seventh century CE on there were instances of Hindu-Buddhist syncretism and hence the presence of non-Buddhist images in Buddhist establishments, since they had already been incorporated into the Buddhist pantheon as protectors or supporters of Buddhism, would not be considered a sacrilege. Susan Huntington was also in the opinion that the Hindu carvings on this temple, due to their incongruous positions, might have been collected

from other sites and reused here; she also speculated that Hindu figures could also represent the minor deities in the outer circles of a Buddhist *mandala* as common in the Vajrayana {Huntington 1984: 24}. Thus, the religious affiliation of Temple 2 at Nalanda is far from being settled.
- Misra also widened Nalanda the Buddhist monastic proper to include numerous peripheral and non-Buddhist sites such as Badgaon, Begumpur, Mustaphapur, Kapatia, Anandpur, and Sarichak; he further included numerous Hindu and Jain images and temples in his discussion of Nalanda and he even chose the image of a Siva *linga* found at Badgaon for the covers of his volumes. His thesis was clearly about Nalanda the Buddhist Mahavihara and therefore these actions were clearly fraught with historical inaccuracies and distortion.
- Misra also hailed the Samudragupta copper plate inscription (c. 325 CE) from Nalanda as 'significant' but it had been found on the upper Devapala (r. 812-850 CE) level; the inscription, which was issued at Anandapura, recorded a grant of the village Bhadrapushkarakagrama to a Brahmana Jayabhati. Thus the content of the plate obviously had nothing to do with Buddhism or the founding of Nalanda and these villages certainly could not positively be identified with Nalanda {Misra 1998 Volume I: 163, 185 / Volume II: 254-255 / Volume III: 131-165, 263-267}.

Returning to the subject of Buddhist arts at Nalanda, most recovered sculptures have been dated between the fifth-twelfth centuries CE; these can be classified as free-standing or decorative components of the architecture and all have been carved in the Gupta-Sarnath Style and Pala Style. The materials are mainly stone, stucco over the brick core, and bronze; the latter two categories probably had polychrome or gilt finishes. The oldest specimens are the Buddha sculptures in the Gupta-Sarnath Style and the stucco torso reliefs belonging to Caitya 3-Phase IV (now hidden from view), all dated in the fifth century CE; the exposed extant stucco sculptures in the niches of Caitya 3-Phase V have been dated stylistically and iconographically between the sixth-seventh centuries CE {Misra 1998 Volume II: 39-195}. The iconography of these sculptures depicts early and late Mahayana subjects (fifth-eighth centuries CE) primarily about Buddha's Life Scenes, *bodhisattva*s, and a rare Dipankara Jataka; the *jataka*s were conspicuously absent at Nalanda. Vajrayana images (ninth-thirteenth centuries CE) like Tara, Vajrapani, Trilokyavijaya, Yamantaka, Heruka, etc. also appeared at Nalanda reflecting diminishing Mahayana influences at the site. Nalanda paintings can also be divided into two categories, namely the illuminated manuscripts and murals; the former were mostly produced in the Pala Dynasty (c. 750-1199 CE) and greatly influenced similar examples in Nepal. Scanty mural fragments, mostly in fading conditions, have also been found in Caitya 14 and Sarai Mound Temple near the site; these were also painted in the Pala Style and probably dated between the tenth-eleventh centuries CE {Nath 1983: xx-xxiv, 13-15, 54, 63-69}.

The huge site of Nalanda **[4.4]** nearly 700' x 1900' was originally surrounded with numerous ponds evidently for the occupation of a large population in the monastery. It composes mainly of a row of eleven *vihara*s or monks' dwellings (1, 1A-1B, 4-11) in the east and south and possibly more if excavations were to be continued further north. These face a row of four *caitya*s or image temples (3, 12-14) on the west directly across an open space of nearly 100' wide; numerous *stupa*s of different periods and sizes are clustered around Caityas 3 and 12. It is evident from the layout of the architectural remains that the plan orientates toward the north where the original entrance to the university has likely been located; from the haphazard positions and modest sizes of the buildings in the southern end, one might conclude that the earliest constructions would be in that area and this has also been corroborated by the archaeological data. The architectural remains at Nalanda can be divided into three categories:

a. *Vihara*s {Misra 1998 Volume I: 69, 185-192 / Volume II: 13 / Volume III: 195-218, 319-320}

These are Vihara 1, 1A, 1B, 4-11 ranging from the smallest 71' x 100' (Vihara 1B) to the largest 178' x 255' (Vihara 11); the small and cruciform-planned building in front of Vihara 1B was probably the earliest *vihara* or temple in Nalanda. Most *vihara*s had been rebuilt by successive kings over a long period of time upon existing foundations, with Vihara 1 having nine strata of occupation; the majority of the ruins on the surface as seen today dated in the Pala Dynasty. These *vihara*s typically have quadrangular plans like Gandhara monasteries **[4.2]** and Ajanta cave *vihara*s **[5.12]** with a projecting entry portico and an image chapel in the back that occasionally has a *pradaksina* path; the interior typically has colonnaded verandahs around a hypaethral courtyard which is surrounded by monk cells on all four sides. Stairs were provided at the four corners and drains were buried beneath the courtyard floor to discharge water to the back of the *vihara*; image chapels, wells, and hearths were also built in the courtyard while meditation cells, built-in beds, and niches were also provided in some of the cells. Service facilities such as kitchen and refectory were reportedly

Part II. Architecture   Monastery . 63

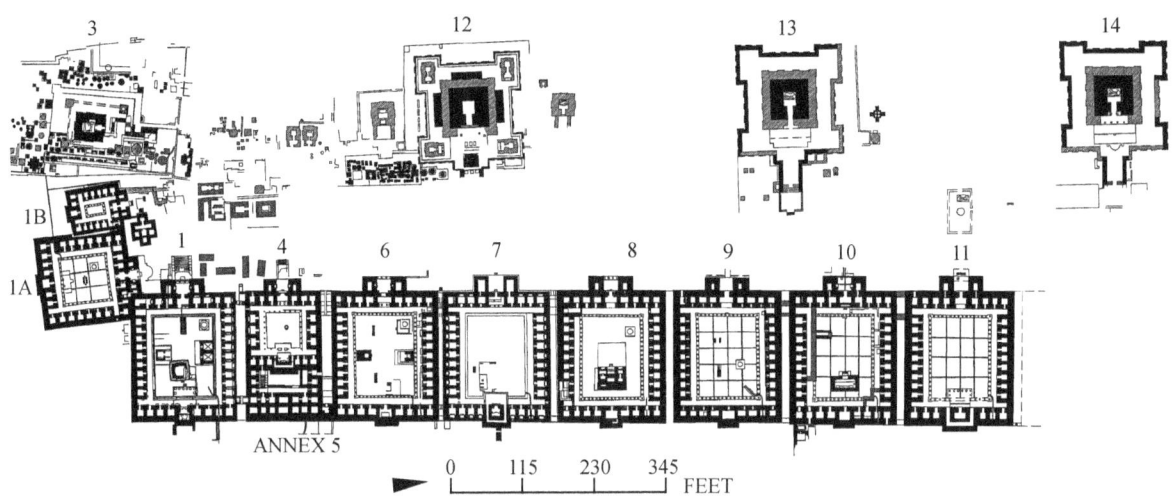

4.4. Site plan. Fifth-thirteenth centuries CE. Nalanda- India

located within these *vihara*s; I-tsing seemed to confirm this arrangement when he stated that the *vihara*s could be regarded as 'a monastic kitchen' and 'raw and cooked food' might also be kept in the cells where food could be consumed {Dutt 1962: 339}. These *vihara*s of probable several stories high were constructed of brick laid in mud mortar and their interior surfaces were originally covered with plaster and might be painted with exquisite murals, polychrome, or gilded. The verandah columns were initially timber but subsequently converted to stone to support heavier loads due to the increase in the stories and to prevent the collapse of the superstructure during conflagration. The roofs were probably flat and might be covered with several layers of brick-and-mud but they could also be pitched and covered with tiles due to the high rain volume in Bihar; corbelled and semicircular vaults have also been reported among the Nalanda *vihara*s. Hsuan-tsang mentioned the names of their builders which provide important clues to their possible construction dates:

> Sakraditya was first to build a monastery at Nalanda. His son and successor Buddhagupta built a monastery to the south of it. To the east of this was built a monastery by Tathagatagupta. To the northeast of this King Baladitya added a fourth monastery. To the west of this monastery Baladitya's son and successor Vajra built his monastery. To the north of this a king of Mid-India afterward erected a large monastery... Siladitya constructed a *vihara* covered with brass-plates by the side of the Nalanda monastery about

100' in height.

Misra chronologically attached these kings to some of these *vihara*s and attempted to link their names with the historical Gupta kings, namely Vihara 4 (Sakraditya for Kumaragupta I), Vihara 1B (Buddhagupta for Skandagupta), Vihara 1A (Tathagatagupta for Purugupta), Vihara 1 (Baladitya for Narasimhagupta), Vihara 5 (Vajra for Kumaragupta II), Vihara 6 (Mid-India king for Purnavarman), and Vihara 7 (Siladitya for Harshavardhana). However other scholars have linked Vajra with Vainyagupta, who was genealogically after Narasimhagupta, since Kumaragupta II was reputedly the predecessor of Buddhagupta and Narasimhagupta {Mookerji 1947: 108-109}; Hsuan-tsang's 'king of Mid-India' has also been identified with Yasodharman by some scholars {Dutt 1962: 330}. In any case, these *vihara*s were undoubtedly constructed between the fifth-mid seventh centuries CE with a period of construction hiatus in the sixth century CE probably due to the lack of patronage and the decline of the Gupta Dynasty caused by the Hephthalite invasions; this brilliant dynasty officially ended in c. 550 CE but some scholars have included Harshavardhana (r. 606-647 CE) as its extension. However, Misra's identification of the *vihara*s with these kings did not tally with the order of the *vihara* locations as given by Hsuan-tsang; for examples Vihara 1B is not south of Vihara 4 and Vihara 5 is not west of Vihara 1. Now if I propose the small 41' x 52' *vihara* in front of Vihara 1B as Sakraditya's then a better order of identification would emerge that closely matches that of Hsuan-tsang's description; also note that I-tsing mentioned the first *vihara* at Nalanda, which was built by Sakraditya, was 50' square and also roughly the same dimension of this small *vihara*. Thus in my opinion the correct construction chronology should be: the small *vihara* in front of Vihara 1B (Sakraditya), Vihara 1B (Buddhagupta), Vihara 1A (Tathagatagupta), Vihara 1 (Baladitya), Vihara 4-ANNEX 5 (Vajra), Vihara 6 (Mid-India king), and Vihara 7 (Siladitya). The position, size, and plan of Vihara 4, as compared with the other early *vihara*s, also do not fit the profile of the earliest *vihara* since the design of these *vihara*s should logically progress from small to large sizes and from the simple to complex. The oldest structures at Nalanda, or Caitya 3 and the surrounding votive *stupa*s, are concentrated in the south-southwest area and it would be natural to build the earliest *vihara*s there; it does not seem logical to construct the large Vihara 4, supposedly the earliest, away from Caitya 3 area and then later built the smaller Vihara 1B next to the latter and far away from the former. Vihara 8 dated between pre-Pala Dynasty to Devapala's reign or between c. 700-850 CE while Vihara 9-11 were all constructed by Devapala (r. 812-850 CE); Devapala likely constructed new *vihara*s over the ruins of earlier ones. Numerous archaeological artifacts have been recovered revealing the names of some of the kings and builders of these *vihara*s; for examples a gold coin of Kumaragupata I and Sakraditya's clay seal were found in Vihara 4 while numerous inscriptions and clay seals of other Gupta kings like Harshavardhana and Pala kings like Dharmapala (r. 775-812 CE) and Devapala were also discovered in Vihara 1. An 847 CE copper plate inscription was found in Vihara 1 mentioning Devapala's construction of a *vihara*, possibly also identified with this *vihara*, on the behalf of the Indonesian King Balaputradeva.

b. *Caitya*s {Misra 1998 Volume I: 185 / Volume II: 12 / Volume III: 229-248, 257, 317-318}

These are Caityas 3, 12-14 aligned in a row on the western side of the site opposite of the *vihara*s. Caityas 3, 12 have quincunxial plans with four smaller towers in the four corners as in the Mahabodhi Temple **[7.10-7.11]** in which the central chapel was likely originally surmounted by a tower; the subsidiary corner towers are conspicuously absent from Caityas 13-14. Each temple is elevated on a low plinth connected by a central stair leading to the inner sanctum, which is entered via a portico; two beautifully carved 7'8" high columns still stand in the southeastern corner tower of Caitya 12. The latter is the biggest temple having a 170' x 194' plan dated between the sixth-eleventh centuries CE while Caityas 13-14 both dated between the sixth-thirteenth centuries CE. Caitya 3, which has seven envelopes reflecting seven phases of construction, was originally a small *stupa* (Phase I-III); it would later be converted to a temple due to the ascendancy of the cult of images and temples over the worship of relics and *stupa*s. This new *caitya* (Phase IV-VII) has been dated between the fifth-eighth centuries CE and what we see today are the ruined four corner turrets of the early sixth century CE (Phase V) and a centrally pyramidal structure of the eighth century CE at the latest (Phase VII). Amalananda Ghosh believed the original *stupa* at the core of this *caitya* must have been laid 'at least two centuries earlier' than the Phase V temple or in the fourth century CE; however this view is untenable and most likely it would date in the fifth century CE like the earliest *vihara*s. The central towers of these *caitya*s may be visualized from A. M. Broadley's conjectural reconstruction of Caitya 12 in the 1872 CE JASB issue and the contemporary Mahabodhi Temple. Similarities between Caitya 3 (Phase V temple), Caitya 12, and the Mahabodhi Temple have already been observed by scholars and also noted by Hsuan-tsang during his stay at Nalanda:

> To the north of this was a large temple [Caitya 12] above 300' high built by King Baladitya. In its size and ornamentation and in its image of the Buddha this temple resembled the one at the Bodhi Tree [Mahabodhi Temple].

By verifying the dimensions of Caitya 12 and the Mahabodhi Temple, one can immediately recognize that both structures have similar proportions; thus Hsuan-tsang's statement was credible. Gold coins of Kumaragupta I and Narasimhagupta have been found in Caitya 3 and a brick inscription (c. 516-517 CE) have also been recovered from the same ruin; thus the foundation of Caitya 3 could be more or less contemporary with the *vihara*s in the fifth century CE.

c. *Stupa*s {Misra 1998 Volume III: 252-260}

All *stupa*s congregate densely around Caityas 3 and 12 where the oldest remains are located. From the remains it is evident that Nalanda, being a Mahayana center, favored *caitya*s and image worship and over *stupa*s since there are no large *stupa*s at the site. The biggest *stupa*s do not exceed 20' high and most are the Votive type; however the *stupa* at the core of Caitya 3 might originally contain important relics. Many who had studied or resided at Nalanda reportedly died here over the centuries and memorial *stupa*s would be raised over their relics. Most *stupa*s had square plinths above which would expectedly be a superstructure consisting of the circular drum, dome, *harmika*, and a timber or stone *yasti-chattra* but these are no longer extant; the dome typically had *caitya*-arched niches containing images of Buddhas and *bodhisattva*s. The finished appearance of these brick *stupa*s, which dated between the fifth-mid eighth centuries CE, could be covered in stucco and probably painted or gilded; stone *stupa*s at Nalanda were generally common in the Pala Dynasty.

Below are abridged descriptions of Nalanda architecture as witnessed by Hsuan-tsang, I-tsing, and Dharmasvamin when they studied here during its heyday and demise; the first was by Hsuan-tsang between c. 637-642 CE {Stewart 1989: 205-206}:

> Then all around [Nalanda monastery] there was built a lofty enclosing [brick] wall with one gate [50' high]...[The *caitya*?] are constructed with extraordinary skills. A three-storied tower is erected at each of the four angles. The beams and projecting heads are carved with great skill in different shapes. The doors, windows, and low walls are painted profusely; the monks' cells [*viharas*] are ornamental on the inside and plain on the outside. In the very middle of the building is the hall, high and wide. These are various storied chambers and turrets of different height and shape, without any fixed rule. The doors open towards the east; the royal throne also faces east... [Hsuan-tsang] took up his residence in the dwelling [*vihara*?] of Buddhabhadra, having four stories...

The next description was by I-tsing between c. 675-685 CE {Stewart 1989: 230-233}:

> [The first Nalanda *vihara*] initially had been built by King Sakraditya for the monk Rajavamsa of North India. The original perimeter of this temple was only fifty paces [125'] square. Subsequently successive kings in emulation built it bigger and bigger [the row of *viharas*?]...The shape of this monastery is roughly that of a square...on the four sides, the edge of the steep, jutting roof forms long covered galleries which go all around the building. All these buildings are of brick; they are three stories high, each story being more than 10' high. Traverse beams are tied together by planks; a walkway [upper verandah?] has been made not of rafters or tiles but of bricks...As for the living quarters of the monks, there are nine each side. Each cell has a surface area of about ten square feet. At the back is a window which goes up to the edge of the roof. Although the doors are high, they are made as a single swinging door so that the monks can all see each other...At the top of one of the angles [corners] is a suspended way [skyway] which permits coming and going in the temple. At each of the four corners there is a room built of brick. These are the cells of the learned and venerable monks...The gate of the temple [*viharas*] faces west. Its top floor goes right into the sky, which quite takes one's breath away. Its marvelous sculptures go to the limits of art and ornamentation. This gate is attached to the building. It was not originally made separately, but two paces [5'] in front of it they have put four columns [a portico]. Although the gate is not very high, its framework is very strong...Inside the monastery [*viharas*] large areas of more than 30' are paved with brick. The smaller spaces of 5'-10' and all the areas which cover the rooms, which are on the roof, in front of the verandah, or in the cells, are paved in the following way. Brick fragments as big as peaches or mangoes are mixed with a sticky paste, and are crust to the same consistency. The builders make a mixture of fibres of hemp to which they add oil with the residue of the hemp and remains of the old hides. They keep it moist for three days. Then they spread this mixture on the place filled the crushed brick mixture. The whole thing is covered in green grass. After about three days they look to see if it has dried. The [dried] surface is rubbed several times with polished stones. They sprinkle [the finished floor] with red earth or a substance similar to sandalwood. Finally, with a greasy mixture they make it smooth and clear like a mirror. All the rooms and the steps of the stairs are made in this way. When it is finished, it will withstand the trampling of feet over a period of ten to twenty years without suffering any damages. It is not like lime which flakes when it becomes wet. They cover the precinct [boundary?] walls with whitewash...There are no less than eight temples [*viharas*] like this. On top of all of them there is a flat terrace [parapet or flat roof] where one can walk...On one side of each temple the monks have chosen a building [courtyard shrines or rear chapels?], sometimes one-storied, sometimes three-storied, for holy images. Or at a certain distance in front of one east side there has been constructed an observatory in the form of a terrace which serves as the room of the Buddha...On the west side of the temple, outside the large enclosure, some large *stupa*s have been constructed and lots of *caitya*s. There are 100 of them. The sacred relics, too many to enumerate, are crowded together. Gold and precious stones for a brilliant ornamentation...When one looks at one of the temples [*viharas*] one sees that the seven others are identical in plan. They all have

flat terraces on top where people can come and go.

The latest description was by Dharmasvamin between c. 1234-1236 CE {Misra 1998 Volume I: 77, 199}:

> Nalanda had seven great pinnacles [*caitya*s] in its center...On the outside towards the north stood fourteen lofty pinnacles. Outside of it there were about eighty small *vihara*s called A-Ri-Kha...They [*vihara*s] were built of brick and many were left undamaged. Two *vihara*s called Dha-Na-Ba and Ghu-Na-Ba were in a serviceable condition. In general, among the eighty-four *vihara*s there were eighty-four human dwellings [cells]...A royal *vihara* containing an image of Khasarpana Avalokitesvara...An image of Tara was painted on the wall of the eastern side of the *vihara*.

The fact that Nalanda arts and architecture were indebted to Gandhara is beyond a doubt; it is apparent that both Nalanda *vihara*s [4.4] and Takht-i-bahi [4.2] have quadrangular plans with hypaethral courtyards, colonnaded verandahs, and wells; the Ajanta cave *vihara*s [5.12] were also hewn in this popular plan. The designs of Nalanda Caityas 3, 12 and the Mahabodhi Temple [7.10-7.11], especially their quincunxial plans and corner towers, could be traced back to Gandhara antecedents [6.14]. Nalanda votive *stupa*s, with their square plans, drums, and image niches on the domes, also show definite Gandhara influence [6.15]; the extensive use of stucco at Nalanda probably also originated in Gandhara. The exclusive iconographical preference of Buddhas and *bodhisattva*s over the *jataka*s at Nalanda suggests an inclination toward Mahayana themes and the continuation of later Gandhara tradition; Nalanda took a more progressive step by replacing large relic *stupa*s with image temples (*caitya*s) which effectively ended the *stupa*'s traditional dominance. This tendency was to be further developed in Somapura [4.8] where its central edifice fused the *stupa* and *caitya* into a new architectural concept, the *stupa*-temple. Somapura plan is obviously an enlarged version of the Nalanda quadrangular *vihara* though with an addition of a huge edifice in the center of its open courtyard, a unique feature already occurred in the Gandhara monastery at Mohenjo-daro [1.1].

4. Horyuji (623-925 CE) - Japan

Buddhism reached Japan in 552 CE from the Korean kingdom of Paekche during one of the latter's many missionaries to the island nation; some Japanese historical sources have further placed the official Buddhist introduction earlier in 538 CE {Washizuka 2003: 25}. Historically Paekche had been instrumental in the creation of early Buddhist arts and architecture in Japan; the kingdom brought to Japan not only monks but also craftsmen, artists, sculptors, architects, and builders who would involve in the creation of the first Buddhist sculptures, pagodas, and monasteries in Japan {Washizuka 2003: 144-145}. As in China upon its arrival Buddhism was immediately caught in the power struggle between the two prominent factions in the Japanese court, namely the pro-Buddhist camp led by the Soga clan and the anti-Buddhist camp led by the Monotobe clan. Soon war broke between them and the pro-Buddhist Soga clan, which was led by the now revered figure in Japanese history Prince Regent Shotoku (574-622 CE), won a decisive victory. The outcomes resulted not only in the rise to prominence of a foreign religion over the native Shinto cult but also the integration of Chinese, and indirectly Indian, culture into every aspect of the Japanese society. Shinto is a Japanese indigenous cult of spirit veneration with its own primitive arts and architecture which were initially deemed not at par with those of the highly civilized cultures of China and India. The continent frequently sent monks and nuns to ordain new Japanese members into the *Sangha* alongwith skill craftsmen and architects to train the Japanese in the art of making Buddha images and constructing pagodas and monasteries. The Japanese imperial house and aristocracy patronized Buddhism generously and they enthusiastically modeled themselves after the continental culture; missionaries and diplomatic envoys were also dispatched to China to bring home the latest trends that were in vogue on the continent at the time. The outcomes of these activities were that the Japanese culture generally reflected that of the continental Chinese culture with minor variations due to the fusion with indigenous elements. The assimilation of Chinese arts and architecture in Japan can generally be divided into three periods:

- Asuka Period (552-645 CE) received the first wave of influences primarily from the northern Chinese dynasties of Northern Wei (386-557 CE), Northern Qi (550-577 CE), Northern Zhou (557-581 CE), and Sui (581-618 CE).
- Hakuho (645-710 CE) and Nara Period (710-784 CE) received the second wave of influences from the Tang Dynasty (618-907 CE). The Japanese Heian Period (784-1186 CE) was a period of crystallization of the Japanese culture though continental ideas continued to flow in uninterrupted.
- Kamakura (1186-1336 CE) and Muromachi Period (1392-1573 CE) received the third wave of influenc-

Part II. Architecture   Monastery . 67

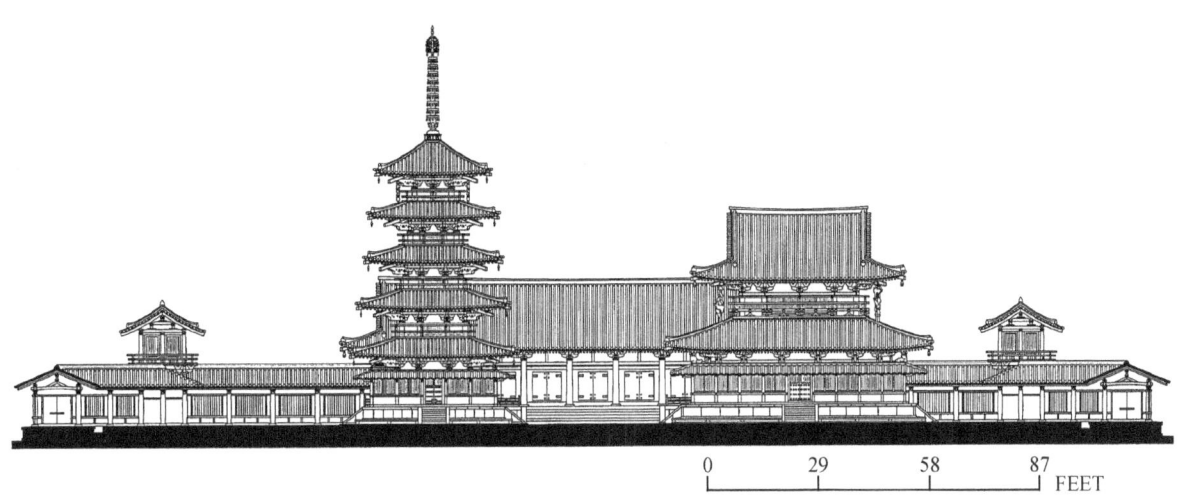

4.5. Elevation-section and plan of Worship Area
623-925 CE
Nara- Japan

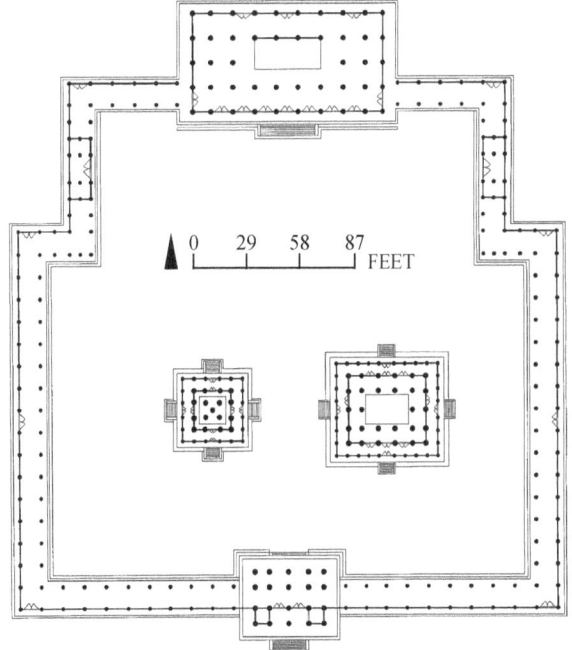

es mainly from the Southern Song Dynasty (1127-1279 CE); this period in Japan was famous for its Zen monasteries and paintings.
- The most glorious period in Japanese Buddhism was around the mid eighth century CE; Emperor Shomu decreed in 740-741 CE that every province in Japan must build a monastery separately for monks and nuns and each should have a seven-storied pagoda {Soper 1959: 18}. Again in 752 CE the gigantic Todaiji monastery was completed with its twin pagodas of 325' high each; its Great Buddha Hall, the largest and oldest surviving timber building in the world, then was 290' wide x 170' deep x 156' high containing the extant 53' high bronze statue of Vairocana Buddha from the period {Soper 1942: 54-55}. Its inaugural ceremony was a spectacle attended by 10,000 monks from many Buddhist countries like China and India.

Horyuji [4.5-4.7, 6.20-6.21] is unquestionably a Japanese national treasure and an East Asian jewel as it is the oldest extant timber structure in the world. The Japanese chronicle Nihon Shoki recorded a total of forty-six temples, monasteries, and nunneries with 816 monks and 569 nuns in Japan by the seventh century CE; among these, seven monasteries had been associated with Prince Shotoku and Horyuji was one of them {Washizuka 2003: 157}. The whole monastic complex of Horyuji is divided

4.6. Pagoda and Golden Hall
623-925 CE
Nara- Japan

4.7. Eave brackets of Golden Hall
623 CE
Nara- Japan

into the East and West precincts consisting of diverse building types including chapels, relic halls, refectories, kitchens, monk quarters, etc.; they are grouped into zones encompassing the worship sector, service area, and residential quarters for monks and nuns. The most important area and representative of Horyuji and also the focus of this discussion is the West Precinct which is the oldest worship sector of the monastery; it includes:

- The Golden Hall (623 CE) **[4.6-4.7]**
- The cloistered galleries (670 CE), the Middle Gate (670 CE), and the five-storied pagoda (670 CE) **[6.20-6.21]**
- Sutra and Bell Pavilions (747 CE)
- Lecture Hall (925 CE)

The history of Horyuji encompasses three most important dates: (1) 607 CE, the first Horyuji called Wakakusadera was erected to house the Yakushi image; this monastery, which was originally located southeast of the current Horyuji, was completely burned down in 670 CE; (2) 623 CE, a year after Prince Shotoku died a mortuary chapel, presumably the Golden Hall, was built to house the Shaka Triad image; (3) 670 CE, after Wakakusadera burned down several new buildings, most importantly the gallery, pagoda, and middle gate, were added to the Golden Hall (the original mortuary Shotoku chapel) to complete the quadrangular precinct {Mizuno 1974: 28-34, 88-89}{Paine and Soper 1981: 294-300}. About 747 CE, the *sutra* and bell pavilions were also added on both sides of the main axis in the immediate area outside the quadrangle in the northern side alongwith a dormitory probably a little further north on the same axis. In 925 CE, this dormitory was burned down and replaced by a lecture hall and consequently new sections of cloistered galleries would be added to connect the *sutra* pavilion, belfry, and lecture hall with the quadrangle. A part of the original northern galleries was chopped off as a result of this reconstruction and its materials might have been salvaged and reused in the new connecting galleries. Thus the current jogging plan of Horyuji apparently dated in the early tenth century CE; in the seventeenth century CE struts of dragon carvings were added to the corners of the Golden Hall, and possibly also the pagoda, to prevent the heavy and wide eaves from collapsing. Besides these historical structures, Horyuji also houses numerous treasures as old as the buildings themselves including relics, small shrines, sculptures, and paintings. Several relic containers and a mirror have been discovered below the pagoda dated about the time of the construction of the pagoda in 670 CE. The small wooden Tamamushi Shrine model with its precious paintings, the oldest in Japan dated around c. 650 CE, show a type of roof construction and brackets similar to the oldest Horyuji buildings, in particular the Golden Hall. Statues of Yakushi (607 CE), Shaka Triad (623 CE), four *lokapala*s (c. 650 CE), are also among the oldest extant Buddhist images in Japan; the two guardians (*dvarapala*s) standing in their ferocious gestures on both sides of the Middle Gate entrance dated in 711 CE; in addition, the murals in the High Tang Chinese Style inside the Golden Hall dated around c. 700 CE. Thus the inventory clearly reveals the Golden Hall and the pagoda as the most important surviving edifices connected with early Japanese Buddhism, and indeed East Asian Buddhism.

The original Horyuji quadrangle consisting of the Middle Gate, galleries, pagoda, and Golden Hall had been constructed about fifty years apart so that their architectural homogeneity is immediately apparent; the entasis of the columns, protruding lever arms, and cloud brackets are the common features among these structures. The Golden Hall is undoubtedly older than the pagoda in its use of the inverted 'V' struts, a feature which is absent in the other structures; among the earliest appearances of the inverted 'V' struts can be found in the Chinese Yungang caves dated around c. 460-505 CE. Above all, the architectural sources for Horyuji originated in China where an earliest construction of a Buddhist monastery was recorded in a literary description dated around c. 190 CE; it told the story of the warlord Chai Jung building the first complete Buddhist monastery in Jiangsu which was evidently a timber one {Soper 1959: 4}:

He erected a Buddha shrine, making a human figure of bronze whose body he coated with gold and clad in brocades. He hung up nine tiers of bronze plates [*yasti-chattra*] over a multi-storeyed pavilion; his covered galleries could contain three thousand men or more.

The passage clearly lists the buildings that are also present in the early plan of Horyuji, namely the Buddha image hall, pagoda, and cloistered galleries; there is no mentioning of the positions of the image hall and pagoda relative to the main axis. In Chinese architecture, a monastery traditionally faces south to maximize the sunlight since Chinese timber buildings virtually has no insulation; the design also presumably satisfies geomantic requirements. The quadrangular plan of the Chinese monastery usually begins with a main gateway in the south, the pagoda in the middle, and finally the image hall in the north while the bell and drum pavilions are located on both sides of the north-south axis. The destroyed Yongningsi Monastery (c. 516 CE) erected during the Northern Wei Dynasty in Luoyang, China is an early example of such plan {Steinhardt 2002: 83-84, fg. 3.21}{Washisuka 2003: 160}. An extant example of this plan can be found in Fugongsi Monastery in Shanxi, China (1056 CE) where the emphasis on axiality, symmetry, and order are paramount and typical in Chinese architecture. An engraving (c. 700 CE) from the Great Wild Goose pagoda also shows a Chinese Tang monastery with the image hall in the center linked with covered galleries on both sides; from these examples, the similarities between a Chinese monastic plan and early Horyuji are unmistaken. Numerous early Tang murals (618-705 CE) in the Mogao caves, as in Cave 172, 220, 217, also depict Pure Land paradises in elaborate architectural complexes consisting of covered galleries, halls, pagodas, etc. amidst the ponds; these were undoubtedly accurate renderings of contemporary Tang monasteries. In Korea, the Chinese plan would again be popularly employed, for examples Kumgangsa (sixth century CE) in Paekche and Hwangnyongsa (c. 553-645 CE) in Silla; the five-storied pagoda in Kumgangsa also had an identical structure as the Horyuji pagoda with a tall pillar in the center rising its entire height. Some Koguryo monastery plans like Kumgangsa (early sixth century CE) had a pagoda in the center and surrounded on the three sides by image halls; this could well be the distant precursor of Horyuji {Washisuka 2003: 158-161}. Paekche architects in turn brought the Chinese plan, or precisely the Sino-Korean 'Kudura' (Paekche) plan, to Japan; this continental plan would once again be implemented in the erection of several earliest Asuka monasteries in Japan including Shintenoji and Wakakusadera, the predecessor of Horyuji. The new Horyuji plan, however, shows clear departure from the continental plan by placing the pagoda and image hall contiguously on both sides of the central axis; it was probably a modified version of the aforesaid Kumgangsa plan of Koguryo. According to Alexander Soper in the early stage of Shintenoji when relics were deemed more important than images, the pagoda was positioned in front of the image hall; in the transitional stage in Horyuji, the side-by-side arrangement of the pagoda and the image hall demonstrated the parity of both relics and images. Still in later monasteries of the Nara Period, such as Kofukuji and Todaiji, the pagoda was entirely placed outside of the quadrangle reflecting the ascendancy of the image cult {Soper 1942: 29}.

The uprooting of the pagoda from the quadrangular plan in later Japanese monasteries also reflected the Gandhara [4.2] and Indian tradition [4.4] where the *stupa*, the Indian equivalent of the pagoda, had rarely been placed inside the monks' *vihara*s, with the exceptions like Mohenjo-daro [1.1] in Gandhara and later Somapura [4.8] in Bangladesh. However, there is no proof that the quadrangular plan of Horyuji was derived from Gandhara since such plan already existed in Chinese architecture before the arrival of Buddhism. The placement of the pagoda in front of the image hall also recalled a similar arrangement in the Taxila Apsidal Temple (c. 30 BCE-50 CE) and Nagarjunakonda (third century CE) in South India where a single or twin *stupa*s were positioned in front of twin apsidal temples {Huntington 1985: fg. 9.27}. Moreover the placement of the pagoda to the side of the image hall in Horyuji or outside the quadrangle would also maintain visual continuity and visitors no longer have to walk around or through the pagoda in order to reach the image hall in the back. There were tendencies in later Buddhist monasteries to expand the size of the quadrangle to gigantic proportions alongwith the fusion of the image temple and *stupa* into a single edifice, a *stupa*-temple, to be positioned in the center of the plan as in Somapura in Bangladesh.

5. Somapura (c. 775-812 CE) - Bangladesh

The earliest people in Bengal, now divided between West Bengal in India and Bangladesh, were the Pundra and Vanga tribes whose neighboring territory was Anga (Bhagalpur district of Bihar), a region under Magadha's powerful clout in Buddha's time. The name Bangladesh, or Bangla-desa (Bangla country), was likely derived from Vanga (seventh-sixth centuries BCE) and later known as Bangala (fourteenth century CE) or Bangla; Pundra and Vanga regions had been mentioned in the Vedas as early as the seventh century BCE. Bengal, due to its extremely soggy, marshy, and alluvial delta drained by the Ganga and Brahmaputra rivers, were not a favorable environment for the people of Middle India; it was probably not until the fourth century BCE when Bengal and its tribes would be brought under the Indian cultural and political sphere {Shamsul Alam 1985: 23-25}. A Maurya Brahmi stone inscription in the third century BCE from Mahasthan in northern Bangladesh mentioned Pundranagara (Mahasthan) evidently as one of India's provinces and among the earliest territories in Bengal. East-southeast Bengal or Samatata (Comilla, Noakhali, parts of Bakerganj and Chittagong) probably remained out of the Maurya control {Shamsul Alam 1984: pl. 1-4} {Shamsul Alam 1985: 30}. Buddhism was likely introduced by Asoka to Bengal and as already mentioned he subjugated Kalinga (Orissa), a neighbor of Bengal, in c. 262 BCE. Numerous Shunga terracotta figurines and a sandstone *yaksi* sculpture have been found throughout Bengal indicating the Shungas' succession over the Mauryas in the area {Shamsul Alam 1984: 8, pl. 5}{Shamsul Alam 1985: 46}. Kushan coins have also been found in Bengali sites like Mahasthan but the Kushans probably did not rule Bengal directly; West Bengal and parts of southwestern Bangladesh between the third-fourth centuries CE belonged to the independent kingdom of Pushkarna {Shamsul Alam 1985: 30}. However the Kushans alongwith Buddhism, Hinduism, and Jainism were likely present in the area from the discovery of a few multi-armed Visnu and Surya images in the Mathura Style in Rajshahi, Bangladesh {Gupta 1961: 23}{Shamsul Alam 1985: 46-53}. The Buddhist presence did not appear to gain strength until the rise of the Guptas who definitely assumed sovereignty over Bengal; Samatata continued its semi-independent status while acknowledging the Guptas' suzerain during which cultural assimilation from central India accelerated in the region. Fa-hsien reportedly sojourned at Tamralipti (Tamluk) in West Bengal in the early fifth century CE, which was then the busiest seaport in northern India for those who planned to embark the sea journeys to southern India, Sri Lanka, Southeast and East Asia; the Chinese monk recorded about twenty-two monasteries in the area. A late fifth century CE copper-plate Gupta inscription was found in Somapura [4.8] testifying the Gupta strength in the whole Bengal. The Theravada, as in India, was likely the earliest Buddhist school in Bengal and followed by the Mahayana; a Gupta inscription (c. 507-508 CE) from Samatata mentioned the grant for the establishment of Asrama Vihara. The Khadga (c. 625-705 CE) and Deva kings (c. 705-900 CE) controlled eastern Bangladesh until succeeded by the Chandras; the latter ruled the territory and Samatata between c. 900-1035 CE where they patronized Buddhism generously with the construction of numerous monasteries. Meanwhile southwest Bengal, now West Bengal in India and then known as Vardhamana, was ruled by the Hindu Sasanka Dynasty (early seventh century CE) while northern Bengal (Varendra) was incorporated into Harshavardhana's empire. Hsuan-tsang toured Pundravardhana, Samatata, and Tamralipti in the early seventh century CE where he reported seventy monasteries in the whole Bengal and thirty monasteries in Samatata with about 2,000 monks; he also commented that the Jains were numerous in the region {Shamsul Alam 1985: 30-33}. The Chinese monk I-tsing entered India via the sea route in Tamralipti where he studied in its famed Varaha Monastery for some times before proceeding to Nalanda. Buddhist Gupta sculptures have been unearthed in Bangladesh though not as numerous as those in the subsequent Pala Dynasty; these dated between the fifth-seventh centuries CE and carved in the lyrical Gupta-Sarnath Style with insignificant local variations. These early examples had mostly been sculpted in stone but gilt bronze also appeared as early as the sixth century CE; the stone reliefs in the base terrace of Somapura main temple were in the transitional style dated between the late Gupta and early Pala Dynasty {Shamsul Alam 1985: 55-127}. The most illustrious dynasty in Bengal was the Pala Dynasty (c. 750-1199 CE) which empire included Bihar, eastern Uttar Pradesh, and possibly Orissa; they were devout Buddhists who founded numerous monasteries in Bengal like Somapura and also in Bihar like the Nalanda *viharas* [4.4] during their long and illustrious reigns. During the Palas' rule, the Vajrayana supplanted the Mahayana as the dominant Buddhist school in Bengal as elsewhere in eastern India. The Varman Dynasty (1035-1150 CE) eventually replaced the Chandras and took control of Samatata while the Senas (1096-1230 CE) seized a large area of the Palas' territory in Varendra {Shamsul Alam 1984: 8}{Shamsul Alam 1985: 36-39}. Under the Hindu dynasties of the Varmans and Senas, Buddhism suffered a decline in patronage and gradually lost their clout in the region; the Palas and Senas, as well as the whole North India, would finally be succumbed to the Muslim onslaughts in the early thirteenth century CE. Bangladesh, with the exception of Chittagong which still retains its Buddhist heritage to this day, eventually converted to Islam in the following centuries. Pala arts, and those of the Senas, were pervasive in Bangladesh where numerous stone and bronze sculptures as well as paintings had been produced; nevertheless indigenous arts also flourished as evident from the folkish terracotta plaques on Somapura central temple. Due the extremely soggy environment of Bengal fragile materials like murals or paintings, which were once certainly abundant in the area, did not survive the ravages of time; Islamic bigotry also contributed to the destruction of ancient Bangladeshi artistic heritage.

From archaeological data, Buddhism did not appear to have a firm foothold in Bangladesh until the Gupta Dynasty; the majority of early Buddhist centers in Bangladesh, and those in eastern Indian states like Bihar and Orissa, was initially Mahayana. In Bihar, there were great Mahayana centers like Nalanda and in Orissa Lalitagiri (third century BCE-thirteenth centuries CE), Ratnagiri (fifth-thirteenth centuries CE), and Udayagiri (eighth-thirteenth centuries CE); all these centers gradually absorbed Vajrayana practices and transformed into great Vajrayana centers from the seventh century CE on. The Palas, after establishing their dominion over eastern India in c. 750 CE, founded new Vajrayana monasteries based on the Nalanda *mahavihara* model; the essential difference with earlier Mahayana monasteries was that these new Vajrayana establishments mainly taught Vajrayana curricula, probably excluding the controversial *yuganaddha* rituals of the *anuttarayoga-tantra*s. Famous Vajrayana centers in Bihar included Odantapura founded by Gopala I (r. 750-775 CE), Vikramasila founded by Dharmapala (r. 775-812 CE), Jagaddala probably founded by Ramapala (r. 1072-1126 CE) in Varendra, and Somapura founded by Dharmapala and probably expanded by Devapala (r. 812-850 CE) in Bangladesh {Dutt 1962: 349-380}. Buddhist monasteries in Bangladesh tend to be distributed on higher and drier grounds avoiding the low-lying, frequently flooded, and marshy areas like the Sunderban delta; they generally dated between the sixth-thirteenth centuries CE. Many of the better documented monasteries in the region have been found around Mainamati (Salban Vihara, Kotila Mura, Ananda Rajar Badi, Charpatra Mura, Mainamati Ranir Badi), Mahasthan (Somapura, Vasu Vihara, Ananda Vihara, Sitakot Vihara), and Samatata (Asrama Vihara). These monasteries generally have two plan types: (a) The smaller *vihara*s, such as Sitakot Vihara, are without a central temple and these are almost identical in size and plan as the Nalanda *vihara*s [4.4] and (b) the quadrangular *mahavihara*s like Somapura [4.8] and Salban all have massive central temples, or precisely *stupa*-temples, of a cruciform plan {Shamsul Alam 1984: 11-12, pl. 15-49}. Plan (b) was certainly later of the two plans and the most popular in Bangladesh but it did not appear to be unique in the region since Vikramasila in Antichak of the Bhagalpur District in Bihar, India also had this identical plan {Huntington 1984: 126}; the square quadrangular plan (b) generally had one or two stories with a main entrance, cloistered galleries, and latrines on the back. The Palas, in their grandiose vision to emulate the *mahavihara* model of Nalanda, constructed numerous monastic universities on even grander scales; these should aptly be termed as '*viharapura*' or monastic city, hence Odanta-*pura* and Soma-*pura*, as town activities would gyrate around these gigantic monasteries. These were likely royal monasteries funded by the state like Nalanda since they had been known to educate scholars and individuals who would later be employed by the government. The fortress-like constructions of these immense monasteries could also be for defensive purposes and places of refuge in the time of war and government soldiers reportedly guarded these monasteries; during the invasion of Bihar, Bakhtiyar Khalji led an audacious assault on Odantapura which he mistook it for a fort as this monastery was then fiercely defended by Indian soldiers {Dutt 1962: 357}. The concepts of a *viharapura* and a defensive monastery

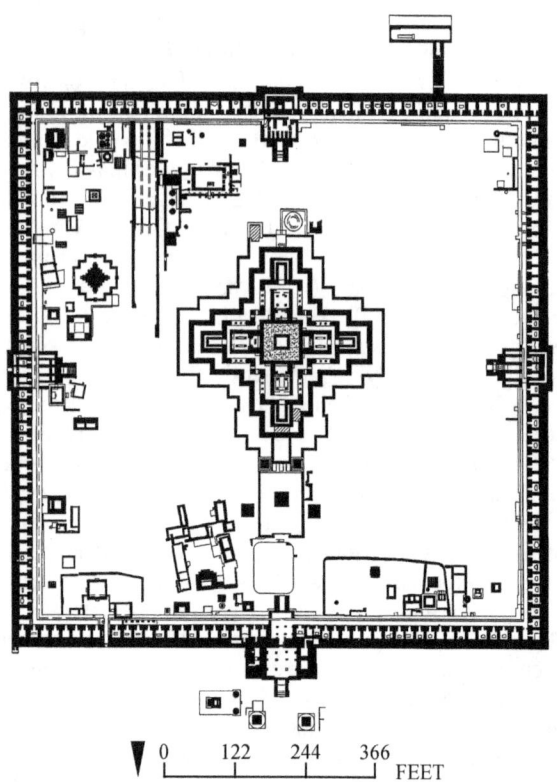

4.8. Plan. c. 775-812 CE. Paharpur- Bangladesh

in the Pala Dynasty already had antecedents in Gandhara where there were recurring warfare and nomadic invasions; this type of a defensive monastery was followed by the fortress/hilltop monasteries in Tibet and the Tibetanized countries.

Somapura **[4.8]** was one of a few Vajrayana *mahaviharas* in Bengal and probably best exemplified the concept of a *viharapura*. The site was first visited and described by Francis Buchanan Hamilton between 1807-1812 CE and followed by Vesey Westmacott in 1875 CE; Alexander Cunningham carried out some initial excavations between 1875-1880 CE. D. R. Bhandarkar's team of Calcutta University started preliminary excavations in 1923 CE and the works were subsequently taken over by the ASI led by R. D. Banerjee in 1925-1926 CE; these were followed by G. C. Chandra in 1930-1932 and completed by K. N. Dikshit in 1933-1934 CE during which the complete plan of the monastery and surrounding areas were finally exposed {Qadir 1963: 1-2}. It is apparent from the scale of the monastery that it had originally been designed for the occupancy of 400-600 monks. From literature and inscriptions, Somapura historically had intimate connections with Bihar monasteries like Nalanda and Vikramasila; Atisa once studied in this great Vajrayana center. The plan is a huge square of 919' east-west x 922' north-south with a massive *stupa*-temple of 359' east-west x 395' north-south in the center which still stands at 70'high above the ground. There are a total of 177 monk cells on all four sides, excluding the main entrance hall on the north side and the three huge image chapels on the other sides. The cells have built-in niches but probably did not have windows since plenty of light could reach the interior via the vast open courtyard; each cell averages about 190 square feet which provided ample space for a single monk. There are ninety-two cells containing image pedestals which had probably been converted into private shrines in later times in response to the growing demands for image worship, the decline in the number of inmates, etc. In front of the cells are 9' wide verandahs once supported by brick piers in the earlier phases but later switched to stone ones; the entire monastery was constructed of kiln-dried bricks laid in mud mortar with the thickness of the back wall between 12'-16'. Stone was mainly for structural use as lintels, door jambs, and door sills while iron cramps were employed to join the different members; the floor of the monastery could be constructed in the same manner as Nalanda of lime concrete. The quadrangle is elevated several feet above the ground level and balustrades would probably be required for the verandahs. The three image chapels and the main entry hall were likely several feet higher than the quadrangle and several stories in height; vaulted tunnel underpasses were provided under these chapels to allow uninterrupted flow of traffic through the verandahs. Most likely the continuous roof of the quadrangle, as in the Nalanda *viharas*, was flat and covered with a thick mud layer spread over a beam-and-plank structure; this, however, does not rule out the possibility of a pitched roof. The monastery has a main entrance through a large pillared hall on the northern side and a secondary postern in the northeastern wing; in front of the main entry are a pair of *stupas* and a small image chapel probably intended for pilgrims or visitors. From the dimensions on the plan, one can deduce that the main entry once had a pair of 4' wide doors which could be locked by a large timber bolt; pockets of 6" x 7 1/2" to receive the bolts are still present on both sides of the jambs. The most dominant feature of the monastery is the massive brick *stupa*-temple in the center of the open courtyard; it has a cruciform plan with two diminishing terraces and above which were once surmounted by a *stupa* superstructure. Visitors proceed to the upper levels via an enclosed courtyard on the northern side having a *stupa* in its center and another two symmetrical *stupa*s outside the enclosure; a pair of *stupa*s also flanks both sides of the main staircase. This massive central edifice consists of four symmetrically projecting image chapels of probably flat roofs constructed around a central block of a hollow core which was once filled with mud to reduce the weight of the structure and increase its load-bearing capacities. These chapels likely once had stone or copper standing Buddha images like the one found in situ at the Rupban Mura Vihara and in later Bagan temples of Myanmar [7.14]; a large bronze torso of a 8'8" high Buddha statue has also been recovered from the site {Shamsul Alam 1985: 78, 162, fg. 18, 60}. The missing upper terminus would likely have a tall drum, dome, solid *harmika*, and a *chattravali* or a *yastichattra* as in somewhat contemporary Sri Lankan *dagaba*s [4.10] and recovered votive *stupa*s in Bangladesh {Shamsul Alam 1984: pl. 39}. The terraces, evidently functioned as *pradaksina* paths for worshippers to perform their religious circumambulation around the image chapels, once certainly had solid balustrades to protect visitors from falling; a drainage system of twenty-two scuppers with 1'6" wide gargoyle ends had been installed throughout the terraces for the proper discharge of excess water. These terraces have cornice projections with decorative motifs like the stepped merlons, lotus petals, and round moldings; their walls are also decorated with stone and terracotta plaques. The hidden section of the first terrace, which is buried under nearly 5' of earth, had sixty-three stone plaques measuring between 1'7"-2'6" high x 8"-2'3" wide; these have stylistically been divided into three groups and dated between c. 600-775 CE or late Gupta to pre-Pala Dynasty. The scenes vary from the sophistication of the Gupta tradition in Group I, to the transitional style between the Gupta Style and indigenous mode in Group II, and the naive folkish style in Group III; the iconography is overwhelmingly Hindu with over sixty panels depicting Siva, Krishna, Agni, Ganesh, etc. The remaining exposed surfaces, or the exposed sections of the first terrace and its balustrades as well as the walls and balustrades of the second terrace, are decorated with more than 2,800 terracotta plaques, of which 2,000 pieces are still in situ but the rest have fallen down. These plaques average 1'2" high x 8.5" wide which display a downright folkish and lively carving style but apparently lack sophistication reflecting a local tradition and workmanship. Their iconographies are also equally divided between Buddhist and Hindu themes in which the former mainly depicts Mahayana and Vajrayana subjects like Buddha, Padmapani, Manjusri, Tara, etc.; local secular folkish scenes are also observed among these plaques. Besides the principal central *stupa*-temple, there are numerous ancillary structures in the courtyard and most of which are located in the north, east, and southeast including a tank, wells, smaller chapels, votive *stupa*s, administration, supporting staffs, etc. The service area including a refectory, kitchen, etc. is concentrated in the southeast while the extremely long rectangular structure could be the great dining hall of the whole monastery; the long extension arm behind the monastery in the southwest corner has been identified as a latrine and washing facility {Gupta 1961: 6-31}{Qadir 1963: 5-26}{Shamsul Alam 1985: 95-127}.

Somapura is a rare example among the Buddhist monuments in having numerous non-Buddhist and Hindu reliefs on the walls of its central temple; the plinth of Caitya 2 at Nalanda also contains numerous Hindu panels, which apparently were not a part of the original Buddhist plan of Nalanda. Since syncretism and mutual tolerance between Hindus and Buddhists grew increasingly common from the seventh century CE on, it might not deem particularly sacrilegious to incorporate Hindu sculptures in Buddhist establishments. Buddha had already been deified as the ninth avatar of Visnu while a four-faced Mahadeva (Siva) statue was also dedicated on the ground of the Mahabodhi Temple during Dharmapala's reign {Ahir 1994: 64-65}. Another plausible explanation is that since Buddhist monuments had been constructed in a region where non-Buddhist religions, like Hinduism, were deep-rooted and constituted the majority of the population, it would therefore be expected to see non-Buddhist elements in these Buddhist establishments as also in the cases of Indrapura in Champa [4.11-4.12] and Bayon of Angkor Thom in Kampuchea [7.16-7.18]. It has been repeatedly suggested that the hidden stone plaques had been collected from the surrounding Hindu or Jain temples and reinstalled on Somapura. The suggestion seems plausible since stone was a precious commodity in the area; as a token of compromise and for the economy of materials, the remaining stones would be collected and reused in the Buddhist edifice. Moreover Somapura might have actually been constructed over the site of a Hindu or Jain temple; a 479 CE copper-plate inscription found in the northeast corner of Somapura mentioned a grant of the land, which was purchased by a *brahmin* couple Nathasarmma, for the purposes of the worship and construction of a resthouse for the Jain teacher Guhanandin presiding in a *vihara* at Vatagohali {Gupta 1961: 2}, which was probably the site of Somapura. The presence of Hindu stone plaques on the first terrace of the central temple may also be explained that the Hindus had probably taken over the original Jain site and built a temple there and the Buddhists in turn constructed their monastery over it. Scholars like Frederick Asher gave an alternative interpretation for the plaque inscription as he believed the word '*nigrantha*' could refer to the Jains but it also literally meant 'a person without attachment to material possessions,' a description which could apply to the Buddhists as well {Asher 1980: 15}. In any case, the fact that the Pala King Dharmapala constructed Somapura is beyond a doubt from the clay seals unearthed from the site containing the legend 'Sri Somapure Sri Dharmapaladeva Mahavihariyarya Bhikshusanghasya' {Gupta 1961: 3}. The Tibetan historian Taranatha stated that Devapala, Dharmapala's son and successor, was the true founder of Somapura but none of his seals or inscriptions has been found {Dutt 1962: 374-375}. Recent excavations have also revealed a monastery of a similar size below Dharmapala's monastery which is believed to be the original Jain *vihara* mentioned in the aforesaid inscription {Alam and Hossain 2004: 14}. I do not accept this suggestion since the Jains were not known to build large monasteries of this size this early in the fifth century CE despite the discovery of a c. 479 CE Jain plaque here; I believe the lower monastery or stratum might actually be Dharmapala's monastery while the one above it probably belonged to Devapala who reportedly completed or renovated his father's enormous monastery with slight modifications. Other inscriptions related to Somapura include an inscribed image (tenth century CE) at Mahabodhi Temple dedicated by Viryendrabhadra from Somapura {Gupta 1961: 4}. Another inscription from Nalanda in the reign of Mahipala I (r. 988-1027 CE) mention Vilulasrimitra who resided at Somapura and where he erected a Tara temple, repaired four cells, and donated a gold ornament for the beautification of a Buddha image. Since Tara images have been found at the main temple in Satyapir Bhita, a site about 900' east of Somapura, it is reasonable to identify this temple as Vilulasrimitra's Tara temple {Gupta 1961: 4, 21}. Lastly, some pillar inscriptions (tenth-twelfth centuries CE) recorded the donation of several pillars at Somapura by Ajayagarbha, Srigarbha, and Dasabalagarbha for 'the gratification of the Three Jewels [*Triratna*] and for the desire of doing good to all good people' {Gupta 1961: 4}{Qadir 1963: 30}.

The conceptual program of a *mahavihara* first popularized at Nalanda would be expanded and metamorphosed into a *viharapura*, in which a gigantic monastery practically became the center of a city, in Bengal during the Pala Dynasty. Its immense size and massive construction seem to have specifically addressed the security concerns where it would effectively be transformed into a great place of refuge in the times of war; this important aspect might also have been imitated by the Tibetans in the construction of their high-walled and fortress-like monasteries on the hilltops. The quadrangular plan of Somapura itself with a central edifice in the center had first been developed in Gandhara, for examples Dharmarajika, Chir Tope D2, Mohenjo-daro [1.1], and Takht-i-bahi [4.2]; it was further refined and enlarged in Kashmir as in Harwan, Ushkur, Parihasapura, and Martand, all constructed during the illustrious reign of Lalitaditya (r. 724-760 CE) {Rowland 1977: 199203}. The plan of Vijayarama [4.9] somewhat echoes Somapura with its two terraces and a long main approach in the south; Benjamin Rowland once suggested that Candi Sewu plan [7.12] had been derived from Somapura {Rowland 1977: 448} but this is only partially true, at least for the cruciform plans of their central *stupa*-temples. However, the most likely precursors of Candi Sewu were Turkistani *stupa*s like Karakhoja Stupa P and Yarkhoto (Chinese Jiaohe) dated in the sixth century CE (see {Yamamoto 1990: 206-207}{TNM 1991: 34}). Further development of Somapura can also be found in the Bayon of Angkor Thom [7.16] in Kampuchea such as its quadrangular plan with galleries, projecting chapels in the cardinal points, long-approached entrance, and a massive cruciform pyramidal temple in the center. The central *stupa*-temple of Somapura is certainly influential from an architectural point of view; the origin of its multi-terraced cruciform plan with image chapels in the four cardinal points could be traced back to Gandhara in examples like Dharmarajika [6.13] and Bhamala [6.17] and the main temple of Sarnath [8.5]. Kesariya Stupa [6.12], with its pyramidal structure and radiating image chapels, also shares similar features with Somapura central temple; Parihasapura Stupa (c. 725-750 CE) in Kashmir also has the multi-terraced and cruciform configuration as Somapura {Huntington 1985: fg. 17.10}. Certain features of Somapura central *stupa*-temple, such as the massive diminishing multi-terraced structure decorated with carved plaques, are also the hallmarks of Borobudur [6.28-6.32]; these features would subsequently be disseminated to Myanmar in monuments like Shwezigon [6.33-6.34] and Ananda Temple [7.14].

6. Vijayarama (eighth century CE) - Sri Lanka

Proto-historical beginning of Sri Lanka, with ancient names as Tambapanna and Sinhala, was in the reign of King Pandukabhaya (fourth century BCE) in the ancient city Anuradhapura; it would not be until the enthronement of his great grandson Devanampiya Tissa (r. 251-209 BCE) that the island nation inaugurated a new epoch in its history. During this period, Sri Lanka received the first Buddhist missionary from the Indian Emperor Asoka after the Third Buddhist Council in c. 249 BCE; the head monk of this council Moggaliputtra Tissa sent Mahendra (Mihinda), Asoka's son-monk, and four other Theravada monks including Itthiya, Uttiya, Bhaddasala, and Sambala to convert the island to Buddhism. After their arrival, Devanampiya Tissa was immediately converted by the Indian missionary at Mihintale, the same location where Mihindra's ashes would later be interred in the Ambasthala Dagaba. On the outskirt of the royal capital Anuradhapura the Sri Lankan king converted his father's pleasure garden, the Mahameghavana, into a rest stop for the Indian monks and dedicated a portion of the land to the newly founded *Sangha* for the construction of new structures for the monks to perform their monastic rites. With a rising number of natives desiring to join the *Sangha*, it was advantageous to build several religious education centers, the *Parivena*s, to ordain and instruct new Buddhist monks into the Buddhist way of life. At the end of the rainy season in the same year, Sri Lanka received Buddha's relics including his right collar-bone and the begging bowl which had been bestowed by Asoka to the island. The bowl was then handed to Mahendra and the collar-bone immediately interred in Thuparama Dagaba [6.26-6.27], the first *stupa* in Sri Lanka. Several months after the construction of Thuparama a second missionary headed by the nun Sanghamitra, Mahendra's sister and Asoka's daughter, and eleven other nuns arrived on the island with a sapling of the *bodhi*-tree taken from the original one in Bodhgaya where Buddha attained Enlightenment; the precious branch was subsequently planted and protected by a boundary wall. Sanghamitra converted several female members of the royal families and many others and in effect founded the first Buddhist nun order in Sri Lanka. Despite the disappearance of Buddhism in India, Sri Lanka steadfastly adhered to the religion of Buddha to the present day; Sinhalese Buddhism also remains the closest to Indian Buddhism and it rightly deserves the title as the preserver of original Buddhism more than any other Buddhist countries in Asia. Succeeding monarchs after Devanampiya Tissa continued to patronize and propagate Buddhism throughout the island. Dutthagamani (r. 161-137 BCE) built Ruvenvali Dagaba and Vattagamani (r. 103-77 BCE) constructed Abhayagiri Dagaba while Mahasena (r. 276-303 CE) erected Jetavana Dagaba, the biggest domed *stupa* in Asia; these colossal edifices are all located in the ancient city of Anuradhapura. The Anuradhapura Period (c. 249 BCE-993 CE) ended with the Chola invasion and occupation from South India between 907-1053 CE; Vijayabahu I (r. 1058-1114 CE) restored Sri Lanka to its native rule in 1070 CE and inaugurated the Polonnaruva Period (eleventh-thirteenth centuries CE) with a new capital at Polonnaruva. Anuradhapura boasted the greatest concentration of excavated Buddhist remains in Sri Lanka and it inaugurated the most important period in arts and architecture on the island. The various accounts of visiting Buddhists to Sri Lanka in the fifth century CE, including well-known names like the Chinese monk Fa-hsien and the Indian Buddhist scholar Buddhaghosa, and the native historical chronicles like the Mahavamsa also testified the flourishing state of Buddhism on the island at the time. Fa-hsien reported 10,000 monks and nuns alone residing in Anuradhapura with 3,000 in the Mahavihara Monastery, 5,000 in the Abhayagirivihara Monastery, and 2,000 at Mihintale {Bandaranayake 1974: 7, 92, 288}.

Within 10,000 acres of Anuradhapura, there are remains of about 4,000 structures including numerous *dagaba*s and temples; these have left a wealth of information on Buddhist arts and architecture that have been accumulating for centuries since the third century BCE. For the most parts, no significant examples of Sri Lankan Buddhist arts and architecture can be dated before the first century CE; no doubt many could have existed earlier in primitive and timber forms but any remaining traces had been obliterated by the ensuing renovations, foreign invasions, and neglect. Between the third century BCE-first centuries CE, the most important remains were the cave residences constructed for monks and the many ancient inscriptions left inside; these inscriptions are in Brahmi and the living proofs of past intimate connections between Sri Lanka and India. The Brahmi script in these rock inscriptions is similar to the one on the Asoka pillars, Sanchi, and Bharhut and their contents are overwhelmingly Buddhist. About thirty-seven out of forty signs in the Asoka's Brahmi edicts also appear in these Sri Lankan Brahmi inscriptions; there are several unexplainable symbols such as the fish recalling the undeciphered Harappa script but possible links between them could not be confirmed {Paranavitana 1970: xv-xvii, xxiii, xxv-xxvi}. In the fields of the arts and architecture, the Sri Lankans have demonstrated their unmistaken indebtedness to India in the way as Japan has been indebted to continental China. The earliest Sri Lankan arts and architecture were predictively in timber while permanent materials like brick and possibly stone were also employed in the construction of the earliest *stupa*s. It was not until the first century CE that arts and architecture on the island began to take shape; much like India, the oldest extant examples are found on the *stupa*s, or *dagaba*s as the Sri Lankans prefer to call them. The frontispieces or *vahalkada*s of Kantaka Dagaba (first century CE) at

Mihintale and Abhayagiri Dagaba (second century CE) at Anuradhapura contain some of the earliest arts and architecture in Sri Lanka; they exhibit a strong resemblance to those on Sanchi, Bharhut, and Amaravati in India as well as Gandhara. Thus the stele pairs erected on the sides of the *vahalkada*s in the four cardinal points, which were crowned with animals like elephants, lions, etc., recall the Asoka pillars, Indian *torana*s, and the *ayaka* pillars in South Indian *stupa*s. The faces of these steles are carved with reliefs of animals, floral scrolls, honeysuckles, and floral vases (*purnaghata*) as well as human and divine figures like *naga*s, dwarfs, *yaksa*s, *yaksi*s, etc; despite their obvious borrowings from India, they were the impetus for subsequent Sri Lankan arts. Sri Lankans also began to sculpt Buddha images as soon as the first Indian prototypes were available on the island some times in the third century CE; these first Buddha images are unmistakably in the Andhra Style of Amaravati in South India while later styles reaching the island from India were the Gupta Style and Pala Style; Sri Lankan Buddhists typically prefer their Buddhas in the standing or sitting posture in the *dhyana-mudra* and rarely deviate from these models. Besides the sculptures, the rare early murals executed inside the Sigiri Cave are among the extant masterpieces of Sri Lankan Buddhist paintings which dated between the sixth-seventh centuries CE; these portray gorgeous celestial female damsels with a style strongly akin to the Vakataka murals of Ajanta in India. Mahayana Buddhism alongwith its arts and architecture also permeated Sri Lanka, a predominantly Theravada territory, where several *bodhisattva* images of Avalokitesvara had been sculpted; the layouts of a few Anuradhapura monasteries were also believed to have been planned by Sri Lankan Mahayanists {Bandaranayake 1974: 70-73}. However, there are no definite proofs that the Mahayana ever held much esteem among Sri Lankan Buddhists since the Theravada had been deep-rooted on the island since the third century BCE; Theravada religious orthodoxy and preeminence in Sri Lanka also extended to the fields of the arts and architecture, particularly the ubiquitously placid immobility of Sri Lankan sculptures and the austere appearance of its monuments. These stand in contrast with the sumptuous decorations in many Indian Buddhist monuments, many of which had been strongly influenced by the Mahayana especially from the Gupta Dynasty on.

Upon the arrival of the Indian Asoka missionary a royal garden, the Mahameghavana, was immediately set aside for Mahendra and other monks which was among the earliest Buddhist establishments in Sri Lanka; the site subsequently grew into one of the three largest monasteries in Anuradhapura, the others being Abhayagiri and Jetavana. Outside Anuradhapura several monasteries were also established at Mihintale, the historical birthplace of Buddhism on the island, including the Mihintalekanda. Between the third century BCE-first centuries CE the concept of well-organized and permanent monasteries, with their multi-functional structures, had yet to be materialized. Instead during this period monks, true to the spirit of early Buddhism, sheltered themselves in various natural and man-made caves; the best of these monastic caves, which were donated by the Buddhist laity, can be found in Mihintale and Vessagiriya. These cave monasteries are especially valuable since they contain numerous Brahmi inscriptions, a total of 1,234, revealing the initial successes of Buddhism on the island; these, however, are small and simple caves compared to contemporary Indian Buddhist caves, which were larger and much more elaborate. Early freestanding Sri Lankan monasteries were typically grouped around a main *dagaba* as in Anuradhapura monasteries like Mahavihara, Abhayagiri, and Jetavana; these have been termed 'organic' by Bandaranayake for their unplanned and natural expansion around the principal *dagabas* and hence they constitute the earliest type of monastic settlements. The remaining three types of Sri Lankan monasteries are the *pancayatana parivena* (Quincunxial Monastic College), *padhanagriha parivena* (Double-platform/Meditation-house Monastic College), and *pabbata vihara* (Mountain Monastery) {Bandaranayake 1974: 33-133}. The principal edifice in the organic type is a *dagaba* with a history usually intimately connected to early Sinhalese Buddhism; these Sri Lankan *dagaba*s would reach monumental scales by the second-third centuries CE. The preeminence of the *dagaba* reflected the universal preoccupation with relics in early Buddhism since it, whether with or without the relics inside, represented the symbolic invisible presence of Buddha and the emblem of Buddhism. In addition to the *dagaba*, the *uposathagriha* (a religious observance house) and *bodhigriha* (*bodhi*-tree house) are also among the most important buildings in an organic monastery {Bandaranayake 1974: 53}. On the third day of Mahendra's arrival the Mahaseema, which was located within the Mahameghavana, was inaugurated at the request of the Indian missionaries as the place for monks to perform important Buddhist rites like the *uposatha* or an observance of the *Vinaya* which would be performed twice a month during the new and full moon days. The arrival of Sanghamitra and a sapling of the *bodhi*-tree also necessitated the construction of a new structure, the *bodhigriha*, to house and protect the precious *bodhi*-tree. In the next centuries as the monks' lifestyle grew increasingly more settled, newer types of buildings emerged such as the *upatthanasala* (assembly hall) and *bhojanasala* (bath house); the last major building type in an organic plan, the *pratimagriha* (image house), had probably been developed in the second century CE to house Buddha images. In the subsequent centuries, buildings catering to the lay Buddhists were also constructed to accommodate the increasing interactions between the laity and Buddhist clergy. The organic plan above all had an early beginning in India in sites like Sanchi [6.3] and Dharmarajika [6.13] in Gandhara. The next important Sri Lankan monastery plan is the *pancayatana parivena* in which a group of four or more smaller buildings is placed symmetrically around a centrally large building or a *pasada*. Examples of this type include Mahasena's Pavilion Monastery, Monastery B, and Kaparama all in the Abhayagirivihara; the others are Monastery L in the Jetavanavihara. This type has a boundary wall to insulate itself from the outside world with a main entrance entered via a formal gatehouse and a long approach; other ancillary buildings essential to the functioning of the monastery include refectories, bathhouses, shrines, ponds, etc. The principal building was probably multifunctional for residential and ceremonial purposes whereas the surrounding four cells were primarily residential in character; this type has tentatively been dated between the sixth-eighth centuries CE or late Anuradhapura Period {Bandaranayake 1974: 94, 99} and its quincunxial plan was common outside Sri Lanka in Nalanda [4.4 (#12)] and Gandhara [6.14]. The central plan of the third *padhanagriha parivena* type composes of a walled-in compound with an imposing building or a *pasada* behind and preceded by a large platform; there is a stone passage linking the platform and the *pasada*. Notable examples of this type are the Western Monasteries A-N attributed to the Pamsukulika Sect of Ritigala constructed in the ninth century CE. According to Bandaranayake {Bandaranayake 1974: 116}:

> The locations of these monasteries outside of the main areas of monastic and secular building, their rigid avoidance of all but the simplest geometrical ornament, the regular practice of their placing their central *pasadas* on a rock outcrop surrounded by a moat, their high enclosure walls and the lack of conspicuous ritual elements such image-houses...

Some unusual features of this type are the construction of a *pasada* directly on a natural rock promontory and the presence of many ornate urinals. The hypaethral platform was probably meant for outdoor congregational activities or the conduct of religious rites and certainly complementary to the imposing *pasada* behind, which was primarily as a residence for monks and the headmonk {Bandaranayake 1974: 131}. The long approach through a formal gateway porch in this plan resembles that in the *pancayatana parivena*; however its highly structured plan and the presence of the moat suggest a later date of probably between the eighth-tenth centuries CE but not earlier than the seventh century CE. The fourth type of monastery plan or the *pabbata vihara* [4.9] has most of the features in the organic and *padhanagriha parivena* plans; these include the *dagaba*, *uposathagriha*, *bodhigriha*, and *pratimagriha*, which are enclosed within and constitute the centrally sacred precinct, as well as subsidiary buildings of residential and service functions. The cross-axiality alongwith several enclosed and distinct precincts, which are organized according to their functions, and the architectural hierarchy are some of the dominant features in this type; the most notable monasteries of this type include Pankuliya, Vijayarama [4.9-4.10], Pacinatissapabbata, Magulmahavihara, Puliyankulam, and Tuluvila. The oldest inscription found in Pacinatissapabbata dated in the fifth century CE but the overall lifespan of the *pabbata vihara* can conservatively be dated between the seventh-tenth centuries CE. In summary the most conspicuous feature of the latter three monastery types, namely the *pancayatana parivena*, *padhanagriha parivena*, and *pabbata vihara*, is the significant decrease in the scale and importance of the *dagaba*, which is a dominant edifice in the organic plan where ancillary buildings would revolve around it. The moat, long approach avenue, multiple precincts, and the elevated terraces are definitely late features dated probably no earlier than the eighth century CE.

A typical monastery of the *pabbata vihara* type is Vijayarama [4.9-4.10]; the site is about 1 1/2 miles north of Jetavana Dagaba in Anuradhapura which was first visited by Ievers in 16th November 1884 then already in ruins much like today. The monastery orientates on the main north-south axis and was demarcated by a large rectangular boundary wall of about 800' x 1100' with a formal entry porch in the south; within this secluded compound, there are distinct precincts separated by walls in which the outer precinct is the service quarter and the middle one for residential, and the inner or central one as a sacred and worship zone. The service quarter provided basic daily needs for monks and included buildings like the refectory, kitchen, and bathhouse behind the southern entrance on both sides of the long approach avenue; the others are privies, a well, and probably buildings for the service staffs or areas where monks could interact with

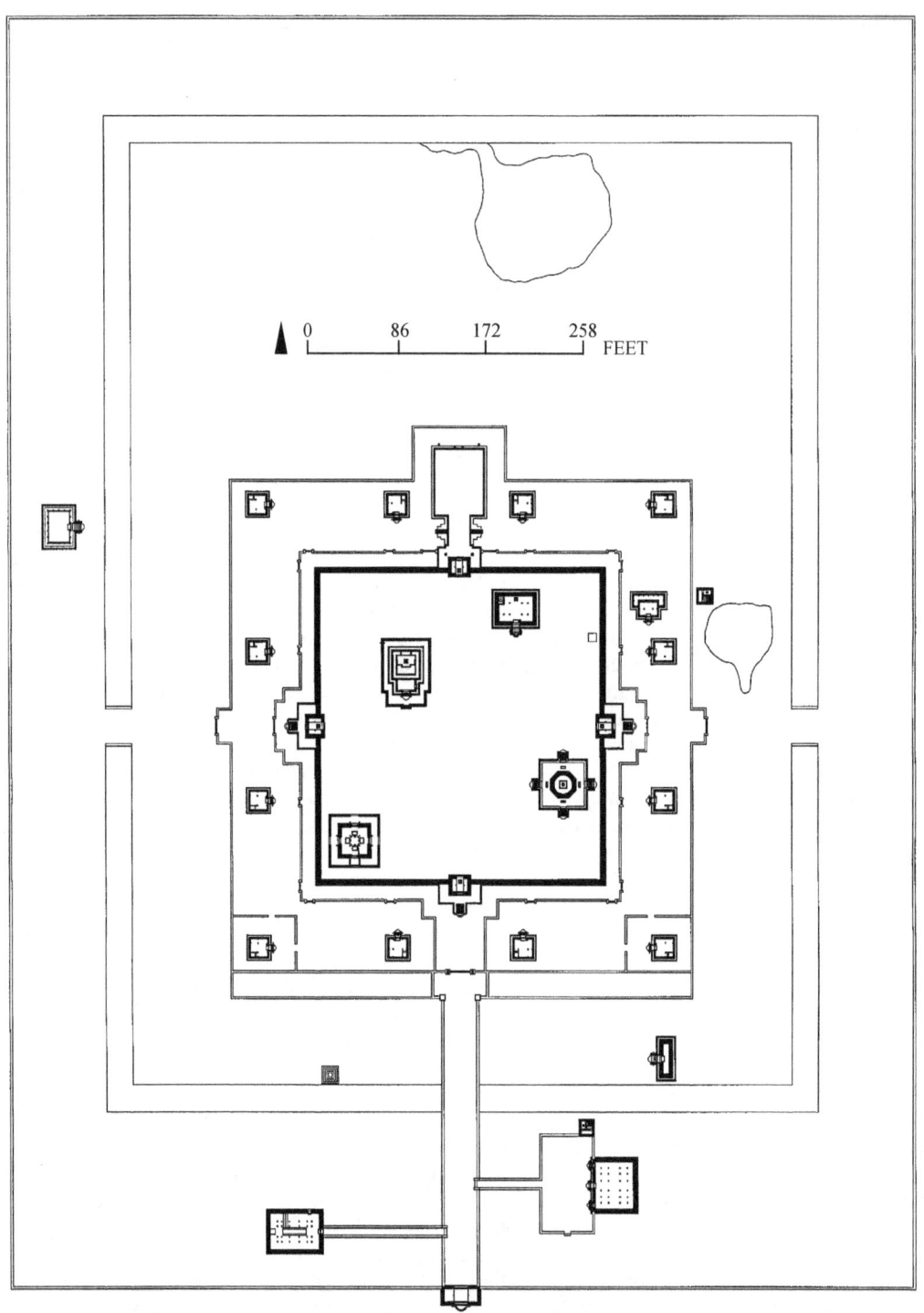

4.9. Site plan. Eighth century CE. Anuradhapura- Sri Lanka

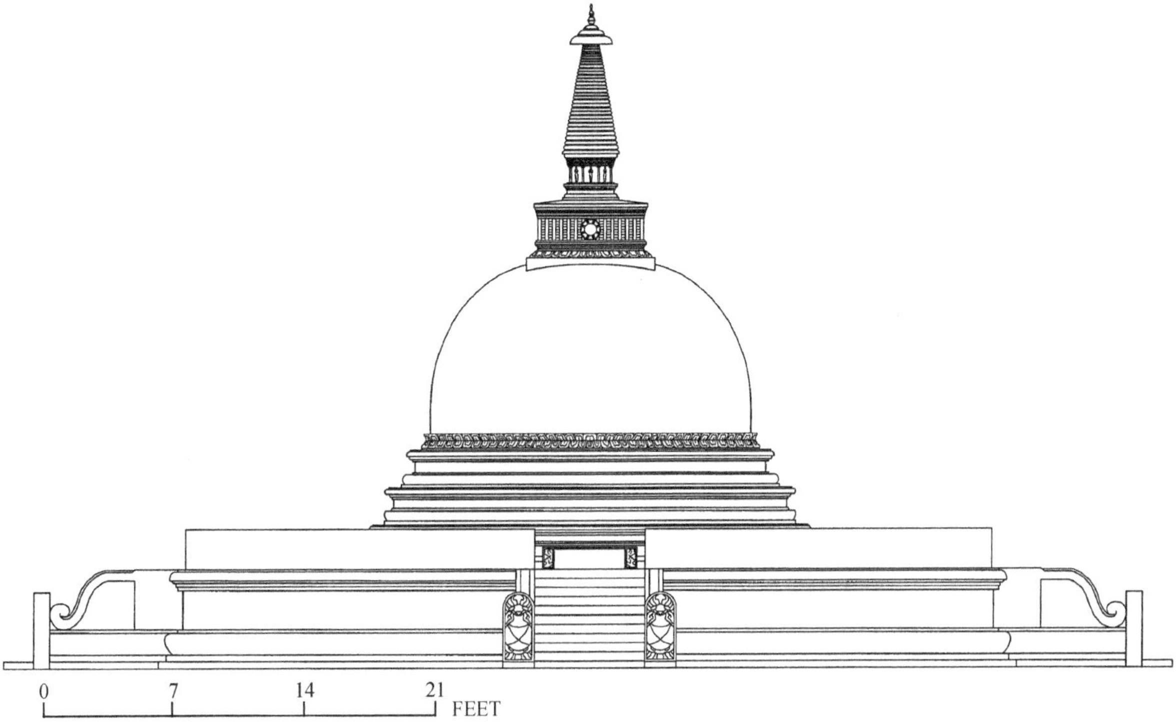

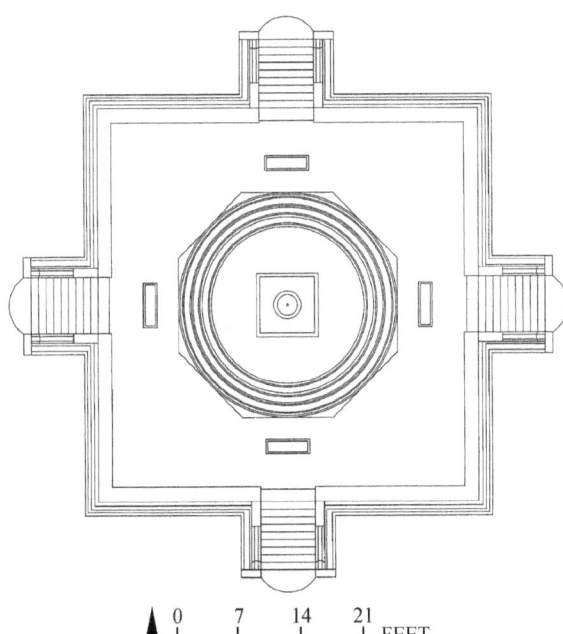

4.10. Stupa elevation (restored) and top view
Eighth century CE
Anuradhapura- Sri Lanka

the laity. The moat and artificial ponds, besides functioning as water reservoirs, create a natural barrier between the service, residential, and sacred quarters. Traces of a second wall of about 435' x 467' can still be discernable surrounding the middle and central precincts which are raised on terraces; there is a pair of crouching humped bulls on pedestals guarding these precincts. In 1896 CE, Wickremasinghe uncovered bronze figures of animals and deities of the four quarters beneath the four entry porches into the sacred precinct; the positions of the animals were the lion (north), elephant (east), horse (south), and bull (west) {Paranavitana 1947: 55} and these animals already occurred in the Sri Lankan moonstones and also the Asoka pillars [3.1-3.6]. The monks' residential quarter is elevated on a 1' high low terrace and has twelve identical square *vihara* cells of 23'7 x 23'9' each; the two walled-in *viharas* in the southeast and southwest corners might be residences of the chief-monk and deputy in charge of the whole monastery. The centrally sacred precinct is elevated on a 6' high terrace and enclosed by a continuous wall punctuated by four entry porches in the cardinal points; in the northern side is a roofed terrace probably reserved for outdoor congregation or the performance of religious rites as in the *padhanagriha parivena*. Within the centrally sacred enclosure of worshiping and ecclesiastical functions are four principal buildings, namely the *dagaba* (southeast) **[4.10]**, *bodhigriha* (southwest), *pratimagriha* (northwest), and *uposathagriha* (northeast) with their principal entrances facing south. The 29' high restored *dagaba* stands on a 45'9" molded square plinth with staircases punctuated in the cardinal points; there are four altars for votive offerings. The *bodhigriha* is a 31'4" square structure surrounded by a 48' square wall with entrances in the cardinal points; its unpaved center of natural earth was likely hypaethral from the presence of a drain pipe beneath it which allowed unimpeded growth of the *bodhi*-tree. Discovered doorsills and columns suggest the existence of a roof {Bandaranayake 1974: 167-169} and there are also four image and offering pedestals in front of the hypaethral center. The 35'5 x 43'8" *uposathagriha* has more decorations than the others; its interior brick floor has a stone basin near the entrance likely for washing and a flat paved area in the back probably intended for an image pedestal or the seat of the head monk. There is an enclosed compartment with doors in its northwestern corner which might once house items for religious rites such as scriptures or sacred objects. The 33'5" x 44' *pratimagriha* is enclosed within a brick wall having an entrance in the south; the foyer, which has a secondary entrance in the east, is attached to the main chamber which contains a pedestal for a Buddha image. It is evident that all buildings in Vijayarama were single-storied and probably had timber structures supporting tile roofs; their walls were brick and covered with plaster finishes, with the exception of the *dagaba* which had a rubble masonry core faced with brick and plaster.

There are several criteria for establishing the construction phases of Vijayarama:
(a) An inscription from Pankuliya, the predecessor of Vijayarama, dated in the eighth century CE {Bandaranayake 1974: 81}; the other six inscriptions on the copper plaques found at the Vijayarama *dagaba* dated in the eighth and tenth century CE {Paranavitana 1947: 98}{ASC Fifth Progress Report 1891: 9}.
(b) The plain guardstones, moonstones, wingstones, *purnaghata*, dwarf *yaksa*s, and *naga*s can be dated between the seventh-tenth centuries CE {Bandaranayake 1974: 328-341}; the plain guardstones occurred in the refectory, *purnaghata* in the *dagaba* and *pratimagriha*, dwarf *yaksa*s in the sacred precinct, south porch, and *pratimagriha*, and *naga*s in the *uposathagriha* and *vihara*.
(c) The plinths of all buildings show considerable stylistic homogeneity of mostly torus moldings, with the exception of the guarding animal pedestals having the torus-and-cyma molding; the latter type dated between the eighth-ninth centuries CE whereas the former type was probably a little earlier in the seventh century CE {Bandaranayake 1974: 313-322}.

Most buildings are brick and coated with plaster with the exception of the *dagaba* which has a rubble masonry core faced with brick and plaster that can be dated in the seventh century CE or later {Bandaranayake 1974: 127-130}. Category (b) is the least reliable method for dating since the degree of ornamentation on a building depended on its status and patronage; thus the refectory, evidently of lesser importance, has been given a plain stair whereas prominent buildings like the *uposathagriha* and *vihara* are appropriately provided with ornate *naga* motifs. The *dagaba* appears to be the earliest edifice while the *uposathagriha*, *vihara*, and guarding animals are the latest; considering (a), (b), and (c) together, Vijayarama can conservatively be dated in the eighth century CE possibly with several renovations after its initial construction.

It is uncommon in Sri Lanka to document a complete quadrangular monastery like Gandhara **[4.2]** and India **[4.4]**, with the exception like Baddhasimapasada in Polonnaruva Period; the closed quadrangular plan is obviously more appropriate in a colder climate than tropical Sri Lanka as it prevents much needed cross ventilation or cool breezes. The most conspicuous feature of Vijayarama is the parity in rank between the *uposathagriha*, *bodhigriha*, and *pratimagriha* with the *dagaba*; the latter had clearly lost its former superior position. This is also similar in Horyuji **[4.5]** wherein its image hall, due to the predominantly Mahayana influence, is positioned contiguously next to the pagoda now essentially reduced to a symbolic structure. As already stated, the immediate predecessor of Vijayarama was undoubtedly Pankuliya; the question remains as whether there was the Mahayana involvement in the planning of Vijayarama in a predominantly Theravada country {Bandaranayake 1974: 70-81} {Paranavitana 1947: 98}. The plaques discovered in the Vijayarama *dagaba* have invocations of Tara, a well-known late Mahayana and early Vajrayana goddess. The incorporation of the *pratimagriha* on the plan concurrent with the decline of the *dagaba* status seems to suggest a Mahayana tendency; however, the presence of the *pratimagriha* in Vijayarama does not suggest a link with the Mahayanists since the Theravadins surely enjoy image worship as much as the former. Another peculiar feature about the sacred precinct of Vijayarama is the apparently haphazard positions of its buildings; this might be attributed to the Indian Pallava influences in the seventh century CE from sites like Mamallapuram; similar random or organic plans are also common in Champa as in Indrapura Monastery **[4.11]**. The symmetrical placement of ancillary cells around a centrally sacred precinct in Vijayarama is also similar to Candi Sewu [7.12]. To a certain degree, the Khmers also learned much from the Sri Lankans in the construction of their massive monuments with an extensive system of moats and reservoirs and a central temple approached via a long avenue [7.16]; these features had already been preceded by Sri Lankan examples some centuries earlier, though in smaller scales.

7. Indrapura (c. 875 CE) - Champa

The once independent country of Champa, which is now located in modern Central Vietnam, corresponds roughly to the coastal strip of land between the eleven to eighteen latitudes or Quang-Binh Province in the north to Binh-Thuan Province in the south. North of Quang-Binh was once the original territory of Vietnam (now North Vietnam) with the Hoanh Son Massif as the natural barrier between the two countries; on the other end of Champa south of Binh-Thuan (now South Vietnam) were Funan and Chenla, once the domains of the Khmers (Kampucheans or Cambodians). It is difficult to trace the exact origin of the Chams but their language belongs to the Autronesian stock akin to Malaysia and Indonesia. Some Vietnamese historians have attempted to link the Chams with the ancient people of Sa-Huynh Culture (c. 2000 BCE-100 CE) but there is no evidence to support such claim {Cao 1988: 186-188}. The Chinese recorded the existence of Lin-yi, the first Cham state, in 192 CE; the Vo-Canh stele inscription found in Nha-Trang, which dated in the second or third century CE, also mentions the foundation of a state by Sri Mara {Coedes 1968: 40}{Cao 1988: 186}{Chihara 1997: 81}. Champa was the smallest of the four preeminent Indianized states in Southeast Asia, the others being Myanmar, Indonesia, and Kampuchea with Sanskrit as the official language and Hinduism the state religion. Indian settlers, traders, and missionaries likely arrived in the coast of Vietnam as early as the beginning of the first century CE and who brought with them the Indian culture. These Indians probably came from South India as evident from the South Indian names of Cham cities like Amaravati (Quang-Nam), Vijaya (Binh-Dinh), Kauthara (Nha-Trang), and Panduranga (Phan-Rang); these correspond to historic South Indian cities in the Krishna River valley in Andhra Pradesh. After its founding, Champa maintained relations with its southern and northern neighbors, or the Khmers and the Vietnamese in the ancient Chinese colony of North Vietnam respectively, while constantly engaged in warfare with both. Among the first historical Cham kings was Bhadravarman (c. 350-400 CE) whose Sanskrit and Cham inscription mentioned his capital as Indrapura which has been identified with Tra-Kieu near Danang. Bhadravarman erected the first Cham temple at Mi-Son in Amaravati, which became the holy land of the Chams, and also the first Hindu temple in Indochina that housed a *linga* named Bradresvara dedicated to the god Siva {Groslier 1962: 66}{Chihara 1997: 82}. The succeeding Cham kings Sambhuvarman (r. 572-629 CE) rebuilt this temple and renamed the *linga* SambhuBradresvara while Prakasadharma (r. 653-686 CE), who descended from King Isanavarman of Chenla, also constructed more temples at Mi-Son {Groslier 1962: 80-82}{Chihara 1997: 82}. Around 758 CE, a new Cham dynasty was founded in Kauthara and Panduranga that lasted until 860 CE; the old name Lin-yi was accordingly changed to Huan-wang and again renamed as Champa (Chan-cheng in Chinese) in 808 CE {Chihara 1997: 187} {Tran: 26}. Champa had reportedly been raided by the Javanese or probably invaded by the powerful Sailendra Dynasty of Java in 774 CE and 787 CE. The intimate relations between the Javanese and the Chams have also been well-documented as the Cham royal family was once reported to have gone on a pilgrimage to Java in 911 CE; marriages between the Cham royal families and the East Javanese Majapahit Dynasty were also recorded while Cham arts and architecture in the tenth century CE have also been influenced by those of the Sailendra and Second Maratam Dynasty {Chihara 1997: 182, 188, 190} {Chutiwongs 2002: 292, 294}. In 860 CE, a new Cham dynasty was founded at Indrapura (Dong-duong), which was not the same as Indrapura of the earlier King Bhadravarman; shortly thereafter King Indrapura II (r. 875-898 CE) founded Indrapura Monastery [4.11-4.12] in c. 875 CE near his capital, the grandest and most important Buddhist monastery in the whole existence of Champa. The ninth-tenth centuries CE were the most prosperous period in Champa and the classic phase of Cham arts and architecture; from the eleventh century CE onward Champa went into a long agonizing decline due to the constant pressure from the newly independent Vietnam in 939 CE in the north and Kampuchea in the south and west. On the southern front, Champa was invaded by the Khmer King Rajendravarman (r. 944-968 CE) and the Cham King Harivarman IV (r. 1074-1080 CE) later retaliated by invading Kampuchea and destroying Sambor, the ancient Khmer capital in the seventh century CE. The Khmers under Suryavarman II (r. 1113-1150 CE) eventually succeeded in subjugating Champa between 1128-1149 CE but the Chams managed to regain their independence, sailed up the Mekong River, and sacked Angkor in 1177 CE. Jayavarman VII (r. 1181-1218 CE), the founder of

Angkor Thom, regained composure for Kampuchea and waged a retaliatory campaign against Champa which was effectively annexed between 1203-1220 CE; however, the Khmer Empire disintegrated soon after Jayavarman VII's death and the Chams once again freed themselves from the Khmers' yoke {Groslier 1962: 120, 133, 194, 197}{Chihara 1997: 139-140, 142, 147, 222}. About the same time as the Chams were fighting the Khmers in the south, they also had to face the formidable Vietnamese in their northern frontier. The Vietnamese under the Early Le Dynasty (980-1009 CE) went on the offensive and destroyed Indrapura in 982 CE so that the Chams' capital and their holy land Amaravati had to be abandoned and moved further south to Vijaya in 1000 CE. The succeeding Ly Dynasty (1010-1225 CE) again invaded Champa in 1044 CE and 1075 CE which resulted in the loss of its three northern provinces north of the Hai-Van Pass, now Quang-Binh and Quang-Tri provinces. There would be more pressures from the Tran Dynasty (1225-1400 CE) as well as from the Mongols who invaded both Vietnam and Champa in 1283-1285 CE but were effectively repulsed. Later the matrimonial alliance between the Vietnamese Princess Huyen-Tran and the Cham King Che-Man (Jaya Simhavarman III) in 1306 CE, probably out of the fear of the looming Mongol threats, again resulted in the loss of Thua-Thien-Hue Province as a dowry gift to the Vietnamese. War resumed again between the Chams and the Vietnamese when the great Cham King Che-Bong-Nga (r. 1360-1390 CE) succeeded in destroying the Vietnamese capital Thang-Long several times but he later died in the battle; from then on the fate of Champa was sealed. The Ho Dynasty (1400-1407 CE) again took possession of Quang-Nam (Amaravati), where the Cham holy land and Mi-Son temples were located, and Quang-Nghia provinces in 1402 CE. By 1470 CE, the Vietnamese under the Later Le Dynasty (1428-1788 CE) occupied Vijaya while Kauthara was lost in 1611 CE and finally Panduranga in 1697 CE; Champa ceased to exist as a nation from then on {Tran: 38, 41, 45, 68, 72-75, 78, 136}{Groslier 1962: 133, 197}{Chihara 1997: 222-224}.

Before the arrival of the Indian religions like Hinduism and Buddhism the Chams were reportedly worshippers of primitive faiths like shamanism, animism, and ancestral cult in the form of the *kut*, or steles venerated as the living manifestations of their deceased relatives {Mus 1975: 38-42}. The Chams, Indian settlers, and their descendents soon embraced Hinduism, which remained the dominant religion of the Chams until the end of their country, after the founding of Champa as evident from its inscriptions; like Kampuchea, Sivaism was the predominant faith of the Chams during its existence. According to Paul Mus, "Of the 128 most important inscriptions found in Champa, 21 are not addressed to any sectarian deity, 92 invoke Siva or Saivite deities, 3 cite Visnu, 5 Brahma, and 7 the Buddha" {Mus 1975: 3}. The Chams, like the Khmers, were ardent worshippers of Siva *linga*s; upon founding a new temple, a *linga* would be installed in its sanctum and given a name after their living king. For example the Siva *linga* installed in the first Cham temple at Mi-Son was named Bradresvara after King Bhadravarman, who was identified with Siva as his living representative on earth. Thus the act of worshipping the *linga* ensured the security of the dynasty, the blessing of the ancestors, and the longevity and prosperity of the country {Mus 1975: 30-31, 38, 43-44, 50-51}. From Cham inscriptions, Buddhism was not popular in Champa but it has been credited for the aforesaid Vo-Canh stele which contains the first Cham inscription dated in second or third century CE; this clearly confirms its early presence at least since the founding of the nation {Mus 1975: 3}. The sophisticated bronze Buddha in the Andhra Style of Amaravati found in Indrapura dated between the third-fourth centuries CE testifies this region as among the earliest Buddhist communities in Champa {Rowland 1977: 364-365}. The Chinese monk-pilgrim I-tsing reported the presence of the Sammitiya and Mulasarvastivada sects of the Theravada in Champa in the late seventh century CE; the Mahayana, mainly in the form of the Lokesvara (Avalokitesvara) cult, later superseded the Theravada between the eighth-tenth centuries CE from the findings of numerous Lokesvara images dated in this period {Chutiwongs 2002: 289-313}. Apparently it was between 875-960 CE, and in the entire Cham history, that Buddhism did make some noticeable successes. King Indrapura II (r. 875-898 CE), a Mahayana follower, founded Indrapura Monastery in c. 875 CE and dedicated to the image of Lakshmindralokesvara; here the king identified himself with Lokesvara and Buddha instead of Siva like his predecessors. He was one of the first kings in Southeast Asia to have instigated the cult of divinized Buddhist kings or *Buddharaja* from the Lokesvara image named after him, the Lakshmindralokesvara; his *Buddharaja* image was perhaps the Buddhist counterpart of the Siva *linga* in Hinduism. Probably in keeping with the popular religion of his people and predecessors, Indrapura II also included the Siva statue inside the monastery; he took a posthumous Buddhist name Paramabuddhaloka but declared his royal status as descended from Siva and thus the Mahayana of the Chams during this period was rather a syncretic form of Buddhism and Sivaism. Indrapura II's successors, probably up to Indrapura III (r. 918-960 CE), also reportedly built more Mahayana temples and possibly monasteries dedicated to the *Buddharaja* cult further south in Quang-Binh Province {Groslier 1962: 138} {Chihara 1997: 189}. The conversion of Indravarman II was not the result of a sudden conversion since his predecessor, King Bhavavarman, had also patronized Buddhism with monastery constructions and Champa had undoubtedly already been saturated with Mahayana ideas by the eighth century CE. The most probable cause for Champa's sudden interest in Buddhism during this period was most likely due to the religious impulse pulsating from the Buddhist Sailendra Dynasty (775-856 CE) in Java or even directly from Orissa and Pala India. Buddhism rapidly faded after Indrapura II and probably reabsorbed into Hinduism; a Buddha head dated in the twelfth century CE has been found in Vijaya but this is a rare occurrence {Cao 1988: fg. 178}.

The history of Cham arts belongs to sculptures and architecture since there are no reports of any paintings or murals; as expected the overwhelming majority of Cham sculptures is Hindu, particularly Sivaite. There are a few Cham Buddhist sculptures and these are mostly Mahayana images like Buddha, Avalokitesvara, and Tara which have primarily been manufactured in the reign of Indrapura II. However, there are earlier Buddhist sculptures in Champa such as the famed Dong-duong bronze Buddha (third-fourth centuries CE) and several Avalokitesvaras also in bronze and stone (late eighth century CE) {Groslier 1962: 83}{Rowland 1977: 364-365}. The materials for freestanding Cham sculptures are mostly sandstone while the architectural ornaments are terracotta plaster (brick); a few Buddhist sculptures have also been casted in bronze as already mentioned. Cham sculptures, including Hindu and Buddhist ones, can be divided into several phases or styles {Groslier 1962: 65-66, 80-84, 133-145, 194-201}{Cao 1988: 196-215, fg. 3-219}:

- Mi-Son E1 (c. 650-750 CE)
- Hoa-Lai (c. 800-850 CE)
- Dong-duong (c. 875-900 CE)
- Tra-Kieu (c. 900-1000 CE)
- Binh-Dinh (c. 1100-1275 CE)
- Po Klaung Garai (c. 1275-1700 CE)

Mi-Son E1 reveals Indian Gupta influences and to a lesser extent the South Indian region of Andhra Pradesh; the Cham Sleeping Visnu tympanum at once recalls the same subject on the Indian Deogarh Temple (c. 500 CE) {Rowland 1977: 224-227}. The flattened arched pediment of Mi-Son E1 is somewhat similar to the contemporary Prei Kmeng Style in Kampuchea and its vomiting *makara*s also resembles a similar motif in the Javanese *candi*s; however the Cham example has, in addition to the *makara*, a hooded cobra curving inward. Hoa-Lai also shares virtually identical features as the Angkor temple Prasat Damrei Krap (c. 800 CE) which most scholars agreed that it must have been constructed by Cham architects. Dong-duong (Indrapura) is also the site of the rare Cham Buddhist monastery and from which the name of the style has been derived; this Cham style characterizes in the wormlike motif, heavy ornaments, thick lips, moustaches, eyebrows, etc. The figures display caricatured countenances yet convey a powerful sense of dignified solemnity and forceful energy. The wormlike carving of the Dong-Duong Style has also been suggested by art historians as unique but in fact it bears a striking resemblance to earlier Indian Buddhist scrollworks from Orissa sites like Ratnagiri and Udayagiri (c. 750-800 CE) {Donaldson 2001: fg. 427, 432, 459}. This suggests a possibility that the Chams might have had direct political and cultural contacts with eastern India besides the Sailendras in Java; all these regions had already been at the peak of their artistic and architectural activities. Returning to Indrapura Monastery, there are numerous Buddha's Life Scenes carved on the image pedestals from the site; probably this was only time in Cham arts that narrative scenes had been decorated in religious sanctuaries. The walls of Cham temples are mostly relieved with floral and isolated figures which generally remain subordinate to the architecture while those in India, Java, and Kampuchea are lavishly illustrated with narrative scenes in sculptures and murals that complement yet compete with the architecture. The main Buddha statue in Indrapura shows traces of Chinese infiltration while the menacing *dvarapala*s holding clubs and the *kala* (monster) masks share similar dispositions as the Javanese counterparts, which could have certainly inspired the Indrapura examples. Perhaps, it was the brutish appearance of the Dong-duong Style that Benjamin Rowland was referring to when he made this highly unjustifiable and erroneous comment {Rowland 1977: 484}:

> This culture, located in the region of modern Annam, flourished for nearly 1,000 years until the ninth century A. D. The architecture and sculpture are a provincial reflection of Cambodian forms with some borrowings from Chinese sources. The brick tower sanctuaries of Mi-son are a prolongation of the isolated *sikharas* of pre-Khmer times. The sculpture, although cast in Indian and Cambodian mould, is characterized by a floridity and barbaric vigour of decoration, such as often distinguishes the best in folk art.

Multi-limbed deities of mostly Hindu type occurred from

the ninth century CE on due to the growing Tantric influences and Pala internationalism in Champa. As already noted the majority of Cham Buddhist images, most of which depict Avalokitesvara, appeared between the eighth-tenth centuries CE. These have been either cast in bronze or sculpted in stone having two to eight arms and share stylistic and iconographic similarities with those in Dvaravati (Thailand), Kampuchea, Java, and India; Chinese elements may also be perceived in the slim and stylized delineation of the forms {Chutiwongs 2002: 295-313}. Passing into the Tra-Kieu Style, there seems to be a completely new artistic direction as the forceful vitality of the previous Dong-duong Style has been replaced with the sensuous grace, sophistication, and warmth comparable to the Indian Gupta-Sarnath Style; this phase was also the pinnacle of Cham arts and architecture. The Binh-Dinh Style shows a slight decline in quality compared to the Tra-Kieu Style in its exaggerated baroque decorations as also observed in contemporary East Javanese sculptures. Few works in the subsequent centuries could be compared to the earlier glorious periods of Cham arts when Champa was still a strong country; this obviously mirrored the rapid decline of the country under numerous devastating wars with the Khmers and the relentless southward advances from the Vietnamese.

The most conspicuous symbol of Champa and Cham architecture is the *kalan* or religious temple; at the first sight, one could be mistaken it for a Khmer temple or a Javanese *candi* due to their formal similarities and common sources in India. The essential difference between the Cham *kalan*, Khmer *prasat*, and Javanese *candi* is that all Cham examples are of the isolated type which has never fully reached gigantic scales as the integrated religious complex or pyramidal mountain temple as in Java and Kampuchea. Even in the rare example like Indrapura, its plan is essentially organic consisting of individual temples that have been randomly erected over the centuries within a walled compound without any logical layout. Thus in Cham architecture, there has never been an unrelenting quest for the axial order on the vast scales as in Kampuchea and Java; the Chams were apparently content with perfecting their modest-sized individualistic and isolated temples and this has been their best accomplishment. In this manner, the Cham *kalan* remains faithful to its Indian predecessors much like the Pallava *ratha* architecture at Mamallapuram in South India and North Indian temples like Bhirtagaon and Deogarh; it also shares many commonalities with early Javanese *candi*s on the Dieng Plateau and the Sambor Prei Kuk temples in Kampuchea {Rowland 1977: 299-306} {Chihara 1997: 77-80, 106-108}. Of the once 250 sites in Champa, only twenty are extant today though in badly damaged conditions; fortunately numerous sculptural and architectural pieces have been salvaged and scattered in the museums of Vietnam, France, and all over the world. Cham architecture, as its arts, is predominantly Hindu and especially Sivaite while Indrapura is the best example of Buddhist architecture and monastery in the entire Cham history. Hindu *kalan*s were often royal temples erected for the benefits of the king and his country whilst Buddhist *kalan*s were probably open to the royalty and commoners alike. Sectarian differentiation in Cham architecture, specifically between a Hindu and Buddhist *kalan*, is typically indicated by the presence of a Siva *linga* or a Buddha statue; the plan of a Cham *kalan* [4.11] invariably consists of a main cella preceded by a projecting portico. Architecturally, a typical elevation of a Cham *kalan* [4.12] has a main squarish body elevated on a low podium and crowned with a superstructure of three diminishing tiers like a multi-terraced roof; the peak is typically capped with a *ratna*-like finial; there are no windows or doors in the upper tiers but false openings are present in the form of blind recesses. The main body is typically divided into vertical bays by pilasters; above the entry opening is a double *caitya*-arched pediment with a tympanum which is the hallmark of Cham architecture traceable to the Indian *caitya*-arch [5.2, 5.8]. Surface ornamentations generally limit to image pedestals and pilasters consisting mainly of motifs like the popular floral scrolls originated in India and isolated figures, which are complementary yet subordinate to the architecture. Narrative scenes had been introduced into the Buddhist Indrapura Monastery on its image pedestals while its walls have been kept free of the crowding reliefs so often present in Indian, Javanese, and Khmer architecture; murals have not been documented in any Cham *kalan*s. All Cham *kalan*s are constructed of brick with sandstone reserved for structural and decorative members like the lintels, columns, pedestals, tympana, and images; the surfaces are typically coated with a special kind of clay plaster whereon ornamentations would be directly carved. The corbelled vault is the typical construction method; the roofs of important structures, especially principal temples and royal pavilions, are brick and coated with a thick plaster layer while secondary buildings could be of timber framing. Po-Hai is the only Cham building constructed entirely of brick {Groslier 1962: 66, 136-137} {Cao 1988: 194} {Chihara 1997: 183, 186, 188}. The earliest Cham architecture and urban planning can be found in Bhadravarman's capital at Indrapura (Tra-Kieu) as recorded in the king's own inscription (c. 350-400 CE) and the Chinese annals (c. 500-550 CE); the excavated site reveals a rectangular brick boundary wall of 1640' north-south x 5577' east-west containing some brick *kalan*s inside {Groslier 1962: 66}{Chihara 1997: 82}. Bhadravarman had also erected the first Siva *kalan* at Mi-Son which was expanded by succeeding Cham kings like Sambhuvarman (r. 572-629 CE) and Prakasadharma (r. 653-686 CE). The site ultimately became the holy land of the Chams like Angkor to the Khmers and the Kedu Plain to the Javanese; it has been thoroughly documented by French archaeologists like Henri Parmentier and Philippe Stern, all specialists in Cham and Khmer arts and architecture, in the early twentieth century CE. The Mi-Son complex has several groups of *kalan*s, each with its own gated boundary wall containing a principal *kalan* that houses a *linga*; this *kalan* is randomly surrounded by ancillary buildings including minor shrines, pavilions, shelters, inscription houses, storehouses, etc. {Chihara 1997: 184-186}. Inventory of extant Cham *kalan*s, like its arts, can also be chronologically classified into several architectural styles {Stern 1942: 4}{Groslier 1962: 80-84, 136-145, 195-201}{Chihara 1997: 187-191, 222-225}:

- Mi-Son E1 (c. 650-750 CE): Mi-Son E1
- Transitional Mi-Son E1 to Hoa-Lai (c. 750-800 CE): Po-Hai, Prasat Damrai Krap (Angkor, Kampuchea), Mi-Son F1
- Hoa-Lai (c. 800-850 CE): Hoa-Lai, Po-Dam, Mi-Son A'1-A'2, F3, C7
- Dong-duong (c. 875-900 CE): Indrapura Monastery **[4.11-4.12]**, Mi-Son B2-4, A10-A13, A'4, E2-E3, E5
- Mi-Son A1 (c. 900-1000 CE): Khuong My, Mi-Son A1, A8-A9, B3-B8, B11, C1-C5, D1-D2, D4, D6
- Transitional Mi-Son A1 to Binh-Dinh (c. 1000-1100 CE): Chien-Dang, Mi-Son E4, Binh-Lam, Silver Towers, Po-Nagar
- Binh-Dinh (c. 1100-1275 CE): Hung-Thanh, Ivory Towers, Copper Tower, Golden Tower, Thua-Thien
- Po Klaung Garai (c. 1275-1700 CE): Po Klaung Garai, Po-Rome

Mi-Son E1 is the oldest *kalan* at Mi-Son but its superstructure is no longer extant while Po-Hai is the oldest surviving *kalan* in Champa built entirely of brick; Prasat Damrai Krap is the only Khmer building in Angkor (Kampuchea) reputedly to have been constructed by Cham architects in the transition to the Hoa-Lai Style. The golden age of Cham architecture was between the ninth-tenth centuries CE with the tenth century CE as its apogee. The Dong-duong Style stands in contrast to the Mi-Son A1 Style in its heroic vitality from its large and assertive double *caitya*-arches, the elegant and precise scrollworks suggesting Javanese Sailendra influence, and the well-proportioned body and crown of its *kalan*.

The Binh-Dinh Style, as exemplified in the Ivory Towers, shows Khmer influences in its distinct tiered and curvilinear crown that terminates in the Khmer-styled *amalaka* finial. In the subsequent centuries after Mi-Son A1, the Cham *kalan* would be increasingly simplified and utterly devoid of the refined ornamentations compared with the earlier *kalan*s and its forms appeared no more than a pile of plain cubical blocks stacking on top of one another. These are not simply signs of a wornout style but symptoms of the depletion of the innovative resources and ideas in a dying nation.

Among the oldest known record of the construction of Buddhist monasteries in Champa was during King Bhavavarman's reign, the predecessor of King Indrapura II (r. 875-898 CE), who built the Pramuditalokesvara Vihara for the monk Nagapuspa. King Indrapura II, certainly the greatest of all Cham Buddhist kings, dedicated the huge Indrapura Monastery **[4.11-4.12]** in c. 875 CE; he also constructed Damaresvara Monastery during his reign which he reportedly made donations to it in 889 CE. The succeeding King Jaya Simhavarman I (r. 898-918? CE) probably built the Ratnalokesvara in Dai-huu while a royal family member, possibly also under his reign, reportedly constructed two *vihara*s Devalingesvara and Vrddhalokesvara. An inscription at Kon-klor mentioned the founding of a temple or *vihara* named Mahindralokesvara in 914 CE by the Cham prince Mahindravarman while another monastery named Indralokesvara was dedicated in 1088 CE at Tranul by King Jaya Indravarman II. The occupation of Champa by the Buddhist Khmer King Jayavarman VII (r. 1181-1218 CE) might have resulted in an upsurge in the construction of more Mahayana monasteries in the country; however no known Buddhist structures of this period have been identified with certainty. On the other hand Suryavarmadeva, who was administering Champa under the Khmer tutelage and a Sivaite, reportedly restored a building called Herukaharmya, evidently a Vajrayana edifice. The names of the aforesaid temples evidently suggest their dedications to the cult of divinized kings in the guise of Buddhist images, mostly Lokesvara; many of these so-called 'monasteries' were probably small *kuti*s (freestanding cells) built for monks around the main temples where the images would actually be housed {Chutiwongs 2002: 291-292}. Returning to Indrapura, it was certainly a preeminent Buddhist and Mahayana monastery in Champa that best represents the Dong-duong Style; unfortunately it has been completely destroyed during the Vietnam War and over centuries of wars and neglect. An inscription dated in c. 875 CE by King Indrapura II mentions the construction of a monastery dedicated to Lakshmindralokesvara, or an image of deified Indrapura II in the form of Lokesvara; it also states that its construction was 'for the usage of the *Sangha* and for the achievement of the propagation of the *Dharma*' {Groslier 1962: 138-141} {Cao 1988: 202-206, fg. 32-54}{Chihara 1997: 186, 189-190}{Chutiwongs 2002: 291}. The main monastery orientates on the east-west axis and is enclosed inside a 509' x 1083' rectangular boundary wall with a main gateway (*gopura*) in the east; one must pass through another three gateways, each of which is guarded by intimidating stone *dvarapala*s, before reaching the main sacred sanctuary in the westernmost end. Inside and outside

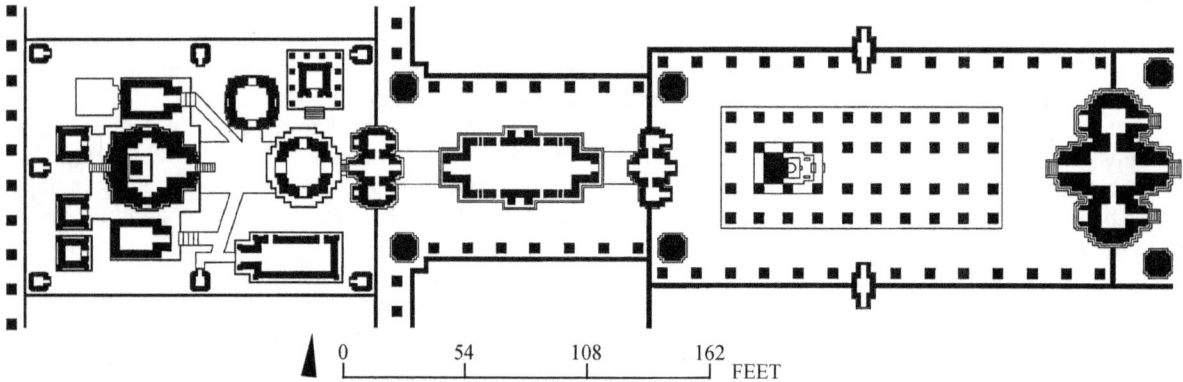

4.11. Plan of sacred precinct. c. 875 CE. Indrapura- Champa. Dong-duong- Vietnam

4.12. Grand east entrance elevation (restored). c. 875 CE. Indrapura- Champa. Dong-duong- Vietnam

the monastery there are large ponds to supply water to the inmates; small fountains in the three enclosed courts probably provided holy water for ceremonial purposes. These three courts shown on the plan measures a total of 137' x 518', each with its own enclosing wall and a gateway; the eastern court dimension is 99' x 203', the central court 77' x 120', and the western court 109' x 154'. In the center of the eastern court is an elevated hall which was once probably sheltered by a timber roof and contained a Buddha image; it was likely a worship or image hall in the monastery. This court, like the others, is flanked by large and tall brick *stupa*s as well as numerous smaller *stupa*s not over 20' high. The grand east entrance pavilion of this court [4.12] is a typical Dong-duong-Styled *kalan* of about 80' high that is flanked on both sides by two 60' high ringed *stupa*s with traces of Gandhara [6.14] and Chinese features [6.24-6.25]. In the middle court is a rectangular building probably monks' dwelling quarter (*vihara*) or an assembly hall; it is also flanked by large and small brick *stupa*s and probably once had timber framing to support a thatch or tile roof. The sacred precinct in the western court encloses the main *kalan*, which once housed an Avalokitesvara image, which is surrounded by eighteen ancillary buildings. The organic plan of this court, which contrasts with the strict order of the rest of the monastery, is typical of Cham religious architecture having, besides the main *kalan* in the back center, minor chapels, royal pavilions, inscription houses, storehouses, and probably seven small meditational cells or ancillary chapels near the boundary wall. In addition to the main images of Buddha and Avalokitesvara, other stone Buddhist sculptures found in the monastery include Tara, *bodhisattva*s, and monks. The rare narrative scenes and hallmark of the Buddhist sculptures in Indrapura are carved on the image pedestals illustrating Buddha's Life Scenes including the Great Departure, First Preaching, Taming the Nalagiri Elephant, *Parinirvana* and Buddha's Cremation, etc. Hindu images like Siva have also been recovered inside this Buddhist monastery and this should not be surprising since Indrapura was a rare and ephemeral flowering of Buddhism in a traditionally and overwhelmingly Hindu country. Though King Indrapura II had been converted to Buddhism for the moment, he probably also worshipped Hindu deities as the protecting gods of his people and kingdom; this peculiar Hindu-Buddhist syncretic phenomenon has also been observed in the central *stupa*-temple of Somapura in Bangladesh and the Bayon of Angkor Thom in Kampuchea. However this does not preclude the possibility of the deliberate placement of these Hindu images inside the monastery after Indrapura II's reign when it might have been converted into a Hindu temple as in the case for the Bayon of Angkor Thom in Kampuchea.

There is no evidence to suggest that this monastery has ever been constructed over any Hindu establishment by Indrapura II; it was a planned Buddhist monastery constructed within his reign. The sources for this original and rare Buddhist monastery in Champa have been a puzzle for scholars but the inspirations likely came from within Champa and abroad. Architecturally, the *kalan*s are characteristically Cham, save for the imposing pagoda-like *stupa*s that seemingly share features of the Gandhara *stupa*s [6.14] and Chinese pagoda [6.24-6.25]; moreover, the entrance gateways flanked by twin edifices already had antecedents in India and Gandhara. Cham architecture, as already noted, also shows similarities with Java and Kampuchea, all are descendants of their Indian precursors. The rectangular and triple-entried plan of the entrance pavilion with its internally linked passages could have been inspired by the Javanese *candi*s like Candi Plaosan and Candi Sari, which might be in turn planned after the Sri Lankan triple-adjoined *pasada*s. The triple-entried *gopura*s of Indrapura seem to be more akin to the Sri Lankan model than the Javanese one since the latter only has one entry. The Indrapura plan evidently combines Cham, as in the Hindu temple complexes of Mi-Son, and foreign sources in the design of its walled-in enclosure punctuated by gateways and guarded by *dvarapala*s and animals; such plans are also known in Indian Buddhist monasteries like the northern monasteries of Sarnath [8.5] and Chinese architecture. The construction of a new monastery after the founding of the Cham capital at Indrapura seems to have also echoed the Pala tradition in India and the Indian concept of a *viharapura* already discussed earlier. On the other hand the organic plan of the western enclosure reflects a traditional Cham plan as at Mi-Son, which also commonly occurs in the Indian *ratha* plan at Mamallapuram {Huntington 1985: fg. 14.21} and to a certain degree Vijayarama [4.9] in Sri Lanka. The remaining plan of the central and eastern courts with their numerous *stupa*s of various sizes, also have precursors in earlier designs like Candi Sewu [7.12] in Java as well as Karakhoja Stupa P and Yarkhoto (Chinese Jiaohe) in Turkistan {Yamamoto 1990: 206-207}{TNM 1991: 34}.

8. Alchi (c. 1175-1300 CE) - Ladakh

In so many ways the western Himalaya region or Trans-Himalaya, which encompasses the Indian Himalaya, western Tibet, Ladakh, Zanskar, Lahaul, Spiti, and upper Kinnaur, can be considered as an extension of the Tibetan cultural sphere since these territories share a common Tibetanized history and culture reaching back as early as the seventh century CE; for the history and discussions on central Tibet see Chapter 6. Before the emergence of the Tibetan empire, western Tibet or Ngari comprised the territory of Zhangzhung, which could extend as far as Ladakh; it was later subjugated by the powerful central Tibetan King Song-tsen-gampo (r. 629-649 CE). Tibetan control and migration to the region likely began since that time as many rock inscriptions (c. 760-840 CE) have been found as far as Alchi in Ladakh containing Tibetan military and official titles {Snellgrove and Skorupski 1977-1980 Volume II: 155-163}. Before the advent of Tibetanization, the region has long been inhabited by many indigenous tribes and foremost among these are the Dard (Ladakh), Mon (Zanskar and Lahaul), Kinnar (Kinnaur), and Kirata (Lahaul, Spiti, Kinnaur). They have already been documented by Indian historians in the Mahabharata, Puranas, and Buddhist literature; their communities were loosely organized under tribal chiefs called *gyalpo* {Handa 2001: 78-89, 100-101}. The earliest official Indian contacts with the Himalaya peoples probably happened during Asoka's reign as he reputedly sent a Buddhist missionary to the Himavanta or probably the Indian Himalaya region; Kashmir and the Kullu region in Himachal Pradesh were then under his suzerain {Handa 2001: 21}. Cultural and political incursions from Kashmir and the Indian plain probably did not reach Ladakh, Zanskar, and other Trans-Himalaya territories until the Early Kushan Dynasty (c. 50-241 CE). Inscriptions in Brahmi and Kharosthi have been discovered in Khalatse (Ladakh) attributed to the Kushan King Kanishka. A *stupa* at the Sani Gompa (Zanskar) is traditionally attributed to Kanishka but likely of a later construction; the plan of its *gompa* (monastery) indeed has a certain Kushan feature like the two round bastions on the side walls {Francke 1977: 72}{Handa 2001: 33, 99-100}{Khosla 1979: 95}. The Kushans' vast territories also included Kashmir and the periphery regions of Kullu and Kangra (Himachal Pradesh); their power and Buddhism would certainly be known to the Trans-Himalaya peoples from then on {Handa 2001: 31-32}. The Sutlej River basin encompassing Spiti, Kinnaur, Kullu, and probably also Lahaul was ruled by the Sen Dynasty between the sixth-seventh centuries CE; the control of Spiti was subsequently transferred to the Ladakhis after the fall of this dynasty in the late seventh century CE {Handa 2001: 101-107}. Ladakh and Zanskar meanwhile had been ruled by petty *gyalpo*s until they were subdued by the Tibetan power in the mid seventh century CE, as did the other Trans-Himalaya territories. Upon the arrival of the Tibetans it can be surmised that increasing traffics, most notably from Kashmir and India, flooded the area alongwith trade, religion, arts, and architecture. Hsuantsang casually mentioned Ladakh as Mi-lo-pho, or the Red Land, when he sojourned in Kashmir in the 630s CE; another Chinese monk-pilgrim Ou-khong while stopping in Kashmir in 757 CE mentioned a route going eastward to Thou-fan (Tibet), which likely crossed over the Zoji-la and passed through Ladakh {Francke 1977: 75, 77}. The fact that the Trans-Himalaya region was teeming with activities from the seventh century CE on has been confirmed by the numerous rock reliefs of mostly Buddhist scattered throughout Ladakh and Zanskar dated between the eighth-tenth centuries CE {Francke 1977: 63-65} {Snellgrove and Skorupski 1977-1980 Volume I: 43, il. 3-5, 109 / Volume II: il. 2, 7-8, 19}. Thus between the Kushan rule in the first century CE to the founding of the Tibetan kingdoms in western Tibet and the Indian Himalaya in the tenth century CE, Buddhism had certainly been known and practiced among the population but it did not yet become an established and predominant religion. The tenth century CE was the true beginning of the western Himalaya countries and the Tibetan arts and architecture in the region and also a crucial period in the renaissance of Buddhism in central Tibet. As mentioned in Chapter 6, the Yarlung Dynasty in central Tibet ended with the assassination of King Lang-darma in 842 CE; one of Lang-darma's two great grandsons, Nyima-gon (r. 900-930 CE), fled to western Tibet and conquered the whole region including the Indian Himalaya. After his death the territory was divided among his three sons, the eldest Pelgyi-gon got Ladakh (from Zoji-la in Ladakh to Rutog in western Tibet), Tashi-gon took Guge and Purang (from Mount Kailash to the Ladakhi border in Tibet), and Detsu-gon got Zanskar, Spiti, Lahaul, and upper Kinnaur (now in Ladakh and Himachal Pradesh); though cultural and ethnically Tibetan, these regions remained politically autonomous from each other. Of the three states, Guge would play a crucial role in inaugurating the second Buddhist transmission and resurgence of Buddhism in Tibet; due largely to Guge's patronage, Buddhism was finally and firmly established in the region as the dominant religion from then on until this day. The most well-known figure responsible for this Buddhist renaissance was King Yeshe-O (r. 967-1040 CE), who was Detsu-gon's son and Tashi-gon's nephew; Tashi-gon died without an heir and his nephew Khor-re (Yeshe-O) from Zanskar was summoned to succeed his throne and the act resulted in the integration of Zanskar, Spiti, and Guge into a single political entity. Yeshe-O, who ruled from Guge with its capital at Tholing, soon abdicated the throne around c.

975 CE and became a *lama* while passing his throne to several more illustrious rulers; some of his successors also became great *lama*s. Meanwhile, Yeshe-O continued to function as the de-facto ruler until his death apparently while he was still a *lama*; he was the certainly the first celebrated *lama*-king in the history of Tibet. Some of the major characteristics and accomplishments of early Guge kings are {Handa 2001: 126-129, 207-224, 266-302}:

- *Lama*-kings. Many early Guge kings were *lama*s who first pioneered a uniquely Tibetan practice of fusing Buddhism and politics which effectively transformed their government into a theocratic institution; it has been well-known that subsequent Sakyapa and Gelugpa sects were able to completely dominate Tibet.
- The second transmission and renaissance of Buddhism in Tibet and the Trans-Himalaya region. This had been a successful enterprise largely due to the assistance of Yeshe-O's most accomplished associate, the great monk-scholar Rinchen-sangpo (958-1055 CE). The first task was to send Rinchen-sangpo and other students to study Buddhism in India who eventually brought back scriptures and thirty Kashmiri craftsmen to Guge to assist in the constructions and decorations of new monasteries; all these activities were patronized by Yeshe-O and his successors with Tholing as the center during this glorious period. Rinchen-sangpo's activities included two missions to Kashmir (976-983 CE and 999-1005 CE), one mission to India (983-989 CE), the founding of new monasteries (989-999 CE), and as the abbot and chief translator of Tholing (1005-1055 CE). Tholing was then modeled after the great Indian Pala *mahavihara*s like Nalanda and Vikramasila which exclusively devoted to Buddhist, and possibly secular, scholarships; this great monastery still stands in the isolated stretch of land in western Tibet. The foundations of another three great monasteries that could surely be ascribed to Rinchen-sangpo are Nyar-ma (Ladakh), Sumda (Zanskar), and Tabo (Spiti); Nyar-ma is now in ruins but Sumda and Tabo still survive with its famed original sculptures and murals. In all, Rinchen-sangpo reportedly founded 108 monasteries and temples all over the western Himalaya during his tenure; the number does not take into account numerous monasteries not directly founded by Yeshe-O and Rinchen-sangpo but associated with the second transmission like Lamayuru and Alchi **[4.13-4.15]** (Ladakh), Karsha and Phugtal (Zanskar), and Lha-lun (Spiti), etc.
- The establishment of new Buddhist sects in Tibet. This happened after the arrival of the eminent Indian monk Dipankara Srijnana or Atisa (982-1054 CE) to Guge between 1042-1045 CE; after the sojourn he proceeded to central Tibet to resume his missionary and where he later died. The inevitable and historic meeting between Atisa and Rinchen-sangpo has been described by subsequent Tibetan Buddhist historians a euphoric tone. Before his arrival, Tibetans were still following the old Nyingmapa sect reputedly founded by Padmasambhava in the eighth century CE; after the complete 'purification' of the Buddhist religion by Atisa, new Buddhist sects would emerge including Kadampa, Kagyupa, Karmapa, Drugpa, Drigungpa, Sakyapa, and later Gelugpa, all had their origins in this second transmission. Drigungpa, Drugpa, and Gelugpa became popular in Ladakh while Sakyapa and Gelugpa, the sect of the Dalai Lama, became the religious and political rulers of Tibet; Drugpa is now predominant in Bhutan. Atisa's arrival gave yet another impetus for the Tibetans to construct more monasteries in central Tibet. A special remark on Tibetan Buddhism is that in the case of Ladakh its kings remained secular throughout its history and unlike Tibet where the *lama*s usurped political power and established a theocratic state; the Sakyapa and Gelugpa were able to rule Tibet directly from their monasteries. The perpetual warfare between the rival monasteries, which have been documented in Tibet, did not occur in the western Himalaya region. The form of Buddhism that the western Himalaya countries initially adopted, as in Tibet, was the Vajrayana of the *yoga-tantra* class; the Guge kings reportedly found some *anuttarayoga-tantra* Tantric practices, like sexual yoga to be too repulsive and they enacted laws to prohibit them {Klumburg-Salter 1982: 76-77}. However the *anuttarayoga-tantra* class, though hardly ever been officially sanctioned, was believed by later Vajrayanists to be the embodiment of the highest Buddhist wisdom; its arts and architecture, which often appeared in Gelugpa monasteries onward, are best exemplified in Tibetan monuments like Kumbum **[6.40-6.41]**.

After c. 1100 CE, Guge began to decline while Ladakh would increasingly exert its dominance over the region; the Mongols imposed its control over Tibet and the western Himalaya between the thirteenth-fourteenth centuries CE. Kashmir and Baltistan would be converted to Islam in the fourteenth century CE and subsequently launched repeated invasions to Ladakh but the Ladakhis managed to maintain their independence and the Buddhist faith. The most illustrious of the Ladakhi dynasties was the

Namgyal Dynasty (1500-1842 CE); meanwhile Zanskar, Spiti, and Guge were reduced to the status of suzerainty of Ladakh but this was ended when the whole region was conquered and incorporated into Ladakh by Sengge Namgyal (r. 1569-1594 CE). The annexation eventually led to the war between Tibet and Ladakh during which the combined Mongol-Tibetan army invaded Ladakh between 1646-1684 CE; the Ladakhis had to appeal for help from the Indian Mughals. The Tibetans were eventually repelled by the Mughal army but they succeeded in taking control of Guge and Rutog from the Ladakhis, who now lost their grips on Kullu, Lahaul, and Kinnaur to the regional pro-Indian factions; Zanskar and Spiti retained their semi-independent status by recognizing the Ladakhis' supremacy. On the other hand the Ladakhis, in repaying the Mughals' military rescue, also had to pay tributes and recognize the Mughals' overlordship over Ladakh as well as building a mosque in Leh. Between 1834-1842 CE the Sikh general Zorawar Singh working under Raja Gulab Singh of Jammu-and-Kashmir invaded the whole region as far as western Tibet; the final outcome of these wars was that the whole western Trans-Himalaya region, with the exception of western Tibet, would be permanently ceded to India {Handa 2001: 130-206}. Ladakh and Zanskar were eventually annexed into the Indian state of Jammu-and-Kashmir while Lahaul, Spiti, and upper Kinnaur were incorporated into Himachal Pradesh; however, the region remains ethnically, religiously, and culturally Tibetan until this day as they were in the past. Historically despite Ladakh's insistence on its autonomy from Tibet, it implicitly continued to recognize Tibet's religious hegemony over its people. So often the Ladakhis would send monks to study in central Tibet where they made numerous generous donations and restorations of its monasteries {Francke 1977: 94, 105, 112, 115}; after all, the Ladakhis' ancestors originally came from central Tibet where the headquarters and parent monasteries of the major Buddhist sects in Ladakh are located.

The arts of the western Himalaya region, which consist of chiefly sculptures and murals, can be divided into three phases based on the stylistic classification of extant archaeological specimens:
- Phase I (pre-Tibetan, second-tenth centuries CE): There are numerous rock reliefs scattered throughout Ladakh and Zanskar; most are Buddhist dated between the eighth-tenth centuries CE {Francke 1977: 63-65}{Snellgrove and Skorupski 1977-1980 Volume I: 43, il. 3-5, 109 / Volume II: il. 2, 7-8, 19}. The earliest Buddhist arts seem to be concentrated in Lahaul where sculptural specimens have been found around Keylang dated between the second-tenth centuries CE {Klumburg-Salter 1982: pl. 85}{Handa 2001: 43-46}.
- Phase II (Indo-Tibetan, eleventh-fourteenth centuries CE): The arts in this phase were associated with the Buddhist renaissance in Guge. Initially the artistic sources came mainly from Kashmir up to c. 1200 CE; afterward new elements, as in the Alchi murals, would have been emanated from Pala India, Nepal, and central Tibet and stylistically these also have many commonalities with some of the later arts at Chinese sites like Mogao and Kharakhoto {Snellgrove and Skorupski 1977-1980 Volume I: 40} {Klimbur-Salter 1982: 88-89, 155-167}{Pal 1988: 20-23, 44-59}.
- Phase III (Tibetan, fifteenth century CE on): This phase came about after the rise of the Gelugpa in Tibet and most examples can be found in monasteries like Spituk, Phiyang, Tikse, Hemis, etc. {Genoud 1978: 64-65, 68-70, 76-86}.

The most conspicuous architectural symbol in the western Himalaya, Tibet, and other Tibetanized countries (Bhutan, Mongolia, and Nepal Himalaya or Mustang) is the *gompa* or monastery. Due to the environmental constraints in the region, in particular the treeless and dry high-altitude landscape, the adobe, loam, and wattle-and-daub construction in combination with the post-and-plank structure are deemed to be the most appropriate method in regional architecture [4.14-4.15]. Another method is the rubble construction, which is also as popular as the sun-dried mud bricks; above all clay and mud are the key materials in both sculptures and architecture while timber is a rare commodity in the region and reserved for high-end constructions like detailed carvings, load-bearing structural members, or in the upper stories to lighten the weight of the superstructure {Khosla 1979: 117-119} {Goepper 1996: 23, 275}. There are minor differences between the western Himalaya and Tibetan architecture; for example the flat-roofed architecture is exclusively found in the former region whereas the tile or gilt pitched roof, which is also known in central Tibet though not as common as the common flat roof, is virtually non-existent here. The development of the Tibetanized monasteries in the western Himalaya can be divided into three phases or types corresponding to the three artistic phases already listed earlier:
- Phase I (pre-Tibetan, second-tenth centuries CE): When Hsuan-tsang visited Kashmir in the 630s CE he already counted about 100 monasteries with 5,000 monks there and about twenty monasteries with 1,000 monks in Kullu. The earliest monasteries in the region are concentrated in Lahaul (Keylang,

Gandhola/Guru Ghantal) and Zanskar (Sani) dated to the Kushans' time; however none of their original forms survives so it is futile to speculate on its earlier designs {Klumburg-Salter 1982: pl. 85}{Handa 2001: 21-22, 43-46}.

- Phase II (Indo-Tibetan, eleventh-fourteenth centuries CE): The new architectural renaissance in the western Himalaya was led by Guge under the sponsorship of Yeshe-O and managed by Rinchen-sangpo; these new monasteries, like the famed Alchi [4.13-4.15], were generally dedicated to the deities of the *yoga-tantra* class. They are typically constructed on the flat grounds with isolated chapels, assembly halls, Tantric initiation halls, *sutra* (Tanjur) halls or libraries, and *chorten*s all enclosed inside a boundary wall whereas the outside belongs to monks' dwellings. Architecturally, these 'ground' monasteries carried on the tradition already developed in earlier Tibetan monasteries like Samye and Kachu; however decorative treatments such as wood carvings, sculptures, and murals were the amalgamation of Indian, mainly Kashimri, and Tibetan elements. The Tibetan plans of these monasteries apparently do not have much commonality with the typical quadrangular *vihara* plan of Gandhara [4.2] and Indian monasteries [4.4]. Tholing (c. 975 CE) founded by Yeshe-O in Guge was the earliest and most preeminent of all monasteries constructed during this glorious epoch; Yeshe-O's protege Rinchen-sangpo also reputedly founded 108 monasteries and temples throughout the western Himalaya but only three monasteries can surely be credited to him, namely Nyar-ma (c. 1000 CE) in Ladakh, Sumda (c. 1000 CE) in Zanskar, and Tabo (996 CE) in Spiti. Numerous other monasteries have also been founded during Rinchen-sangpo's time, which can definitely be indirectly attributed to him or his time, including Wanla (eleventh century CE), Lamayuru (eleventh century CE), and Mang-gyu (eleventh century CE) in Ladakh, Karsha (c. 1050-1100 CE), Phugtal (c. 1050-1100 CE), Dzongkul (eleventh century CE), and Thongde (eleventh century CE) in Zanskar, and Lha-lun (eleventh century CE) in Spiti. Monasteries would continue to be constructed in line with Rinchen-sangpo's specifications after his death including Hunder (early twelfth century CE) and the famed Alchi monastery (c. 1175-1300 CE) in Ladakh {Snellgrove and Skorupski 1977-1980 Volume I: 19-80 / Volume II: 37-69}{Khosla 1979: 29-73} {Goepper 1996}{Handa 2001: 213-217}{Sharma 2003: 122-123}.
- Phase III (Tibetan, fifteenth century CE on): Another prominent monastery type is the imposing fortress/hilltop monastery which was likely emanated from Tibet; this type seems to be a design response to the threats from foreign invasions and internal fighting between rival monasteries. In the early days of Tibetanization a fort would usually be constructed where a monastery was located as in the cases of Alchi, at Shey the ancient capital of Ladakh, Basgo, and sTing-mo-sgang in Ladakh. Gradually the fort and monastery merged into an integrated unit in response to the political, religious, and military challenges at the time; these resulted in the elaborately planned monasteries perching precariously on the hilltop like imposing fortresses. The most important chapels in these monasteries, specifically the *dukhang*, typically dominate the surrounding buildings while those of lesser importance are located lower down the hill. Other subsidiary units in these monasteries are the *zimchung* (head abbot's room), *gonkhang* (room for guardian deities), *sutra* room, storage, service quarter (kitchen, refectory, scullery, etc.), and monks' cells; the *chorten*s are usually erected at the entrance approach in the base of the hill. The buildings are interconnected via zigzag passages built into the hillside; they are designed to facilitate the integration of the monastery into a single self-sufficient unit so that it can easily repel the enemies and survive longer when attacked or under a protracted sieged. In the past, these hilltop monasteries also owned the lands below where the peasants tilled and portions of the harvest would become payments to the monasteries; this made them wealthy and luring targets for attack and hence their fortress and inaccessible appearance. Thus the fortress/hilltop monastery was not only the lifeblood of the town but also the focus of the religious and cultural activities in the community, which generally occurred in the spacious courtyards of these monasteries just like the present day. Hilltop monasteries had already been prevalent in Gandhara [4.2] while the concept of a *viharapura*, with the monastery as the center of the town, could also be traced back to the Indian *mahavihara*s [4.4, 4.8]. Most likely, the hilltop/fortress monastery had first been developed in Tibet at least in the thirteenth century CE and subsequently transmitted to the western Himalaya in the fifteenth century CE. Some of the well-known monasteries of this type in the latter region include Spituk (fifteenth century CE), Tikse (fifteenth century CE), Likir (fifteenth century CE), Diskit (1420 CE), Ma-tho (sixteenth century CE), Phiyang (mid sixteenth century CE), Stakna

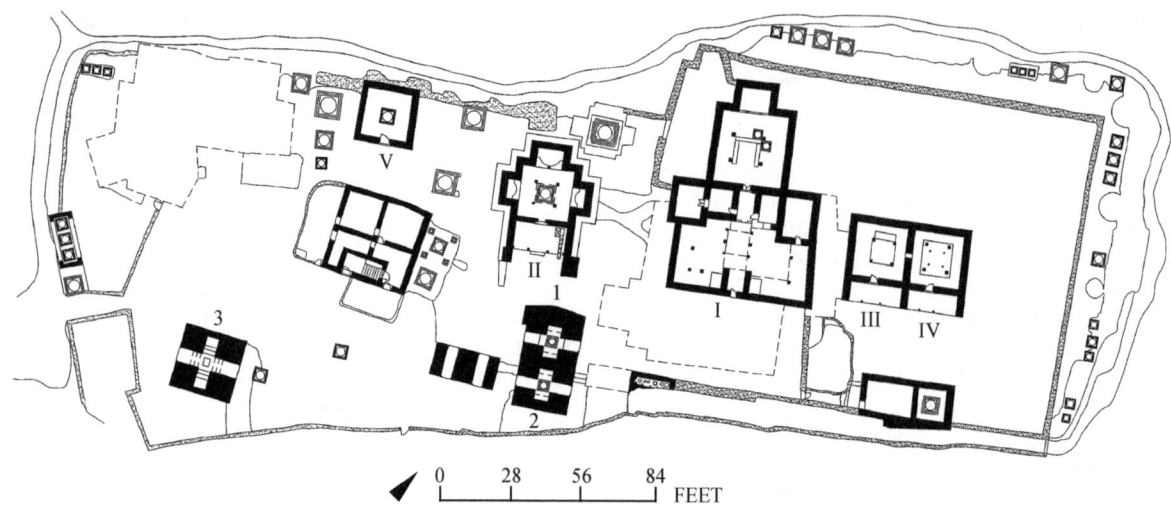

4.13. Site plan. c. 1175-1300 CE. Alchi- Ladakh. Jammu and Kashmir- India

(late sixteenth century CE), Hemis (early seventeenth century CE), Chemdey (early seventeenth century CE), Hanle (early seventeenth century CE), and Ri-dzong (1872 CE) in Ladakh, and Bardan (seventeenth century CE) and Rangdum (eighteenth century CE) in Zanskar {Snellgrove and Skorupski 1977-1980 Volume I: 81-104, 105-133 / Volume II: 55, 57}{Khosla 1979: 75-100}{Sharma 2003: 120-121}.

Alchi **[4.13-4.15]** is a famed and historic monastery in Ladakh constructed during the mature Phase II of the second Buddhist renaissance in the western Himalaya; due to its miraculously preserved conditions dating back to its founding, it is extremely valuable to the study of the evolution of regional Tibetan architecture, Vajrayana iconography, and the extinct Kashmiri or Indo-Kashmiri Style of Buddhist paintings. The founder of this monastery was a Buddhist monk named sKal-ldan-shes-rab from his inscription discovered inside the Dukhang or Assembly Hall (I), which is undoubtedly the oldest building at the site; the discovered fourteen inscriptions in Alchi have also shed much light into its history and founders {Snellgrove and Skorupski 1977-1980 Volume II: 119-154}:

> In that best of continents, southern Jambudvipa [India], at this spot, the hermitage of Alchi in sPu-rgyal's Tibet, land of pure ground and high mountains, I have built a precious temple with devoted veneration! To look on the wood carvings and paintings... Composed by the Buddhist monk sKal-ldan-shes-rab [Inscription 1]

> His [sKal-ldan-shes-rab] birthplace is Sumda...His residence is Alchi...His lineage [clan] is 'Bro...He built a temple as a place of meditation and study [Inscription 2]

> He [sKal-ldan-shes-rab] studied at Nyar-ma in Mar-yul [Ladakh]...He is wealthy...He built a fort and bridge [at Alchi]...In pursuance of the request to his father, he built this great *vihara* here at Alchi [Inscription 3]

The construction of the Sumtsek Temple (II) **[4.14-4.15]** has been ascribed to another Buddhist monk Tshul-khrims'od, possibly the brother of sKal-ldan-shes-rab as mentioned among the inscriptions inside this temple.

> That patron and monk, Tshul-khrims'od...[Inscription 6]

> In the north part of Jambudvipa [India] is the Land of Snows, the country of sPu-rgyal's Tibet with its high mountains and pure ground, filled with religious practitioners who possess the Thought of Enlightenment. The patron who founded this precious tiered *vihara* [Sumtsek] here at Alchi of Ladakh, in Lower Mar-yul of Upper Nga-ri [western Tibet] was the teacher Tshul-khrims'od. He was of the great and aristocratic 'Bro lineage'...As the sun and the moon together ornament the sky, so did the two great 'Bro brothers' [sKal-ldan-shes-rab and Tshul-khrims'od could be brothers] [Inscription 7]

Some repairs have already been carried out to the Sum-

4.14. Sumtsek elevation-section. c. 1200 CE. Alchi- Ladakh. Jammu and Kashmir- India

tek during Tashi Namgyal's reign (r. 1532-1560 CE) (Inscription 10); recently discovered inscriptions Number 13-14, also written by Tshul-khrims'od, are crucial in establishing a more accurate chronology for the individual buildings at the site. Number 14 found on the south wall mural on the third story of the Sumtsek recorded the lineage names of nine Indian and Tibetan monks and specifically mentioned the name of the monk Jig-

4.15. Facade of Sumtsek
c. 1200 CE
Alchi- Ladakh
Jammu and Kashmir- India

ten Gonpo (1143-1217 CE) who was the founder of the Drigungpa sect {Goepper 1996: 18, 211-212, 216-217}. Some scholars believed the names on the inscription had been added later to an earlier mural and thus making the identification and chronology conjectural; however, the date between c. 1175-1200 CE for the construction of the Dukhang and Sumtsek seems credible which is also corroborated by the styles of the murals. The Sumstek was probably erected around Jigten Gonpo's time whereas the Dukhang was a little earlier based on the style of its murals and inscriptions. Anyhow, Drigungpa was presumably the sect with which Alchi was associated when it was first founded; nowadays the monastery is in the custodian of the Gelugpa monks residing in the nearby Likir Monastery. The rectangular site of Alchi measures 160' x 430' which is bounded by a mud wall enclosing encloses the original buildings inside alongwith their sculptures and murals. The original buildings include the Dukhang (I), the Sumtsek (II), the attached twin temples of Lotsawa Lhakhang (III) and Manjusri Lhakhang (IV), Soma Lhakhang (V), and Chortens 1-3 (1-3); the other buildings were of later additions including houses, *chorten*s, shrines, *sutra* halls, etc. From the inscriptions and styles of the murals, the various dates for the most important buildings at the site can be established, namely the Dukhang (c. 1175 CE), Sumtsek (c. 1200 CE), Chortens 1-3 (c. 1200 CE), Lotsawa Lhakhang (c. 1200-1250 CE) and murals (c. 1250-1300 CE), Manjusri Lhakhang (c. 1200-1250 CE), Soma Lhakhang (c. 1250-1300 CE) and its murals (c. 1250 CE) {Snellgrove and Skorupski 1977-1980 Volume I: 23-80 / Volume II: il. 82}{Khosla 1979: 54-68}{Pal 1988: 46-62}{Goepper 1997}.

a. Dukhang

It is certainly the oldest building at the site with a 58' x 79' plan measuring and like the other buildings, with the exception of the three-floored Sumtsek, it has a single story with a flat roof and a parapet painted in a continuous red band as in all other buildings; its wooden entry portal is elaborately carved like the Sumtek. The interior contains a single Vairocana image inside the niche at the back while the surrounding walls and those in the courtyard are completely covered with murals of mostly Buddhist themes and a few secular ones depicting royal banquets. The most important murals are the seven *mandala*s of Vairocana, Manjusri, and Prajnaparamita; these are some of the earliest painted *mandala*s in the western Himalaya and Tibet. The oldest extant *mandala* paintings in the world, which are in the scroll format, came from the Chinese Mogao caves in Dunhuang and Japan dated in the ninth century CE {Klimburg-Salter and Others 1982: 115, pl. 68-69}. Above the door of the Dukhang is a mural of the protecting deity Mahakala as in the other buildings; all deities depicted in the Dukhang murals belong to the *yoga-tantra* class with Vairocana as the principal deity in the center of the *mandala*.

b. Sumtsek [4.14-4.15]

Sumtsek is probably the most important in terms of its Tantric iconographies and symbolisms; it is a three-storied temple with a 47'4" x 34'7" plan about 42'4" high. Its highly ornate portico, which also contains murals but much faded due to exposure, is supported by fluted timber columns and half-columns or pilasters in the Indo-Kashmiri Style that faintly resemble the Greek Ionic order and also the Ajanta columns [5.10, 5.12]; the triangular trussed-like pediments on the entablature, besides serving as decorative elements, also function as braces to strengthen the structure against earthquakes. The interior, which contains a large *chorten* of a later date in the center, also employs the same fluted timber columns as the exterior to support the mud floors. The three niches on the first floor house three huge standing polychrome clay and four-armed *bodhisattva*s wearing five-pointed tiaras with the tallest image of Maitreya in the back, Avalokitesvara on the left, and Manjusri on the right; their heads reach all the way to the second story where openings are cut through the walls in front of their faces so they can look out to the second floor. On the first floor there are murals on Maitreya's *dhoti* depicting Sakyamuni's Life Scenes while those on Avalokitesvara's *dhoti* are quasi-religious and secular scenes probably of Buddhist pilgrimage centers in Kashmir and Manjusri's *dhoti* contains scenes of the Eighty-four Siddhas. The surrounding walls are murals of Akshobya, Amitabha, and Manjusri as well as secular and religious personages including the royalty, celestial beings, musicians, etc. The second floor is also completely filled with murals including ten *mandala*s of Vairocana, Aksobhya, Amitabha, Amoghasiddhi, Ratnasambhava, Vajrasattva, and their various manifestations including female ones; the others depict paradises of Aksobhya, Amitabha, Amoghasiddhi, and Ratnasambhava. Above Maitreya's head are murals of Sakyamuni, above Avalokitesvara's is his multi-limbed manifestation, and above Manjusri's is the multi-limbed Prajnaparamita. The third floor has three *mandala*s of Manjusri, Sakyamuni, and Prajnaparamita; the remaining murals are pictorial eulogies to the lineage of Buddhist monks, both Indian and Tibetan, who were responsible for the introduction and founding of the various Vajrayana sects in Tibet. Above the doors of each floor are murals of ferocious guardian deities with the one on the first floor depicting Mahakala, the second Yamantaka, and the third Acala; these are the *dharmapala* deities like the one above the entry doorway of the Dukhang. The ceiling of the top floor is constructed in the lantern roof common in Central Asia [5.16-5.17] whereas the ceilings of the lower floors are completely covered in murals of decorative patterns and non-religious themes. Thus the architectural and iconographical program at Sumtsek appear to represent a symbolic spiritual progression from the lower to the higher levels of enlightenment and the Mahayana to the Vajarayana from the lowest floor to the upper floors. The highest third floor symbolically consecrates pilgrims and Tantric initiates who have completed their spiritual journeys by ascending up the floors or literally entering different *mandala*s. These symbolic levels of spiritual enlightenment, as embodied in the arts and architecture, and the ritualized consecration of the initiates have also been suggested for Borobodur [6.28-6.29] and Kumbum [6.40-6.41]; these are common Vajrayana themes throughout the Buddhist world dated as early as the eighth century CE and certainly not unique in Alchi. Among the earliest cases of the implementation of a combined sculptural and architectural program to portray the concept of an architectural *mandala* occurred in the Elora caves in India (c. 700-730 CE) wherein each of the three floors of Elora Cave 12 had been conceived as a *mandala* with *bodhisattva* sculptures flanking both sides of a central Buddha {Malandra 1993: 18-19, 75-90}. This *mandala* arrangement would later be repeated in many western Himalaya monasteries like the Tabo *dukhang* (996 CE) and here in the Sumtsek of Alchi; this concept was subsequently transmitted to central Tibet where it became the imprint of Vajrayana rituals in the multi-tiered architectural *mandala* of Kumbum. The inscriptions at Alchi also suggest such esoteric or Tantric schemes for its buildings {Snellgrove and Skorupski 1977-1980 Volume II: 147}{Goepper 1997: 271-272}

> That patron and monk, Tshul-khrims'od…set up these reliquaries of Body, Speech, and Mind. In order to remove bodily impurities and obtain a 'human' Buddha-Body, he set up Manjusri as a body-image. In order to remove vocal impurities and obtain a 'glorious' Buddha-Body, he set up Avalokitesvara as a speech-image. In order to remove mental impurities and obtain an 'absolute' Buddha-Body, he set up Maitreya as a mind-image [Inscription 6]
> From the sky of the non-originated Dharmakaya [Absolute Body] the unobstructed Sambhogakaya [Celestial Body] appears like a cloud and the active Nirmanakaya [Physical Body] like incessant rain [Inscription 13]

Manjusri was associated with Body and 'human' Buddha-Body, Avalokitesvara with Speech and 'glorious' Buddha-Body, and Maitreya with Mind and 'absolute' Buddha-Body; thus the 'human,' 'glorious,' and 'absolute' Buddha-Body can be equated respectively with Nirmanakaya (Physical Body), Sambhogakaya (Celestial Body), and Dharmakaya (Absolute Body).

c. Lotsawa Lhakhang

This building measures 24'6" x 31'6" and shares a common wall with Manjusri Lhakhang as both have obviously been constructed about the same time and have simple porticos. The mural-filled interior is also supported by fluted timber columns like in the Sumtsek with its central bay opens to a loft story above; in the back end is the main polychrome Sakyamuni statue. The walls contain murals of Avalokitesvara and Amitabha *mandala*s, Ringchen-sangpo, Lokesvara, Amitabha, and Mahakala above the door while the remaining spaces are painted with repeated rows of the Thousand Buddhas theme; the iconography of the deities in these murals belong the *yo-ga-tantra* class as in the Dukhang and Sumtsek.

d. Manjusri Lhakhang

This chapel measures 23'11" x 31'6" and also has a simple entry portico like its immediate neighbor Lotsawa Lhakhang; it also has a loft story projecting beyond the roof above the central bay. This bay is elevated on a high plinth and has four polychrome clay images of Manjusri on the four sides, each of which is painted in gold, white, blue, and red according to their proper directions. Unfortunately the murals have been completely ruined from rain seepage and they most likely, as one might guess, have similar stylistic and iconographic contents as those in the Lotsawa Lhakhang.

e. Soma Lhakhang

This so-called 'new' temple of a single-storied flat roof measures 22'2" x 22'6" and in the center is a *chorten* probably added at a later time. The murals on the interior walls are filled with deities of the *yoga-tantra* and *anuttarayoga-tantra* class arranged in rows, a scheme which appears more formal and rigid than the murals in other buildings; the three *mandala*s of Amitayus, Sakyamuni, and Vairocana are painted on the left wall alongwith Sakyamuni's Life Scenes, which have clearly diminished in popularity. Historic personalities like Santaraksita and Padmasambhava are also among the figures in the murals; Mahakala is once again found above the door as a protecting deity.

f. Chortens 1-3

Chorten 3 measures about 23'8" square while the combined dimension of Chortens 1-2 measures 20'11" x 38'6"; the small *chorten*s inside Chortens 1-2 were probably later additions. It has been suggested that these hollow *chorten*s were originally constructed to frame the entries into the Dukhang and Sumtsek; however due to their odd positions relative to the surrounding buildings, this suggestion seems unconvincing. These *chorten*s are constructed of rubble cores and coated with several layers of clay; Chorten 3 is unique in having four miniature *chorten*s in the corners conceptually derived from Gandhara [6.14] and India [4.4 (#12), 7.10-7.11]. The interiors of these *chorten*s also contain murals that have been determined to be contemporary with those in the Sumtsek; their iconographies include *mandala*s, historical figures like Rinchen-sangpo and Indian Buddhist masters, the Five Jina Buddhas, rows of *chorten*s similar to those in the Bamiyan murals, and decorative motifs.

The murals of the Dukhang and Sumtsek are the acme of the Buddhist Kashmiri or Indo-Kashmiri Style while the style of their sculptures has also been derived from Kashmiri bronzes; the Soma Lhakhang murals have been painted in the international Indian Pala Style. The Lotsawa Lhakhang murals, which fuse the Kashmiri and Pala Style, are believed to have been painted later than those in Soma Lhakhang {Snellgrove and Skorupski 1977-1980 Volume I: 40}{Klimburg-Salter 1982: 88-89, 155-167}{Pal 1988: 20-23, 44-59}. The Alchi murals are painted in several modes with slight shading and highlighting to render volume, without shading using lines to define forms, or the combination of both. The first mode was characteristic of the Indian artists at Ajanta whereas the second mode was favored by the Chinese at Mogao; above all the Alchi murals show an eclectic mixture of different styles rather than the predominance or preference over any particular style. Some of the most conspicuous elements in the Alchi murals, such as the lantern roof, *mandala*s, painted *chorten*s, pearl medallions, alongwith the postures and dresses of many figures, are of Central Asian origins; the exaggeratedly pinched waists and mannerisms of the paired female dancers also recall the females of the Begram ivories from Afghanistan and Andhra sculptures of Amaravati and Nagarjunakonda. Possible Chinese infiltration from Mogao may also be surmised such as the murals of the pairs of female dancers, the acrobatic dives of the *apsara*s with feet swinging awkwardly backward and the Thousand Buddhas theme. The use of pastiglia in the Alchi murals would subsequently be employed in the Kumbum murals in Tibet; the Alchi Style might have also influenced later Indian paintings after the disappearance of Buddhism in India. The plans of the Dukhang and Sumtsek with their principal image niches in the back can be traced back to the classic plan of the Indian Mahayana caves like Ajanta [5.12]. A few architectural elements such as the trefoil triangular pediments, the Indo-Kashmiri pseudo-Ionic columns, etc. also had earlier Kashmiri precursors. However, the overall forms of all Alchi buildings conform to the traditional Tibetan architecture and one must also be careful not to attribute all the woodworks to Kashmir since wood carving is also the traditional craft of the peoples in the Himalaya and Tibet. Above all, the concepts of utilizing architecture as a religious instrument and medium in the process of Tantric initiation and consecration and an aid to spiritual enlightenment are the cornerstone of the Vajrayana as exemplified in the Indian Elora caves, the Dukhang of Tabo in Spiti, the Sumtsek here at Alchi, and later Kumbum [6.40-6.41] in Tibet.

Chapter 5. Rock-hewn Cave

Buddhist rock-hewn caves, which are essentially monasteries like their freestanding counterparts, are especially prevalent along the Silk Road linking India with Central and East Asia; in India most caves are concentrated in the Deccan in Maharashtra and a few earlier ones in Bihar. Buddhist caves are virtually non-existent in South India and Southeast Asia with a few exceptions in Sri Lanka but even these are pale in comparison to the sumptuous grandeur of the Indian caves. The humid and rainy conditions in southern Asia provide plenty of timber for the construction of freestanding timber structures; probably because of this reason that man-made caves were not popular in the region and moreover cave habitation in such a tropical environment is certainly not a comfortable experience for most. On the other hand the hot and dry desert landscapes in northern Asia, where timber is a rare and precious commodity, are perfectly suited for the construction of caves and preservation of their murals. Expectedly, the material of choice for the sculptures in Central Asia and China is mud or clay plaster reinforced with vegetal matters as appropriate for the region where hard rocks are generally scarce while the abundance of permanent materials like stone and brick in South and Southeast Asia is evident in their sculptures and architecture; caves hewn straight from hard stone are common in India and a single exception of Seokguram [5.24-5.25] in Korea. Besides the obvious dissimilarity and limitation in the choice of materials due to geographical and environmental constraints, Indian caves also differ from Central and East Asian ones in many aspects. Indian Buddhist caves are both Aniconic and Iconic types, or sometimes referred to as Theravada and Mahayana respectively, while the Aniconic type is non-existent in Central and East Asia. The Aniconic caves in India generally phased out before the first Iconic caves were hewn; the latter type predominated in Central and East Asia due to the late arrival of Buddhism in the region. Indian caves also manifested early Vajrayana tendencies as early as the sixth century CE; Vajrayana caves are found numerously in the western Himalaya like Saspol in Ladakh, Dungkar and Piyang in western Tibet dated in the Guge Period (tenth-sixteenth centuries CE) and a few in China like some late Mogao and Binglingsi caves. Architecturally, the Vajrayana caves do not differ much from their Aniconic and Iconic counterparts except for their iconography which is dedicated to Vajrayana deities {Snellgrove and Skorupski 1977-1980 Volume II: 74-81}.

Indian caves generally adhered to the long tradition of architectural orthodoxy as observed in the recurrence of the colonnaded apsidal plan with a *stupa* in the back or the *caityagriha* [5.4-5.5] and its characteristic *caitya*-arched facade [5.8]. Furthermore, cave residences for monks, or the *lena*, were always built in the quadrangular *vihara* plan with cells surrounding a central hall [5.6] and pillars in later caves [5.12]. Such strict adherence to the Indian models in Central and East Asia has not been the norm due to geographical limitations and localization where experimentations with new forms of artistic and architectural expressions that reflected the local conditions and preferences have probably been deemed more advantageous. In Central Asia, the octagonal plan and lantern roof [5.14-5.19] were the defining characteristics while in China traditional Chinese architecture had also been incorporated into its caves [5.25]; thus the further away from India the lesser the influences of the Indian designs and Indian Buddhism upon the local architecture became. Nevertheless, a few Central and East Asian caves have exhibited certain Indian features, particularly the placement of important devotional objects like *stupa*s and Buddha images in the back of the caves [5.14-5.15, 5.18-5.25]. Regardless of their locations, murals generally cover the interior surfaces of Buddhist caves; the iconographical and narrative themes in the murals and sculptures began with Aniconic/Theravada (second century BCE-third centuries CE), Iconic/Mahayana (fourth-sixth centuries CE), and Vajrayana (seventh century CE on). Theravada and Mahayana caves were generally built, besides utilitarian purposes, for worship; on the other hand Vajrayana caves, like Elora in India, often employed sculptures and paintings alongwith the architecture as an integrated program in the ritualized consecration and spiritual advancement for the Tantric initiates. The following sections trace the evolution of Buddhist cave architecture in India and its subsequent transformations in Central and East Asia.

A. India

The study of rock-hewn caves is crucial not only in the comprehension of the architectural relationships between the monolithic *stupa*s in these caves [5.3] versus structural ones like Sanchi [6.3] but also the development of the Buddhist monastery in particular. Indian Buddhist caves are essentially freestanding monasteries, which have already been discussed in Chapter 4, in principles and configurations which accommodate and serve the religious needs of the *Sangha* and its followers. Both have similar plans, compare [4.4] and [5.12], in which the essential difference between them is that one is a freestanding structure and the other is a cave. The fact that these caves, especially the earlier Aniconic ones, were faithful replications of contemporary freestanding timber architecture is well attested; however due to the choice of stone in their construction, most caves have survived intact while their freestanding timber counterparts have long since perished. The development of rock-hewn architecture has also been deemed to be a perfect compromise between keeping the ancient ascetic tradition on the one hand and yielding to the comfortable environment of a settled lifestyle in a freestanding monastery on the other. The permanence (less prone to earthquake damages, vandalism, destruction from wars), ease of maintenance, security (shelter from heat, rain, wild beasts), and safety (free from risk of fire) of rock-hewn caves are some of the foremost factors that contributed to their popularity. In addition to the *stupa*s (Chapter 6), these caves also contain some of the earliest Indian and Buddhist arts and architecture; nearly all Indian caves are concentrated in two main areas:

- Area I is in Bihar near Gaya and Rajir which only has a few caves [5.1-5.2]; these all dated in the late Maurya Period (c. 257-214 BCE) or particularly in the reigns of Asoka and Dasaratha (r. 214-206 BCE).
- Area II is in the Deccan in Maharashtra and near Mumbai which has over 1,000 caves [5.3-5.13]; these were generally commenced between c. 200 BCE-800 CE.

Most caves in Area I were built by Asoka and Dasaratha for the Ajivika sect but a few, like Lomas Risi [5.1-5.2], could have been constructed for the Buddhists. The caves in Area II generally concentrate along the old trade route running southwestward from ancient Magadha, then the seat of the Maurya Empire; Buddhism also spread in this direction as the great Buddhist center at Sanchi lies directly north-northeast of Area II and to the northeast of Sanchi is Bharhut. The disintegration of the Maurya Empire and the fall of the pro-Buddhist government first inaugurated by Asoka would be succeeded by the Shunga Dynasty (184-72 BCE) and which founder Pushyamitra reportedly persecuted Buddhism. Probably in such adverse conditions in Magadha, Buddhism found a more favorable environment in the Deccan concurrent with the rise of the tolerant Andhra Dynasty (c. 228 BCE-225 CE) in the region; the genealogy of the late Andhra kings can be found among the inscriptions in the Nasik and Karla caves. There was a brief interlude (119-124 CE) when Area II was under the control of *Ksatrapa* Nahapana whose inscriptions can also be found alongside with the aforesaid Andhra inscriptions in the Nasik and Karla caves. The Abhira Dynasty (c. 248-416 CE) held sway over the region for a while and was succeeded by the Vakataka Dynasty (c. 250-505 CE) in which the latter's rise to prominence actually happened in the fifth century CE; some of the most beautiful caves and murals in Ajanta had been executed during this enlightened dynasty. The next dynasty which ruled the area was the Asmaka Dynasty (sixth-seventh centuries CE) and later the Rashtrakuta Dynasty (c. 735-982 CE) when the last of the great Indian Buddhist caves at Elora was excavated. Cave construction activities mostly ended by the ninth century CE with Hinduism superseding Buddhism in the area; from then on eastern India and Bangladesh, which were ruled by the Pala Dynasty (c. 750-1199 CE), became the last prominent Buddhist region in the whole India until the demise of Buddhism in c. 1200 CE.

Seventy-five percent of the 1,000 caves in Area II or about 750 caves are Buddhist while the remaining caves are Hindu and Jain caves or eighteen percent and seven percent respectively. The Buddhist caves in Area II were generally hewn between c. 200 BCE-750 CE while Hindu and Jain caves had a late start around c. 500 CE. Some of the most well-known Hindu caves are Aihole (c. 500-550 CE), Badami (c. 550-579 CE), and Elora caves (c. 600-725 CE); however, the Buddhists hewed the first caves at Elora and they continued to build more caves alongside with the Hindu and Jain caves in the same site. Some Hindu sites like Mamallapuram (c. 625-700 CE) in Tamil Nadu and Kailasha Temple (c. 725-800 CE) in Elora are strictly not caves since these are actually freestanding monolithic temples carved directly out of rock and stand in the open. The Jains also hewed a few caves but these were not as well-known or early as the Buddhist caves; a few notable examples are Indra Sabha (c. 750-800 CE) and Jagannatha (c. 800-850 CE) in Elora. Hindu and Jain caves have also developed their own characters reflecting their respective faiths; nevertheless they show conspicuous architectural borrowings from the Buddhists who had an earlier and influential tradition of rock-hewn cave architecture before the other faiths. In the Buddhist case owing to the initial patronage from Emperor Asoka, Buddhism subsequently became immensely popular among the population in the Deccan as evident in an overwhelming number of Buddhist caves here. The numerous inscriptions in these caves have revealed their donors, sex, social status, and relative positions within the Buddhist *Sangha* and the Indian society. Out of 222 inscriptions, the merchants top the list of donors with thirty-five percent (forty-six donations), royalty twenty-three percent (thirty donations), government officials twelve percent (sixteen donations), Buddhist *bhiksu*s and *bhiksuni*s twelve percent (sixteen donations), farmers and craftsmen ten percent (fourteen donations), and even foreigners like the Greeks or *Yavana* eight percent (ten donations); thirty percent of all these donations had been made by women {Nagaraju 1981: 26-27, 32}.

Buddhist caves were typically hewn straight into the vertical rock faces in secluded and picturesque areas and clustered in groups, each sometimes is over 100 caves like the 120 caves of Kanheri; some of the biggest and most important caves in Area II are {Nagaraju 1981: 97-325}{Fergusson and Burgess 1969: 109, 367-384}:

- Bhaja (late third century BCE-first centuries CE) **[5.4-5.6]**
- Junnar-Tuljalena (late third century BCE-first centuries CE)
- Kanheri (second century BCE-third centuries CE... fifth-seventh centuries CE)
- Kondivte (second century BCE-second centuries CE... fifth-seventh centuries CE) **[5.3]**
- Ajanta (second century BCE-first centuries CE... fifth-seventh centuries CE) **[5.10-5.13]**
- Pitalkhora (second century BCE-second centuries CE... fifth-seventh centuries CE)
- Kondane (second century BCE-first centuries CE)
- Nasik (second century BCE-third centuries CE... fifth-seventh centuries CE)
- Bedsa (first century BCE-first centuries CE)
- Karla (first century BCE-second centuries CE... fifth-seventh centuries CE) **[5.7-5.9]**
- Kuda (second-third centuries CE)
- Elora (fifth-mid eighth centuries CE)

These Deccan caves generally commenced in c. 200 BCE or after the last of Dasaratha's caves in Bihar had been hewn; Nagaraju maintained that some of the earliest rudimentary caves in Bhaja, Jivadan-Virar, Junnar-Tuljalena, and Kanheri dated as early as c. 250 BCE as if they were an independent development apart from the Bihar caves {Nagaraju 1981: 309-310, 312-314}. This seems to be an impossible proposition for if these caves were contemporary with the Bihar caves then the Deccan cave builders must have known about these contemporary Maurya caves and probably already incorporated the Maurya features into their new caves. But these earliest Deccan caves are apparently crude and stylistically unrelated to the Bihar caves which could be due to the initial lack of patronage as Buddhism was still new in the area. On the other hand, a comparison between the Maurya caves in Bihar **[5.1-5.2]** and some of the earliest Deccan caves **[5.3]** will clearly demonstrate the architectural continuity between them; new features are evident in the Deccan caves possibly owing to the increasing patronage and fresh innovations. The lack of the characteristic shiny Maurya polish in the Deccan caves suggests their later dates and patronage from the commoners; thus the c. 200 BCE date would be more plausible for the commencement of the Deccan caves. Cave construction activities in the Deccan did not go on uninterrupted as there seems to be a hiatus between the second-fourth centuries CE; this coincided precisely with the rise in great artistic centers in the Krishna River valley like Amaravati and Gandhara. A few centers like Kanheri and Kuda remained active until the third century CE probably due to the strong momentum pulsating from Amaravati. Hewing activities resumed again after the decline of the Krishna River valley centers and Gandhara and concurrent with the preeminent rise of the Guptas and the Vakatakas in the fifth century CE; Buddhist rock-hewn architecture in India also reached its peak splendor during this second renaissance. For the convenience of the chronological and stylistic identification, Buddhist caves are generally divided into two main phases: Aniconic (c. 200 BCE-300 CE) and Iconic (c. 400-750 CE) or Theravada and Mahayana respectively. I prefer the Aniconic-Iconic designation since it also corresponds to the two phases of Buddhist sculptures and paintings. Aniconic caves depicted Buddha images as symbols whereas Iconic caves contained numerous images of Buddhas and *bodhisattva*s in anthropomorphic forms. More often Aniconic and Iconic caves were hewn within the same site as in Ajanta, Kondivte, Karla, etc. with the time lapse between the caves sometimes over several centuries suggesting their reoccupation or refurbishment at a later time. It is also incorrect to label all later caves as Mahayana since caves with Vajrayana manifestation also appeared late in the scene and it is no longer tenable to consider the Vajrayana as a part of the Mahayana. No known Indian caves had exclusively been hewn for the Vajrayana but some late Mahayana caves like Ajanta (2, 4, 26), Kanheri (14, 41), Elora (8, 11/Do Thal, 12/Tin Thal), and Aurangabad (2, 9) displayed Vajrayana inclination such as the multi-limbed figures, *sakti*s, *mandala*-like arrangement of the decorative and architectural programs. Vajrayana tendencies in the late Indian Buddhist caves were likely due to the influences from early Hindu caves like Aihole, Badami, and Udayagiri as well as Hindu Tantricism. The strict division of Buddhist caves into the Aniconic and Iconic phases has also led to several false impressions and myths; the first is that the Aniconic caves had been mysteriously abandoned during the transitional 'dark period' between the second-fourth centuries CE. Most likely Theravada monks continued to inhabit their caves but the construction activities would be halted possibly due to the decrease in patronage and the rise of the renowned Buddhist centers in the Krishna River valley and Gandhara; no doubt some Theravada caves might have been abandoned and would be reoccupied later by Mahanaya monks from the presence of Mahayana decorations in some of the earlier caves. The second myth is that the Iconic caves were reserved for Mahayana monks. In reality, Theravada and Mahayana monks could certainly have lived side by side within the same monasteries or caves apparently without any sectarian problems; the presence of Buddha images in later Mahayana caves did not necessarily mean the absence of Theravada monks therein since the latter apparently enjoyed image worship as much as the Mahayanists. The account of the Chinese monk-pilgrim I-tsing (683-727 CE) traveling in India in the late seventh century CE reported Indian monasteries housing both Theravada and Mahayana monks; according to him those who worshipped the *bodhisattva*s and read Mahayana *sutra*s were the Mahayanists while those who did not were the Theravadins. The truth is that probably only the Buddhist caves at Elora are considered as 100 percent Mahayana or early Vajrayana whereas the majority of the other caves are Aniconic/Theravada or about seventy percent of all Buddhist caves while the remaining caves contain a mixture of both Theravada and Mahayana designs and themes {Nagaraju 1981: 309}.

Indian Buddhist caves can be divided into three important types based on their functions {Nagaraju 1981: 68-71}:
(a) *Caityagriha* [5.3-5.5, 5.7-5.11].
 It is basically a rectangular hall with a semicircular apse in the back and a continuous colonnade dividing the interior into two symmetrical aisles and a nave in the middle; a monolithic *stupa* is typically erected in the back. A ubiquitous and dominating feature in this cave is the horseshoe *caitya*-arched facade on the exterior [5.5, 5.8, 5.11]; the interior has a barrel-vaulted ceiling merging with the quadrantal apse in the back whilst both aisles have quadrantal vaults. The ceilings and aisles in some early caves are flat [5.3] and a few do not have the semicircular apse but these are exceptions rather than the rule; some early *caityagriha*s like Bhaja 12 [5.4-5.5], Ajanta 10, and Karla 8 [5.7-5.9] have wooden ribs which have been completely replaced with stone ones in the later caves. The *stupa*, an archetypical feature of the *caityagriha*, was the first element to be incorporated into the plan due to the rise in the popularity of its cult; these cave *stupa*s typically develop in the verticality and have an elongated drum body due to the limited space in the nave. The introduction of columns in the interior, besides imitating timber architecture, would transform the aisles into *pradaksina* paths for religious circumambulation around the *stupa* while the columns themselves were comparable to the *vedika*s in contemporary freestanding *stupa*s. It is no coincidence that the plain octagonal pillars in Bhaja 12 and the ground *vedika* of Sanchi [6.3] are essentially similar in forms and therefore contemporary. The *stupa* in the *caityagriha* might have been the Relic type since relics were discovered in some caves (Pitalkhora 3, Karla 8) while most are the Symbolic type. Relics had often been interred in smaller *stupa*s in a different location outside the *caityagriha* (Bhaja) but sometimes they were also found inside the interior columns (Karla 8); it is apparent that only relics of eminent monks would be interred inside the *caityagriha stupa*s {Nagaraju 1981: 73, 98, 229-230, 285}. Thus the *caityagriha*, with its *stupa* symbolizing Buddha's invisible presence, is indeed a holy chapel and a place of worship for the public and monks; it was probably in these halls that important and solemn rites and ceremonies would be conducted by monks and functionally it was the equivalent of the later Mahayana *pratimagriha* (image temple). A few rare rock-hewn *caityagriha*s, such as Bhaja 24/26, Junnar-Tuljalena 3, Guntupalli, and their freestanding counterparts like Bairat Temple [7.1] have circular plans which were direct translations of contemporary timber prototypes. Toward the later years of the Aniconic Phase (c. 100-300 CE), a few caves (Shelarwadi 8) fused the *caityagriha* and *lena* plans so that the *stupa* and monks' cells were now located in the same cave; contemporary freestanding Gandhara monasteries also had this plan as in Mohenjo-daro [1.1].

(b) *Lena* [5.6, 5.12-5.13]
 The *lena* had been referred to as a *guha* for older caves but eventually the former began to supplant the latter term; it is essentially a rock-hewn cave *vihara* or a residential dwelling for monks in which the earliest caves had simple single cells and were gradually enlarged to accommodate more occupants. A fully developed *lena* in the Mahayana period typically has a quadrangular plan with cells surrounding a central hall in the interior which is divided into aisles on all four sides by a closed colonnade. The cells in the Aniconic caves often have built-in stone couches and niches for monks whereas Iconic caves do not; virtually all Aniconic/Theravada *lena*s do not have interior columns but Iconic/Mahayana ones typically

have columns in the interior. Almost all *lena*s have flat ceilings with the exception of Pitalkhora 4 which has barrel-vaulted ceilings in its cells and Bhaja 22 has a quadrantal ceiling in its verandah while Bedsa 11 is a unique *lena* having an apsidal end and a vaulted ceiling like the *caityagriha*. Unlike the *caityagriha*, a *lena* does not have a *caitya*-arch on its facade; the open space in the center of a *lena* might have had dual purposes for the congregation of monks to discuss religious matters and possibly sharing their meals together. On the other end of a *lena* deep inside the cave is a cell or chapel that houses a large Buddha statue carved straight out of the rock; this is the quintessential feature of the Iconic/Mahayana caves. The quadrangular colonnaded plan of the *lena* with a central space is typical of Indian architecture which can be traced back to the Indus sites like the Great Bath of Mohenjo-daro [1.2-1.3].

(c) *Matapa*

These subsidiary caves often have benches running along the back walls and like the *lena* they have flat ceilings; in the early days of Buddhism when monks were still begging for food these were probably reserved for pilgrims or lay Buddhists. Gradually and probably beginning in the Common Era, as monks adopted a more sedentary lifestyle with increasing interactions between the laity and *Sangha*, these *matapa*s would also function as the service quarter of the monastery encompassing the refectory, kitchen, pilgrim rest areas, assembly and meeting between monks and the laity, Buddhist education for the laity, etc. {Nagaraju 1981: 220-221}. Many water cisterns or *podhi* were also present in these monasteries for the occupants' usage as well as for sanitary and hygienic purposes.

Some fundamental chronological and stylistic development in Indian Buddhist rock-hewn caves from the Aniconic to Iconic phase can be perceived:

- A *caityagriha* without a *stupa* in the interior [5.1-5.2].
- A *caityagriha* with a *stupa* in the interior [5.3].
- The great *caitya*-arch is the defining characteristic of the *caityagriha* and early Indian Buddhist architecture in general [5.2, 5.5, 5.8, 5.11].
- The presence of a screen-wall and verandah [5.3, 5.6, 5.12] to block the monsoon rain, diffuse harsh tropical sunlight, and prevent outside intrusion.
- The incorporation of columns in the interior as a structural precaution due to the gradual increase in the scale and height of the cave, which varies from single to multiple stories up to three like Elora 11-12, and also as the decorative components of the architecture [5.4-5.5, 5.7, 5.9, 5.10, 5.12].
- The embellishment of sculptures and murals in the exterior and interior, especially Buddha and *bodhisattva* images in the Iconic caves, as decorative treatments and complementary to the architecture [5.6, 5.8, 5.10, 5.12].
- Projecting porticos generally in Iconic/Mahayana caves [5.10, 5.12].

There are unique features that differentiate between earlier Aniconic and later Iconic caves. Aniconic/Theravada caves are significantly smaller than Iconic/Mahayana caves typically having single-storied and their surfaces devoid of Buddha and *bodhisattva* images; the *caityagriha stupa*s in Aniconic caves have timber or stone *harmika*s and timber *yasti-chattra*s but these would be completely replaced with stone ones in the Iconic caves. Aniconic caves have plain octagonal and pot-shaped columns with sculptured capitals, timber and stone ribs on the ceilings or the combination of both, timber and stone screen-walls or the combination of both, slanting door jambs, and built-in benches in the halls and cells. The exterior often contains decorative motifs such as brackets, stepped cornices, merlons, double-crescents, and moonstones (*chandrasila*); the lotus-medallion *vedika*s and *chandrasila*s found in Kanheri 3 and Nasik 3 were late Andhra features dated in the early second century CE. On the technologies and construction methods for these caves, once a site of sufficiently hard rock without defects had been selected the mason with his pick axes and chisels hew the caves from front to back and top to bottom to avoid falling rocks from above while hewing {Griffiths 1983 Volume I: 3}{Somathilake 2002: 350-352}. All Maurya caves like Lomas Risi typically had a mirror-like polish in the interior whereas the interior of the Deccan caves were only smoothened or troweled with plaster if the surfaces were to be painted later on {Nagaraju 1981: 66-67}{Gupta 1980: 205-209}{Mitra 1956: 9}. Hewing a cave might have taken less time and resources than constructing a freestanding stone temple of the same size as Fergusson once suggested since stone was plentiful and did not require long distant transportation {Fergusson and Burgess 1969: 167}. A rock-hewn cave also blended perfectly into the surroundings and became an integral part of the landscape which was ideally suited for the contemplative lifestyle of Buddhist monks. Mistakes however could be very unforgiving as observed in the large natural cracks inside Lomas Risi; it therefore demanded great skills on the part of the mason and his accurate judgments on the structural strength of the rocks before the commencement of the hewing activities as a successful completion of a cave would be an eternal reward that continues to be prided by Buddhists to this day.

1. Lomas Risi (c. 257-250 BCE)

As already stated, the oldest rock-hewn caves in India dated to the time of Asoka and his grandson Dasaratha; these are all located in Bihar with one group on the Barabar and Nagarjuni hills about sixteen miles north Gaya and the other in Rajir. These caves have been visited and studied by Major Markham Kittoe who published his accounts in the May 1847 CE ASB issue. The Barabar group, which includes Sudama, Visvakarma, Karna Chopar, and Lomas Risi [5.1-5.2], has Asoka's inscriptions with the exception of the undated Lomas Risi has also been attributed to Asoka; the Nagarjuni group includes Gopika, Vadathi, and Vapiya, all have Dasaratha's inscriptions. The Rajir group consists of Sitamarhi and Son Bhandar which have no inscriptions but have been tentatively dated in the late Maurya or Dasaratha's reign from their gleaming polish {Fergusson and Burgess 1969: 45-49}{Gupta 1980: 190}. All these Bihar caves share similar features that are also characteristics of Maurya cave architecture:

- Most plans have rectangular antechambers and with or without the attached circular chambers in the back. A variation of this plan in Gopika fuses the rectangular antechamber with the circular chamber to create an integrated plan having an apsidal end as in Jivakavanarama [4.1]; it was evidently the predecessor of the Deccan *caityagriha*s [5.4].
- Most have barrel vaults in the antechambers and domes in the circular chambers. The apse of Gopika has a quadrantal vault and Visvakarma has a flat ceiling while the vaults of Vadathi and Sitamarhi spring directly from the floor; Sitamarhi has a pointed arch vault and the oldest of its kind in India.
- All have plain interiors but are compensated by the glistening polish as in contemporary Asoka pillars and the characteristic of Maurya architecture.
- Imitation and translation of contemporary timber architecture are evident in the designs of these caves, for examples their hut-like forms, the timber-like facade of Lomas Risi [5.1], and the socket holes in the entrance floors of Visvakarma and Vadathi suggesting the presence of wooden screen walls and doors.
- All have slanting door jambs, which are also present in the early Aniconic caves in the Deccan but never in later Mahayana caves; Son Bhandar is the only exception having a window.
- Most caves are entered from the sides but a few have direct frontal entries.

Many of Barabar and Nagarjuni caves contain inscriptions of Asoka and Dasaratha which are crucial in determining their construction dates and religious affiliations of the occupants {Cunningham 1871: 40-53}{Buhler 1891: 361-365}{Hultzsch 1969: xxviii, 181-183}{Gupta 1980: 189-202}:

a. Barabar Group
- Sudama
"When King Priyadarsin had been anointed twelve years, this Nigoha [Banyan tree] Cave was given to the Ajivika." This cave dated in c. 257 BCE.
- Visvakarma
"When King Priyadarsin had been anointed twelve years, this cave in the Khalatika Mountain was given to the Ajivika." This cave also dated in c. 257 BCE.
- Karna Chopar
"When King Priyadarsin had been anointed nineteen years, this cave in the very pleasant Khalatika Mountain was given by me for [shelter during] the rainy season." This inscription also contains symbols of a swastika and a dagger in the end; this cave dated in c. 250 BCE.
- Lomas Risi [5.1-5.2]
"Prince Maukhari Anantavarman installed a statue of Krishna in this cave in the Pravaragiri." This Gupa inscription dated in the mid fifth century CE; Pravaragiri is evidently the ancient name of the Barabar hill.

b. Nagarjuni Group
- Gopika
"The Gopika [Milkmaid] Cave, an adobe lasting as the Sun and Moon, was caused to be excavated by Devanampriya [Beloved of the Gods] Dasaratha on his ascension to the throne as a hermitage for the most devoted Ajivika." It dated in c. 214 BCE and like Lomas Risi it also contains an Anantavarman inscription (mid fifth century CE) recording the installation of the Katyayani statue in the cave.
- Vadathi
Same as the Gopika inscription except for the name of the cave; it also has an Anantavarman inscription (mid fifth century CE) as in Lomas Risi and Gopika.
- Vapiya
Same as the Gopika inscription except for the name of the cave; Vapiya or Well Cave probably alludes to the well in front.

With the exceptions of Karna Chopar and Lomas Risi, all others were definitely constructed for the Ajivikas, a sect founded by Makkhali Gosala who was a former disciple of Mahavira the founder of Jainism and a contemporary of Buddha. Karna Chopar was donated by Asoka but the received sect was not recorded in the inscription; however the presence of the swastika, which was often a Buddhist symbol, and the description of the cave as a shelter for the rainy season strongly allude to the traditional annual Buddhist *vassavasa* (rain retreat) and hence these suggest a Buddhist affiliation. Moreover, Asoka specifically mentioned the Ajivikas in the Sudama and Visvakarma inscriptions but not in Karna Chopar and thus the latter could very well be a Buddhist cave.

Lomas Risi [5.1-5.2] is architecturally the most important of the Bihar caves as it exhibits the earliest features and precursors of the Deccan *caityagriha*s [5.3]; regrettably it has no Maurya or Asoka inscriptions so that it is not possible to confirm its donors or religious affiliation. Otherwise its plan is identical with Sudama and the main difference between them is the finely chiseled *caitya*-arched facade on its entrance [5.1]; this grand *caitya*-arch became the defining characteristic of all Buddhist *caityagriha*s in the subsequent Deccan caves [5.5, 5.8] and pre-Mahayana architecture [7.1-7.3]. The dimension of the antechamber is 36'5" wide x 18'9" deep x 11'2" high with an entry of about 5'7" high; the diameter of the circular rear chamber should have been 17'9" in its original plan but it was left to its currently unfinished elliptical shape due to the incompletion or abandonment of the cave. Lomas Risi also has all the aforesaid features of a Maurya cave such as the rectangular antechamber attached to a circular chamber, barrel and dome vaults, the lustrous polish interior, slanting door jambs, and a side entrance. Imitation of contemporary timber architecture may also be deduced in the hut-shaped circular chamber and the great *caitya*-arched facade with its slanting posts, exposed rafters, finial, and carved reliefs of lattice-and-lotuses on the upper arch, and elephants-and-*makara*s on the lower arch. The conceptual relationships between the Lomas Risi facade, Bharhut *torana* [6.7], Pitalkhora 4 {Dehejia 1972: pl. 25}, and Bhaja 12 [5.5] are evident in the depiction of animals marching toward the center from both sides and the great *caitya*-arch. The interior of Lomas Risi was partially finished and only the walls of its antechamber was polished shiny while the outer wall of the circular chamber was smoothened but not polished; the remaining surfaces in the circular chamber and the floor and ceiling of the antechamber were left rough. Most likely due to its incomplete conditions, Lomas Risi had not been provided with an inscription. Various theories have been put forward about the incompletion of the cave from structural failures due to the large cracks in the interior {Gupta 1980: 209-211} to the sudden collapse of the Maurya Dynasty in c. 184 BCE that abruptly halted all constructions {Gupta 1980: 215}. There are sugges-

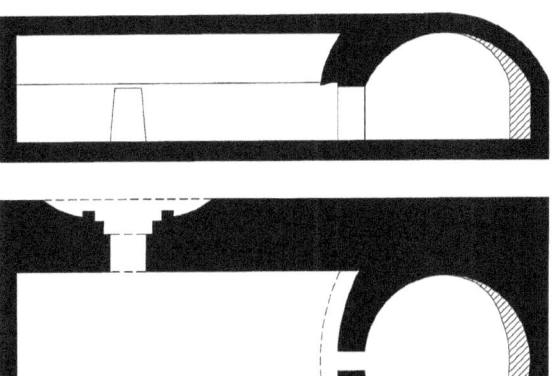

5.1. Section and plan
c. 257-250 BCE
Gaya- India

5.2. Entrance
c. 257-250 BCE
Gaya- India

tions that the cave had initially been hewn in the Maurya Dynasty while the elaborate *caitya*-arched facade was carved at a later time as late as the Gupta Dynasty {Gupta 1980: 211-215}. This is clearly a groundless theory since it seems unreasonable from an aesthetic viewpoint to carve such an intricate facade when the interior was already in a ruinous condition with noticeable fissures; moreover the facade, with a slanted doorway and a side entrance, stylistically did not belong in the Gupta Dynasty. Fergusson suggested this cave to be a contemporary of Sudama and had possibly been donated by Asoka since both had identical designs but without the ornate facade in Lomas Risi {Fergusson and Burgess 1969: 38}; others, due to the presence of the seemingly incongruous facade, gave Lomas Risi a post Dasaratha date {Gupta 1980: 215}. However its plan, the mirror-like polish in the interior, and the faithful copy of the timber eave of the circular chamber are all identical with Sudama; thus Lomas Risi must be at least contemporary with Sudama or slightly later but undoubtedly within Asoka's reign between c. 257-233 BCE. Another important step in these Maurya caves was the gradual abandonment of the fully closed circular chamber beginning with Karna Chopar; thus the date for Lomas Risi can be further narrowed down between c. 257-250 BCE. Karna Chopar has already been attributed to the Buddhists and could Lomas Risi also have been constructed for the Buddhists? With the patronage of a Buddhist emperor like Asoka the Buddhists could certainly have had plenty of wealth to construct Lomas Risi and its ornate facade. Perhaps one may question as why Asoka built Sudama and Visvakarma for the Ajivikas earlier and Lomas Risi and Karna Chopar for the Buddhists at a later time. It is well-known from Asoka's rock and pillar inscriptions that he only became a zealous Buddhist emperor later in his reign and so Sudama and Visvakarma could have been built before he devoted his full attention to Buddhism; perhaps he also decided to construct the caves for the Buddhists, just like he did for the Ajivikas, concurrent with the erection of his pillars. Had the *caitya*-arch been the special feature of the Ajivikas' caves, the Buddhists would probably not copy it in their Deccan *caityagriha*s and in the same token no Hindu or Jain caves copied it because they knew it was a quintessential Buddhist feature; thus Lomas Risi and its celebrated facade could have been a Buddhist invention. Another curious anomaly in these Maurya caves is the conspicuous absence of the *stupa* inside the circular chamber and apsidal end, a feature which is always present in the Deccan *caityagriha*s. Fergusson stated that the circular chambers in the Bihar caves, which functioned as sacred chapels in the subsequent Deccan caves, might have had 'a wooden or metal *dagaba* [*stupa*] or relic shrine' {Fergusson and Burgess 1969: 41-42}. A portable shrine, though not necessarily containing relics, would be more plausible since it was obviously not possible to bring a solid timber or stone *stupa* through the narrow doorway of the circular chamber. My hunch is that the *stupa* was probably not present in these Maurya caves since its cult was still in infancy and some of the earliest Deccan *caityagriha*s like Bhaja 20, 24 also did not have *stupa*s inside their chambers; thus the incorporation of the *stupa* inside Buddhist caves likely happened at a later time starting with the Deccan caves. The Maurya caves appear to be multi-functional having the circular and apsidal ends as sacred shrines while the antechamber was probably reserved for the communal activities of the occupants like sharing meals, meditation, etc.

2. Kondivte (second century BCE-third centuries CE... fifth-seventh centuries CE)

The next important phase in the evolution of Indian Buddhist caves was commenced in the Deccan around c. 200 BCE; though Bhaja, Jivadan-Virar, Junnar-Tuljalena, and Kanheri contain the oldest caves in the region, Kondivte [5.3] is considered the crucial transition between the Bihar and Deccan caves and in particular the development of the *caityagriha*. The *caityagriha*s of Kanheri 2e and Junnar-Tuljalena 3 are also very similar to Kondivte; Nagaraju placed Kanheri 2e and Junnar-Tuljalena 3 earlier than Kondivte from the forms of the *stupa*s inside these caves {Nagaraju 1981: 66-67}. However the conclusion can be misleading since Kanheri 2e does not have a circular chamber and Junnar-Tuljalena 3 has a colonnade, features that are absent in Kondivte and the Maurya caves. There are about twenty caves in the Kondivte group with only one *caityagriha*; about five caves belong to the Aniconic/Theravada type and the remaining caves are Iconic/Mahayana.

The *caityagriha* plan of Kondivte [5.3] is an open rectangular antechamber with a flat ceiling and a circular domed chamber in the back that contains a *stupa* of 8'1" diameter and 11'11" high; this *stupa* has a carved *vedika* on its drum and a thin protrusion on its dome having four holes probably to affix a timber *harmika* and *yasti-chattra*. The cylindrical form of the *stupa* is unlike contemporary freestanding domed *stupa*s [6.3] due to the spatial constraint of the cave; however, its elongated form became the precursor of later Gandhara *stupa*s [6.15] which typically had multi-tiered drums. The circular chamber of the cave has grille openings imitating wooden lattice windows and a wooden screen-wall in the entrance no

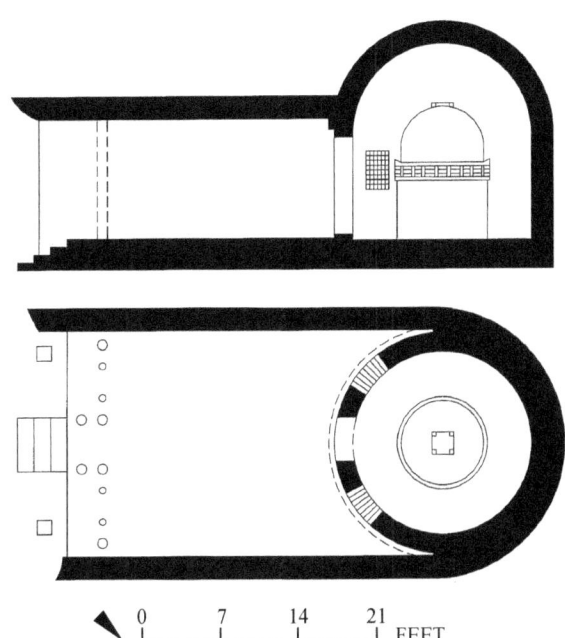

5.3. Section and plan
c. 200 BCE
Kondivte Cave 9, Kondivte- India

longer extant from the remaining mortised holes on the floor; there are three stone steps leading to the cave. It is hard to conjecture what this wooden screen-wall might have originally looked like; most likely it resembled the facade of Lomas Risi [5.1] and therefore maintained the architectural continuity between the Bihar and Deccan caves. Many early Deccan caves did not have stone screen-walls probably due to the initial lack of patronage and early stage of architectural development. At the top of the outer wall of the circular chamber is a stone band recalling the overhang projection of Lomas Risi; unlike the latter, the interior of Kondivte had been smoothened but unpolished which was also a characteristic of all Deccan caves. Without features like the unpolished interior, *stupa*, and grille windows, one can easily be mistaken Kondivte for a Maurya cave; on the other hand caves with direct frontal entries, wooden screen walls, and even windows were not unknown in the Maurya caves in Bihar as in Visvakarma and Son Bhandar. The right wall of Kondivte contains an anachronous carving of Buddhas, *bodhisattva*s, and attendants obviously inserted during the Mahayana ascendancy which likely dated in the seventh century CE. There is an inscription (mid second century CE) above one of the grille windows recorded the patronage of the cave by 'a Brahman of the Gautamagotra, an inhabitant of Pachikamayi.' It is not known if this Kondivte *stupa* originally had any relics and so it might be a Symbolic type that reminded monks and pilgrims of Buddha's *Parinirvana* and the transitoriness of life so they must steadfastly strive for their own salvation.

3. Bhaja (late third century BCE-first centuries CE)

Bhaja has about twenty-nine caves and is one of several groups in the Deccan that remained untouched by later Mahayana constructions unlike some of other caves; all hewing activities seemed to have ceased after the second century CE. Cave 12 [5.4-5.5] and Cave 26 are *caityagriha*s while Cave 24, probably the earliest, has a circular plan without a *stupa* which was possibly as a chapel; Cave 20 consists of a group of *stupa*s built in the memory of deceased monks and likely contained their relics. Most other caves are *lena*s [5.6], a few are *matapa*s, and there are some *podhi*s; Caves 9-11 are on the upper level and can be reached via staircases or ladders in the ancient days. There are a total of eight inscriptions found in Cave 6, 17, 20 (*stupa*s 6-9) and over the rock cisterns between Cave 14, 17; these recorded donations to the Bhaja monastery by the laity and names of the deceased monks interred in their respective *stupa*s.

The most important cave at Bhaja must be Caityagriha 12 [5.4-5.5] wherein several new features in the Indian Buddhist rock-hewn architecture can be observed. Compared to Kondivte [5.3], the interior of Bhaja has been totally opened up by eliminating the wall separating the circular chamber and the rectangular antechamber which create the characteristic U-shaped apsidal plan; the Gopika cave in Bihar and Jivakavanarama [4.1] already had such plan which was common in early Indian timber architecture. The flat ceiling of Kondivte has also been transformed into a barrel-vaulted one in Bhaja, a feature already occurred in the Bihar caves [5.1]. The newest feature is a continuous colonnade of octagonal stone columns dividing the interior into quadrantal-vaulted aisles and a barrel-vaulted nave in the middle; these columns are unique in that they slightly taper and rake inward toward the top as if imitating timber buildings to counteract the thrust of the vault, which is obviously structurally redundant in stone architecture. The barrel-vaulted nave springs directly above the 5'9" high triforium which is in turn rested directly on the 11'6" high columns, some of which have carvings of archaic aniconic symbols such as the *triratna*, taurine, *dharmacakra*, etc. as also found in Bharhut and Sanchi. The presence of socket holes in the entry suggests the existence of a wooden screen-wall

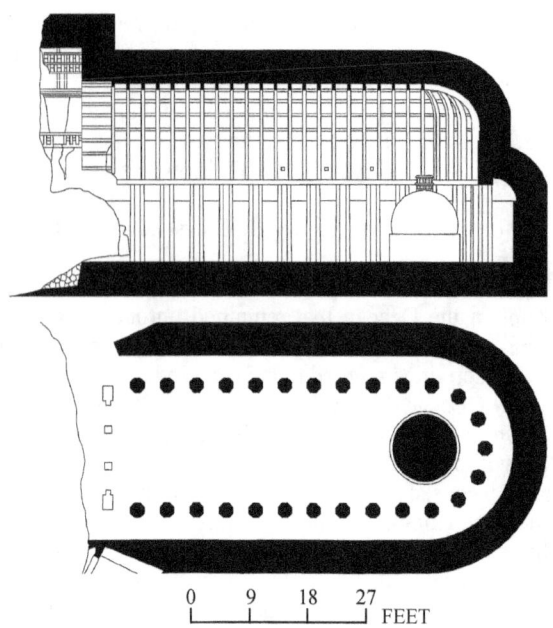

5.4. Section and plan
c. 175 BCE
Bhaja Cave 12, Lonavala- India

5.5. Exterior
c. 175 BCE
Bhaja Cave 12, Lonavala- India

that is no longer extant; the dimension of the nave from these socket holes to the end of the apse is 62'9" and its width 27'2" with 3'3" wide aisles, while the total height from the floor to the apex of the nave is 26'3". At the apsidal end is a *stupa* having a stone *harmika*, another

advance from the wooden *harmika* in Kondivte; it probably did not have relics since *stupa*s containing monks' relics had been collectively placed in Cave 20. Other new elements are the carved ribbed beams in the nave and aisles intersected perpendicularly by purlins, all were undoubtedly faithful replications of timber architecture; moreover these ribs are timber and amazingly still remain in situ after the centuries. The facade of this cave is a huge horseshoe *caitya*-arch with huge beam sockets on the side walls; it must have originally been attached with a wooden screen-wall from the floor to the ceiling and which form should closely resemble that of the slightly later and extant Ajanta Cave 10. Above and on both sides of the great arch are decorative treatments including *vedika*s, small *caitya*-arches, brackets, and merlons alongwith a few tiny figures of possibly *mithuna*s and *yaksi*s. The overall architectural meaning of this *caity-agriha* suggests a celestial palace and Buddha's abode inhabited and guarded by divine beings; functionally it was also a chapel for religious ceremonies and worship. The introduction of a colonnade surrounding the *stupa*, a practice likely imitating contemporary freestanding *stupa*s like Sanchi [6.3-6.4], was to create a *pradaksina* path for monks and visitors.

The completely stone Lena 22 [5.6] is decisively an important development from earlier plain single-celled dwellings for monks; it not only has large figural carvings inside but also new column orders. The cave, which is composed of a porticoed verandah and an open hall inside without columns, is 29' wide x 35'6 deep from the back of the cells to the outside face of the verandah columns. It has cells on the right and back of about 5'6" wide x 6'6" deep each and some have built-in stone benches as characteristic of the Aniconic/Theravada caves; the left wall has no cells but is elaborately carved with *caitya*-arched niches and figural reliefs, all of which are set above an elevated platform. The verandah has three new column orders including the square-and-chamfer, the octagonal double-pot on top and bottom with an animal capital, and the square-and-chamfered with a bell-shaped animal capital; the latter is a pilaster and not a column. The right side of the verandah is provided with a built-in stone table, probably an altar or pedestal for some cult objects; to its right and above is a lattice window already occurred in Kondivte [5.3]. The verandah, more so than the interior, also contains profusely carved reliefs of *dvarapala*s (door guardians) on the entry wall while on the right wall are royal couples riding a richly caparisoned four-horsed chariot and a stately elephant; the scene on the left wall depicts a bull fight and men, many of whom riding richly caparisoned horses. The controversial royal scenes have

Part II. Architecture   Rock-hewn Cave . 107

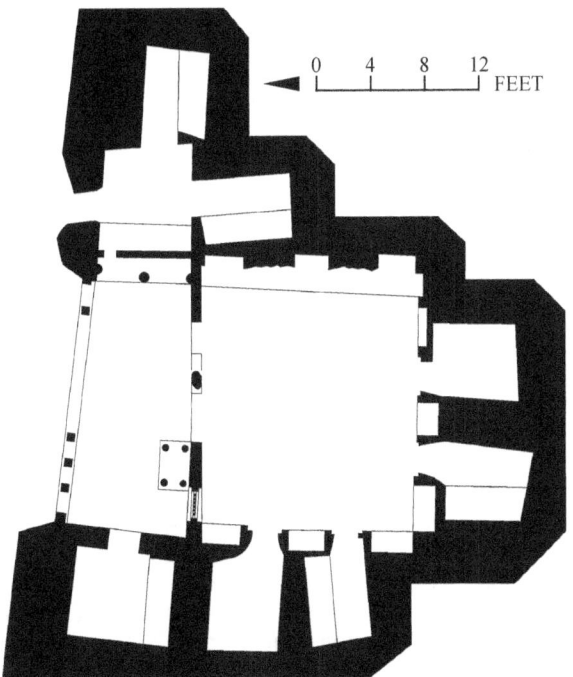

5.6. Section and plan
c. 150-100 BCE
Bhaja Cave 22, Lonavala- India

been identified by scholars as Surya riding the chariot and Indra riding the elephant {Fergusson and Burgess 1969: 522}{Rowland 1977: 88-89}; however these could also be scenes in a *jataka*, secular royal couples and donors, or some unidentified Buddhist stories since similar depictions also occurred on Sanchi and Bharhut *stupa*s. Behind the left wall is an annex of two cells with a small opening linking it with the verandah; much of this wall has since collapsed but was probably present in the 1880s CE when James Fergusson's *'Cave Temples'* was published. The 11' high interior ceiling is flat whereas the 14' high verandah ceiling is quadrantal with stone ribs and purlins and not timber as in Cave 12, which is another important step in eliminating the remaining vestiges of timber architecture in Buddhist caves. Some scholars opined that this *lena* had been constructed in several phases based on the style of the decorations alongwith its haphazard and asymmetrical plan, which is obviously less developed than Mahayana *lena*s [**5.12**]. Nagaraju placed the constructions in the hall and cells, verandah, verandah entry and right walls, and the right doorway (first), the verandah carvings (second), and the verandah left wall, columns and pilasters, left doorway, lattice window, annex (third); he dated the cave between c. 150-140 BCE {Nagaraju 1981: 125-126, 129} but there are problems with this view. First if the annex cells had been hewn after the hall, would it make more sense to hew them out of an already existing blank and un-celled left wall of the interior hall? I believe the annex cells must have already existed before and behind the left wall of the hall so that the builders had to adorn the latter with carvings to distract attention and beautify the interior; thus the annex cells must logically date before the left wall of the interior. Second, the figures on the left wall of the hall stylistically appear more archaic than those of the verandah and nearer to those on Sanchi Stupa II *vedika* (c. 125 BCE); the verandah figures show greater sophistication in style and composition while its columns and pilasters are closer to the Bharhut *vedika* reliefs (c. 125-100 BCE). On the other hand, some of the cells in the hall could have existed before the cave was expanded and so the first excavations were probably in the mid second century BCE. It also appears that the right and back cells of the hall, annex, and verandah cell had been excavated first, followed by the carvings on the left wall of the hall, and finally the verandah. Taking into account of Sanchi and Bharhut, I would place most of the carvings between c. 125-100 BCE and c. 150-100 BCE for the whole cave since the carvings were generally later than the architecture.

4. Karla (first century BCE-second centuries CE... fifth-seventh centuries CE)

There are about sixteen caves in this group, of which three are Mahayana caves; most are *lena*s with Cave 14 constructed above Cave 13. An inscription of the Andhra King Vasisthiputra Pulumavi (r. 130-158 CE), which was found in Caityagriha 8 [5.7-5.9] and dated in the seventh year of his reign (137 CE), mentioned the ancient name of Karla as 'Valuraka' monastery. There are about twenty-two inscriptions discovered in Karla and almost all have been found in the great Caityagriha 8, which clearly demonstrate the importance of this cave. They recorded the usual donations by lay Buddhists, monks and nuns, merchants, bankers, royalties, and even a *Yavana* (foreigners, Asiatic Greeks). The Andhra kings' inscriptions in the early second century CE mostly recorded land donations to Karla so that the generated revenues could be used for its maintenance. The impeccable Caityagriha 8 certainly stands out among the undistinguished caves of Karla and it is undoubtedly the most refined of all Aniconic/Theravada caves. There were several stages in the architectural experimentation and refinement of numerous earlier *caityagriha*s, chronologically from Kondivte 9 [5.3], Bhaja 12 [5.4-5.5], Ajanta 10, Pitalkhora 3, Kondane 1, Ajanta 9, Nasik 18, and Bedsa 7, before the final perfection in this great *caityagriha* {Nagaraju 1981: 312-317}. Nearly 150 years had elapsed between Kondivte 9 and Karla 8; after Karla 8, the *caityagriha* architecture and cave construction in general experienced a steep decline in both quantity and quality as observed in Kanheri 3, which was stylistically after Karla 8. There would be no more coherent *caityagriha*s after the first century CE until the emergence of the opulent Iconic/Mahayana *caityagriha*s between the fifth-sixth centuries CE [5.10-5.11].

Karla 8 [5.7-5.9] is among the biggest rock-hewn caves in India and decidedly the most impressive of all Aniconic/Theravada caves; one inscription mentioned this great *caityagriha* as 'a rock-mansion -the most excellent in Jambudvipa [India]' and it surely fits the description. The plan consists of the usual U-shaped nave measuring 129'9" deep x 47'10" wide and a 19'7" deep x 57'6" wide screened verandah. Outside on the left is a huge 39' high freestanding pillar with a bell-shaped capital crowned with four addorsed lions recalling the Asoka pillar at Sarnath [3.3, 3.6] and it might have originally been surmounted with a *dharmacakra*; the interior walls are bereft of sculptures. There are thirty sturdy 'double-pot' columns, as already occurred in Bhaja 22 verandah, flanking both sides of the nave; their capitals contain sculptures of individuals or couples riding on addorsed elephants and horses that anticipated a similar style within the next decade in the Sanchi *torana*s [6.4]. At the apsidal end and behind the *stupa* are seven plain octagonal columns but these and the nave columns no longer taper and rake inward like Bhaja 12; they are visually blocked by the *stupa* and therefore of no visual value to the viewers. The 17'10" high aisles has flat ceilings whereas the 43'9" high nave retains the traditional barrel-vaulted ceiling and timber ribs as in earlier Bhaja 12 as wooden arches are also present in the great *caitya*-arch; clearly remnants of timber architecture still remained strong even after nearly two centuries of existence in cave architecture. The *stupa* of 13'4" diameter x 30'7 high to the tip with a still extant original wooden *yasti-chattra* is a grand edifice in the back of the nave; the underside of the *chattra* is beautifully carved with concentric circular motifs and a multi-petaled lotus. Henry Cousens discovered a square hole beneath it full of saw dust which he concluded that the compartment originally contained relics {Nagaraju 1981: 229}; however such saw dusts could have belonged to the carpentry activities during construction. On the other hand, this cave indeed housed the relics of some eminent monks from a discovered inscription that clearly stated 'a pillar containing a relic, the gift of Svatimitra, a preacher of the venerable Dhamutariyas [Dharmottariya Sect], from Soparaka' {Burgess 1964: 91, note #3}; a hole cut into the fifth column on the

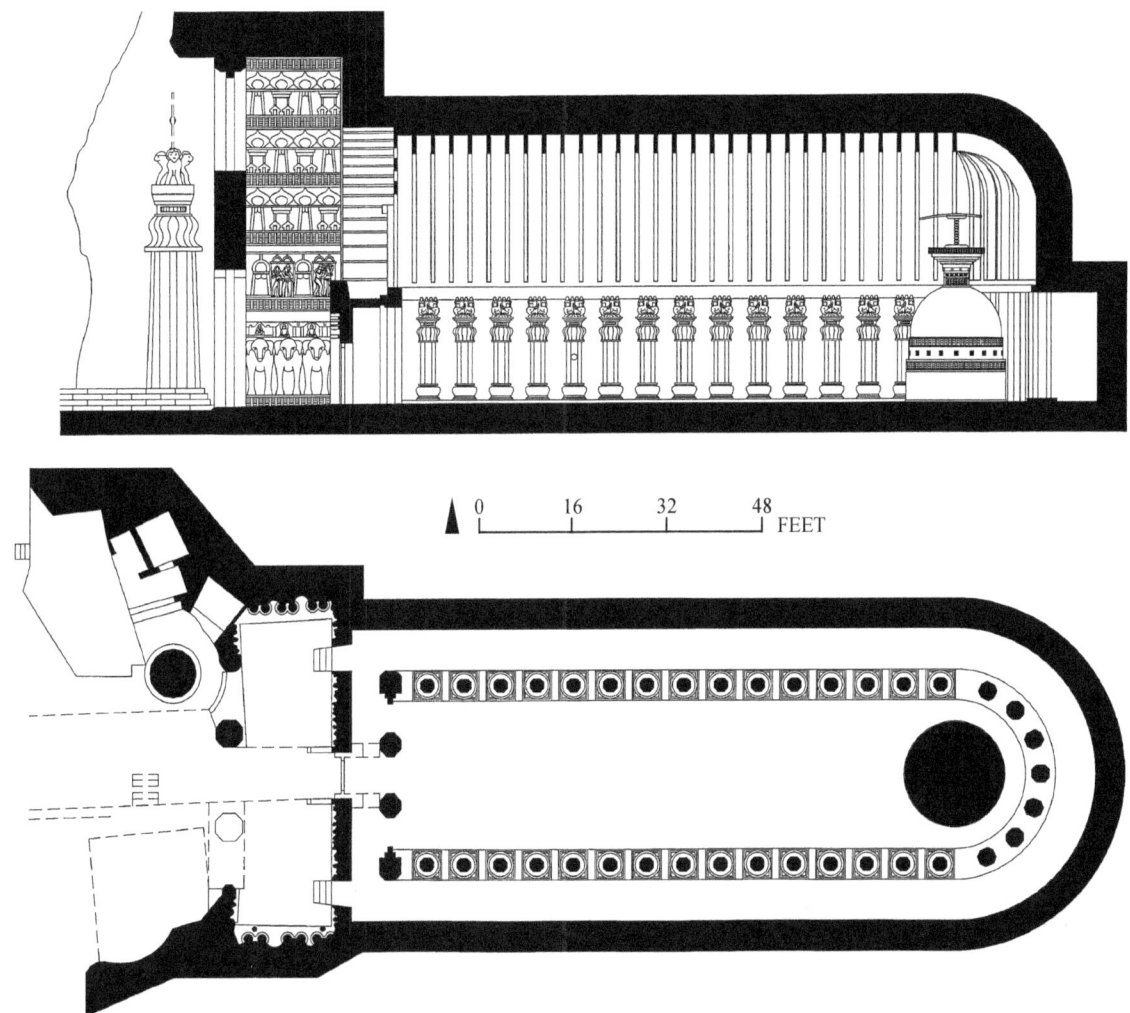

5.7. Section and plan. c. 60-50 BCE. Karla Cave 8, Karli- India

left row was obviously originally intended for the placement of this relic but is now empty of its contents. Such a relic column was rather unusual but the practice has been reported in many Gandhara *stupa*s. The construction of the lion pillar in front of a holy sanctuary like Karla, and also in Kanheri, seems to suggest the resurgence in the popularity of the Asoka pillars; Mathura and Gandhara subsequently also incorporated freestanding Asoka-typed pillars into their *stupa*s **[6.14]**. There are two inscriptions of King Pulumavi (mid second century CE) mentioning a land grant and dedication of Karla 8 nave to the Mahasanghika sect {Burgess 1964: 112-114}. Thus it is possible that Mahasanghika and Dharmottariya monks, the latter had also been recorded in a Junnar inscription proving their presence in the second century CE, were living alongside in Karla possibly as joint guardians as in the case of Amaravati where donative inscriptions of several different sects have also been recorded. An outstanding masterpiece in this *caityagriha* is its elaborate verandah **[5.8]** with its dominant horseshoe or ogee arch carved with numerous smaller *caitya*-arches and *vedika* ornamentations stacking in rows above one another probably replicating multi-storied timber buildings. Compared to the Lomas Risi arch **[5.1]**, this great Karla *caitya*-arch is elevated high above the ground at the level of the vault while the wall below is provided with three doorways; there are finely sculpted standing elephants on the left and right walls near the ground level. Perhaps its most

5.8. Verandah elevation of great *caitya*-arch
c. 60-50 BCE
Karla Cave 8, Karli- India

5.9. Interior
c. 60-50 BCE
Karla Cave 8, Karli- India

conspicuous sculptures are a set of carved *mithuna*s (loving couples) on its walls with their semi-nude and sexually suggestive bodies standing in *tribhanga*s and engaging in seemingly unBuddhist behaviors such as touching one another and dancing joyfully. However voluptuous females were common in early Buddhist *stupa*s as *devata*s and *yaksi*s guarding and protecting sacred sanctuaries; these *mithuna*s were considered divine couples in Indian folk mythology and their presence in Buddhist sanctuaries were considered auspicious. The *devata*s, *yaksi*s, and *mithuna*s constituted the uniquely Aniconic arts but they eventually disappeared in later Mahayana arts and caves; moreover, the luxurious and joyful figures in this cave represented the blissful celestial world of the *deva*s which mirrored the terrestrial world of the royal families. Above all, the female nude was an integral part of the Indian artistic tradition dating back to the Indus Civilization; Notice the numerous Iconic/Mahayana carvings of Buddhas and attendants between the *mithuna*s on the verandah wall have been inserted during the Mahayana ascendancy or reoccupation of Karla which provide a great opportunity to compare the differences between Theravada and Mahayana iconography.

5. Ajanta (second century BCE-first centuries CE... fifth-seventh centuries CE)

Ajanta was first discovered by British officers in the Madras army in 28th April 1819 CE during which an inscription by John Smith was carved on a column in Cave 10. The cave was again visited in 1824 CE by Lieutenant James E. Alexander who subsequently wrote its first official account in the 1829 CE RAS issue; from then on, Ajanta has been eulogized by countless scholars and continues to receive a constant stream of visitors annually. While Karla 8 is the jewel among the Theravada caves Ajanta is considered the epitome of elegance and sophistication of Mahayana cave architecture. One does not have to go to any other caves in the Deccan to study rock-hewn architecture since Ajanta has all types of caves dating from the earliest of the Aniconic/Theravada caves to the latest of the Mahayana caves. Its illustrious 800-year long history witnessed the triumphant heyday of Buddhism in the Deccan and the beginning of the Buddhist demise in the region from the late seventh century CE on. Out of a total of thirty caves, twenty-four belong to the Iconic/Mahayana period, which confirm Ajanta to be one of the greatest Mahayana centers in India. An inscription in Cave 16, which was donated by a minister of King Harisena (r. 470-505 CE) of the Vakataka Dynasty, mentioned the old name of Ajanta monastery as 'Mandara' {Burgess and Indraji 1976: 69-73}. The Chinese monk-pilgrim Hsuan-tsang probably referred to Ajanta in his travelogue in the early seventh century CE {Burgess 1964: 132-136}{Mitra 1956: 5}:

Part II. Architecture   Rock-hewn Cave . 111

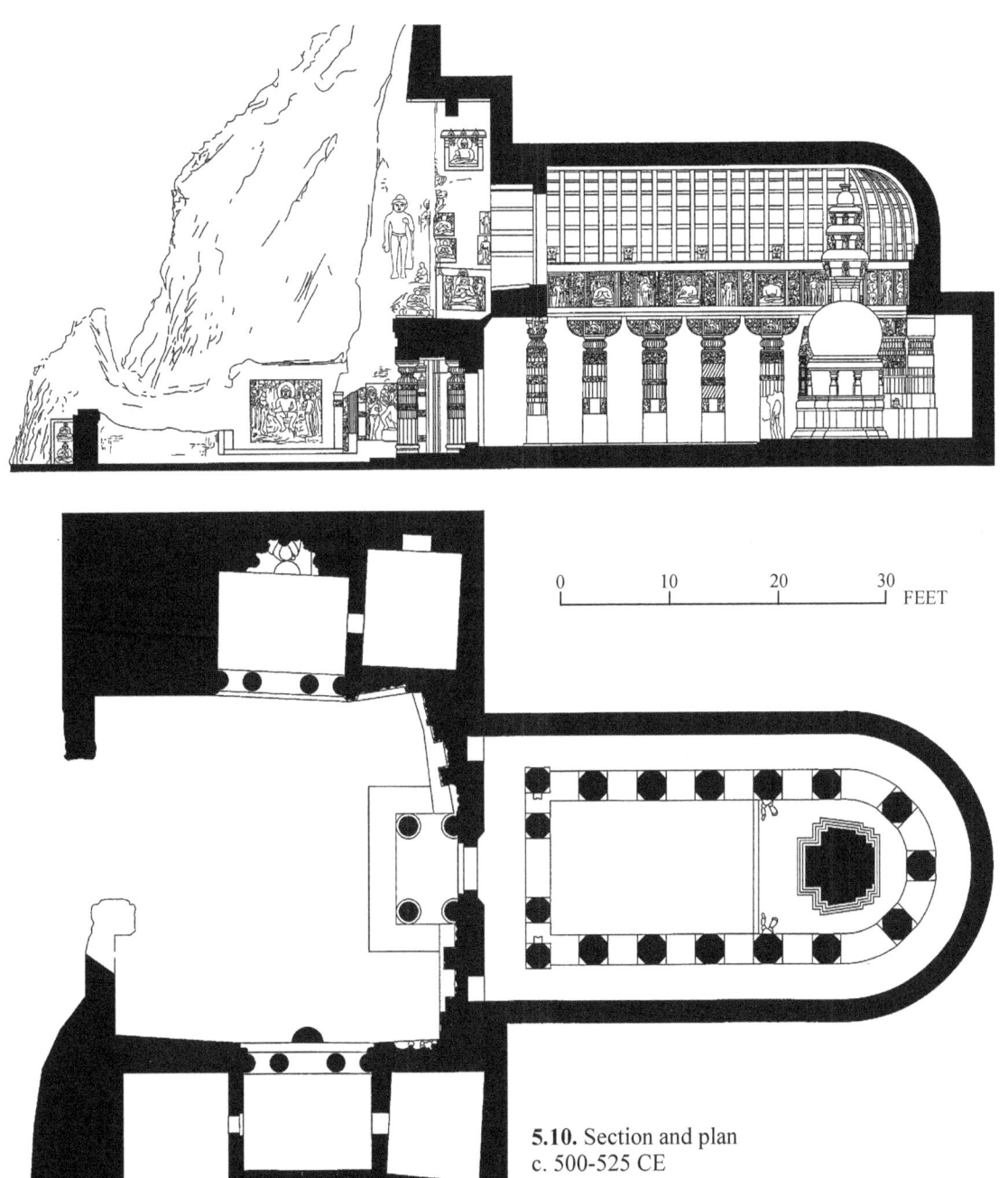

5.10. Section and plan
c. 500-525 CE
Ajanta Cave 19, Ajanta- India

In the east of this country Mo-ha-la-cha [Maharashtra] was a mountain range, ridges one above another in succession, tiers of peaks and sheer summits. Here was a monastery the base of which was in a dark defile, and its lofty halls and deep chambers were quarried in the cliff and rested on the peak, its tiers of halls and storied terraces had the cliff on their back and faced the ravine. This monastery had been built by the A-che-lo of West India.

5.11. Exterior
c. 500-525 CE
Ajanta Cave 19, Ajanta- India

The description clearly tallies with the location of the Ajanta caves which have been hewn along the horseshoe crag and ravine overlooking an idyllic stream and waterfall. Most importantly a crucial piece of evidence is an inscription in Cave 26 dated in the early seventh century CE mentioning Achala, a Theravada monk who built several *lena*(s) at Ajanta and closely matched Hsuan-tsang's 'A-che-lo.' Evidently Theravada monks were involved in the construction of many Ajanta caves and this also confirms an observation by the Chinese monk-pilgrim I-tsing that Theravada and Mahayana monks were living together in the same monasteries in India {Dutt 1962: 175-176}. Of the thirty Ajanta caves, there are four *caityagriha*s with two belonging to the Aniconic/Theravada Phase (Cave 9, 10) and two in the Iconic/Mahayana Phase (Cave 19 **[5.10-5.11]**, 26). The remaining caves are *lena*s with Aniconic/Theravada caves (Cave 8, 12, 13, 15a, 30) and Iconic/Mahayana caves (Cave 1 **[5.12-5.13]**, 2-7, 11, 14-18, 24-25, 27-29). Lena 6 is the only two-storied cave at Ajanta while Cave 14 is located at a higher level above Cave 13 and Cave 30 is further down near the stream bed. Architecturally, Cave 11 is considered the transition between the Theravada and Mahayana caves; Cave 28-29 are unfinished while most of the others are complete and in decent state of preservation. The following list proposes a conservative chronology for the Ajanta caves based on epigraphic and stylistic grounds {Williams 1982: 181-187}{Somathilake 2002: 174-181}; note that oldest Aniconic caves are located in the center of the cliff and the numerical designations for the caves are only for the counting expediency and do not reflect any chronological order:

- Cave 30 (second century BCE)
- Cave 8-10, 12-13 (second-first centuries BCE)
- Cave 11 (second-third centuries CE, c. 400-450 CE)
- Cave 5-7 (c. 450-475 CE)
- Cave 14-18 (c. 450-500 CE)
- Cave 1-2, 19-20 (c. 500-550 CE)
- Cave 21-24, 26 (c. 550-600 CE)
- Cave 3-4, 25, 27-29 (c. 600-650 CE)

The Mahayana caves in Ajanta, which certainly contain the finest and rarest Buddhist murals in India, were constructed during the classic period of Indian arts and architecture under the Vakatakas and Asmakas who were the contemporaries of the equally refined Guptas in North India. Overall there are nine rock inscriptions and thirty painted epigraphs in Ajanta, of which the two earliest ones are in Prakrit and written in the Brahmi script dated between the second-first centuries BCE (Cave 10, 12) while the remaining caves are in Sanskrit dated in the Iconic Phase {Burgess 1964: 116, 124-138}{Burgess and Indraji 1976: 67-88}. The historic inscriptions recording the lineage of the Vakataka kings have been discovered in Cave 16 and of the Asmaka kings in Cave 17, 26; the latter kings appeared to acknowledge the Vakatakas' supremacy only up to the early sixth century CE.

Cave 19 **[5.10-5.11]** is certainly the finest and quintessential Iconic/Mahayana *caityagriha*; its familiar U-shaped plan is entered via a prostyled and pilastered projecting portico after passing through a spacious open courtyard in front. The large hall in the interior measures 47'2" deep x 23'7" wide which is divided into a central nave and two symmetrical aisles by a sturdy and continuous colonnade; its 11'5" high columns are typically square at the bottom turning multi-sided in the upper parts, capped with the *amalaka*s, and finally crowned with curved bracket capitals. As usual, in the back of the nave is a tall monolithic stone *stupa* having a bulbous dome, a three-tiered *yasti-chattra*, and crowned with a

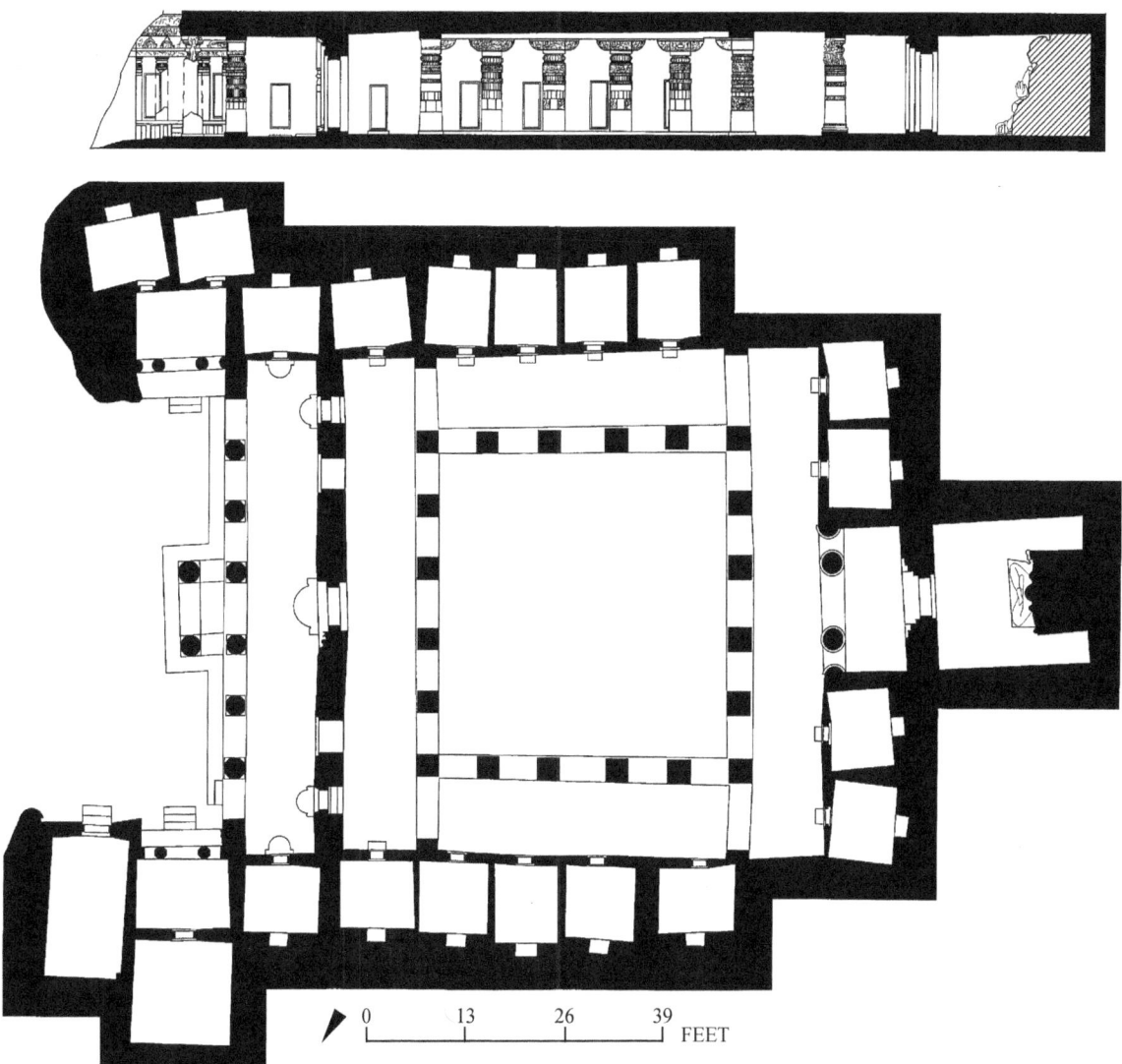

5.12. Section and plan. c. 500-525 CE. Ajanta Cave 1, Ajanta- India

finial nearly touching the ceiling. The front of this *stupa* is carved with a standing Buddha in the Gupta-Sarnath Style inside a *makara*-and-pilastered niche, which was to become a popular architectural device in later Indian architecture and throughout Buddhist Asia; this *stupa* might be a Symbolic type since it is impossible to determine whether relics had ever been interred in it. The 3'2" wide aisles have flat ceilings whereas the nave has a barrel-vaulted ceiling with stone ribs springing directly above the richly decorated triforium, which in turn rests on the colonnade. Small sculptures of stone lions were inserted above the triforium as if guarding the sacred sanctuary below; the aisle walls and ceilings were once painted with murals but in very fragmentary conditions. Compare between the facade of Ajanta [5.11] and Karla [5.8] will make clear that the great horseshoe *caitya*-arch has been significantly reduced in size while the repeating miniature *caitya*-arched and *vedika* motifs have also been entirely eliminated to be replaced with pilasters and image niches. The apex of this Ajanta *caitya*-arch is also decorated with a popular Mahayana motif or the *kirtimukha* (demon face) spouting jewelries, which is also

5.13. Exterior
c. 500-525 CE
Ajanta Cave 1, Ajanta- India

prevalent in Javanese *candi*s as the *kala-makara* (monster mask); the *mithuna*s in Karla have also been entirely replaced with Buddhas and *bodhisattva* images. The elimination of the verandah in this Ajanta *caityagriha*, which allows direct sunlight into the nave, and the introduction of a projecting portico are also two important features in the Mahayana caves. On either sides of the courtyard are cells with porticoed entries, most probably as secondary chapels for pilgrims or rooms for guardian monks; these could also be used as rest and preparation areas of the cave. The courtyard was once certainly closed off with a gate but no longer extant today; on the rock face to the right side of the left courtyard chapel is the carvings of a *naga* king and his queen. Compare between Ajanta 19 and the earlier *caityagriha*s in Kondivte [5.3], Bhaja [5.4-5.5], and Karla [5.7-5.9], the austere simplicity in the earlier Theravada caves have been substituted with sumptuous Mahayana decorations in Ajanta, particularly in the conspicuous Buddha and *bodhisattva* sculptures and murals that virtually cover all available surfaces of the cave. The Theravada caves in Ajanta (Cave 9, 10) have also been decorated as lavishly as the Mahayana caves; however they are typically restrained in appearance than the Mahayana caves. Despite the excessive embellishments, the Mahayana caves never appear distasteful as they are extremely refined and pleasing to the senses which could have strongly appealed to the worldly outlook of the Mahayanists and their followers than the emotionally controlled and ascetic predilection of the Theravadins. Furthermore the Mahayana caves, after experiencing a long architectural evolution from earlier caves, have finally managed to shake off the hangover of timber architecture so often present in the Theravada caves.

One of the most noticeable changes from the Theravada to Mahayana *lena*s is the dimensional increase in the latter; among the biggest of the Mahayana *lena*s is Ajanta 1 [5.12-5.13] which is completely stone like Cave 19; it is certainly most famous for its murals though it has no inscriptions. The plan is typical of a Mahayana *lena* having a nearly square central hall of about 63' deep x 65' wide with a flat ceiling; this hall is divided into 9'4" wide cloistered aisles by a colonnade of curved bracket columns similar to those in Cave 19. There are monks' cells on the three sides, each having a flat ceiling and a niche in the back for storage or display but without the stone beds as in the Theravada caves since the monks might have switched to portable wooden beds as monastic rules grew increasingly less stringent; these rectangular cells are approximately 8' wide x 10' deep and have 2' wide doorways. Compared to Theravada *lena*s like Bhaja 22 [5.6], Ajanta 1 appears highly organized and symmetrical with a large chapel in the back of about 18'6" wide x 20'2" deep that is preceded by an columned and pilastered antechamber; the main Sakyamuni image in this chapel is carved straight out of the rock and flanked possibly by Maitreya and Vajrapani. The 9' deep verandah of this cave has cells on both sides probably reserved for guardians and low-ranking monks or for pilgrims and the laity who might be providing the supporting services for the monks inside; in the center of the verandah a flat-roofed projecting portico as in Cave 19. The ceiling height of this cave is about 13' throughout, a slight increase from Bhaja 22; the tremendous depth of the cave created a space 88' wide x 114' deep from the verandah columns to the back of the image chapel, or about three times the size of Bhaja 22. Such a large space probably required stout pillars in the interior as a precaution against the potential collapse of the cave especially during earthquakes; the columned interior is another distinct characteristic of the Mahayana *lena*s compared to the empty interior of the Theravada *lena*s. All available surfaces of this cave have been sumptuously embellished with sculptures and murals of Buddhas and *bodhisattva*s as typical of the Mahayana caves; these are obviously different from the aniconic iconography in the Theravada caves.

B. Afghanistan, Central Asia, Turkistan

The region traditionally identified as Central Asia encompasses Afghanistan, the five Central Asian republics of Kazakhstan, Kyrgyzstan, Tajikistan, Uzbekistan, and

Turkmenistan as well as Turkistan (Chinese Xinjiang); Buddhism was one of the earliest religions in the area. Central Asia had long been inhabited by and under the influences of the Iranian-speaking peoples whose religion was Zoroastrianism, a Persian religion founded by Zoroaster in the seventh century BCE in Balkh in northwestern Afghanistan; another Iranian religion, Manichaeanism, founded in the third century CE was also very influential in the region. Since the earliest times the region had been repeatedly subjected to recurring invasions, cultural infiltration, and nomadic migrations and this resulted in some of the most culturally and ethnically diverse in Asia. In the past it was wedged between the three great ancient cultures and powers in Asia with the Chinese in the east, the Iranian (Persian) in the west, and the Indian in the south. By the fourth century BCE a completely new culture would be introduced from the West by the Greeks after the invasion of Alexander the Great and again from the Romans in the beginning of the Common Era owing much to the international trades along the Silk Road. Perhaps there were no other places in Asia where the artistic impacts of the Greeks and Romans had been felt stronger than in Gandhara and Bactria where their syncretic cultures have often been termed by scholars as an eastern extension of the Greco-Roman culture. Buddhism was first introduced to Gandhara and Afghanistan by Asoka in the third century BCE as several of his edicts were engraved on numerous boulders (Shahbazgarhi, Mansehra, Laghman, Pul-i-Darunta, Shar-i-Kuna, Kandahar) and on a pillar in Taxila. These edicts were written in many languages, specifically Aramaic, Greek, and Kharosthi, suggesting the cultural and ethnic diversity in the region. According to the Sri Lankan Mahavamsa, after the Third Buddhist Council in c. 249 BCE missionaries were dispatched throughout the known world including Kashmir and Gandhara, Aparantaka (probably southeastern Afghanistan, southeastern Pakistan/Sindh, and western India/Gujarat), and the *Yona* (Greek) country (possibly Bactria in northern Afghanistan). From Gandhara and Afghanistan Buddhism gradually spread as far as Turkmenistan, the other Central Asian countries, and Turkistan in the Kushans' rule, which controlled a vast empire encompassing much of Central Asia, Afghanistan, Pakistan, Turkistan, and northwestern India. The eleventh century CE Muslim historian Al-Biruni reported that Buddhist monasteries were present as far as Syria before the advent of Islam {Berzin 2003}. With the wane of the Kushan power and the ferocious Hephthalite persecutions around c. 500 CE, Buddhism began to decline in the region; when Hsuan-tsang passed through Samarkand (Uzbekistan) around c. 630 CE he noticed the two Buddhist monasteries in the city had been deserted and the local Zoroastrian population was hostile toward Buddhism. However, Buddhism would once again be revitalized with the rise of the Western Turks during Turki-Shahi Dynasty (552-744 CE) in Central Asia and Afghanistan alongwith the Chinese overlordship of the latter and Turkistan between 659-737 CE. The Korean monk Hui-chao again passed through Samarkand around c. 727 CE and saw only a monastery with a single monk in charge; however at Bamiyan in Afghanistan he observed Buddhism flourishing under the rule of an Iranian king {Dupree 1967: 58-59}. Thus the Buddhist golden ages in Central Asia were under the Kushans and later the Western Turks; in the subsequent centuries Afghanistan and Gandhara were ruled by the Hindu-Shahi Dynasty (744-1000 CE). With the arrival of Islam in the late seventh century CE and its final conversion of Afghanistan, Central Asia, and Turkistan in the eleventh century CE, the fate of Buddhism in the region was doomed.

A special note on the arts and architecture of Central Asia, there were certain thematic and stylistic commonalities between them that had been strongly influenced by Gandhara since the Kushan Dynasty. In many cases, sites like Gyaur-kala (Turkmenistan), Termez (Uzbekistan), and Miran (Turkistan) were as contemporary as those in Gandhara during the paramount Kushans' rule in the region. The perpetual impetus behind Gandhara arts and architecture might have been emanated from Bactria as this was originally a Greek colony where sites like Ai-khanum have been discovered containing probably the earliest Greek arts and architecture in Asia. In the early years, as already mentioned, Gandhara was an amalgamation of the Greco-Roman and Indian tradition with the latter as the driving force behind Buddhist arts and architecture; in the years after the Iranian invasions and occupation of Gandhara, Sassanian influences also permeated Gandhara's artistic milieu. Thus it was the Greco-Roman, Iranian, and Indian traditions that were the sources for Gandhara and Central Asian arts and architecture. The Chinese tradition also infiltrated Central Asia at a later time, generally from the seventh century CE on; however their spheres of influences were mainly limited to Turkistan. Furthermore, scholars have also observed the stylistic similarities in the murals across Central Asia, for examples the Miran sites (Turkistan) with Gandhara and Hadda (Afghanistan) as well as the cave murals at Bamiyan (Afghanistan), Kizil (Turkistan), and early Mogao caves {Rowland 1974: 33-44}{Rowland 1977: 185-198}; these would be considered in later discussions.

* * *

Afghanistan has been a country with a disputed and contradictory culture, at least before its conversion to Islam, that contains many different layers of history, arts, and architecture, which for the most parts have been written by foreigners through recurring migrations, invasions, and colonization since the earliest times. First came the Aryans (c. 1500-1200 BCE), then Persians (c. 558-326 BCE), Greeks (c. 326-90 BCE), Indians (c. 323-185 BCE), Sakas (c. 90 BCE-25 CE), Parthians (c. 25-50 BCE), Early Kushans (c. 50-241 CE), Sassanians (241-390 CE), Later/Kidara Kushans (390-454 CE), Hephthalites (454-552 CE), Western Turks or Turki-Shahi Dynasty (552-744 CE), and Hindu-Shahi Dynasty (744-1000 CE). After several centuries resisting with the Arabs, Afghanistan was finally converted to Islam in the eleventh century CE and it remains the dominant religion to this day. Several Indian scholars, for political reasons, maintained that Afghanistan culturally and geographically belonged to India since the earliest of times {Warikoo 2002: 56-57}. However historically the Persians were the first ruler of Afghanistan and Gandhara while archaeological data also confirm that Iranian influences (Persians, Parthians, Sassanians) were as strong as the Indian. In spite of it being the center of cultural and ethnic migrations in the past, Afghanistan presents many sites with surprisingly great antiquities such as Fullol (c. 2600-1700 BCE) in Bactria and Mundigak (c. 4000-1500 BCE) in Kandahar {Tissot 2006: 12-19}{Mizuno 1964: 194, 202-207}; the latter site shows possible cultural communications and trade with Iran and the Indus Civilization. The invasion of Alexander brought the Greeks and the Western Civilization to Central Asia in the fourth century BCE; the remaining Greeks founded their kingdom in Bactria north of the Hindu Kush along the Amu Darya (Oxus) River. A wealth of Greek artifacts have been uncovered at Ai-khanum, which has been identified as the Greek capital in Bactria, thus confirming the existence of a thriving Hellenistic culture from Alexander's time to the end of the Greek rule in Central Asia or between c. 326-90 BCE {Tissot 2006: 23-48}. The influence of this Hellenized culture in Bactria upon the Asoka arts in India, especially the Asoka pillars, has been proven to be a likely possibility. Another great site in Bactria is Dilberjin near Balkh which was occupied since the late Greek period to the early Kushans and Sassanians or between c. 189 BCE-390 CE {Tissot 2006: 73-93}. Among the findings are a huge citadel containing a Dioscuri Temple, possibly Zoroastrian, built in several stages and pseudo-Greek figurines as well as traces of Greek and Indian paintings of Siva and Parvati; these might be tentatively dated between c. 189 BCE-241 CE. A small chapel in the northeast corner of the Citadel has also been identified as a Zoroastrian temple, which contained some of the earliest paintings in Central Asia in the Sassanian Style and precursor of later Bamiyan murals; this temple and its murals can be tentatively dated after the Sassanian invasion or between c. 241-390 CE. Zoroastrian temples had probably been erected as far as Taxila in Gandhara such as the Jandial Temple described by John Marshall. Another well-known temple in Bactria was the multi-terraced Surkh Kotal erected by King Kanishka in the second century CE as his royal temple {Tissot 2006: 51-69}{Mizuno 1964: 215-221}. The presence of Buddhism in Bactria in the Early Kushan Dynasty can be inferred from the Buddhist sites of Lili-tepe, Cham Qala, Ahangaran, and Chaqalaq-tepe {Tissot 2006: 94-104}. Thus Bactria and Central Asia were probably the domains of Zoroastrianism but they also tolerated the presence of Buddhist monasteries, which were generously patronized by the local royal houses. The area south of the Hindu Kush had practically been dominated by the Gandhara culture since the early Kushans; Gandhara arts and architecture under the Kushans, whether in Afghanistan or Pakistan, showed identical workmanships albeit insignificant variations. The classic heavy-robed Gandhara Buddhas in Pakistan and the Afghan Buddhas from Shotorak and Paitava obviously had a common origin in Gandhara. Numerous Buddhist sites have been documented throughout Afghanistan dated in the early to late Kushans (c. 50-454 CE) mostly around the cities of Hadda, Kabul, Kapisa (Begram), Parvan, and Ghazni; the site of Bamiyan [5.14-5.17] was traditionally believed by many scholars to have been commenced during the Kushan Dynasty but it has now been ascribed to a much later date mainly between the fifth-seventh centuries CE. In Kapisa an important hoard of treasures has been unearthed containing numerous items like glass, ivory-bone carvings, lacquerware, plaster medallions, and bronze figurines, all exhibiting Greco-Roman, Indian, and even Chinese elements {Mizuno 1964: 208-214}{Tissot 2006: 134-305}. These have been dated between the first-second centuries CE, which coincided with the rise of the cosmopolitan Gandhara, and confirmed the site as a flourishing center of trade and cultural interactions with other parts of the world. Surprisingly a few Hindu temples have also been constructed in Afghanistan as at Tagao, Khair Khana, Skandar-tepe, and Gardez dated between the fifth-ninth centuries CE {Tissot 2006: 342, 355-358, 472}{Warikoo 2002: 23-28}; however, Hinduism was not as deep-rooted as Zoroastrianism or widespread like Buddhism in Afghanistan and Central Asia.

* * *

The five Central Asian countries together formed one of

the earliest civilized settlements in the world dated as early as the fifth millennium BCE; sites like Dzheytun and Anau in Turkmenistan have been dated around c. 5000 BCE {Frumkin 1970: 129-130}. In the sixth century BCE much of Central Asia, like Gandhara, had been subjected to the Persian rule which was to be vanquished by the Greeks in the late fourth century BCE. The remaining Greeks subsequently based their center of power in Bactria until they too were annihilated by repeated invasions from Central Asian tribes like the Sakas and the Kushans. The latter succeeded in ruling a vast empire encompassing much of Central Asia between the first-third centuries CE; between c. 241-454 CE Central Asia was under the Sassanians' control after they destroyed the Kushan power. The Hepthalites, who were well-known for their anti-Buddhist persecutions, displaced the powers of the Sassanians and Later/Kidara Kushans from Central Asia and ruled the region between 454-552 CE. It took the combined forces of the Western Turks and Sassanians to finally destroy the Hephthalites' power; the confederation of the Western Turks afterward controlled Central Asia, Afghanistan, and Turkistan between 552-659 CE. The Western Turks would in turn be defeated by the Chinese, whose paramount rule over the region centered in Kucha, Turkistan lasted between 659-737 CE. The defeat of the Chinese in the hands of the Arabs in 751 CE at the Battle of Talas effectively ended their power in Central Asia and Islam began to take hold in the region from then on.

Much of Central Asia before the 1990s CE were parts of the Soviet Union and had been thoroughly examined and documented by Russian archaeologists like Boris Litvinsky and Galina Pugachenkova; their works confirmed the existence of Buddhism in the region as early as the first century CE. It is well-known that Zoroastrianism was the predominant religion in Central Asia but there were other religions in the region with Buddhism as the most popular one followed by Hinduism, Manichaeanism, and Nestorian Christianity; monuments of the latter three religions were few and not as ubiquitous as those of Buddhism. The Nestorians, whose presence has been documented as far as Turkistan and western China, reportedly built a few Christian churches in the Chu Valley (Kyrgyzstan), and Samarkand and Khorezm (Uzbekistan). One of the Kyrgyz churches dated in the eighth century CE "combines a Syrian cross-cupola structure with a Central Asian open courtyard and "aivans" along the walls" {Frumkin 1970: 38, 79, 91}; the design recalls Type 9 in the Bamiyan caves **[5.15 (D)]** but the latter certainly had an earlier origin. Another contribution to Central Asian arts was the existence of the influential regional school of painting in Sogdiana (c. 400-760 CE), a region now encompassing eastern Uzbekistan and western Tajikistan. The murals of this Sogdian School mainly depict secular subjects with figures dressing in Central Asian attires; its sites are located in Tajikistan (Pandjikent) and Uzbekistan (Balalyk-tepe, Kara-tepe, Varakhsha, Afrasiab, Khalchayan) {Frumkin 1970: 54-127}. The reverberation of this influential school could be felt as far as Afghanistan in the murals of Bamiyan East Buddha Cave and Turkistan in the Kizil caves. Central Asia might have been exposed to Buddhism before the Common Era but it was not until the Kushan rule in the first century CE that it had a firm foothold in the region; in all likelihood, Buddhist arts and architecture in Central Asia and Turkistan did not flourish until the reign of Kanishka (r. 128-151 CE). Buddhist centers in the region continued to function until about c. 1000 CE when Central Asia converted to Islam; Buddhism in Turkmenistan and Uzbekistan probably perished earlier starting in the seventh century CE likely due to the competition with Zoroastrianism and the devastating impact of Islam later on. Literary testimonies from pilgrims like Fa-hsien and Hsuan-tsang in the fifth and seventh century CE respectively mentioned the predominance of the Mahasanghika and Sarvastivada in Central Asia; both were prominent Theravada sects with Mahayana inclination {Klimburg-Salter 1989: 51-53}. Numerous notable remains of Buddhist monastic sites have been unearthed in Turkmenistan (Gyaur-kala), Uzbekistan (Fayaz-tepe, Kara-tepe, Zar-tepe, Zang-tepe, Termez, Airtam, Dalverzin-tepe, Kuva), Tajikistan (Adzhina-tepe), Kyrgyzstan (Krasnarechka, Dzhul, Saryg, Suyab, and Ak-Beshim all in the Chu Valley, Novo Pakrovskoe, around Lake Issyk-Kul), and Kazakhstan (Semirechiya, Talas Valley) {Warikoo 2006: 40-56}{Berzin 2003}{Frumkin 1970: 37-39, 44, 63-66, 110-113, 115-116, 147-149}. Buddhist caves in the five Central Asian republics are virtually non-existent with a single exception of Kara-tepe (second-fourth centuries CE) in Uzbekistan.

* * *

Turkistan was an important trade and communication link between China, India, and the Western World and it had often been subjected to recurring military conquests from powerful neighbors who sought to control this strategic region. The territory, variously termed as Serindia, East Turkistan, Chinese Turkistan, or Xinjiang, was intermittently under the Huns' rule in the Early Han Dynasty (206 BCE-25 CE); these same Huns who earlier displayed the Yueh-chi tribe, or the Kushans, from the area in the second century BCE. Between 139-119 BCE, the Han emperor sent Zhang Qian (Chan Chien) to the western region to seek an alliance with the Yueh-chis against the Huns; the attempt failed but he succeeded in reaching Parthia, Bactria, Sogdiana, and Ferghana via Turkistan where he reported thirty-six kingdoms beyond the Chinese border. Between c. 73-300 CE Turkistan was subjected to the Chinese rule and it probably enjoyed a semi-independent status between c. 300-435 CE while recognizing the Chinese overlordship by paying annual tributes. Between 435-552 CE Turkistan was once again subjected to the control of various Chinese dynasties including Former Chin, Northern Liang, and Northern Wei; western Turkistani principalities like Khotan were reportedly under the Hephthalites' sway as reported by Sung-yun in the early sixth century CE {Bell 2000: 35}. The Western Turks succeeded in ruling Turkistan and Central Asia between 552-650 CE after displacing the Chinese and the Hephthalites from the region. The assertive Chinese Tang Dynasty subsequently destroyed both the Eastern Turks and Western Turks, in 650 CE and 659 CE respectively, and became the overlord of Central Asia ruling the vast region from their nucleus of power in Kucha, Turkistan. The Tibetans also managed to briefly rule Turkistan between 670-690 CE after defeating the Chinese and again between 781-847 CE when they occupied the strategic Chinese town of Dunhuang; the struggle between these two Central Asian superpowers did not cease until the peace treaties between them in 821-823 CE. The Uygurs found their own dynasty in Turkistan between c. 745-1000 CE and finally converted to Islam around c. 1000 CE; Buddhism perished in Turkistan from then on. Turkistan, and virtually the whole Asia, would be subjugated by the Mongols between 1227-1368 CE but it regained some measures of independence afterward but was once again re-conquered and annexed by Manchu China in 1759 CE {Klimburg-Salter 1989: 51-53} {Rowland 1974: 20-21}.

Turkistan, like Central Asia, was a region dominated by international and non-Chinese religions like Zoroastrianism, Manichaeanism, Nestorian Christianity, Hinduism, and certainly Buddhism; the latter remained predominant in the area since the Kushans' infiltration in the first century CE. A painting on wood of the Iranian god Rustam dated between the sixth-seventh centuries CE was found at Dandan-uilik in Khotan proving the existence of the Iranian religion in the region. Manichaeanism, another Iranian religion once adopted as the state religion of the Uygurs, was also present in Turkistan and especially strong in the vicinity of Turfan; numerous Manichean illuminated religious texts have been found at Khocho dated between the eighth-ninth centuries CE. At Khocho and Turfan, remains of a purportedly Nestorian Christian church was also discovered and among the ruins were fragments of murals depicting Christian worship themes all dated in the ninth century CE. The presence of Hinduism was also evident in Turkistan from the finds at Balawaste and Dandan-uilik both in Khotan; these were paintings of multi-limbed Hindu deities like Siva dated between the sixth-seventh centuries CE, possibly the oldest extant evidences of Indian Tantric paintings in Asia confirming an early presence of Tantricism outside India. According to some sources, Buddhism had been introduced to Khotan, and therefore Turkistan, as early as c. 59 BCE {Yamamoto 1990: 165}; evidently Buddhism was simultaneously established in Central Asia and Turkistan in the early Kushans from Margiana (Turkmenistan) in the west to Lou-lan (Turkistan) in the east. An-shih-kao, a Parthian prince and Buddhist monk from Margiana, went to China in 148 CE to propagate Buddhism and translate Theravada scriptures; another Parthian monk An-hsuan stayed in Luoyang, China in 181 CE to translate Mahayana *sutra*s there. The great Kucha monk-translator Kumarajiva spent the latter half of the fourth-early fifth centuries CE in China translating many Sanskrit Mahayana texts into Chinese. From the testimonies of Chinese pilgrims like Fa-hsien and Hsuan-tsang, the sites along the northern Silk Road were primarily Theravada whereas those in the southern Silk Road were predominantly Mahayana {Yamamoto 1990: 164-165} {Rowland 1974: 22}. Beginning in the seventh century CE, there were signs of Indian Tantricism and some of the earliest manifestations of the Vajrayana in Turkistan. A few murals in the Bezeklik caves (ninth-tenth centuries CE) in Turfan also contained some of the earliest Vajrayana murals in Asia; no Vajrayana paintings before the eleventh century CE survive in India to date.

The history of exploration in Turkistan by Western explorers has been well documented and often synonymous with Western imperialism and colonialism; taking advantage of the political weakness of the Chinese Qing Dynasty (1644-1911 CE) Europeans, Russians, Americans, and Japanese flocked into Turkistan between the late nineteenth-early twentieth centuries CE {Rowland 1974: 23-24}{MMA 1982: 24-46}{Le Coq 1929: 25-28}. Between 1875-1899 CE, Russians like Nikolai Prejevalsky, Albert Regel, and Dimitri Klementz first ventured in Turkistan and started collecting souvenirs from the numerous ruins in the area; next was restless Swedish Sven Hedin who explored Turkistan between 1895-1899 CE. Then there was the Hungarian-British Aurel Stein in Turkistan between 1900-1915 CE, the Germans led by Albert Grunwedel and Albert von Le Coq between 1902-1914 CE, the Japanese led by Count

Otani Kozui between 1902-1909 CE, and the French Paul Pelliot between 1906-1909 CE. These archaeologist-treasure hunters pillaged rare relics, mostly Buddhist, from the innumerable and unguarded ruins of Turkistan under the guises of archaeology and 'rescuing' artistic heritage from the bigoted Muslims; their activities would not have been successful had they not bribed the local officials as well as taking advantage of the poverty, lawlessness, and power vacuum in the region. The first German expedition carted away forty-six chests of 3,802 pounds, the second expedition 103 cases of 353 pounds, the third expedition 128 cases of 176 pounds, and the fourth expedition 156 cases of 176 pounds; these totaled to two tons of precious relics but unfortunately forty percent of these finds would forever be destroyed in World War II. The most heinous acts had been committed by Le Coq as he described in details how he sawed off a whole ancient mural from one of the Kizil caves:

> To begin with, the picture must be cut around with a very sharp knife…to the proper size for the packing-cases…Next, a hole must be made with the pickaxe in the wall at the side of the painting to make space to use the fox-tail saw…Then this painting is sawn out…

In spite of these unforgiving acts, gratefully he and other explorers have resurrected the ghostly relics of Buddhism from the ruins along the Silk Road, most of which had long been buried beneath the desert sands for centuries. However they also destroyed and uprooted the treasures from their original locations in the process and effectively cut them off from their glorious heritage. Ironically Le Coq's infamous treasure-hunting career was shamelessly knighted by the British monarchy as stated at the end of his notorious book 'Buried Treasures of Chinese Turkestan.'

Turkistan boasts a wealth of Buddhist arts (sculptures and paintings) and architecture (monasteries, temples, *stupa*s, structural *caityagriha*s, rock-hewn caves) that rival even those in Gandhara and other Central Asian countries {MMA 1982: 46-55}{Yamamoto 1990: 164-219}. Turkistani Buddhist arts fused diverse elements from Gandhara, Iran, India, and to a lesser extent China; Miran and Lou-lan were probably the earliest sites with surviving artifacts, many of which are paintings, dated between the third-early fourth centuries CE that show marked affinities with Gandhara. Virtually all pre-Islamic architecture in Turkistan is in dilapidated conditions but records from early European explorers have clearly portrayed the picture of a brilliant architectural past.

Buddhist sites in Turkistan are numerous from Kashgar in the west to Lou-lan near the edge of the Chinese proper; the monasteries at Miran were mostly mud-brick and often incorporated the *stupa*s and *pratimagriha*s into their plans. The site also had Miran also had many circular freestanding *caityagriha*s (Site 3, 5) in which the *stupa* was typically positioned in the center of a domed structure that created an interior *pradaksina* path between the *stupa* and the exterior wall. The *stupa* base was often covered with sculptural reliefs and the surrounding walls were completely covered with Buddhist murals; this type of structural circular *stupa*-temples obviously originated in the Indian *caityagriha*s [7.1]. Similar *stupa*-temples have also been found in Khocho Temple Y and A which also had rectangular plans and visitors could enter the interiors and perform *pradaksina* around the *stupa* in the back {Yamamoto 1990: 203}{MMA 1982: 54-55}. From the plans of the Miran temples, it may be conjectured that the *stupa* in the back and their surrounding walls could be several stories or tiers in height and certainly tower above the one-story anteroom; similar buildings might have already existed in Gandhara like the Jandial Temple in Taxila and this type was likely the precursor of the Indian Hindu *sikhara*. Another type, as in Khocho Temple Y, was a multi-terraced pyramidal *stupa* with four cardinal stairs in the base and image niches in the faces of the terraces {MMA 1982: 54-55}; it probably dated in the fifth century CE. The forerunner of this type can be sought in the terraced *stupa*s of Gandhara [6.16-6.18]; the Great Goose Pagoda in Xian, China also belongs to this category of *stupa*s. A unique and latest development of Turkistani *stupa*s was Karakhoja Stupa P and Yarkhoto (Chinese Jiaohe), each having a central tower *stupa* that was symmetrically surrounded by four groups of twenty-five smaller towers each as well as four cardinal stairs {Yamamoto 1990: 206-207}{TNM 1991: 34}; it might tentatively be dated in the sixth century CE. This design, which was certainly an elaborated version of the quincunxial plan of Gandhara [6.14] and India [4.4, 7.10-7.11], would be extremely influential in the subsequent temple architecture in Java and Kampuchea, Hindu and Buddhist alike, as in Candi Sewu [7.12] and the Bayon of Angkor Thom [7.16]. Another notable design was the quadrangular *vihara* plan of Karakhoja with a *stupa* in the center of its courtyard {Yamamoto 1990: 210}; it likely evolved from Gandhara monasteries [1.1] and dated at least in the seventh century CE. This plan would be employed in the Indian Pala monasteries like Vikramasila, Ratnagiri, and Somapura [4.8]. The three-tiered Miran Temple 1 had a square base plan, an octagonal middle tier with squinch arches in the corners, and a dome at the top {Yamamoto

1990: 169}; this type recalls Types 2 **[5.15 (C)]** and Type 3 **[5.15 (A, F)]** in the Bamiyan caves, which probably originated in Iran. Temple V at Karakhoja, the city identified with Hsuan-tsang's Kao-chang and the old Uygur capital between c. 326-1000 CE, probably dated in the sixth century CE; it was a tunnel-vaulted freestanding edifice similar to the design of Kizil Cave of the Painters **[5.18-5.19]** {Yamamoto 1990: 207-211}. This type also recalls the tunnel-vaulted temples prevalent in Bagan, Myanmar **[7.14]**; in fact Turkistan was the only known region anterior to Bagan, the exception being earlier Indian temples **[7.1]**, where the vault, arch, and dome had commonly been employed in architecture. Most Buddhist sites in Turkistan were usually constructed near the trading centers in the oases along the northern and southern Silk Road. The southern route, which was traversed by Fa-hsien on his departure and Hsuan-tsang on his return, has some of the earliest sites in Turkistan as in Khotan (Rawak, Balawaste, Ak-terek, Farhad-beg-yailaki, Khadalik), Keriya (Dandan-uilik), Niya, Endere, and Charkhlik (Miran, Lou-lan). These sites had later been deserted in favor of the northern route due to many reasons such as the desert encroachment, the desiccation and disappearance of oases and lakes, changes in the river courses and the mountain glaciers that fed them, and also the Tibetan menace from the south beginning in the seventh century CE. The northern Silk Road also has many important sites, most dated later than the southern ones, around Kashgar (Kanui, Mauri Tim), Maralbashi (Toquz Sarai, Tomshuk), Kucha (Duldur Aqur, Subashi, Siksin, Kirish, Kumtura, Achik-ilek), Korla (Shorchuk, Karashahr), and Turfan (Yarkhoto, Karakhoja, Khocho, Asana, Sengim Auz, Chikkan Kul, Murtuk). The scarcity of water, the dry and hot desert of Turkistan where trees, water, and hard rock were rare commodities had obviously inhibited the construction and sustenance of large freestanding stone monasteries compared to Gandhara. Cave monasteries were therefore a more practical alternative than structural ones and they had exclusively been constructed along the northern Silk Road, the route that Hsuan-tsang traveled on his departure. The most important groups of Turkistani caves along this route began chronologically from its western end in Kashgar (Uch-meravan, Sanxian), Kucha (Kizil **[5.18-5.19]**, Kumtura, Kirish, Shimshin, Mazar-bech, Kuzulgaha), Korla (Shorchuk), and Turfan (Bezeklik, Toyuk). The convergence of the Silk Road in its eastern end at Dunhuang, the traditional frontier town in old China, is the location of the great Chinese Mogao caves **[5.20-5.23]** which will be discussed later.

1. Bamiyan (mid third-seventh centuries CE) - Afghanistan

Afghanistan also built freestanding monasteries and *stupa*s like Gandhara but these were rarely documented unlike the preeminence of its surviving caves; Gandhara, however, has no rock-hewn caves, with the exception of the natural caves of Kashmir-Smast, whereas Afghanistan has numerous caves probably spanning from the Kushan Dynasty to the end of Buddhism or between the second-tenth centuries CE. The three principal groups of Afghan caves are situated near the Pakistani border (Jelalabad), north of the Hindu Kush (Nigar, Haibak), and south of the Hindu Kush (Bamiyan **[5.14-5.17]**, Kakrak, Fondukistan, Foladi). The monumental survey of the Bamiyan caves completed by the Japanese team of Kyoto University counted about 751 caves {Higuchi 1984: 3} and the total number of all Afghan caves could certainly be over 1,000 caves; all caves were once painted with exquisite murals but now in severely dilapidated conditions or totally destroyed. The Bamiyan caves, the most important group of all Afghan caves, form a conglomerate of contiguous groups of caves linking each other via internal passages and external stairs; a group typically consists of interconnected cells and there is no evidence of the division into distinct zones as in the Indian caves. The caves, which are connected with one another via internal linkages, may have a common vestibule, an assembly hall, public or private chapels, monk cells, and possibly pilgrim or guest areas with refectories for travelers since Bamiyan was a major reststop on the Silk Road at the foot of the Hindu Kush. The two great Buddha caves **[5.14-5.15]** and their towering statues were once the centerpieces at Bamiyan; their colossal dimensions must have provided great solace for pilgrims and travelers before and after their perilous journeys crossing the high passes of the Hindu Kush. The Kyoto University team has classified the Bamiyan caves into fifteen principal types based primarily on their plans {Higuchi 1984 Volume III-IV: 56-60, 96}.

(a) Square Plan (SP)
- Type 1: SP with a domed ceiling and a horizontal band **[5.14 (A, F)]**
- Type 1a (my addition): SP with a domed ceiling and a central platform (Cave J6 or #385)
- Type 2: SP with a domed ceiling and a tambour **[5.14 (B), 5.15 (C)]**
- Type 3: SP with squinch arches **[5.15 (A, F)]**
- Type 3a (my addition): SP with squinch arches and a central platform (Cave G or #51)
- Type 4: SP with a lantern ceiling **[5.14 (A), 5.16-5.17]**
- Type 5: SP with a flat ceiling **[5.14 (J)]**

(b) Octagonal Plan (OP)
- Type 6: OP with a domed ceiling and a horizontal band [5.15 (H)]
- Type 7: OP with a domed ceiling and a tambour [5.14 (C-E, G)]
- Type 8: OP with a lantern ceiling [5.15 (E)]
- Type 9: OP with a cross-vaulted ceiling [5.15 (D)]

(c) Circular Plan (CP)
- Type 10: CP with a domed ceiling [5.14 (H-I), 5.15 (G)]

(d) Rectangular Plan (RP)
- Type 11: RP with a flat ceiling (Cave #210)
- Type 12: RP with a vaulted ceiling (Cave #220)
- Type 13: RP with a lantern ceiling (Cave #38)
- Type 14: RP with a cross-vaulted ceiling (Cave #140)

(e) Niche Plan (NP)
- Type 15: NP with a vaulted ceiling [5.15 (B)]

Caves with elaborate designs having octagonal plans, multi-tiered niches, lantern and coffer ceilings, sculptures, etc. are in the minority; these were naturally reserved for important religious functions as image chapels, assembly halls, and possibly residences for high-ranking monks and probably the latest and certainly most sumptuously decorated at Bamiyan. The majority of the Bamiyan caves are Type 11-12 without paintings or sculptures; the Japanese team believed these were monks' quarters or storage facilities due to their plain appearances and probably among the earliest at Bamiyan {Higuchi 1984 Volume IV: 57}. Other possible functions for these simple caves might be for Buddhist education, areas for interactions between the *Sangha* and the laity, pilgrims' shelters, and reststops for travelers; it is not improbable to imagine the entrepreneurial monks charging travelers for overnight stays. Extant examples of Type 1a, 3a have ruined platforms in the center which scholars believed to be the bases for *stupa*s but they could be pedestals for Buddhist images or offering altars; this plan recalls Mogao Cave 285 [5.20]. Some of the unique features of Bamiyan and Afghan caves are:

- Lantern [5.16-5.17], squinch-arches, cross-vaulted and coffer ceilings (Cave XI or #605). The lantern ceiling, however, was not unique to Afghanistan as numerous examples have also been found throughout Central Asia, in the Eastern Han tombs in Yinan, Shandong (second century CE) and early Buddhist caves in China, Koguryo tombs in Korea (fourth-seventh centuries CE), Indian temples [7.2], Turkistan [5.18-5.19], and the Sumtsek in Alchi, Ladakh (c. 1200 CE); the earliest occurrence was reportedly in the Nisa Palace (third century BCE) in Ashkhabad, Turkmenistan {Higuchi 1984 Volume III-IV: fg. 98, 58}. The squinch-arched ceiling might have originated from Sassanian Iran as in the Firuzabad Palace (third century CE) {Higuchi 1984 Volume III-IV: fg. 97, 57}. A few scholars have suggested the Roman influence for the coffered ceiling and Byzantine Christian inspiration for the cross vault {Rowland 1977: 174}{Higuchi 1984 Volume III-IV: fg. 100, 69}. Roman architecture is certainly filled with examples of coffered ceilings such as the Pantheon, Basilica of Trajan, Basilica of Constantine, Bath of Caracalla, and Bath of Diocletion {Fletcher 1975: 288-289, 291-292, 296-297}{Higuchi 1984 Volume III: fg. 100}. However, the cross design also occurred in early Buddhist *stupa*s like Nagarjunakonda having cross-shaped walls in the interior of its dome {Sarkar 1966: fg. 23} and many Buddhist *stupa*s also have cross or cruciform plans [6.17-6.18].
- Octagonal and square plans [5.15 (A, C, F)]. The circle-and-square plan is believed by some scholars as derived from Byzantine and Sassanian (Iranian) architecture {Higuchi 1984 Volume IV: 59-60}; however, such plan already occurred earlier in Indian [6.1-6.2] and Gandhara *stupa*s [6.14-6.15]. The octagonal plan also occurred among early Indian *stupa* reliefs [7.4] {Agrawala 1968: fg. 21-22} and it became very popular in China as the ideal plan for its pagodas [6.22, 6.24].
- Caves with giant Buddha statues standing frontally in the entrances [5.14-5.15]. Many contemporary Indian caves also had large sculptures on their verandahs as in Ajanta and Kanheri; however none of their sculptures were placed frontally in the cave entrances in monumental scales as these Bamiyan Buddhas, which have unfortunately been destroyed by the Talibans in 2001 CE.
- Caves with *pradaksina* paths around Buddha images [5.14-5.15] and image shrines (Type 1a, 3a), which are typically located in the center or the back of the cave. The ability to circumambulate around and behind the objects of worship, usually a *stupa* or a cult image, had been a long tradition in the Indian *caityagriha*s [5.3, 7.1].

It is evident from the Japanese reports that Bamiyan had no *caityagriha*s or colonnaded *lena*s like the Indian caves; Type 10-12 were undoubtedly derived from the Indian cave and structural *caityagriha*s but they had no columns due to the soft rock common throughout Bamiyan and Central Asia. On the other hand, there are similarities between the Afghan and Indian caves in the profusion of decorations and the Buddhist iconographies of their sculptures and paintings. Some Bamiyan caves also had low benches and shallow depression in the center reminiscent of the Indian caves; the great Buddha caves [5.14-5.15] were conceptually derived from the Indian *vihara* plan [5.12] in the manner that the individual cells or caves were organized around an open space. Like the Indian caves, Bamiyan caves were also painted with exquisite murals; the ground of these murals consisted of an undercoat of clay, topped with coat of plaster, and lastly covered with a fine thin layer of white plaster before the execution of the paintings {Higuchi 1984 Volume IV: 60}.

The most preeminent group of all Afghan caves is none other than Bamiyan Cave 620 and 155 or Great (West) and Small (East) Buddha respectively [5.14-5.15]; numerous scholarly studies have been devoted to these famed caves and they have generated a great deal of controversies regarding the chronologies and styles of their murals and the two destroyed giant Buddha statues. Several archaeological teams from different countries have performed critical surveys and produced valuable publications on these sites including the French (1920s-1930s CE), Japanese (1960s-1970s CE), and the Afghan archaeologist Zemaryalai Tarzi who published his findings in 1977 CE. Bamiyan has sadly suffered the same misfortunes as other Buddhist sites elsewhere in Afghanistan during many of its iconoclastic Islamic regimes since the eleventh century CE as well as the incessant warfare in the country and recurring acts of vandalism in modern times by Afghans and foreigners. Corrosion caused by wind-blown particles, water seepage deteriorating the plaster, and natural disasters like earthquakes have also contributed to the damages. Parts of the Bamiyan caves had been seriously damaged during the Mongol attack by Genghis Khan in the thirteenth century CE and by the Indian Muslim Emperor Aurangzeb firing his canon at the Great Buddha destroying parts of its legs {Higuchi 1984 Volume IV: 69}. The damaged faces of the Buddhas could also be the works of the Muslims but others believed they once had been covered with masks; I will come back to this point later. The Indian ASI team conducted a major restoration on the statues between 1969-1977 CE which stabilized much of the weakened spots and extended their lifespan {Warikoo 2002: 142-149}. Unfortunately the Muslim Taliban regime destroyed these two tallest and oldest Gandhara-Styled Buddha statues in the world in March 2001 CE despite much protests and sanctions from the world community.

The taller West Buddha [5.14] once stood majestically at 180' high possibly on two lotus cushions inside a squarish 81' deep niche of a trefoil shape. There are ten caves of Type 1-2, 4-5, 7, 10 dug around the feet of the statue; these, the largest of which or Cave D measures 34' wide x 32' high, are larger in size than those below the East Buddha and many have image niches arranged in tiers. An internal stair begins in Cave H and continues up to the height of 65' where it ends in a dead-end opening looking out the valley below. It appears that the original plan intended to build a *pradaksina* path tunneling around the statue and passing around his head, as in the East Buddha cave, but this was abandoned halfway; possibly there was once an external wooden stair continuing upward from this point. Instead a new corridor was dug on the west side of the rock face to halfway up the cliff, which might have at one time been connected with external scaffolded stairs where pilgrims could ascend to the top and around the statue. Openings, projecting balconies, and scaffolds were probably built around the head for construction purposes or for closer viewings of Buddha's giant head and the splendid murals on the vault; a similar projecting balcony is also present in the Ajatasatru Cave of Kizil in Turkistan {Yamamoto 1990: 193}. The badly mutilated image now completely destroyed was in the Gandhara Style like the smaller East Buddha with patches of wavy hairs still visible on the head and it was cladded in a *sanghati* (a monk's robe) having multiple string-like folds; both Buddhas still retained the characteristic Gandhara pleats below the right hands, which further helped in determining their dates. On the construction method, the rough shape of the statue was first hewn out of the rock upon which wooden pegs would be driven into its body to be attached with ropes to serve as guides for shaping the folds of the *sanghati*. A layer of mud-straw mixture were then applied over the rope lines and the rock core and finally covered with a fine coat of lime-plaster; the image was lastly painted and gilded or possibly covered with brass and sparkling ornaments as described by Hsuan-tsang {Klimburg-Salter 1989: 87-89}. The caves below Buddha's feet must have been filled with sculptures and exquisite murals but only scanty patches remained; the statue and murals have unfortunately been destroyed by the Talibans. Unlike the trefoil niche of the West Buddha, the 125' high East Buddha [5.15] stood in a tapering arched niche having eight caves of Type 2-3, 6, 8-10, 15 hewn around its feet; these caves are significantly smaller and simpler than those of the West Buddha with few niches for images and therefore chronologically earlier. The great niche had a completely internal stair tunneling all the way to the head and around the statue but it did not have a projecting balcony at the head level like the West Buddha Cave. The construction technique was nearly identical as the latter except that here the plaster was applied directly over the

Part II. Architecture   Rock-hewn Cave . 123

roughly shaped rock core without the guiding ropes. The caves in Buddha's feet once contained images and completely covered with murals but they are all gone now; as in the West Buddha, this niche had also been embellished with murals but they were completely destroyed along-with the statue in 2001 CE.

Unlike the Indian caves, Afghan caves virtually had no inscriptions or records, which made the task of ascertaining their construction dates more difficult; scholars had to rely on stylistic comparisons between the caves and literary accounts from foreign pilgrims like Hsuan-tsang and Hui-chao for more accurate chronological reconstructions. Hsuan-tsang's travelogue described in great details about Bamiyan in c. 632 CE {Klimburg-Salter 1989: 77}{Dupree 1967: 55-57}:

> There are more than ten convents and more than 1,000 priests. They belong to the Little Vehicle [Hinayana], and follow the school of the Lokottaravadins.
> To the north-east of the royal city there is a mountain [Hindu Kush], on the declivity of which is placed a stone figure of Buddha, erect, in height of 140 or 150 feet. Its golden hues sparkle on every side, and its precious ornaments dazzle the eyes by their brightness [West Buddha].
> To the east of this spot there is a convent, which was built by a former king of the country. To the east of the convent there is a standing figure of Sakya Buddha, made of metallic stone [teou-shih], in height 100 feet. It has been cast in different parts and joined together, and thus placed in a completed form as it stands [East Buddha].
> To the east of the city twelve or thirteen li [3.7-4 miles] there is a convent, in which there is a figure of Buddha lying in a sleeping position, as when he attained Nirvana. The figure is in length about 100 feet or so [*Parinirvana* Buddha].

Another pilgrim, the Korean monk Hui-chao who passed through Bamiyan in c. 727 CE, described a still flourishing Buddhist culture in the area {Dupree 1967: 58-59}:

> The king is an Iranian...For clothing, the people wear shirts of cotton, cloaks of fur, coats of felt, etc....The kings, the chiefs, and the people are very devoted to the Three Jewels; monasteries and priests are in abundance; they practice the Great [Mahayana] and Little Vehicle [Hinayana or Theravada]...They clip their beards and cut their hair...

In the seventh century CE the country was still following

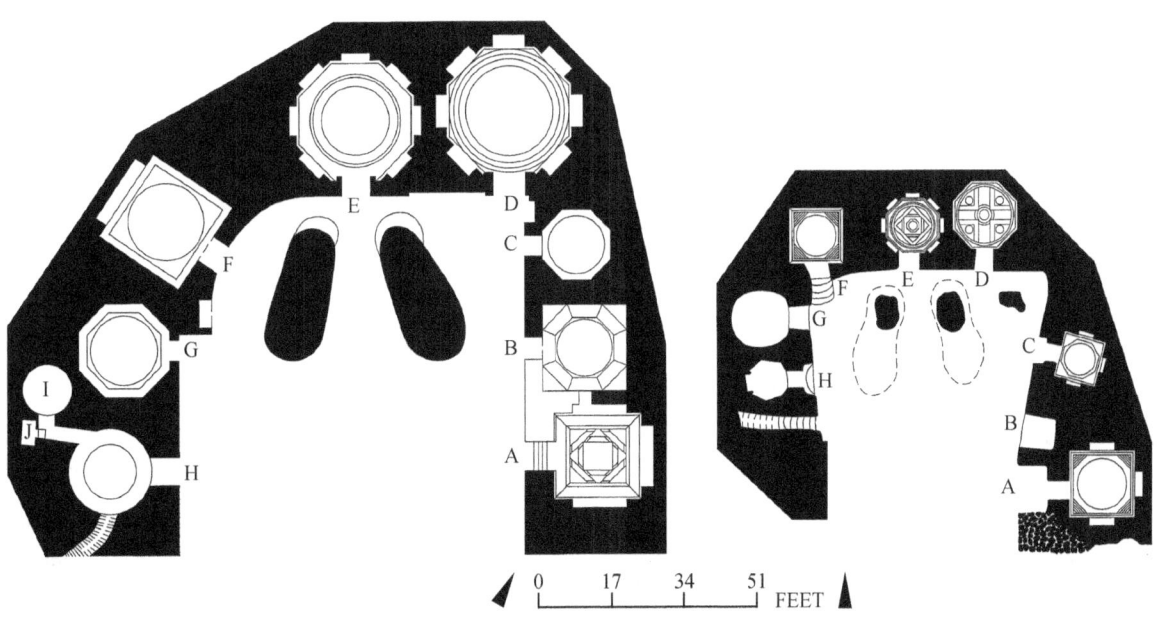

5.14. Great/West Buddha niche plan
c. 500-550 CE
Bamiyan Cave 620, Bamiyan- Afghanistan

5.15. Small/East Buddha niche plan
c. 400-450 CE
Bamiyan Cave 155, Bamiyan- Afghanistan

the Theravada and specifically the Lokottaravada, a sect with Mahayana inclination; however the rise of the Mahayana in Bamiyan in the eighth century CE was evident from Hui-chao's description. Hsuan-tsang also described a monastery in front of the caves and remains of a ruined *stupa* can still be recognizable in the vicinity. He also named the East Buddha as Sakyamuni and the western one simply as a Buddha; most importantly he mentioned a third *Parinirvana* (reclining) Buddha statue but there is no trace of it today. The East Buddha was described by Hsuan-tsang as 'made of metallic stone' and 'cast in different parts and joined together;' scholars have interpreted this description to mean the exposed parts (head, hands, feet) were once made of metal or brass {Klimburg-Salter 1989: 88}. The cutoff face of this Buddha, and the West Buddha, was believed by some as having been covered with a brass mask supported by a wooden armature in the same way as the hands {Klimburg-Salter 1989: 88-89, 205}. I disagree with this view since carving the Buddha image with a cutoff face, even when covered with a golden mask afterward, would appear to be a sacrilege and there is no logical explanation for this. The most acceptable hypotheses are the images might have been defaced by early Muslim invasions or damaged by natural fractures and subsequently rebuilt by the Buddhists with a mask to cover the damaged face; possibly only the hands and feet were once supported with wooden frameworks. Traces of red paint, which might have served as the primer for the gilding of the whole body, were found on the feet of the sculpture; patches of blue paint still adhered to the surfaces of the *sanghati* while the exposed parts of the image and foot cushions certainly also gilded. The West Buddha's left shoulder had multiple mortised holes that have been interpreted as wooden frameworks for the shoulder flames as typical of Afghan Buddha images such as those from Shotorak and Paitava {Klimburg-Salter 1989: 90}. There are a few publications that might help in visualizing the original appearances of these two giant Buddhas {Higuchi 1984 Volume III: fg. 103}{Tissot 2006: 309, 330, 339, 354}. Due to the probable presence of the shoulder flames, the West Buddha has been identified by scholars as Dipankara {Klimburg-Salter 1989: 115-117}; Benjamin Rowland also concluded that {Rowland 1974: 106}:

> We have observed that certain iconographic and stylistic elements in the 'Sassanian' cycles of painting and sculpture surrounding the 35-meter Buddha point to a date in the sixth and seventh centuries. Roughly the same period has been suggested for the more Indian style of the 53-meter colossus and the wall paintings of the giant niche. It is obvious, of course, that all of these schemes of decoration were completed before the visit of Hsuan-tsang in 622 [632 CE to be exact].

Deborah Klimburg-Salter believed that "probably the two extant colossal statues of the Buddha at Bamiyan can be dated no earlier than ca. A.D. 600" while the patron of these colossi could be the Western Turk ruler T'ung Shih-hu (r. 618-630 CE); she also claimed that the statues could have been completed 'within a few decades' in the latter's rule {Klimburg-Salter 1989: 90-92}. Lokesh Chandra adhered to the traditional dates of second-third centuries CE for the East Buddha and fourth-fifth centuries CE for the West Buddha; he also identified the East Buddha as Maitreya and West Buddha as Vairocana and believed the statues should date anterior to the colossi in the Chinese Yungang caves {Warikoo 2002: 1-10}. In my view, Sakyamuni and Dipankara would be more plausible for these Buddhas since Maitreya had often been depicted in a princely robe, wearing a crown, and sitting on a throne while Vairocana was a much later Vajrayana (Tantric) Buddha who was not known to have shoulder flames. Furthremore, there are important historical events that greatly facilitate the process of determining the chronology of the Bamiyan caves and the two Buddha colossi:

- Expansion on the Afghan side of Gandhara, as in the sites like Hadda, Shotorak, Paitava, and possibly Bamiyan, could be dated in the Later/Kidara Kushans between 390-454 CE.
- Numerous Gandhara monasteries were destroyed and Buddhism persecuted in the wake of the ferocious Hephthalite invasions around c. 500 CE; this possibly made cave monasteries a more attractive alternative to freestanding ones. However freestanding monasteries dotted the landscape of Gandhara between the first-fifth centuries CE whereas cave monasteries were virtually absent in Afghanistan during this period; thus the rise of the Afghan caves almost certainly occurred from the fifth century CE and after.
- The renaissance of cave construction in India in the fifth century CE possibly stimulated the cave construction activities in Afghanistan. The construction of the Indian caves and mural decorations peaked around c. 500 CE and realistically it should take several decades for Indian influences to appear in the Central Asian murals but certainly not until the mid seventh century CE as Klimburg-Salter suggested.
- The rise of the Turki-Shahis' tolerant regime in the latter half of the sixth century CE could be the height

of cave construction in Afghanistan.
- Changes in the international trade routes, which shifted further west to Bamiyan possibly after it had been selected as a new capital and the site for a new royal monastery of the Turki-Shahi Dynasty. Fa-hsien who pilgrimaged to India in the early fifth century CE did not mention or traveled to Bamiyan but Hsuan-tsang stopped over and described it as a flourishing international Buddhist center; thus conservatively Bamiyan likely flourished in the sixth century CE.
- The styles and proportions of the two Buddhas and the murals in their niches are discernibly different and do not appear to be of a homogeneous style; in all likelihood, the interval between them was certainly not less than fifty years. Thus it is not credible to suggest, as Klimburg-Salter did, that all three Buddhas and their murals were commenced between c. 600-630 CE.
- The Bamiyan caves and murals appear to have a parallel chronology as those of the Kizil caves which certainly also flourished more or less contemporarily between c. 500-700 CE, at least for their murals.

Stylistically the two Buddhas could not possibly date between the second-third centuries CE since their thin string-like folds were very close to the Shotorak and Paitava Buddhas and the Indian Gupta-Mathura-Styled Buddhas. The East Buddha, the earliest of the two, could be dated in the Later/Kidara Kushans or c. 400-450 CE while its caves and Central Asian-Styled murals showed the first wave of influences from Sassanian Iran or possibly the Sogdian School; these murals could have been painted slightly later around c. 450-550 CE when Iranian influences in Bamiyan were probably at its peak. These dates also satisfy the questions of Sassanian influences and the relationships between the Bamiyan Buddhas and contemporary Indian Gupta-Mathura Buddhas as well as the probable inspirations for the colossal Buddhas in the Chinese Yungang caves. The West Buddha was much more well-proportioned while its caves and murals also demonstrated a higher level of maturity than those of the East Buddha and therefore of a later date. This colossal statue was possibly carved between c. 500-550 CE and its Central Asian-Styled murals showed the second wave of influences from India and probably dated anywhere between c. 550-600 CE. The great reclining *Parinirvana* Buddha that Hsuan-tsang saw at Bamiyan (current location unknown) was probably completed between c. 550-600 CE or before his sojourn there in c. 630 CE. Another controversial issue was when precisely the Hephthalites' Buddhist persecutions occurred in Gandhara and whether these could have affected or prevented the construction of the Bamiyan caves. Some scholars believed the Hephthalites actually turned hostile toward the Buddhists in c. 515 CE {Berzin 2003}; Miharakula (r. 515-533 CE), who initiated this great persecution, was the son of Toramana who was active between c. 500-515 CE {Marshall 1951 Volume I: 397}. The former reportedly fought with the Indian King Bhanugupta in c. 511 CE and Yasodharman in c. 533 CE when he was finally defeated and expelled from India {Williams 1982: 101-102}. John Marshall held the view that the Hephthalites' ferocious persecutions of Buddhism happened between c. 475-500 CE since there were fragments of a burned birch-bark Buddhist manuscript found in Cell 29 of Jaulian Monastery possibly dated between c. 450-475 CE {Marshall 1951 Volume I: 387, 397}. Some scholars also proposed that the Hephthalites' Buddhist persecutions actually happened later between c. 520-552 CE since Sung-yun did not mentioned this famous calamity to Buddhism in his travelogue that dated about c. 520 CE and Hsuan-tsang mentioned it in c. 630 CE {Bell 2000: 35}. Above all, the Hephthalites' persecutions probably involved only the destruction of the prosperous monasteries in Gandhara and they might have left the small Buddhist community at Bamiyan unscathed.

Parts of Cave 733 **[5.16-5.17]** have been damaged but a substantial amount of architectural details remains in situ that enable the reconstruction of its original appearance; it is among the most sophisticated and elegant of all lantern-ceiling caves in Bamiyan. Architecturally the cave is divided into three tiers: (a) A plain base of 14' square, (b) the pilastered middle tier consists of two types of pilasters carved out of the rock that are set on a continuous shelf; of which Type 1 is multi-sided and plain similar to Bhaja 12 columns **[5.4-5.5]** and Sanchi *vedika* **[6.3-6.4]** while Type 2 is plain consisting of two adjoined circular shafts recalling the pillars of the Bharhut *torana*s **[6.7]** that are capped with a semi-rounded capital etched with the rope motif, and (c) the lantern ceiling has five tiers of diminishing squares of stone beams or planks alternately placed at forty-five degrees and is capped with a small dome at the top. The total height of this cave from the floor to the apex of the dome is about 17'10" in which the illusion of space is further enhanced due to the inclination of the walls and the gradual diminution of the lantern ceiling; the effect is comparable to sitting in a Central Asian yurt, which could be the actual prototype for this cave. The cave was originally covered with a plaster layer and might have been profusely painted like most Bamiyan caves but no murals remain today. What were the religious functions of this elegant cave? Its high

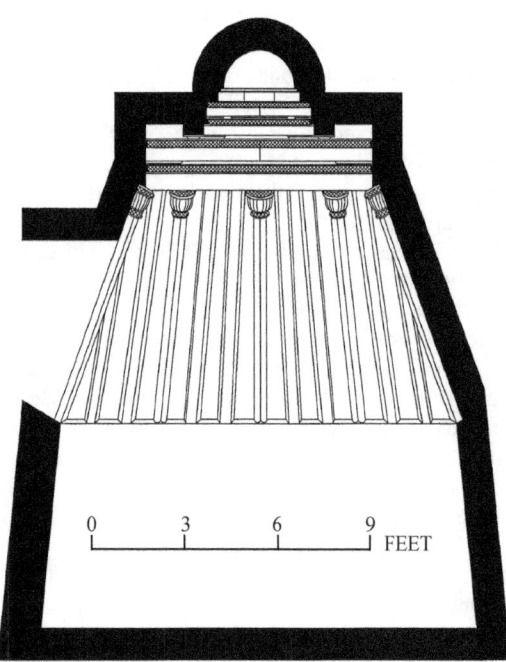

5.16. Section and ceiling plan
c. 400-450 CE
Bamiyan Cave 733 (XV), Bamiyan- Afghanistan

5.17. Interior (restored) (*above right*)
c. 400-450 CE
Bamiyan Cave 733 (XV), Bamiyan- Afghanistan

location above and to the west of the West Buddha seem more suitable as a meditation cell than a chapel and there were no image niches inside. Its floor level is 6'4" below the opening to the next cave (Group XIVa), which further substantiates the theory of its meditational function; it might also be the sleeping quarter for important or high-ranking monks. Stylistically, the presence or absence of the dome above the lantern ceiling is useful in determining the chronology for this type of caves; earlier lantern caves, like East Buddha Cave E **[5.15 (E)]**, had domes but later caves, like West Buddha Cave A **[5.14 (A)]**, had flat ceilings instead of domes. Cave 733 is also similar in design to the next door Cave XIVa but the latter has no dome and therefore of a later date; thus it dated somewhere between the East Buddha Cave E, Cave XIVa, and the West Buddha Cave A or c. 400-450 CE. As stated earlier, the lantern ceiling was common throughout Asia with Turkmenistan apparently as the earliest instance, followed by China, Korea, Turkistan, India, and Ladakh; Bamiyan Cave 733 was certainly among the most elegantly designed of its kind.

2. Kizil (fourth-seventh centuries CE) - Turkistan

Kizil **[5.18-5.19]** is an important group of caves near the oasis town of Kucha in Turkistan on the northern Silk Road that exhibits mostly Central Asian features without visible Chinese influences, which generally did not permeate the region until 650 CE when the Eastern Turks' power were destroyed by the Chinese. Hsuan-tsang mentioned Kizil in c. 629 CE as having about 100 monasteries and over 5,000 monks, all belonged to the Sarvastivada sect of the Theravada {Bell 2000: 51}. The third German expedition and their treasure-hunting entourage

Part II. Architecture   Rock-hewn Cave . 127

led by Albert Grunwedel and Albert von Le Coq stopped by Kizil where they camped for awhile; their 'archaeological' rampages destroyed many Kizil caves and their beautiful murals that had been existing for over a thousand years. The 236 Kizil caves are distributed across the cliff overlooking the Muzart River, which is a quiet and convenient location suitable for a contemplative lifestyle and close to the source of water as essential for the survival in the desert environment. Kizil and other Turkistani caves can be categorized into five basic types {MMA 1982: 50-53}{Howard 1991: 69-70}:

(a) A simple rectangular plan having a barrel-vaulted ceiling; this is essentially Bamiyan Type 12.
(b) A single monk cell or a group of cells of a rectangular plan arranged around an open passage with an entrance in one end; these cells have flat ceilings and are provided with built-in stone benches or hearths; the design is similar to the Indian cave *vihara*s [5.12] though without the interior column and Mogao Cave 285 [5.20].
(c) Two oblong chambers separated in between by a screen wall with openings for windows and a doorway; the ceiling in the rear chamber is barrel-vaulted whereas the anteroom ceiling is pyramidal. This type probably combined features of the Indian cave *vihara*s [5.12] and the pyramidal lantern ceiling in the Bamiyan caves [5.16-5.17].
(d) A square plan having a domed ceiling that was often provided with an image pedestal in the center and it is similar to Bamiyan Type 1, 1a [5.14 (A, F)] and Mogao Cave 285 [5.20]; this type might include an antechamber in front of the main rear chamber.
(e) This is the *stupa*-pillar cave and the most common of the Turkistani caves [5.18-5.19] consisting of an entry hall, an anteroom, and a rear chamber; the *stupa*-pillar in the back is an image shrine in the form of a shaft merging with the ceiling. A barrel-vaulted *pradaksina* path tunnels around and behind this shaft, which is a popular convention originated in the Indian *caityagriha*s [5.4-5.5]; the ceiling of the anteroom might be of a lantern, dome, or barrel vault. The image shaft here replaces the *stupa* reflecting the popularity of cult images in Central Asia; this type has been the Turkistani rendition of the Indian *caityagriha* and which counterparts can be found in Mogao [5.22] and Yungang caves in China.

Kizil Types (a-c), which likely served as monks' private quarters, arrangements for the laity, and the service or utility quarters, often have plain interiors whereas the assembly halls and image chapels or Type (d-e) are lavishly decorated with sculptures and murals.

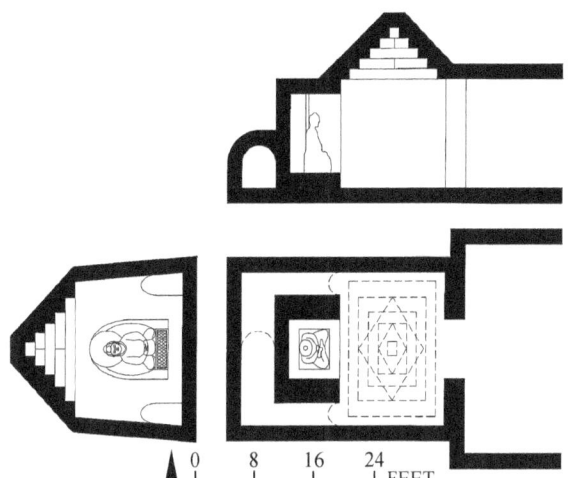

5.18. Sections and plan
c. 500-550 CE
Kizil Cave of the Painters, Kucha- Turkistan
Xinjiang- China

5.19. Interior
c. 500-550 CE
Kizil Cave of the Painters, Kucha- Turkistan
Xinjiang- China

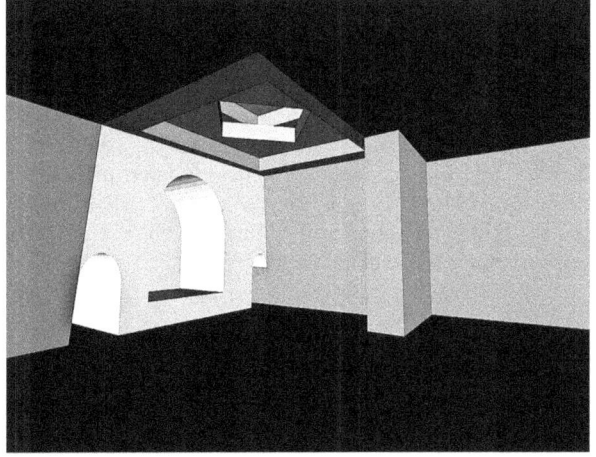

Parts of the ceiling in Kizil Cave of the Painters [5.18-5.19] have collapsed and its walls, possibly also the sculptures, stripped of the murals by the Germans. Architecturally, the cave is Type (e) with the side walls of the antechamber raking inward and terminating in a pyramidal lantern canopy as in Bamiyan Cave 733 [5.16-5.17]; unlike the latter this lantern ceiling is simpler without a dome or stone beams, a design more akin to the Chinese caves and Korean tombs than Central Asian ones. The missing image in the niche was likely Sakyamuni of polychrome clay or gilded wood like similar examples found in the nearby caves. The Kizil murals, as in other Turkistani caves, are certainly more captivating than the architecture or sculptures; they originally covered all the surfaces but only one extant mural remains depicting the visit of Indra and Pancasika the harp player to Buddha's cave to receive his teachings. Originally the right wall had nine scenes of Buddha preaching to an assembly of monks and kings with flying *deva*s hovering above; one of these flying figures placed his fingers in his mouth in the whistling gesture, a peculiar gesture first observed among the Bharhut relief panels **[7.6]**. Buddha's shoulders in this scene issued flames as in the Bamiyan murals while the figures were also provided with haloes regardless of their ranks and they dressed in Central Asian attires with mustaches and plaited hairs over the shoulders wearing triple-medallion crowns and flowing scarves; however, their plump physiques and dreamy eyes were clearly in the Indian convention as in the Ajanta murals. Out of a total of nine scenes on the left wall, there was a scene of a *naga* rising out of the sea to pay homage to Buddha and a group of five monks, which might be an unidentified *jataka*. The vaulted tunnel on the left side portrayed scenes of the war over Buddha's relics in Kushinagar and the subsequent peaceful division of his relics by Brahmin Drona; the right tunnel depicted an unidentified scene of a monk preaching to a group of reverential men under a blooming tree. The scenes in the murals were divided into panels by floral scroll bands in between and there was an inscription reading 'the painter Tutuka' that has been paleographically determined to be around c. 500 CE {Yamamoto 1990: 187}{MMA 1982: 56, pl. 14-15}; the style of the murals in this cave closely approximates those in the nearby caves.

C. China

As in India, Afghanistan, Central Asia, and Turkistan, Chinese Buddhists also devoted a great deal of time and resources to construct elaborate caves for their religion; in so many ways their caves were even more numerous, better preserved, and as much as splendid and grand as their foreign Buddhist counterparts. Chinese tolerance and religious piety toward Buddhism have historically shielded its monuments from destruction over the centuries compared to the dilapidated conditions of Central Asian caves which have utterly been decimated under the rules of the iconoclastic Muslims. The Chinese have also proven to be as much competent as the Indian Buddhists in rock-hewn cave construction. It is no accident that Buddhist caves were more popular in northern and western China than in the south due to the environmental constraints (hot and dry desert, etc.) and architectural expediency (abundance of soft rock for economical and speedy constructions ready materials like soft rocks without inordinate pre-construction processing which spare precious desert trees from being cut down, etc.). It is certain that the construction of Buddhist caves became widespread in China from the fifth century CE, which was as early or probably contemporary with Bamiyan and Kizil. It is estimated that there are between 1,000-2,000 Buddhist caves in China; the most important groups, according to their proper chronology, are Mogao **[5.20-5.23]**, Binglingsi, Maijishan, Yungang, Xumishan, Longmen, Kung-hsien, and Tienlongshan, all in northern China. There is an isolated group in southern China, the Dazu caves in Sichuan, but it dated much later than those in northern China. According Chinese historical records, the earliest Mogao caves were hewn out of the cliff in 366 CE but not a trace of these remains today; Binglingsi Cave 169 is the oldest dated cave in China with in situ inscriptions on its murals dated in 420 CE. Often Chinese caves have an entry foyer that might be sheltered with a traditional timber roof **[5.22]**; the main hall, where a main image chapel or a pillar-pagoda is located, is generally entered via an elongated doorway. The ceiling might be truncated pyramidal (dipper) **[5.20-5.21]**, flat, lantern, vaulted, coved at the cornices, or most popularly in the Chinese-styled gable ceiling. Variations of the Indian *vihara* and *caityagriha* designs can also be found in Chinese caves as in Mogao Cave 285 **[5.20-5.21]** and Cave 427 **[5.22-5.23]** respectively; the *vihara*-typed cave was likely used as meditational cells rather than actual living spaces for monks and nuns. The decorative schemes in Chinese caves typically involve polychrome clay sculptures, which generally occur in the Gansu caves, or stone sculptures wherever feasible as in the Longmen caves; the interior is typically completely covered with magnificent murals in brilliant colors while the floor might be laid in decorative tiles.

1. Mogao (366-1368 CE)

As a Chinese scholar rightly observed that "In China, grotto art is synonymous with religious art, or, even more precisely, Buddhist art" {DICR 1981: 3}. Certainly no other Chinese caves exemplify this than Mogao **[5.20-5.23]**, which no doubt is the Ajanta of all Chinese Buddhist caves. It is the oldest, best preserved, and the most magnificent of all Chinese caves; it also has the longest lifespan spanning over a millennium that contains virtually the whole artistic lineage of Chinese Buddhist sculptures and paintings. It is located about fifteen miles southeast of Dunhuang oasis in Gansu on the cliff running north-south along the Daquan River and facing Mount Sanwei on the opposite bank where the ruins of tall *stupa*s of past eminent monks still stand. Mogao is located in the vicinity of Dunhuang and the westernmost group of all Chinese caves in the traditional geo-political proper; the strategic location of the town is beyond question when it was founded in 111 BCE by Emperor Wudi (r. 140-87 BCE) of the Han Dynasty (206 BCE-220 CE) as one of the four garrisons guarding China's western frontier. Earlier between c. 139-119 BCE, Wudi sent Zhang Qian to the western countries to seek alliance with the Yueh-chis (Kushans) against a common enemy, the Huns; the ultimate outcome of these epic trips was the formation of what would later be known as the Silk Road as a vital trade and communication link between China and the western region. Dunhuang, its ancient name Shazhou and later renamed Dunhuang in 742 CE, was the traditional gateway to the west or east depending on your point of reference and the first border town inside the Chinese territory. Situated in a green oasis between the western end of the Gobi desert and the eastern end of the dreaded Taklamakan desert, it was the ideal halting place for all caravan traffics before embarking on the dangerous journey westward or after crossing the inhospitable desert wastelands before reaching the edge of the Chinese civilization. Trade tariffs, pilgrims, traders, etc. provided huge sources of income to the locals so that they could channel their abundant resources into the construction of the Mogao caves; similar situations have also been observed in the oases along the Silk Road like Kizil and Bamiyan. Remains of Han defensive walls, evidently extensions of the Great Wall, can still be found north of Dunhuang; over thirty-one miles to the northwest and southwest of the town are ruins of the two famed ancient Chinese border posts at Yumenguan and Yangquan respectively where all caravans entering and exiting China in the past must pass through these checkpoints. The central Silk Road once passed through Yumenguan and continued northwesterly passing through Lou-lan to the northern Silk Road in Kucha and meeting at Kashgar while the traffic along the southern Silk Road departed at Yangquan southward toward Miran and Khotan and finally meet the northern Silk Road also at Kashgar. The central road via Lou-lan had probably been abandoned as early as the fifth century CE, which was initially due to the demise of this ancient town and later the Tibetan threat from the south, in favor of an alternative or northern route through Hami and Turfan likely after the Chinese reconquered the western region in 650 CE. Dunhuang had been ruled by successive Chinese dynasties down to the Early Liang (313-376 CE) when the first Mogao caves were reputedly hewn; the Northern Liang (397-439 CE) did not establish in Dunhuang until 421 CE when the oldest surviving Mogao caves and murals were built. Constructions of new caves would subsequently be commenced by every ruling dynasty at Dunhuang, powerful local warlords and families, Chinese and foreign, including Northern Wei (439-535 CE), Western Wei (535-557 CE), Northern Zhou (557-581 CE), Sui (581-618 CE), Early Tang (618-781 CE), Middle Tang or Tibetan Occupation (781-847 CE), Zhang Yichao family or Late Tang (847-920 CE), Cao Yijin family or Song (920-1036 CE), Xi Xia (1036-1227 CE), and Yuan (1227-1368 CE). The Tibetans, Xi Xia (Tanguts), and Yuan (Mongols) were non-Chinese rulers who succeeded in occupying Dunhuang in several occasions; cave construction ceased after the Yuan Dynasty. With the rise of the Ming Dynasty (1368-1644 CE), Chinese borders with the western region were effectively sealed off, international trades completely halted, and the once fabled Silk Road fell into oblivion as the sea trade routes began its renaissance. The once restless town of Dunhuang and its legendary caves gradually faded from memory, fell into disrepair, and in danger from being buried by the desert sands. While some repairs and refurbishments of the caves had already happened in the Five Dynasties (907-960 CE), Song (960-1036 CE), and Xi Xia (1036-1227 CE), it was not until the Qing Dynasty (1644-1911 CE) reconquered Turkistan in 1715 CE that some real repairs were initiated at Mogao. Between 1962-1965 CE the Chinese government completely renovated the caves and opened them to the public.

Being an important center of Buddhism the bustling town of Dunhuang and certainly the Mogao caves had attracted a great number of distinguished monks, pilgrims, and devotees since the earliest days. Many foreign monks arrived in the town and translated Buddhist scriptures into Chinese before continued on to central China where they made great contributions to the propagation of Buddhism in the foreign land {Dutt 1962: 294-316} {Tan 1994: 46-48}. The Yueh-chi (Kushan) monk-translator Dhamaraksa (c. 231-308 CE), who was regarded as the 'Dunhuang Bodhisattva' and whose master was an Indian *thera*, was born in Dunhuang where he translated many *sutra*s into Chinese before moving on to Changan and Luoyang in the Chinese heartland. Other monk-translators also visited Dunhuang and briefly stayed here including the Indo-Kuchan Kumarajiva (c. 344-413 CE), the Indians Dharmamitra (c. 357-442 CE), Dharmaksema (c. 385-433 CE), Gunabhadra (c. 394-468 CE), and Dharmagupta who arrived in Dunhuang in 590 CE; these monks were instrumental in introducing the Mahayana into China. The famed Indian monk Amoghavajra (705-774 CE) and his master Vajrabodhi (671-741 CE), who brought the latest Vajrayana School to China, also passed through Dunhuang. Among the most famous Chinese monk-pilgrims who spent their time in Dunhuang were Fa-hsien (c. 377-422 CE), who stayed here for a month on his departure, and Hsuan-tsang (c. 600-664 CE), who received a grand reception in Dunhuang in c. 644 CE after his legendary sixteen-year sojourn in India. Another eminent Chinese monk in Dunhuang was Hongbian (died in c. 850 CE) active during the Tibetan occupation and whose Mogao Cave 17 was constructed in his honor with his lifelike statue inside. This was the infamous Library Cave where Aurel Stein and Paul Pelliot hauled cartloads of ancient manuscripts between 1907-1908 CE to Britain and France after bribing the Daoist priest Wang Yuanlu. From available records and artistic evidences in Dunhuang and Mogao, the site itself was Theravada in the early years (c. 366-600 CE) and turned predominantly Mahayana afterward; Vajrayana manifestations appeared sporadically as early as the seventh century CE but particularly strong in the Yuan caves owing to the heavy patronage for Tibetan Buddhism by the Mongol regime.

As in Turkistan, the disgraceful history of Western explorations and plunders of Mogao deserved special attention especially in the early twentieth century CE when China was severely weakened by European powers. The first Europeans to have visited Mogao in 1878 CE were Hungarians Szechenyi Bela, Lajos Loczy, and Gustav Kreitner and they produced the first engraved views of Mogao; they were followed by Russian Nikolai Prejevalsky in 1879 CE. Then the clouds of disaster began to swirl around Mogao after the Daoist priest Wang Yuanlu discovered the Library Cave in 1900 CE; the cave was originally built around c. 850 CE to commemorate the death of the chief monk Hongbian and housed his statue inside. It had been sealed up and covered with murals between c. 1002-1035 CE to hide the contents inside probably in anticipation of the gathering threats from Xi Xia or Islam. When opened nine hundred years later, the cave was packed from the floor to ceiling with thousands of manuscripts, *sutra*s, official documents, silk paintings, banners, etc., all dated before its closure. Having heard of the news and smelling treasures in the air, Aurel Stein rushed to Mogao in 1907 CE during his second expedition in the region. Seeing Wang Yuanlu was literally opening his illegal antique shop using the available treasures straight out of Mogao and seizing the power vacuum in the region as well as using bribing tactics, Aurel Stein was able to bring back to Britain thousands of priceless artifacts all from Library Cave 17. The shipment was packed in twenty-four crates of 7,000 old Buddhist manuscripts including the oldest printed book in the world dated in 868 CE and five crates of 500 paintings; he later returned in 1914 CE and again took away additional several hundred scrolls. More archaeologist-looters flocked to Mogao for their shares including Paul Pelliot's expedition in 1908 CE who took back to France over 6,000 scrolls, scriptures, etc.; next the Japanese Tachibana Zuicho and Yoshikawa Koichiro were able to obtain 300 scrolls from Wang Yuanlu's 'private collection' in 1911 CE. The Russian Sergei Oldenburg descended to Mogao between 1914-1915 CE and took away more scrolls, silk banner paintings, and removed some of the murals from the caves. About 900 White Russian soldiers fleeing the Bolsheviks between 1920-1921 CE took refuge inside the Mogao caves where they cooked and the soots blackened many murals; they also scribbled graffiti on the murals causing much damage. The American Langdon Warner of Harvard University arrived at Mogao between 1923-1924 CE with a clear hidden agenda of removing relics from the caves for the Fogg Art Museum; his disingenuous defenses of 'rescuing' and 'preserving' cultural relics were typical of earlier explorer-looters. He stripped the murals from some of the caves (Cave 324, 328) and removed a fine Early Tang statue from Cave 328; he returned again in 1925 CE but was prevented by the locals from taking away more precious relics. It must be remembered that these were not only eminent explorers but also renowned Buddhist scholars and eminent Orientalists; many of the removed items have unfortunately destroyed during World War II in Europe and some were later sold to different owners.

The history of Mogao is certainly well-known and it will briefly be reiterated here; according to many historical accounts, the first cave was hewn by Lezun (Yuezun) in 366 CE after having a vision of a thousand Buddhas. This story has been unanimously confirmed by various sources, for examples in Li Junxiu's book 'Fokan Ji' written during Empress Wu's reign (r. 684-704 CE), on a stele inscription 'Restoration of the Mogao Grottoes' in Cave 332 dated in 698 CE, in 'Mogaoku Ji' dated in 860 CE, and in an inscription in Cave 300 dated between c. 907-923 CE. However, a similar account in the 'Shachou Ti Chih' gave a slightly earlier date for the founding of Mogao which stated that the first cave was opened in 353 CE {Akiyama and Matsubara 1969 Volume II: 10-11, 14}{DICR 1981: 1, 3-4, 250}{Tan 1994: 29}; in any case, the first cave was undoubtedly hewn in the second half of the fourth century CE. Soon after the completion of Lezun's first cave, the monk Faliang from eastern China constructed another cave next to it; no descriptions have been given on the designs of these caves or their exact locations among the numerous Mogao caves, most likely they were very simple. There were about 1,000 caves hewn during the lifetime of Mogao but only 492 caves are still extant and well-preserved today; the majority of the Mogao caves were hewn during the prosperous Tang Dynasty {Tan 1994: 289-290}. The caves were evidently completed within a very short amount of time, for instance Cave 98 had been completed in one year and Cave 156 in three years {Whitfield 1995 Volume II: 327, 334}. The caves are grouped into two distinct zones; to the north are simple and undecorated caves and in the south are more elaborate and lavishly decorated caves. Roderick Whitfield suggested the northern zone might be workshops and craftsmen quarter {Whitfield 1995 Volume II: 267} but it could also be the service quarter catering to the laity, pilgrims and travelers, or reststops similar to Bamiyan. The southern zone was obviously the worship sector where the caves would be served as meditation halls [5.20-5.21], image chapels [5.22-5.23], and assembly halls. The monks' residential quarter might be located among the caves in the northern zone or off-site monasteries on the opposite bank of the Daquan River; in the medieval time there were reportedly about fifteen monasteries and nunneries near Mogao {Whitfield 2000: 123}. The caves generally had small dimensions in the early years and greatly expanded in the heyday of Mogao during the Tang Dynasty; they were originally accessed and linked with ladders and overhang walkways. Cave 268, 272, 275 are the oldest extant caves all constructed during the Northern Liang, which also contain the oldest murals and sculptures in Mogao. Caves 96 (695-705 CE), which has a nine-tiered facade, and Cave 130 (713-741 CE) were the biggest ones housing two colossal Buddhas, both believed to have depicted Maitreya; Cave 158 (781-847 CE) sheltered the biggest reclining *Parinirvana* Buddha statue in Mogao. A typical decorated cave consists of sculptures and murals; there are three basic types of caves {Tan 1994: 94-95}:

(a) This type [5.20-5.21] is a variation of the Indian *vihara* [5.12] having cells arranged around a central hall; these cells are small and likely for meditational purposes rather than as monks' actual habitation. There are three known caves of this type in Mogao in which Cave 268 is the earliest and Cave 285 is the largest and most developed of this type.

(b) This type [5.22-5.23] is the Chinese assimilation of the Indian *caityagriha* [5.10] and parallel examples can also be found in Kizil [5.18-5.19]; it first appeared in the early Northern Wei Dynasty like Cave 257 and generally phased out after the Sui Dynasty. Its dominant feature is a pillar-pagoda in the back with a *pradaksina* path around it and preceded by an intermediate space; a passageway links the main chamber with the verandah, which might have a timber roof as in traditional Chinese architecture supported by timber columns as in Mogao Cave 427.

(c) This is the most popular type of the Tang caves, which has a large image niche in the back that might be flanked by additional niches on the side walls. A large space in the center has a truncated pyramidal ceiling, which sometimes also occurs in the ceiling of the main niche, and Cave 272 is the oldest example of this type.

The abandonment of the pillar-pagoda plan Type (b) beginning in the Tang caves clearly reflected the growing symbolic and religious importance of cult images over the pagoda. A similar situation also occurred throughout the Buddhist world where the earlier popularity of the *stupa* gradually receded into the background and virtually eclipsed by the cult of images, all echoing the Mahayana ascendancy. The designs of the Mogao caves overall translate, transform, and fuse local and foreign elements. The popular lantern ceiling, which first appeared in the Northern Liang caves probably under Central Asian influences, was lastly abandoned in the late Sui Dynasty (c. 600 CE); this was concurrent with the introduction of Chinese architecture into the caves such as the gable ceiling. Initially sculptures of Sakyamuni, Maitreya, and Prabhutaratna were common with *bodhisattva*s painted on the side walls; gradually the latter would be molded in sculptural reliefs. Eventually a unified iconographical program consisting of sculptures of Ananda, Kasyapa, *lokapala*s, and *dvarapala*s became a standard group from the Sui caves on. Mogao sculptures were typically reinforced with vegetal matters and covered in clay to be painted or gilded. Northern Liang and early Northern Wei sculptures were particularly influenced by Gandhara and Turkistan; however these would gradually be Sinicized during the Western Wei and Northern Zhou Dynasty. Sui and Tang sculptures, though essentially exhibited a mature Chinese Style, displayed a cosmopolitan style reflecting a new wave of artistic penetration from Gupta India in their mannerist postures alongwith the plump, fleshy, and feminized figures. Cave 45 is the epitome of this elegant international Chinese Style and the acme of Buddhist sculptures in Mogao and China; a parallel development can also be observed in the Mogao murals.

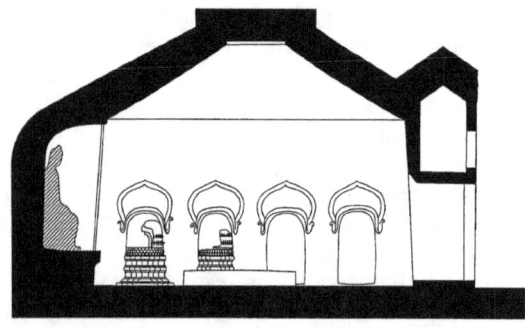

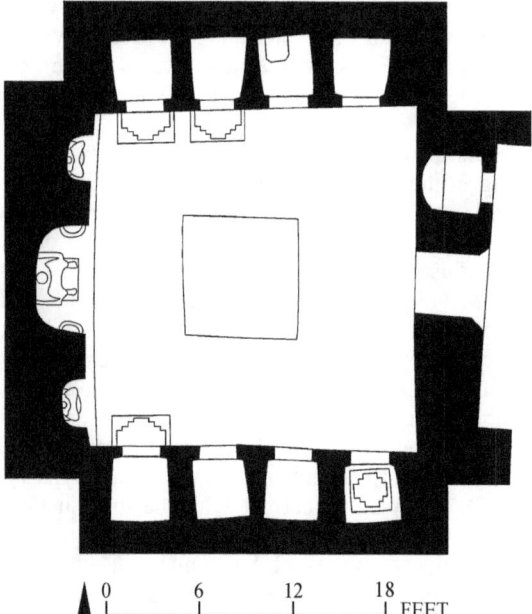

5.20. Section and plan
c. 525-539 CE
Mogao Cave 285, Dunhuang- China

5.21. Interior
c. 525-539 CE
Mogao Cave 285, Dunhuang- China

Cave 285 **[5.20-5.21]** is unique among the Mogao caves as an amalgamation of Indian, Central Asian, and Chinese elements; it also contains dated inscriptions and thus an important stylistic reference point in the establishment of the chronology of the Mogao caves as well as other Central Asian caves like Kizil and Bamiyan. Its design is a more developed form from the earlier Cave 249 with unmistaken influences from the Indian *vihara* plan **[5.12]**. Its plan is nearly square of 29' east-west x 30' north-south having two rows of eight cells in the north and south walls; each cell is nearly 3'8" square and 4'6" high, which likely functioned as meditational cells rather than monks' dwellings {Akiyama and Matsubara 1969 Volume II: 210}. The concept of a meditation cave, to my knowledge, had no parallel in India but it also occurred in Turkistani caves; this type, however, could be traced back to Gandhara in the meditational compartments of Takht-i-bahi **[4.2 (D)]**. The west wall of this cave has three niches elevated over 2' above the floor with the central 7'9" high niche containing three polychrome clay sculptures of Sakyamuni and two now damaged *bodhisattva* attendants in high reliefs; the two adjacent smaller niches contain sculptures of probably Sakyamuni's chief disciples Sariputra and Maudgalyayana. In the center of the cave is a 1' high offering platform; the cave is entered through a doorway in the east wall while a single cell outside and to the north of this doorway is Cave 287. The section reveals a 15' high space with slightly sloping walls on all sides and a truncated pyramidal ceiling; the molded lantern ceiling much popular in earlier Mogao caves has instead been painted here. The overall Central Asian feel of the cave is evident when compared with

5.22. Section and plan. c. 581-600 CE. Mogao Cave 427, Dunhuang- China

Bamiyan Cave 733 [5.16-5.17], in particular the sloping walls and lantern ceiling. Indian elements [5.8, 5.12] are also conspicuous such as the *vihara* plan and the ogival *caitya*-arches above the cell doorways which are otherwise painted or molded in the main niche. In the Yuan period, the openings of some of these cells were sealed off by *stupa*s while *stupa*s containing relics of eminent monks were also raised in some of the cells with traces of Yuan paintings still extant inside {Akiyama and Matsubara 1969 Volume II: 210}{Whitfield 1995 Volume II: 285}. The practice of placing relic *stupa*s inside monks' cells was extremely rare in India but certainly known in Gandhara monasteries as in Dharmarajika, Kalawan, and Mohra Moradu {Marshall 1951 Volume I: 361}. The murals in this cave, which cover all surfaces except the floor, are probably more interesting and eye-catching than the architecture or sculptures; here the Central Asian Style and Chinese Style were painted side by side likely within the same span of time. Scholars agreed that the earliest murals had been painted in the rear (west) wall, followed by the left (south) wall and the ceiling, and finally the right (north) wall and the entry (east) wall {Akiyama and

5.23. Interior
c. 581-600 CE
Mogao Cave 427, Dunhuang- China

Matsubara 1969 Volume II: 209- 211}{Whitfield 1995 Volume II: 284-287}{Tan 1994: 113-115}. The west mural is the only one painted in the red background and shows obvious Central Asian influences; the murals in the ceiling and other walls have white backgrounds and painted in the Chinese Style. The figures in the west mural dress in typical Central Asian attires, particularly the triple-medallion crowns and haloes, bare upper bodies and Indian *dhoti*s below, long flowing scarves, etc.; these are also present in Bamiyan and Kizil. Possible infiltration from Bamiyan may also be discerned in the way that the figures have been painted contiguously in medallions and the scenes of Surya riding the four-animal chariots driven by shielded figures. The murals on both sides of the main niche depict the four-armed Visnu and Siva alongwith lesser Hindu gods like Ganesh, Kumara, Indra, Brahma, and *lokapala*s, all are minor deities attending Buddha on his preaching occasions; a band of arabesque common in Indian architecture is below the niches. The ceiling has been painted to represent a giant jeweled canopy floating in the heavenly sky filled with twisted clouds, flying spirits, mythical beings, fantastic beasts, and monsters, which complement the pyramidal shape of the ceiling. The theme portrays ancient Chinese mythological themes, possibly Daoist, including the divine couple Fuxi and Nuwa, four celestial animals (tiger, phoenix, dragon, tortoise), Gods of Thunder, Lightning, Rain, etc. Above the intersection of the ceiling and walls are continuous rows of hermits meditating in mountain caves and below are knotted curtains reminiscent of the Bamiyan murals. The left wall is divided into three registers, of which the top one depicts continuous flying *apsara*s and the bottom register or dado contains large *yaksa*s; the middle register portrays in bird's-eye view perspective the Five Hundred Bandits Jataka who were converted by Buddha. The north wall is also divided into three registers with the uppermost one depicting Seven Manusi Buddhas and Prabhutaratna and donors, the middle showing Buddhas and *bodhisattva*s some in conversation, and the bottom or dado with large menacing *yaksa*s; the uppermost register contains inscriptions dated in 538 CE and 539 CE. The entry wall has two mural registers with the upper one depicting two large Buddhas' preaching scenes with donors below. In the center of each scene is Amitayus, or possibly Sakyamuni, surrounded by four Mahayana *bodhisattva*s (Avalokitesvara, Mahasthamaprapta, Aksayamati, Manjusri) and four Theravada *arhat*s (Ananda, Kasyapa, Sariputra, Maudgalyayana), according to Paul Pelliot's readings of the accompanied cartouches. Such a group of figures had already occurred in Gandhara in Kalawan Monastery that was subsequently transmitted to China via Central Asia and Turkistan {Marshall 1951 Volume I: 338}; the theme would be transformed into the paradise scenes extremely popular during the Tang Dynasty. The bottom register or dado of this wall originally depicted the usual *yaksa*s but were subsequently painted over by donor figures probably during the rule of the Cao Yijin family (920-1035 CE). The murals show noticeably stylistic and iconographical transitions, hence their chronology, from Central Asian Style (west wall) to Chinese Style (ceiling and remaining walls) and from the Theravada (south and north wall) to Mahayana themes (east wall). From the inscriptions on the north wall murals, Cave 285 apparently began some times before its completion in 539 CE; historical records indicated that Prince Dongyang arrived and ruled Dunhuang between 529-542 CE after the collapse of the Northern Wei Dynasty. Thus Phase II decorations (ceiling and south, north, east walls) were probably completed during his rule while Phase I (west wall) might have been finished shortly before his arrival. The lapse in time expectedly resulted in the stylistic changes in the murals, which were likely caused by the hiatus in patronage due to the dynastic change; thus a suitable date for this cave would be between c. 525-539 CE.

Cave 427 **[5.22-5.23]** is among the most developed of all Mogao and Chinese *caityagriha*s, which was constructed as the religious significance of the cult of images would gradually be superseded by the pillar-pagoda. Its foyer of 13'8" deep x 26'4" wide x 17'2" high is covered with a roof supported by a Chinese timber structure consisting of four columns and a four-tiered bracketing system. There are six standing reinforced polychrome clay guardians with the four *lokapala*s on the north and south walls trampling on demons and two *dvarapala*s in front of the entry doorway. These menacing statues, like the remaining sculptures inside, are typical of the Sui sculptures in their stunted bodies, large heads, and fleshy figures reflecting growing Indian influences and transition to the mature Tang Style; the murals behind these guardians and the Chinese roof were executed in 970 CE during a restoration. The short passageway into the main chamber has lifesize murals of Cao Yuanzhong and his wife, whose family ruled Dunhuang between c. 945-974 CE, and each is accompanied by his or her own entourage; a few travelers have left their graffiti here in 1103 CE, 1724 CE, 1736 CE, and 1743 CE {Whitfield 1995 Volume II: 293}. The main chamber of 40'9" deep x 28' wide has a pillar-pagoda in the back end; the eastern side of the pillar has a polychrome and gilded triad of a Buddha (Amitabha) and two *bodhisattvas* (Avalokitesvara and Mahasthamaprapta) all standing on lotus pedestals. These sculptures are the first ones in the round since the opening of Mogao; some has pearl medallions on their dresses, a popular motif in Central Asia {Whitfield 1995 Volume II: 294-295}. The remaining sides of the pillar are three groups of polychrome triads (Sakyamuni Buddha, Ananda, Kasyapa) inside *caitya*-arched niches 5'6" above the floor with dragon pilastered frames, which was obviously a Chinese substitute for the popular Indian *makara* niche; the spaces between the pillar and walls create a continuous *pradaksina* path having a 17'6" high flat ceiling. The anteroom in front of the pillar is a 21' high simulated Chinese gable roof, which completely replaces the lantern ceiling in the earlier caves that first appeared in Cave 254 in the early Northern Wei Dynasty; in the center of this space is the outline of an offering platform. On both sides of the gabled walls are two groups of polychrome and gilded triads of Buddhas and *bodhisattvas* also standing on lotus pedestals similar to the pillar group in style and iconography. Like the other Mogao caves, this one has also been completely painted with murals, in particular the Thousand Buddhas theme filling up the ceiling and walls of the main chamber **[5.23]**; there are two isolated panels of Buddha's preaching scenes on the north and south wall inserted in between. The pillar-pagoda and its niches also contain murals of *bodhisattva*s, acolytes, and attendants to complement the sculptures. The design of Cave 427 could be traced back to early Northern Wei caves like Mogao Cave 254 and Yungang caves; this type of pillar-pagoda cave is also common in Turkistani caves like Kizil **[5.18-5.19]** with its ultimate source in the Indian *caityagriha* **[5.10-5.11]**. The most conspicuous feature in Cave 427 is the huge standing statues that virtually eclipse the pillar-pagoda, which has obviously lost its religious importance with the rise of the Mahayana cult of images. The incorporation of monumental images into Buddhist caves also echoed a similar trend that had already been happening throughout Indian and Central Asian caves like Bamiyan **[5.14-5.15]**. The latest evolution in the Indian *caityagriha* after Mogao Cave 427 was the Seokguram cave **[5.24-5.25]** where the Buddha image finally and completely replaced the pagoda as the main object of worship and a preeminent feature in the cave.

D. Korea

1. Seokguram (751 CE, 760-790 CE)

Koreans attributed the beginning of their race and nation in 2333 BCE to the mythical being Tangun who was an offspring of the god and a bear-woman; a later legend told the story of ethnic and cultural migration from China to Korea led by Kija in the end of the Chinese Shang Dynasty (c. 1600-1100 BCE). By the second century BCE, there was a small country called Choson in the area of the Yalu River on the Chinese and Korean borderland; meanwhile the Mahan tribe inhabited in the south of the Korean peninsula while the Chinhan and Pyonhan tribes occupied in the east. In 108 BCE the Han Emperor Wudi conquered Choson and established four military outposts, one of which was Lo-lang (108 BCE-313 CE) with its territory encompassing much of modern North Korea from the Yalu River to the Taedong River. In 204 CE another Chinese colony called Tai-fang was set up below Lo-lang stretching from the Taedong River to the Han River. Eventually the Korean tribes consolidated and formed four separate states:
- Koguryo (37 BCE-668 CE) encompassed much of North Korea and Manchuria in China with its capitals near Paektu-san and Pyongyang.
- Paekche (18 BCE-660 CE) included the western half of South Korea with its capitals in Seoul, Kongju,

and Puyo.
- Silla (57 BCE-668 CE) encompassed much of the eastern half of South Korea with its capital in Kyongju.
- Karak/Kaya (42-562 CE) situated in the southeast of South Korea with its capital in Kimhae. Karak/Kaya was an insignificant state probably under the Japanese sway but culturally and possibly ethnically it was considered a part of the Korean sphere; it was absorbed into Silla in 562 CE {McCune 1962: 71}.

The three kingdoms of Koguryo, Paekche, and Silla were constantly fighting each other since the beginning while maintaining economic and cultural relations with the Chinese through Lo-lang and Tai-fang; the latter colonies would eventually be conquered by the increasingly powerful Koguryo and Paekche in 313 CE. The final showdown between the three states were in the late seventh century CE when Silla, while allying with the Chinese Tang Dynasty, succeeded in destroying Paekche in 660 CE and Koguryo in 668 CE and finally united the whole Korean peninsula into one nation; however this time Manchuria, which had been grappled from Koguryo by the Chinese since 645 CE, remained firmly in China. Unified Silla (668-935 CE), like the contemporary Chinese Tang Dynasty, was one of the most brilliant periods in Korean arts and architecture and also the height of Buddhism in Korea; the succeeding Koryo Dynasty (935-1392 CE) consolidated the Korean cultural identity after centuries under Chinese influences. Between 1234-1368 CE, Korea was subjected to repeated Mongol invasions and eventual subjugation; the Yi Dynasty (1392-1910 CE) was a long period which lasted until the early twentieth century CE when Korea was colonized by Japan between 1905-1945 CE.

As in China and other East Asian countries, the form of Buddhism that ultimately prevailed in the Korean peninsula was the Mahayana; geographical and political domains in the Korean peninsula actually determined the route of the Buddhist transmission to Korea. Koguryo, being in the north, received the first direct official introduction of Buddhism in 372 CE from the Former Qin (357-385 CE) of the Chinese Northern Dynasties (317-589 CE); Shundao and Ado were the Chinese monks during this missionary. In 375 CE a monastery Sumunsa along-with a Buddhist learning and preaching center were constructed for these Chinese monks and these were the first monasteries in Korea. Paekche, due to its control of the western sea coast as its northern land route was blocked by Koguryo, received the first Buddhist missionary in 384 CE via the sea route from the Eastern Jin (317-420 CE) of the Chinese Southern Dynasties (317-589 CE). This missionary was led by the Turkistani *thera* Marananda and in the next year monasteries were constructed on Hansan where ten Korean monks were ordained into the *Sangha*; Silla, where its land and sea access to China were both blocked by Koguryo and Paekche, received Buddhism at a later date than the other kingdoms. In 424 CE and later in the same century, the 'black monk' Mukhoja and the monk Ado, both from Koguryo, made the first Buddhist missionary to Silla but their effort was unsuccessful; it was not until 527 CE that Buddhism was officially accepted and the earliest documented Silla monastery Hungnyunsa (527-544 CE) was constructed immediately after this missionary. Around thirty monasteries were built in and around Silla capital at Kyongju between 527-668 CE; the period after the Korean unification by Silla saw the construction of another 173 monasteries in Korea.

The finds of Stone Age (c. 1000-200 BCE), Bronze and Iron Age (c. 200 BCE-0 CE) in Korea are meager with insignificant artistic values; the most notable ones are the megalithic dolmens and simple tombs of timber and other permanent materials {McCune 1962: 27-37}. The most significant impact on the Korean heritage was the Chinese culture, which had been absorbed by the Korean kingdoms over centuries of contacts with Lo-lang and to a lesser extent Tai-fang. The sophisticated levels of Lo-lang arts have been confirmed in over 10,000 tombs found all over North Korea and which recovered artifacts show remarkable achievements in the provincial Chinese style. Earlier tombs (c. 108 BCE-100 CE) were generally subterranean, single chamber, and primarily built of timber while later tombs (c. 100-313 CE) were typically constructed of brick on the ground level and had multiple chambers of flat and vaulted ceilings {Eckardt 1929: 43-44, Inset Plate H}{McCune 1962: 42-48}. An important highlight of Lo-lang arts is numerous Chinese paintings on lacquered baskets in Tomb of the Painted Basket (first-second centuries CE); faint traces of murals have also been found on the walls of this tomb. Tombs containing lacquer paintings have also been discovered throughout central and eastern China during the Han Dynasty such as the famous Mawangdui Tomb (early second century BCE) in Hunan, China. Native Koreans subsequently fused the Lo-lang Chinese culture with their own during the Three Kingdoms Period to broaden the boundaries of their cultural experiences and expression. Koguryo was particularly credited for creating the first Korean, or Sino-Korean, arts and architecture; it also had the highest technological achievements in tomb constructions with over 10,000 tombs discovered within its territory. Paekche and Silla also built tombs but these paled in comparisons to the splendor and larger dimensions of the Koguryo tombs. The latter, like Lo-lang tombs, were constructed for aristocrats and kings having vaulted main chambers but unlike the Lo-lang tombs they were stone (granite) and generally covered with murals in the interior; the plan of a Koguryo tomb typically consists of an anteroom connected with the main chamber, which houses the tomb, via a narrow corridor. There are basically two periods and types of Koguryo tombs: (a) The stepped pyramid tombs (c. 313-400 CE), which are mostly located on both sides of the Yalu River in Manchuria, China and North Korea and have no murals and (b) the tumulus tombs (c. 400-668 CE) are near the Yalu River inside Korea and in the vicinity of Pyongyang. The zenith of the Koguryo tombs was in the sixth century CE and these usually contained murals painted on a thin plaster layer or directly on a smoothened rock surfaces, which were painted in the Chinese color schemes and depicted mythical themes derived from Han and Northern Wei paintings. Early Buddhist influences can also be discerned in a few tombs having lotus, floral arabesque, and *purnaghata* (floral vase) motifs as well as images of Buddhas and *bodhisattva*s; the oldest Buddhist mural is in Jangcheonni Tomb Number 1 in Tonggu (fifth century CE). Another unique and conspicuous feature in many of these tombs is the lantern ceiling suggesting possible contacts and influences from Central Asia via China {Eckardt 1929: 42-45, Inset Plate H}{McCune 1962: 72-79}{Kang 2005: 12-13, 18}. In summary early Buddhist arts and architecture in Korea, as transmitted from China, can be divided into three phases:

- Phase I (c. 372-500 CE) belonged to pre-Northern Wei influences and surviving specimens are rare; a gilt bronze Buddha sculpture is among the earliest pieces dated in the fifth century CE {Kim and Lee 1974: pl. 32}.
- Phase II (c. 500-668 CE) was the beginning of Buddhist expansion in Korea which was mainly emanated from the Northern Wei Dynasty; the oldest extant pagodas in Korea in stone and brick dated in the sixth century CE. Buddhist sculptures like the pensive Maitreya, which first originated in Gandhara and India and later disseminated to China, were prevalent during this period; it would subsequently be exported to Japan where it also became immensely popular in the seventh century CE.
- Phase III (c. 668-935 CE) received the latest wave of influences from the Chinese Tang Dynasty; Korean Buddhist arts and architecture reached its peak magnificence in the eighth century CE, which also corresponded to the contemporary High Tang period in China.

Seokguram Cave [5.24-5.25] is situated in the Pulguksa Monastery, which was first founded in 535 CE, and the only Buddhist cave in Korea; it is certainly the last of the Indian *caityagriha*s and the farthest Buddhist cave beyond India since no man-made Buddhist caves exist in Japan. In the tenth year of King Kyongkok's reign (751 CE), Prime Minister Kim Taesong completely rebuilt and enlarged the monastery and during this occasion Seokguram was also inaugurated. The 'Memorabila of the Three Kingdoms' stated that *"Kim Dae-seong built Pulguksa Temple for his parents in this life and Seokbulsa Temple for his parents in his former life."* {Kang 2005: 245, footnote #31}. Seokbulsa or Temple of the Rock-Buddha was the original name of Seokguram or Temple of the Rock-Cave. It has been visited and written by several German scholars in the early twentieth century CE like Gottsche and Andreas Eckardt; the latter found a section of the dome already fell down when he visited the cave in 1913 CE. Soon the Japanese colonial government took notice and intermittently restored the cave between 1913-1923 CE; it was again restored by the Korean government in the 1960s CE when a roof was constructed over the entry vestibule to shelter the cave from the elements. Situated on the mountain high above Pulguksa and faces east-southeast, the cave is highly structured and elegant in design and execution; it was constructed entirely of coarse-grained granite. Originally it had an entry vestibule of 12'2" deep x 22'6" wide x 13'9" high now protected by a roof, the middle barrel-vaulted passage of 9'2" deep x 11'11" wide x 16'11" high, and the main domed chamber of 24'7" diameter rotunda x 30'1" high. This rotunda houses a huge Buddha image sitting on a lotus-petaled pedestal with the combined height of about 17'8"; it is positioned slightly off-center and further back that creates a 3' wide *pradaksina* path at the narrowest point in the back. The cupola is structurally secured by a lotus keystone at the apex and further reinforced with over 6' long key-blocks spaced alternately at regular intervals. This sacred rotunda is symbolically separated from the mundane world by an arched gateway of 22'1" high supported by two octagonal pillars of 2'8" wide each; structurally unlike the other Buddhist caves, Seokguram was not hewn directly out of the rock since the rotunda was constructed entirely of prefabricated slabs about 9'1" high x 1'2"-1'11" thick. With the exception of the main Buddha image, which is in the round, all other images are in high reliefs on slabs; originally their lips were painted red with faint traces of the pigment can still be seen. There are a total of thirty-eight extant sculpted figures, of which two have already been lost, including (1) a large Buddha in the round in the center, (29) large standing

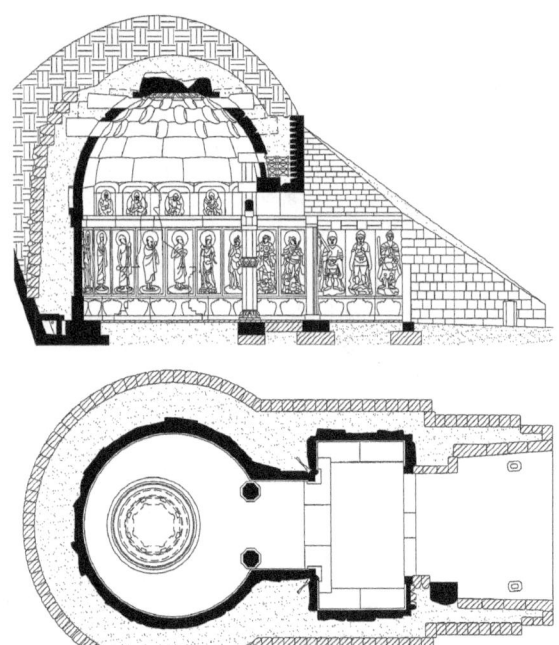

5.24. Section and plan
751, c. 760-790 CE
Gyeongju- Korea

5.25. Interior (*right*)
751, c. 760-790 CE
Gyeongju- Korea

figures in reliefs, and (8) small sitting statuettes in the niches at the spring of the dome or the triforium level. The iconographies of these figures have already been substantially established by scholars with the exception of a few figures that have not been properly identified {Moon 2000}{Kang 2005: 125-180}:

- Entry Hall
(2) *Dvarapala*s or door guardians.
(8) *Dharmapala*s or protectors of Buddha's teachings (*garuda, mahoraga, yaksa, deva*, dragon or *naga, gandharva, kinnara, asura*). These images are the only ones without halos on their heads due to their lower ranks in the Buddhist pantheon; the *garuda* is smaller than the other figures while the *asura* is incomplete. Scholars believed that these *dharmapala*s, due to their location originally exposed to the elements and of low-quality carvings, had been added some times in the late eighth century CE after the initial completion of the cave in 751 CE, which probably only included the rotunda and the middle passage serving as the entrance {Moon 2000: 11} {Kang 2005: 137-138}.
- Middle Passage
(4) *Lokapala*s or heavenly guardians of the four corners of the world (Dhartarastra, Vaisravana, Virupaksa, Virudhaka).
- Rotunda
(1) Sakyamuni.
(10) Sakyamuni's great disciples or *arhat*s (Sariputra, Maudgalyayana, Kasyapa, Subhuti, Purna, Anaruddha, Katyayana, Upali, Ragora, Ananda).
(2) Hindu *deva*s (Indra, Brahma) as audiences of Buddha's preaching sessions.
(3) Great Mahayana *bodhisattva*s (Avalokitesvara, Samantabhadra, Manjusri).
- Triforium Niches
(8) *Bodhisattva*s. A few have been tentatively identified by scholars as Avalokitesvara, Ksitigarbha, Sa-

mantabhadra, Manjusri, and Vimalakirti; one of the images is incomplete.

Scholars believed the sculptural program in the cave probably represented Buddha's preaching scene in the Lotus Sutra when he was being surrounded by an entourage of attendants and celestial beings; it might also portray one of Buddha's many preaching sessions on the Gijjhakuta {Kang 2005: 27-28, 172-175}. However it could also depict the moment when Sakyamuni attained *Bodhi* in Bodhgaya due to the fact that the statue displays the *bhumisparsa-mudra* or the earth-touching hand gesture associated with Sakyamuni in the eve of his enlightenment. He is also surrounded by images of Theravada *arhats* and Mahayana *bodhisattva*s suggesting the syncretism and harmonization of these two Buddhist schools. Early signs of the Vajrayana iconography in Korea are also present such as the Eleven-headed Avalokitesvara behind the Sakyamuni statue and the multi-armed *asura* in the entry hall; these, however, were isolated cases and should not necessarily signify the presence of the Vajrayana in contemporary Korea.

The basic configuration of the cave, which consists of the main chamber and an anteroom, could be traced back to the Lo-lang tombs; the two conspicuous gateway pillars of Seokguram were also an architectural adaptation of similar examples in the secular Tomb of the Twin Pillars (sixth century CE) in Koguryo {Eckardt 1929: Inset Plate H, fg. 70}{McCune 1962: fg. 47}. It is apparent that the style and iconography of the sculptures were strongly influenced by Tang China, in particular the High Tang as in Longmen Fengxiansi Cave (c. 672-675 CE) and Mogao Cave 45 (c. 713-755 CE). Architecturally, the design of Seokguram also suggests influences from the Indian caves, especially the classic plan of the Indian *caityagriha* [5.10-5.11] and earlier freestanding temples [7.1]. However, Seokguram essentially differs from the Indian *caityagriha* in the replacement of the *stupa* with Sakyamuni as the principal cult image; this reflected a transplantation of worshiping practices from the relic *stupa* to the image cult. The gradual abandonment of the *stupa* in favor of images in the Buddhist caves already happened in Elora (India), Bamiyan (Afghanistan), Kizil (Turkistan), and Mogao Cave 427 [5.22-5.23] (China); the *stupa* or pillar-pagoda would finally be replaced with images in the Chinese Tang caves and Seokguram. Interestingly, there is a strong resemblance between Seokguram and the Indian domed *stupa*s [6.3-6.4]. The arched gateway symbolically separating the outside world from the sacred chamber in Seokguram appears to replicate the Indian *torana* while its domed rotunda also recalls the Indian hemispherical dome; thus the form of Seokguram could be an architectural transformation and symbolic representation of the Indian *stupa*.

Chapter 6. Stupa

To a neophyte the Buddhist *stupa* (Sanskrit) or *thupa* (Pali), which is etymologically derived from '*stup*' meaning 'to heap,' may seem mystical and exotic due to its ancient beginning but it is undoubtedly the most important type of all Buddhist edifices with forms and functions originally developed in India. Since its first commencement on the Indian soil, the *stupa* is now found in virtually every Buddhist establishments throughout Asia where it is known in various local names as the *caitya* (Nepal), *dagaba* (Sri Lanka), *candi* (Indonesia), *zedi* or *chedi* (Southeast Asia), *chorten* (Tibet), and most popularly the *t'a* or pagoda (East Asia). The Kalingabodhi Jataka already listed three main types of *caitya*s (sacred shrines), which encompassed the *stupa*, including *sarika caitya* (relic shrines), *paribhagika caitya* (article and object shrines), and *uddesika caitya* (memorial shrines) {Krishan 1996: 14}. There are five principal types of Buddhist *stupa*s according to their forms and functions: Relic, Object, Commemorative, Symbolic, and Votive.

(a) Relic Stupa

It was originally commenced as the burial place for the corporal remains of Sakyamuni after his cremation in Kushinagar; in addition to Sakyamuni's, the remains of other Buddhas, his disciples, and even lay saints, including non-historical ones, have also been interred in *stupa*s. These are the reasons why the Relic Stupa is the most venerated of all Buddhist monuments; it is also the earliest and most common of all *stupa* types. Piprahwa **[6.1-6.2]** and Sanchi **[6.3-6.4]** are the exemplary examples of this type as they reportedly contained Sakyamuni's relics and those of his contemporary disciples and later Theravada saints.

(b) Object Stupa

Important items or personal belongings of Buddhas and his disciples, such as the begging bowls, monks' robes, Buddhist scriptures, etc. might also be interred in the *stupa*. Kesariya **[6.12]** is an excellent example of this type which reportedly encased Buddha's begging bowl; Hsuan-tsang also mentioned Kanishka Stupa **[6.18]** as having been originally erected over Buddhist scriptures inscribed on copper plates after the conclusion of the Fourth Buddhist Council {Handa 2001: 27}.

(c) Commemorative Stupa

*Stupa*s were also built to commemorate important events in the lives of Buddhas and his disciples. After his Buddhist conversion, Emperor Asoka made numerous pilgrimages to the places associated with Buddha's life and in each place he erected a *caitya* (holy shrine) to commemorate such event. The Asoka Stupa on the ground of the Mahabodhi Temple in Bodhgaya **[8.3]** and Dharmarajika Stupa in Sarnath **[8.5]** are typical examples of this type.

(d) Symbolic Stupa

A *stupa* was also specifically built to remind Buddhists the invisible presence of Buddhas and his *Dharma*. Type (a) had originally been constructed to inter Buddha's relics and it eventually became the ultimate symbol of Buddha's *Parinirvana*, whether with or without his relics inside, that reminded Buddhists of the impermanence of life so they must constantly strive for their own liberation; the *stupa*s in the Indian *caityagriha*s **[5.3]** and freestanding counterparts like Bairat **[7.1]** are common examples of this type. In the subsequent centuries, the architecture of the *stupa* increasingly embodied the complicated doctrines of different Buddhist schools. Thus architecturally, Borobudur **[6.28-6.29]** might symbolize the Three Worlds (*dhatu*) and the spiritual stages (*bhumi*) in a Mahayana *bodhisattva*'s career or a Vajrayana *mandala* in stone; Swayambhunath in Nepal **[6.37-6.38]** is another magnificent example representing the complex Vajrayana ideas in the form of an architectural *mandala*.

(e) Votive Stupa

These *stupa*s were often erected at important pilgrimage centers and monasteries by pilgrims or devout Buddhists to gain merits and better *karma*s or to commemorate their special visits; they are usually small and diverse in forms and often cluster around a large *stupa* or temple. *Stupa*s of this type can be found numerously on the grounds of major pilgrimage centers like Lumbini **[8.1]**, Bodhgaya **[8.3]**, Sarnath **[8.5]**, and Kushinagar **[8.7]**.

A classic Indian *stupa* **[6.3-6.4]** typically has a hemispherical dome that is continuously enclosed by an ornate railing (*vedika*) punctuated by elaborately carved gateways (*torana*) in the four cardinal points; these contain among the earliest religious and Buddhist arts in India commonly referred to as the *stupa* or Aniconic arts. Many *stupa*s in the neighboring countries of Gandhara (Pakistan) **[6.13]**, Sri Lanka, and Nepal **[6.37-6.38]** also retained the characteristic Indian dome and *vedika*s. In other countries, the large dome of the Indian *stupa* would gradually be reduced and the railing eliminated while its height was emphasized by stretching its body and elevating it on a high plinth; these were characteristics of a classic Gandhara *stupa* [6.15, 6.18]. The East Asian pagoda [6.20-6.21, 6.24-6.25], which was partly shaped by the native architectural tradition, also developed along the line of the Gandhara *stupa* in its emphasis on the verticality; it also delivered the most radical and certainly unique design of all *stupa* types in its complete elimination of the dome. Southeast Asian countries favor another important and widespread form of *stupa*s, the multi-terraced and galleried *stupa* mostly found in Indonesia [6.28-6.29], Myanmar [6.33-6.34], and Tibet [6.40-6.41]. Perhaps the most refined and innovative of all Buddhist *stupa*s is Shwedagon [6.35-6.36] in Myanmar in its ingenious design that fuses and harmonizes diverse architectural elements of a traditional *stupa*, particularly the multi-tiered and receding terraces with the dome, to create a unified and logical form. In most cases a *stupa* can not be entered as in the case of South [6.3-6.4] and Southeast Asian *stupa*s [6.28-6.29]; however in other types of *stupa*s such as the Tibetant *chorten* [6.40-6.41] and East Asian pagoda [6.20-6.21, 6.24-6.25], there are multiple entries in the cardinal points at the base where worshippers can enter the hollow interior and exit out the other sides. In the late stages of the Indian Buddhist *stupa*, its form would sometimes fuse features of the *stupa* and temple into a single structure or the *stupa*-temple as in the central temple of Somapura [4.8]. The architectural evolution of the Buddhist *stupa* in India and Asian countries also reflected the sectarian development in Buddhism itself. Thus early Indian *stupa*s like Bharhut [6.6-6.7] adhered to the original model of the *stupa* as a sepulchral monument dedicated to Buddha; its surfaces were exclusively decorated with narrative reliefs about Buddha's life and the *jataka*s as consistent with the orthodox Theravada worldviews. Overtime religious tenets and symbolisms grew increasingly complex that resulted in the corresponding modifications of the decorative schemes and architectural forms of the *stupa*. Thus Borobudur [6.28-6.32] might embody the Mahayana *bodhisattva* ideal of unrelenting religious quest for enlightenment by passing through the various stages of spiritual perfection or as an early form of a Vajrayana architectural *mandala*. Stupas like Swayambhunath [6.37-6.38] and Kumbum [6.40-6.41] represented the latest phase in the *stupa* symbolisms in their incorporation of highly abstract and esoteric Vajrayana concepts into the architecture which became the medium for expressing religious ideas such as ritualized consecration. In order to better understand the intricate relationships between the Indian *stupa* and their Asian derivatives, it is crucial to study its origin and development starting from the land of its conception in India.

A. Indian Stupa

Besides sharing similar religious functions with other Asian *stupa*s, the Indian *stupa* ultimately served as an architectural model for the latter in the process of experimenting with new forms and functions; architecturally, a fully developed Indian *stupa* [6.3-6.4] composes of four distinct components:

- Stone railing (*vedika*)
  A *vedika* punctuated by gateways (*torana*) in the four cardinal points encircles the *stupa* at the ground level to form a circumambulating *pradaksina* (religious procession) path; it functions like a physical barrier or a fence which symbolically separates the mundane from the spiritual world and guides pilgrims to the path around the *stupa* for the proper worship of the sacred relics inside. The practice of thrice clockwise circumambulation around the *stupa* base is explicitly mentioned in the Mahaparinirvanasutra; it is also an ancient Indian tradition of showing reverence to a *caitya*. This ground *vedika* consists of and is held together by vertical pillars (*stambha*) and horizontal bars (*suchi*) spaced at regular intervals and capped with a cope (*usnisa*); with the exceptions of the stair and *medhi vedika*s having two *suchi*s, all other *vedika*s have three *suchi*s. During the peak of its construction, Amaravati [6.9] even reportedly had four *suchi*s but this was a rare occurrence. The ground *vedika* is set directly into the ground on a stone footing whereas the stair, *medhi*, and *harmika vedika*s are inserted into stone mortised holes.

- Base (*medhi*)
  The Indian *medhi* or berm is generally circular whereas Gandhara *medhi*s are typically square; two flights of stairs (*sopana*) connecting with the upper terrace and *pradaksina* path project out of the *medhi* face usually in the main entrance. In later *stupa*s small shrines, offering platforms, or image chapels have also been placed in the four cardinal points in the base so pilgrims could leave their offerings. Obviously the substructure or foundation, which supports the *stupa* superstructure, must be of strong load-bearing materials like stone or brick to be able to bear the tremendous loads pressing down from above particularly from a massive solid dome.

- Dome (*anda*)
  The middle and conspicuous portion of the *stupa* is the dome (*anda*) usually truncated at the top where relics would be deposited into its core before being

closed by a heavy lid from the top; the bowl-shaped or hemispherical dome is very typical of Indian *stupa*s. The *medhi* typically wraps around the *anda* and forms an elevated terrace; it has a *vedika* to protect pilgrims from falling so they can safely perform *pradaksina* around the dome. In Indian *stupa*, the dome springs directly from the ground level whereas in a Gandhara *stupa* it is built directly upon the *medhi*, which in this case functions like a plinth.

- Crown (*harmika*)
  The crown (*harmika*) is a square balustrade (*harmika vedika*) on top of a truncated dome and which form replicates the ground *vedika*. In the center of the *harmika* is an umbrella shaft (*yasti-chattra*) consisting of a shaft (*yasti*) attached with several disc-like parasols (*chattra*) to be sunk into the *stupa* interior; the parasol was a traditional Indian emblem of royalty was transformed into the *yasti-chattra* to symbolically shelter relics of holy men like Buddha. In some Indian *stupa*s, especially Andhra ones like Amaravati [6.9], an octagonal post (*yupa*) replaced the *yasti-chattra*; in the subsequent centuries, a solidly tapering spire (*chattravali*) replaced the *yasti-chattra* in Sri Lanka [6.26-6.27], Indonesia [6.28-6.29], and Myanmar [6.33-6.36].

The terminologies above generally apply to Indian and Gandhara *stupa*s and so too is the word *stupa* itself; it is necessary to distinguish between a *stupa* versus a *caitya* since these terms have frequently been employed often interchangeably in Buddhist literature. A *caitya* generally encompasses any sanctified religious entity or edifice including religious shrines, temples, sacred trees, etc. as well as the *stupa*. A *stupa*, however, specifically refers to a special category of *caitya* that is erected exclusively for the purpose of interring holy relics, often bones and ashes of Buddha, his disciples, Buddhist monks, and even lay Buddhist saints. Many Buddhist edifices in the past have been known to display relics in the interior and these are strictly not *stupa*s but as temples; South Indian *stupa*s have at times been known as *caitya*s, the term which is more common in Southeast Asia.

The list of controversial theories regarding the origin of the Indian *stupa* is substantial and many are without factual bases; Benisti described in details these hypotheses as proposed by different scholars in which the alleged forerunners of the *stupa* included the primitive round hut, the hut for fire worship in Vedic Hinduism, Vedic caves, and Vedic tumulus tombs {Benisti 2003: 8-14}. Dome-shaped huts and caves were certainly numerous in the Vedic Period and in Buddha's time and many might have been adapted in Buddhist architecture as early as the third century BCE [7.1]; however, there are very few commonalities in either forms or functions with the Buddhist *stupa*. The tumulus burials of the Vedic Period came very close to the earliest Buddhist *stupa*s in forms but functionally the latter was a Buddhist creation to enshrine Buddha's relics where his followers could worship and gain good *karma*s; on the contrary, Hindu cremated ashes and remains were generally not buried as they were typically scattered into the various holy rivers throughout India. Possibly the form of the Vedic tumulus had initially been adapted as the Buddhist *stupa* but they essentially differed in religious functions and architectural symbolisms. B. M. Barua had a somewhat convincing theory about the Bramanical (Hindu) *smasana* or 'fire-altar tumulus,' as the transitional model to the Buddhist *stupa*; according to him the *smasana* chronologically evolved in different stages {Barua 1979 Book III: 12-20}:

(a) The remaining bones after cremation were buried in a tumulus.
(b) The deceased was ritually cremated alongwith a she-animal and their remains were in turn collected and buried in a pit with the bones arranged limb by limb and laid over with thirteen 1' bricks. The site was then covered up in a mound of earth in the shape of a four-cornered fire-altar of several feet high and enclosed with a stone barrier.
(c) The cremated remains were collected inside a vessel and buried in an earthen mound not unlike in (b).
(d) A jar containing the crusted remains of bones and ash were 'probably buried,' in Barua's own words, while the rituals of cremating the body with the she-animal in (b) were all dispensed with; this stage belonged to the Ramayana or late Epic Period.
(e) The Buddhist stage emerged when the relics would be interred in the *stupa* as described in the Mahaparinirvana-sutra.
(f) In the last stage, the relic jar of bones and ashes would be thrown into the river, obviously should be a holy one like the Ganga River.

The initial impression suggest superficial similarities between the Buddhist *stupa* and the *smasana* such as the ancient Indian tradition of cremating and collecting remains in a container to be buried in an earthen tumulus, which was to be protected by some forms of barriers, that is a *vedika*. However, there are is archaeological evidence confirming the use of a stone enclosure in this early stage and most likely a wooden one was employed prior to its conversion into stone. There are also vast incompatibilities between Buddhist and Brahmanical burial rituals; in the Buddhist case, the cremation and interment of sacred relics involving animal sacrifices would be sacrilegious whereas for the *Brahmana*s this was the norm. My main objection is Barua's placement of the Buddhist stage (e) within the evolution of the *smasana* and after (d) since the Buddhist *stupa* was not a replication of the Brahmanical *smasana* and apparently earlier than the Ramayana stage (d). There are no known *smasana*s in India compared to the prevalence of the Buddhist *stupa*s in early Indian architecture; possibly the only known depiction of a *smasana* was on the east *torana* of Sanchi Stupa I but this could be a primitive form of the Buddhist *stupa* {Oki and Ito 1991: pl. 80}.

1. Piprahwa Stupa (fifth-third centuries BCE)

Earliest Buddhist *stupa*s, besides those raised over the ashes of Buddha's disciples Sariputra, Maudgalyayana, and Ajnata-Kaundinya dated in Buddha's lifetime, were constructed over Buddha's ashes and remains immediately after his cremation in Kushinagar in 487 BCE; the Mahaparinirvana-sutra in the Digha-nikaya eloquently described this poignant episode in the last days of his life {Walshe 1995: 264-265, 275-277}. Before his impending death, Buddha recommended four types of distinguished individuals 'worthy of a *stupa*,' namely a Buddha or an *arhat*, a Pratyeka or private Buddha, a Buddha's disciple, and a *cakravartin*; according to him, those who paid their reverence to these *stupa*s would attain heaven after death. Buddha enjoined the responsibilities of arranging his funeral and building *stupa*s afterward to the Buddhist laity while the monks needed only concerning with their religious liberation {Walshe 1995: 264}; his wise injunction obviously intended to deter monks from involving in worldly affairs. Buddha not only instructed his followers to erect *stupa*s over his remains but also endorse the worship of these holy edifices; thus the practice of building *stupa*s, where lay followers could pay homage to and earn good *karma*s, was likely a Buddhist one. It was also due to the nature of Buddhism in which the pious devotion to a single charismatic leader would fuel the desire to construct lasting memorials for veneration; Buddha's cremation was led by the honorable Brahmin Drona and the remains were divided equally into eight portions for eight delegates with the urn and embers given to the remaining parties; *stupa*s would subsequently be constructed over the precious relics and the urn {Walshe 1995: 275-277}. The list of those arriving to claim their portions of Buddha's sacred earthly remains included:

(1) King Ajatasatru of Magadha Republic. A *stupa* was built for the relics in Rajagriha.
(2) The Licchavis of Vaishali. A *stupa* was built for the relics in Vaishali.
(3) The Sakyas of Kapilavastu. A *stupa* was built for the relics in Kapilavastu.
(4) The Bulayas of Allakappa. A *stupa* was built for the relics in Allakappa.
(5) The Koliyas of Ramagrama. A *stupa* was built for the relics in Ramagrama.
(6) The Mallas of Pava. A *stupa* was built for the relics in Pava.
(7) The Mallas of Kushinagar. A *stupa* was built for the relics in Kushinagar.
(8) Brahmin of Vethadipa. A *stupa* was built for the relics in Vethadipa.
(9) Brahmin Drona. A *stupa* was built for the urn used in dividing Buddha's relic at an unknown location.
(10) The Moriyas of Pippalavana. A *stupa* was built for the embers in Pippalavana.

The forms of these eminent Buddhist *stupa*s are not known and probably they were tumuli or mounds of natural earth or stones with *pradaksina* paths and perhaps they were also protected by wooden *vedika*s; there could be one or more entrances in the cardinal points and possibly offering platforms. These *stupa*s likely had circular plans like many extant early *stupa*s such as the one in Vaishali; circular plans were probably initially adopted to conform to the ritual of clockwise circumambulation around the funeral pyres in accordance to the ancient Indian rites. Buddha also suggested ways for his followers to pay homage to *stupa*s {Walshe 1995: 264}:

> And whoever lays wreaths or puts sweet perfumes and colours there with a devout heart, will reap benefit and happiness for a long time.

This became an enduring Buddhist tradition and in later *stupa*s the flower garlands would be translated into actual sculptural motifs on the *anda* of the *stupa* **[6.9]**; Stupa Number 9 was special since it had not been erected over Buddha's remains but over the urn used in the division of Buddha's relics and it was obviously the first Object *stupa* in India.

What were the fates of these ten Buddhist *stupa*s? Up to now only five have been tentatively identified by archaeologists, namely Rajagriha, Vaishali, Ramagrama, Kushinagar, and Kapilavastu; among these the Kapilavastu Stupa has proven to be the most controversial since its exact location, or more precisely the location of the city of Kapilavastu where the *stupa* was first constructed, is still a disputed question. Many scholars believe that Piprahwa Stupa **[6.1-6.2]** and its surroundings at Ganwaria on the Indian side of the Indo-Nepalese border are the site of the Kapilavastu Stupa and the original location

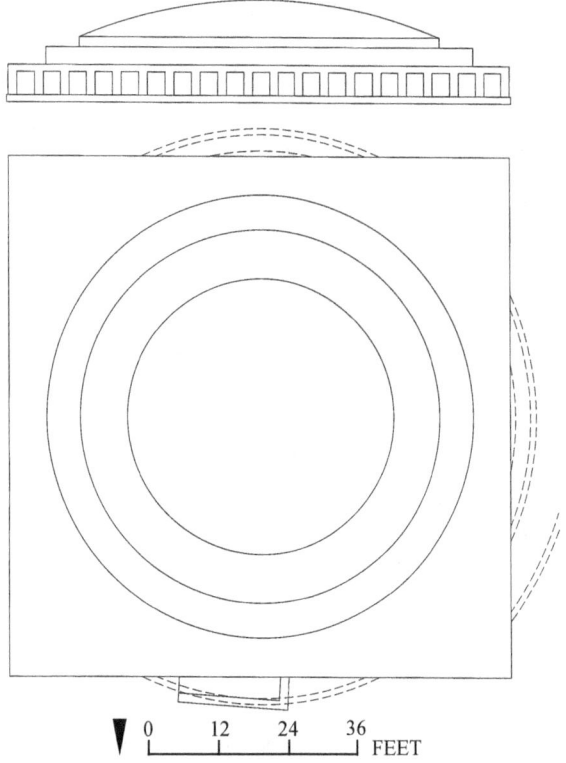

6.1. Elevation (restored) and top view (*above*)
Fifth-third centuries BCE
Third century BCE (final form)
Piprahwa- India

6.2. Stupa view (*below*)
Fifth-third centuries BCE
Third century BCE (final form)
Piprahwa- India

of the Sakya capital where Prince Siddhartha Gautama spent twenty-nine years of his youth before becoming a Buddha. As controversial as Piprahwa and Ganwaria are, nevertheless this *stupa*, and the Vaishali Stupa, is certainly among the oldest extant *stupa*s in India; it was probably constructed in three phases {Srivastava: 48-51}:

- Phase I (fifth century BCE): A tumulus of natural earth, which reportedly contained Buddha's sacred relics, was encased inside two brick chambers; a brick retaining wall also enclosed the base of the *stupa* and *pradaksina* paths were also paved with bricks during this phase.
- Phase II (fourth century BCE): The *stupa* was expanded by essentially enveloping the earlier remains while the two-tiered flattened dome was also covered in bricks; more relics were deposited into the *stupa* core during this phase.
- Phase III (third century BCE): A square plinth wrapped around the circular structure of the earlier phases and an offering platform(s) was also provided which is still visible on the plan; another relic casket was deposited into the *stupa* during this phase.

In its current dimensions Piprahwa has an 86' square base rising nearly 20' high from the ground level to the apex of its tumulus-shaped dome. The *stupa* was constructed entirely of brick with rectangular recesses spaced at regular intervals on each face where offering lamps might be left by worshipers that would create a magical religious atmosphere filled with lights; similar lamp niches were also reported on the *medhi* of Bharhut **[6.6]**. The square base of Piprahwa seemed to echo the four-cornered *smasana* already mentioned earlier but it was discontinued in subsequent Indian *stupa*s **[6.3, 6.6, 6.9]**, all had circular *medhi*s; the square-and-circular plan would later be adopted in Gandhara *stupa*s **[6.15]**. The two circular brick *pradaksina* paths in the *stupa* base might also have been encircled by wooden *vedika*s and there are several features suggesting an early date for this *stupa*; its low tumulus-shaped dome is clearly different from later *stupa*s which typically have hemispherical domes. It lacks other elements like a *vedika*, *torana*s, *harmika*, and *yasti-chattra* that are the hallmark features of later *stupa*s; moreover, it is completely plain and without inscriptions. Lastly, the Phase II relic vase has an early Brahmi inscription dated in the fourth century BCE that reads, "This receptacle of relics of the Blessed Buddha of the Sakyas is the pious gift of the brothers of Sukuti, jointly with their sisters, with their sons and wives" {Srivastava 1986: 59}.

Is this *stupa* one of the original ten *stupa*s and the Kapilavastu Stupa? To answer this question the original site of Kapilavastu must first be firmly established. From current archaeological data, scholars have proposed two possible sites for Kapilavastu, namely Tilaurakot in Nepal and Piprahwa-Ganwaria in India; these sites have been arousing much political passion and archaeological controversies because Tilaurakot lies in Nepal and Piprahwa-Ganwaria is situated inside India. The governments of both countries clearly want to claim their site as the original Kapilavastu and Buddha's homeland for the obvious reasons of economic gains from tourism, fame as an eminent site, race, territory, and history. Putting disputes aside, there are some important historical facts on Kapilavastu that are valuable in its identification and for accurate assessments of the historical validity of Tilaurakot and Piprahwa-Ganwaria.

a. Kapilavastu

Its location was mentioned in Buddhist scriptures as southeast of Sravasti, the capital of Kosala which was then the overlord of the Sakya Republic; to the north of Kapilavastu was the Himalaya while Lumbini, the birthplace of Buddha, lied to the east. Originally Kapilavastu was likely a provincial town with a small population lying on the bank of a lake or near Bhagirathi River as water would be essential for any city; it was surrounded by a moat and a city wall with gates in the cardinal directions. The city was probably divided into administrative, commercial, and residential quarters wherein its buildings would be ranked according to their size, class, and proximity to the king's quarter in the center {Schumann 1989: 13-21, 24-29}. Buddhist literature also told the story of the vengeful King Virudhaka of Kosala annihilating Sakya Republic in c. 485 BCE and by the mid fifth century BCE North India were united under the Magadha Empire; by this time Sakya had long ceased to exist and the Sakyas dispersed and absorbed into the larger North Indian population. In c. 249 BCE Emperor Asoka made a pilgrimage to Buddha's natal town and erected three stone pillars in Lumbini, Nigali Sagar, and Gotihawa that are still extant but in damaged conditions (Chapter 3); these historical pillars further help in narrowing the original territory of Sakya and Kapilavastu. Fa-hsien and Hsuan-tsang, who were celebrated Chinese pilgrim-monks traveling to India between 399-414 CE and 629-645 CE respectively, reportedly visited Kapilavastu and also documented in details what they saw; the Kapilavastus they visited were already in ruins with numerous *stupa*s and monasteries constructed in the city center over earlier foundations. According to Fa-hsien, Kapilavastu was fifty li (15 1/2 miles) west of Lumbini and about 1 1/2 *yojana*s (13 1/2 miles) northeast of Krakucchanda Buddha Stupa and pillar. According to Hsuan-tsang, Kapilavastu was thirty li (9 3/10 miles) northwest of the Arrow Spring and fifty li (15 1/2 miles) north of Krakucchanda Buddha Stupa and pillar; the Arrow Spring was situated eighty to ninety li (24 9/10 to twenty-eight miles) southwest of Lumbini {Deeg 2003: 46-55, 73-77}. Both travelers' descriptions slightly agreed on the current locations of Lumbini and Krakucchanda Buddha Stupa and pillar relative to Kapilavastu and that Lumbini was easterly of Kapilavastu while Krakucchanda Buddha Stupa and pillar was southerly of Kapilavastu.

b. Tilaurakot {Rijal 1996: 21-48}

The site of Tilaurakot is about 17 2/5 miles west-northwest of Lumbini and close to the Banganga River inside Nepal; its extensive ruins have been excavated by P.C. Mukherji, Japanese archaeologists, and a host of other Indian and Nepalese archaeologists around the turn of the twentieth century CE. The large site is surrounded by an ancient moat with several levels of occupation possibly dating back to the Vedic Period with brick foundations still in fine conditions. Plans of the ruins appear closer to administrative (palaces) than religious types (monasteries, *stupa*s, temples); these have also been confirmed by Fa-hsien's and Hsuan-tsang's testimonies. Tumulus-shaped brick *stupa*s have also been discovered northeast of the site at Dhamnihawa; a host of other uncovered items include pre-Maurya and Maurya figurines, potteries, and a large quantity of coins like silver punch-marked coins dated in the fifth century BCE. One terracotta token has an inscription reading 'Token of the Sakyas;' northeast of Tilaurakot in Nigali Sagar lies the Asoka pillar originally erected for Kanakamuni Buddha and another one in the southwest in Gotihawa reputedly constructed for Krakucchanda Buddha.

c. Piprahwa-Ganwaria {Srivastava 1986: 38-79}

This site is about nine miles south-southwest of Lumbini inside India encompassing two distinct sites or zones of Piprahwa and Ganwaria about 3/5 mile apart. Piprahwa boasts an impressive *stupa* already discussed [6.1-6.2], monasteries with plans identical to Nalanda *vihara*s [4.4], and temples; the site is clearly a monastic settlement and, together with Ganwaria, is relatively small compared with the larger Tilaurakot. There are two important items recovered from Piprahwa that have significantly elevated its status as one of the contenders for the original Kapilavastu. The first is a relic vase containing a Brahmi inscription dated in the fourth century BCE already mentioned earlier and the second is twenty-two sealings with inscriptions stated 'the Community of Buddhist Monks of Kapilavastu.' Besides the seals and sealings, the list of the discovered items at Piprahwa-Ganwaria also includes coins, terracotta figurines, sculptures, potteries, personal items, and rudimentary weapons; like Tilaurakot, habitational stratifications of Piprahwa-Ganwaria can also be dated back in the Vedic Period.

Regarding the scholarly controversies on Tilaurakot and Piprahwa-Ganwaria, P.C. Mukherji maintained that Tilaurakot was the original Kapilavastu {Rijal 1996: 2, 85} while Vincent Smith concluded that "Piprava is the Kapilavastu of Fa-hsien, whereas the city around Tilaura-Kot is the Kapilavastu of Hsuan-tsang" {Rijal 1996: 64}. Krishna Srivastava, obviously an ardent Indian supporter of Ganwaria-Piprahwa as the original site of Kapilavastu, believed Ganwaria was the central township of Kapilavastu while Piprahwa was the monastic site and its *stupa* as one of the first ten *stupa*s that originally interred Buddha's original relics {Srivastava: 61}. Hans Schumann further distinguished the Old Kapilavastu as Buddha's youthful home before its annihilation in the hands of the Kosala King Virudhaka and Piprahwa-Ganwaria as the New Kapilavastu after its destruction and the new settlement for the remnants of the Sakyas {Schumann 1989: 17}. Above all, does either Tilaurakot or Ganwaria-Piprahwa match the profile of the original site of Kapilavastu as listed in (a)? In terms of geography, location, historical descriptions, and extant archaeological remains Tilaurakot is clearly a better match as the original site of Kapilvastu than Ganwaria-Piprahwa; it lies close to the Banganga River, north of Krakucchanda Buddha Stupa and pillar, and 17 2/5 miles west of Lumbini, which comes close to the 15 1/2 miles given by Fa-hsien. Moreover, archaeological remains of Tilaurakot apparently resemble the site of a township than the mainly monastic Piprahwa-Ganwaria, which is relatively small and without a river nearby. Piprahwa-Ganwaria also lies about nine miles southwest of Lumbini; Hsuan-tsang's Arrow Spring, however, was about 24 9/20 to twenty-eight miles southwest of Lumbini and my calculation results in his Kapilavastu of about twenty-eight miles west-southwest of Lumbini. It is clear that there is no current archaeological site that can match Hsuan-tsang's Kapilavastu; Piprahwa clearly does not tally with Hsuan-tsang's distance between Lumbini and the Arrow Spring. Though an obvious agreement between Fa-hsien's and Hsuan-tsang's Kapilavastu was its location of about 15 1/2 to twenty-eight miles west to west-southwest of Lumbini. Fa-hsien's descriptions of Kapilavastu are, in my view, more trustworthy since he arrived in this city in the early fifth century CE or more than two centuries before Hsuan-tsang. However, both travelers heavily depended upon local Indian guides for directions to Kapilavastu, a town which had long since vanished nearly nine centuries before Fa-hsien's arrival, and therefore their descriptions might not be entirely reliable. Tilaurakot is a better match than Piprahwa-Ganwaria since it is situated near the Banganga River and close to the Asoka pillars in Gotihawa and Nigali Sagar; this region must have been the heart of Sakya territory and the location of its capital Kapilavastu. What about the famous inscribed relic vase of Buddha's relics found inside Piprahwa Stupa and the Kapilavastu sealings? First, it is impossible to believe in the authenticity of Buddha's relics obtained by the Sukuti brothers almost two centuries after his passing. There was a well-known story in the Mahavamsa, the Sri Lankan chronicle, about the redistribution of Buddha's relics twenty years after the interment of his remains by King Ajatasatru. The latter reputedly opened and collected the relics from all eight original *stupa*s, with the exception of Ramagrama Stupa, and reburied them in a single *stupa* southeast of Rajagriha; about two centuries later, this *stupa* was again reopened by Emperor Asoka and its relics redistributed in 84,000 *stupa*s erected all over India {Cunningham 1854: 30}. Thus I believe the purported Buddha's relics in the hands of the Sukuti brothers were not authentic. On the Kapilavastu sealings, the monks might have decided to name their settlements as 'Kapilavastu' after this famous place associated with Buddha's life and inscribed them on the sealings, many of which actually dated in the Kushan Dynasty long after Buddha's death. Another possibility is that a few remaining Sakyas regrouped in Piprahwa-Ganwaria after the destruction of their homeland by King Virudhaka and renamed the area after their former natal town.

My conclusion is that Tilaurakot is comparatively a better match for Kapilavastu than Piprahwa-Ganwaria but it may not be taken for Kapilavastu; the obvious discrepancies between Fa-hsien and Hsuan-tsang's descriptions of Kapilavastu have raised the likelihood that the original Kapilavastu may still remain buried in the area. As in the fates of many other ancient Indian cities, the original Kapilavastu could have been buried deep under new foundations thus making it impossible to ascertain the remains. Above all, there needs to be more thorough explorations of the region between Lumbini and Banganga River in Nepal as well as the immediate areas north and south along the Indo-Nepalese border since this region was certainly the heart of the Sakya territory and Buddha's homeland. Lastly Piprahwa, though an extremely significant edifice in the evolution of the Indian *stupa*, does not exhibit the qualification as one of the original ten *stupa*s, the Kapilavastu Stupa, since the Piprahwa-Ganwaria ruins have not been irrefutably proven as the original site of Kapilavastu.

2. Sanchi Stupa I (c. 241-50 BCE)

Sanchi [6.3-6.5] boasts some of the oldest religious and Buddhist arts and architecture in India; most of these arts are carved reliefs on the ground, *medhi*, and *harmika vedika*s on the Sanchi *stupa*s. An Asoka pillar, which was erected by Emperor Asoka around the mid third century BCE containing his inscription, still stands in front of the south entrance of Stupa I though only its stump remains; the foundational remains of Temple 40 dated in the third century BCE is also among the earliest freestanding apsidal temples in India. The first informative surveys of Sanchi and nearby monuments in the area was carried out by Alexander Cunningham and Frederick Maisey in 1851 CE; Cunningham later wrote a pioneering book 'Bhilsa Topes' documenting all *stupa*s and their famous Buddhist relics in the region. Dozens of major *stupa*s have been discovered in Sanchi, Sonari, Satdhara, Bhojur, and Andher containing remains of Buddha's most distinguished disciples Sariputra and Maudgalyayana in Sanchi Stupa III and Satdhara Stupa II alongwith relics of numerous Buddhist saints in the other *stupa*s. The most important evidence that links Sanchi to Emperor Asoka and confirms its preeminence as a Buddhist site is his pillar erected in the south entrance of Sanchi Stupa I between c. 241-233 BCE. This 42' high pillar erected on the holy Sanchi hill was a testament to the emperor's imperial grandeur; it possibly marked the boundary of his empire and a monument proclaiming his allegiance to Buddhism. Prior to becoming a paramount ruler in India, Asoka was once a viceroy in the nearby town of Ujjain where he married a local banker's daughter whom had two sons and a daughter. One of his sons Mahendra and daughter Sanghamitra later joined the *Sangha* and led the first missionaries to Sri Lanka after the conclusion of the Third Buddhist Council in c. 249 BCE; before his departure, Mahendra visited his mother in Vedisa where she led him to stay in a monastery at a place called Chetiyagiri or Holy Hill {Marshall 1983 Volume I: 14}. The abundance of important archaeological remains and Buddhist relics unearthed on the Sanchi hill strongly suggests the site as Chetiyagiri. From the inscriptions found on the remains, Sanchi was known as Kakanava or Kakanaya in the second century BCE, Kakanadabota in fifth century CE, and Bota-Sriparvata in the seventh century CE; coincidently a modern village in the foothills of Sanchi is also called Kanakheda, which is undoubtedly derived from the ancient name of Sanchi. The extensive artistic and architectural remains at Sanchi dated between the third century BCE-twelfth centuries CE; afterward, Sanchi lied dormant on the isolated hill for the next six centuries until reawaken in the beginning of the nineteenth century CE by the British.

The discovery and rebirth of Sanchi in the nineteenth century CE was not only a tragic tale for modern India, and particularly the Buddhists, but it also exposed the arrogance of the British colonial power. Between 1818-1819 CE, Sanchi witnessed the first visits by British colonists, first by General Taylor in 1818 CE and Captain Fell in 1819 CE during which they reported the remarkable conditions of the *stupa*s with the exception of the already fallen south *torana* of Stupa I. The unwanted exposure that Sanchi had received and the subsequent unwelcome streams of British visitors soon contributed to its doom as wanton destructions of the *stupa*s began in earnest. Tales of ancient treasures buried inside these magnificent monuments lured British adventurers to Sanchi to dig out for these supposedly hidden riches and many came under the guise of archaeological explorations. The first plunder was committed by Captain Johnson in 1822 CE when he caused a large breach on the western side of the *anda* of Stupas I that resulted in the collapse of the west *torana* and parts of the southwest quadrant of the ground *vedika*; he also demolished portions of Stupa II-III. A second plunder happened in 1851 CE by the well-known 'father of Indian archaeology' General Cunningham and his partner Captain Maisey. Cunningham was also the official archaeologist of Bharhut [6.6-6.8] in 1873 CE where he behaved more responsibly in this *stupa* thanks to the accumulated experiences twenty-two years after his blunder at Sanchi. During this 1851 CE visit, Cunningham and Maisey made several disastrous excavations at Sanchi and nearby *stupa*s at Sonari, Satdhara, Bhojur, and Andher; at Sanchi they utterly destroyed Stupa II-III and they continued their ongoing ransacks of the *stupa*s at the other locations. From one *stupa* to the next, Cunningham repeatedly described his disastrous manner of excavation in his now infamous phrase 'a shaft was sunk down the centre of the Tope' as he searched hysterically for the hidden contents inside these *stupa*s {Cunningham 1854: 269-350}. He and Maisey indeed succeeded in recovering a large number of relic containers and corporal remains of past famous Buddhist saints; it is obvious that they were after the treasures and not because of any wish to restore the artistic heritage of India. To quote from Cunningham's own words {Cunningham 1854: xi}:

> I would also venture to recommend that the two fallen gateways of the Sanchi Tope should be removed to the British Museum, where they would form the most striking objects in a Hall of Indian Antiquities.

The value of these sculptured gateways will, I feel confident, be highly appreciated after the perusal of the brief account of them contained in this work; while their removal to England would ensure their preservation.

Obviously Cunningham was a British colonist who systematically robbed the Indians and the Buddhists of their own cultural heritage for the glory of the British Empire; he also employed the classic colonial justification for archaeological lootings by declaring his egregious actions as ensuring 'preservation.' Have any of these treasures ever been returned to India to prove their sincerity about preserving Indian antiquities? No. The only things the British had returned were the bones and ashes of the Buddhist saints and replicas of their relic boxes while they kept the priceless original containers in the Victoria-Albert and British Museum. Fortunately, the heavy and ornate Sanchi *torana*s remained in India but these again caught the attention of the world in 1869 CE when the French Emperor Napoleon III requested the east *torana* of Sanchi Stupa I to be sent to him; the Indians, who had become smarter by now, sent the replicas instead. Coming back to Cunningham's 1851 CE excavations, his discoveries of the precious relics of the Buddhist saints in these *stupa*s, which would later be published in his famed 'Bhilsa Topes' book, shook the Buddhist world {Cunningham 1954}:

- Sanchi Stupa II: Brahmi inscriptions on the relic containers reveal the names of the Buddhist monks who participated in missionary activities after the Third Buddhist Council in c. 249 BCE. These names were Kasapagota, Majjhima, Haritiputa, Vachi-Suvijayita, Mahavanaya, Apagira, Kodiniputa, Kosikiputa, Gotiputa, and Moggaliputa. Note that this Moggaliputa is not Moggaliputa Tissa the president of the Third Buddhist Council since the former was likely three generations younger than the latter and probably a lower-ranking monk {Marshall 1983 Volume I: 291-293}.
- Sanchi Stupa III: Brahmi inscriptions reveal the names of Buddha's most famous disciples, Sariputra and Maudgalyayana.
- Sonari Stupa II: Brahmi inscriptions reveal the names of some of the Buddhist monks already found in Sanchi Stupa II, namely Kasapagota, Majjhima, Kosikiputa, Gotiputa, and Apagira; this *stupa* and Stupa I nearby can be dated as contemporary with Sanchi Stupa II or c. 125-100 BCE.
- Andher Stupa I: Though this *stupa* did not yield any relics, it is important to the study of the *stupa* evolution as it is the only one having a 13" wide x 15" high *usnisa* erected directly on the *medhi* as a protecting barrier instead of the usual *vedika* {Cunningham 1854: 343, pl. XXVIII}; probably the *medhi* initially did not have a *vedika*. This *stupa* may be dated around c. 150 BCE.
- Andher Stupa II: Brahmi inscriptions reveal the names of some of the Buddhist monks already found in Sanchi Stupa II, namely Vachi and Moggaliputa, alongwith a new one Kodinagota.
- Andher Stupa III: A Brahmi inscription reveals the same Buddhist monk Haritiputa already found in Sanchi Stupa II.

Notice that the simultaneous presence of the relics in different *stupa*s tallies entirely with the Buddhist tradition of splitting up the remains among different *stupa*s. The inscribed names of the monks also confirm the stories in the Buddhist chronicles that the monks, who had been sent as missionaries to foreign countries after the Third Buddhist Council, did indeed historically exist. Sanchi finally began its renaissance when the first restorations were carried out by a few responsible British led by Major Cole between 1881-1883 CE; he successfully reconstructed the fallen south and west *torana*s and filled the large breach in the dome of Sanchi Stupa I. He also restored the sole *torana* of Stupa III; however, his operations swept away numerous old votive *stupa*s once clustering around Stupa I {Marshall 1983: 47}. Due to his lack of experience some lintels of Stupa I and III architraves, in particular the top and bottom lintels of the south *torana*, the bottom two lintels of Stupa I west *torana*, and the top lintel of Stupa III, had been wrongly reerected back to front {Marshall 1983 Volume I: 233}; until now no attempts have been made to reverse these lintels back to their original positions. A second restoration between 1912-1919 CE was executed by the eminent archaeologist John Marshall when he succeeded in reconstructing the *anda* and *medhi vedika* alongwith the southwest quadrant of the ground *vedika* of Stupa I; Stupa II-III were also reconstructed from the ground up. The whole site was then cleared up of the accumulating debris whilst the establishment of Sanchi Museum was inaugurated to house the unearthed artifacts; among the displayed items in the museum were the relics of Sariputra and Maudgalyayana recently returned from Britain. A few mistakes were made during this restoration like some *suchi*s of Stupa I had been turned upside down from the odd positions of inscriptions on them; though these did not in any way affect the overall architecture of the *stupa* {Marshall 1983 Volume: 301-383}.

Among the earliest forms of Indian and Buddhist

arts were mostly found on the *vedika*s of *stupa*s, temples, and certainly on any *vedika*s protecting a holy sanctuary; these arts collectively formed the Aniconic School or Phase of Buddhist arts in which Buddha were depicted as symbols instead of anthropomorphic forms. The most important early *vedika*s belonged to Sanchi Stupa I-III, Bharhut Stupa, Mahabodhi Temple, Mathura *stupa*s, and South Indian *stupa*s like Amaravati. It is therefore imperative to establish the construction chronologies for these *vedika*s, which are primarily based on stylistic and epigraphic analyses.

a. Sanchi Stupa I [6.3-6.5]

The ground and *harmika vedika*s of this *stupa* are completely plain whereas the outer faces of the *stambha*s of its *medhi vedika* contain reliefs of half-medallions on top and bottom and a medallion in the center; all *usnisa*s and *suchi*s are plain. The most elaborately carved are the corner *stambha*s of the *medhi vedika* depicting *yaksa*s and *yaksi*s while the reliefs on the medallions and half-medallions are mainly lotuses, animals, and fantastic beasts like griffins, winged lions, centaurs, and *makara*s {Marshall 1983 Volume II: pl. 8a-8f}; the style of these reliefs is crude and archaic and the subject matters straightforward without being referenced to any specific Buddhist story. On the epigraphic ground, N. G. Majumdar proposed the date of c. 175-125 BCE for the unadorned ground and *harmika vedika*s and c. 125-100 BCE for the *medhi vedika* while the *torana*s of this *stupa* were dated much later around c. 50 BCE {Marshall 1983 Volume I: 263-281}. Taking into accounts of the Deccan caves (Chapter 5), a more precise date would be c. 175-150 BCE for ground and *harmika vedika*s and c. 150-125 BCE for the *medhi vedika*. Stylistically, the reliefs on the latter appear identical to those of Sanchi Stupa II; however the subjects on Stupa I reliefs are limited to a few animal and floral motifs whereas Stupa II reliefs, in addition to the motifs already occurred in Stupa I, also depict the Four Events in Buddha's life (Nativity, Enlightenment, First Sermon, Decease) and possibly a first known *jataka* {Marshall 1983 Volume I: 180-181}. Evidently the *medhi vedika* of Stupa I is stylistically the oldest of all carved *vedika*s and certainly earlier than those of Sanchi Stupa II, as also emphatically agreed by Alfred Foucher {Marshall 1983 Volume I: 170}.

b. Sanchi Stupa II

The reliefs gradually expanded in terms of contents, quantity, and quality having the usual medallions and half-medallions on both faces of the *stambha*s of the ground *vedika*; the *medhi vedika*, as in Stupa I, only has reliefs on the outer faces of *stambha*s. All *usnisa*s and *suchi*s are still plain, with the exception of the *harmika vedika* showing a row of fully bloomed lotuses on its *usnisa*s though its *stambha*s and *suchi*s are still unadorned. There is a wider range of representations including animals, fantastic beasts, floral motifs, and the *triratna* symbol alongwith the Four Events; the style is still archaic but with a higher degree of sophistication than Stupa I as one can now connect the scenes and symbols on the reliefs with the major events in Buddha's life. Thus the scene of a pillar surmounted by a wheel with deer in the base can be identified as Buddha's First Sermon and the two elephants pouring water over a queen's head might symbolize Buddha's Nativity, as Foucher has ingeniously pointed out. In the Buddhist context, the queen in the latter scene shall be identified as Mayadevi and not Goja-Lakshmi as many scholars have proposed {Marshall 1983 Volume I: 183-186}. N. G. Majumdar dated all the *vedika*s of this *stupa* between c. 125-100 BCE {Marshall 1983 Volume I: 263-281} but considering Sanchi Stupa III and Bharhut these *vedika*s may aptly be dated around c. 125 BCE; this *stupa* does not appear to have any *torana*s like the others.

c. Sanchi Stupa III

The reliefs are similar to those on Stupa II but here the *stambha*s of the *harmika vedika* have medallions and half-medallions while its *usnisa*s and *suchi*s now have a row of fully bloomed lotuses in the spaces created by an undulating line. This decorative device also occur on the Bharhut *vedika* and this Sanchi *harmika vedika* suggests a definite transition to the latter; the remaining *usnisa*s and *suchi*s of the ground and *medhi vedika*s are still plain; epigraphically, N. G. Majumdar proposed c. 125-100 BCE for the *medhi* and *harmika vedika*s and c. 50 BCE for the ground *vedika* {Marshall 1983 Volume I: 263-281}. Stylistically the lotuses on the ground *vedika* are similar to Bharhut though at a slightly later date, perhaps c. 75 BCE but not as late as c. 50 BCE; the single *torana* in this *stupa* was likely contemporary with Stupa I *torana*s in c. 50 BCE.

d. Bharhut Stupa [6.6-6.8]

This *stupa* displays great artistic and architectural advancements from Stupa I-III as literally all available surfaces on its *vedika*s are completely covered in reliefs; all *suchi*s are now decorated with medallions. There are numerous *jataka*s and narrative scenes mostly about Buddha's life with accompanied glosses for proper identifications; thanks to these labeled inscriptions, many of the scenes on the early *stupa*s have now been identified with great certainty. N. G. Majumdar dated this remarkable *stupa* between c. 125-100 BCE for its *vedika* and c. 100-75 BCE the extant east *torana* {Marshall 1983 Volume I: 263-281}; stylistically, the dates might be c. 100

BCE for the former and c. 75 BCE for the latter since this *stupa* is definitely later than the *vedika*s of Stupa II-III.

e. Mahabodhi Temple [7.8]

A definite affinity between this *vedika* and Bharhut is evident though the former is likely of a later date or around c. 60 BCE as given by Majumdar {Marshall 1983 Volume I: 263-281}; stylistically its carvings are inferior to Bharhut.

f. Amaravati [6.10-6.11]

Amaravati is certainly the most preeminent of all South Indian *stupa*s with its elaborately carved *vedika*s dated between the first-second centuries CE, though many of its scenes dated as early as the second century BCE.

g. Mathura

There are a few *stupa vedika* specimens between 4'-5' high belonging to Buddhist and Jain *stupa*s; unfortunately none of these Mathura *stupa*s remain intact to be able to ascertain their sectarian affiliation. Stylistically there are two types in which the *stambha*s of the first type have two to three medallions in the center and two half-medallions on the top and bottom; their reliefs encompass decorative motifs such as lotuses, undulating foliate creepers, and the *jataka*s {Agrawala 1966: 3-5, pl. 1-12} and stylistically recall Bharhut and the Mahabodhi Temple *vedika* and can be dated between c. 125-60 BCE. In the later second type, which dated between the first-third centuries CE or during the Kushan Dynasty, its *stambha*s are carved with the provocative and sexually suggestive *salabhanjika*s (she who plucks the *sala* flowers) having robust breasts and exaggerated swaying hips {Agrawala 1966: 5-12, pl. 13-28}; these belong to a class of gorgeous and voluptuous female nudes like the *yaksi*s and *devata*s in early Buddhist arts.

Sanchi Stupa I [6.3-6.5] marked the mature phase of the *stupa* architecture and Aniconic arts in India; with the exception of its archaic *vedika*s and the Asoka pillar dated between c. 241-125 BCE, it is chronologically positioned between Bharhut and Amaravati. It is in a remarkable state of preservation especially its ornate *torana*s, compared to the destroyed Bharhut and Amaravati, thanks to the combined restorative talents of Major Cole in the late nineteenth century CE and John Marshall in the early twentieth century CE. Compared to the smaller Stupa II-III half way downhill, it dwarfs them in scales and decorations; while relics of important Buddhist saints have been recovered from the former two *stupa*s, only a large stone lid once covered the empty relic box of this *stupa*. John Marshall believed the presumably lost relics must have been of Buddha himself due to the huge size of this *stupa*, the presence of the Asoka pillar in front of it, and the recovered relics of his disciples in Stupa II-III {Marshall 1983 Volume I: 32}.

A. Architecture

Architecturally the stone *stupa* [6.3-6.5] has all the typical features of a mature Indian *stupa* including the *hamika* and *yasti-chattra* in the summit, the hemispherical *anda* in the middle, and the circular *medhi* in the base; it is enclosed by a ground *vedika* that is punctuated by four ornate *torana*s. The *anda* was enlarged during the Shunga Dynasty (184-72 BCE) which encased a smaller original brick core with neatly dressed ashlar stone blocks; this core had likely been constructed during Asoka's reign from the presence of his pillar to the right of the south *torana*. John Marshall noted the *anda* sprang directly from the foundation below the ground level and the *medhi* only encircled it, which created an upper *pradaksina* path and buttressed the massive *anda* against its tremendous outward thrust {Marshall 1983 Volume I: 29-30}. This structural method might also be a necessary measure against earthquake, as this area was and is still prone to, since without it the tall and massive dome of stone blocks could crumble under the violent shaking movement during an earthquake. The height of the *stupa* from ground to top of the *harmika vedika* is about 60' and the diameter of the *anda* is about 120' at the base; the *medhi* does not have lamp niches like Piprahwa [6.1] and Bharhut [6.6] but it has four Buddha shrines in the four cardinal entries which were installed in the Gupta Dynasty (c. 320-647 CE). The bulge in the south entrance, which is obviously the main entry from the presence of the Asoka pillar, was evidently planned to accommodate the staircases, each of which has 17" treads and 7" risers; the stair *vedika*s are over 3' high and the *medhi vedika* is over 4' high. These ancient dimensions closely match those in modern staircases and it is obvious that Sanchi architects have devoted a great deal of preplanning before erecting the *stupa*; the ground *pradaksina* path is paved with massive rectangular slabs of 6'8" x 3'4" x 3" thick and many have donative inscriptions on them. John Marshall noticed the orientation of the south entrance was offset fifteen degrees due west in order to provide enough clearance for the Asoka pillar, which had already been standing when the ground *vedika* was erected. The plain ground *vedika* stands at an astounding height of 10'7" and is punctuated by four 28' high and ornately carved *torana*s in the four cardinal points. At Sanchi, the architects apparently corrected a design flaw of the Bharhut plan [6.6] by moving the *torana*s outside of the ground *vedika* so they could erect them without

Part II. Architecture   Stupa . 151

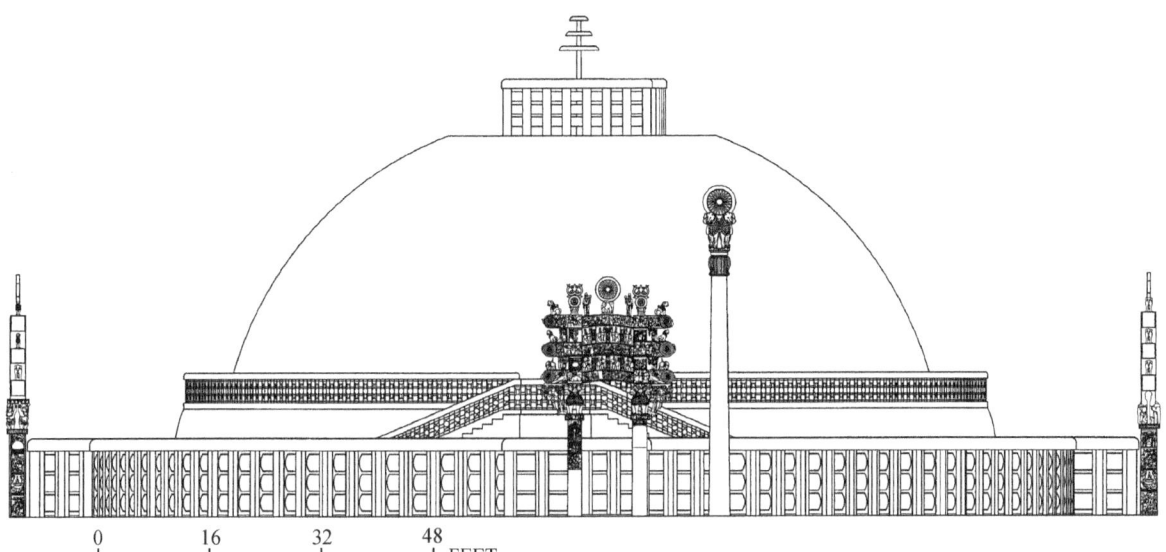

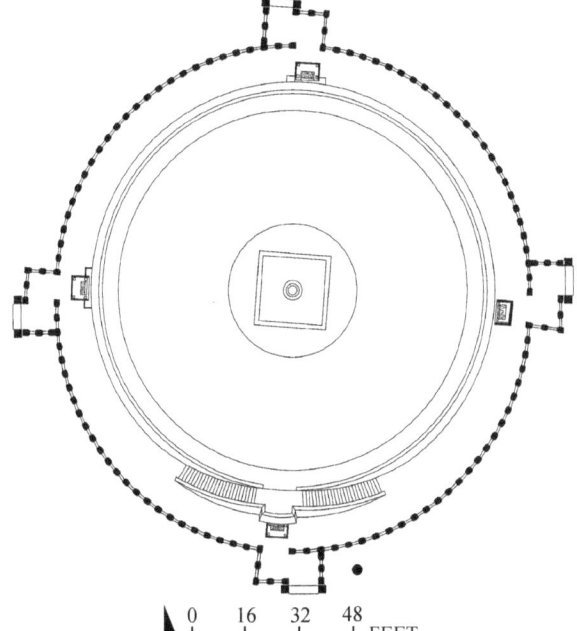

6.3. Elevation and plan
c. 241-50 BCE
Sanchi Stupa I, Sanchi- India

having to disturb the already standing *vedika*. The design of the Sanchi *torana*s is similar to Bharhut but with minor differences; the Sanchi posts are square and the projecting cantilever ends of the architraves are decorated with volutes instead of the *makara*s in Bharhut. According to John Marshall, the order in which the Sanchi *torana*s had been erected was chronologically and stylistically south, north, east, and west {Marshall 1983 Volume I: 36-37}; the north and east *torana*s are the best preserved and have stood in their positions for over two millennia. There are evidences suggesting the men erecting this *stupa* had previous experiences in timber construction and carving-related professions such as ivory or miniature carvings; apparently the sculptor simply transferred his expertise into the stone works, which obviously required additional practice due to the difficulties in carving stone. In fact, the Sanchi *torana*s were constructed probably much like their timber precursors complete with joints in mortises and tenons {Marshall 1983 Volume I: 33}; a crucial inscription on the south *torana* categorically stated that the 'carving done by the ivory-workers of Vedisa' {Marshall 1983 Volume I: 120-121, 342}. This clearly suggests that timber prototypes might have actually existed before their transference into the stone *torana*s and the Indian sculptors had already accumulated sufficient skills at his disposal to proficiently carve such elaborate masterpieces evidently without the help of foreign craftsmen; the presence of 'stain' to protect the stone surfaces as if wood treatment also suggests the Sanchi mason were experienced in timber architecture {Marshall 1983 Volume I: 163}. Stylistically the oldest extant *torana* is Bharhut **[6.7]** and followed by Sanchi **[6.4]** while South Indian *stupa*s have no *torana*s; the classic arched design of these North Indian *torana*s have been imitated as far as Kampuchea in the Sambor and Prei Kmeng Style {Chihara 1997: 90}. Base on epigraphic and stylistic grounds,

6.4. North *torana*
c. 241-50 BCE
Sanchi Stupa I, Sanchi- India

there were about five construction phases for this *stupa*:
- Phase I (c. 241-233 BCE): The small original core of the *stupa* and the Asoka pillar were probably erected at the same time late in Asoka's reign from style of the pillar and his Brahmi inscription; this Asoka inscription or Schism Edict, and which counterpart on the Sarnath pillar **[3.3, 3.6]** also carried a nearly identical message, stated {Hultzsch 1969: 160-161}:

  > [The *Sangha* can not] be divided. The *Sangha* both of monks and of nuns is made united as long as [my] sons and great-grandsons [shall reign and] as long as the moon and the sun [shall shine]. The monk or nun who shall break up the *Sangha*, must be caused to put on white robes and to reside in a non-residence [expel from the *Sangha*]. For my desire is that the *Sangha* may be united [and] of long duration.

- Phase II (c. 175-150 BCE): The ground and *harmika vedika*s were erected in the early Shunga Dynasty but without the *torana*s; the plain octagonal *stambha*s of the ground *vedika* are similar to the columns in Bhaja 12 **[5.4-5.5]** and they were likely contemporary; the new constructions also involved the enlargement of the *stupa* which encased its original core.
- Phase III (c. 150-125 BCE): The *stupa* was again enlarged in the middle to late Shunga Dynasty including the *anda*, *medhi* and *harmika* alongwith their *vedika*s; the sculptural programs and their narrative contents were greatly expanded.
- Phase IV (c. 50 BCE): The four ornate *torana*s were erected in the four cardinal entries, chronologically south, north, east, and west.
- Phase V (fifth century CE): The four Buddha shrines in the four cardinal entries were installed in the Gupta Dynasty.

According to John Marshall, the time required for the erection of the homogenous ground *vedika* was between five to six years and not over a century as some scholars believed {Marshall 1983 Volume I: 34}; the numerous inscriptions by donors suggest plenty of funds were available to finance the project which certainly hastened its completion. In its final form, the *anda* was probably covered in a 2"-5" layer of plaster as patches are still visible today and it would certainly be whitewashed with lime; reliefs of garlands might decorate its dome as in Amaravati **[6.9]** {Marshall 1983 Volume I: 30}. The *torana*s and *vedika*s would be covered in two coats of red stain, the first coat transparent and the second opaque {Marshall 1983 Volume I: 162-163}; the beauty of stone would evidently be obscured in the process. Imagine it must have greatly awed the pilgrims to see the *stupa* for the first time covering in the dazzling red and white colors.

B. Sculpture

This *stupa* contains the archaic and oldest carvings on the stair and *medhi vedika*s which have stylistically been dated before Bharhut; the *torana*s, however, demonstrate a great leap beyond the archaism of Bharhut to the mature phase of early Aniconic arts. The ornate north *torana* **[6.3]** is the best preserved of all Sanchi *torana*s and its carvings on both faces are among the most intricate surpassing even those of Bharhut **[6.7]**. Besides the obvious intention of making a strong impression on the visitors, these elaborately carved *torana*s also tell many Buddhist stories that are imbued with great religious significance and symbolisms; there are two basic categories of sculptures:
- Aniconic symbols of Buddha including the *triratna*, *dharmacakra*, *stupa*, *bodhi*-tree, *vajrasana*, *Buddhapada*, etc.
- Sculptures of *yaksa*s, *yaksi*s, animals, fantastic beasts, people, etc.

Many of these sculptures were also present in Bharhut; nonetheless the Sanchi *torana*s, which were erected later than Bharhut, show a higher degree of technical proficiency and quality in the carvings of a manifestly mature style. The round modeling of the *yaksi*s hanging on the tree branches as brackets clearly demonstrates the Indi-

6.5. War for Buddha's relics (south *torana*). c. 50 BCE. Sanchi Stupa I, Sanchi- India

ans' technical expertise in this area. The *triratna* symbol, which had already appeared on the Bharhut *torana*s and elsewhere, was repeated again on the Sanchi *torana*s but with the additional 'taurine' in its center; Mirelle Benesti already discussed this constantly evolved decorative motif and it needs not be repeated here {Benesti 2003 Book I: 159-201 / Book II: pl. I-XVI}. Let's now take a look at the distribution of the sculptures on these *torana*s; their square posts, with capitals of addorsed animals and dwarfs, are minutely carved with narrative scenes about Buddha's life, a few scenes of heavens, Eight Manusi Buddhas, the *jataka*s, etc. As in Bharhut, the *lokapala*s (celestial guardians of the four world corners) also stand guard the four cardinal entrances but without the animal vehicles (*vahana*) under their feet. The sculptural pieces between the architraves and their end cantilevers depict aniconic symbols, animals, *yaksa*s, *yaksi*s, worshipers, and attendants, all expertly carved in the round. The architrave dies between the architraves and the end cantilevers depict pairs of crouching and standing animals, many of which are fantastic beasts with or without riders facing in opposite directions. The remaining intermediate dies, or the square blocks sandwiched between the architrave dies, portray aniconically the Four Events in Buddha's life (Nativity, Enlightenment, First Sermon, Decease). Unlike Bharhut, there are very few *jataka*s in Sanchi and only five have been identified with certainty, namely Chaddanta, Mahakapi, Rishyasringa, Syama, and Visvantara, and possibly Horse-headed Fairy Jataka {Marshall 1983 Volume I: 181-182, 223-226}. The Mahakapi Jataka already occurred in Bharhut while the lengthy Visvantara Jataka, which has the largest carving area, is depicted continuously from front to back of the bottom architrave of the north *torana*. Other notable scenes presumably include many historical scenes such as Asoka's visit to the Mahabodhi Temple, episodes in-

timately linked with Sakyamuni's life, and rare genre scenes possibly depicting *mithuna*s engaging in sensual delights such as drinking and holding one another. There are several paradise scenes of the *deva*s and possibly Indra's Mount Meru Paradise on the bottom architrave of Stupa III *torana*; a few scenes have been repeated on the other *torana*s and purely decorative scenes on the back sides of the *torana*s.

The scene depicting the war for Buddha's relics on the back of the bottom architrave of the south *torana* [6.5] clearly demonstrates a higher degree of technical and stylistic advancement than Bharhut. This architrave is among the finest reliefs at Sanchi which have accidentally been put in reverse from front to back during Major Cole's restoration; the story continues in the two end cantilevers of this *torana*. This famous story is well-known in the last pages of the Mahaparinirvana-sutra about the fierce competition among the eight contemporary kings and clans in North India for their shares of Buddha's cremated remains. Brahmin Drona averted the potential conflict at the last moment by giving each king an equal portion of the relics; they all returned to their kingdoms happy and eventually enshrined Buddha's relics in *stupa*s in their respective countries {Walshe 1995: 275-277}. In the center of the scene is the fortified town of Kushinagar, which was the Mallas' domain and Buddha's cremation place; it is obviously besieged from all sides with the contesting armies poised for an epic battle for Buddha's relics. The Mallas' town is obviously overwhelmed with the massive forces outside their fortification while the residents are shown raising their bows and ready to throw stone in the defense of their town; some residents appear to converse with the soldiers probably trying to convince them not to fight while others stand shoulder to shoulder praying for peace. But not a single fight has happened; in the center of the scene there is a man, no doubt a very important person, appearing to toss the flowers in his hands to the hostile soldiers below. Could this man be Brahmin Drona or the Mallas' leader calling for peace to all parties to stop fighting and ready to receive their share of the relics? The next scenes on both sides of the panel and the end cantilevers show the incoming armies begin their triumphant departure from Kushinagar and each with their happy share of the relics, which are placed inside caskets that are honorably mounted on top of their state elephants. Like its predecessors in Lomas Risi [5.1] and Bharhut [6.7], all the movements in the scene converge to the center; however in Sanchi the actors are simultaneously moving in both directions to indicate their arrival and departure from Kushinagar. Compared to the archaic episodes in the Bharhut scene, which jump disconnectedly and incoherently from one episode to the next in a circular manner, the Sanchi episodes are smoothly synchronized in a harmonious pictorial orchestra that imparts a strong sense of purpose and meaning in the actors in the scene. Instead of filling in the background with trees and buildings as in Bharhut, the Sanchi carver chose to insert more actors into the relief who apparently acted in unison in various movements to heighten the realism and dynamism and intensify the drama in the scene; the juxtaposition of different scales and actions in the figures as manifested in the lively stream of people and animals energetically coming and going is so expertly planned and integrated such that they all appear to completely melt into one scene. Thus the viewers get to perceive only one and dominant scene in this Sanchi relief, which is the war for Buddha's relics, which has been achieved by the conscious suppression of the individual episodes for the holistic effect in the scene. The Sanchi sculptor was also an expert in solving the problem of perspective the skewed ground in Bharhut and the viewers here are also looking at the scene from the eye-level rather than the bird's-eye view as in Bharhut; this effectively draws them to participate in the scene as if active participants and not as outsiders looking dispassionately in. There are overwhelming senses of drama and tension in the atmosphere and the actors freely move around in the scene unlike the Bharhut actors who appear calm, detached, and unemotional as if they are not able to move about or be expressive. The Sanchi sculptors also reached greater proficiency in carvings which are so minute and meticulous as if the relief had been carved out of wood than stone. In fact, an inscription on the left post below this architrave states that the "carving done by the ivory-workers of Vedisa" {Marshall 1983 Volume I: 342, #400}. The natural and fleshy modeling of the figures in conjunction with the variation in the depth of the carving creates strong interplays of light and shadow that achieve greater realism.

There are still lingering questions on foreign influences. How does one explain the apparent disparity between the impeccable Asoka arts, especially the glistening Asoka pillars, and the arts of early Buddhist *stupa*s as exemplified in the *vedika*s of Sanchi Stupa I-III? It is not difficult to trace the technical and stylistic progress from the *vedika*s of Sanchi Stupa I-III to Bharhut and finally the *torana*s of Sanchi Stupa I, all apparently within a century or so. However when comparing the transition from the flawless Asoka pillars to the crude and archaic reliefs on the *vedika*s of Sanchi Stupa I-III, one can not help but wonder if the Asoka arts have suddenly become extinct after the fall of the Maurya Dynasty. The most convincing theory was put forward by John Marshall that Asoka employed foreign craftsmen, particularly the Bactrian Greeks, to sculpt his majestic pillars and after the collapse of the Maurya Dynasty they simply left causing the extinction of the Asoka arts {Marshall 1983 Volume I: 91}. Evidently John Marshall has made two assumptions:

- Foreign artists were employed by Asoka. If foreign artists built the pillars then they must also be the builders of the Lomas Risi cave [5.1-5.2] since both had been constructed and patronized during Asoka's reign and also had the same lustrous polish. In my view, Lomas Risi was undoubtedly constructed by the Indians and they, with the ingenuity and financial backing from Asoka, were entirely capable of erecting any monuments including the pillars. Moreover, the gleaming polish typical of the Asoka pillars apparently did not become extinct after the Maurya Dynasty as in the case of the famed Didarganj Yaksi sculpture (first century CE) which also had an identical shiny polish.
- Foreign artists left after the Maurya Dynasty collapsed. There was no reason for them to leave after the Maurya Dynasty ended since the succeeding Shungas could as well employ and utilized their expertise and there were certainly plenty of projects lying around.

As already mentioned, Asoka arts were essentially imperial with all its royal sanctions while the arts of the Buddhist *stupa*s were religious belonging to the common people; both were dictated by different sets of artistic parameters. It would take an inconceivable amount of resources and time for the common religious folks to duplicate the lustrous polish and perfection of the Asoka pillars for all members of a huge Buddhist *stupa*; moreover, the conservative Theravada monks probably would not approve such ostentatious displays of opulence in a religious setting. John Marshall also believed the availability of Greek objects, such as the Bactrian Greek coins, facilitated the dissemination of Western modeling and relief techniques into India {Marshall 1983 Volume I: 157-158}. How could the tiny Bactrian Greek coins and motifs be compared with or serve as the model for the complicated layouts of the Sanchi *torana* reliefs? The accumulated experiences in timber construction and technical proficiency in wood carvings of Indian craftsmen and builders, such as the reputed ivory-carver guild of Vedisa, would certainly qualify for the tasks without the technical assistance from foreigners. Even Marshall failed to explain how the Bactrian Greeks, who left no outstanding monuments of their own except for Ai-khanum, could have played a dominant role in influencing early Indian arts or if there were any commonalities between them; he also did not take into the account of the existence of the Indus Civilization long before the Greeks (Chapter 1). On the other hand, this does not mean that early Indian arts were completely free of foreign elements, especially Near Eastern like the fantastic beasts such as the winged lions, griffins, cantauers, addorsed winged animals, decorative motifs, etc.; however their influences upon early Indian and Buddhist arts were insignificant and mostly confined to the decorative role.

C. Epigraph {Marshall 1983 Volume I: 263-396}

Sanchi inscriptions are the treasure-trove for linguists and valuable not only in examining the long and complex history of India and Buddhism but also useful tools in dating their monuments and construction phases. Sanchi inscriptions, which dated from Emperor Asoka's time in the third century BCE to the ninth century CE, reflect the long history of the site as an important center of Buddhism, Buddhist arts and architecture in India; like other Indian sites, Sanchi certainly continued to function until c. 1200 CE when Buddhism ceased to exist in India. Between the third century BCE-first centuries CE the inscriptions were written in Brahmi, the first historical Indian script, while the spoken dialect in these inscriptions was Prakrit. Between the first century CE-mid fourth centuries CE or the Kushan Dynasty, a mixture of Prakrit and Sanskrit was used in the inscriptions; Sanskrit was chiefly used from the mid fourth century CE on or the Gupta Dynasty. There are a total of 842 inscriptions in Sanchi as described by Majumdar, which can chronologically be classified in the followings:
(1) An Asoka inscription on his pillar in the south entrance of Sanchi Stupa I contains the Schism Edict similar to those on the Allahabad-Kausambi and Sarnath pillars.
(2-14) These are inscribed on the relic containers stating the names of various Buddhist *arhat*s and among these were Buddha's famous chief disciples Sariputra and Maudgalyayana.
(15-827) These inscriptions are inscribed on Stupa I-III and a few other pre-Kushan monuments.
(828-831) These are Kushan inscriptions and many have been inscribed on Buddha and *bodhisattva* statues.
(832-840) These are Gupta inscriptions, of which the most famous one recorded the installment of the four Buddha shrines in the four cardinal entrances of Stupa I.
(841-842) These are post-Gupta inscriptions and among these recorded the last known pre-modern name of Sanchi as Bota-Sriparvata.

Unlike Bharhut, where many scenes especially the *jataka*s were duly labeled, the Sanchi reliefs have no informative labels so scholars have to rely on Bharhut for identifications. The majority of Sanchi inscriptions have donative contents often recording the initiation of new projects or installations of sculptures, etc.; the others are about donors making contributions to Sanchi for feeding monks and maintaining lamps. A few are imprecatory inscriptions, particularly on the north, east, and west *torana*s of Sanchi Stupa I, cursing those who dare to damage or transfer these precious *torana*s to other monasteries and that violators shall incur the five heinous Buddhist sins and "live in dirt." Several inscriptions also record identical donors making multiple donations in different *stupa*s which further narrow down their relative construction dates. Sanchi inscriptions, like Bharhut, have also revealed a multitude of people making their concerted contributions that enable the erections of these superb and costly monuments. Asoka was the founder of Sanchi as evident from his pillar, followed by royal families, then monks, nuns, the Buddhist laity, artisans, and commoners; the ivory-carver guild of Vedisa, which undoubtedly carved and possibly donated the south *torana*, was certainly among the most skillful craftsmen in contemporary India. A single foreigner, an Asian Greek, was reported among the donor suggesting the universality of Indian Buddhism.

The Buddhist stories as told on the stone surfaces of Sanchi began on the stair and *medhi vedika*s of Stupa I and ended in its *torana*s; the style of the sculptures suggests the transition between the imperial arts of Asoka and that of the common people. No longer was there the centralization of artistic creations dictated by an all powerful personality like Asoka as average Indian citizens could now carry out their individualistic artistic visions and reaped the religious rewards of good *karma*s. Sanchi art also demonstrated the increasingly liberal outlook in Buddhism in the closing years of the first century BCE; thus there are a few scenes in Stupa I depicting the *mithuna*s engaging in self-indulgent and decadent activities such as drinking, cosmetic concerns, and caressing one another. These are some of the early instances of seemingly secular subjects in religious sanctuaries possibly reflecting the growing influences of the merchants and women in Buddhism who were important patrons and contributors in these great endeavors. The prominent positions of the *mithuna*s in early Aniconic arts virtually disappeared in the Gupta Dynasty and after to be superseded with the cult of Buddha and *bodhisattva* images.

3. Bharhut Stupa (c. 175-75 BCE)

Alexander Cunningham discovered this *stupa* **[6.6-6.8]** in 1873 CE and resurrected it from oblivion in his now classic book 'Stupa of Bharhut.' Unfortunately by the time of his arrival, the *stupa* had already been pillaged for hundreds of years by the locals for stones and bricks to be used in the constructions of their dwellings or in any other purposes they deemed fit; the remains of the *stupa* was then covered in a 4' high mound of debris. This has also been the sad fate for most Buddhist monuments in India after the disappearance of Buddhism in c. 1200 CE since there were no Buddhist caretakers around to protect them. However, Cunningham was fortunate enough to salvage pieces of the southeast quadrant and the elegant east *torana* from the ruins; even with the meagerly available materials, he and later scholars have been able to accurately reconstruct its history. The discovered remains can be classified into three categories: architecture, sculptures, and epigraphs.

A. Architecture

The *stupa* originally composed of the main plaster-coated brick structure in the center having a hemispherical dome, a *harmika*, and a *yasti-chattra*; it was surrounded by a stone *vedika* punctuated by four entry projections and four stone *torana*s in the four cardinal points. Cunningham's excavations revealed the diameter of the *medhi* about 67'9" and the inner diameter of the ground *vedika* (called 'Inner Railing' by Cunningham) about 88'5" {Cunningham 1962: 4-14, pl. III-VI}. The 10'4" wide ground *pradaksina* path was paved with hard lime; the *medhi* had light alcoves of 14" top x 5" bottom spaced at regular intervals. The flat-topped mound of earth, bricks, and some foundation stones was what remained of the *anda* as the relic casket had been taken away by a local *raja* and its whereabout is unknown; most recovered bricks measured 12" x 12" x 4" or larger. The east *torana* and the southeast quadrant of the 9' high ground *vedika*, with its usual *stambha-suci-usnisa* form, were all that could be salvaged from the ruins. The ground *vedika* continued with the Return Railings or the entry projections to form the entrances, each having a sejant lion on top of the *usnisa* facing the visitors. The 20' high east *torana* **[6.7]**, the oldest and most complete of its kind, consisted of a pair of conjoined octagonal posts to be spanned with three arched architraves; each post was crowned with a pair of addorsed humped bulls (seen from outside) and lions (seen from inside). Cunningham reasonably argued that originally there were four entrances at the four cardinal points since pieces of the individual *torana*s had been collected from the site {Cunningham 1962: 128-130}. Cunningham also recovered a 3'3" high *vedika* which he believed to have belonged to the Outer Railing outside of the main ground *vedika*; its construction, he believed, was to prevent the construction encroachment to the ground of the main *stupa*. He also dug up a 3'1" wide stone staircase in the west entry and seven 10" wide treads which he believed to have originally descended down to the *stupa* court 6' below the ground level {Cunningham 1962: 12-13, pl V}. However, John Marshall have since corrected this mistake that this 'Outer Railing' was no other than the *medhi vedika* and the staircase was one of a pair leading up to the upper *pradaksina* path as in Sanchi {Barua 1979 Book II: preface}. According to Barua, the east and west *torana*s had octagonal posts whereas the south and north *torana*s had square posts; he further stated that the south and north *torana*s were freestanding pillars without the arched architraves and erected before the other two *torana*s, which are conceivably incorrect and not typical of early Indian *stupa*s {Barua 1979 Book I: 5-7}.

From the available data supplied by Cunningham and other scholars {Cunningham 1962: pl. III, V}{Oki and Ito 1991: fg. 261, 264}{Coomaraswamy 1956: fg. 64, 65} in conjunction with studying the Bharhut reliefs and the Sanchi *stupa*s, I was able to draw the restored plan and elevation of Bharhut **[6.6]**. The restored elevation shows the approximate height of the *stupa* from the ground to the top of the *harmika* of about 45'. Bharhut must also have a main entrance just like Sanchi; B. M. Barua plausibly argued that the main entrance must be in the east but I believe it should originally be in the west since a staircase was discovered there. A donative inscription on the first *stambha* located on the northern side of the southeast quadrant next to the southern post of

Part II. Architecture　　　　　　　　　　　　　　　　　　　　　　　　　　　　　　　Stupa . 157

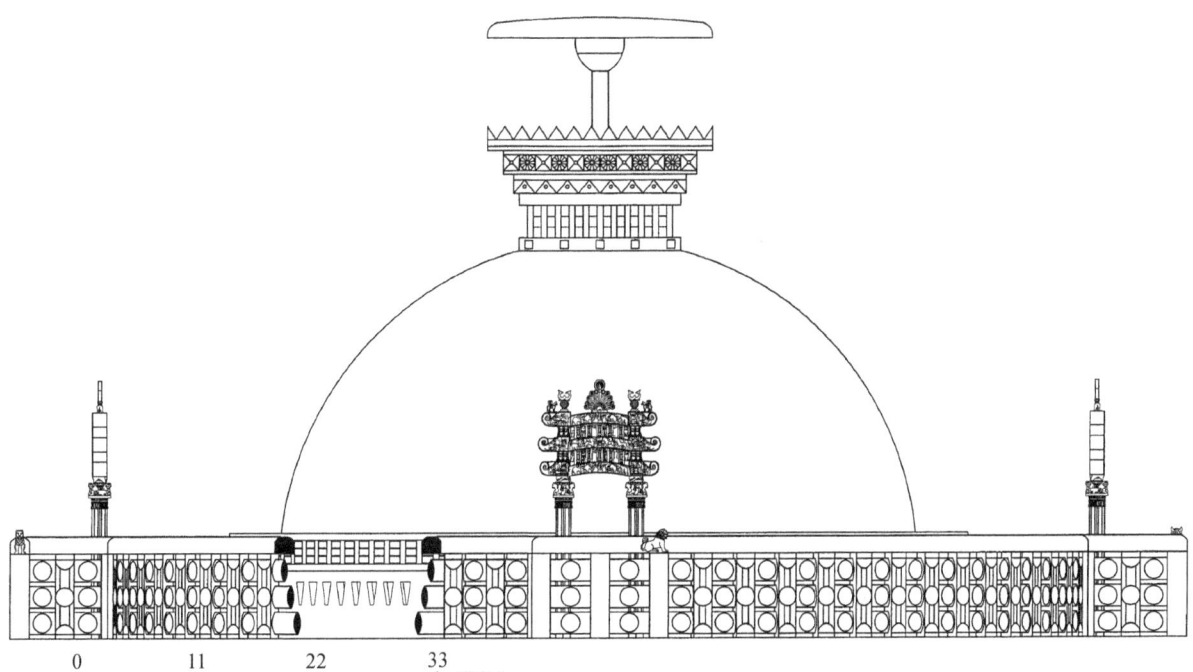

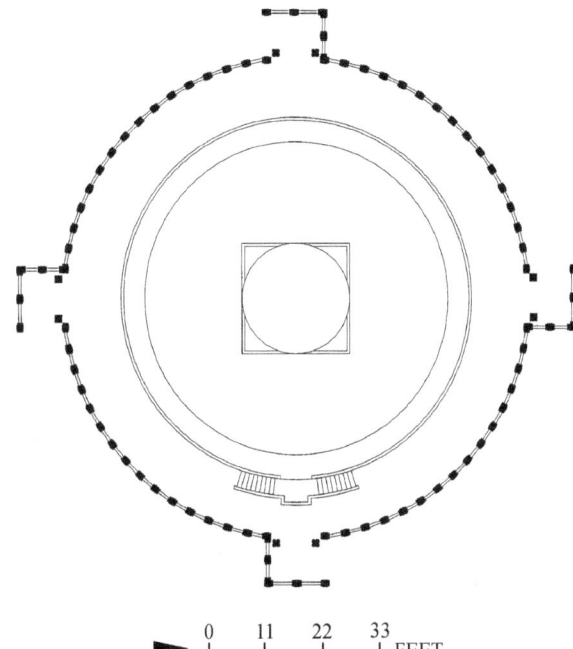

6.6. Elevation and plan (restored)
c. 175-75 BCE
Bharhut- India

the east *torana*, which depict a royal entourage carrying a relic urn to be deposited into the *stupa*, clearly states that it was the 'first pillar' {Barua 1979 Book I: 5-6}{Luder 1963: 26, pl. XXVII A34}. Most scholars placed the date of the final form of the *stupa* in the Shunga Dynasty (184-72 BCE); an inscription on the east *torana* states that during the reign of the Shungas the gateway was erected with the patronage of King Dhanabhuti {Cunningham 1962: 128-129}{Barua 1979 Book I: 41}. The original core of the *stupa* had probably been commenced in the early Shunga Dynasty or possibly late Maurya Dynasty from its use of large-sized bricks; it is impossible to ascertain whether Asoka was involved in its initial construction but he had certainly initiated the construction and expansion of Konakamuni Buddha Stupa in c. 249 BCE and Sanchi Stupa I. Cunningham dated Bharhut between c. 250-200 BCE but there was no evidence of Asoka or Maurya arts in this *stupa* to substantiate his conclusion. Other scholars presented two methods of narrowing down the construction timeframes for Bharhut by studying the evolution of its Brahmi inscriptions and the style of its sculptures. Based on his analyses of the Brahmi inscriptions, Buhler placed the overall date for the *stupa* in c. 150 BCE while N. G. Majumdar dated it between c. 125-75 BCE {Luder 1963: xxx-xxxiv}; from the sculptural techniques, B. M. Barua placed Bharhut between c. 150-100 BCE {Barua 1979 Book I: 29-36 / Book III: 31-32}. I believe N. G. Majumdar's conclusions of c. 125-75 BCE for the *vedi-*

6.7. East *torana*
c. 125-75 BCE
Indian Museum, Kolkata- India

was entirely possible that every new construction or expansion such as the erection of new *torana*s would require the ground *vedika* to be dismantled, reassembled, enlarged, or rebuilt entirely. There were about three construction phases for Bharhut:

- Phase I (c. 175-125 BCE): The *stupa* was enlarged, which entombed its original core of possibly early second century BCE, concurrent with the erection of the *medhi vedika*.
- Phase II (c. 125-100 BCE): The ground *vedika* was erected without the entry projections (Cunningham's Return Railings). The carvings, I believe, were executed on the ground and erected segment by segment, that is *stambha-suchi-stambha-usnisa* that slowly progressed toward the entrances to complete the railing; I can not imagine the sculptors erecting scaffolding in order to carve the stone reliefs directly on an already standing *vedika*.
- Phase III (c. 100-75 BCE): The *torana*s and entry projections were erected at the same time and these obviously required the partial and temporary dismantlement of the already standing ground *vedika* to allow enough clearance spaces for the erection of the tall *torana*s; this construction problem and design flaw might be the reason why the Sanchi *torana*s would eventually be erected outside the ground *vedika*. The square posts of the south and north *torana*s mentioned by Barua suggest a definite transition to the Sanchi *torana*s and therefore probably the latest to be erected.

Bharhut, like Sanchi, has decidedly progressed beyond the architectural archaism of Piprahwa **[6.1-6.2]**. The stone *vedika*s and ornate *torana*s in the four cardinal entries are the new features while the newly hemispherical dome rises higher to be crowned with a *harmika* and *yasti-chattra*; the square base of Piprahwa has evidently been eliminated to be replaced with a circular *medhi*. There are countless theories regarding the symbolisms of the Buddhist *stupa*, some of which are valid while many others are purely fanciful speculations. For examples, the Buddhist *stupa* has been associated with the Vedic 'Golden Stupa of Agni' with the *yupa* (a Vedic sacrificial pillar) sunk into its center as allegedly found in the Lauriya-Nandangargh tumulus {Cunningham 1962: i-iii}; however, it is now firmly established that the edifice is in fact a Buddhist *stupa* and the wooden post was unquestionably the remain of the *yasti-chattra* {Mitra 1971: 84}. As previously stated, the Vedic tumulus might have been transformed into the Buddhist *stupa* but both had different forms and functions just like the differences between the Asoka pillar and the Vedic *yupa*. The *stupa* plan was

*ka*s and the east *torana* are the most acceptable if taken the Sanchi *stupa*s into account {Marshall 1983 Volume I: 263-281}; evidently all scholars agreed that the *stupa* had been constructed in successive stages, specifically the *stupa* and *medhi vedika* first, the ground *vedika* next, and finally the *torana*s. B. M. Barua described some illogical construction methods for Bharhut in his book that the ground *vedika* had been erected before the *torana*s and some works were carved directly on already standing members while some parts were taken down and put up again either as replacements or new carvings {Barua 1979 Book I: 32-35}. It is difficult to visualize how the Bharhut builders could have erected a heavy 20' high *torana* right next to an already standing *vedika* without destabilizing the ground and causing it to collapse. Thus digging a hole next to a standing *vedika* in order to erect the *torana*s would likely cause the collapse of the *vedika*; in other words there were no construction clearances. It also popularly believed to resemble a swastika, an Indian symbol of auspiciousness, and the entry projections were thought of as the arms of the swastika. However, these returning arms of the entry projections were meant to direct pilgrims into the clockwise *pradaksina* path around the *stupa* for proper worship and therefore had nothing to do with the swastika symbolisms. Cunningham's casual comparison between the plain ground *vedika* and the Stonehenge in Britain could potentially mislead readers to think that somehow the two were related {Cunningham 1854: v-vi, pl. II}; clearly there was no connection whatsoever between them. Barua also constructed a controversial theory explaining the symbolisms of the east *torana* and its carvings {Barua 1979 Book I: 9-10 / Book III: 25-26, 28}:

> A parapeted bridge [architrave] over the river of life with hungry crocodiles that lie in wait on its two banks, the bridge being the dharmasetu made by the Buddha.

This was obviously Barua's own mental projections as nowhere in Buddhist scriptures had suggested such symbolisms. The *torana* were undoubtedly architectural replications of actual traditional timber models, which must have been prevalent in Indian architecture from the beginning as in the Lomas Risi facade **[5.2]**.

B. Sculpture

All available surfaces of the ground *vedika* and east *torana* are completely covered in sculptural reliefs. Investigations have revealed several important types of surface decorations having different iconographic and narrative contents; many reliefs have accompanied labels for proper identifications:
- Contemporary historical scenes. The conspicuous scene on the *stambha* of the east entrance shows a royal procession carrying a relic box on a state elephant obviously to be interred in the *stupa*; the scene undoubtedly depicts a contemporary Buddhist funerary rite and also carries a Brahmi inscription identifying the *stambha* as 'the first pillar' {Luder 1963: 26, pl. XXVII}. This first pillar was probably an architectural device to instruct pilgrims to begin their *pradaksina* here or it could actually be the first pillar of the ground *vedika*; in any case, it probably marked the east as the main entrance of the *stupa*.
- Scenes of Eight Manusi Buddhas, of which those of Sakyamuni occurred most frequently and often lavishly decorated.
- Religious narrative scenes. The most commonly depicted scenes are the *jataka*s (Buddhist moral folklores) retelling past reincarnations of Buddha; these are often accompanied by moral implications to inculcate ethics in the Buddhist clergy and laity as well as for the general public and one of these moving tales is Miga or Ruru Jataka **[6.8]** {Barua 1979 Book II: 136-138, pl. LXXXV 126}{Luder 1963: 51, 125-126/pl. XLI}. The Bodhisattva, or Sakyamuni in his past incarnations before becoming a Buddha, was once born as a Ruru deer and the leader of a herd of deer who once saved a distraught man from drowning himself in the river. Unfortunately, the ungrateful and disgraceful man returned the favor by revealing the secret location of the golden deer to the *raja* of Benares for a large reward. The *raja*, led by the traitorous man, eventually arrived at the deer's forested dwelling and about to shoot his arrow at the innocent deer but the latter suddenly spoke to him about the perfidious story of the rescued traitor; the *raja*, deeply moved by the deer's compassion, granted a boon of protection for all living creatures. The archaic

6.8. Miga Jataka
c. 125-100 BCE
Indian Museum, Kolkata- India

pictorial representation only depicts the abbreviated main episodes in the *jataka* including: (1) The deer saves the man's life from drowning by carrying him on its back, (2) the *raja*, with his informant pointing at the deer, raises his bow and about to shoot at the deer, (3) the couchant Bodhisattva deer tells the betrayal story and requests the king to refrain from killing living beings as the latter listens reverently and attentively. The archaic and clumsy sculptural technique in this medallion is immediately apparent; at the first glance the whole scene appears to be fragmented that lacks coherence and cohesion while the contents of the story are hard to decipher without first consulting the *jataka* in Buddhist scriptures. The actors in the scenes seemingly have a difficulty standing on the steep tilted ground while the viewers survey the scene from the bird's-eye perspective as if a detached outsider's viewpoint and not an active participant as in Sanchi. Evidently the Bharhut sculptor was trying to portray the story by compressing all the episodes into one scene in a small medallion at the detriment to the holism of the story; the style and technique appear rudimentary and folkish compared to the later Sanchi *torana*s **[6.5]**. On the other hand, there is a certain degree of simplicity and naivete in the relief that the viewers can not possibly doubt the religious sincerity of the story and its actors; an overwhelming feeling of inner serenity and spiritual devotion is pervasive throughout the scene and these are the accomplishments of the Bharhut sculptors. Compared to the Indus seals nearly two millennia before, the Bharhut style apparently did not improve much from the technical point of view; however, its religious contents significantly progressed especially in narrative storytelling. This typical *jataka* also reveals some underlined commonalities in all Buddhist *jataka*s in which it primarily espouses the pan-Indian theory of rebirth, most importantly how one's past *karma*s will affect future reincarnations, and the glorification of Buddha as a compassionate teacher and leader; the story extols the virtues of self-sacrifice and compassion for others with a strong emphasis on inculcating ethical conducts to listeners. There are about 550 *jataka*s in the Pali *Tripitaka*, most presumably to have been told by Buddha himself; in these *jataka*s, he typically appears in human and animal forms and is addressed as 'Bodhisattva;' the religious model of a compassionate and selfless *bodhisattva* subsequently became the hallmark of the Mahayana.

- Many medallions also depict images of donor couples or possibly *mithuna*s and *stupa*s in their contemporary architectural forms that enable the reconstruction of Bharhut.
- There are also depictions of guardian deities of the *stupa* such as the *yaksa*s, *yaksi*s, *deva*s, *devata*s, and *naga*s who zealously and reverently guard in the entrances and sanctity of Buddha's shrine and ward off evil spirits. These are gods, demi-gods, and spirits in the popular Indian cults who have been pacified by Buddha and absorbed into the Buddhist pantheon but they are generally in subservient positions.
- Plants, animals, repetitive patterns and motifs. The majority of the reliefs are simply decorative motifs such as garlands, bells, parapeted merlons, *purnaghata*s, and lotuses; the Bharhut sculptors were especially fond of depicting scenes of aquatic life, fauna, and flora not only because they were abundant but they also appealed to the Indian senses of beauty and life. A few floral motifs have evidently been borrowed from the Near East such as the honeysuckles **[Backcover]** but these are insignificant compared to an already abundant and diverse decorative repertoire in Indian arts.
- Aniconic symbols representing Buddha and the Three Jewels including most notably the *triratna*, *bodhi*-tree, *Buddhapada*, *vajrasana*, *dharmacakra*, and *stupa*.
- Sculptures as integral parts of the architecture such as the bulls and lions crowning the *torana* posts, which have been adapted from the Asoka pillars into architectural usage.

Stylistically, Cunningham observed that the carvings on the east *torana* was more superior than the *vedika*s {Cunningham 1962: 8} while Barua suggested the stylistic progress of Bharhut sculptures from the earliest in the *lokapala*s, *yaksa*s, and the *medhi vedika* to the latest in the Prasenajit Pillar {Barua 1979 Book I: 35 / Book III: 31-32}. Persistent speculations still remain pertaining to the origins and possible intrusions of non-Buddhist and foreign elements into the Bharhut sculptures. Some scholars thought that celestial and supernatural beings like the *yaksa*s, *deva*s, *naga*s, etc. were of Hindu origins but these were pre-Aryan indigenous deities that were generally non-sectarian in characters; Vedic and Aryan Hindu gods like Brahma and Indra have also been depicted among the scenes but often of inferior status as Buddha's attendants. Cunningham's bias in identifying some Bharhut reliefs with the popular Hindu Ramayana story of Rama and Sita {Cunningham 1962: 99, pl. XLI #5} has been rejected by Barua who believed these depicting the Buddhist *jataka*s {Barua 1979 Book II: 126-

127, pl. 120}. Another well-known controversy is about the so-called 'Goja-Lakshmi or Sri Lakshmi' scenes depicting a goddess, sometimes with or without a lotus in her hand, standing on a fully bloomed lotus between two elephants that anoint her with water {Coomaraswamy 1956: fg. 122-123}; these commonly occur in Bharhut and also in Sanchi. Barua identified her as a heavenly nymph and one of the four daughters of Indra {Barua 1979 Book II: 74-75} but Foucher plausibly argued that the scene represented Buddha's Nativity in the Buddhist context and the goddess was no other than Mayadevi and not Goja-Lakshmi as many scholars would like to believe {Marshall 1983 Volume I: 183-186}. Among the minor foreign elements in Bharhut imported from the Near East include the animal-crowned pillars which also occur in the Asoka pillars **[3.1-3.6]**, honeysuckle motifs, human-faced sphinxes which also already appeared in the Indus seals, fantastic beasts such as winged animals, parapeted battlements, etc. Several sculptors' Kharosthi marks on the east *torana* implicated the employment of Gandhara craftsmen in the construction of Bharhut; however these intrusive foreign elements were negligible and the *stupa* remained essentially an Indian monument built and supervised exclusively by zealous Indian Buddhists.

C. Epigraph

The most unique feature distinguishing Bharhut from other Indian *stupa*s has been the use of inscriptional labels, which are mostly in the post-Asoka Brahmi script, for the precise identification of the scenes; these are mostly found on the *vedika*s and *torana*s. As stated earlier, Cunningham also discovered several sculptors' marks in Kharosthi on the east *torana* which he rightly suggested the presence of Gandhara craftsmen in the construction of Bharhut. There are two classes of inscriptions: donative and labeling.

- Donative Inscriptions {Luder 1963: 1-65}
  Donative inscriptions identified and credited donors who had made contributions to the construction of Bharhut; a typical inscription spelled out the title, name, location, and occupation of the donor. These generous patrons included members of the royal family such as kings, queens, and princes as well as the Buddhist clergy like monks and nuns. The most famous donor of Bharhut was King Dhanabhuti who financed the east *torana* and was probably a feudal of the Shungas; many others were lay Buddhists and ordinary folks while a donor was reportedly also the sculptor of his relief.
- Labeling Inscriptions {Luder 1963: 66-181}

Many *jataka*s carry labeled inscriptions that facilitated the identification and demystification of their contents; scholars have been able to identify the scenes in the reliefs with great accuracy by cross-referencing with their literary sources in the Buddhist scriptures. The ground *vedika* bears many inscriptions and the most important one is on a *stambha* mentioning it as the 'first pillar.'

What were the purposes of the inscriptions? The majority was about the acknowledgment of the individual donors in the most auspicious occasion of constructing the *stupa* so they could earn good *karma*s; any Buddhists would certainly dream to have their names inscribed on a famous Buddhist monument like Bharhut for eternity. The labeled inscriptions for the *jataka*s also served to expound Buddhism to a wider audience as one could visualize the scene where Buddhist monks stood before the awe-inspiring reliefs, with the help of the glosses, explaining the wonder and exalted morality of the *jataka*s to Buddhist pilgrims and visitors. The inscriptions also confirmed an important truth about Bharhut that its construction had been completed with the generous donations from pious benefactors; the *stupa* was possibly completed with the help of many volunteers and likely without the use of forced labor or slaves which would be deemed contrary to the spirit of Buddhism.

The story of Bharhut exemplifies the development of Buddhism, its arts and architecture. No longer was Buddhism confined to Bihar since it now had new converts from all over India as evident from the inscriptions and it practically became the most successful religion at the time with the generous patronage from the royalty like King Dhanabhuti in the new territories. Its adherents were influential and wealthy enough to organize major construction projects like Bharhut compared to the paucity of the monuments in other contemporary Indian religions. The visual arts also played an ever crucial role in strengthening the religious and communal bonds between the *Sangha* and lay worshippers while attracting new converts to Buddhism, who were naturally more drawn to straightforward imageries than its detached and abstract philosophy. The explosion of sumptuous decorations and the complex form of Bharhut compared to the simplicity and plainness of Piprahwa **[6.1-6.2]** and Sanchi Stupa I-III *vedika*s, with the exceptions of the latter's ornate *torana*s, clearly demonstrated the growing sophistication in Buddhist arts and architecture.

4. Amaravati Stupa (c. 200 BCE-250 CE)

The region in the valley along the banks of the Krishna River and toward its mouth in the Indian Ocean in Andhra Pradesh can rightly be claimed as the fourth most important Buddhist centers after Bihar, the birthplace of Buddhism, the Deccan in India, and Gandhara in Pakistan. It is also considered as the origin of the Mahayana as it was here that Nagarjuna, the great Mahayana philosopher, rose to eminence in the second century CE; the Nagarjunakonda Stupa, which was erected in his honor, is also located in this region. According to Taranatha, the great fifteenth century CE Tibetan monk-historian, Nagarjuna reputedly erected a section of the ground *vedika* of Amaravati {Sivaramamurti 1956: 6}. A fragment of an Asoka inscription was also found in Amaravati confirming the early presence of Buddhism in the region in the third century BCE; by the third century CE the region would be dotted with *stupa*s as it became a major center of Buddhist arts, architecture, and scholarship in South India. In addition to Amaravati [6.9-6.11], there are other important *stupa*s scattered throughout the Krishna River valley such as Bhattiprolu (second century BCE), Jaggayyapeta (second-first centuries BCE), and Nagarjunakonda (third-fourth centuries CE). While sharing similar features as their North Indian counterparts, Andhra *stupa*s like Amaravati have also developed their unique features:

- The *ayaka* platforms and *ayaka stambha*s.
- The *yasti-chattra* was occasionally substituted by an octagonal pole or *yupa-yasti* while the ornate *torana*s in the North Indian *stupa*s were completely replaced with freestanding animal-crowned pillars.
- Wheel-shaped structural walls radiating from the *stupa* core with their interstices filled with compacted earth; this method is also present in Gandhara *stupa*s suggesting its widespread employment in the construction of large *stupa*s {Sarkar 1966: 88-90}. This structural design had undoubtedly been introduced to support the massive dome, which increasingly grew into tremendous scale and height, and reduce potential subsidence; it also enabled the economy of materials by reducing the amount of bricks used in construction, which otherwise completely filled the solid domes in earlier *stupa*s.
- A few *stupa*s like Nagarjunakonda Site 20 also have swastikas in the base and center of the dome; the swastika in these cases was likely an auspicious symbol and might also represent Buddha aniconically.

Amaravati was undoubtedly the oldest *stupa* in the region and the grandest of its kind in the whole India; during its peak expansion in the second century CE it was one of the biggest *stupa*s in Asia and its size even rivaled the biggest of Gandhara *stupa*s. Amaravati also developed a unique artistic style that was the representative of South India collectively named Andhra Style; the style became profoundly influential in the subsequent arts in India, Sri Lanka, and Southeast Asia. Architecturally, Amaravati was a brilliant synthesis and advancement from Bharhut and Sanchi; it was no coincidence that the biggest *stupa* in the region was located in Amaravati since this was once the eastern capital of the Andhra Empire (c. 228 BCE-225 CE). The Andhras or Satavahanas ruled west central India, which included Sanchi, until the beginning of the second century CE when they expanded their territory to encompass east central India with their new capital in Dhynakataka or Dhanakataka, the old name of Amaravati. An inscription in the Early (Western) Andhras has also been found on one of the Sanchi *torana*s while the Nasik and Karla caves in the Deccan also contain numerous inscriptions of the Late (Eastern) Andhras. The massive *stupa* in Dhynakataka had been known to the locals as Dipaldinne (Hill of Lamps) as late as the eighteenth century CE when it was visited by the British. It was still an active Buddhist center in 1344 CE when Dharmakirti, possibly a Sri Lankan monk and teacher of the Bengalese monk Vanaratna, restored a two-storied temple here; Vanaratna later sought for instructions from two monks, Sabari dBanphyug and Nagabodhi, who were also residing in Dhynakataka between c. 1410-1415 CE {Mitra and Bhattacharya 1989: 190}. By the late eighteenth century CE, Dhynakataka was changed to Amaravati when a local *raja* Vasu Reddi Nayudu set up his new seat of government here; the *stupa* must have been in good conditions in 1796 CE when the irresponsible *raja* ordered his men to pillage it for building materials to be used in the construction of his new town. A year later, Colonel Mackenzie arrived and inspected the ruins for himself and he returned again with competent assistants in 1816 CE to survey the remains and make accurate drawings of the sculptures; he carried off a number of sculptured slabs during his stay. The customary pattern of antiquity looting, first making the surveys then carted the precious pieces away, continued unabated by the British until the beginning of the nineteenth century CE when there was virtually nothing left of this formerly celebrated *stupa*. The names of the involved individuals, besides the initial demolition by the local *raja*, included Robertson, Walter Elliot, Robert Sewell, James Burgess, and Alexander Rea; most of the fine pieces taken away were eventually shipped to the British Museum where they remained until this day while the others were housed in the Chennai Museum and the remaining members became the construction materials for the nearby Hindu temples. Like Sanchi and Bharhut, Amaravati also had a long history with the earliest inscription dated back in the Maurya Dynasty in the third century BCE and the latest in the twelfth century CE. While pillaging the *stupa* for building materials, Raja Vasu Reddi Nayudu also recovered a stone casket in the center of the dome and inside was a crystal box containing a small pearl, gold leaves, and likely relics; these were then shipped to the Chennai Museum. The remains of Amaravati can also be divided into three categories: architecture, sculptures, and epigraphs.

A. Architecture

At the first glance Amaravati **[6.9-6.11]** has all the familiar features of an Indian *stupa* including a ground *vedika* punctuated by four cardinal entries, a *medhi*, and a hemispherical *anda* crowned with a *harmika* and a *yupa-yasti* at the summit; besides these, this South Indian *stupa* also exhibits new features that distinguish itself from its cousins in the North. First, the tremendous increase in its size and dense surface ornamentations are immediately apparent; the huge diameter of the *medhi* is 162' compared to 120' for Sanchi and 68' for Bharhut while its diameter at the intersection of the *medhi* and *anda* is 138'. The inner diameter of the ground *vedika* is 192' and Amaravati rises to an amazing height of over 90' from the ground level to the top of the *harmika*. The identical entries in the four cardinal points are approached frontally rather than from the sides as in North Indian *stupa*s; each entrance has a semi-cicular half-lotus slab that also serves as one of the treads leading to the 15' wide *pradaksina* path, which is elevated 2' above the outside ground level. The 'moonstone' slabs common in Sri Lankan architecture likely originated in these Amaravati semicircular slabs. The ornate *torana*s typical of North Indian *stupa*s at Sanchi **[6.3]** and Bharhut **[6.6]** have been eliminated in South Indian *stupa*s to be replaced with pairs of lion-crowned pillars serving as formal gateways; there are eight couchant lions on top of the *usnisa*s facing the visitors at the four entries as in Bharhut. The massive limestone ground *vedika* **[6.10]** is over 13' high and at the peak of Amaravati both faces of its *stambha*s must have had two medallions and two half-medallions as well as two medallions on both faces of the *suchi*s as in Bharhut; the Amaravati *anda* was probably not truncated at the top like Sanchi and the *harmika* would fit on the curvature of the *anda*. A *yasti* or *yupa-yasti* is planted into the interior of the *anda* in the center of the *harmika* while *chattra*s are provided in the corners; I suspect in most South Indian *stupa*s the *yupa-yasti* probably replaced the *yasti-chattra* altogether. The *medhi* is about 6' high without a *vedika* and it has 6' x 28' curved projections (*ayaka*) in the four cardinal

points; each *ayaka* has a set of five 33' high pillars having square bases, octagonal in the middle, and rounded at the top. The elimination of the *medhi vedika* from the *stupa* was likely linked with the abandonment of the upper *pradaksina* path; this might have been influenced by Gandhara *stupa*s which typically did not have *medhi vedika*s or *torana*s **[6.13, 6.15]**. The obstruction of the upper *pradaksina* path due to the presence of the five imposing *ayaka* pillars alongwith the absence of the staircases and the *medhi vedika* clearly preclude the need for an upper *pradaksina* path; thus Sivaramamurti's belief in the existence of an upper *pradaksina* path is without bases {Sivaramamurti 1956: 26}. I also want to comment on the three well-known conjectural reconstructions of Amaravati by Jouveau Dubreuil {Sivaramamurti 1956: 25-26}, Percy Brown {Brown 1965: 37-38, pl. XXXV}, Douglas Barrett {Barrett 1954: 28}, and Robert Knox {Knox 1992: 24). Dubreuil's reconstruction, from which those of Barrett's and Knox's have been based on, seems the most logical except that his drawings shows all the *stambha*s having four medallions and there are no ninety degrees return railings at the entries. The four-medallion *stambha*s occurred only in a few segments of the ground *vedika* while the return railings were clearly shown on the Amaravati slab in the Chennai Museum {Brown 1965: pl. XXXVI fg. 2}; his drawing also shows the *anda* slabs curved when it should probably be straight. Brown's well-known reconstruction incorrectly shows the *stupa* having a solid *medhi vedika* since the latter was evidently absent in the *stupa* slabs {Stone 1994: pl. 104}. The sculpted slabs at the foot of the dome were meant to be viewed from below and a solid *medhi vedika*, as shown on Brown's drawing, would obstruct this view; he also erroneously shows the *yupa-yasti* as square when it should be octagonal. Barrett's reconstruction shows the *anda* a little too deflated or half-elliptical shape when it should be hemispherical while his *ayaka* pillars are too short and out of proportion to the massive dome behind. My own reconstruction of the *stupa* elevation and plan **[6.9]** is very similar to its actual reconstruction model now housed in the Chennai Museum; notice this Chennai model shows the *harmika* as solid when there should be spaces between the members as typical of Indian *stupa*s. The ornamentations on the *stupa* have also become extravagant and excessive compared to earlier Indian *stupa*s as literally every available surface, including the *anda* and *medhi*, is now covered with sculptural reliefs. During the mature phase of Amaravati in the second century CE, the upper part of the *anda* was relieved with a plaster (stucco) band of medallions and simulated jeweled swags whilst a continuous ring of sculpted stone

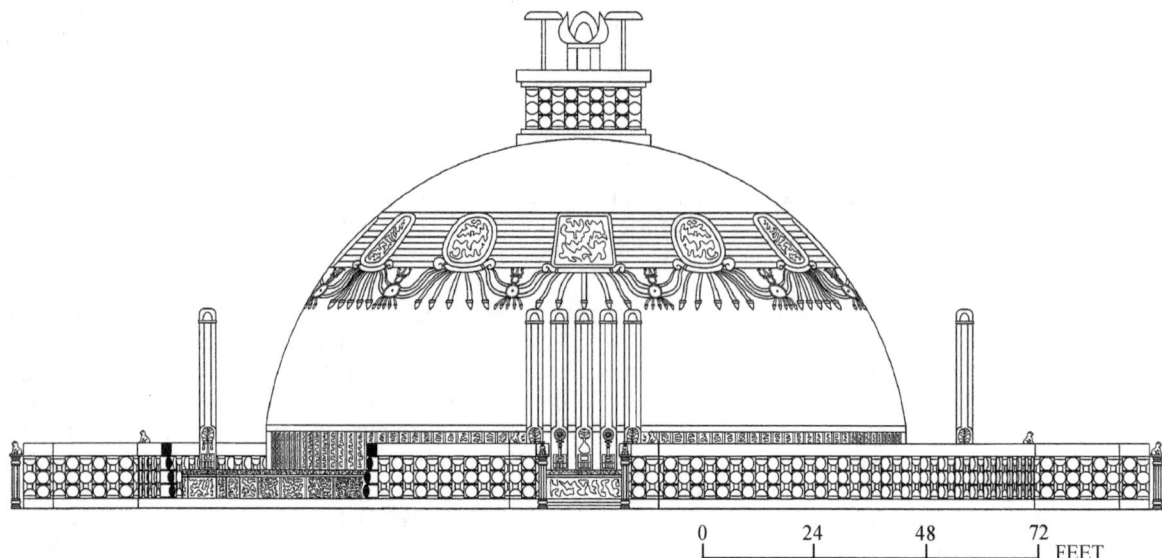

slabs completely encircled its base, probably with the exception of the surfaces behind the *ayaka* pillars. The expansion of decoration to include the *anda* and *medhi* might be credited to Gandhara influence [6.14-6.15]; the stucco coating on the *anda* and it reliefs could be the diffusion from Gandhara where stucco modeling was widespread since the first century CE {Varma 1985: 21-22}. The highest dimension of the Amaravati *anda* slabs is about 8'2" and each consists of two to three separate panels stacking above each other whilst the *medhi* slabs consists of single panels, the highest of which is about 5'8" or the height of an average man. Thus the different sizes of the sculpted scenes, the smaller on the *medhi* and the larger on the *anda*, directly correlate to the distances between the viewers and the viewed scenes on the slabs. The *anda* slabs were meant to be viewed from below and this was why their sizes were bigger than the *medhi* slabs, which would be viewed at the eye level; this clearly suggests that there was not an upper *pradaksina* path or a *medhi vedika* as Brown and Sivaramamurti believed {Sivaramamurti 1956: 26}. Thus pilgrims could circumambulate the *stupa* and view the sculpted scenes from below without interruption, hence the absence of stairs. The ground *vedika* was completely and minutely carved on both faces; a few *stambha*s had four medallions instead of the usual three while the spaces between these medallions, which had previously been left blank, were now tightly packed with sculpted scenes [6.10]. Like Bharhut, Amaravati also had small lamp niches on the *usnisa*s and *anda* slabs where pilgrims could leave their votive offerings and lamps; this was probably the reason why the *stupa* was aptly called by the locals as 'Hill of Lamps'

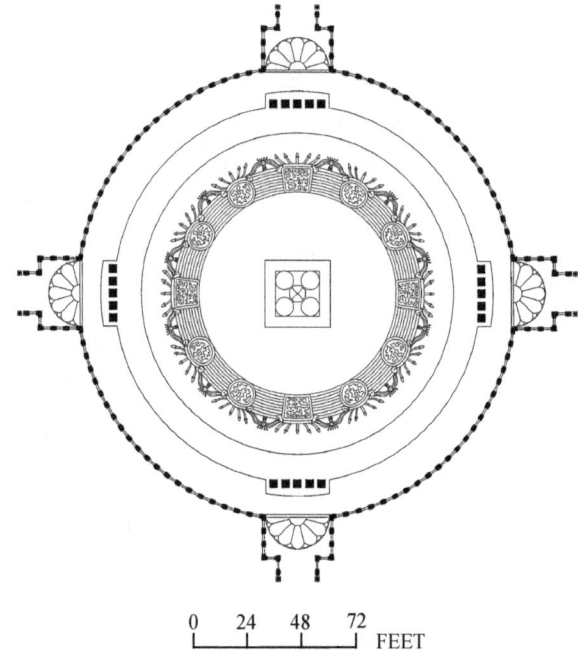

6.9. Elevation and plan (restored)
c. 100 CE
Amaravati- India

{Roy 1994: 118}.

Construction materials for Amaravati are similar to Bharhut and Sanchi; its core and foundation were constructed of oversized bricks about 20" x 10" x 4". Due to its tremendous size and large span, the dome interior probably had numerous structural brick walls crisscrossing one another and radiating outward from the center to bear the loads of the massive dome; the interstices between the walls would be filled with compacted earth. This was a unique technology in South Indian *stupa*s as also found in Nagarjunakonda Stupa {Stone 1994: pl. 17-18}; similar intersecting walls have also been discovered in Gandhara *stupa*s like Taxila Block E' Stupa (first-second centuries CE) and Dharmarajika (second century CE) [6.13]. On the other hand, the material for the slabs in the *anda* base and *medhi* was marble faced over brick; this was probably the earliest employment of marble in Indian architecture. The technique of facing marble slabs over the brick core prompted scholars to speculate that the Indians had borrowed this technology from the Romans {Stone 1994: 10}. I do not believe this was the case since the Indians already knew how to face the brick core of their *stupa*s with plaster and ashlars in Sanchi and it would not be too difficult to figure out how to face Amaravati with marble slabs. Moreover, due to the immense size of the *stupa* it would be preferable to prefabricate the pieces and assemble them together for the sake of architectural expediency and ease of transportation. Some marble slabs had subsequently been pulled down to have their back sides recarved; thus the manufacture and erection of the stone slabs in separate pieces were perfectly suited for the never-ending process of design modifications. The *vedika* was mainly sculpted out of limestone and granite was initially used in the carvings but it would eventually be abandoned in favor of the softer limestone, which was obviously more suited for minute carvings. As one may guess, the construction of the *vedika* again utilized the traditional mortise-and-tenon technique to join different members together as already observed in Sanchi and Bharhut.

It is now the moment to discuss the architectural functions and religious symbolisms of Amaravati. A few scholars have attempted to link the *yupa-yasti* with the Vedic sacrificial post (*yupa*) and Indra's peg {Roy 1994: 105-107}, both connotations I find incompatible in the Buddhist context. In the Sri Lankan chronicles a post, which was also termed '*yupa*' but apparently without any relationships with the Vedic *yupa*, was used to mark the center of the spot where the *stupa* would eventually be raised; possibly over times it became an integral architectural member of the *stupa*. The Amaravati slabs also reveal that in most cases the *yupa-yasti* resembles a giant octagonal parasol, an emblem of sovereignty {Brown 1965: pl. XXXVI fg. 2}{Stone 1994: pl. 144-146, pl. 148, pl. 150-151, pl. 153}. Architecturally, the choice of the *yupa-yasti* over the *yasti-chattra* would simplify the construction since the builder no longer had to build the complicated and tall multi-disc crown. Dubreuil proposed that the *ayaka* platforms and the *medhi* were flat to effectively shed water running down the dome {Sivaramamurti 1956: 26}; some also suggested that these were built so as pilgrims could leave their flowers or other offerings {Roy 1994: 95} but over 6' high *ayaka*s and *medhi* were obviously out of sight for the latter purpose. The *ayaka* platforms function as bases for the five imposing pillars, which visually unify the immense dome with the ground; without these pillars the massive dome would completely dwarf the viewers from the ground level. Moreover, the *ayaka* platform and its five pillars correlate to the width of the entrance and thus it is logical visually to erect five pillars instead of only one. It is also tempting to suggest these pillars as a conceptual transformation of the Asoka pillars, which were also commonly erected in front of Buddhist *stupa*s [6.3, 6.13]. They also indirectly evoke the *torana*s in North Indian *stupa*s [6.4, 6.7] and curiously they are nearly similar in heights; probably these *ayaka* pillars were South Indian equivalents of the North Indian *torana*s. The presence of imposing pillars as integral members of the *stupa* architecture was not unique in South India since comparable examples were also prevalent in Mathura and Gandhara *stupa*s [6.14] as early as the first century CE; probably the *ayaka* pillars of Amaravati had been influenced by the latter. These *ayaka* pillars also have carvings in their square bases depicting, from left to right, a tree, wheel on pillar, *stupa*, wheel on pillar, and tree. Fergusson believed these five pillars as representing the five Manusi Buddhas of the present *kalpa*, the Five Jina Buddhas, Five Elements, or simply as worshipping pillars {Benisti 2003 Volume I: 129}; Dubreuil also wrote "as there were four projections, it made twenty Buddhas, a known number according to religious texts {Benisti 2003 Volume I: 130}. Longhurst speculated that these symbols represented the five events in Buddha's life, namely Nativity, Great Departure, Enlightenment, First Sermon, and Decease {Benisti 2003 Volume I: 131}. Benesti believed each pillar as symbolically representing a Buddha and five pillars corresponding to the five Manusi Buddhas (Krakucchanda, Kanakamuni, Kasyapa, Sakyamuni, Maitreya); the five Buddhas in the four cardinal points were manifestations of the fifth 'noumenal Principle' in the center {Benisti 2003 Volume I: 133-145}. I will respond to these theories regarding the symbolisms of the five *ayaka* pillars. First, the aforesaid aniconic symbols on these *ayaka* pillars, the *bodhi*-tree, *dharmacakra*, and *stupa*, also commonly occur in Sanchi and Bharhut; they aniconically represent Buddha's Enlightenment, First Sermon, and Decease respectively. Second, actually there are Eight Manusi Buddhas as already depicted in Bharhut; Benisti seemed to have conveniently dropped the other three Buddhas to fit her theory. Her speculations about the pillars as symbolically representing the five Manusi Buddhas and manifestations of the 'noumenal Principle' are too fanciful and subjective to be accepted as valid. Dubreuil's quick mathematical calculation resulting in the total of twenty Buddhas is purely fantastic; the scholars' suggestion of the five Manusi Buddhas and the Five Jina Buddhas for these five *ayaka* pillars are also without factual bases. Moreover, the concept of the Five Jina Buddhas in the four cardinal directions and center alongwith the incorporation of their religious symbolisms in the *stupa* architecture did not occur until the eighth century CE in Vajrayana arts and architecture as in Orissa *stupa*s. Third, each of the five events in Buddha's life should have been represented as a unique symbol but the carved symbols on these pillars, namely two *bodhi*-trees, two *dharmacakra*s, and one *stupa*, were obviously repeated. Thus there were only three events representing Enlightenment (*bodhi*-tree), First Sermon (*dharmacakra*), and Decease (*stupa*) and not five according to Longhurst; these three events, alongwith the fourth for Nativity, would subsequently be depicted anthropomorphically in Andhra and Gandhara sculptures. Moreover the three symbols did not necessarily represent Buddhas since each was depicted without a parasol, which is an aniconic symbol typically denoting the invisible presence of Buddha.

According to Barrett, Amaravati had been constructed in three phases between c. 200 BCE-250 CE while Roy and Sivaramamurti believed there were four phases in the same period {Barrett 1954: 40-56}{Sivaramamurti 1956: 26-32}{Roy 1994: 113-116}. However their construction phases did not take into accounts of Sanchi and Bharhut; I do not believe Amaravati could have dated any earlier than these North Indian *stupa*s. Moreover, the fragment of the supposedly Asoka pillar containing a South Indian Brahmi inscription are doubted to be the work of Asoka; it probably dated in the late Maurya and post-Asoka or c. 200-175 BCE. The early granite *stambha*s were probably contemporary or later than the ground *vedika* of Sanchi Stupa I or c. 175-150 BCE; some of the archaic reliefs of Amaravati recall the *medhi vedika*s of Sanchi I-III and can be dated between c. 150-100 BCE. Later works of Phase I may be placed in the period between late Bharhut to the *torana*s of Sanchi Stupa I, probably between c. 75-50 BCE or slightly later. Besides, the archaic appearance of some early Amaravati reliefs was not indicative of an early date since the Amaravati carvers might not have sufficiently mastered the carving skills or they probably preferred to carve in an archaic style. Some late Amaravati sculptures also contain early inscriptions suggesting that these had been recarved at a later time and in fact the back sides of many Phase I slabs had been recarved during Phase III; other scholars, however, suggested the possibility of the archaism of the old script {Roy 1994: 180-184}. In my view the construction of Amaravati from architectural, sculptural, and epigraphic evidences appears to have been executed in four main phases {Roy 1994: 113-116}:

- Phase I (third-first centuries BCE): Possibly an Asoka pillar was first erected on the site of a small *stupa* and followed by a few granite *stambha*s, all dated in the third century BCE. Between the second-first centuries BCE the *stupa* was expanded with limestone replacing granite as the material for the ground *vedika*, which was probably plain without much decorations, and a few stone *medhi* slabs were also installed; the *harmika* and *yasti-chattra* or *yupa-yasti* were probably timber.
- Phase II (first century CE): The *stupa* continued to expand with new additions and the *vedika* would be carved with medallions and half-medallions; more marble slabs were installed on the *medhi* and the *anda* which were sculpted with narrative friezes and plaster swags.
- Phase III (second century CE): This was the mature phase of Amaravati and the peak of the construction activities with the erections of the great ground *vedika*, *ayaka* platforms and pillars; probably the *yupa-yasti* replaced the *yasti-chattra* during this phase.
- Phase IV (early third century CE): Construction activities decreased significantly; however, numerous small votive *stupa*s were also built around the main *stupa* with forms replicating the latter.

B. Sculpture

Sivaramamurti divided Amaravati sculptures into four phases {Sivaramamurti 1956: 26-32}:
- Phase I (c. 200-100 BCE): Some pieces displayed an archaic style similar to the *medhi vedika*s of Sanchi Stupa I-III and subsequent sculptures of *yaksa*s, *yaksi*s, etc. also exhibited a style akin to Bharhut. Toward the end of this phase, there emerged a new style comparable to the Sanchi *torana*s and parallel

to Barrett's Early Phase {Barrett 1954: pls. I, V, IXb-IXd, XIVb, XXXVIII-XXXIX, XLVI-XLVIII}.
- Phase II (c. 100 CE): The appearance of Buddha in the human form began late in this phase; however his aniconic representations, in particular the flaming pillar, remained popular.
- Period III (c. 150 CE): The production of Amaravati sculptures reached its peak as the carvings were generally refined, graceful, and also manneristic in behaviors and postures; many *stambha*s of the ground *vedika* had four medallions and were densely carved in the spaces between them [6.10].
- Phase IV (c. 200-250 CE): The sculptures gradually degenerated in numbers and quality as the main artistic center in the Krishna River valley shifted from Amaravati to Nagarjunakonda, now the seat the new Iksvaku Dynasty (225-325 CE). The scenes were tightly sculpted with numerous restless human figures and in many cases their depictions degraded into merely elongated stick figures resembling ivory carvings.

I would place Phase I between c. 175-0 BCE or in the second-first centuries BCE as I believe none of the Amaravati reliefs could have been dated between c. 250-200 BCE. Sivaramamurti arbitrarily placed Phase II in c. 100 CE leaving a century gap between Phase I-II and therefore I would date Phase II for the entire first century CE; Amaravati mature Phase III should span the whole second century CE and Phase IV probably did not immediately cease in c. 250 CE or about the rise of the Iksvakus and therefore should be dated in the third century CE. On the styles and themes of the Amaravati sculptures, Phase I displays similar characteristics as those of Sanchi and Bharhut; in closer scrutiny, Amaravati appears to share more common features with Bharhut than Sanchi. Thus the *makara* issuing an undulating garland on the *usnisa* of Amaravati [6.10 (left)] strongly suggests the continuation of Bharhut. The serpentine line resembling a garland in Amaravati, which was initially carried by dwarfish *yaksa*s in Phase I and later by *deva*s or men, is much thicker and heavier than Bharhut; the depiction of men carrying an undulating garland probably originated in the West and it also occurred in Gandhara and Khmer architecture. The ground *vedika* of Amaravati with numerous lotus medallions and half-medallions on both faces evidently carried on the Bharhut tradition [6.7-6.8]. As in Bharhut and Sanchi, there were familiar appearances of *yaksa*s, *yaksi*s, *deva*s, *devata*s, *naga*s, *triratna*s, *makara*s, and winged animals as well as aniconic symbols of Buddha like *Buddhapada*, *bodhi*-tree, *dharmacakra*, etc.; the flaming pillar, however, was new and unique in Andhra sculptures. Depictions of Buddhist monks in Amaravati, which were conspicuously absent in Bharhut and Sanchi, suggest Gandhara influence. On the other hand the Mayadevi or 'Goja-Lakshmi' scenes, which were ubiquitous in Bharhut and Sanchi, were conspicuously absent from Amaravati and it might have lost its religious appeal. There are depictions of the elephant-faced dwarfish *yaksa* without the long trunk which Sivaramamurti believed to be the forerunner of the popular Hindu god Ganesh; the squarish crown worn by Indra among the Amaravati reliefs also became the model for Visnu's crown {Sivaramamurti 1956: 77, 85, pl. VII fg. 8, XV fg. 2}. The checker-patterned *sanghati* worn by Buddhist monks among the Amaravati reliefs can be found as far as East Asia; a few figures also wore the short skirt resembling the Roman dress, which had probably been introduced via trade with the Roman Empire since a Hadrian coin has been found in the Krishna River valley {Sivaramamurti 1956: 119, pl. IX fg. 14-15, LIX fg. d}. Some exceptionally naturalistic depictions of the acanthus-leaf motifs on the *vedika* suggest an indirect influence of the Greco-Roman technique likely via Gandhara. The thematic distribution of the sculptures reveals the perpetual popularity of Buddha's Life Scenes and the *jataka*s seem to have experienced a resurgence in Amaravati after its temporary abatement in Sanchi. There are several innovations in the Amaravati sculptures, particularly the pre-fabricated or pre-carved marble slabs on the *anda* and the continuous friezes on the *medhi*; the latter type is conceptually similar as the architrave reliefs on Sanchi *torana*s [6.5]. The scenes on the *anda* slabs are separated by pilaster-like bands, a technique already used to frame the scenes in Bharhut. The friezes are typically depicted continuously and the scenes are separated by medallions and pilasters with *mithuna*s inserted in between; for the first time, the *mithuna*s are found on the *anda* in such a conspicuous location. The *mithuna*s' rise to prominence in Amaravati virtually eclipsed the *yaksa*s and *yaksi*s previously common in Bharhut and Sanchi as *dvarapala*s; the most erotic of these *mithuna*s were found in Nagarjunakonda Stupa. Indeed, women in the Amaravati reliefs and Andhra arts are generally treated with the utmost carving skills and there are senses of poise and mannerism their behaviors; they are beautifully portrayed often standing about and looking languorously into the dreamy space. They are lavishly adorned with exquisite jewelries, beautiful dresses, and sumptuous head crowns; their worlds are full of external beauty and refined tastes bordering on aristocratic mannerism. Amaravati sculptors apparently devoted inordinate attention in depicting the curvaceous bodies of these gorgeous women and they

6.10. Ground *vedika*, outer face (left), inner face (right)
c. 150 CE
Chennai Museum, Chennai- India

6.11. Buddha tames the Nalagiri elephant in Rajagriha
c. 175-200 CE
Chennai Museum, Chennai- India

all appeared to exude certain exhibitionistic seduction about them. The exaggerations of their limbs became even more pronounced in later sculptures as their long slender legs were purposely juxtaposed with their robust hips, extremely narrow waists, and round firm breasts. These scenes would pave the way to the eventual climax of Indian and Buddhist arts in the Gupta Dynasty as observed in the superb Gupta-Styled sculptures and the Ajanta murals. With the decline of Amaravati in the third century CE, its sculptures manifested an extreme propensity toward excessive carvings as the scenes were minutely and densely carved with figures in perpetual motion and many also displayed extreme emotions; this tendency was even more pronounced in Nagarjunakonda sculptures.

One of the typical scenes of the mature phase of Amaravati is a medallion depicting the well-known incident in Buddha's life or the taming of the fuming Nalagiri elephant [6.11]; the animal was set loose as a part of the plot by Devadatta, the jealous cousin-monk and Buddha's rival, to kill him. The scene is portrayed twice in which the first one shows the large beast issuing from the city gate on the left and charging wildly on the street of Rajagriha toward Buddha and his attendants standing on the right while the second depicts the actual episode of taming the mad elephant. In the first episode the beast can be seen throwing the mahout off its body who is about to be trampled under its huge feet as spectators on the balconies and street look on in horror. The petrified woman in the upper center leans to the right with her arm grasping tightly to her man for protection; the mahout again tries in vain to control the savage beast. The intense terror in the first episode is strongly contrasted with the pervasive tranquility in the second episode where the wild beast is finally pacified by Buddha's magical and spiritual power; the elephant is seen prostrating below the charming presence of Buddha, who is clearly unaffected by all the commotion before him. The differences between this scene and Bharhut [6.8] are in their styles and contents; in the Amaravati scene there is a strong inclination toward the juxtaposition of dissimilar elements to dramatize the scene, particularly the deliberate contrasts between the wild beast and the superhuman Buddha as well as the suspenseful terror in the spectators and Buddha's great spiritual equanimity. These are further intensified by the sculptor's manipulation of the interplay of light and shadow which is brought out by varying the depth of carving. Conversely, the Bharhut scene characteristically displays a pervasive detached calmness which is further reinforced by the stiff and frozen demeanors of its actors; the apparent flatness and archaic style of Bharhut clearly did not attain the high level of sophistication as in Amaravati. The mastery of perspective also reaches maturity in Amaravati in which its scenes are typically viewed from the eye-level while the actions are crystallized in single episodes rather than multiple episodes to be viewed from the bird's-eye level as in Bharhut. Andhra arts continued for two more centuries in Nagarjunakonda (third-fourth centuries CE) though the style was already in its waning years.

C. Epigraph

Amaravati inscriptions reflected its long history spanning between the late third century BCE-twelfth centuries CE which confirmed the site as an important Buddhist center that certainly rivaled Sanchi. The earliest inscription is on an alleged Asoka pillar presumably dated in Asoka's time or possibly late Maurya Dynasty (c. 249-184 BCE); its six-line text is too effaced with only a few readable words like *vijaya* (victory) but overall the paragraph does not make any sense {Roy 1994: 15-17}. There are parallels between Amaravati and Sanchi inscriptions, in particular their script and the spoken dialect; between the third century BCE-first centuries CE, the southern variant of the Brahmi script was used in Amaravati inscriptions and the language was Prakrit. Between the second-fourth centuries CE, a modified version of the southern Brahmi script continued in the inscriptions while the spoken dialect was a mixture of Prakrit and Paisaci, the official language of the Andhras. From the Gupta Dynasty to the twelfth century CE, Amaravati inscriptions primarily employed local South Indian scripts and dialects like Telugu; the last inscriptions were in the Nagari script and the language Sanskrit. Sivaramamurti listed more than 100 recorded inscriptions and certainly higher if all the remains have been accounted for {Sivaramamurti 1956: 271-304}. Donative inscriptions, like Sanchi and Bharhut, contain names from the royalty to the common folks, from an individual to the whole town, and from the religious such as monks and nuns to lay devotees. There are names of different Buddhist sects among the inscriptions and the most influential one is the Caityaka (Worshippers of Caityas) of the Theravada. Clearly by this time the Buddhist *stupa* became immensely popular so that a wholly new sect was founded to devote exclusively to its worship and construction; many monks of this sect likely specialized in the *stupa* design and construction as project superintendents. Many inscriptions also mention the name of Amaravati as Mahacaitya (Great Sacred Monument) and Southeast Asian *stupa*s are also commonly known as *caitya*s. Amaravati inscriptions usually start out with a typical prayer like "Sidham! Namo Bhagavato!" (Success! Adoration to the Buddha!) and many end with the usual phrase 'for the welfare and happiness of the whole world.' One important inscription reveals various sects controlling different areas of the *stupa* ground and reads 'a pious gift of *dharmachakra* at the Western gate, the property of the Caityaka School' {Sivaramamurti 1956: ins. #51}. A few Amaravati scenes also contain labeled inscriptions but not as prevalent like Bharhut which suggests that the practice has probably fallen out of favor. The longest inscription in c. 1100 CE mentioned King Simhavarman's visit to Amaravati where he made offerings to the *stupa*; from then on the Buddhist presence in Amaravati and South India gradually disappeared.

Amaravati was the last of the greatest Old School Buddhist *stupa*s in India; as in North Indian *stupa*s like Sanchi and Bharhut, Amaravati sculptures continued to rely on archaic aniconic symbols to represent Buddha even as his anthropomorphic image had already been depicted for over two centuries. The Amaravati Style was profoundly influential as an artistic foundation for the subsequent flowering of the brilliant Gupta Style in North India and the Vakataka Style in the Deccan caves; its classic Buddha had been emulated as far as Sri Lanka, Java, Champa, and Kampuchea. Amaravati was the most representative of Andhra arts that was to be succeeded by Nagarjunakonda between the third-fourth centuries CE; South India was historically among the longest Buddhist centers in India where sporadic production of Buddhist sculptures at Nagapattinam occurred as late as between the sixteenth-seventeenth centuries CE.

5. Kesariya Stupa (third century BCE-seventh centuries CE)

Kesariya [6.12] was among the latest and biggest *stupa*s ever constructed in India; it was discovered by Alexander Cunningham in the nineteenth century CE but its excavation did not begin until 2001 CE by K. K. Muhammad's team. The reason for its late resurrection was probably due to its relative obscurity compared to other well-known *stupa*s like Sanchi, Bharhut, and Amaravati. Before the excavation it was covered with a mound of earth and vegetation and like many other Indian Buddhist *stupa*s it had also been pillaged for bricks for construction usage. A huge earthquake in 1934 CE reduced its already ruined height from 123' to 104'; in its original height the *stupa* is estimated to be 150' from base to the tip of the *yasti-chattra* {Muhammad 2002: 19}. During his pilgrimage to India in the early fifth century CE, Fa-hsien mentioned a *stupa* constructed over Buddha's alms-

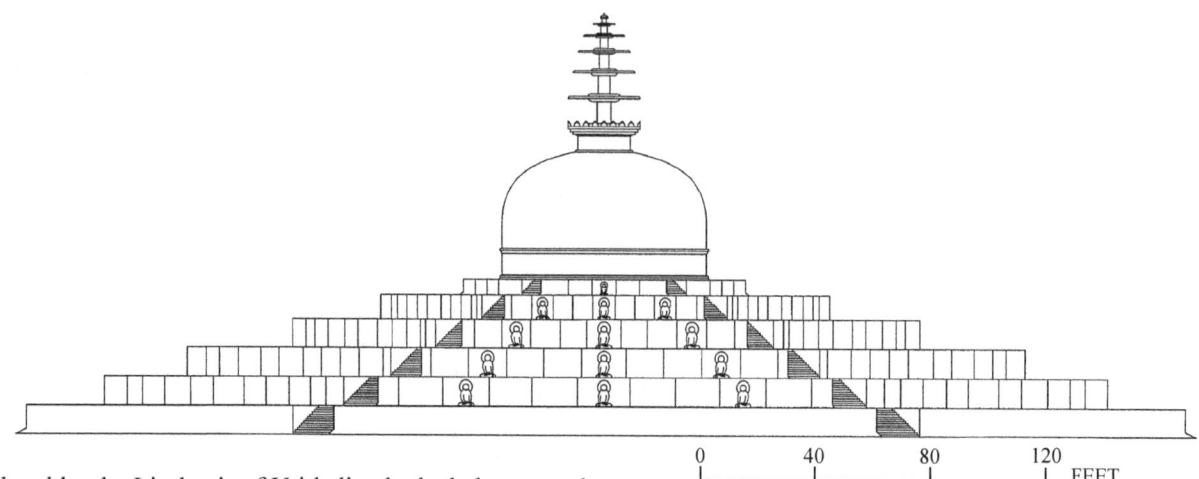

bowl by the Licchavis of Vaishali, who had also erected a stone pillar engraved with an inscription {Beal 1869: 94-95}; this is undoubtedly the description of Kesariya and its Asoka pillar, which lion capital was found here in 1862 CE. Another Chinese pilgrim-monk Hsuan-tsang also documented this same *stupa* in the seventh century CE but he gave no specific details about the site {Beal 1905 Volume II: 73-74}. The Mahaparinirvana-sutra told a well-known story of Buddha spending the night in Bhognagara during his last journey toward Kushinagar; the town lied somewhere along the Vaishali-Kushinagar road probably near modern Kesariya {Walshe 1995: 255-256}. During this occasion Buddha was reportedly followed by the people of Vaishali knowing that this would be his last journey before his imminent death in Kushinagar. Buddha, who was unable to convince the Vaishalis to turn back, decided to hand over his begging bowl to the distressed people in Kesariya; they, in honoring this great personal belonging of Buddha, subsequently constructed a *stupa* for it to commemorate this poignant event. The Majjhima-nikaya mentioned a certain town called Kesaputta which was also associated with one of Buddha's initial spiritual teachers Alara Kalama; one of Buddha's most important discourses was addressed to the Kalama people also in Kesaputta {Rahula 1974: 2}. A local legend unrelated to Buddhism told the story of Raja Bena who died grief-stricken upon hearing the death of his wife Kamalavati; he and his family were subsequently buried alongwith in the Kesariya mound, then known as Deora or Raja Bena ka Garh. This was obviously a later legend unrelated to the Buddhist *stupa*, which is not a royal tomb. Parts of the *stupa* still remains hidden under the mound as continuing efforts are being made to excavate it and completely expose the site; governmental plans are already on the table to transform it into a tourist

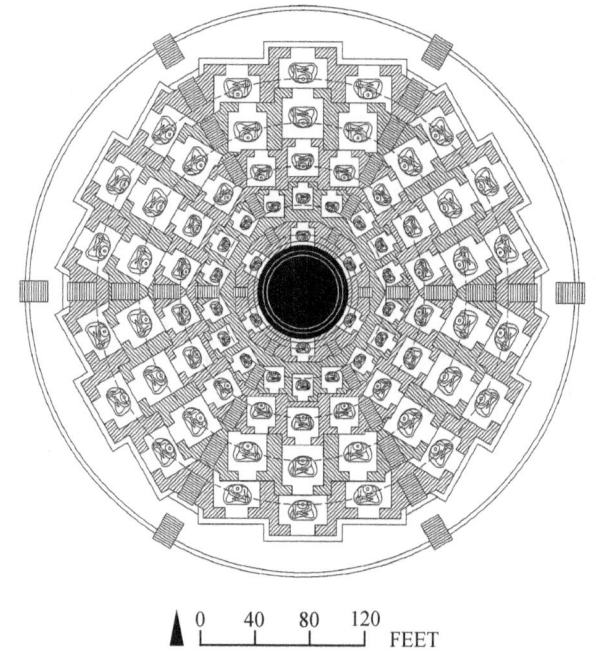

6.12. Elevation (restored) and plan
Sixth-seventh centuries CE (final form)
Kesariya- India

and pilgrim center.

The brick *stupa* **[6.12]** has a large 403'6" diameter base and its height to the top of the current ruin is about 104'; there are six sets of thirty-six staircases radiating from the center and divide the plan into six equal segments. There are six terraces with the lowest one circular and the upper five hexagonal; each of the upper five terraces have three squarish *vihara*-typed cells that diminish in scales and numbers so that the uppermost terrace has only one cell. Each of these cells once had a stucco Buddha image seated on a cushion gesturing the *bhumisparsa-mudra*; on the stylistic ground, the sculptures might be dated in the post-Gupta Dynasty or between the sixth-seventh centuries CE. The upper cells are set back from the ones below by a distance of about 4'-5' which creates a narrow but wide enough *pradaksina* path for pilgrims to circumambulate the upper terraces. The back sides of these cells have been constructed over earlier foundations of larger and better quality bricks suggesting the construction of the *stupa* likely dated before the Gupta Dynasty (c. 320-647 CE); most Kesariya bricks have geometric patterns, floral designs, and *kirti-mukha*s typical of the Gupta designs. On the top terrace stands a massive *stupa* of 72'2" diameter and 32'10" in its current height having moldings in the base and on the body; its restored elevation likely has a drum as in Gandhara *stupa*s with the characteristic small dome and a solid *harmika* crowned with a multi-tiered *yasi-chattra*. An Asoka pillar with a sejant lion capital was discovered here by Captain Markham Kittoe in 1862 CE proving beyond a doubt that Kesariya could have been founded by Asoka in the third century BCE {Singh 2003: 246-247}. In its current conditions, a comprehensive picture of Kesariya is far from being complete but some basic construction phases may be deduced from its initial excavations:

- Phase I (third century BCE-third centuries CE): The core of the *stupa* likely existed in Asoka's time, if not founded by him, as a capital of his pillar was found here; initially it might have started out as a small and simple *stupa* like Sanchi which would gradually be enlarged in the subsequent centuries.
- Phase II (fourth-fifth centuries CE): It was again expanded possibly having a multi-terraced circular or cruciform plan surmounted by a *stupa* superstructure with four staircases as also in vogue among contemporary Gandhara *stupa*s **[6.17]**.
- Phase III (sixth-seventh centuries CE): The *stupa* was again modified from a circular or cruciform terraced plan to a circular hexagonal terraced form; the Buddha sculptures in the cells were probably sculpted in the post-Gupta Dynasty or seventh century CE.

The massive brick Buddhist *stupa* from Lauriya-Nandangarh (third century BCE-seventh centuries CE), with its three polygonal bases surmounted by three circular ones, seems to be the precursor of Kesariya {Mitra 1971: 83-85}{Deva 1995: 27}. Among the Mathura reliefs (c. 100 BCE) are depictions of *stupa*s having multiple terraces and thus the form of multi-terraced *stupa*s like Kesariya might have been conceived at least in the first century BCE {Quintanilla 2007: fg. 21}; *stupa*s having two or three terraces with Buddha niches were not uncommon in Gandhara **[6.17-6.18]**. Descendants of Kesariya can be found as far as Java in the famed Borobudur **[6.28]**; however the plain and massive form of Kesariya is architecturally less refined than Borobudur.

B. Development of the Indian Stupa

The Indian *stupa* was not an inflexible form as it continued to evolve in different temporal and geographical contexts that were functionally determined by local requirements; availability of local materials, climate, tradition, cultural milieu, etc. would ultimately shape its forms. Thus in India its classic dome-shaped form prevailed as in Sanchi **[6.3]** while in Indonesia it metamorphosed into a multi-terraced monument like Borobudur **[6.28]**. Further in East Asia, it would be transformed into the ubiquitous multi-tiered pagoda like Songyue **[6.24]** while in Myanmar it became the epitome of the Buddhist architectural elegance in the shimmering golden pinnacle of Shwedagon **[6.35]**. Despite its multiplicity in forms and functions, its fundamental spirit remains essentially unchanged as a holy edifice for interring Buddhist relics; above all, the Indian *stupa* was the original impetus and inspiration for later generations of Asian *stupa*s. The following sections will delve into the classification of the forms and symbolisms of the Buddhist *stupa* beyond the Indian proper.

1. *Stupa* - Pakistan, Afghanistan, Central Asia, Turkistan

In the case of Gandhara, there is not a completely extant *stupa* that can be compared with the outstanding conditions of the Indian *stupa*s like Sanchi since most have utterly been flattened that only their plans can be discerned. Fortunately in a few cases, parts of their superstructures still remain and with a number of surviving votive *stupa*s and reliquary models it is still possible to restore the original forms of Gandhara *stupa*s. The initial form of Gandhara *stupa*s strongly exhibited the characteristic Indian hemispherical dome **[6.13]**. However unlike the typically hemispherical dome in the Indian *stupa*, the Gandhara *stupa* would be subjected to several innovative modifications that ultimately diverged greatly from their Indian predecessor within several centuries of its existence [6.14-6.18], most notably in its emphasis on the verticality. Sung-yun, a Chinese pilgrim in India in c. 520 CE, reportedly saw the Kanishka Stupa [6.18] rising to a staggering height of over 560'; the travelogues of Fa-hsien (fifth century CE) and Hsuan-tsang (seventh century CE) gave it a 400' height. A comparison between a classic Indian *stupa* [6.3] and a typical Gandhara *stupa* [6.15] will elucidate the obvious differences between them; the followings will elaborate on these dissimilarities as well as the types and characteristics of Gandhara *stupa*s:

- A typical Gandhara *stupa* [6.15] composes of three distinct parts: (a) A square plinth generally serves as a base for the superstructure while the *medhi* of the Indian *stupa* encircles the dome which springs directly from the ground up, (b) the body has several tiers of circular drums stacking on top of each other that are capped by an insignificant dome, (c) the solid *harmika* is crowned with an imposing multi-tiered *yasti-chattra* of an astonishing proportion equal to height of the base and body combined; the emphasis of Gandhara *stupa*s on the elongated drum and multi-tiered *yasti-chattra* is clearly evident in the Kanishka Stupa [6.18].
- The *vedika*s and *torana*s typical in Indian *stupa*s are conspicuously absent in Gandhara *stupa*s, with the exception like Saidu Sharif Stupa I [6.14] which has *vedika*s but without *torana*s; eventually all *vedika*s would be eliminated from Gandhara *stupa*s.
- Gandhara *stupa* generally emphasizes on the verticality [6.18] and its towering appearance was achieved by piling up several tiers and levels consisting of plinths, drums, *harmika*, and the tall *yasti-chattra*; the latter sometimes had over ten *chattra*s and could reach half the height of the *stupa*.
- Gandhara builders also experimented with new designs, some of which would be repeatedly emulated in later *stupa*s throughout the Buddhist world, such as the quincunxial [6.14] and terraced pyramidal designs [6.16] and the cruciform plan [6.17].
- From the second century CE on, the Gandhara *stupa* increasingly emphasized on the four cardinal directions, each having an image chapel containing Buddhist images [6.13].
- Gandhara *stupa*s conspicuously employed many Greco-Roman elements such as the Ionic and Corinthian pilasters, acanthus leaves, dentils, etc. along with Westernized sculptures to profusely decorate its plinths and drums.
- The materials and construction technologies of Gandhara *stupa*s were also very different from their Indian counterparts with stone as the main material; the *stupa* core consisted of rubbles that were faced with neatly cut stone pieces known as diaper or ashlar masonry. Gandhara *stupa*s were typically covered in several layers of plaster or stucco as this was the most economical and speediest construction method. Stucco could easily and quickly be molded into a variety of shapes that produced smoother and sharper looks in their final forms than stone; it also took surface coatings such as paint and gilt, which most Gandhara *stupa*s had, better than stone.
- In two rare cases of Mohenjo-daro and Kalawan A4 *stupa*s, their relic chambers were accessible and possibly had never been closed {Marshall 1951 Volume I: 323-324}. The purpose was probably to allow pilgrims direct and instant access to important relics inside, which were otherwise typically buried in other *stupa*s, so as to stir up deep religious fervor; a hollow interior would also reduce the loads of the structure and construction materials as Gandhara *stupa*s grew increasingly tall and massive. This type of Gandhara *stupa*s with accessible interiors is common in the northern Buddhist countries in East Asia [6.20-6.21, 6.24-6.25] and Tibet [6.40-6.41].
- Relics were sometimes deposited into columns like Column Number 24 of Saidu Sharif Stupa I [6.14] which effectively transformed it into a *stupa*.

The westernmost presence of Gandhara *stupa*s has been reported at Gyaur-kala in Turkmenistan and the easternmost in Turkistan such as Rawak in Khotan and the Miran groups reaching all the way to the Chinese western frontier in Dunhuang. It is much more difficult to precisely date Gandhara *stupa*s as most have been damaged beyond recognition and the recovered materials, unlike the Indian *stupa*s, lack sufficient inscriptions for proper identifications. On the other hand hoards of coins, which usually contain dates and titles of the reigning kings, have been excavated from Gandhara monasteries and *stupa*s and these help significantly in dating the structures in which they were buried. Another useful method for dating Gandhara *stupa*s is based on the types of masonry used in their constructions; John Marshall have identified four masonry types {Marshall 1951 Volume I: 260-261, pl. 55}: (a) Rubble (sixth century BCE-25 CE), (b) Diaper (c. 25-150 CE), (c) Single diaper-ashlar (c. 150-300 CE), and (d) Double diaper-ashlar (c. 300-460 CE). There was evidently another masonry type that he overlooked or the large ashlar blocks (c. 30 BCE-25 CE) found in Dharmarajika D2 {Marshall 1951 Volume I: pl. 55 #1}, Chakpat {Behrendt 2003: fg. 114}{Fergusson 1910: fg. 23}, and Saidu Sharif Stupa I {Faccenna 1995: pl. 23-31, 224-225}; it should typologically and chronologically be between Type (a) and Type (b). Large ashlar blocks had already been used as facing stones in Sanchi Stupa I and the Gandhara builders probably inherited this type from the Indians. There are several types of Gandhara *stupa*s, with the earliest type exhibiting strong Indian influences that could have been commenced as early as Asoka's time.

a. Neo-Indian Stupa

This was certainly the earliest form of Gandhara *stupa*s and a direct descendant of the Indian *stupa* as exemplified in Dharmarajika [6.13]; it retained the dominant hemispherical dome in the Indian tradition as in Sanchi [6.3], Bharhut [6.6], and Amaravati [6.9]. Besides Dharmarajika, there are several similar examples in Gandhara like Chakpat, Manikyala, and Butkara I; Dharmarajika had been looted and damaged numerous times until excavated by John Marshall in 1913 CE. Its name was possibly a combination of '*Dharma*' (Buddha's Teachings) and '*raja*' (king), meaning 'the *stupa* of the *Dharma* king or Buddha.' Moreover in the Asokavadana, Asoka also reputedly erected 84,000 *dharmarajika*s (monuments of religious piety) throughout his empire and for this pious act the Buddhists dearly venerated him as a *dharmaraja* (virtuous king). These *dharmarajika*s were originally erected by Asoka not only over Buddha's relics but also as shrines and temples (*caitya*) to commemorate the special events in Buddha's life. Asoka was once the governor of Gandhara in Taxila and expectedly that he must have also built some monuments in this great cosmopolitan city; thus Dharmarajika could be one of his many *dharmarajika*s {Marshall 1951 Volume I: 234-235}. There are no relics or surviving inscriptions to ascertain its construction dates and only careful examinations of its remains will shed some lights on its history. The *stupa* was originally surrounded by image chapels or cells (*pratimagriha*), which architecturally replaced the ground *vedika* in the Indian *stupa* and created a 12' wide ground *pradaksina* path; there were gaps between these cells that created natural entrances into the *stupa* ground and so the Indian *torana*s were no longer needed. The incorporation of the *pratimagriha*s on the *stupa* plan reflected the growing cult of images in Gandhara; a similar arrangement of radiating *pratimagriha*s encircling a principal *stupa* could also be found in Butkara I

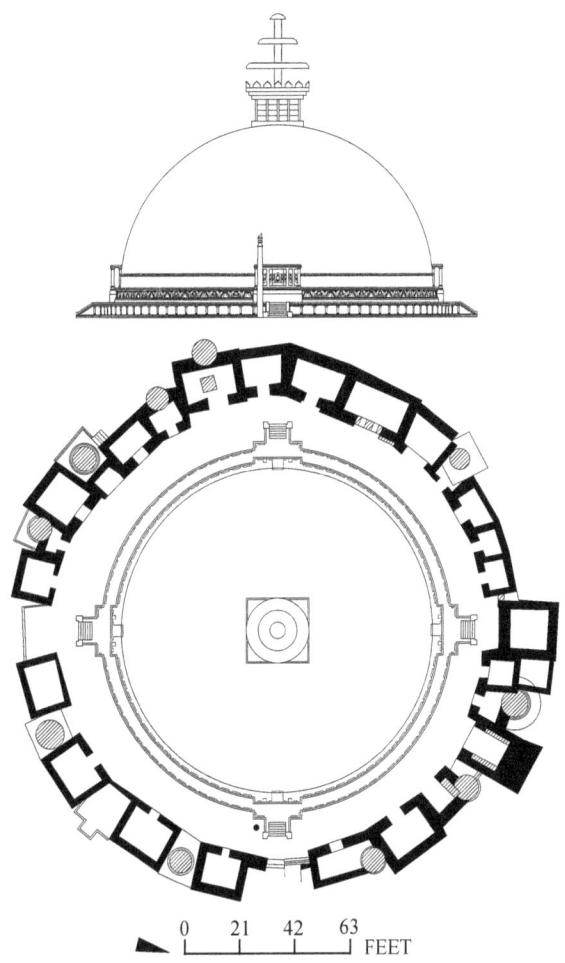

6.13. Dharmarajika Stupa elevation (restored) and plan
c. 100 BCE-500 CE
Fourth-fifth centuries CE (final form)
Taxila- Pakistan

and Jamalgarhi. The *harmika* of Dharmarajika was lost and the *anda* badly damaged but fortunately its base is still extant to facilitate the reconstruction of its plan and elevation with a certain degree of confidence. The symmetrical plan shows remarkable similarities to Amaravati with its *anda* dimension of nearly 120' diameter or about the same diameter as the Sanchi *medhi*. The *anda* is elevated on a 5' high circular *medhi* that creates an upper *pradaksina* path and the *stupa* has four staircases in the four cardinal points connecting with the upper level; the original height of the *stupa* from the ground level to the top of the solid *harmika* is estimated at about 80'. It is uncertain if this elevated *pradaksina* path was meant for religious circumambulation around the *anda* since there was not a *vedika* to protect pilgrims from the danger of falling off the narrow walkway, which is 4'9" wide and 5' above the ground. On the eastern stair there was a pillar of kanjur stone, which is the local soft sandstone unrelated to the Chunar sandstone of the Asoka pillars; this 2'2" diameter and about 30' high pillar might be contemporary with the original *stupa*. There were four large image chapels containing Buddhist sculptures in the four cardinal points; originally there were image niches with sculptures between the Corinthian pilasters at the base of the *anda* as the *medhi* only had dividing pilasters. Dharmarajika also had sixteen rubble walls radiating outward from its core that resembled a *cakra* (wheel) plan; the interstices between these walls were completely filled with rubbles no doubt to support the massive dome. This *cakra* plan, or *dharmacakra* in the Buddhist context, might also be interpreted as the symbolic representation of Buddha as a *dharmacakravartin* or a universal and religious *Dharma* monarch who turned the Wheel of Truths that radiated Buddha's *Dharma* throughout the four corners of the world, hence also the four image chapels in the four cardinal points. Similar *cakra* plans with radiating structural walls have also been found in Sirkap Block E' Stupa and South Indian *stupa*s like Nagarjunakonda; the exterior of Dharmarajika was originally faced with single diaper-ashlars, which would most likely be coated with several plaster layers to be painted or gilded.

According to John Marshall, the construction of this *stupa* might be divided into five phases {Marshall 1951 Volume I: 234-95}:

- Phase I (c. 100-50 BCE): The *stupa* was presumably commenced by Asoka in the third century BCE but it is impossible to confirm this. The first foundation was probably laid down contemporary or later than Shunga *stupa*s in India like Bharhut where masons' marks in Kharosthi, the language of Gandhara, have been discovered on the east *torana*; this strongly suggests that there were artistic exchanges between the two regions and this period was indeed the beginning of the rise of Gandhara architecture. Only the partially ruined rubble dome of Dharmarajika is still extant while all other traces of its early constructions have been completely obliterated by later reconstructions and it is not possible to reconstruct its original form.
- Phase II (c. 50 BCE-25 CE): The dome and the plain circular drum were enlarged alongwith the addition of a ring of small *stupa*s surrounding the principal *stupa*. A few of these small *stupa*s, such as D2, were constructed of rubbles and ashlars similar to Sirkap Block F-G *stupa*s and they could be freestanding pedestaled pillars as in Butkara I, a *stupa* in Swat contemporary with Dharmarajika.
- Phase III (c. 25-150 CE): Initially a few *vihara*s were inserted between the aforesaid small ring *stupa*s for guardian-monks and caretakers of the site or possibly as pilgrim reception halls. Probably it was not until King Kanishka's reign (c. 128-151 CE) that the *pratimagriha*s were also added to house images of Buddha and *bodhisattva*s; all these new additions were in the new diaper masonry. John Marshall concluded that all these new cells were *pratimagriha*s but some could be *vihara*s; the lion pillar in front of the *stupa* could be erected during this phase with a form resembling the contemporary Saidu Sharif Stupa I pillars [6.14].
- Phase IV (c. 150-300 CE): The circular plinth and its lower band of pilasters were constructed alongwith four staircases in the four cardinal points; these were in the single diaper-ashlar masonry.
- Phase V (c. 300-500 CE): The four image chapels were added in the four cardinal points. The band of Corinthian pilasters was built into the drum with trapezoidal portal and *caitya*-arched niches in between, all originally attached with Buddhist images; the whole monument was then replastered and given a new coat of lime or gild.

Swayambhunath [6.37-6.38] in Nepal seemingly echoes Dharmarajika having image chapels in the cardinal points, a solid *harmika*, and the conspicuous absence of the Indian *torana*s; the transitional sub-type in the Jamalgahri main *stupa* had two similar circular drums and a larger lower one alongwith a significantly smaller dome. The emphasis on the verticality in Jamalgahri became more apparent alongwith the disproportionate increase in the height of the *yasti-chattra* in relation to the *stupa* body; these transitional features paved the way to the eventual emergence of the mature Gandhara *stupa*.

b. Pillared and Quincunxial Stupa

This stage marked a significant development toward the mature Gandhara *stupa* and an excellent example is Saidu Sharif Stupa I [6.14]; this *stupa*, which was a part of the Saidu Sharif monastery (first-fifth centuries CE), has been thoroughly excavated by the Italian team lead by Dominico Faccenna for nearly thirty years since the 1950s CE. The approach to the main entry of the *stupa* in the north is symmetrically flanked on both sides with freestanding pedestaled pillars of similar forms as those on the main *stupa*. The nearly square 64' x 69' plinth

Part II. Architecture   Stupa . 175

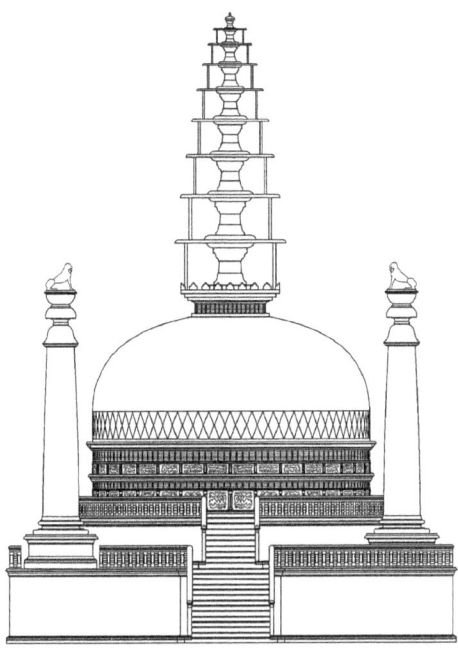

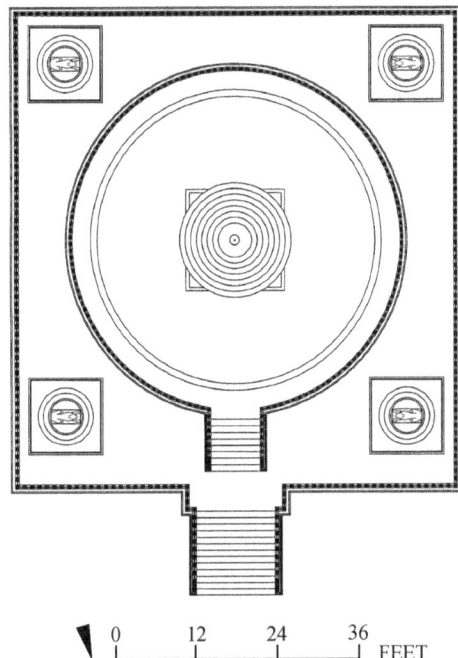

6.14. Saidu Sharif Stupa I elevation and top view (restored)
First-third centuries CE
Saidu Sharif- Pakistan

serves as the foundation for the massive upper superstructure consisting of the circular plinth about 50' diameter; there are two staircases connecting the two levels on the north side. There are four imposing pedestaled pillars of about 43'7" high in the hybrid Indian and Greco-Roman style that are symmetrically positioned in the four corners of the plinth; they are surmounted by four lions facing one another toward the *stupa* in the center. The square plinth is protected by a *vedika* but the 2'9" wide clearance between the pillared pedestals and the circular drum is evidently too narrow to have originally functioned as a *pradaksina* path; the 3'8" wide *pradaksina* path on the circular plinth is also protected by a *vedika*. The obvious commonality with the Indian *stupa*s is the presence of the upper and lower *vedika*s of 3' and 3'3" high respectively; however these chamfered Gandhara *vedika*s are much shorter and devoid of decorations unlike the sumptuous Indian *vedika*s and soon all *vedika*s would disappear from Gandhara *stupa*s. The *stupa* superstructure consists of five tiers with the first a square plinth, the second a circular plinth, the third and four the two circular drums, and the fifth the dome; it is surmounted by a solid *harmika* and an exceedingly tall multi-tiered *yasti-chattra*. The two circular drums of the third and fourth tiers were originally decorated with Corinthian pilasters alternated with narrative relief panels undoubtedly about Buddha's life and many of which are now housed in the nearby Swat Museum; the dome might also have been decorated with stucco reliefs. The Gandhara architects seemed to have consciously proportioned their *harmika*s to be of an equal height as the *stupa* body; the towering dimension of the 40' high *yasti-chattra* further increased the total height of the *stupa*, which was about 90' from the ground level to top of the *yasti-chattra*. These enormous *chattra*s, the largest being 16' diameter, are supported by stone rods and hollow circular stone tubes enveloping a solid *yasti* inside. As in the majority of Gandhara *stupa*s, Saidu Sharif Stupa I was originally coated with several layers of fine plaster to shield it from water penetration and give it a smooth appearance. The plaster coatings also served as underlayment to receive paint and gilding, which have been reported among the recovered remains; the dome was likely washed with white lime so that the *stupa* would dazzle and inspire pilgrims and visitors {Faccenna 1995: 125-126, 133-134}. Relic caskets have been recovered from the *stupa*, which once certainly contained Buddhist remains, and in some of the nearby *stupa*s. The majority of the relic chambers in Gandhara *stupa*s were located at the level of the top of the square plinth; in a rare instance, a recess containing relics have also been discovered inside Column Number 24.

There are a few notes about my revised elevation drawing of this *stupa*, which is based on Dominico Faccena's research. First, from his excavated artifacts there was evidently another set of *vedika stambha*s {Faccenna 1995: fg. 196 # b} which unquestionably belonged to the square plinth while the shorter one in Faccena's drawings belonged to the upper *vedika*. Second, Faccenna also had problems determining the exact locations of the set of sculpted Registers A-B on these drums; however there certainly existed another set of registers {Faccenna 1995: fg. 263, 264 # b} and together there should be two different sets of registers on the two drums. Third, based on the recovered fragments of the stone parasols I have also added the tall multi-tiered *yasti-chattra*. In all, my reconstruction adds the sculpted registers on the drums, the upper *vedika*, and the *yasti-chattra* to Faccenna's elevation. There are no inscriptions at the site and therefore the chronology of this *stupa* has chiefly been based on the masonry type and stylistic comparisons with similar *stupa*s. Saidu Sharif Stupa I was constructed in the soapstone ashlars, a masonry technique similar to Sirkap Block G Stupa, and therefore both were probably constructed between c. 0-25 CE {Faccenna 1995: 92}. Moreover the discovered Kushan coins of mostly Huvishka (r. 151-185 CE) and Vasudeva (r. 200-234 CE) alongwith many schist reliefs on the drums, which were common from the second century CE on, suggest that there were new renovations between the second-third centuries CE. In summary, there were probably three construction phases in this *stupa*:

- Phase I (first century CE): The *stupa* was constructed including all the major architectural features but without the reliefs.
- Phase II (second-third centuries CE): The *stupa* was again renovated during the peak of Gandhara with the schist reliefs installed on the drums.
- Phase III (fourth-fifth centuries CE): The *stupa* might be coated in plaster to be painted or gilded during the ascendancy of the Kidara Kushans.

The prevalence of square-based *stupa*s in Gandhara has led many scholars to speculate that the type must have originated there {Behrendt 2004: 52}; however, it already existed at a very early stage in India as in Piprahwa [6.1-6.2]. The characteristic drum superstructure of Gandhara *stupa*s, the emphasis on the verticality, and the reduction in the size of the dome already appeared in many *caityagriha stupa*s in the Indian caves like Kondivte [5.3], Bhaja [5.4-5.5], and Karla [5.7, 5.9]. Pillared *stupa*s were not uncommon in Gandhara such as Sirkap Block G Stupa (c. 25 CE) and have also been documented as far as Merv in Turkmenistan in the Gyaur-kala Stupa (second-fourth centuries CE) {Faccenna 1995: pl. 273 # d}. This type has certainly been constructed in India since several Mathura plaques, which have tentatively been dated between c. 25 BCE-100 CE and probably anterior or contemporary with their Gandhara counterparts, also depict this type of pillared *stupa*s; however, these Mathura examples have *torana*s in the main entry {Faccenna 1995: pl. 284 # a, b}{Quintanilla 2007: fg. 165-168}. There are many extant architectural models of these Gandhara pillared *stupa*s in the museum collections throughout the world as in the New York Metropolitan Museum and the Art Institute of Chicago. The incorporation of pillars into Gandhara and Mathura *stupa*s certainly dated before the five *ayaka* pillars of Amaravati Phase III [6.9]; as already noted, the tradition of erecting pillars in or near Buddhist *stupa*s were first credited to Asoka as in Sanchi [6.3]. The four animals on the capitals seem to symbolically represent the four guardian animals of the *stupa*; the lion probably symbolizes Buddha's *Dharma* roaring to the four corners of the world since his teachings are known as the 'Lion's Roar.' Saidu Sharif Stupa I fused elements from different sources including Asoka (the animal-crowned pillars [3.1-3.3]), Mathura (the pillared *stupa*), and Greco-Roman (Corinthian pilasters, pseudo-Ionic pillared pedestals). Its quincunxial plan was an original Gandhara creation probably derived from similar Mathura pillared *stupa*s; it became very influential in later Buddhist and Hindu architecture in India and all over Asia as in the Nalanda *caitya*s [4.4 (#3, 12)] and Mahabodhi Temple [7.10-7.11] in India, Ruvenvali Stupa in Sri Lanka, Chedi Phra Paton in Dvaravati Thailand, the central temples of Candi Sewu [7.12-7.13] in Indonesia, and Bayon of Angkor Thom [7.16-7.17] of Kampuchea. The single stair projection on one side of the plinth in Saidu Sharif Stupa I was characteristic of early *stupa*s and generally occurred between the first-third centuries CE; later *stupa*s often had cruciform plans with four staircases in the four cardinal points [6.17-6.18]. The four-pillared and quincunxial design in Buddhist *stupa*s is probably one of the most important contributions to Islamic architecture, the others being the pointed and ogee arches. Islamic mosques and mausolea are often flanked by four tall minarets in the four corners and I know of no Islamic or Christian monuments having this feature that can be dated earlier than the pillared *stupa*s of Gandhara and Mathura. One only has to glance at the Taj Mahal and immediately recognizes the overall formal similarities with Saidu Sharif Stupa I despite their 1,500 years apart.

c. Classic Gandhara Stupa

Part II. Architecture   Stupa . 177

A small but well-proportioned schist votive *stupa* from Loriyan Tangai **[6.15]** represents the mature phase of Gandhara *stupa* architecture; its height to the top of the *harmika* is about 4'6". Though the staircase is not present in this *stupa*, it was certainly a standard in larger Gandhara *stupa*s; while it has most of the features as Saidu Sharif Stupa I **[6.14]**, there are noticeable differences. All vestiges of the Indian *vedika*s have been eliminated and there is a large *caitya*-niche for images that integrates the dome and the drum below. The *stupa* is also profusely decorated with schist reliefs which were in vogue during this period; it was also the height of Greco-Roman influences in Gandhara as evident in the employment of Corinthian pilasters and dentils in the *stupa*. Indian features significantly diminished concurrent with a strong emphasis on the verticality in Gandhara *stupa*s by multiplying the number of tiers and drums and the imposing height of the *yasti-chattra*.

The use of schist in construction and decorative reliefs alongwith the abundance of sculptures as indicative of the opulence and culture in contemporary Gandhara suggest the probable date for this *stupa* in the mature Kushan Dynasty, or specifically in the reigns of Kanishka and Huvishka in the second century CE. The Guldara Stupa in Afghanistan and many Turkistani *stupa*s are manifestly in the same category as this type of *stupa*; it became the emulated form for the majority of later Indian votive *stupa*s **[8.9]**.

d.   Pyramidal Stupa

Another important stage in the evolution of Gandhara *stupa*s was the development of the pyramidal design; its examples were numerous as in the votive Stupa A16 from Jaulian Monastery **[6.16]**. A relic casket was discovered in this *stupa* containing potteries, gold and copper cylinders, bone fragments undoubtedly of Buddhist monks, and two Vasudeva coins. Its core consists of rubbles that are faced with large diaper-ashlars, coated with several layers of stucco, and probably painted or gilded; it has several diminishing tiers resembling a truncated pyramid. The upper tiers have identical *caitya*-arched and trapezoidal portal image niches alternated between pilasters that contain stucco Buddhas attended by pairs of devotees; the base dado is decorated with figures alternated between atlantes, elephants, and lions that are apparently compressed under the massive weight above. The body of this pyramidal structure was no doubt originally crowned with the usual circular drums, a solid *harmika*, and a *yasti-chattra* as typical of Gandhara *stupa*s; these drums probably had image niches between pilasters like

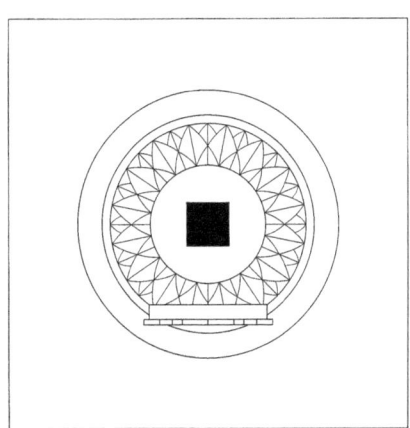

6.15. Loriyan Tangai Stupa elevation and plan
c. 128-185 CE
Loriyan Tangai- Pakistan
Indian Museum, Kolkata- India

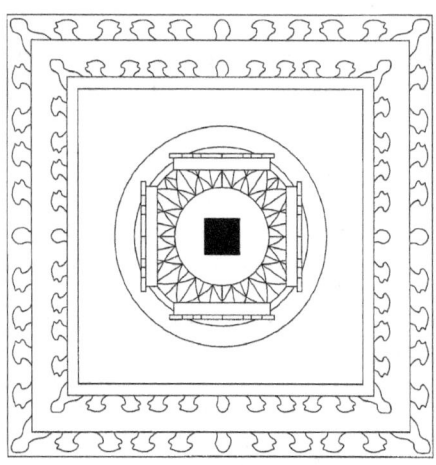

6.16. Stupa A16 elevation and plan (restored)
Second-fifth centuries CE
Jaulian Monastery, Taxila- Pakistan
Jaulian Monastery Museum, Taxila- Pakistan

the extant niches below. The presence of Vasudeva coins suggest that this type probably appeared in the early third century CE whilst the diaper-ashlar masonry and the stucco images belonged to later renovations between the fourth-fifth centuries CE.

The uniquely pyramidal design of this small votive *stupa* was a wholly Gandhara innovation that certainly appeared at least in the second century CE from a similar design in the Kushan plaque from Kumrahar of the Mahabodhi Temple **[7.9]**. Its decorative schemes derived from several sources, primarily Indian and Greco-Roman; the Corinthian pilasters and dentils originated in Greco-Roman architecture while *caitya*-arched niches were typical in Indian architecture. A nearly identical counterpart of this *stupa* was the Ali Masjid Stupa on the Khyber Pass in the Pakistani-Afghan border. The celebrated Mahabodhi Temple **[7.10-7.11]** and the Kumrahar plaque are essentially the architectural amalgamation of the verticality of Gandhara tower *stupa*s **[6.18]** and the pyramidal *stupa*s.

e.   Cruciform Stupa

Among the latest and most important types of Gandhara *stupa*s is the cruciform plan and a typical example is Bhamala Stupa in Sirkap **[6.17]**; it was constructed in Bhamala Monastery having a still discernable plan but the superstructure had long been destroyed. There are several new features in this *stupa* including the uniquely cruciform plan, which differs from Shah-ji-ki-dheri **[6.18 (plan)]** in the absence of the corner bastions, and the pairs of lions or elephants guarding the entrances as in Indian *stupa*s. The 58' square plinth is 9'6" high having a 3' wide terrace skirting its base which provides a *pradaksina* path so pilgrims could circumambulate and simultaneously view its continuous narrative reliefs; this innovation is also the hallmark of Borobudur **[6.28]**. In this late Gandhara *stupa*, stucco began to replace schist as the main facing material and in the decorative reliefs; the plinth likely had trapezoidal portal and *caitya* niches for Buddhist images as in Dharmarajika Phase V **[6.13]** and a relief of the *Parinirvana* scene was still extant in the eastern side of the south staircase. The paramount role of the narrative relief panels in Buddhist *stupa*s had been significantly diminished due to the decline in the popularity of Buddha's life stories and the *jataka*s; these would be replaced with Buddha and *bodhisattva* images in later monuments reflecting the Mahayana ascendancy. John Marshall dated this *stupa* between the late fourth-fifth centuries CE from the numerous coins from the period recovered at the site {Marshall 1951 Volume I: 393}; its late single diaper-ashlar masonry type, stucco reliefs, and

Part II. Architecture   Stupa . 179

6.17. Bhamala Stupa elevation (restored) and plan
Fourth-fifth centuries CE
Taxila- Pakistan

cruciform plan also corroborate its construction between the fourth-fifth centuries CE.

The cruciform plan, occasionally having a skirting terrace in the base, was common in later Gandhara *stupa*s like Shah-ji-ki-dheri [6.18 (plan)] and Sahri Bahlol in the Peshawar Valley, Guldara and Tope-i-rustam in Afghanistan, Rawak in Turkistan, the central temples of Somapura [4.8], Candi Sewu [7.12], Bayon of Angkor Thom [7.16], and Sarnath [8.5] as well as Borobudur [6.28-6.29] in Java, and Horyuji pagoda in Japan [6.20-6.21], and Ananda Temple [7.14]. The emphasis on the four cardinal directions already had antecedents in earlier Indian *stupa*s [6.3, 6.6, 6.9], which were ingeniously transformed into the cruciform plan in Gandhara.

f.   Tower Stupa

In its peak phase, the Gandhara *stupa* evolved into a towering monument emphasizing on the verticality and the region was certainly dotted with many skyscraper *stupa*s then. Fa-hsien in the early fifth century CE mentioned the 'highest of all the towers in Jambudvipa' built by King Kanishka now identified with the Shah-ji-ki-dheri mound near Peshawar [6.18 (plan)]. Another Chinese pilgrim Sung-yun, who passed through Gandhara in c. 520 CE, also documented the same tower reaching 560' high having a timber superstructure, assuming the original stone structure had been destroyed by the White Huns between the late fifth-early sixth centuries CE and subsequently rebuilt in timber. It was reportedly crowned with an iron *yasti-chattra* having thirteen gilded copper *chattra*s as the switch from stone to metal enabled the increase in the tiers and numbers of *chattra*s. The plan and elevation of this tower may be deduced from the excavated plan of Shah-ji-ki-dheri [6.18 (plan)] and the Stupa A11 reliquary model from Jaulian Monastery [6.18 (elevation)]; the huge plan of Shah-ji-ki-dheri near Peshawar has been identified with Kanishka Stupa where his reliquary had also been uncovered. The plinth of its square plan measures 175' wide if counting the staircases the total dimension would be 272' wide; the conspicuous features in this *stupa* are the symmetrically cruciform plan with four median staircases in the four faces alongwith its mighty height. The plan with the four corner bastions composes of possibly mini-*stupa*s or animal-crowned pillars had already been documented in Ai-khanum (c. 326-90 BCE) and Sirsukh (c. 50 CE); these bastions probably evolved into the four corner pillars as in Saidu Sharif Stupa I [6.14]. The superstructure of this great *stupa* can be surmised from the imposing verticality in Stupa A11 model, which has been achieved by simply multiplying the tiers

of the drums and the height of the *yasti-chattra* that terminates in a finial; the four *caitya*-arches in the four cardinal points of the dome, which has inlays of precious stones, would be meant for image niches in constructed *stupa*s. Like its previous predecessors, Shah-ji-ki-dheri was certainly adorned with numerous Buddhist sculpted reliefs on the plinth and drums; from the dimension of the plan, its height was probably in the 400' range counting the *yasti-chattra*. It was no doubt the tallest of all Buddhist *stupa*s in contemporary Asia and among the highest, if not the highest, skyscrapers in the ancient world. Dating Shah-ji-ki-dheri is still controversial and the recovery of the Kanishka reliquary in it does not imply that its construction were started in Kanishka's reign since there were several Kushan kings in this name; its cruciform plan, towering form, and stucco images in the base push its construction back to a later date between the fourth-fifth centuries CE. Above all it had probably been commenced after Kanishka's death (c. 151 CE) as his memorial *stupa* by one of his successors, possibly Kanishka II, and subsequently rebuilt and expanded several times; it probably had four construction phases:

- Phase I (c. 151-300 CE): It might have been commenced in c. 151 CE as the *stupa* for Kanishka's relics with its original form probably resembling Loriyan Tangai [6.15] and schist reliefs was installed on its plinth and drums.
- Phase II (fourth century CE): The renovated *stupa* was probably converted into a cruciform plan having four staircases with four corner bastions and a towering form in the beginning of the fourth century CE.
- Phase III (fifth century CE): Stucco images probably replaced earlier schist reliefs reflecting the contemporary popularity of Buddha and *bodhisattva* images.
- Phase IV (early sixth century CE): The original stone superstructure was reconstructed in timber as documented by Sung-yun after its destruction under the White Huns.

This type of tower *stupa* was influential and a great contribution of Gandhara to Buddhist architecture; it unquestionably became the precursor of the tower *stupa*s in Turkistan [6.22] and early Chinese brick pagodas like Songyue [6.24-6.25]. The Mahabodhi Temple [7.10-7.11] and the subsequent Hindu *sikhara*s certainly inherited the verticality of this type; however, tall towers were also prevalent in early Indian [7.4-7.5] and Chinese architecture [6.19]. The cruciform plan was also among the most important type created by the Gandhara architects as in Bhamala [6.17] and throughout Asia; the nearest resemblance to the bastioned plan of Shah-ji-ki-dheri must

6.18. Stupa A11 reliquary elevation and Kanishka Stupa plan
Fourth-fifth centuries CE
Jaulian Monastery Museum, Taxila- Pakistan (elevation)
Shah-ji-ki-dheri, Peshawar- Pakistan (plan)

be Nalanda Caitya 3 **[4.4 (#3)]** though the latter only has one staircase.

2. *T'a, T'ap, Tháp, To* - China, Korea, Vietnam, Japan

Any study of Buddhist arts and architecture in East Asia, specifically the pagoda, naturally starts with China where Buddhism first arrived in the early years of the Eastern Han Dynasty (25-220 CE), then Vietnam (first-second centuries CE), Korea (372 CE), and Japan (552 CE). The latter three countries have thoroughly assimilated the Chinese culture to such an extent that their arts and architecture, including the Buddhist, are hardly distinguished from the Chinese and together they all share a homogeneous Sinicized culture. In the case of Buddhism, once it had already been absorbed into the Chinese mainstream other East Asian countries in turn inherited its arts and architecture from the Chinese. The official version of the Buddhist transmission into China told that in 67 CE the Han emperor Mingdi (r. 58-75 CE) dreamt of a 20' tall golden man with a large halo on his head appearing in his dream; his ministers later informed him of what he saw was Buddha. The emperor immediately dispatched his messengers to the west to seek for Buddha's teachings; they returned the same year with two Indian monks, Dharmaratna and Kasyapa Matanga, who also brought along Buddhist *sutra*s and an image of Sakyamuni. A year later in 68 CE the first monastery in China, or the White Horse Monastery named after the horse that carried Buddhist *sutra*s to China, was built to house Buddhist icons and for monks who stayed and translated the *sutra*s; by now Buddhism was more than a popular Indian religion as it also became an important tool in international diplomacy between Asian countries. The route that Buddhism entered China from India passed through Gandhara, Central Asia, and Turkistan; it was the Buddhist arts and architecture from these regions that became the immediate sources for China. Buddhism probably reached southern China in the first century CE via the sea route as it was during this time that Indian traders and settlers also reportedly arrived in Southeast Asian nations like Indonesia, Kampuchea, Champa, and North Vietnam. Kang Senghui was a Sogdian monk born in Chiao-chih, now North Vietnam then a Chinese colony, who was active in the first half of the third century CE; his parents followed Indian traders by the sea route and settled in China. The Chinese monk Fa-hsien pilgrimaged to India and came back to China in the early fifth century CE via the sea route; however the land route, popularly known as the Silk Road, was more accessible and less dangerous in the earlier centuries than the sea route since cartloads of religious objects like sculptures, paintings, and Buddhist *sutra*s could easily be carried on horsebacks on land than ships. In the formative years, Buddhist missionaries continued to pour into China to feed the increasingly curious and religious minds among the Chinese population; many foreign monks came and resided in the country to translate Buddhist *sutra*s. The confusing body of Buddhist literature from different sects also compelled many Chinese monks to travel to India to seek the truths and bring back more newer Buddhist *sutra*s alongwith Buddhist arts and architecture from the western countries and India. Gradually Buddhism won many converts from the Chinese populus, the aristocracy, and the royal families; its profound philosophy and promises of salvation alongwith a great artistic and architectural tradition easily appealed to all classes of Chinese. Buddhism in its initial years on the foreign land was not without enemies since the Chinese already had deep-rooted religious or socio-religious institutions of their own, particularly Confucianism and Daoism, that existed at least since the sixth century BCE. Chinese history documented numerous persecutions that Buddhism had suffered from time to time by pro-Confucian emperors who felt threatened by the newly alien and influential religion. The three greatest persecutions of Buddhism occurred in 445 CE during the Wei Dynasty (386-557 CE), 574 CE during Northern Zhou Dynasty (557-581 CE), and 845 CE during Tang Dynasty (618-907 CE); surprisingly there were virtually no Buddhist persecutions in Vietnam, Korea, and Japan during its lifespan. Buddhism was periodically purged in China due to its incredible wealth and hypnotic sway over the Chinese masses; its monasteries in China increased dramatically and grew more powerful that potentially threatened and weakened the powers of the Chinese emperors. By the time of the Sui Dynasty (581-618 CE) and Tang Dynasty (618-907 CE), Buddhism was thoroughly assimilated into the Chinese society that it was no longer considered as an alien religion. Historically Chinese emperors generally adopted a pendulous attitude toward Buddhism from the start and used it to their own advantage; they ardently supported it for awhile then fiercely persecuted it when it was deemed threatening to the imperial throne. Many emperors of the Wei Dynasty in northern China patronized Buddhism generously and they also brought Buddhist arts and architecture to prominence throughout China and East Asia; the Southern Liang Dynasty (502-557 CE) was also a great patron of Buddhism in southern China. In the initial years, the Buddhists found it imperative to solicit and maintain patronage from the monarchy in exchange for their backings of various emperors, whom they aptly and flatteringly elevated to the level of Buddhist saints. This was the familiar symbiotic relationships between the Buddhist *Sangha* and the monarchy as already observed in the cases of Asoka and Kanishka; despite numerous severe persecutions, Buddhism ultimately survived and continued to prosper due to the supports of the majority of the Chinese population.

It is well-known that China had a long history of secular and perhaps religious arts and architecture before the arrival of Buddhism including most importantly timber architecture, bronze production, gilding, lacquerware, jade, sculptures, paintings, etc. Some of China's most famous early sites are the Terracotta Army sculptures in the tomb of Emperor Qin-shih-huang (r. 221-210 BCE) in Shaanxi and the paintings in Mawangdui Tomb (early second century BCE) in Hunan. These are just some exemplary examples of the antiquity of the Chinese culture and tracing the arts and architecture in pre-Buddhist China is beyond the scope of this book. Before the arrival of Buddhism, China virtually had neither organized religions nor systematic religious arts and architecture that could be compared to or rivaled those of subsequent Buddhism. Confucianism and Daoism, though having existed over half a millennium in China before Buddhism, were systems of moral codes (Confucianism) and mysticism (Daoism) and not organized religions in the Chinese context. Buddhism, on the other hand, not only had a well-established system of ethics but also a profound philosophy revealing deep insights into the field of human psychology. It also came to China with an appealing pantheon of ideal saints and compassionate deities like the *arhat*s and *bodhisattva*s ready to instruct and rescue all sentient beings from misery in this very life and the next life. It introduced a completely new monkish lifestyle and a fellowship of monks and nuns (*Sangha*) all unified in the collective ideals and efforts to end all sufferings in the world. Moreover Buddhism also presented an irresistible afterlife and a chance of a glorious rebirth in the next life; *Nirvana* and Amitabha's Western Paradise were the magical and heavenly realms that the Chinese had not experienced in their native Chinese religions before the advent of Buddhism. Above all what Buddhism offered to the Chinese was more than mere words and empty promises as it also came to China with magnificent works of arts and monumental architecture to which every Chinese could emulate, devote, and contribute their resources to earn good *karma*s; Buddhism was historically the greatest impetus behind Chinese religious arts and architecture with the majority of extant examples belonged to Buddhism. During the Western Jin Dynasty (265-317 CE) there were 180 monasteries in its twin capitals at Luoyang and Changan {Wei 2000: 118}; a Northern Wei Dynasty census in 476 CE recorded a total of 6,478 monasteries and 77,258 monks and nuns in its territory. The great Northern Zhou persecution in 577 CE recorded over 40,000 monasteries and 3,000,000 monks and nuns in North China alone {Soper 1959: 100, 118}; during the southern dynasties of Song, Chi, Liang, and Chen (c. 420-589 CE) there were over 8,000 monasteries and 180,000 monks and nuns {Wei 2000: 118}. These statistics clearly confirmed North China as the dominant Buddhist center, five times greater than the South, and it is here that numerous remains of early Chinese Buddhist arts and architecture are located. The categories of Chinese Buddhist arts and architecture consist of pagodas, monasteries, rock-hewn caves, sculptures, and paintings. Among the oldest surviving pagodas are Songyue [6.24-6.25] and Sakya; the best preserved caves are Mogao [5.20-5.23], Binglingsi, Maijishan, Yungang, and Longmen containing great masterpieces of early Buddhist sculptures and paintings in China. Buddhist arts and architecture in China can be divided into three periods:

- Period of Importation (c. 68-475 CE): This beginning period received foreign influences primarily from Gandhara and Turkistan. The oldest extant Buddhist arts in China dated in the late second century CE on Mount Kongwang in Lianyungang of Jiangsu which depicted Mahasattva Jataka in rock reliefs {Bell 2000: 158}; the Mahao Cave in Sichuan also has rock reliefs of Buddha images dated contemporary with the Mount Kongwang site. The collision and fusion of different Buddhist cultures of Indian, Gandhara, Central Asian, and Chinese origins can be observed in early Chinese Buddhist caves like Mogao, Binglingsi, and Yungang.
- Period of Transition (c. 475-618 CE): Chinese elements occurred in greater frequency whilst foreign features would gradually be Sinicized or replaced with Chinese ones; the most typical examples of this transitional style are the austere Northern Wei sculptures and the subsequent fleshy sculptures in the Northern Qi and Northern Zhou Dynasty {Watson 1995: 128-151}.
- Period of Assimilation (after 618 CE): This period completed the transformation and assimilation of Buddhism to reflect the Chinese temperament as Buddhist arts and architecture took on decisively Chinese characters. Foreign features that deemed inappropriate or incompatible with the Chinese sensibility like the domed *stupa*, the nudity and sexual nuances common in Indian arts, etc. would be discarded altogether. A wave of fresh influences swept

through China during this period primarily from Gupta India with its characteristic plump figures in *tribhanga* (three bents at head, waist, and feet) and the conveyance of refined spirituality in these images. The climax of Buddhist arts and architecture in China was undoubtedly during the Tang Dynasty, particularly the High Tang in the reign of Emperor Xuanzong (r. 713-755 CE), as observed in the Mogao caves of the period.

The pagoda is certainly the most ubiquitous symbol of East Asian Buddhist architecture; the terms *t'a* (China), *t'ap* (Korea), *tháp* (Vietnam), and *to* (Japan) popularly denoting the East Asian pagoda are unquestionably derived from *thupa*, a Pali word for Sanskrit *stupa*. The word 'pagoda' itself could be the European translation of the Portugese word *pagode*, which is a transliteration of Tamil *pagavadi* that originated from Sanskrit *bhagavat* meaning 'blessed.' The pronunciation of 'pagoda' even phonetically suggests the Sri Lankan word *dagaba* both referring to the same type of Buddhist monuments, the Indian *stupa*. There are three major types of East Asian pagodas based on their forms and construction materials: timber **[6.20-6.21]**, masonry **[6.24-6.25]**, and the combination of both; there are also stone pagodas and unusual materials like bronze and iron but these are not as popular as the other types. Extant masonry pagodas in China are more numerous than timber ones and these commonly have octagonal plans; on the other hand, Japan built none of the masonry pagodas on their land and most Japanese pagodas have square plans but it produced the oldest extant timber pagoda in the world. Whatever the materials of a pagoda might be, its form is essentially a multi-tiered tower that decidedly emphasizes on the verticality and instantly recalls the ruined brick towers in Turkistan and the tower *stupa*s of Gandhara **[6.18]**.

A. Timber Pagoda

From the evidence extracted from historical and Buddhist literature alongwith architectural remains, it is conclusive that the timber pagoda was the first to appear in China before the masonry type. The historical 'Record of the Three Kingdoms' (220-265 CE) stated that Chai Jung (Zhai Rong), the warlord of Jiangsu, built a monastery in 190 CE which had covered galleries and a multi-storied pavilion crowned with a spire hung with nine tiers of bronze plates, evidently a *yasti-chattra*, that could pack over 3,000 men inside {Soper 1959: 4}. This pavilion was clearly the earliest description of a Buddhist timber pagoda in China but functionally it was probably not a *stupa* since it housed a Buddha image and not relics with

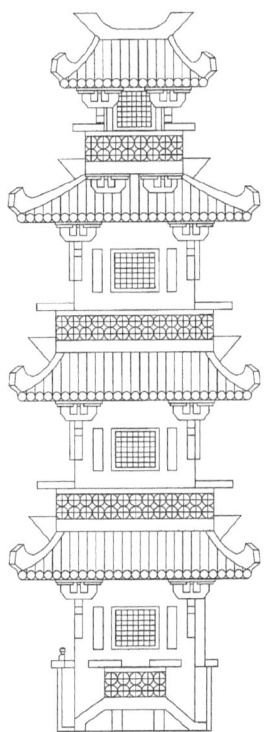

6.19. Pottery model of a Han tower
First-second centuries CE
Shandong Museum, Shandong- China

an accessible interior. In this early stage of Chinese Buddhist architecture, its builders were obviously ignorant of the religious functions and symbolisms of the Indian *stupa*; it was only at a later time that Buddhist relics began to be interred in the pagoda and essentially transformed it into a *stupa* in accordance to the Indian Buddhist tradition. This pavilion and monastery were certainly constructed in timber as in contemporary Chinese architecture; however, the description did not give any details regarding the original form of its pagoda. Most likely its design had been directly adopted from secular pleasure pavilions and watch towers found numerously as small pottery models buried inside many Eastern Han tombs **[6.19]**; these were unquestionably miniature architectural models of contemporary structural towers that unfortunately have not survived to this day. This pottery model shows a vertical tower having diminishing stories; its form strongly suggests the material might be of timber, or less likely a brick core attached with timber members as in later Chinese pagodas, from its distinct bracketing system supporting the tile roofs. If constructed for defensive

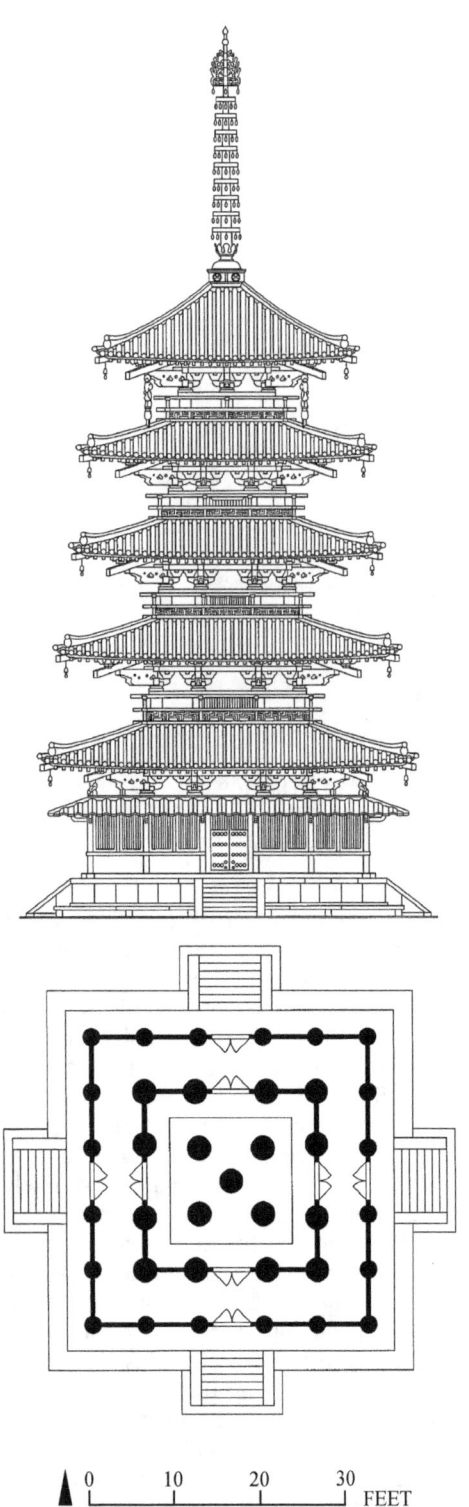

6.20. Pagoda elevation and plan (*left*)
670 CE
Horyuji, Nara- Japan

6.21. Pagoda (*above*)
670 CE
Horyuji, Nara- Japan

purposes, for which many Han towers have been known, such a tall tower could be constructed in brick and stone like later Chinese pagodas since this would provide better fire protection and military defense than timber. Had this Han pavilion been constructed, it would likely have stairs in the interior connecting the upper floors; also visible from the model are the entry staircases from both sides, lattice windows to allow light into the interior, and balconies protected by balustrades on the upper floors. Another similar pottery model from Fucheng in Hebei dated in the Eastern Han period also shows a multi-tiered watch tower enclosed by a wall rising in the center of a gated and walled compound {Steinhardt 2002: fg. 2.12}. Thus the form of Chai Jung's pagoda was undoubtedly modeled after the native Chinese secular pavilion and the attribution is more palpable when compare between the Han tower [6.19] and Horyuji pagoda [6.20-6.21]. Chinese craftsmen were already very experienced in building such tall pavilions by the time Buddhist architecture arrived in China and they simply added the *yasti-chattra*s to the top of the pavilions to complete the familiar form of the Buddhist pagoda with a few minor structural modifications like the addition of the central pillar to bear the weight of the spire and allow secondary members to be attached to it for maximum structural stability.

It is unfortunate that none of the extant timber pagodas in China can be dated before the eleventh century CE; this was not only due to the perishable nature of timber but also the ravages of wars and destructions under many anti-Buddhist emperors who were at times compelled to eradicate the alien religion from their land. The massive octagonal Sakya Pagoda constructed during the Liao Dynasty (907-1125 CE) is the only oldest and largest extant timber-and-brick pagoda in China dated in 1056 CE; to date, the most reliable materials for studying early Chinese architecture and pagodas are mostly found in the murals of the Mogao caves. And fortunately, many extant pagodas and monasteries dated back in the Chinese Tang Dynasty (618-907 CE) have survived in Japan; among these the Horyuji pagoda [6.20-6.21] inside of Horyuji Monastery [4.5-4.7] is evidently an elegant Chinese-styled Japanese pagoda and also the oldest best preserved timber pagoda in the world. Its plan is a five-bay square 32'4" center to center of the outermost interior columns and a smaller three-bay square in the interior 20' center to center of the outermost columns. In the center of the plan are five columns with the central one being cut from a single tree rising from the floor of the plinth to the roof apex, a feature recalling the identical structure of the five-storied Kumgangsa pagoda (sixth century CE) in Paekche {Washisuka 2003: 159}. The entire pagoda is elevated on a 38"4" square stone plinth with four median staircases in the four cardinal points and skirting this plinth is a 2'2" wide low terrace; the plan strongly recalls the cruciform plan of Bhamala [6.17]. The 100' high elevation of the pagoda is divided into three distinct sections: (a) The 4'5" high plinth, (b) the 68'1" high main body consisting of a five-tiered module that is covered with a low-pitched and gracefully curved tile roof on each tier as characteristic of Chinese and East Asian pagodas, and (c) a 27'5" high spire (*yasti-chattra*) attached with nine circular bronze discs and a coronet finial. The pagoda is also hung with numerous bronze bells on the eave and spire which generate tinkling soothing sounds under the wind and further contribute to the magical and holy atmosphere in the monastery. The timber structure of the pagoda, with its uniformly tiered bracketing system, can be traced back at least in the Chinese Qin Dynasty (221-206 BCE); it consists of:

- A post-and-beam system composes of vertical members such as posts and horizontal members like beams that are tied together to form a rigid frame. In the pagoda center is a sturdy timber pillar sunk 9'10" below the floor of the plinth that rests on a stone footing; it rises to the rooftop to bear the loads of the spire and to be attached with secondary structural members such as joists, rafters, etc. for structural stability. The Han pavilion [6.19] probably did not require this central pillar since it did not have a spire; thus these new innovations (central pillar, *yasti-chattra*) were undoubtedly introduced by Chinese Buddhists.
- Secondary framing members consist of floor joists, rafters, bracing members, brackets, and lever arms (*ang*). Floor joists and rafters mainly bear the loads of the floors and roofs and they are tied to the core pillar to form a rigid structure against the potentially dangerous sway of wind and earthquake. Brackets and *ang*s are designed to spread the loads evenly and support the excessively wide eaves, which extend 12'9" from the center of the interior column to the edge of the lowest eave in the Horyuji pagoda; from an aesthetic viewpoint, the bracketing system also enhances the appearance of elegance and complexity in the East Asian pagoda. In later centuries, the size of the brackets and *ang*s in Chinese buildings would greatly be reduced and their functions diminished to merely ornamental and non-structural uses {Liang 1984: 72, fg. 32}.

There are several noticeably unusual features in the Horyuji pagoda as, for example, the penthouse with its double roof was possibly originally erected as an afterthought to create a roofed-in space for the *pradaksina* path; for the original appearance of the pagoda before this alteration see {Watson 1995: fg. 296 B, C}. Probably the central podium for the image altar was widened to such an extent that it necessitated the construction of the penthouse and the *pradaksina* path; thus the enlargement of the altar podium and the construction of the penthouse probably happened about the same time. Another hidden feature is the false upper 'stories' since from the exterior the pagoda appears to have five stories when in fact only the lowest story is accessible; its interior ceiling is coffered to hide the framings above and thus the upper tiers, balconies, railings, and windows are merely decorative. In 1926 CE a relic chamber was discovered beneath the core pillar; the relics were first placed in a glass bottle which was in turn placed inside four other diminutional containers containing gold, silver, bronze, and beads alongwith a mirror of vine, animal, and hunter design {Mizuno 1974: 101-102}{Washizuka 2003: 179-180}; the manner of burying Buddhist relics by placing them in containers of diminishing sizes was typical of the Indian Buddhist tradition. The four plastered walls surrounding the core pillar were built like grottos which contained sculptures depicting the four Buddhist scenes of Buddha's *Parinirvana*, the division of his relics, Maitreya (Miroku)'s paradise, and the dialogue between Manjusri (Monju) and Vimalakirti (Yuima); these dated in 711 CE. The chronology of Horyuji monastery and its pagoda was once plagued with controversies but has now been settled beyond doubts. It should be reiterated that the new monastery Horyuji had been rebuilt in 670 CE after a conflagration destroying the original monastery Wakakusadera; this reconstruction involved new additions to the Shotoku's chapel (Golden Hall) first constructed in 623 CE including the pagoda, the Middle Gate, and the cloistered corridor all added in 670 CE {Mizuno 1974: 28-34, 88-89}{Paine and Soper 1981: 294-300}. The pagoda was constructed in the style of the adjacent Golden Hall; the penthouse of the latter was probably added in 711 CE or about the same time as the grottoed walls. There are other early features distinguishing Horyuji from later Japanese architecture such as the low-pitch roof, the cloud brackets, the inverted 'V' struts, the sarato plate between the capitals and shafts of the columns, and the pronounced convex entasis of these columns; the inverted 'V' struts can also be found among the pagodas in the Chinese Yungang caves [6.23].

The architecture of the Horyuji pagoda is ultimately derived from the Chinese Han pavilion [6.19]. However, it fundamentally differs from the latter in the incorporation of the core pillar to bear the loads of the *yasti-chattra* and where other secondary structural members could be tied to; this strengthens the structural integrity of the pagoda and permits the increase in the numbers of stories or tiers and height. The Chinese pagoda had also been slightly modified on the Korean soil before transmitted to Japan but there are subtle differences between the Japanese and continental pagodas. For examples, the Japanese seemed to prefer timber and thatch for their pagodas in contrast to the Chinese preference for masonry-and-tile pagodas; the Chinese apparently preferred the octagonal over square plans common in Japanese pagodas. Japan also constructed many elegant modest pagodas of one to two stories in height compared with the monumental scales of the Chinese pagodas; the Japanese pagoda is evidently more symbolic than utilitarian since only its lowest story can be occupied while the upper tiers are inaccessible. The Chinese *yasti-chattra*s are usually short and bulky whereas their Japanese counterparts are tall and slender which render the pagodas more graceful and proportional. The plan of Horyuji pagoda is reminiscent of the cruciform plan of Gandhara *stupa*s [6.17] while its solid capping box or *harmika* and multi-tiered *yasti-chattra* have apparently been derived from Gandhara *stupa*s [6.14-6.15, 6.18]; other than these pan-Asian features inherited from the Buddhist *stupa*, the Japanese timber pagoda is essentially Chinese in form.

B. Masonry Pagoda

The masonry pagoda of brick and stone is probably the most common type in China with many extant examples thanks to the choice of permanent materials that have prolonged its lifespan; perhaps more than its timber counterparts, the masonry pagoda bears a striking resemblance to the tower *stupa*s of Gandhara [6.18] and Turkistan [6.22] in forms and functions. The architectural development of the Chinese masonry pagoda can be divided into two main phases:

- Phase I (c. 68-618 CE): This phase began with the wholesale imports of the Buddhist *stupa* architecture primarily from Gandhara and Turkistan. As already stated, in the early years of Chinese Buddhism the Chinese adapted the Han pavilion into the Buddhist usage which resulted in the timber pagoda. However it was probably not until a later time that they began to attempt the construction of masonry pagodas in conforming to the traditional and internationalized forms of the Buddhist *stupa*; probably initially the Chinese did not know how to build tall masonry towers but evidences seem to suggest their competency in accomplishing such feats.
- Phase II (after 618 CE): This would be the period of complete Sinization during which the initial foreign forms would be modified and assimilated to suit the Chinese contexts. In the initial years between the fifth-mid tenth centuries CE or from the Northern Wei to Tang Dynasty, the masonry pagoda was built with corbelled eave projections and their forms strongly resembled Gandhara [6.18] and Turkistani tower *stupa*s [6.22]. Beginning in the Song Dynasty (960-1279 CE) or certainly earlier, the Chinese masonry pagoda, besides having a masonry core, also incorporated a timber structure for its floors and tile roofs complete with timber balconies and railings as well as a wooden bracketing system to support

6.22. Model of a *stupa* or pagoda (*left*)
428 CE
Gansu Museum, Lanzhou- China

6.23. Cave pagoda (*right*)
c. 460-505 CE
Yungang Cave 39, Datong- China

the wide eaves. In many cases the Chinese had also attempted to faithfully replicate their timber pagodas in masonry or even iron with simulated wooden brackets; this was clearly a conscious effort to assimilate foreign elements in the Buddhist *stupa* into the mold of the traditional Chinese architecture. Examples of the exact translations of timber buildings into stone ones already existed since the Eastern Han Dynasty such as the stone gateway of the Gao Yi tomb in Sichuan and later in the numerous stone pagodas in early Chinese Buddhist caves **[6.23]**. The gradual Sinization of the Buddhist *stupa* had already been occurring since the fifth century CE from the stone pillar-pagoda in Yungang Cave 39 **[6.23]** which has a square plan and an elevation of five diminishing tiers and each a smaller copy of the one below. Its emphasis on the verticality and monotonous repetition of the Buddha niches still strongly evoked Gandhara models **[6.16]** and contemporary regional towers **[6.22]**; however the replication of tile roofs and a system of posts, beams, and brackets as in traditional timber architecture were indicative of the Chinese attempt to naturalize foreign elements. This Yungang pillar-pagoda was undoubtedly the forerunner of the destroyed nine-storied Yongningsi Pagoda (516 CE) in Luoyang, China originally constructed in timber that rose to staggering height of 528' {Steinhardt 2002: 83-84, fg. 3.21}.

Current inventory of existing masonry pagodas suggest that they were probably not built until the latter years of the Northern Wei Dynasty in the sixth century CE; however they certainly had an early beginning from the numerous stone votive models of pagodas found in the Jiuquan district of Gansu **[6.22]** and Turkistan {MMA 1982: 64-65}. The base story of the Gansu model is octagonal and has incised *bodhisattva* figures while the tier above is roundish and incised with Buddhist texts in Chinese characters. The third tier is a drum capped with an insignificant lotus-petaled dome that has *caitya*-arched niches containing Buddha images; the pagoda is crowned with a six-tiered and gracefully curved pinnacle that terminates in a half-domed finial. The towering form of this miniature pagoda or *stupa*, with its Buddha niches and multi-tiered *yasti-chattra*, obviously emulated Gandhara *stupa*s **[6.18]**. Its octagonal plan and emphasis on the verticality also recall early Indian multi-storied towers among Amaravati and Mathura reliefs **[7.4-7.5]** and Kushan temples **[7.9]**; it also has a similar configuration as the *caityagriha stupa* in Ajanta Cave 19 **[5.10]**. Perhaps an important innovation in this votive model is its holistic design that dissolves the tripartite division of base, body, and crown typical of Indian and Gandhara *stupa*s to form a unified and seemingly tierless vertical tower. I have no doubt that this was the model of an actual contemporary masonry pagoda and therefore among the earliest of its kind in China and a precursor of later brick pagodas like Songyue.

The oldest masonry pagoda in China and East Asia is undoubtedly the brick Songyue **[6.24-6.25]** constructed in 523 CE; the site once served as a temporary residence of the Northern Wei emperors which was later converted into a monastery in 520 CE. The pagoda has a dodecagonal plan of about 37' wide with a tower superstructure elevated on a low 3'3" high plinth; it soars gracefully about 130' high from the plinth base to the top of the finial. There are four openings in the four cardinal points where visitors can enter and exit the other sides, a common feature in East Asian pagodas that already occurred in Gandhara and Turkistani *stupa*s. The elevation has four two-storied high *caitya*-arched entries with a plain base story while the upper story has shallow niches and abstract reliefs divided by hexagonal pilasters. Above the main body is an elliptical cone rising in fourteen diminishing tiers with simulated eaves creating a 2' wide cornice; corbelled niches and false windows are also in-

6.24. Songyue pagoda elevation and second floor plan
523 CE
Dengfeng- China

6.25. Songyue pagoda
523 CE
Dengfeng- China

serted in the faces of each tier. The apex is capped with a finial in the shape of an inverted lotus bud and a stunted mast of incised discs resembling a *chattravali*. The interior of the pagoda is open and at one time timber floors and staircases were probably provided so visitors could climb up and worship in the second story as well as enjoy the surrounding views {Liang 1984: 134}. I believe only the bottom two stories were originally accessible as the spaces in the upper conical tiers were too narrow and without window openings; the open space in the center of the bottom floor most likely originally displayed Buddhist images or possibly relics.

Some scholars have asserted that the form of Songyue could have originated in India; Alexander Soper confidently declared that the pagoda "represents an exceptionally faithful reproduction of some Indian model of the contemporary Gupta style" {Soper 1968: 391}. Another thought that the Indian *sikhara* "influenced the development of the Chinese pagodas" {Pirazzoli-t'Serstevens

1970: 137} since the graceful conical profile in the latter apparently resembles the Hindu *sikhara*s. First of all, I am not aware of any Gupta temples that were the exact model for Songyue; the oldest extant Indian Hindu *sikhara*s, particularly the northern Nagara type like the Durga Temple at Aihole with its graceful curvilinear tower dated in the seventh century CE, are definitely later and without the distinct tiers of Songyue. The Indian *sikhara* typically has a *mandapa* (hall) in front of the main sanctum which is crowned with a curvilinear (Hindu) or pyramidal tower (Buddhist); thus its designs do not have much commonality with the isolated towers like Songyue. In my view, the characteristic curvilinear profiles of the North Indian Hindu Nagara *sikhara*s and Songyue probably emulated the curvilinear profiles of the tall multi-tiered *yastichattra*s in Gandhara [6.14, 6.18] and Turkistani *stupa*s [6.22]; the mature prototype of a *sikhara* had probably been crystallized in Turkistan in the third-fourth centuries CE and possibly earlier in Gandhara in the Jandial Temple. The octagonal plan popular in Chinese pagodas and their emphasis on the verticality and multi-tiered forms also had antecedents in early Indian temples [7.4-7.5, 7.9-7.11] and Gandhara *stupa*s [6.18 (elevation)]. However the immediate predecessor of Songyue should be sought in the votive model *stupa*s [6.22], which were unquestionably modeled after Turkistani towers that are still standing half-ruined throughout Xinjiang.

3. *Dagaba* - Sri Lanka

As already discussed (Chapter 4), monasteries and *stupa*s were constructed soon after Buddhism arrived on the island of Sri Lanka in c. 249 BCE; as one might have guessed that these earliest Buddhist edifices were very much Indian in forms and functions which were likely small and circular in plans constructed in brick or stone. A common designation for the Indian *stupa* in Sri Lanka is *dagaba* derived from the Sanskrit words *dhatu* (relics) and *garbha* (womb, chamber, receptacle, house); in Sri Lanka the *thupa*, a Pali word, is more widely known and accepted than Sanskrit *stupa* and can be used interchangeably with *dagaba*. Many *dagaba*s were greatly expanded in Dutthagamani's reign and these were chiefly limited to the enlargement of the dome; it was not until the second-third centuries CE that the image chapels (*vahalkada*) were added in the four cardinal points of the *dagaba* following the continental trend. Gandhara was famous for its pioneering constructions of the tallest *stupa*s in Asia while Sri Lanka built the largest domed *stupa*s and among the biggest structures in the ancient world surpassing even Amaravati, which was about half the size of the biggest Sri Lankan *dagaba*s. These colossal *dagaba*s were erected in the three biggest monasteries in Anuradhapura, namely Mahavihara, Abhayagirivihara, and Jetavanavihara; their imposing dimensions easily dwarfed the low clusters of buildings in the surroundings and dominated the skyline from afar. The first of these gigantic *dagaba*s, Ruvenvali or Mahathupa, has two receding square terraces with a 475' wide base and above which are the massive white dome crowned with a solid *harmika* and a *chattravali*; its original height stood at 300'. There are staircases connecting the terraces, which have four miniature *dagaba*s in the four corners of the upper terrace and four *vahalkada*s in the four cardinal points; all these features recall Gandhara *stupa*s between the second-fifth centuries CE [6.14, 6.18]. The Mahavamsa told a story about a Sri Lankan king who made a *bodhi*-tree out of many precious materials such as gold, gems, coral, silver, etc. and placed inside the relic chamber of this *dagaba*, which also contained many Buddhist murals and statues. Occasionally and before the closing of the relic chamber, the king would take these statues out and showed them to his subjects to inspire religious devotion {Vacissara 1971: 113-122}. The story seems too fanciful but it is clear that the construction of such magnificent monument demanded a great concerted effort and resources from the devotees and especially the financial backings from the monarchy. The second great *dagaba* is Abhayagiri again having almost identical configurations; its huge base terrace is 587' wide and its height originally reached 350'. The Jetavana Dagaba, the biggest domed brick *stupa* in Asia and the third biggest structures in the ancient world after the Egyptian pyramids, measures 590' wide at the base and rises to a staggering height of 400'. These colossal monuments were epic endeavors by the Sri Lankan kings probably to compete with similar oversized Buddhist *stupa*s in Andhra and Gandhara.

Ruvenvali, Abhayagiri, and Jetavana *dagaba*s belonged to a family of Indo-Gandhara *stupa*s as they evidently combined the Indian dome [6.3, 6.6, 6.9] with the multi-terraced design, the cruciform plan, and the verticality of Gandhara *stupa*s [6.17-6.18]. In old Sinhalese literature, Sri Lankan *dagaba*s were categorized into six types according to the shapes of their domes: the bell, pot, bubble, heap-of-paddy, lotus, and *amalaka* (an elliptical and fluted crown in Hindu and Buddhist *sikhara*s resembling an *amalaka* fruit) {Paranavitana 1947: 27-28}; the *amalaka*, pot, and lotus shapes were virtually unknown in Sri Lanka. There are three known Sri Lankan *dagaba*s having the heap-of-paddy form, namely Ottapuva, Kalani, and Thupurama [6.26-6.27]; however these have been greatly modified over the centuries, especially the latter, so that their domes are no longer in their original forms. All known massive Sri Lankan *dagaba*s discussed earlier, Ruvenvali, Abhayagiri, and Jetavana, have bubble-shaped domes and are easily recognized as the most Indianized among Sri Lankan *dagaba*s. Finally, the bell shape is the most common in Sri Lanka and Southeast Asia, which certainly existed in the third century CE from a rock engraving in Kahandagala {Paranavitana 1947: 40-41}.

Among the most important types of Sri Lankan *dagabas* must be the *vatadage* or a circular relic house, a word derived from *vatta* (round), *dhatu* (relic), and *griha* (house). Numerous Sri Lankan *vatadage*s like Ambasthala, Attanagalla, Lankarama, Silacatiya, Rajangane, Tiriyaya, Midirigiriya, Thuparama **[6.26-6.27]**, and Polonnaruva, have been constructed in the Anuradhapura and Polonnaruva Period and many are still standing today though in less than perfect conditions; Thuparama is certainly the most eminent and oldest of all Sri Lankan *dagabas* and *vatadage*s. Originally the dome of Thuparama had been constructed in the heap-of-rice shape but was carelessly restored and given the current bell shape in 1842 CE based on other Anuradhapura *dagaba*s; before this restoration, its *harmika* and *chattravali* were missing. The illustrious account of Thuparama construction was retold in the Mahavamsa and Thupavamsa; it was during the dialogue between the Indian monk Mahendra and King Devanampiya Tissa near the end of the first rainy season in c. 249 BCE that the construction of Thuparama was initiated {Vacissara 1971: 64-68}:

> "Great King, it is a long time since we have last seen the Perfectly Enlightened One, there is no object to which salutation and homage, devotion and honor can be paid; hence we are disappointed."
> "But, Sir, have you not said that the Perfectly Enlightened One has passed away in perfect nibbana?"
> "Great King, even though he passed away in perfect nibbana, his bodily relics, however, remain."
> "Sir, I have understood it. I will establish a thupa, and may you select a site…"

And when the king inquired Mahendra about the shape of the *stupa*, the latter replied:

> "Great King, in the shape of a heap of paddy."

It was then clearly specified that Thuparama was to be constructed over Buddha's relics and in the form of a heap of paddy; the site was immediately chosen on the south side of the royal capital in Anuradhapura. The right collar-bone, as it has been told, was subsequently obtained from the Indian Emperor Asoka to be interred in Thuparama and it was the first *dagaba* in Sri Lanka. The above passage also made it clear that the *dagaba* symbolized Buddha's invisible presence and constructed, besides interring Buddha's relics, to inspire religious devotion. It originally had a rubble core, faced with bricks, coated with hard plaster, and finally whitewashed with white lime; its construction technique was essentially identical as the Vijayarama *dagaba* **[4.10]** and also recalled a similar technique in Gandhara *stupa*s. Thuparama has two entrances with the east apparently as the main one; in its current state the *dagaba*, or precisely a *vatadage*, is elevated over a 164'6" diameter and 11'4" high plinth with pilasters spaced at 8' intervals. Its height is about 67' above the plinth level and has 7'7" x 15'11" projections in the four cardinal points probably originally intended as offering platforms; these rectangular projections instantly evoked the *ayakas* of Amaravati **[6.9]** though without the imposing pillars. In old Sinhalese texts dated between the second-third centuries CE, there are three technical words *ayaka, adimukha,* and *vahalkada* denoting these projections {Paranavitana 1947: 8, 57-60}. The *ayaka* and *adimukha* likely referred to these low projections with the former of an Andhra origin and the latter Sinhalese; the *vahalkada* is an image chapel projecting from the dome and dated later than the other two. Returning to Thuparama, its bell-shaped dome is elevated on a two-tiered molded circular podium of a 62'5"diameter at the base; it is crowned with a solid square *harmika*, which was originally relieved with the sun and moon symbols in the center of its faces, and terminates in a solidly molded tapering spire (*chattravali*) and a copper finial. Among the intrusive elements on the plan is an elongated image chapel in the southwest constructed after the thirteenth century CE; the plinth of the *dagaba* might at one time have a solid balustrade but the current picket-fence railing belonged to a recent restoration.

Besides the *chattravali*, there are other conspicuous features that distinguish Thuparma from other Indian and Gandhara *stupa*s. The first one is a set of architectural elements in the staircases common in Sri Lankan architecture consisting of the wingstone or a solid foliate scroll and *makara* balustrade, the guardstone or a gravestone-like baluster at the foot of the staircase, and the moonstone or a highly ornamental semicircular slab at the landing. Other decorative elements consisting of the *purnaghata, naga,* dwarfish *yaksa, makara* and floral motifs, etc. obviously originated in early Indian *stupa*s. The moonstone in Thuparama, which is profusely decorated with flora and animals like the bull, lion, horse, elephant, and goose, is

Part II. Architecture   Stupa . 191

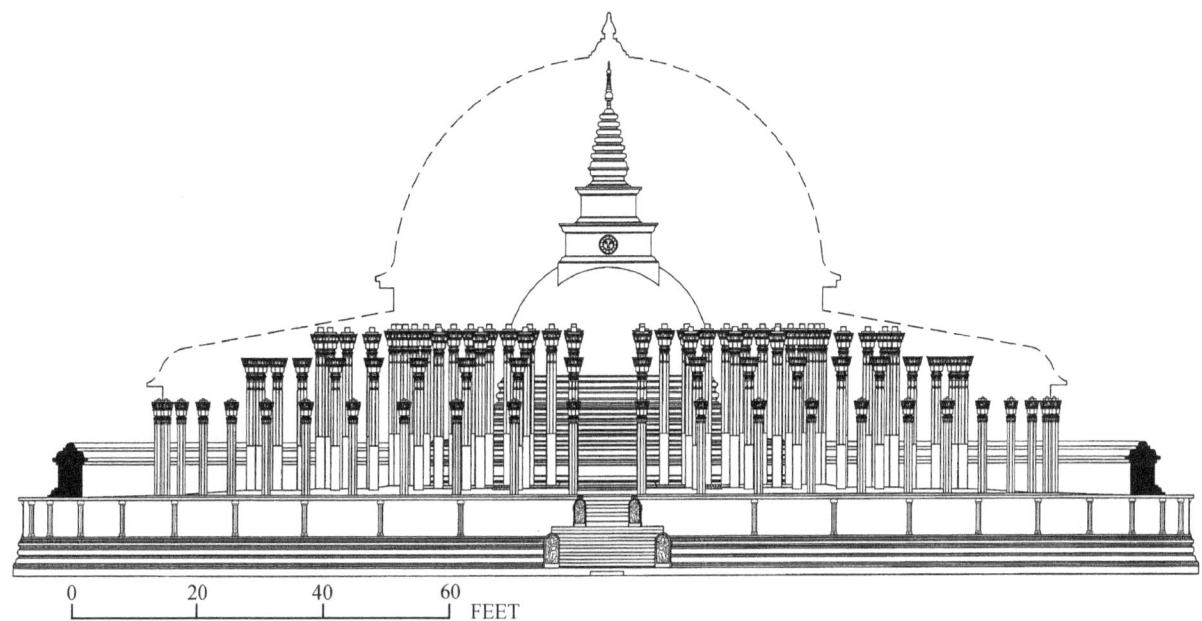

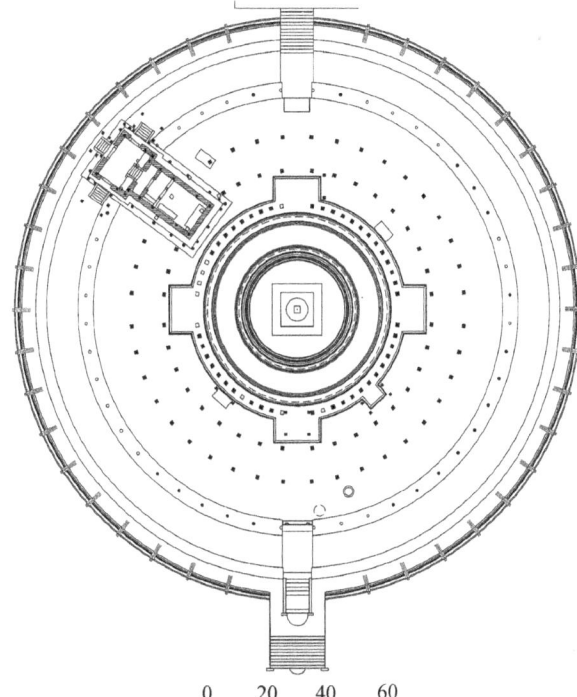

6.26. Thuparama elevation and plan
c. 249 BCE-1842 CE
Eighth century CE (final form)
Anuradhapura- Sri Lanka

6.27. Thuparama
c. 249 BCE-1842 CE
Eighth century CE (final form)
Anuradhapura- Sri Lanka

also of Indian origins. This *vatadage* has 176 stone columns arranged concentrically in the four circles around the main *dagaba*; their heights from the innermost ones outward are 22'10", 21'3", 19'9", and 14'. Each column is square in the base, octagonal in the upper section, and is capped with a lotus-bud capital, which is secured to the column shaft in the mortise-and-tenon technique; this ornate capital has motifs of flowers and dwarfs in various postures. Paranavitana convincingly theorized that these columns were once structural members supporting a timber roof; more specifically, he proposed that the innermost columns supported a hemispherical dome while the outer ones carried a low pitch sloping roof as shown in the elevation {Paranavitana 1947: 83-96, fg. 13}. Such a curved roof would probably be covered with sheet copper much like the Lohapasada as mentioned in Sinhalese chronicles. He also noticed the tenons above the columns as having been designed to tie them to the timber roof framing or brackets; traces of a brick wall, which was once probably the outer wall of the *vatadage*, have been found near the outermost columns. The latter standing just outside this brick wall would probably have been fitted with wooden brackets to support the eave; remains of a door sill were also present among the ruins suggesting the *dagaba* had once been enclosed with a wall and covered with a timber roof. The recovered tiles among the debris have also raised questions as whether the roof was originally pitched in the rectilinear conical shape or a dome as suggested by Paranavitana. Bandaranayake suggested a tile pitched roof, which certainly deem more appropriate in the tropical climate of Sri Lanka and in conforming to its timber architectural tradition, instead of a domed one. Such a rectilinear tile roof would also come closer to the *srikoil*, a type of Hindu temples having conical roofs in Kerala as in the Irinnalakuda Temple {Bandaranayake 1974: 154, 362-378, pl. LIV}; however the central roof might have a dome and the outer roof could be pitched as shown on the elevation. From the available data, the construction and renovation of Thuparama can be divided into several phases:

- Phase I (c. 249 BCE): In the inceptive year of Buddhism in Sri Lanka, a simple heap-of-paddy *dagaba* was raised over the collar-bone of Buddha; it was probably a small and tumulus structure much like Piprahwa [6.1-6.2].
- Phase II (second century CE): King Vasabha (r. 126-170 CE) reportedly erected a *thupaghara* or *vatadage* in Thuparama; the new structure was undoubtedly timber, which enclosed the *dagaba* in the center, and its form was likely similar to Bairat [7.1] in India. Notice the current diameter of the Thuparama plinth is 164'6 compared to the 162' diameter of Amaravati; probably the plinth and the *vatadage* had been enlarged in the second century CE or contemporary with Amaravati. The spire probably still retained the Indian form with its characteristic multi-tiered *yasti-chattra*.
- Phase III (eighth century CE): King Aggabodhi VI (r. 721-761 CE) restored a rotted door of the *vatadage* and probably also replaced its timber pillars with stone ones; the *chattravali* probably occurred earlier in the seventh century CE {Paranavitana 1971: 43-44}. The wingstone, guardstone, and moonstone in the eastern stair alongwith the cyma-and-torus molding of the plinth can also be dated in the eighth century CE {Bandaranayake 1974: 319-320}.
- Phase IV (twelfth century CE): King Parakramabahu I (r. 1153-1186 CE) again initiated another restoration which probably replaced the lotus moldings in the base of the dome, as in the Vijayarama Dagaba [4.10] and a common feature in late Anuradhapura monuments, with plain ones prevalent in the Polonnaruva Period; the pilasters on the plinth almost certainly dated to this restoration.
- Phase V (nineteenth century CE): The *dagaba* was restored in 1842 CE and the dome reshaped into the bell form to be crowned with a solid *hamika* and *chattravali*; this restoration was based on Polonnaruva *dagaba*s.

Many freestanding and rock-hewn *caityagriha*s in India also have a circular and colonnaded plan with a domed roof and a *stupa* in the center and the most well-known examples are Junnar and Guntupalli caves and Bairat Temple [7.1]; the Sri Lankan *vatadage* was undoubtedly a direct translation of the Indian circular *caityagriha*s. Thus Paranavitana's domed roof covering the *dagaba* seems plausible but this does not completely rule out the possibility of a rectilinear tile roof, as proposed by Bandaranayake, also common in the Polonnoruva Period. A few Sri Lankan *dagabas*, like some Gandhara *stupas*, also have the Indian-typed *vedikas* as in Midirigiriya and Abhayagiri; Ruvenvali certainly had a *vedika* at one time but was obliterated by later renovations. Sri Lankan *dagaba*s have been strongly influenced by Gandhara [6.13-6.14, 6.17-6.18] such as the multiple terraces containing pilasters and moldings alongwith the cruciform and quincunxial designs. However the bell-shaped dome, *chattravali*, and lotus moldings were characteristically Sinhalese and these had strong impacts upon the forms of subsequent Southeast Asian *stupa*s [6.28-6.29, 6.33-6.34].

4. *Candi* - Indonesia

The Indonesian archipelago, ancient name Suvarnadvipa, composes mainly of four largest islands Sumatra, Java, Kalimantan, and Sulawesi; Indonesia together with Myanmar, Kampuchea, and Champa were the oldest Indianized countries in Southeast Asia. What these countries absorbed from India were Hindu and Buddhist civilizations that had been brought over by Indian settlers, traders, and missionaries since the beginning of the first century CE. This complex process of Indianization had been accomplished not by military conquests but through peaceful and gradual assimilation as well as intermarriages between the Indians and natives. There were two basic routes through which Indian ideas would be disseminated to Southeast Asia, namely the land route via Bengal and the sea route across the Indian Ocean and the South China Sea. Meanwhile in the first century CE, Buddhism also reached the East Asia via the land route along the Silk Road where the Chinese civilization remains dominant as distinguished from the Indianized countries of Southeast Asia. The single exception is Philippines which did not appear to be Sinized or Indianized in the past but it was converted to Catholicism in the sixteenth century CE. Thus Asia is geographically divided between two spheres of cultural influences with the Chinese predominating in the north and the Indians in the south; this, however, does not take into account Tibetan influences mainly in Mongolia, Bhutan, and the Himalaya region. It is also a similar case for Buddhism in which the Mahayana is predominant in North Asia whereas the Theravada is the principal Buddhist school in South and Southeast Asia while the Vajrayana generally prevails in Tibet and the Tibetanized countries. Initially Hinduism was the chief religion in the southern region but it never had a firm foothold in the north like Buddhism; countries like Kampuchea had historically been Hindu for most of its early history until it was converted to the Theravada in the thirteenth century CE. The differences also extended into the fields of arts and architecture in which the northern architecture primarily employs timber and overwhelmingly Chinese in style whereas the southern countries employ predominantly brick and stone in construction and essentially Indian in style. Tibetan-styled architecture is, on the other hand, mostly a combination of adobe and timber. Coming back to Indonesia, there are numerous Indian Sanskrit inscriptions and artifacts found on the archipelago testifying to the early presence of the Indian civilization; the '*varman*' suffix common in the names of Southeast Asian monarchs ultimately originated in India. Seven Sanskrit edicts in the Grantha script of the South Indian Pallavas, among the oldest in Southeast Asia, have been discovered in Kutei, Kalimantan which were issued by King Mulavarman and dated in the mid fifth century CE. Another four Sanskrit inscriptions also in the Grantha script have been found near Jakarta in Java mentioning the name of a certain King Purnavarman who ruled the country of Turama (fifth-seventh centuries CE); these may be dated in the mid fifth century CE. Recent archaeology has indeed confirmed Turama as the oldest kingdom on the Indonesian archipelago with its center of power near Jakarta in western Java where Hindu and Buddhist sites of Cibuaya (seventh-eighth centuries CE) and Batujaya (sixth-eleventh centuries CE) respectively are located. A few inscriptions from Palembang in Sumatra dated at a later time between c. 683-684 CE and these were written in the Old Malay script. Another Old Malay inscription from Sojomerto in central Java probably dated in the seventh century CE; the oldest dated Javanese inscription in 732 CE is from Gunung Wukir in central Java where famed monuments like Borobudur **[6.28-6.32]** were later built. It appears that the preeminent rise of old Indonesian kingdoms began in the early seventh century CE; first, there was Srivijaya (c. 600-1250 CE) founded in Sumatra around Palembang and included parts of the Malay peninsula. However, some scholars also suggested Kedah in Malaysia as the real center of Srivijaya {Chihara 1996: 87}; remains of Buddhist *stupa*s and Hindu temples have been unearthed in Kedah with the levels of occupation dated between the fifth-fourteenth centuries CE. The cradle of Indonesia lied in central Java where the classic Central Javanese Period between the eighth-tenth centuries CE produced some of the most brilliant monuments in Southeast Asia and many are still standing today such as Borobudur, Candi Sewu **[7.12-7.13]**, and Candi Loro Jonggrang. Important dynasties during this period were the First Maratam or Sanjaya Dynasty (c. 600-775 CE), Sailendra Dynasty (c. 775-856 CE), and the Second Maratam Dynasty (c. 856-928 CE); the Maratams were mostly Hindus and Sivaite whereas the Sailendras were Buddhists. Some scholars believed the Maratams and Sailendras as essentially belonged to one Sailendra Dynasty; the above Sojomerto inscription already mentioned the name of a certain Selendra dated in the seventh century CE. The Sailendras were initially Hindus but later converted to Buddhism in the late eighth century CE and they were again reconverted to Hinduism in the mid ninth century CE {Chihara 1996: 93-94}. The marriage between the Hindu Maratam King Pikatan and Buddhist Sailendra Princess Pramodavardhani resulted in the construction of the Buddhist Candi Plaosan and Candi Loro Jonggrang in the mid ninth century CE. The former was the last great Buddhist monument in Indonesia and from then on Hinduism prevailed as the Sailendras also mysteriously disappeared from Javanese history. Whatever the case, the Sailendras and Maratams were undoubtedly responsible for the constructions of many grandiose monuments during the classic Central Javanese Period. After 928 CE, the seat of the political power shifted to eastern Java as the former glories of central Javanese monuments would be left to ruin; the three important dynasties during the East Javanese Period were Kediri Dynasty (1050-1221 CE), Singosari Dynasty (1221-1293

CE), and Majapahit Dynasty (1293-1530 CE). Eastern Javanese temples, despite of their small scales compared with the earlier huge central Javanese monuments, display a considerable originality and refinement in designs and executions. Hinduism and Buddhism, though essentially rivals in early Indonesian history, appeared to coexist peacefully and even in syncretic forms during the East Javanese Period; from the sixteenth century CE on Islam gradually replaced Hinduism, with the exception of Bali, and remains the dominant religion in Indonesia to this day.

The arts of the Indonesian archipelago began in the Bronze Age around the third century BCE and probably lasted until the arrival of the Indian civilization in the first century CE; among the common items in this period were human figurines, vessels, ceremonial axes, and large drums all in bronze {Kempers 1959: 7}. The latter has been found not only in Indonesia but also throughout Southeast Asia in Thailand, Vietnam, and Yunnam in China; overall the sophisticated designs of these drums are very similar to one another. China has been known to cast bronze items as early as the Shang Dynasty in the second millennium BCE and probably from which the Bronze Age then spread throughout Southeast Asia. With the arrival of Hinduism and Buddhism from India, continental arts began to flourish in Indonesia; early works exhibited a variety of Indian styles infused with indigenous elements. Sources of influences for Indonesian arts were mainly derived from the Gupta Style and Pala Style in North India, the Pallava and Chola styles in South India, and to a lesser extent from Sri Lanka. In the case of Buddhism, there are several bronze Buddha images in the Andhra (Amaravati) Style discovered in Sulawesi and eastern Java and similar images have also been found in Sri Lanka, Thailand, and Champa; another early Buddha image have also been discovered in Sumatra and some Buddha statuettes from the western Javanese site of Batujaya. All these can conservatively be dated between the third-seventh centuries CE suggesting an early propagation of Buddhism in Indonesia. The Mahayana grew increasingly popular on the archipelago in the eighth century CE and with it the production of Mahayana images like Avalokitesvara, Manjusri, Maitreya, Tara, etc. Between the ninth-tenth centuries CE or slightly later, the latest wave of Indian Buddhism or the Vajrayana swept throughout Indonesia alongwith its Tantric deities like Vajrasattva, Vajrapani, Jambhla, etc; the acme of Indonesian Buddhist iconography is indisputably the superb image of Prajnaparamita dated in c. 1300 CE. It appears that the Vajrayana prevailed over all other Buddhist schools in Sumatra and Java during the East Javanese Period whereas in the earlier Central Javanese Period the Mahayana was predominant. Fa-hsien, who previously spent several years in Sri Lanka before returning to China via the sea route, reportedly stayed in Java (c. 414 CE) for about seven months; he mentioned the island was predominantly Hindus with a small Buddhist community. Another Chinese monk I-tsing (683-727 CE) sojourned in Sumatra around c. 690 CE and saw the island as a flourishing center of the Theravada; other Indian monks like Vajrabodhi (671-741 CE) and Amoghavajra (705-774 CE) also passed through Sumatra in the eighth century CE en route to China. Cultural exchanges certainly flowed in both directions as records have indicated that the Indian Pala King Devapala (r. 812-850 CE) built Vihara 1 in Nalanda **[4.4 (#1)]** in 847 CE on the behalf of the Indonesian King Balaputradeva.

The term *candi* in Indonesia denotes any religious or sacred monuments including temples and *stupa*s, most often temples; it could be derived from the Indian word *caitya*, a word that also has many variations throughout Southeast Asia as *zedi* (Myanmar), *chedi* (Thailand, Laos), and *chedei* (Kampuchea). The oldest architecture in Indonesia to date are the foundational remains of isolated Hindu and Buddhist *candi*s near Jakarta at Cibuaya (seventh-eighth centuries CE) and Batujaya (sixth-eleventh centuries CE) respectively; the latter encompasses twenty-four Buddhist sites of temples and *stupa*s which were originally constructed of brick foundations and timber superstructures. Some of the remains have square plans and a few have square corner bastions and four staircases in the four cardinal points reminiscent of Gandhara *stupa*s **[6.17-6.18]** and Nalanda Caityas 3, 12 **[4.4 (#3, 12)]**; their superstructures are no longer extant. The bases of these structures have torus moldings and regularly spaced dentils very similar to the Mahabodhi Temple **[7.10-7.11]**. Architectural activities subsequently shifted to central Java on the Dieng Plateau where the oldest extant group of eight isolated Hindu stone *candi*s was constructed below the western slope of Mount Ungaran; these are all Sivaite temples. The older *candi*s in this group are Arjuna, Semar, and Srikandi dated between c. 675-732 CE while Puntadeva, Sembodro, Gatotkoco, Darawati, and Bhima dated between c. 732-775 CE. A typical plan of these *candi*s consists of a square or rectangular cella with a projecting porch and staircase on one end; the one-storied porch is roofed over with a rectilinear or curvilinear pediment. The main structure has three sections, namely the plinth, the body, and the roof with the latter having a three-tiered crown and terminating in a finial. These *candi*s, particularly Candi Puntadeva, are decorated with *kala-makara* motifs (Indian *kirti-mukha*) on the entry architraves and side niches; other prominent Indian themes are also conspicuous such as reliefs of guardians, Hindu gods, etc. and motifs like the *purnaghata*s, foliate scrolls, and mythical animals such as *kinnara*s, *naga*s, etc. Indonesian *candi*s, whether Hindu or Buddhist, can be classified into several types:

(a) Isolated one-storied buildings. This was the earliest type as in the Jakarta and Dieng groups that persisted in later Hindu and Buddhist *candi*s throughout the Central and Eastern Javanese Period.
(b) Multiple-storied or multi-tiered buildings. These, to my knowledge, are the only type found in Buddhist *candi*s like Candi Sari and Candi Plaosan Lor; the second story was timber that could be reached by a wooden staircase, all have vanished due to the perishable material.
(c) A group of buildings elevated on terraces with a central temple. This type exemplifies in large temple complexes like Candi Sewu [7.12-7.13] and Candi Loro Jonggrang; it became the precursor of the multi-terraced pyramidal temples during the Angkor Period in Kampuchea.

All central Javanese *candi*s show a marked degree of maturity as indicative of their previously long exposure and evolution from timber architecture; in fact, the foundations of the Batujaya *candi*s, Candi Bhima, Candi Sewu, and Candi Mendut were all brick while their superstructures were likely timber; these have also been the case for many pre-Angkor temples of Kampuchea. The prevalence of brick foundations in early Hindu and Buddhist *candi*s strongly suggests that they were probably contemporaneous in date; by the early seventh century CE experiments with permanent materials like stone began to be implemented in architecture. The architecture of earlier brick *candi*s at Batujaya appeared to have their sources in the North Indian Gupta temples while later stone *candi*s on the Dieng Plateau were likely inspired by the South Indian Pallava *ratha*s as in Mamallapuram. The unique form of the stone Candi Bhima architecturally imitated the Bhirtagaon Temple in India though the latter was built of brick. The Batujaya and Dieng *candi*s also served as architectural models for later *candi*s regardless of their religious affiliations; however there are fundamental differences between Hindu and Buddhist *candi*s. The latter typically has miniature *stupa*s crowning their roofs with their decorative schemes and cult images Buddhistic whereas Hindu *candi*s are crowned with *ratna* (jewel) or *amalaka* finials with the *linga*s or images of Hindu gods installed in their cellas. In rare instances, Hindu pseudo-*ratna* finials also appeared in Buddhist monuments like Borobudur and conversely pseudo-*stupa*s also occurred in Hindu ones like Candi Loro Jonggrang. With the rise of the Buddhist Sailendra Dynasty in the late eighth century CE, administrative and artistic center in central Java shifted away from Dieng Plateau to the Kedu Plain; this was the golden age of Buddhism in Indonesia and the classic period in Javanese arts and architecture. The Sailendras built massive and influential Buddhist *stupa*s and *candi*s like Borobudur and Candi Sewu; their splendid achievement, which was certainly inspired by the colossal scales of Sri Lankan *dagaba*s as well as Indian and Bangladeshi monuments like Kesariya [6.12] and Somapura [4.8], could only be matched by the Khmers a few centuries later. The first important Buddhist *candi* on the Kedu Plain was Candi Kalasan (778 CE), followed by Candi Sewu, Mendut, Pawon, Ngawen, Borobudur, Sari, Plaosan Lor/Kidul, Sajiwan, and Banyjunibo; some of these are *stupa*s like Borobudur. The construction of these gigantic monuments within the seventy-five-year period probably hastened the collapse of the Sailendra Dynasty. The succeeding Second Maratam Dynasty erected an equally massive Hindu monument Candi Loro Jonggrang (856 CE); this masterpiece was obviously a modified design of Candi Sewu. With the exhausted energy of the Central Javanese Period, later *candi*s of the East Javanese Period were noticeably smaller yet elegant for their scales; Buddhist *candi*s during this period showed strong signs of syncretism fusing both Hindu and Buddhist elements as in Candi Jawi. In retrospect, the extravagant stone monuments of the Central Javanese Period are comparable to those of the Angkor Period in Kampuchea much like the isolated brick *candi*s of the East Javanese Period to the brick *kalan*s of Champa.

Early Hindu *candi*s like Candi Arjuna usually had a Siva *linga* in its cella, which would subsequently be replaced with images of Hindu gods like Siva, Brahma, and Visnu as in Candi Loro Jonggrang. Indonesian kings, like their Khmer and Cham counterparts, often built new *candi*s housing *linga*s or images of Hindu gods to commemorate their enthronement and legitimatize their rules. The features of these gods are generally believed to have been modeled after the reigning king and when installed in temples to be worshipped by his subjects they would accordingly be considered as the divine manifestations, living representatives, and embodiments of the gods on earth. The idea of divine incarnations of Hindu gods, which would be manifested in the human forms as *devarajas* (god-kings) on earth, certainly originated in India as many of its Hindu monarchs also considered themselves as reincarnations of Visnu or Siva; this belief and cult were also widespread among the Khmer and Cham kings. The Buddhists also believed in a similar concept with an essential difference in that their Buddhist kings were called *dharmaraja*s who uphold and defended Buddha's *Dharma* but rarely were they considered as Buddha's reincarnations; the most famous Buddhist *dharmaraja* was no other than Emperor Asoka. A central Javanese *candi* might also have a shaft directly below the enshrined image of the Hindu god wherein a foundation deposit box would be dropped. This box typically contained a small *pripih*, or a fabricated object or dummy in which the gods could be animated and manifested during religious occasions; other deposited items in the box also included metal, semiprecious stones, seeds, and important objects. Similar foundation shafts have also been discovered beneath the cellas of Khmer temples like Angkor Wat though not necessarily for depositing sacred objects but possibly as a linkage to the underworld. It has been proven that the Javanese *candi*, whether Hindu or Buddhist, has never been a sepulchral monument for the interment of human relics {Soekmono: 14, 37, 49, 102-103, 116-122}.

A few notes about materials and construction technologies that the earliest *candi*s had timber superstructures elevated on brick plinths and foundations. New constructions eventually completely employed stone (andesite) beginning in the late seventh century CE and throughout the Central Javanese Period; East Javanese *candi*s generally employed brick and stone or the combination of both. The *candi*s are basically held together by interlocking stone blocks using various technologies and devices such as dowels, I-cramps, mortises-and-tenons, key blocks, and shiplapping. These are also preventive measures to minimize the swaying movement which will especially be detrimental to the structures in a strong earthquake zone like Indonesia. A *candi* exterior is made up of neatly dressed stone blocks that are faced over a roughly dressed stone core and the whole monument were probably covered in a fine layer of plaster as in Candi Kalasan and might be painted or gilded {Kempers 1959: 50, pl. 102}; the *candi*s were constructed in the corbel-arched technique as true semicircular or pointed arches were unknown in Indonesia. There were possible participations of foreign craftsmen from other Southeast Asian countries in the constructions of several central Javanese *candi*s; for examples, the *makara* head in one of the exterior niches in Candi Kalasan curves inward, which was a common occurrence in Cham architecture (Mi-son E1) but rarely in Java. A relief on the wall of Candi Plaosan Lor shows a foreigner resembling a Khmer royal personage paying tribute to a Javanese king; possibly Khmer craftsmen were present in Java working under the tutelage of the Sailendras.

Buddhist monasteries certainly existed in Indonesia but none survives likely due to the perishable timber construction; such timber monasteries have been found alongwith several brick *stupa*s on the north side of Candi Mendut and to the northwest of Borobudur. It is important to distinguish between the temple-*candi*s, which house religious icons or *linga*s inside a hollow cella, and *stupa-candi*s, which inter relics and are closed off from all sides. The latter type is the *stupa* and not as common as the former in Indonesia; some of the oldest Indonesian *stupa*s have been constructed at Batujaya as early as the sixth century CE and as late as the East Javanese Period. The bell-shaped dome is the most typical in Indonesian *stupa*s while the rarer type is cylindrical *stupa*s like Sunberawan in eastern Java and Maligai in Sumatra; the *chedi-tong*, a type of Thai *stupa*s, is probably derived from the latter type. There are three basic types of *stupa-candi*s in Indonesia:

(a) These are usually small in various shapes and sizes crowning the roofs of *candi*s that are the integral and complementary components of the *candi*s as in Candi Sewu **[7.12-7.13]**.

(b) These are typically isolated and small structures which encompass votive *stupa*s; examples of this type are the Batujaya group and Candi Plaosan Lor/Kidul.

(c) These are large to colossal freestanding *stupa*s which are rare in Indonesia; the most exemplary model of this type is Borobudur **[6.28-6.32]** and lesser known ones like Sunberawan and Maligai in Sumatra.

The most preeminent of all Indonesian *stupa-candi*s and among the most unique and influential of all Buddhist *stupa*s in Asia is Borobudur **[6.28-6.32]**; it is situated on the Kedu Plain in central Java virtually forgotten for over a millennium. Indonesia had been a Dutch colony since the late seventeenth century CE and was briefly transferred to the British during the Napoleonic war in the nineteenth century CE. Thomas Stamford Raffles, then a British colonial administrator of Java, sent H. C. Cornelius to conduct the first survey and clearing the ruins in 1814 CE. Even after its discovery, the monument continued to be ransacked; the side of the main *stupa* was broken into and a teahouse was built on its summit in 1844 CE as a rest-stop for visitors to enjoy the surrounding views! In 1886 CE a Dutch archaeologist discovered the hidden gallery behind the massive base terrace; it was temporarily disassembled and put back together in 1890 CE by a Dutch engineer J. W. Ijzerman so an Indonesian photographer could photo the entire hidden gallery. The monument was so famous that another plunder occurred in 1896 CE

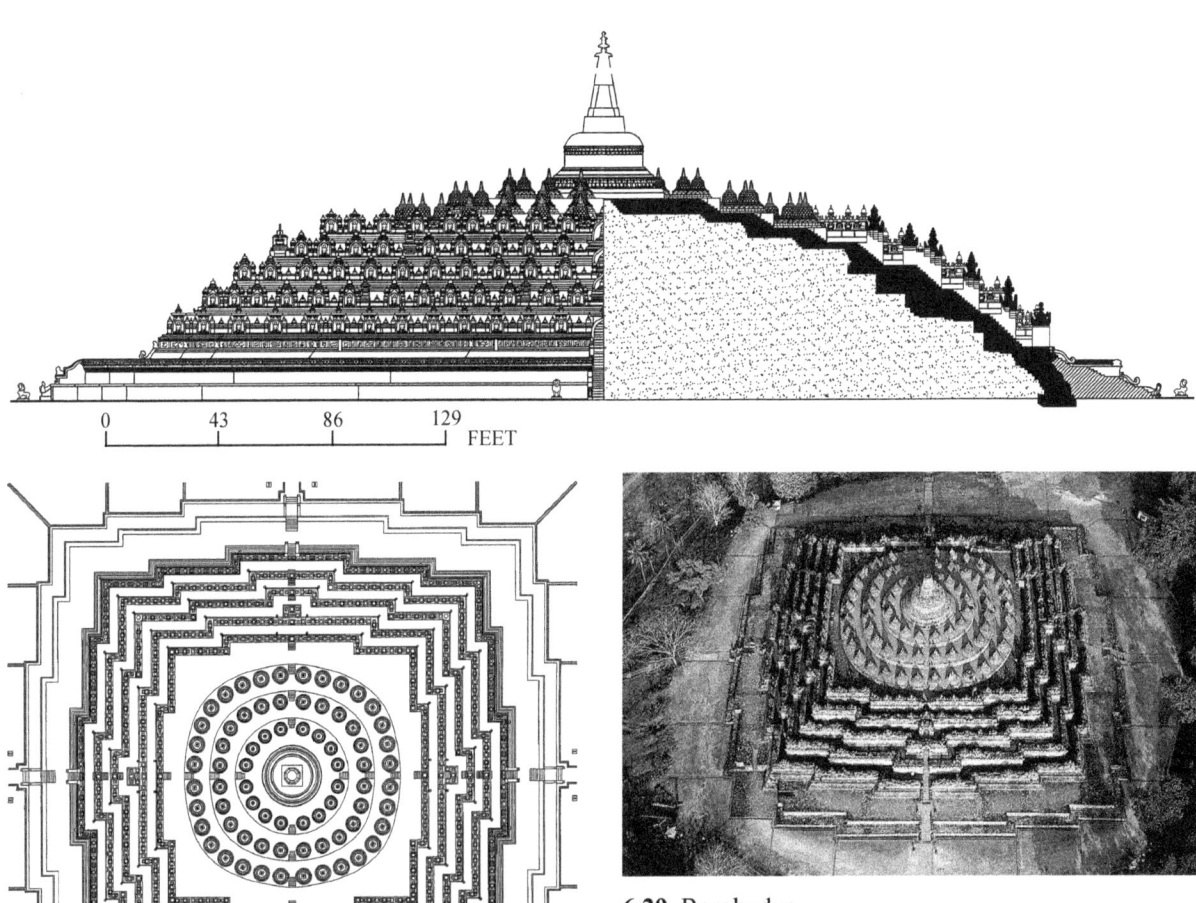

6.28. Borobudur elevation-section and top view
c. 792-842 CE
Magelang- Indonesia

6.29. Borobudur
c. 792-842 CE
Magelang- Indonesia

when the Thai King Chulalongkorn stopped by and allowed to take home eight cartloads of sculptures from Borobudur as gifts. The first major restoration was initiated by the Dutch engineer Thadedus van Erp between 1907-1911 CE; he successfully reerected the ruined upper *stupa* terraces and filled the openings in the paving to prevent water from seeping into the ground which had been the primary cause of subsidence. Another major restoration would subsequently be carried out by UNESCO between 1973-1983 CE; this time the relief galleries and balustrades were reinforced and a new drainage system installed for the proper discharge of water away from the monument. There were numerous contentions about the name Borobudur as early twentieth century CE scholars like N. J. Krom called it 'Barabudur' which he believed to have been originated from *bara* (holy) and *budur* (Buddha). Stutterheim thought the name was derived from Javanese *boro* (monastery) and *budur* (hill) and a Javanese chronicle mentioned a rebel hiding in the 'mountain Bara-Budur' after his defeat; considering all the views, Borobudur seems to suggest 'Mountain of the Buddhas.' In any case, the massive *stupa* was constructed directly on top of a natural hill taking full advantage of the topography; first the hilltop was leveled, infilled, and tamped to be served as a firm foundation for the *stupa* before its construction could begin. Borobudur essentially

composes of three distinct divisions:
- The plain bottom two terraces, which essentially are *pradaksina* paths, also function like sturdy retaining walls buttressing the monument from its tremendous outward thrust. Initially these terraces were probably not present but seemed to have been added later for some undetermined reasons; they effectively covered and hid the lowest relief gallery from view but a section of it is currently exposed in the southeast corner.
- The middle five terraces are zigzag outdoor relief galleries, which include the solid balustrades to protect pilgrims from falling, depicting Buddhist stories and where pilgrims can perform their religious procession and appreciate the monument at the same time.
- The top three terraces have almost circular plans as bases for the small *stupa*s, of which only the uppermost one is perfectly circular whereas the lower two are slightly oval; the summit is surmounted by a large bell-shaped *stupa* having a solid *chattravali* now partially broken.

The monument has four entries and median staircases in the four cardinal points with the main entrance facing east as common in Buddhist architecture; there are pairs of animals guarding the entrances at the landings. The *stupa* was constructed by piling up millions of 9" high stone blocks; its base measures approximately 417' square, 346' at the foot of the first balustrade, and 168' at the base of the lowermost circular *stupa* terrace. The most exquisitely decorated sections of the monument are the continuous narrative relief panels on the five balustrades, with the exception of the back side of the uppermost balustrade which is plain. There are a total of 1,300 carved panels with a combined length of 1 1/2 miles; the hidden gallery also contains additional 160 panels and this gives a grand total of 1,460 relief panels. It has now been established among the scholars that the sources for these reliefs have been based on several Buddhist texts, though precise identifications of all scenes remain highly speculative and controversial in many cases. All the panels are to be viewed from right to left starting from the eastern staircase in the southern wing in accordance to the usual clockwise *pradaksina* path.

A. The Hidden Gallery

Each panel of the hidden reliefs is about 2'2" high x 6'6" wide; the gallery is believed to have been based on the Mahakarmavibhanga (Great Classification of Actions), which list the consequences of one's *karma*s as either a

6.30. Scene of pleasurable indulgences
c. 792-842 CE
Borobudur Hidden Gallery, Panel 20
Magelang- Indonesia

reward or a punishment usually in the form of a higher rebirth (good *karma*s) or a lower rebirth and hell (bad *karma*s). Many of the reliefs depict scenes of violence, hell, punishment, quarrels, pleasurable indulgences, rewards for a virtuous life, etc. and one of such panel depicts a scene of pleasurable indulgences **[6.30]** now exposed in the southeast corner of Borobudur; it appears to show a group of hedonists playing music, enjoying dancing and drinking to the point of intoxication. This is contrasted with the calm scene on the extreme right seemingly about a virtuous family where its members appear dignified and in control of their behaviors; it is separated from the left scene by a tree, also a common compositional device in Indian Buddhist reliefs. The scene exemplifies a classic Buddhist story of extolling virtues while condemning immorality that eventually leads to a destructive life and a low rebirth in the next life; scenes like these in the hidden gallery seem to portray the debased world at the lowest levels of existence devoid of spirituality as described in the Mahakarmavibhanga. In closer scrutiny, the hidden gallery also virtually has no grand palace scenes as in the upper galleries, which are typically carved with the most intricate details; at least five panels were either left unfinished or the carvings abruptly ceased halfway for some unknown reasons. Some panels have Old Javanese inscriptions resembling sculptors' marks that enable the ascription of the construction date for Borobudur in the Central Javanese Period and during the Sailendra Dynasty. A small section in the southeast corner of the monument was originally exposed in 1943 CE by Y. Furuzawa of the occupying Japanese Army and the public can now visualize the hidden gallery and the massive terraces that cover it.

B. The Upper Four Galleries and Five Balustrades

These 14'-16' high galleries, which contain a few sculp-

6.31. Prince Sidhartha and Four Signs of Suffering (above) and King Sibi Jataka (below)
c. 792-842 CE
Borobudur Wall Gallery I, Panel 56
Magelang- Indonesia

tors' marks, are on the walls and balustrades containing relief panels that average between 1'10"-3'3" high x 6'2"-8'2" wide and Buddha niches of 4' high x 3 1/4' wide x 2 1/2' deep; the back side of the uppermost balustrade is uncarved due to various reasons. All balustrades are capped with pseudo-*ratna* finials on the first balustrade and mini-*stupa*s on the remaining four balustrades; there are 432 Buddha images in niches that crown these balustrades all facing outward and are grouped in the four wings on the monument in according to their unique iconographical features. These Buddhas gesture different *mudra*s: the *abhaya-mudra* for Buddhas in the north wing, *varada-mudra* for Buddhas in the south wing, *bhumisparsa-mudra* for Buddhas in the east wing, and *dhyana-mudra* for Buddhas in the west wing. The single exceptions are the Buddhas in the uppermost fifth balustrade all gesturing the *vitarka-mudra* while the seventy-two Buddhas in the terrace *stupa*s gesture the *dharmacakrapravatana-mudra*. Louis Frederic attributed each *mudra* to a Buddha, namely *abhaya-mudra* for Amoghasiddhi, *varada-mudra* for Ratnasambhava, *dhyana-mudra* for Amitabha, *bhumisparsa-mudra* for Aksobhya, and *vitarka-mudra* for Samantabhadra Bodhisattva {Frederic 1996: 178-184}; however the iconography of the images on the fifth balustrade is clearly a Buddha not Samantabhadra Bodhisattva as Frederic stated; I will return to this point later. The outside face of Balustrade

Gallery I facing visitors is carved with guardian figures separated by pilasters; its inner face, like Wall Gallery I, is unique in having two registers of narrative reliefs separated in between by a narrow decorative band while the individual scenes in these panels are divided from one another by a tree. Scholars have identified the panels in the upper registers of Wall Gallery I as illustrating scenes from Sakyamuni's life as told in the Lalitavistara; the other panels, up to Balustrade Gallery II, portray the *jataka*s and *avadana*s. For example, a panel in the upper register of Wall Gallery I **[6.31 (above)]** depicts an episode where Prince Siddhartha encountered an old man on the eastern gate as he was riding outside his Kapilavastu palace; this was one of the Four Signs of suffering (birth, old age, sickness, death) that eventually drove him to adopt the an ascetic life before ultimately becoming a Buddha. Prince Siddhartha is shown here sitting on his carriage and surrounded by his royal entourage; on the extreme left is an old man with a cane in his hand who can only manage to walk with the guide and help of his grandson. The lower register in the same panel **[6.31 (below)]** is a moving *jataka* about King Sibi sacrificing himself to save a dove from being killed by a falcon {Krom 1927 Volume I: 275-278}. Indra (Sakra) king of the gods decided to test the shining virtues of King Sibi by disguising himself as a falcon and Vicvakarman as a dove. The terrifying dove, when pursued by the falcon, would seek protection from King Sibi who was famed for saving the lives of all living creatures; the falcon demanded that it would only release the dove in exchange for the king's own flesh of an equal weight as the dove's, a proposition that King Sibi magnanimously agreed to. The king in the scene is shown sitting on an elaborate throne on the right as the dove rests next to his right shoulder as the falcon perches on the tree branch. Further on the left is a scale with a dove on one side and a lump of flesh in the other as exactly told in the Buddhist *jataka*; the king's retinue is apparently profoundly touched by the poignant and holy moment. Scenes like these were generally common throughout the Buddhist world due to their rich narrative contents, strong religious and moral values. Other famous *jataka*s depicted on Borobudur already occurred in early Indian Buddhist *stupa*s like the Miga Jataka **[6.8]** (Wall Balustrade Gallery I, Panel 94-98) and Mahakapi Jataka (Wall Balustrade Gallery I, Panel 99-102) in Bharhut, and Visvantara Jataka in Sanchi (Balustrade Gallery I, Panel 35-39, upper register). The panels from Wall Gallery II to Balustrade Gallery IV are believed by scholars to have depicted scenes in the Gandavyuha, a Mahayana text describing the spiritual quest of the youth Sudhana who was the son of a rich Indian merchant in search for

6.32. Stupa terraces and central *stupa*
c. 792-842 CE
Borobudur, Magelang- Indonesia

Buddhist teachings and enlightenment. Along the journey he met many Buddhas, wise teachers, and *bodhisattva*s like Manjusri, Avalokitesvara, and Maitreya; finally he met Samantabhadra Bodhisattva who enlightened the inquisitive youth through his wisdom. The uppermost Wall Balustrade Gallery V presumably depicts the last section in the Gandavyuha text, or the Bhadracari, in which Samantabhadra made the vows to lead all sentient beings toward enlightenment and Buddhahood. The scenes on these panels seem to portray the various meetings between Sudhana and his spiritual teachers while those near the end of the gallery contain many Buddhas, which appear to tally with the Bhadracari. The appearance of numerous Buddhas on these panels seem to prepare visitors for the dramatic and climactic encounter with the seventy-two Buddhas in the terrace *stupa*s above; however the identification of these last galleries with the Gandavyuha remains far from fully settled. Stylistically, the carvings on the galleries and balustrades are the most refined, and have broader themes than the hidden gallery; the depictions of luxurious palaces in these panels strongly suggest actual portrayals of contemporary court scenes of the Sailendras.

C. The Three Stupa Terraces

Leaving the relief galleries and balustrades behind, visitors continue to ascend to the upper three *stupa* terraces which contain seventy-two perforated *stupa*s that are utterly bereft of decorations [6.32]; these are distributed in groups of thirty-two, twenty-four, and sixteen concealing seventy-two Buddha sculptures inside that amount to a grand total of 504 Buddha images for the whole *stupa*. The practice of placing Buddha images inside *stupa*s certainly originated in India as an inscription on a Mathura Buddha image referred to its dedication and installation inside a *stupa*; the excavation of Devnimori Stupa in Gujarat (fourth-seventh centuries CE) also uncovered nine Buddha images inside {Lohuizen-de Leeuw 1949: 182-183}{Khandalavala 1991: 83-84}. The lower two terraces have oval plans and *stupa*s between 11'-13' high all having solid square *harmika*s and tapering *chattravali*s. The uppermost terrace is perfectly circular containing sixteen smaller *stupa*s about 13' high; the massive 40' high central *stupa*, which is also elevated on the same terrace as the other sixteen *stupa*s, has a solid *harmika* and a tapering *chattravali* already broken off. Some scholars have conveniently counted the central *stupa* as a separate terrace or level to justify their theory of the *bodhisattva*'s multi-stages of enlightenment and I will come back to this point later; the current height of Borobudur from the ground level to the tip of the broken spire is about 115'. All seventy-two Buddha images inside these perforated *stupa*s gesture the *dharmacakrapravatana-mudra* and have been identified as Vairocana by Frederic {Frederic 1996: 180}:

> This mudra, i.e. *dharmacakrapravartana mudra*, represents the first sermon preached by the Sakyamuni Buddha to his five disciples in the Deer Park at Sarnath. It is characteristic of Vairocana, the supreme Buddha, who dwells at the zenith.

In this case it is impossible to reconcile the symbolisms of Sakyamuni (a Theravada Buddha) and Vairocana (a Vajrayana Buddha) since both have the *dharmacakrapravatana-mudra* as their special attribute; this is further complicated by Frederic's identification of the fifth Buddha on the fifth balustrade as Samantabhadra, who is actually a Mahayana *bodhisattva* not a Buddha. The religious meanings of Borobudur became more convoluted when an unfinished statue in the *bhumisparsa-mudra*, an attribute of Aksobhya, was discovered inside the main *stupa* in 1842 CE; all these problematical issues and scholarly hypotheses alongwith the complex symbolisms of the *stupa* will be considered in the following discussions.

Borobudur is such a preeminent monument that numerous theories have been proposed regarding its constructions and symbolisms since it was first discovered by Europeans in the early nineteenth century CE; many are no more than fanciful speculations which have further confused than elucidated the meanings of the monument.

a. Construction
- A domed *stupa* {Chihara 1996: 114-118}
Henry Parmentier proposed that a giant dome equal to the diameter of the largest bottom terraces must have once crowned Borobudur. This massive dome probably proved to be a heavy load for the *stupa* so that the architect decided to replace it with a lighter and smaller central *stupa* and seventy-two small *stupa*s with their shells perforated and interiors hollowed out. In any case, the proposal of a huge dome bearing on the *stupa* is clearly illogical from the structural standpoint and aesthetically incompatible with the balustraded relief galleries below. Probably a bell-shaped dome was more plausible than a hemispherical one but it is impossible to verify whether originally there was a dome or not.
- A Buddhist *candi* {Chihara 1996: 114-118}
A. Hoenig hypothesized that a *candi* or temple must have once stood at the summit in the place of the *stupa* terraces; indeed similar Hindu pyramidal terraced temples have been built a little later than Borobudur such as Bakong (881 CE) and Phnom Bakheng (890 CE) in the Angkor Period of Kampuchea. However many Buddhist multi-terraced structures in Myanmar like Shwezigon [6.33-6.34] were also crowned with *stupa*s and so should Borobudur.
- Constructed over an abandoned Hindu *candi* {Dumarcay 1986: 27}
This theory was proposed by Jacques Dumarcay:

> The decline of Hinduism had left a stepped pyramid which was far from complete. Only the first and second terraces were finished but the walls were bare and the outlines of the building were uncarved. This huge stone mass could have been abandoned, for it was difficult to adapt to Buddhism. However, leaving in evidence such an obvious manifestation of Hinduism was probably not judged politically prudent, and the work was taken up again, most likely just after 790, adapting as best as possible the forms and the iconography already introduced at Candi Sewu.

Now, was it more 'politically prudent' to build over a Hindu monument belonging to a religion that had been as powerful and deep-rooted as Buddhism? Even at the height of Buddhism during the Sailendras, there was no evidence of Buddhism ever replacing Hinduism or a Buddhist monument had been constructed over a Hindu one. Moreover the obvious design changes or inconsistencies in Borobudur such as the unfinished panels of the hidden gallery, the double registers in the first gallery, and the *ratna* finials in the first balustrade contrasting with the rest of the monument do not necessarily suggest a conversion of a Hindu monument to a Buddhist one. Above all the lowest hidden gallery of Borobudur, which clearly depicts Buddhist themes, is the overwhelming proof that its foundation was originally Buddhist; furthermore, no Hindu monuments in the Central and East Javanese Period have ever been constructed in the multi-terraced pyramid like the Buddhist Borobudur. Thus Dumarcay's alleged theory about Borobudur's religious and architectural conversion from a Hindu to Buddhist one has no factual bases.
- Location relative to other Buddhist *candi*s {Chihara 1996: 127-129}{Frederic 1996: 85-86}.
According to Y. Iwamoto and Daigoro Chihara, Borobudur, Pawon, and Mendut might have been conceived as a group to form a sacred pilgrimage path or as a conceptual map leading to the location of the Sailendras' royal palace. They theorized that as Mendut faced northwest and Borobudur faced northeast and the place where these diagonal lines intersected could be the location of a buried royal palace; the area where the intersection occurs has been thoroughly excavated and yet nothing conclusive has turned up. In reality Borobudur, Pawon, and Mendut do not lie on the same east-west axis but rather in the northwesterly direction while their entrances also have different orientations; therefore they are not considered as in alignment with each other. The theory is thus highly conjectural and without any factual supports.
- Mount Merapi {Frederic 1996: 39}
Louis Frederic stated that Borobudur was a man-made symbolic mountain as an answer to the natural volcano Mount Merapi in the distance. First of all, there are many other volcanoes besides Mount Merapi visible from Borobudur such as Mount Merbabu and Mount Sumbing and I am not certain with which mountain Borobudur should spiritually be associated. This theory is therefore highly subjective.

b. Symbolisms
- Ten *bhumi*s {Chihara 1996: 119}{Soekmono 1995: 57-60}
This theory was first espoused by De Cadparis based essentially on the Sri Kahulunnan inscription in 842 CE which stated that:

> At the time Her Majesty the Queen dedicated

the village of Teru I Tepusan, under the Queen's jurisdiction, as a freehold belonging to kamulan i bhumisambhara.

Since 'bhumisambhara' denoted a terraced hill and *bhumi* in Mahayana literature also meant a spiritual stage(s) that a *bodhisattva* must traverse before becoming a Buddha, De Casparis concluded that 'kamulan i bhumisambhara' was actually referring to Borobudur; these ten Mahayana *bhumi*s are giving, morality, forbearance, energy, meditation, wisdom, means, vow, strength, and knowledge. Chihara gave a different translation of 'kamulan i bhumisambhara' as 'place of origin of provisions of the earth;' in any case, the translation and exact meaning of the term were far from being settled. Most importantly, do these ten *bhumi*s architecturally correspond to the ten terraces of Borobudur? What *bhumi* does the hidden gallery represent? Only the third to fifth balustrades and the third to fourth galleries have been tentatively associated with the Gandavyuha about Sudhana's spiritual quest for enlightenment; even these do not appear to correlate to the ten *bhumi*s. Thus Borobudur could not have been constructed to specifically represent the ten *bhumi*s.

- Ten *paramita*s and design changes {Chihara 1996: 119-122}
This theory by Daigoro Chihara was based on De Casparis' ten *bhumi*s theory already discussed but he substituted these with ten *paramita*s (perfection). He also suggested that the design changes in Borobudur, such as the additions of the bases and upper *stupa* terraces, reflected the introduction of new religious ideas from India like the concepts of the ten *bhumi*s or ten *paramita*s. However, some of the design modifications were obviously practical solutions to minimize the potential structural problems like subsidence and lateral forces from the massive loads of the superstructure and earthquakes; moreover, it is also impossible to precisely correlate any particular terrace with a specific *paramita*.

- Mount Sumeru {Dumarcay 1986: 89-91} {Chihara 1996: 25-26}
This cliched idea has been around for a long time in which the concept of Mount Meru (Hindu) or Mount Sumeru (Buddhist) represents a cosmic mountain that has four summits surrounding a central one; in the base is the seven circular mountain chains separated by seven oceans and beyond the seventh ocean in the eighth ocean is Jambudvipa with Lake Anavatpa in its center. Another slightly different version of the Mount Meru myth is that it rises in the center of Jambudvipa with the gods inhabiting its slopes and summits according to their proper ranks; Jambudvipa is traditionally associated with our world, or more precisely India, and Mount Meru and Lake Anavatpa with Mount Kailash and Lake Manasarovar in western Tibet. The idea of Borobudur as representing the cosmic Mount Sumeru does not tally exactly with the architecture or the contents and iconographies of the reliefs and sculptures.

- Ancestor cult {Frederic 1996: 79-86}
Louis Frederic was among the proponents of this hypothesis:

> The pyramidal shape of Borobudur also testifies to a combination of native Javanese cults of ancestor worship, whose observances included the use of a stepped pyramid, with a staircase at the center of one side leading to the summit. These layered pyramids, dedicated to the cult of ancestors, are widely found in Java.

He was probably thinking of the terraced pyramidal Hindu temples in the Angkor Period of Kampuchea, which were mostly dedicated to the *devaraja* cult, when he made this statement; however the cult has nothing in common with Borobudur, which is obviously a Buddhist *stupa*. He also did not specifically list any Javanese 'layered pyramids' that were dedicated to the cult of ancestors to support his claim; moreover, the terraced pyramidal *stupa*s like Borobudur are exceptionally rare and not 'widely found' in the whole Indonesia let alone Java.

- Numerology {Frederic 1996: 75-78}
Another far-fetched theory was about the purportedly numerological logics of Borobudur also proposed by Louis Frederic:

> In its present form, Borobudur has five square platforms (those of the four galleries and another supporting the round terraces). The processional plinth cannot be counted in this number, as it serves only as part of the ritual *pradaksina*. If we add the three round terraces to the five square platforms, we arrive at a total of eight, the most sacred of all numbers, symbolic of infinity…The number 8 is a symbol of infinity and limitless… it is also a symbol of cosmic equilibrium…

The author simply picked and chose the architectural

elements to fit his grand theory about the supposedly esoteric and numerical symbolisms of Borobudur. Which ancient texts, Hindu or Buddhist, stated Number 8 as 'the most sacred of all numbers' and a 'symbol of infinity and limitless'? He apparently excluded the central *stupa* in the summit and the hidden gallery from his numerical scheme.

- *Kamadhatu, rupadhatu,* and *arupadhatu* {Kempers 1959: 43-45}{Chihara 1996: 26, 115, 118-119}
This straightforward theory has frequently been cited by many scholars as symbolizing the three tiers of the Buddhist cosmology in which *kamadhatu* represents the World of Desire, *rupadhatu* the World of Ordinary Form or Physical Manifestation, and *arupadhatu* the World of Formless or Highest Existence. *Kamadhatu* supposedly corresponded to the hidden gallery, *rupadhatu* the five balustrades and galleries, and *arupadhatu* the three *stupa* terraces while the central *stupa* symbolized the highest realm, the Void (*Sunya*) and Enlightenment. This theory is certainly very convincing but it too has drawbacks. If the central *stupa* symbolizes *Sunya*, why was there a Buddha image reportedly present inside it? Why were the four Jina Buddhas located in *rupadhatu*? This theory is also incompatible with the *mandala* theory.

- A Vajrayana *mandala* {Rowland 1977: 458-460} {Frederic 1996: 69-72}
This theory seems convincing but it did not properly address the issues of the hidden gallery, the fifth Buddha in the fifth balustrade or Samantabhadra Bodhisattva according to Frederic, and the sixth Buddha in the seventy-two terrace *stupa*s or Vairocana according to Frederic. According to the *yoga-tantra*, the Vajradhatu Mandala consists of the Five Jina Buddhas and their *prajna*s, Vajrabodhisattvas, Sacrificing and Commanding Taras, and *dvarapala*s (Chapter 2). With the exception of the Five Jina Buddhas, the remaining deities are nowhere to be found in Borobudur and thus it is evidently not a Vajradhatu Mandala. There is a group of small bronze figures from Ngandjuk which have been identified as a complete set of deities of the Vajradhatu Mandala dated in the Kediri Dynasty (1050-1221 CE), or at least a century later than Borobudur; thus the height of the Vajrayana in Java did not appear to be contemporary with the construction of Borobudur. Despite all these views, the Javanese architects were probably aware of the basic conceptual and architectural configuration by the late eighth century CE. It must be reminded that the idea of an architectural *mandala* had already been pioneered by the Indians in the Buddhist Deccan caves like Elora as early as the late seventh century CE. Some Orissa *stupa*s had also been constructed in accordance to the *mandala* principles of the *yoga-tantra* class in the early eighth century CE in which the four Jina Buddhas were positioned in the four cardinal directions of the *stupa* with Vairocana in the center. As already mentioned, the Vajradhatu Mandala and Garbhadhatu Mandala also appeared in Japan in the early ninth century CE or about the time when Borobudur was constructed. If indeed Borobudur was originally conceived as an early form of a Vajrayana *mandala*, it seems to resemble certain features of the Garbhadhatu Mandala, particularly the hierarchical organization of its deities from the highest to lowest realms with Buddhas in the center or the top of the *stupa* and the lower and demonic beings in the fringes or the base of the *stupa* {Grotenhuis 1999: 58-77}. Thus the Garbhadhatu Mandala might theoretically correspond to *kamadhatu* and *rupadhatu* or the relief galleries and balustrades, the Vajradhatu Mandala to *arupadhatu* or the three *stupa* terraces, and the *stupa* in the summit symbolizing *Sunya* or Enlightenment at the highest level of religious experience. Moreover, if there was a sixth Buddha in the central *stupa* as reported then Borobudur might also represent an early form of an *anuttarayoga-tantra mandala* with the Five Jina Buddhas and a sixth Aksobhya Buddha, Mahavairocana, or Adi-Buddha in the center. However, this advanced form of a *mandala* did not appear in India until the late ninth century CE and therefore the theory might not apply to Borobudur. Despite the missing numbers of the required deities in Borobudur to complete the Vajradhatu Mandala, the *stupa* seems to represent an inceptive form of a Vajrayana *mandala*.

Above all, Borobudur needs not have all the complicated and hidden symbolisms as espoused by the scholars above; it is probably a Symbolic *stupa* since no relics have been recovered. It is evident that Theravada subjects are concentrated in the lower galleries (*jataka*s, *avadana*s, Sakyamuni's Life Scenes), the Mahayana in the upper galleries (the Gandavyuha, *bodhisattva*s), possibly an early Vajrayana architectural *mandala* in stone (the five or six Jina Buddhas), and finally the dissolution of all concepts in the central summit *stupa* (*Sunya* or Enlightenment). Borobudur is thus a synthesis of all Buddhist schools as embodied in its form; it represents a philosophical and religious progression from the basic (the *jataka*s, etc.) to the most complex Buddhist thoughts (*mandala* and *Sunya*). It is imperative to analyze the monument from an empirical standpoint to better understand its history; there are a number of architectural peculiarities and inconsistencies about Borobudur that have already been noted by many scholars:

(a) The hidden gallery is covered by massive terraces.
(b) The Buddha niches in the first balustrade have *ratna* finials whereas the others have *stupa* finials.
(c) The first gallery is unique in having two registers of reliefs.
(d) The first and second *stupa* terraces have oval plans and their *stupa*s have square *harmika*s whereas the uppermost terrace has a perfectly circular plan and its *stupa*s have octagonal *harmika*s.
(e) The central *stupa* and uppermost sixteen *stupa*s are on the same circular terrace.

How can these anomalies be explained? Was the *stupa* completed in one or several phases reflecting new design changes? Borobudur was the first and only multi-terraced pyramidal *stupa* in Indonesia to have been constructed on a massive scale seemingly without past architectural antecedents. However, the Javanese had already accumulated centuries of experiences in *candi* construction and they subsequently applied their knowledge to the construction of Borobudur though with a few imperfections as observed; architecturally, Borobudur conjures up the form of a flattened *candi*. As in contemporary or earlier Buddhist *candi*s like Candi Kalasan and Candi Sewu [7.12-7.13], Borobudur also has three distinct divisions, namely the plinth (the base terraces), the body (the five balustrades and four galleries), and the crown (the three *stupa* terraces with a central *stupa* in the summit); the multi-terraced relief galleries were evidently the invention of Javanese architects. The Javanese certainly looked toward India and Sri Lanka for inspirations; the massive scale and multi-terraced form of Borobudur might have been inspired by colossal Sri Lankan *dagaba*s like Jetavana and Kesariya [6.12] in India. Adding the retaining terraces in the base, Item (a), would successfully solve the potential structural problems and created the elevated *pradaksina* paths skirting the base as in continental *stupa*s [6.17]. The crowns of the image niches in the first balustrade with its distinct *ratna* finials, Item (b), were probably added to an originally shorter balustrade after the latter had been converted into a relief gallery. The two relief registers in the first gallery, Item (c), might originally belong to the first balustrade, which would subsequently be transformed into the second balustrade after the conversion of the lowest first balustrade into a gallery; probably the two-register design demanded greater planning and time to execute so that it was later replaced with a one-register type in the upper galleries. All three

stupa terraces and their *stupa*s probably originally had octagonal bases and *harmika*s; the lower two terraces were converted to oval shapes and their *stupa harmika*s to square forms, Items (d-e), during construction or later renovations. Notice the crowns of many Javanese *candi*s and the bases of some Sri Lankan *stupa*s [4.10] also had octagonal plans. These design changes had likely been implemented after the monument was near its completion, with a few unfinished panels in the hidden gallery; they were probably carried out by a new group of inexperienced architects and builders who then made a few inconsistent modifications that failed to match with the rest of the monument as already observed. What were the reasons behind these changes or architectural anomalies? These might not be due to fresh introductions of new religious theories from the continent as De Casparis and Chihara believed. Probably Borobudur suffered partial damages caused by an earthquake, subsidence, temporary dynastic disturbances, or some unknown destructive calamities and immediately rebuilt or restored under the supervision of a new and inexperienced team. In summary, the construction of Borobudur probably involved two main phases and not four as Dumarcay proposed:

- Phase I (c. 792-817 CE): Borobudur probably commenced about the same time as Candi Sewu at the height of the Sailendras who had sufficient power and resources to complete the immense project without interruption. It was probably finished within twenty-five years since the complex restoration of Borobudur by UNESCO, which completely dismantled and reassembled the *stupa*, only took ten years. A few inscriptions in the hidden and first galleries enable the dating of this monument in the Sailendra Dynasty.
- Phase II (c. 817-842 CE): Some times after its completion, the monument was disturbed or damaged for various reasons (earthquake, subsidence, conflicts, latest renovations reflecting fresh continental ideas, etc.). A new architect was appointed to restore the monument and he, who was probably guided by new design challenges, built the massive base terraces to buttress the tremendous lateral thrust of the monument and the heavy loads of the superstructure. This transformed the first balustrade into the first gallery to be crowned with *ratna* finials while alterations was also being made in the upper *stupa* terraces; these latest changes did not synchronize with the existing architecture of the monument and were probably completed toward the end of the Sailendra Dynasty in the mid ninth century CE.

Borobudur was a late Buddhist *stupa* par excellence that

drew creative inspirations from diverse sources yet still retained its Javanese originality. The themes and motifs of its myriad continuous narrative relief panels followed the Indian *stupa* tradition of Sanchi [6.5], Bharhut [6.7-6.8], and Amaravati [6.10-6.11] as well as Gandhara *stupa*s [6.15]. Borobudur sculptures and relief panels show Gupta and Sri Lankan influences in their refined and graceful style; however their style and iconography apparently do not surpass earlier Indian precursors. Architecturally, Borobudur was a distant derivative of the Indian Kesariya Stupa [6.12] and Gandhara *stupa*s like Bhamala [6.17] but with a higher degree of sophistication and execution in forms and contents; its form, however, was conceptually modeled after the native *candi* architecture like Candi Sewu [7.12-7.13]. The central temple of Somapura [4.8] and the cruciform *stupa* in the southeast corner could provide fresh inspirations for Borobudur since the Sailendras no doubt had intimate relations with the Indian Palas; the employment of sculptural panels and solid balustrades are also evident in Somapura and Borobudur. Javanese architects were also following the tradition of Gandhara *stupa*s in reducing the size of the domes of their *stupa*s while emphasizing the plinth and terraced galleries. The *stupa*s on the upper terraces of Borobudur all have bell-shaped domes, solid *harmika*s and *chattravali*s, and lotus-cushioned bases; these features might have been derived from Sri Lankan *stupa*s as in Vijayarama [4.10]. Massive multi-terraced pyramidal *stupa*s like Borobudur was the first to be constructed in Southeast Asia; this type continued to evolve in other Asian countries such as Bakong (881 CE) in Kampuchea, Shwesandaw and Shwezigon [6.33-6.34] in Myanmar, and Kumbum [6.40-6.41] in Tibet.

5. *Zedi, Chedi, Chedei, That* - Myanmar, Thailand, Kampuchea, Laos

Myanmar (Burma) was the earliest Southeast Asian country to have reportedly received a Buddhist missionary from Asoka in c. 249 BCE after the conclusion of the Third Buddhist Council. This missionary, which was headed by Sona and Uttara, was sent to Suvarnabhumi or the Land of Gold and probably the ancient name of lower Myanmar; together Myanmar, Sri Lanka, Kampuchea, Thailand, and Laos shared the conservative Theravada School. The greatest epoch in Buddhist arts and architecture in Myanmari history began in the eleventh century CE compared to Kampuchea (late twelfth century CE), Thailand (late thirteenth century CE), and Laos (early sixteenth century CE). Due to its strategic location on the land trade route between India and southwestern China and its proximity to Bengal, Myanmar repeatedly received and absorbed the religious and artistic impulses from India in the past and especially those of Buddhism. Geographically, in the center of Myanmar is the Irrawaddy River flowing from the northern highlands down to the southern lowland deltas around Yangon before emptying into the Indian Ocean; it is the main riverine artery between the various regions in Myanmar. The history of Myanmar was essentially the story of its three main ethnic groups, the Pyu, Mon, and Mranmar and from the latter is the name Myanmar derived from; the Pyus and Mons historically founded the earliest settlements in the country. The Pyus once occupied an area roughly of central Myanmar from Shwebo in its northern end to Prome in the south and they built great early cities like Halin, Beikthano, and Sriksetra between the first-seventh centuries CE; meanwhile, the Mons also inhabited the area south of the Pyus' territory in the river deltas of the Irrawaddy and Salween River as well as in western and southern Thailand. As already stated, the Sri Lankan chronicles Dipavamsa and Mahavamsa recorded that the Asoka Buddhist missionary led by the monks Sona and Uttara arrived in the Mon territory of Suvarnabhumi and landed near Thaton {Luce 1969: 21}; thus the Mons were probably the earliest people in Southeast Asia to have reputedly been converted to Buddhism. The Mons in Myanmar founded Ramannadesa in the first century CE, a territory encompassed Yangon, Pegu, and Thaton reaching all the way to the Thai border; at a later time, the Mons on the Thai side founded the kingdom of Dvaravati in the sixth century CE. The power of the Pyus gradually waned with the decline of their great capital at Sriksetra in the eighth century CE and after the sack of Halin in 835 CE by the Sinicized Nanchao Kingdom. Probably taking advantage of the political situations, the Mranmars descended from east central Myanmar and founded Tampbadvipa, an ancient name of upper central Myanmar; this territory composed of seventeen administrative centers (*kharuin*) encompassing Kyaukse and Minbu. Next, the great city of Bagan was founded in 849 CE and from then on the power of the Mranmars was on the ascent; the artistic and architectural heritage of Myanmar was also intimately linked with this single most important historic city. King Aniriddha (r. 1044-1077 CE) completed the conquest of the whole Myanmar with the captures of Sriksetra and Thaton, both fell during his military campaigns around c. 1057 CE. These southern campaigns were reputedly punishments of the Mon kingdom for refusing to surrender Buddhist scriptures to Aniriddha but in reality they were obviously territorial expansions. The captured Mon royal family and Theravada monks were brought to Bagan where they reputedly erected many early buildings like Manuha and Nanpaya temples; the Pitakat-taik Library was also constructed to house the captured Buddhist scriptures. Contacts with Sri Lanka, and with it Sinhalese Theravada Buddhism, had also been initiated during Aniruddha's reign; he reportedly sent expeditionary forces to assist the Sri Lankan King Vijayahabu I in his struggle to drive out the Indian Chola invaders. With over half a century under the rule of the Cholas, who were Hindus, Buddhism suffered serious decline in Sri Lanka and at the request of Vijayahabu I Mon monks from Ramannadesa were sent to revitalize Buddhism on the island; an inscription in Polonnaruva also confirms this event {Luce 1969: 38-40}. Thus the historical introduction of Theravada Buddhism to Bagan was undoubtedly led by Mon and Sri Lankan monks and the school was on the rise in the whole Myanmar beginning in Aniruddha's reign. Being close to eastern India and Bengal, the remaining strongholds of Buddhism in India during the Pala Dynasty, Bagan also received a great deal of influences from these regions, in particular the Mahayana and Vajrayana schools. The Mahayana already made its presence in Sriksetra in the seventh century CE and it reached its peak influences in Bagan as many of its temples were decorated with Mahayana images. Tantric elements of the Vajrayana also appeared among Bagan temples; Abeyadana, the chief queen of King Kyanzittha (r. 1084-1113 CE), was an ardent Vajrayana devotee who constructed the Abeyadana Temple that was embellished with numerous Vajrayana images. And wherever there was Buddhism, Hinduism was also present and this was especially true in other Southeast Asian countries like Indonesia, Kampuchea, and Champa; Bagan reflected this multifarious religious atmosphere with many of its temples dedicated to the worship of Visnu. Many of Kyanzittha's official ceremonies and dedications of new construction projects, which often involved the propitiation of the Indian *naga*s, were conducted and blessed by both Hindu priests and Buddhist monks. A few important Bagan temples have obvious Hindu decorations such as Nat-hlaung-gyaung and Nanpaya that are primarily dedicated to Visnu. The peaceful co-existence of foreign religions like Buddhism and Hinduism happened concurrently with the incorporation of the native cult of spirits or *nat* into their pantheons. The latter, like the Indian *yaksa*, is frequently found in Bagan sites and throughout Myanmar in Shwezigon and Shwedagon as guardians of sacred sanctuaries; the lord of all *nat*s was Bo-bo-gyi and by Kyanzittha's reign the cult of Thirty-seven Nats was already widespread among the population. Buddhism shrewdly incorporated these indigenous *nat*s into its ever-expanding pantheon to facilitate the conversion of the native population. Bagan fell into decline after the Mongol invasion in 1287 CE; Myanmar was afterward ruled by several northern and southern dynasties like Eva (1287-1531 CE), Pegu (1287-1531 CE), Toungoo (1531-1753), Konbaung (1753-1824 CE), and Mandalay (1824-1885 CE). The country succumbed to British colonialism in 1885 CE and did not regain its independence until 1948 CE.

The arts of Myanmar can be divided into the Pre-classic Period or Pyu (c. 0-1057 CE) and Mon (c. 0-1057 CE), and Classic or Bagan Period (849-1287 CE); archaeological specimens are meager for Pyu and even rarer for Mon but numerously for the Bagan Period. Most Pyu and Mon examples, which likely dated no earlier than c. 400 CE, are in a variety of forms such as votive tablets, plaques, slabs, and statues; the materials vary from terracotta to stone and also bronze with a few gilded ones. The iconographies include themes from both Buddhism and Hinduism such as Sakyamuni in the *bhumisparsa-mudra* and *dhyana-mudra*, Maitreya, and Avalokitesvara for Buddhism and mainly Visnu for Hinduism. On stylistic and inscriptional grounds, Pyu and Mon arts fused elements from South India, particularly Andhra and Pallava, as well as Gupta, Orissa, and Pala in North India {Stadtner 1999: 13-36}. Bagan arts, which are primarily in sculptures and paintings, are overwhelmingly Buddhist and predominantly Theravada; Pala India exerted paramount influences upon Bagan due to the latter's geographic proximity to India. The popularity of the terracotta plaques, which were carved with numerous *jataka*s, continued to be elaborated in Bagan where they were often incorporated into the terraces of Bagan *stupa*s and the interiors of its temples; Pala stone steles depicting the Eight Scenes in Sakyamuni's life were especially common in Bagan. The majority of Sakyamuni sculptures in Myanmar assumed the characteristic *bhumisparsa-mudra*, immobile posture, and placid composure and they outnumbered all other types. Besides the stone material already occurred in Pyu and Mon sculptures, Bagan sculptors also employed stucco over brick or stone core; the surface would typically be painted or gilded. Bagan temples were unique in Southeast Asia with interiors painted with splendid murals over a prepared stucco base, as in the Abeyadana Temple; the dry climate of Bagan is evidently ideal in preserving these paintings, which can still be seen today. Stylistically, these murals form a part of the wider painting tradition of the Pala Style and Vajrayana Style in India, Ladakh, Nepal, and Tibet.

The earliest architecture in Myanmar can be found

at Beikthano where there are traces of a brick ramparted city and an Andhra-typed *stupa* having four *ayaka* platforms in the four cardinal points as in Amaravati {Chihara 1996: 61-62}. A profound architectural revolution were later initiated by Pyu architects in Sriksetra that would prove to be extremely influential in later Bagan architecture; the site contains the oldest extant brick buildings and earliest Buddhist architecture in Southeast Asia dated back between the fifth-seventh centuries CE. The cylindrical *stupa* of Bawbawgyi and the conical dome of Payagyi and Payama *stupa*s are instantly recognizable as uniquely different from Bagan *stupa*s. These *stupa*s are elevated on multiple terraces and have elongated drums recalling the Dhamekh Stupa [8.6] at Sarnath; however the elimination of the *harmika* in these *stupa*s, which enables the body to rise continuously to the apex, is the hallmark of Myanmari *stupa*s. Another three temples in Sriksetra, Bebe, Lemyethna, and East Zegu, are as old as the aforesaid *stupa*s; their oblong plans consist of a central cella preceded by a projecting porch and an entry hall. The elevation consists of the main body that is covered in a diminishing terraced roof or sometimes crowned with a *sikhara*-typed mass. Architectural inspirations for these early temples might ultimately be sought in the Indian Gupta temples but their final forms were essentially Pyu. Perhaps the single most important and innovative feature in these Sriksetra temples is its structural system composing of thick masonry walls, arches, and vaults to support the superstructure. Myanmar was the only country in Southeast Asia to have heavily employed this arch-vault technology in its architecture as demonstrated in Sriksetra and subsequently Bagan; on the other hand, other Southeast Asian countries like Indonesia, Kampuchea, and Champa employed exclusively the corbelled arch in their buildings. This structural system had already been employed in load-bearing in Takht-i-bahi [4.3] in Gandhara, Jivakavanarama [4.1], Nalanda [4.4], Bairat Temple [7.1], Mahabodhi Temple [7.9], Ratnagiri Monastery 2, and Bhirtagaon Temple in India. It was the Bagan architects who further developed, refined, and crystallized Pyu architecture into a national style unique to Myanmar; Bagan was certainly the single greatest site in old Myanmar and also the classic period in Myanmari architecture. The monumental 'Inventory of Monuments at Bagan' by Pierre Pichard listed over 2,000 buildings from the site in various conditions; the original number could well exceed 4,000 as documented in a fifteenth century CE count by King Mohnyin of Eva {Pichard 1992 Volume I: 3}. Most of the remains dated between eleventh-thirteenth centuries CE with a few as recent as between the nineteenth-twentieth centuries CE. The majority of its buildings are Buddhist with a few Hindu or quasi-Hindu ones like Nat-hlaung-gyaung (Pichard # 1600) and Nanpaya (Pichard # 1239). Bagan encompasses a diverse collection of building types primarily *stupa*s, temples, and monasteries constructed above (Pichard # 1147) or also underground (Pichard # 171, 297); a few are cave-temples (Pichard # 172), libraries (Pichard # 1587), Sri Lankan-typed *uposatha*, etc. The buildings are of various sizes and stories from an isolated type to a large complex of several buildings, sometimes with several different types in the same site, and from one to multiple stories such as the imposing four-storied and 210' high That-byin-nyu Temple (Pichard # 1597), the biggest and tallest building in Bagan. Most Bagan buildings were constructed of bricks to be bonded by a thin layer of mortar consisted of clay and organic additives {Stadtner 1999: 73-74} while a few were constructed in stone and many were timber that had perished over centuries of exposure and neglect; the buildings were typically coated with several layers of plaster which served the surface for painting or gilding. A typical Bagan building was crowned with a *stupa* or a curvilinear *sikhara* tower that was supported by a body of a solid core (Pichard #2171) [7.14], solid walls (Pichard #1580), and pier-and-arch walls or arcade (Pichard #1239). Bagan architects were more daring in pushing construction technologies to a new high by employing exclusively the wall-arch-vault system first observed in Sriksetra; this structural system consisted of:

- The massive perimeter wall distributing the upper loads to the ground and buttressing the outward thrust of the arches.
- A system of arches including the relieving arch (Pichard #728), pointed arch (Pichard #1597), flat arch (Pichard #386), semicircular arch (Pichard #1192), and occasionally corbelled arch (Pichard # 1123); this system opened up the interior and allowed stairs to be located within large walls (Pichard #744). The Ma-nu-ha-hpaya Temple has the greatest arch span in Bagan of about 30'10" and probably also the longest barrel vault of 94'6".
- The vault, including the relieving vault (Pichard #803), barrel vault (Pichard #2171), barrel vault hipped at one end or both ends (Pichard #690), cloister vault (Pichard #577), and diaphragm vault (Pichard #771).
- The cupola (Pichard # 684).
- The pier-and-arch or an arcade (Pichard #1239). The Nan-hpaya probably had the most technological advanced and daring design of all Bagan buildings with a system of piers-and-arches forming a square plan of four arcades in the center to support a heavy

sikhara above; this unique design has not been observed anywhere in mediaeval Asia and certainly the crowning achievement of Bagan.

This wall-pier-arch-vault system obviously allowed effective distributions of structural loads to achieve wider spans and spacious interiors as well as permitted larger fenestration and more light into the interiors. Above all, massive walls were vital in resisting earthquakes, which were and still are a common occurrence in Myanmar. On the other hand, there was no true dome, groin vault, or pure arcaded designs in Bagan as in Byzantine, Romanesque, and Gothic architecture in the West and mediaeval Europe where the emphases on expansive spaces, light structures, and the economy of materials were paramount. Bagan architects had obviously experimented with designing spacious interiors but their buildings still retained the massive characteristic probably due to the fear of earthquakes or they probably did not dare to implement more radical designs as in Gothic architecture.

The Buddhist *stupa* is known as *zedi* in Myanmar, *chedi* in Thailand, *chedei* in Kampuchea, and *that* in Laos; the first three terms were evidently derived from *caitya* while the last probably originated from *dhatu* or *thupa*; besides the employment of the wall-pier-arch-vault structural system as the temples, the forms of Bagan *zedi*s were generally not conformed to the Indian Buddhist models. First, the architect eliminated the *hamika* in Bagan *zedi*s so that the dome fused seamlessly with the *chattravali* to create a continuously integrated spire [6.33-6.34]; only China is known to have similarly adopted such a radical and innovative step for its pagodas [6.24-6.25]. Second, Bagan *zedi*s also blurred the distinction between a *stupa* and a temple as well as between a Hindu and Buddhist type; thus a superstructure of a Bagan building, whether a temple or a *zedi*, could be crowned with a curvilinear Hindu *sikhara* [7.14-7.15], a straight-edged pyramidal *sikhara*, or a Buddhist *stupa* so that it is difficult to discriminate their sectarian affiliation. Third, many Bagan *zedi*s also had temple plans with deep recesses for icons and accessible or hollow interiors so that some have been erroneously labeled as temples by Pichard (Pichard #467, #1479). In these cases, over half of the plan area is solid and there are no windows or *pradaksina* corridors in the interiors which certainly put them in the category of *stupa*s or perhaps *stupa*-temples like the central edifice of Somapura [4.8]. *Stupa*s with limited or fully accessible interiors were also common in Gandhara *stupa*s like Mohenjo-daro [1.1] and Kalawan A4, East Asian pagodas [6.20-6.21, 6.24-6.25], and a few Tibetan *chorten*s like Kumbum [6.40-6.41]. Bagan *zedi*s [6.33-6.34] basically consists of three sections, namely the multi-terraced plinth with four median staircases in the four cardinal points generally occurred in larger *stupa*s, the bell-shaped dome, and the *chattravali*. The absence of a *harmika* between the dome and *chattravali*, which smoothly unifies the different sections of the *zedi* into one integrated and logical structure, is unique to Myanmari *stupa*s. However, *stupa*s with *harmika*s in Bagan were also as common as those without and in a rare instance the *chattravali* was replaced with a straight-edged pyramidal spire (Pichard #1193) like the Indian Mahabodhi Temple [7.10-7.11]. Bagan *zedi*s can chronologically be divided into several types based on the shapes of their domes or *sikhara* superstructures:

(a) Cylindrical (Pichard #1632, #1657) or c. 900-1000 CE in the pre-Bagan Period up to the reign of Caw Rahan (r. 956-1001 CE).
(b) Bulbous (Pichard #1038-1041, #1603) or c. 1000-1100 CE encompassing the reign of Klon-phlu-man (r. 1001-1044 CE).
(c) Drum-to-bell or transitional (Pichard #772, #1023, #1030-1031, #1328, #1568) or c. 1044-1084 CE in Aniriddha's reign.
(d) Bell (Pichard #1924, #2217) or c. 1084-1113 CE in Kyanzittha's reign; this was the most common type of Bagan *zedi*s.
(e) Pseudo-*ratna* or ribbed (Pichard #394) or c. 1113-1287 CE.
(f) Pyramidal (Pichard #492) or c. 1084-1287 CE; this was probably the rarest type in which the dome had been replaced with a straight-edged pyramidal tower that seemingly transformed the *zedi* into a temple-like structure.

Type (a) was architecturally derived from the native models like Bawbawgyi in Sriksetra and ultimately in foreign precursors in Gandhara [6.18] and Dhamekh Stupa [8.6] in India; Type (b) originated in the *caityagriha*s *stupa*s in the Indian caves [5.3-5.5, 5.7, 5.9-5.10] while Type (d) was likely derived from Sri Lankan *dagaba*s [4.10, 6.26-6.27]. The source of Type (e) might be found in early Mathura temples [7.4-7.5], Mamallapuram in South India, and Candi Loro Jonggrang in Java. Type (f) was certainly inspired by the straight-edged pyramidal tower of the Mahabodhi Temple in India [7.10-7.11].

One of the most typical and well-preserved of all Bagan *zedi*s is Shwezigon [6.33-6.34] which has been praised by Gordon H. Luce as 'the most national of all Burma's pagodas.' Kyanzittha's inscriptions on the two pillars in the east entrance mentioned its original name as 'Nirbbana-mula-bajra-parya-mahaceti' or 'The Great Caitya, Circle of Adamant, Nirvana's Root,' which was built on the site called 'Jayabhumi' {Luce 1969: 268}.

Part II. Architecture   Stupa . 209

6.34. Shwezigon
c. 1084 CE
Bagan- Myanmar

6.33. Shwezigon elevation and top view
c. 1084 CE
Bagan- Myanmar

It was likely constructed by Kyanzittha in the beginning of his reign in c. 1084 CE from his aforesaid Mon pillar inscriptions; others, however, attributed the three terraces to his predecessor Aniriddha between c. 1059-1060 CE. The Myanmari Glass Chronicle also reported Aniriddha constructed Shwezigon to enshrine the relics taken from Sriksetra and a duplicate of Buddha's tooth from Sri Lanka {Luce 1969: 268}. Many of Bagan large buildings were built in a very short time like That-byin-nyu in five years and Shwezigon in 7 1/4 months and thus Kyanzittha could have easily completed this *zedi* during his reign. Shwesandaw in Bagan attributed to Aniriddha have five terraces and a Type (c) dome and likely dated earlier than Shwezigon; therefore he was probably not the builder of the latter. On the other hand, it is possible that the original smaller *zedi* was built by Aniriddha and later enlarged by Kyanzittha but there is no evidence to support this. Numerous inscriptions from the site testify to the historical and architectural importance of Shwezigon including King Kyanzittha between c. 1084-1100 CE, Queen Saw Mi Phwa in 1261 CE, King Narapathisithu in 1381 CE, King Bhayinnaung between 1551-1581 CE, and King Bodawpaya in 1785 CE alongwith other unidentified inscriptions in 1356 CE, 1368 CE, 1392 CE, 1399 CE, and 1843 CE {Pichard 1992 Volume I: #1}. The main *zedi* is located in the center of two enclosed boundary walls, of which only the outer one remains, with the main entrance in the east where Kyanzittha's pillars stand; all entrances, including the four median staircases of the *zedi* terraces, are guarded by pairs of crouching stone lions. Within the walls, there are numerous ancillary buildings around the main *zedi* including smaller *zedi*s, temples, and pavilions housing various Buddhist images, Indra, *devapala*s, and guardian *nat*s. The four temples in the four cardinal points of the *zedi* house four colossal gilt bronze images of the Manusi Buddhas (Krakuchandra, Konagamana, Kasyapa, Sakyamuni) all gesturing the *abhaya-mudra*; they average between 12'-13' high and might have been installed during Kyanzittha's reign. The Shwe-bon-tha and Hti-taw-kyauk-sa-gu (Pichard #3, #22) also contain murals dated between the seventeenth-eighteenth centu-

ries CE; all buildings in the Shwezigon compound, including the main *zedi*, have been constructed over a long period between the eleventh-nineteenth centuries CE. The main *zedi* composes of three sections:
- The three diminishing square terraces forming the plinth are punctuated by four median staircases in the four cardinal points; the largest base terrace measures 170' across and has four gateways. There are mini-*stupa*s and *makara* gargoyle spouts in the four corners of the terraces and in the foot of staircases to properly discharge excess water. The three terraces have 597 recesses containing green glazed terracotta plaques, each 13 1/2" x 14 1/2" with a few stone ones, that illustrate all 547 or 550 *jataka*s in abbreviation; obviously some *jataka*s have been repeated to fill the extra recesses. These plaques should be viewed beginning likely in the base of the eastern stair going clockwise and upward in accordance to the direction of the *pradaksina* path.
- The bell-shaped dome rests on an octagonal terrace and contains several molded bands of lotuses and decorative motifs; it has recently been regilt in the nineteenth century CE.
- The *chattravali* terminates in a double-lotus bud and metal finials of a recent date.

The *zedi* is approximately 156' high from the ground level to the top of the metal finial. A conspicuous feature is the absence of a *harmika* so that the *chattravali* appears in smooth transition and an extension of the dome rather than a distinct part as in traditional Buddhist *stupa*s; this radical innovation is characteristic of Myanmari *stupa*s and already occurred in Sriksetra *stupa*s. Shwezigon is constructed of brick like the majority of Bagan buildings, covered in several layers of fine plaster, and finally gilded to a dazzling golden hue. It has been constructed during the Theravada ascendancy in Bagan as evident from its overwhelmingly Theravada iconography with a special preference for the *jataka*s and Sakyamuni's Life Scenes; there is no hint of the Mahayana, Vajrayana, or Hinduism in the *zedi*. The decoration is simple yet effective in conveying the Theravada austerity in contrast with the usually sumptuous decors in contemporary Mahayana buildings like Abeyadana Temple. Shwezigon is the amalgamation of the features in earlier *zedi*s, most notably Shwesandaw (1060 CE) (Pichard #1568) and Hpetleik (Pichard #1030-1031), and in its use of narrative carved plaques in the recesses. The type of multi-terraced pyramidal *zedi*s decorated with Buddhist stories in reliefs recalls Somapura central temple [4.8] and Borobudur [6.28-6.32]. The tendency of Myanmari builders to splendidly gild their monuments is also at par with Thai and Lao *stupa*s; such an extravagant practice has most likely been pioneered in Gandhara. Shwezigon is one of the first Myanmari *zedi*s to have departed from the strict tripartite division of the Indian *stupa* in its complete elimination of the *harmika*; however the division between the base (terraces or plinths) and the superstructure are still clearly demarcated. It would be in Shwedagon [6.35-6.36] that the architectural beauty of the Buddhist *stupa* has finally been realized in its smooth fusion of the traditionally three distinct divisions of base, body, and crown into one graceful and soaring edifice.

Shwedagon [6.35-6.36] is the epitome of the architectural elegance and perfection of all Buddhist *stupa*s as no other *stupa*s in Myanmar and Asia can surpass its design ingenuity and extravagance. One can certainly appreciate its soaring golden spire glowing mysteriously against the deep blue sky, saturated sunset, and dark night and it is easy to imagine why this *zedi* is a national monument. In the past, Shwedagon has regularly been a rallying location for the independence movement from the British led by Bogyoke Aung San between 1945-1946 CE. It was also intimately linked with the many legends on the founding of Yangon; the name of the latter is derived from the word 'Dagon' or Mon 'Dgun' which was associated with ancient Okkala founded by the legendary King Okkalapa in the sixth century BCE. This king learned in a vision that the Shwedagon or Singuttara Hill contained the buried relics of the three Manusi Buddhas, or the twenty-fifth to twenty-seventh Buddhas in Myanmari Buddhism, namely Krakuchandra (a staff), Kanakamuni (a water-dipper), and Kasyapa (a bathing garment); these objects had presumedly been interred separately in the Sule, Botataung, and Hmawbi *zedi*s around Yangon. The king also wished to obtain relics of Sakyamuni, the last of the Manusi Buddhas and the historical founder of Buddhism, to be buried in the hill alongwith those of the other three Manusi Buddhas. Sakyamuni psychically understood King Okkalapa's devout wish and conveyed the vision to the two merchant brothers in Okkala named Tapassa and Bhallika, who then immediately set out to India to obtain the relics. During their meeting, Sakyamuni gave the brothers eight hairs in the fifth day in July 532 BCE or two months after his Enlightenment in Bodhgaya; these would be later brought back to Myanmar and interred in a *stupa* on the Shwedagon Hill {Moore 1999: 126, 132, 140-143, 158-159}. For this reason the hill and its *zedi* are known as the Four-relic Sacred Shwedagon after the four relics of the four Manusi Buddhas. The first historical inscription in Mon and Mranmar mentioning the name Shwedagon was in 1485 CE by King Dhammaceti; it described the founding story of the 'Kesa-

Part II. Architecture   Stupa . 211

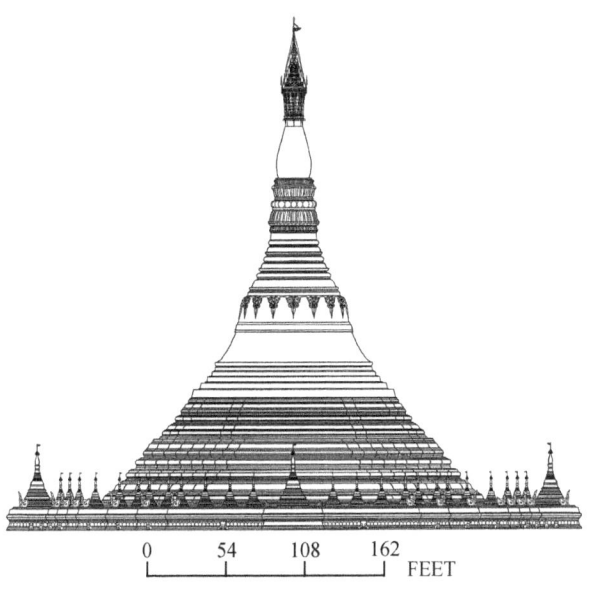

6.36. Shwedagon
1372, 1472, 1774 CE
Yangon- Myanmar

dhatu-chetiya' or 'Hair-Relics Zedi' as the old name of Shwedagon.

The site of Shwedagon contains an assortment of buildings including *zedi*s, pavilions, halls, temples, etc., all clustering around the main *zedi*, which reputedly interred the original eight hairs of Sakyamuni. A medium-sized *zedi* in the northwestern corner called Naung Daw Gyi had presumably been raised on the spot where the hairs were originally placed by the two brothers when they first reached Yangon. The main *zedi*, which is 339' high from the base of the plinth to the apex, is elevated on a 17' high plinth of 351' north-south x 363' east-west; it is surrounded by a ring of sixty-four smaller *zedi*s of about 40' high of about 23' high and four medium-sized *zedi*s in the four cardinal points. In 1906 CE, the outer ring of seventy-one image chapels and four timber pavilions dedicated to the four Manusi Buddhas were constructed in the four cardinal points; these chapels had originally been painted red until 1980s CE when they were repainted yellow. Outside this outer ring is the marble *pradaksina* path encircling Shwedagon. Notice the tiny shrine in the base of the main *zedi* in the eastern side, which shelters the Ruby-eyed Mya Shin Buddha image, was originally built in 1852 CE to cover up the tunnel dug by Major Fraser during the second Anglo-Myanmari War. This image has also been associated with Bo Bo Aung *weiza* or a magician-immortal while some believe it represents Maitreya {Moore 1999: 125}; this shrine and the upper inner *pra-*

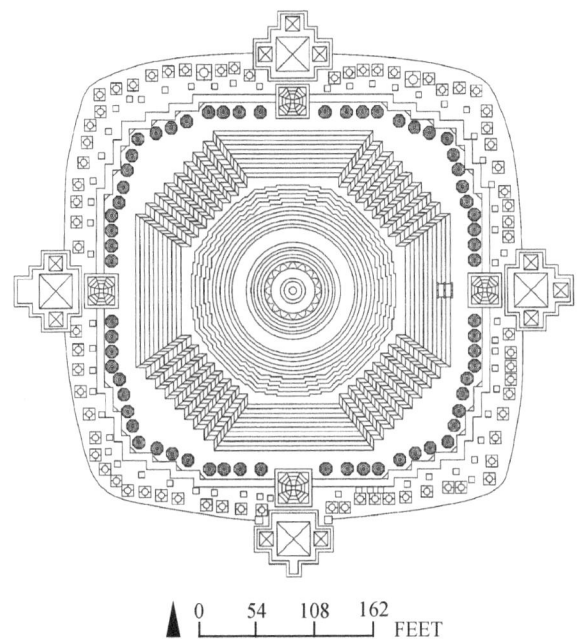

6.35. Shwedagon elevation and top view
1372, 1472, 1774 CE
Yangon- Myanmar

daksina path surrounding the main *zedi* are only reserved for men and therefore off-limit to women. In Shwedagon, the architect took a radically innovative step in smoothing out the distinct divisions of base, body, *harmika*, and *yasti-chattra* in a traditional Indian Buddhist *stupa* **[6.3]**. It was also an ingenious leap beyond the conventional multi-terraced pyramidal *stupa*s like Kesariya **[6.12]**, Borobudur **[6.28]**, and Shwezigon **[6.33]** like a sharp pinnacle piercing the sky in a gradual and graceful upsweeping curve; the ring of small *zedi*s around the base is architecturally a design compliment to the main *zedi* in the center. Shwedagon is constructed entirely in bricks and plastered over with fine stucco and the whole monument is then gilded; above all the *zedi* is more than an elegant design since it has also been adorned with countless precious materials. The incredible amount of extravagant adornments on Shwedagon clearly demonstrates its historic significance {Moore 1999: 138, 185-186}:

1451 CE Queen Shin Saw Bu was the first to gild the pagoda using her own weight in gold (40 kg)…
1485 CE King Dhammaceti…measures his weight and his queen's weight, i.e. Queen Shin Saw Bu, in gold and with four times their weight overlays the pagoda with scrollwork and tracery…
1769-1775 CE King Hsinbyushin's restoration… included 3,538 gold plates, over 5,000 silver plates, over 10 million bricks, 100,000 brass screws and 100,000 iron screws. The gilding from top to base took 77 kg of gold equivalent to the king's body weight…The *hti*, i.e. umbrella, the cone, the jeweled vane and diamond orb were plated with 44 kg of gold…15,038 diamonds and gems…356 gold and silver bells…and 32.9 kg of gold and silver bells…600 gold Buddha images and over 7,700 silver images
1871 CE 214 kg of gold
1872 CE 18,000 packages of gold leaf

A recent inventory of priceless items includes:

1956 CE 9,272 gold plates…
Hanging from the rungs of the cone are gifts of jewelry and gold and silver bells. Four angled spheres, *zoom*…hung with bells and jewels. Next is the vane, decorated with more than 1,100 diamonds, equaling 278 carats, and more than 1,300 rubies, sapphires and other gems. At the very top is the orb, a 10-inch sphere, signifying Nirvana. Made of gold, it is decorated with gems: 4,351 diamonds weighting 1,800 carats and 93 other stones. On the tip is a 76-carat diamond.

Shwedagon is also gilded in intervals with gold leaves covering up to the level of the moldings and plated with gold above this point.

The construction phases of this famous *zedi* are among the most well-documented in Myanmar; earlier phases were mostly legendary or semi-historical and it was not until the fourteenth century CE when the first historical record was documented:

- Phase I (c. 532 BCE): An earliest and obviously fabricated account recounted the construction of Shwedagon to inter the eight sacred hairs of Sakyamuni.
- Phase II (c. 249 BCE): Another certainly fabricated account about Sona and Uttara, who were actually the historical leaders of the Asoka missionary to Myanmar, reputedly cleared the jungles around Shwedagon and repaired it for the first time.
- Phase III (fifth century CE): The Pyu King Duttabaung of Sriksetra left an *hti* at the site. The story might be regarded as proto-historical since no *zedi*s have yet to be discovered in the Mon territory in lower Myanmar that can be dated in the pre-Bagan Period or before the eleventh century CE; though this event could conceivably be the manifestation of Shwedagon. The *zedi*, if it had ever been constructed at all at this time, was likely small and any trace of its original form has since vanished during many reconstructions and enlargements.
- Phase IV (eleventh century CE): The Bagan King Aniriddha paid homage to the *zedi* with a silver *hti* and constructed a shrine at Shwedagon during his southern conquest of the Mons in the mid eleventh century CE. In my view Shwedagon was probably constructed during this time, which was contemporaneous with the emergence of Myanmari arts and architecture; the original *zedi* was likely small in size.
- Phase V (1372 CE): Byinnya U raised the height of Shwedagon to 68'.
- Phase VI (1436-1451 CE): During the period of three kings Byinnyayan, Byinnyawaru, and Byinnyakyan, the *zedi* was rebuilt to its present plan and elevation.
- Phase VII (1492-1526 CE): During his reign, King Byinnyayan constructed a ring of forty-eight small *zedi*s to commemorate his forty-eighth birthday; the additional sixteen *zedi*s were likely added at a later time.
- Phase VIII (1769-1775 CE): A major reconstruction was completed under King Hsinbyushin and the cur-

rent moldings, lotus petals, and banana bud could be dated in this phase; Shwedagon was also lavishly decorated with countless precious objects and materials.

- Phase IX (1871-1872 CE): Another renovation was initiated by King Mondon involving the replacement the *hti* and addition of new jewels; the *zedi* was once again regilt.
- Phase X (1906 CE): The outer ring of seventy-one image chapels and four timber pavilions were constructed, which enclosed the main *zedi* and its sixty-four mini-*zedi*s.
- Phase XI (1970 CE): A major renovation involved new donations and regilding of the *zedi*.
- Phase XII (1998 CE): The most recent regilding of the whole monument was initiated.

The tendency to smooth out disparate sections in a traditional Buddhist *stupa* as observed in Shwedagon was as old as Myanmari architecture itself and certainly earlier than Bagan; the elimination of the *harmika* already began in Sriksetra *zedi*s and early Bagan *zedi*s like Shwezigon [6.33-6.34]. In Ananda Temple [7.14-7.15], features that would eventually become the precursors of Shwedagon began to appear such as the emphasis on a large base and the gradual diminution in the scales of the individual parts in relation to the height and their architectural fusion or, in other words, the suppression of the individual sections for an integrated and holistic mass. It was in Shwedagon that the synthesis and crystallization of all these earlier features would finally be achieved in an edifice of elegance and ingenious design in which the abrupt transition between the various sections of the *zedi* has been completely eliminated so that they now appear to melt mellifluently into one another as a single entity. Above all the holistic design and beauty in the elementary form of Shwedagon in conjunction with its extravagant decorations have undoubtedly contributed to its strikingly elegant architecture. The Chinese pagodas [6.20-6.21, 6.24-6.25] represent another class of Buddhist *stupa*s that also radically deviates from the traditional form of the Indian *stupa*; however it is less logical and graceful than Shwedagon due to its emphases on the static verticality and monotonous repetition of the architectural elements alongwith its utter refrainment from lavish embellishments like gilding. Shwedagon is an architectural gem with many imitations in Myanmar and abroad as in the post-Bagan *zedi*s like Shwesandaw in Prome and Shwemawdaw in Pegu; similarities with Shwedagon are also evident in That Laung (sixteenth century CE) in Laos. On the other hands the design of Shwedagon, with its smaller *zedi*s encircling the main *zedi*, is not unique to Myanmar as it has already occurred in Borobudur [6.28-6.29] and also Changspa (thirteenth-fourteenth century CE) in Ladakh.

6. *Caitya* - Nepal

Nepal is a beautiful and diverse country sandwiched between India and Tibet with the towering Himalaya in the north and the lowland Terai in the south, which is an extension of the Indian Gangetic plain; the country has been inhabited by numerous tribes and ethnic groups since the time immemorial. In the heart of the country is the Kathmandu Valley, the cradle of Nepal, with its three most important and historic cities Kathmandu (Kantipur, Kasthamandapa), Patan (Lalitpur), and Bhadgaon (Bhaktapur). The oldest city is Patan founded around c. 400 CE by Vrsadeva, Bhadgaon in 889 CE by Raja Anandamalla, and Kathmandu in 950 CE by Gunakamadeva {Korn 1976: 8-10}. When historians speak of Nepalese arts and architecture they are generally referring to those in the Kathmandu Valley and so are most of the contents of my discussions in this section. The regions outside of the valley were once independent principalities held by various princes and kings loosely affiliated with India as their ancestral homeland. It was not until 1769 CE when the Gurkha King Prthivi Narayan Shah from west of the Kathmandu Valley conquered its cities, founded the Shah Dynasty (1769-2008 CE), and expanded the territory of Nepal to its current size. The historical founder of Buddhism Sakyamuni Buddha was also born in Lumbini now a part of Nepal; Lumbini and Kapilavastu (possibly Tilaurakot) once belonged to the ancient Sakya Republic, which was once a part of the ethnic and cultural sphere of North India. Asoka came to this part of Nepal in c. 249 BCE and left three commemorative stone pillars in Lumbini, Nigali Sagar, and Gotihawa where their broken stumps still stand today (Chapter 3). Between the sixth-fifth centuries BCE the area beyond the hills south of the Kathmandu Valley likely belonged to the Vajji Federation, which encompassed Videha in the north and Licchavi in the south, with its twin capitals in Mithila (Janakpur) and Vaishali respectively; between Sakya and Vajji were the territories of the Moriyas, Koliyas, and Mallas {Schumann 1989: 3-5}. Janakpur was also the holy site mentioned in the great Hindu epic Ramayana where King Janak married his daughter Sita to Rama of Ayodhya. The Kathmandu Valley meanwhile was inhabited by indigenous peoples like the Kiratas and Newars between c. 600 BCE-100 CE much like today; ancient Indian literature mentioned a flourishing trade between India and Nepal, including the Kathmandu Valley, as early as the sixth century BCE {Pal 1978: 3}. For the most parts the penetration of the Indian culture into the Kathmandu Valley began around the second century CE, which were brought into by the Licchavis (c. 100-880 CE). They were undoubtedly no other than the Licchavi clan of the Vajji Federation in India who introduced the Indian language and culture into Nepal, in particular Sanskrit, Hinduism, and Buddhism as well as the arts and architecture associated with these two prominent Indian religions. The Licchavis left the oldest Sanskrit stone inscriptions in Nepal, which were mostly about the foundings of Hindu and Buddhist establishments. Stories have also been told in Nepalese chronicles about this early period in Nepalese history; the Gopalarajavamsavali chronicle mentioned Vrsadeva, the first known Buddhist king in Nepal, constructing Swayambhunath monastery and *caitya* **[6.37-6.38]** in the beginning of the fifth century CE {Gutschow 1997: 86}{Shakya 2004: 87-88}. Sankaradeva, son of Vrsadeva, left a Sanskrit inscription in the lime-making pit near Swayambhunath mentioning the construction of probably the first Buddhist monastery in Nepal {Shakya 2004: 89-91, 577}. Manadeva I (r. 464-505 CE), great grandson of Vrsadeva, also left his inscription on a pillar dated in 464 CE at the Hindu temple Changu Narayan; this king also left an inscription on a stele in Swayambhunath no longer extant. It is evident that Hinduism and Buddhism were firmly established in the valley by the fifth century CE but sculptural evidences confirmed the early presence of the Licchavis and Indian civilization in Nepal in the second century CE {Pal 1974: pl. 54}. Licchavi Nepal had certainly been a vassal of Gupta India until the reigns Amsuvarman (r. 605-621 CE) and Narendradeva (r. 645-685 CE) when measurable independence and recognition were achieved. Amsuvarman secured an alliance with Tibet with the marriage of his daughter Bhrkuti to the powerful Tibetan King Song-tsen-gampo (r. 629-649 CE). Narendradeva also received several Chinese ambassadorial delegations, most notably that of Wang Hsuan-tse; evidently during the latter's two tours of the Kathmandu Valley in the seventh century CE Nepal was already well developed as a separate state. Many Licchavi kings like Sivadeva II (r. 694-705 CE), son of Narendradeva, and Jayadeva II (r. 713-733 CE), grandson of Narendradeva, also took Indian wives in their intelligent schemes to seek political alliances and maintained independence at the same time. The post-Licchavi period or Thakuri Period (c. 880-1200 CE) has often been dubbed are 'the dark age' by Nepal historians as only a few inscriptions, arts, and architecture were produced during this period; most likely, Nepal was in the process of consolidating its identity as separate from India and to a lesser extent Tibet. The Licchavis, like their Indian neighbors, used the Saka Era (began c. 78 CE) whereas the Thakuris employed the new Nepal or Newar Era (began c. 880 CE). The Newars, like the Kiratas, were the indigenous inhabitants in the valley and many were many gifted craftsmen and builders; they created some of the most beautiful works of arts and architecture in Nepal that can still be seen throughout the valley. Sanskrit continued to be used alongwith Newari as the official languages until Yaksamalla (r. 1428-1480 CE) replaced Sanskrit with Newari. Many illustrated religious manuscripts had been produced in Nepal during the Thakuri Period and some of which could rival those of Pala India in term of artistic quality. During the Thakuri Period, Laksikamadeva I (r. 1039?-1069 CE) reportedly patronized the construction of Shalu Monastery in Tibet; Sankaradeva (r. 1069-1080 CE) was the successor of this king {Vitali 1990: 96}{Ricca and Lo Bue: 1993: 24}. The Thakuri Period was followed by the illustrious Malla Period (c. 1200-1769 CE), which is generally divided into two sub-periods or early Malla (1200-1480 CE) and late Malla (1480-1769 CE). In the subsequent years after the strong reign of Yaksamalla ended in 1480 CE, the Kathmandu Valley would be broken into three independent and often competing city-kingdoms of Kathmandu, Patan, and Bhadgaon. Most of the surviving architecture in these cities, particularly the elaborate palaces (*durbar*) and elegant multi-storied temples, has been constructed in the late Malla Period. Some early Malla kings came from western Nepal and settled in the Kathmandu Valley in the thirteenth century CE. Ripumalla (late thirteenth-early fourteenth centuries CE), the great grandfather of Prithvimalla (r. 1354-1358 CE) who was the son of Punyamalla (r. 1333-1339 CE), came from western Nepal and who had his inscriptions carved on the Asoka pillars in Lumbini and Nigali Sagar during his visits there. The early Malla kings were rulers of Purang and Yartse in the border regions of southwestern Tibet, western Nepal, and India; the Italian scholar Giuseppe Tucci stated that the Mallas had already established a dynasty there by the tenth century CE {Handa 2001: 208}. Meanwhile Jayabhimadeva (r. 1258-1271 CE) controlled the valley before Anantamalla (r. 1274-1310 CE) and whose rule also extended over the Kathmandu Valley; it was the former who sent the famed artist Arniko to Tibet in 1260 CE {Vitali 1990: 103, 105}. Buston (1290-1364 CE), who was the great Tibetan abbot-scholar of Shalu Monastery, reportedly received steady backings from Punyamalla {Vitali 1990: 102}. On the other hand, Sthitirajamalla or Jayasthitimalla (r. 1382-1395 CE), the grandfather of the powerful Yaksamalla, also came from a noble family in Mithila and probably had an Indian ancestry {Pal 1978: 7}. And then there were the well-known Mallas in Uttar Pradesh who were mentioned in ancient Buddhist scriptures as the people in charge of arranging Buddha's funeral and division of his relics {Schumann 1989: 4, 247-254}; the Indian and Nepalese Mallas might certainly have had a distant connection but no scholars have yet to prove beyond doubts. Evidently some of the early Mallas, like the Licchavis before, were not native of the Kathmandu Valley but soon after their arrivals they mingled with the locals, most notably the Newars, to form a distinctly Nepalese culture as observed today.

Buddhism and Hinduism were probably unknown in the Kathmandu Valley until the arrival of the Licchavis in the second century CE. The Newars, who were among the native inhabitants of the Kathmandu Valley and from whom the name Nepal was most likely etymologically derived from, were reputedly the earliest people to have embraced Buddhism; many have their family names as 'Sakya' proclaiming their purported ancestry with Sakyamuni {Pal 1974: 1-2}. Hinduism was probably the dominant religion in the valley from the start and the status it continues to enjoy to this day; Sivaism and Visnuism had equal shares among the population but the latter seems to have an upper hand as it produced some of the most refined and oldest Visnu sculptures in Nepal. Nepalese kings also worshipped *linga*s and named their temples with the suffix '*esvara*' much like the kings of Java, Kampuchea, and Champa; they, starting with Sthitirajamalla, also regarded themselves as incarnations of Narayana (Visnu) {Wiesner 1978: 21}. Meanwhile Buddhism continued to co-exist peacefully with Hinduism in the valley though probably as a minority; the Theravada was certainly the oldest Buddhist school in Nepal but it was the Mahayana and the Vajrayana that became the dominant Buddhist schools in the country. Since the early period Nepal was the transit hub for Indian Buddhism en route to Tibet, especially after the matrimonial union between the Tibetan king and a Nepalese princess in the seventh century CE. Nepalese Buddhism educated some of the most outstanding monks like Buddhabhadra (c. 358-429 CE) and Santaraksita (c. 747-792 CE); the former, born in Kapilavastu, reportedly followed Fa-hsien to China where he stayed and translated Buddhist *sutra*s while the latter founded the great Samye Monastery in Tibet in 779 CE. Santaraksita, alongwith Padmasambhava (c. 735-792 CE), was instrumental in the early transmission of the Vajrayana into Tibet in the eighth century CE. Some celebrated Mahayana and Vajrayana monks also reputedly came and taught in Nepal like Vasubhahu (fourth century CE), Pamasambhava (eighth century CE), Atisa (eleventh century CE), and Ratnaraksita (twelfth century CE). Atisa, during his missionary to Tibet at the age of sixty after leaving his abbotship at Vikramasila Monastery, reportedly visited Swayambhunath before proceeding to Tibet; the episode not only demonstrated the importance of this Nepalese *caitya* as a Buddhist center but also the contributory role of Nepalese Buddhism in shaping Tibetan Buddhism. From the tenth century CE on, the Vajrayana superseded the Mahayana as the dominant force in Nepalese Buddhism, though Mahayana deities remained popular as well {Pal 1978: 5}. There is a considerable degree of syncretism between Hinduism and Buddhism in Nepal today and Hindu practices have exerted great influences on the latter. In Nepalese Buddhism, as practiced by the Newars, monks are either married or celibate and they are generally divided into two castes, the Vajracarya and Sakyacarya; the former belongs to a higher caste than the latter and they generally prefer to marry within the same caste. In performing certain rituals for Swayambhunath, only the Dongol farmer caste is allowed to climb the *caitya* while the Tibetans are forbidden to complete such a task despite their heavy presence around the *caitya* since the seventeenth century CE. A new construction of a *caitya* usually requires a consecratory rite to be performed by the Vajracaryas to render it 'live' as a living deity ready for worship. In a similar fashion, renovations of a *caitya* also demand special rituals to extract its living spirit inside, or to render it 'dead' so to speak, so that the construction tasks can be carried out; once the project has been completed, a consecratory ritual is once again performed to bring it back to life {Gutschow 1997: 11, 68-74}. Such esoteric practices in Nepalese Buddhism are unique among the Buddhists countries and in a way it resembles the *pripih* rituals in Javanese *candi*s. Some deities are also popularly worshipped by Hindus and Buddhists alike; Matsyendra (Avalokitesvara) is the protecting deity of Nepal who is both a Hindu god and a Buddhist *bodhisattva* {Wiesner 1978: 27-28} and so is Kumari, the living goddess and incarnation of Durga chosen from a Newari prepubescent girl belonging to the Buddhist Sakya caste. This belief in a living incarnation of the god also has its parallel in Buddhist Tibet where the Dalai Lama is also considered the living incarnation of Avalokitesvara and living *lama*s are also believed to be reincarnations of past *lama*s; this religious belief no doubt originated in India and might have passed to Tibet via Nepal. The increasing presence of Tibetan Buddhism in Nepal since the seventeenth century CE has stimulated the revitalization of Nepalese Buddhism as well as its arts and architecture; to the Tibetan credits, they have made numerous renovations to Swayambhunath, which was time and again in dilapidated conditions. Recently in 1942 CE, Theravada monks from Sri Lanka also introduced this orthodox Buddhist school to Nepal where they built a monastery and a replica of Thuparama in the southwestern base of Swayambhunath hill {Shakya 2004: 558-562}; Gutschow further stated that "Theravada Buddhism is now a powerful, influential, and dynamic part of the Newar Buddhist scene" {Guschow 1997: 12}.

Nepalese arts can be divided into the categories of sculptures and paintings; the materials for Nepalese sculptures are primarily stone, gilt bronze, and wood; the latter is usually reserved for decorative architectural members. Judging from the inventory of extant specimens, the classic period of Nepalese sculptures was in the late Licchavi and early Thakuri Period or between c. 600-900 CE. Among the most popular subjects in early Hindu sculptures are Striding Visnu, Supine Visnu, Visnu Riding Garuda, Garuda, Mahesvara-Uma (Siva-Parvati), and Siva *linga*s. The two sculptures of Striding Visnu from Tilganga and Lajimpat, which were commissioned by King Manadeva I with accompanied inscriptions dated in 467 CE, are the oldest dated sculptures in Nepal {Pal 1974: 17-20, 40, pl. 1-2}. Buddhist sculptures in the Licchavi and Thakuri periods belonged to the Mahayana and early Vajrayana with typical subjects like Sakyamuni, Buddha and *bodhisattva* triads, Avalokitesvara, Maitreya, Manjusri, Hariti, Tara, and Vajrapani. During the Malla Period wrathful Tantric deities of the late Vajrayana type began to appear such as Mahakala and Samvara-Nairatmya in *yuganaddha*. On the stylistic ground, extant Nepalese Buddhist sculptures possibly dated earlier than their Hindu counterparts; for examples, sculptures of a *bodhisattva* and two Haritis have been dated as early as between the second-third centuries CE by Pal {Pal 1974: pl. 54, 58-59}. There are fragments of narrative architectural relief panels found in Buddhist monasteries; these are more numerous and the forerunners of the carved wooden reliefs in Malla architecture. Nepalese sculptures, whether Hindu or Buddhist, are stylistically and iconographically derived from the vast repertoire of Indian prototypes. There are four main phases of stylistic influences emanated from India as observed in Nepalese Buddhist sculptures, namely Mathura Style, Gupta Style of Mathura and Sarnath, Pala Style, and Vajrayana Style. Buddhas in the refined Sarnath-Gupta Style were extremely favored in Nepal and they were sculpted as late as the seventeenth century CE whereas the Pala Style appeared to hold less sway in Nepal {Pal 1974: 162-165}; there was no detection of the Gandhara Style in Nepal. Stylistically, Nepalese sculptures are scarcely distinguished from their Indian prototypes albeit minor differences suggesting the Nepalization of foreign features. There is a greater degree of stylization, linearization, and reduction in volumetric modeling in the figures, which are generally thinner with visibly Mongoloid features. The classic *tribhanga* common in the Indian nude females is less pronounced in Nepal while Nepalese female nudes appear slimmer and elegant compared with the plump and hypersexual figures in their Indian counterparts.

In the field of Nepalese paintings, a mid fifth century CE inscription stated that a Buddhist temple was decorated with murals {Pal 1978: 1-2}; however, there are no extant paintings dated before the eleventh century CE. Like its sculptures, Nepalese paintings are both Hindu and Buddhist types with the latter constitutes the majority of surviving examples; most examples are religious paintings while the secular types are rare and mostly painted in the late Malla Period and Shah Dynasty. The development and classification of extant Nepalese paintings can stylistically and chronologically be divided into three phases and/or types {Pal 1978}:

(a) Illuminated Manuscripts (eleventh-fourteenth centuries CE): These are religious *sutra*s written and painted in the miniature formats by master copiers; the most frequently copied Buddhist scriptures are Prajnaparamita-sutra and Pancaraksa-sutra. In the early years they were made of palm leaves and later replaced with paper as the latter became more available; often the pages or leaves depict images and stories of Buddhas and *bodhisattva*s and many have annotations identifying the figures. The sources for these Nepalese manuscripts likely originated in similar examples that had been produced numerously in eastern India and Bangladesh during the Pala Dynasty coeval with the Nepalese examples.

(b) *Paubha* (thirteenth-sixteenth centuries CE): A *paubha* is a form of Newari religious paintings typically on rectangular cotton cloth; it exhibits unique characteristics in terms of color, composition, and exquisite rendering comparable to the early *thangka* paintings of Tibet. Compositionally, the surface of a *paubha* is usually occupied by a large figure in the center that is placed inside a shrine sometimes of trilobate forms and surrounded by registers of smaller figures on the sides; the background is usually filled in with natural elements such as rocks rendered in abstract patterns. The color is often deep and subdued with subtle shadings of the figures and exquisite renderings of details that are the hallmarks of early Nepalese *paubha*s; the subjects consist of Buddhas and Mahayana *bodhisattva*s as well as Vajrayana deities and their *mandala*s.

(c) Narrative and Secular (seventeenth century CE on): The formats of these paintings include four different types, namely the scroll in either horizontal or vertical format with its surface divided into two or more registers, picture book (*kalapustaka*), folio album, and painted murals in religious and secular establishments. Unlike the *paubha*s of the earlier period, the main figure in the composition has been considerably reduced in size and sometimes positioned off-center; numerous surrounding figures and busy background elements now compete for attention with the main figure. There were increasingly stylistic penetration from Mughal-Rajput India and Tibet in Nepalese paintings during this period and there was a general decline in quality in these later paintings. The classic period in Nepalese paintings was evidently during the early Malla Period (c. 1200-1480 CE).

Nepalese paintings were especially influential in Tibet as intimate relations between the two countries had been documented since the seventh century CE. Many Nepalese craftsmen and artists were routinely invited by Tibetan monks to assist in the decorations of their monasteries; the celebrated Nepalese artist Arniko (1244-1306 CE) and eighty craftsmen were reportedly involved in the constructions and decorations of the Sakya monasteries in Tibet between 1261-1262 CE {Pal 1978: 145-147} {Guschow 1997: 87}. Under the order of Kubilai Khan in 1263 CE, Arniko then traveled to the Mongol Yuan court in Beijing where he worked on numerous projects in architecture, paintings, and metal castings {Vitali 1990: 103-105}.

From the beginning, the Nepalese were masters of timber architecture as evident in the myriads of intricately carved temples found throughout the Kathmandu Valley; however, not a vestige of this early architecture survive today due to the perishability of timber, repeated renovations, recurring foreign invasions, and internal conflicts. The Islamic army of Bengal led by Sultan Shams-ud-din reportedly invaded the Kathmandu Valley in 1350 CE and laid waste to its cities and temples; Kathmandu, Patan, and Bhadgaon alongwith Swayambhunath were utterly destroyed {Shakya 2004: 129-130}. Most surviving buildings as seen today in the valley, with the exception of small votive objects like the Licchavi *caitya*s, generally dated after the mid fourteenth century CE. Nepalese architecture can be divided into two categories: religious, typically Hindu or Buddhist, and secular; in Nepal, Hindus built exclusively temples (*dega*) and priest houses (*math*) while Buddhists specialized in the construction of *caitya*s and monasteries. Secular architecture encompasses royal palaces (*durbar*) and communal public resthouses {Korn 1976}; the *durbar*s of Kathmandu, Patan, and Bhadgaon as seen today dated between the sixteenth-nineteenth centuries CE. There are about 400 Buddhist monasteries in the Kathmandu Valley and the majority is located in Patan; in contrast to the conspicuous *caitya*s, they are probably the hardest to spot 'due to its integration into the surrounding architecture,' according to Korn {Korn 1976: 26}. This may also be due to the weak and inconspicuous institution of the Buddhist *Sangha* in Nepal as celibate and shaven-headed Nepalese monks are not a common sight in Nepal as in other Buddhist countries. There are two different types of Nepalese monasteries depending on the marital status of the residing monks; the *bahil* is reserved for celibate monks whereas the *bahal* is for married monks, who are either the Vajracaryas or Sakyacaryas living together with their family. Needless to say the *bahal* is a later type; Cabahil in Kathmandu is among the oldest monasteries in Kathmandu Valley dating back in the Licchavi Period. Generally Nepalese religious architecture is virtually indistinguishable from the secular architecture and the essential difference between them is in the absence of religious imageries in the latter. Most Nepalese temples are Hindu with the exception of a few syncretic Hindu-Buddhist temples like Matsyendranath in Patan and Kathmandu, both dated in the sixteenth century CE. All Nepalese temples can be classified as either Indian (*mandir*) or Nepalese (*dega*) based on the materials and architectural forms. The *mandir*s are exclusively Hindu with many fine examples in Patan and Bhadgaon and these are built entirely in stone and typically in the Indo-Mughal style; the Mahabauddha Temple (c. 1564-1610 CE) in Patan modeled after the Mahabodhi Temple in India is the only known Buddhist temple in the *mandir* form. The *dega*s, in contrast, are uniquely Nepalese creations with numerous excellent examples throughout the Kathmandu Valley. They usually have square plans with a brick-and-timber body elevated on a brick or stone terrace(s) and covered with a gilt metal or tile roof or the combination of both; the peak typically terminates in a gilt metal finial (*gujar*). Its structural system essentially consists of load-bearing walls and timber framing for the roof with angular struts supporting deep overhangs; the appearance of multiple stories in the *dega*s are misleading since only the ground floor is habitable as in the Japanese pagodas **[6.20-6.21]**. There is a great deal of speculations by scholars regarding the origin of the Nepalese *dega*; the most commonly cited sources for the *dega* are China, Karnataka and Kerala in southwestern India, Kashmir, Himachal Pradesh, and extinct Indian timber temples {Wiesner 1978: 34-38}

{Banerjee 1980: 86-95}. However, there are virtually no architectural examples in any of these countries that can be considered as the prototype for the Nepalese *dega*; above all the *dega* seems to have fused diverse elements from some of these countries not to mention those primarily originated in the vernacular architecture of Nepal. For examples the multi-terraced plinth in the Nepalese *dega* is also common in the Buddhist architecture of India [6.12], Gandhara [6.17], Java [6.28-6.29], Myanmar [6.33-6.34], etc; the intricate carvings and style of its timber members also reveal unmistakably Indian influences. Its multi-tiered roofs strikingly resemble the East Asian pagodas [6.20-6.21]; however the diminishing rate for the roof in the latter is lesser than the Nepalese *dega*. The multi-tiered roofs and deep overhangs of the Nepalese *dega*, which are supported by a complex timber structure consisting of struts, exposed rafters, and king struts, are also the hallmarks of East Asian timber architecture; however, the roofs of the Nepalese *dega* are straight whereas the roofs of the East Asian pagoda are elegantly curved. Further away in Bali (Indonesia) the *meru* tower also has a similar design as the Nepalese *dega* but both apparently have no historical connections. Above all, the *dega* might have certainly evolved from earlier antecedents in Nepalese architecture as early as the Licchavi Period; the travel account of the Chinese ambassador Wang Hsuan-tse in the seventh century CE and the history of the Chinese Tang Dynasty left a vivid picture of contemporary Licchavi Nepal and its architecture {Pal 1974: 6-7}:

> Their houses are constructed of wood. The walls of these are sculptured and painted...In the middle of the palace there is a tower of seven storeys roofed with copper tiles. Its balustrade, grilles, columns, beams, and everything therein are set with fine and even precious stones...In the capital of Nepal there is a construction in storeys which has more than 200 *tch'eu* (200 feet) of height and 80 *peu* (400 feet) of circumference. Ten thousand men can find place in its upper part. It is divided in three terraces and each terrace is divided in seven storeys. In the four pavilions, there are sculptures to make you marvel. Stones and pearls decorate them.

Thus it is clear that Nepalese architecture and especially the *dega*, with its multi-storied towers of metal roofing decorated with precious materials, already had an early beginning in the valley; moreover the Nepalese evidently also absorbed foreign elements, particularly from India, to suite their own aesthetics and local contexts. Another important point is about Pasupatinath, the most important Siva temple in Nepal; according to Wiesner this temple is the earliest and the prototype for later, if not all, Nepalese temples {Wiesner 1978: 1-9}. This is obviously an exaggeration since Changu Narayan might have dated even earlier from a historical inscription by Manadeva I in 464 CE; Pasupatinath, on the other hand, was mentioned in a much later Amsuvarman inscription (early seventh century CE) and the site itself only had one inscription by Jayadeva II (eighth century CE). In the light of these points Changu Narayan should have been the prototype rather than Pasupatinath but this is only a conjecture; to pursue this discussion further about the origins of the Nepalese *dega* would be straying far away from the subject of the Nepalese Buddhist *caitya*.

Caitya, which is the Sanskrit variation of Pali *cetiya*, is a word for all religious edifices and in Nepal it generally denotes a Nepalese Buddhist *stupa*. Any extant structures qualified as architecture or having architectural forms that could be dated in early Nepalese history it would be the Licchavi *caitya*s; they are crucial in the study of the evolution of the Nepalese *caitya*. The question as whether these Licchavi *caitya*s should be classified as architecture or votive sculptures has already been pondered by Gutschow since they appear to exhibit the characteristics of both {Gutschow 1997: 246-247}. Architecture is above all differentiated from a sculpture by its size and utilitarianism; the height of a typical Licchavi *caitya* is equal or shorter than an average man and it is generally erected by pious individuals or a family as a personal commemorative memorial or a votive *caitya*. It is not specifically designed to accommodate the religious needs of the general public and not necessarily imbued with the complicated symbolisms as bigger *caitya*s like Swayambhunath; thus a Licchavi *caitya* is essentially and precisely an architectural sculpture. Also according to Gutschow, there are about 263 Licchavi *caitya*s in the Kathmandu Valley and many are often accompanied with dedicatory inscriptions that greatly facilitate their identifications and chronologies. Overall the Nepalese *caitya* [6.37-6.38] exhibits these fundamental characteristics:

- Nepalese *caitya*s are not commonly known to have been erected over Buddhist relics and they are likely Votive, Symbolic, or Commemorative type.
- There are no *torana*s or *vedika*s as in Indian *stupa*s.
- The use of gilt metal for image chapels, *harmika*, and *yasti-chattra*.
- The *yasti-chattra* or *chattravali* typically has a pronounced bulge in the lower end, which is traceable to late Gandhara *stupa*s and among the *stupa*s depicted in the Bamiyan murals. The *chattravali* is in the form of a diminishing pyramidal spire, as in Bodhnath

Stupa, originated in the Licchavi Period {Gutschow 1997: 99, 112-113}; a similar spire have also been documented among Turkistani *stupa*s in Kharakhoto {Stein 1981 Volume IV: pl. 19}.
- The presence of the shields (*halapau*) above the *harmika*. The latter is solid and typically painted with pairs of eyes, abstract noses, and *urna*s on the four sides; these are repainted yearly in October as in Swayambhunath.
- Many incorporate Vajrayana iconographies and symbolisms, most importantly the Five Jina Buddhas and their *prajna*s as in Swayambhunath; these *caitya*s belong to the Tantric type and among the latest development in the Buddhist *stupa*s.

Gutschow's monumental study and inventory of the Nepalese *caitya*s have identified fourteen different types ranging from the small Licchavicaitya of a few feet high to the supersize like Swayambhunath and Bodhnath more than 100' high {Gutschow 1997}:

(a) Great Size
1. Asokacaitya (attributed to Asoka in third century BCE).
   These are the four tumulus-shaped *caitya*s in Patan situated in the northwest, northeast, southeast, and southwest corner of the city; their low domes recall Piprahwa Stupa **[6.1-6.2]** but do not necessarily suggest an early date. There is a well-known legend among the Nepalese Buddhists that Asoka, led by Upagupta, alongwith his wife Tishyaraksita and daughter Carumati visited the Kathmandu Valley in c. 250 BCE; the emperor reputedly visited Swayambhunath and built these four Patan *caitya*s. His daughter presumably married a Nepalese named Devapala Ksetri and remained in Nepal where she later became a nun and founded Cabahil, the first Buddhist monastery in the country {Shakya 2004: 75-78}. Indeed Asoka historically visited the Nepalese Terai in c. 249 BCE and erected several pillars there but there is no evidence suggesting he ever visited the Kathmandu Valley. Moreover, no discovered artifacts in the valley can be dated earlier than the second century CE; the oldest inscription in the northwest *caitya* dated in 1455 CE and the latest renovations in the other *caitya*s dated in 1878 CE. Thus in my view the foundations of these four *caitya*s likely did not date any earlier than the Licchavi Period.
2. Mahacaitya (fifth-twentieth centuries CE).
   The most representative of this type is Swayambhunath **[6.37-6.38]** and Bodhnath, both founded in the Licchavi Period; these are not only the biggest and oldest but also the archetypical of all Nepalese *caitya*s.

(b) Medium Size
3. Monumental Caitya (fifteenth-nineteenth centuries CE).
   These are between 6'7"-32'10" high and their forms undoubtedly evolved from earlier examples like the Licchavi *caitya*s (Type 4); there are about 140 extant examples in the Kathmandu Valley such as Kathesibu and Dharmadeva in Kathmandu.

(c) Small Size
4. Licchavicaitya (fifth-eighth centuries CE)
5. Caturvyuhacaitya (fifth-twentieth centuries CE)
6. Ramyakutagaracaitya (seventeenth century CE)
7. Sikharakutacaitya (seventeenth-nineteenth centuries CE)
8. Vimsatikonacaitya (seventeenth-nineteenth centuries CE)
9. Padmavalicaitya (seventeenth-nineteenth centuries CE)
10. Neo-Licchavicaitya (seventeenth-twentieth centuries CE)
11. Jalayharyuparisumerucaitya (seventeenth-twentieth centuries CE)
12. Sumerucaitya (nineteenth-twentieth centuries CE)
13. Jvalavalicaitya (nineteenth-twentieth centuries CE)
14. Tibetan *caitya-chorten* (eighteenth-twentieth centuries CE)

These small *caitya*s are 5'11" high maximum; there are about 263 *caitya*s in the Kathmandu Valley in which the Licchavicaitya (Type 4) is the oldest while a Caturvyuhacaitya (Type 5) in Swayambhunath courtyard has also been dated in the early Licchavi Period. Some of the most conspicuous features in the later types as distinguished from earlier Licchavi *caitya*s are multiple plinths, frequent occurrences of one or more lotus thrones or pedestals (*padmasana*), the reduction in the size of the dome, and lavishly decorative schemes. There are evidences of the *padmasana* and *chattravali* in the Licchavi *caitya*s but these appear to be the exception rather than the norm {Gutschow 1977: 167-168}; the *caitya*s in the Licchavi and Thakuri periods seemed to favor the *yasti-chattra* over the *chattravali* {Gutschow 1997: 192-193}.

The most representative of all Nepalese *caitya*s is undoubtedly Swayambhunath **[6.37-6.38]**; notice the elevation drawing in Gutschow's book was incorrectly mirrored {Guschow 1997: fg. 185}. This magnificent *caitya* exhibits the hallmark traits of a Nepalese Buddhist *caitya* and its construction has also been intimately linked with the legendary founding of the Kathmandu Valley and its cities, as told in the Swayambhu Purana; its illus-

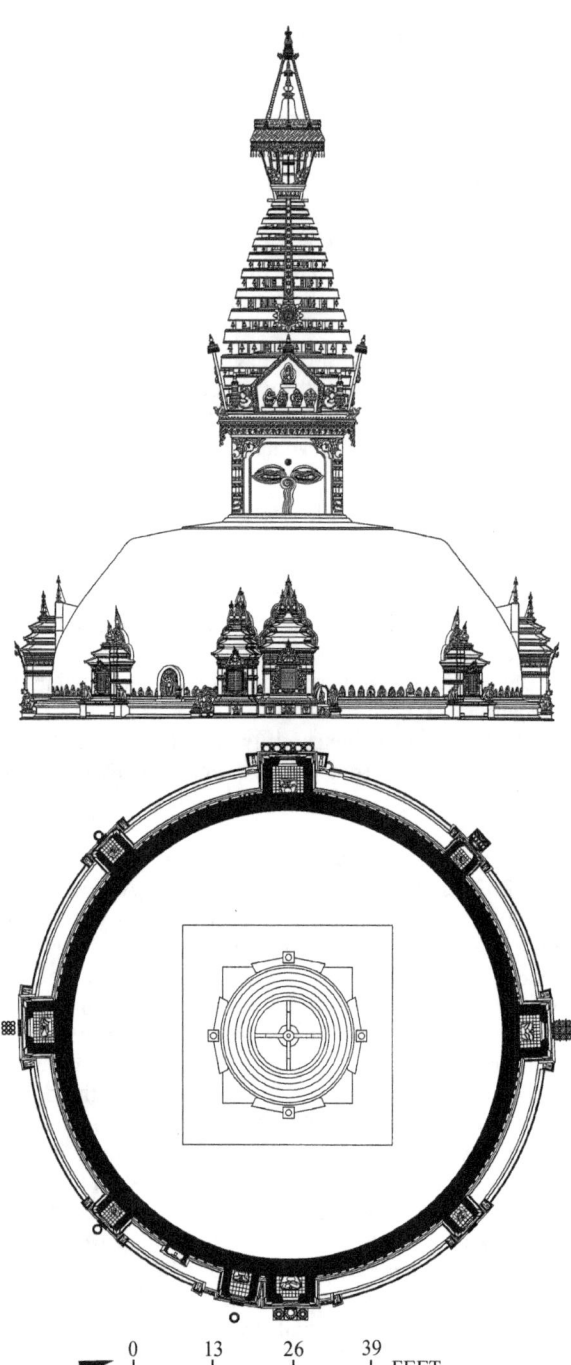

6.37. Swayambhunath elevation and plan
c. 400-1918 CE
Seventh-sixteenth centuries CE (final form)
Kathmandu- Nepal

6.38. Swayambhunath
c. 400-1918 CE
Seventh-sixteenth centuries CE (final form)
Kathmandu- Nepal

trious history has been studied by Nepalese scholars like the Newari scholar Hem Raj Shakya in his exhaustive volume 'Sri Swayambhu Mahacaitya' {Shakya 2004}. A legend told that in the days of yore the Kathmandu Valley was the beautiful Lake Nagahrada; one day Vipasyin Buddha came and scattered a lotus seed in the lake which instantly bloomed into a splendid thousand-petaled lotus and on which was seated the primordial Adi-Buddha. The sacred lotus emitted brilliant light of five colors from which there manifested the Five Jina Buddhas and their five *prajna*s, namely white (Vairocana Buddha, Vajradhatvesavri), blue (Aksobhya Buddha, Locana), golden (Ratnasambhava Buddha, Mamaki), red (Amitabha Buddha, Pandara), and green (Amoghasiddhi Buddha, Tara). Since the lotus was a self-born one it was called Swayambhu, or also Adi-Buddha, and because it emitted luminous light it was called Jyotirupa. According to Shakya, the full name of Swayambhunath should be 'Adi-Buddha Jyotirupa Swayambhu Dharmadhatu Vagisvara;' the latter two words mean 'Dharmadhatu Mandala' and 'Gnostic Body' respectively {Shakya 2004: xxxii-xxxiii}. Then Manjusri Bodhisattva from Mount Wutai in China came and by using his magical sword he cut through the surrounding hills to create a gorge which drained Lake Nagahrada. The lake now became a dry lakebed, or the Kathmandu Valley, and Manjusri founded Manjupattana, a town at the foot of Swayambhunath stretching from here to the Guhyesvari Temple near Pasupatinath; he next crowned King Dharmakara, the first Nepalese king and undoubtedly a Buddhist one. Subsequently kings, gurus, *bodhisattva*s, and Buddhas from all corners visited and paid homage to the lotus Swayambhu until one day Santikaracarya decided to build a *caitya* to cover this shining self-arisen lotus so that it could properly be worshipped. Presumably when Santikaracarya constructed the *caitya* the land below the lotus immediately turned into a hill like today that became the foundation for the *caitya*. The form of this very first Swayambhunath, according to the story, was exactly like the one we see today complete with the ten image chapels, dome, *harmika*, and thirteen-tiered *yasti-chattra*. Then Sakyamuni Buddha visited Swayambhunath after spending some times in Lumbini; this event presumably happened in the sixth century BCE when he was still alive. Next Emperor Asoka came and worshipped Swayambhunath, which presumably occurred in the third century BCE; this would be followed by the visits of the great Indian Buddhist philosophers Nagarjuna and Vasubandhu in the third and fourth century CE respectively. Naturally if you are a devout Buddhist then you would surely believe the above legend that the *caitya* had been constructed long before Sakyamuni and Asoka; even great scholar like Shakya was adamant about the historicity of this legend {Shakya 2004: xxxix-xl}. Obviously, there is no evidence suggesting this early existence of Swayambhunath in the Kathmandu Valley; Shwedagon in Myanmar also had a similar legend about its ancient foundation. The first truly historical and oldest document in Nepal is a Sanskrit inscription by Sankaradeva (early fifth century CE) in the lime-making pit at Swayambhunath mentioning the construction of probably the oldest dated Buddhist monastery and *caitya* in Nepal {Shakya 2004: 89-91, 577}. The Gopalarajavamsavali chronicle also mentioned Vrsadeva, the first known Buddhist king in Nepal, constructing Swayambhunath *caitya* and monastery in the beginning of the fifth century CE, which were then called Singhu or Samhegu {Gutschow 1997: 86}{Shakya 2004: 87-88}. Vrsadeva was in fact the father of Sankaradeva and this has been corroborated by an inscription of Jayadeva II at Devapattana near Pasupatinath {Shakya 2004: 87}; it is also possible that the foundation of Swayambhunath and monastery had originally been commenced by Vrsadeva and later expanded or completed by Sankaradeva. In all likelihood, this early *caitya* was initially of a modest size and subsequently enlarged over the centuries to its current form; new renovations have been recorded well into the twentieth century CE. Swayambhunath perches on top of a prominent knoll a little west of Kathmandu and commands a sweeping view of the city and the Kathmandu Valley below; the great *caitya* has amassed an impressive collection of artifacts and inscriptions over the centuries reflecting its historical importance and antiquity. There are 313 inscriptions between c. 400-1976 CE testifying its long history including (2) Licchavi, (3) Thakuri, (80) Malla, and (228) Shah; these are in Sanskrit, Nepalese, Tibetan, and even English; the *caitya* itself is literally surrounded by an assortment of subsidiary buildings including monasteries, temples, shrines, votive *caitya*s, etc. There are 274 lesser *caitya*s mostly of the votive type scattered throughout the site and in the base of the hill; there are additional structures associated with the site including Tibetan and Sri Lankan monasteries like the Tibetan Kimdol Monastery (1687 CE) and the Sri Lankan Ananda Kuti Vihara (1942-1949 CE). The *caitya* on the hilltop is reached via a main approach on the east by ascending a 318-step stone staircase (1909-1914 CE) inaugurated by Nepalese Nhuche Tej and Tirtha Raj Manadhar. The main gate and prayer wheel shrine (1976 CE) at the foot of the staircase were originally commissioned by the Tibetan Lama Svennam Simha with the design and construction by Nepalese Nhuche Raj Vajracarya. There are Tibetan-styled *chorten*s and huge Buddha statues just pass the main entrance gate; among these the Aksobhya or Sakyamuni statue (1637 CE) is the oldest. Higher up on both sides of the staircase are a variety of minor sculptures (late Malla) of various deities, *devapala*s, and five *vahana*s (vehicles or animal mounts) of the Five Jina Buddhas, namely lion (Vairocana), elephant (Aksobhya), horse (Ratnasambhava), peacock (Amitabha), and *garuda* (Amoghasiddhi). Just off the last step on the hilltop and in front of the eastern side of the *caitya* is a huge gilt thunderbolt or *vajra* (1668 CE) by Jayapratapamalla (r. 1641-1674 CE) resting on the Dharmadhatu Mandala stone drum. Other conspicuous buildings in the immediate area around the *caitya* are the two whitewashed *sikhara*s Anantapura and Pratapapura (1655 CE) by Pratapamalla (r. 1641-1674 CE), the Karmaraja Gompa (1947-1959 CE), Hariti Temple (late Malla), the miracle-performing Santipura believed to have been founded by Santikaracarya, the votive *caitya* courtyard (fifth-twentieth centuries CE), etc. A votive Caturvyuhacaitya in the *caitya* courtyard has been dated by scholars as the oldest *caitya* in Nepal in the fifth century CE {Gutschow 1997: 175}. The plan of Swayambhunath is 87' diameter with ten image shrines projecting across the plinth and dividing it into eight equal sections. These gilt metal shrines are dedicated to and contain gilt images of the Five Jina Buddhas and their five *prajna*s; these are, clockwise starting from the eastern shrine, Aksobhya Buddha, Vairocana Buddha, Vajradhatvisvari (Prajnaparamita), Locana, Ratnasambhava Buddha, Mamaki, Amitabha Buddha, Pandara, Amoghasiddhi Buddha, and Tara. Prajnaparamita, who is the *prajna* of Vairocana symbolizing Emptiness (*Sunya*), is aniconically represented as an empty hole in the small stone shrine barely visible on the plan and elevation. There are pairs of guardian lions on both sides of the image shrines and an additional 114 minor niches encircling the dome above the plinth with votive plaques inside. The ring of Tibetan prayer wheels encircling the *caitya* (1917-1918 CE) contains *mantra*s of Avalokitesvara, Manjusri, and Vajrapani in the Nepalese script; a pair of stone Buddha images also flanks both sides of Aksobhya and Vairocana shrines. The 107'9" high elevation of the *caitya* consists four distinct sections as in the Indian and Gandhara *stupa*s including the molded plinth base, the bowl-shaped and slightly truncated dome, *harmika*, and the thirteen-tiered *yasti-chattra*; the latter terminates in a *gujar*, a lotus *amalaka* finial, and a *chattra*; the section above the dome are completely gilt with the exception of the *harmika*, which is covered in gilt sheet metal. The construction material of the *caitya* is mainly bricks that are plastered over and whitewashed with several coats of lime; there is no evidence of Buddhist relics ever interred inside this *caitya* and it is therefore considered as a Symbolic type. A unique and ubiquitous feature in this Nepalese *caitya* is the presence of the painted eyes, an *urna*, an abstract nose on the *harmika*, and the four *halapau*s as well as the bulging of the *yasti-chattra*; similar features have already appeared in many Buddhist *stupa*s throughout Asia. For examples, the sun and moon symbols also occur on the *harmika*s of Sri Lankan *dagaba*s [6.26], the *halapau* on some Gandhara *stupa*s and Amaravati slabs, and the bulge of the *yasti-chattra* among the *stupa* reliefs of Borobudur; the mysterious painted eyes on the *harmika* of Swayambhunath also appear in the Tibetan Kumbum Chorten [6.40-6.41], which was undoubtedly under Nepalese influence. A mural in Shalu Monastery in Tibet, which was reportedly painted by Nepalese artists and dated between 1333-1335 CE, also depicts a *chorten* with a pair of eyes on its *harmika* {Vitali 1990: pl. 74}. A gilt copper *stupa* model from Kashmir dated in 714 CE clearly shows an incised eye on its dome while an Indian Pala votive *stupa* in the Indian Museum (ninth-tenth centuries CE) also has carved eyes on its *harmika* alongwith the *halapau*, the bulging *yasti-chattra*, and *gujar* {Pal 2003: 106-107, fig. 63} {Sharma 2004: fig. 53}. The *halapau* and *chattravali* also appeared among the Nepalese reliefs of the Licchavi *caitya*s {Gutschow 1977: 167-168} while the imposing multi-tiered *yasti-chatta* were common in Gandhara [6.14, 6.18].

The complex Vajrayana symbolisms of Swayambhunath are profoundly manifested in its architecture as the legendary tales of its founding shroud the *caitya* in a thick mystical air. The Nepalese scholar Hem Raj Shakya asserted that the full name of Swayambhunath as 'Adi-Buddha Jyotirupa Swayambhu Dharmadhatu Vagisvara' {Shakya 2004: xxxii-xxxiii}, which alludes to its intimate connection with the story of the resplendent lotus Swayambhu. There is no doubt that Swayambhunath is an important surviving representative of all early Vajrayana *caitya*s from the presence of the Vajrayana deities enshrined in its ten niches including the Five Jina Buddhas and their five *prajna*s; the *caitya* itself is the embodiment of Adi-Buddha. The Nepalese specifically refers to the *harmika* as a neck (*gala*) while the combination of the *halapau* and the thirteen-tiered *yasti-chattra* represents the crown of the exalted Swayambhu Adi-Buddha with his ever compassionate eyes gazing at the world below. The thirteen discs also symbolize the thirteen *bhumi*s of the Mahayana *bodhisattva* path and the thirteen *paramita*s associated with this path {Gutschow 1997: 21, 23, 86-87}. The giant *vajra* symbolizes the non-dual state of enlightenment while the *caitya* represents the self-born Adi-Buddha, Vajrasattva, or Vajradhara in early Vajrayana iconography; both represent an abstract and esoteric Tantric reality in the Vajrayana that is embodied and manifested in the architectural form. At the heart of the Vajrayana are the concepts of *upaya*, which represents compassion and male with the *vajra* (thunderbolt) as its symbol, and *prajna*, which represents wisdom and female with the *padma* (lotus) and/or *ghanta* (bell) as its symbols; the union of *upaya* and *prajna* is the attainment of the highest enlightened state or *Vajra*. Thus the luminous lotus Swayambhu represents *prajna* and the huge *vajra* in front of the *caitya* represents *upaya*; the ritualized consecration of Swayambhunath is none other than the symbolic union of *upaya* and *prajna*, which symbolizes and embodies the non-dual enlightened state of *Vajra*. Changes in the designs and complex symbolisms of Swayambhunath have also mirrored the evolution of Nepalese Vajrayana Buddhism itself, from early Vajrayana (Five Jina Buddhas), to middle Vajrayana (Five Jina Buddhas and five *prajna* shrines, the sixth Adi-Buddha), and late Vajrayana (the huge *vajra* symbolizes the non-dual state of Enlightenment or *Vajra*, the union of *upaya*/*vajra* with *prajna*/the lotus Swayambhu). Moreover the idea of a living Buddha, who can be manifested in Swayambhunath, itself an architectural medium, through a complex process of ritualized consecration, is also a purely Tantric concept that has been exclusively practiced by the Vajrayanists and Nepalese Buddhists {Gutschow 1997: 11, 68-74}. One bogus theory proposed by John Irwin stated Swayambhunath as the 'Primordial Hillock floating on the Primordial Ocean' and the central timber shaft, which is actually a structural member supporting the thirteen-tiered *yasti-chattra*, as 'Indra's mythic pillar, the axis of the world' {Gutschow 1997: 90, 92}. These fantastic speculations had no place in Nepalese or Vajrayana Buddhism and the Swayambhu Purana mentioned no such symbolisms. They also do not reflect the actual architecture and symbolisms of the *caitya*, which are about Swayambhu Adi-Buddha, and the Five Jina Buddhas and their five *prajna*s; in other words, Swayambhunath is a Vajrayana architectural *mandala*.

The architecture and religious symbolisms of Swayambhunath evolved considerably over the centuries and the *caitya* has also been subjected to destructions by foreign invasions and repeated renovations so that it is difficult to ascertain its original forms and chronology. However despite the repeated involvement of foreign Buddhists in the process of shaping its forms, most notably the Tibetans in the thirteenth century CE and from the late seventeenth century CE on, Swayambhunath still retains the fundamental features of a Nepalese *caitya*; it has also been well documented that many of its construction phases and earlier forms might be deduced with certainty. The followings list the most important construction phases excluding many trivial repairs that often involved the replacement of the central timber shaft.

- Phase I (legendary and before the sixth century BCE): Santikaracarya built a *caitya* to cover the bright lotus Swayambhu; its form, as it has been told, was exactly as its current form complete with the ten image shrines, dome, *harmika*, and the thirteen-tiered *yasti-chattra*. Obviously this was the final form of the *caitya* dated to the time when Swayambhu Purana, in which the legend was told, was compiled in the sixteenth century CE.
- Phase II (early fifth century CE): According to the Gopalarajavamsavali chronicle, Vrsadeva built Singhu monastery and *caitya*; however a Sanskrit inscription in the lime-making pit at Swayambhunath clearly mentions Sankaradeva, Vrsadeva's son, as the one who constructed a Buddhist monastery and *caitya*. In both cases, the commencement of Swayambhunath was evidently in the beginning of the fifth century CE. The early form of this *caitya* was probably a small hybrid Indo-Gandhara *stupa* like Dharmarajika [6.13] with an Indian hemispherical dome and a multi-tiered *yasti-chattra*; it might also have four niches in the four cardinal points like Gandhara *stupa*s.
- Phase III (seventh century CE): An inscription in the Dharmadevacaitya of Cabahil dated in the seventh century CE mentioned the installation of four shrines in the four cardinal points to house four Buddha images {Gutschow 1997: 171}; thus the four Buddha shrines were probably present in Swayambhunath around this time.
- Phase IV (eleventh-twelfth centuries CE): A seventeenth century CE manuscript mentioned the earliest renovation during this period but it is difficult to verify this {Gutschow 1997: 87}. However, a twelfth century CE inscription in the base of Swayambhunath recorded a definite renovation by Sakyabhiksu Maitricandra with the involvement of Theravada monks or the Sravakas {Shakya 2004: 125-126}; the painted-eyes on the *harmika* and the *halapau*s presumably occurred during this phase.
- Phase V (c. 1362-1372 CE): After the Islamic army of the Bengali Sultan Shams-ud-din completely destroyed Swayambhunath in 1350 CE, the *caitya* was totally rebuilt under the direction of Rajaharsa Bhalloka {Shakya 2004: 131-132}; an inscription confirms this devastated invasion and the subsequent reconstruction of the *caitya*. The prominent bulge in the lower end of the curvy *yasti-chattra* as characteristic of Nepalese *caitya*s probably also occurred during this phase since a 1015 CE manuscript still showed the *yasti-chattra* in a straight conical profile without the bulge {Gutschow 1997: 192-193}.
- Phase VI (sixteenth century CE): The fifth Vairocana shrine and the five *prajna* shrines were probably added during this phase concurrent with the compilation of the Swayambhu Purana, which was written in the same century mentioning all the architectural features as we see today including all ten image shrines. Gutschow, however, dated the installation of Vairocana and five *prajna* shrines in the early sixteenth and the seventeenth century CE respectively {Gutschow 1997: 32, 51-55}. In any case, these modifications reflected a new iconographical program and changing symbolisms of the *caitya* based on the Vajrayana tenets; they highlighted the philosophical transition from the *yoga-tantra* (Five Jina Buddhas) to *anuttarayoga-tantra* (Five Jina Buddhas and their five *prajna*s and Adi-Buddha). The construction of these shrines might occur even earlier since a painting dated in 1416 CE clearly showed an unidentified *caitya* having four cardinal and four intermediate image shrines {Pal 1978: pl. 79}. Apparently the occurrence of the image shrines in Swayambhunath

was quite late since Dhamekh Stupa **[8.6]** at Sarnath in India already had eight image niches a millennium before.
- Phase VII (1595 CE): A golden umbrella was installed on the apex of the *caitya* by Sivasimhamalla (r. 1583-1620 CE) in 1595 CE {Shakya 2004: 144-148}.
- Phase VIII (1668 CE): Jayapratapamalla installed a huge gilt *vajra* on the eastern side of the *caitya*, which completed the Vajrayana symbolisms of the *caitya*; it now symbolically represented the union of *upaya* (the *vajra* and male) and *prajna* (the lotus Swayambhu and female) in a non-dual enlightened state of *Vajra*. The *caitya* would in effect be transformed into an architectural *mandala*.
- Phase IX (1917-1918 CE): The latest important renovation was initiated by Lama Dharma Man Tuladhar during which the image shrines previously rested on the molded plinth were expanded and projected across the latter; Buddha images and guardian lions were added on both sides of the image shrines and a ring of Tibetan prayer wheels encircling the *caitya* was also installed {Gutschow 1997: 88, 92}{Shakya 2004: 313-322}. Though it is not possible to determine precisely when the 114 plaque niches above the molded plinth have been commenced, they probably occurred in this renovation; formerly these niches were at the plinth level and not above it.

Swayambhunath is among the most innovative Nepalese *caitya*s containing many newly symbolic and esoteric features such as the painted eyes on the *harmika*, the *halapau*, and the shrines of the Five Jina Buddhas and their *prajna*s. These are unique to the Nepalese *caitya* reflecting the latest Tantric phase of the Buddhist *stupa* in which the architecture embodies Vajrayana principles and as a medium, an architectural *mandala*, in the process of attaining Enlightenment; this type of esoteric architecture has already been suggested for the Indian Elora caves and Borobudur **[6.28-6.29]** in Java. Like the Sri Lankan *dagaba*, the Nepalese *caitya* also strongly adheres to the Indian tradition **[6.3]** in its hemispherical dome slightly truncated in the top. However in closer examinations, Swayambhunath evidently perpetuates the architectural features of Gandhara *stupa*s **[6.13, 6.18]** in the incorporation of image shrines in the cardinal points, the solid *harmika*, and the tall multi-tiered *yasti-chattra*. Nepal was historically an intermediary between India and Tibet and it is expected to find Nepalese elements in the latter; the famed Kumbum **[6.40-6.41]** also exhibits many Nepalese features, most notably the painted eyes on the *harmika* and the gilt *gujar*.

7. *Chorten* - Tibet, Indian Himalaya, Bhutan, Mongolia

Unlike Southeast and East Asia where the Theravada and Mahayana predominate, Tibet, Mongolia and the Himalaya countries are the domains of the Vajrayana; the Tantric phase of Buddhism manifested strongest in Tibet and even more so than Nepal especially after the demise of Indian Buddhism after c. 1200 CE. From Tibet, the Vajrayana fountain head in the region, the Tibetan branch of the Vajrayana, sometimes known as Lamaism, subsequently spread to Mongolia and Bhutan. It is thus natural to begin the discussions with Tibet and in particular its local form of the Indian *stupa*, or the *chorten*. The once immense territory of Tibet composed of five provinces of Ngari (western Tibet), U (central Tibet), Tsang (west-central and southern Tibet), Kham (eastern Tibet), and Amdo (northeastern Tibet). Parts of Kham and Amdo later became Qinghai and were absorbed into Gansu, Sichuan, and Yunnam provinces of China after Tibet was conquered by the latter in 1950 CE. Ngari was once the traditional territory of Zhangzhung and a stronghold of Bon, a native Tibetan belief before the arrival of Buddhism in the seventh century CE. Bon is a shamanistic and animistic cult of nature, spirits, demons, and gods involving elaborate rituals like animal sacrifice and mystical dances to propitiate these fearful agents {Francke 1977: 82-86}{Handa 2001: 254-262}. Namri-tsong-tsen (r. 607-629 CE) and his powerful son Song-tsen-gampo (r. 629-649 CE) of U conquered Zhangzhung, founded the Yarlung Dynasty (c. 607-842 CE), and a vast Tibetan empire in the early seventh century CE. Song-tsen-gampo commanded respect and fear among his neighbors such that the Chinese and Nepalese had to send their princesses, Wenchen and Bhrkuti respectively, to secure political matrimonies with him. During Song-tsen-gampo's reign the Tibetan script, which was modeled after the Kashmiri alphabet, was created in 632 CE by the scholar-minister Thonmi Sambhota. He reportedly spent some times studying at Nalanda and Kashmir before returning to Tibet; this was probably the earliest official contact between India and Tibet {Dutt 1962: 342}{Ricca and Lo Bue 1993: 108}{Misra 1998 Volume I: 306}. The Tibetans also managed to rule Turkistan between c. 670-690 CE and became a formidable force in Central Asia until the mid ninth century CE. Buddhism is believed to have been officially introduced into Tibet by the aforesaid princesses; Wenchen reportedly brought with her the Jobo Sakyamuni statue from China and Bhrkuti brought the Aksobhyavajra image from Nepal. Subsequently the temples of Jokhang (c. 638-639 CE) and Ramoche (c. 641 CE) were constructed in Lhasa to house Aksobhyavajra and Jobo Sakyamuni respectively. A popular story related that in the early eighth century CE Kong-co, the Chinese queen of Khri-lde-gtsug-rtsan (c. 712-755 CE), swapped the Jobo Sakyamuni with Aksobhyavajra where they remain to this day {Vitali 1990: 7, 74-75, 78}. Kong-co reputedly built Kachu Monastery (728-739 CE), probably the first in the country, for Khotanese monks who were taking refuge in Tibet after being expelled from Khotan {Vitali 1990: 4, 6-11}; they were again expelled from Tibet in 739 CE. Buddhism was briefly outlawed in 755 CE and Bon was on the ascendance after the assassination of Khri-lde-gtsug-rtsan. His successor was the great Tibetan king Tri-song-detsen (r. 755-797 CE) who successfully occupied the Chinese town of Dunhuang, where the famed Mogao caves are located, between c. 781-847 CE; he also sacked Changan in 763 CE, then a great city and capital of the Chinese Tang Dynasty. Tri-song-detsen reinstated Buddhism and proclaimed it the state religion of Tibet in an inscription on a stele at Samye Monastery (779 CE), which was reportedly founded after the arrival of the eminent monks Padmasambhava (c. 735-792 CE) and Santaraksita (c. 747-792 CE) from Kashmir and Nepal; Padmasambhava reportedly founded the Nyingmapa, the oldest and one of the six Vajrayana sects in Tibet. At Samye, a great debate was initiated by Tri-song-detsen to determine whether Tibet should follow the Indian or Chinese branch of Buddhism; to no one's surprise, Indian Buddhism was chosen for obvious political reasons {Kossak and Singer 1998: 4}. The official royal patronage of Buddhism over the native Bon religion would become the main source of antagonisms between them for the next decades. The last great king of Tibet was Re-pa-chen (r. 815-838 CE) who brought the Tibetan empire to its greatest extent from Sichuan (China) in the east, Baltistan (Pakistani Kashmir) in the west, Khotan (Turkistan) in the north, and Nepal in the south; a peace treaty with China between 821-823 CE also brought short-lived stability. Re-pa-chen elevated Buddhism to an exalted status in the Tibetan society where Buddhist monks occupied important positions in the government and the Buddhist precepts were imposed on the Tibetans while tax collections would be designed to favor the *Sangha* {Vitali 1990: 18}. The last Yarlung King Lang-darma (r. 838-842 CE) decided to persecute Buddhism and supported Bon and his action prompted the Buddhist faction to assassinate him in 842 CE; his death brought an end of the powerful Yarlung Dynasty and Tibet never again recovered its former glory. From the end of the Yarlung kings in 842 CE to the menace of the Mongols in the thirteenth century CE, the political scene shifted for awhile to Ngari with the rise of Guge (Chapter 4).

This kingdom then under the leadership of the Lama-King Yeshe-O (r. 967-1040 CE) was especially instrumental in inaugurating the second phase of Buddhist diffusion into Tibet. Another momentous event was the arrival of the Indian monk Dipankara Srijnana (982-1054 CE), alias Atisa then the abbot of Vikramasila Monastery in India, who traveled to central Tibet in 1045 CE after a three-year sojourn in Guge; the golden age of the Vajrayana in Tibet began during this time. With this newly religious impetus from India, soon new monasteries would be constructed all over Tibet like Shalu (1027 CE), Yemar (1037 CE), Reting (1056 CE), Sakya (1073 CE), Drathang (1081-1093 CE), Thil (1158 CE), etc.; some of the oldest Tibetan religious paintings on cotton (*thangka*) and murals were commissioned soon after the arrival of Atisa. Another four important Buddhist sects and numerous sub-sects emerged during this second transmission, namely the Kadampa, Kagyupa, Karmapa, and Sakyapa. The latter, soon after its collaboration with their Mongol overlord, became the first ever religious authority to rule Tibet in the mid thirteenth century CE, with dire consequences in the centuries to come. Due to the apparent lack of a strong centralized and secular government in this period, the monasteries grew increasingly powerful. This led to the rise in the mutual cooperation and joint-ruling of the political institution between the regional clans and their respective monasteries; expectedly the Buddhist abbots would often populate their monasteries with members of their own clans while lineage successions were rarely handed to outsiders. This symbiotic relationship maintained economic, political, and religious powers in the hands of the regional clans and their monasteries, which further weakened Tibet and also led to the mutual hostilities and frequent clashes between rival monasteries {Kossak and Singer 1998: 20}. Between 1285-1290 CE, there was open warfare between Sakyapa and Drigungpa monasteries over the Mongol patronage; the Sakyapa eventually triumphed and the monasteries of Drigung and Densatil were burned to the ground. The sack of rival monasteries continued to be documented in Tibet well into the twentieth century CE as vividly told in his book 'Seven Years in Tibet' by Heinrich Harrer. Needless to say, the prospect of Buddhist monks resorted to armed conflicts has been unprecedented in the history of Buddhism; the imposing and fortress-like constructions of Tibetan monasteries were evidently the product of the conflicts between the monasteries and also the threats from foreign invasions. Another unique system of selecting a successor, or a reincarnated *lama* (*tulku*), had also been developed during this second phase of Tibetan Buddhism. Rangchung Dorje (1284-1339 CE), the third Karmapa, started the *tulku* tradition by prophesying his own reincarnation {Kossak and Singer 1998: 21}; the practice survives to this day in the well-known reincarnation selection of the Dalai Lama adopted by the Gelugpa sect. While there is nothing unusual about reincarnation since many Hindu kings also proclaimed themselves to be incarnations of Visnu, the Tibetan *tulku* system is unique in that the reincarnated-*lama*-to-be actually predicts and selects his next reincarnation before his death thus preventing succession disputes. From the thirteenth century CE onward, the political and religious history of Tibet was often interwoven since the Buddhist *Sangha* effectively became the state; this was Buddhist theocracy at its best in Asia. In 1249 CE, Sakya Pandita (1182-1251 CE) of the Sakyapa was appointed a viceroy of Tibet by the Mongols, who were in control of a vast empire at the time. The move averted bloodsheds and the Mongols were in effect converted to Tibetan Buddhism; the Mongols, like the Tibetans, could not choose Chinese Buddhism for obvious political reasons. The Mongol patronage brought immense wealth and power to the Tibetan monasteries and especially the Sakyapas, who in turn channeled their immense wealth into new artistic and architectural endeavors. Artists, craftsmen, and architects from countries like Nepal flocked to Tibet where they assisted in the constructions and decorations of Sakyapa monasteries; as already mentioned, one such prestigious group was the eighty Nepalese artists headed by the multi-talented Arniko working in Tibet between 1261-1262 CE. During the Sakyapa Period (c. 1249-1400 CE), a revered Tibetan *lama* named Buston (1290-1364 CE) ascended to the abbotship of Shalu Monastery in 1320 CE; he translated and systematized the Tibetan version of the Indian *Tripitaka*, known as Kanjur and Tanjur. The next successors of the supreme monk-ruler class in Tibet after the Sakyapa were the Gelugpa sect founded by Tsong-khapa (1357-1419 CE); the Gelugpas also founded some of the largest monasteries in Tibet like Ganden (1409 CE), Drepung (1416 CE), Sera (1419 CE), and Tashilunpo (1447 CE). The zenith of their power was when Sonam-gyatso (1543-1588 CE), then the abbot of Drepung, had been bestowed the title Dalai Lama (Ocean of Wisdom) in 1578 CE by the Mongol Altan Khan. He became the third Dalai Lama while his earlier predecessor dGe.'dun.grub (1391-1474 CE) accordingly became the first Dalai Lama; even Altan Khan's grandson was also selected as the fourth Dalai Lama. Lopsang-gyatso (1617-1682 CE), the great fifth Dalai Lama, constructed the Potala (1645-1648, 1690-1694 CE) in Lhasa which was obviously an enormous palace for a king than as a monastery; it was renovated and expanded from the original seventh century CE building. Chinese influences in the fields of the arts and architecture gradually gained strength in Tibet during the Gelugpa Period (c. 1400-1720 CE). Among the most distinguished personalities during this time was Lama Taranatha (1575-1634 CE) who wrote a great history on Indian Buddhism. Unfortunately, the Buddhist theocracy was more suited in governing a peaceful Tibet than confronting the mighty military threat from China. Tibet would effectively be conquered and annexed into Manchu China in 1720 CE and it was not until 1911 CE that the country again broke free from China due to the latter's internal revolution; the Dalai Lama institution was instantaneously reinstated. However as soon as the Chinese civil war was over, Tibet was immediately invaded in 1950 CE and thereafter made a province of China; the 1959 CE Tibetan revolt sent the fourteenth Dalai Lama into exile in India where he remained until this day.

Since the defeat of Bon in the eighth century CE Buddhism became the dominant religion in Tibet; an overwhelming body of Bon religious literature as well as its arts and architecture have been borrowed from Buddhism to such an extent that there are hardly distinctions between them. It is also likely that the Tibetan Vajrayana also incorporated many Bon rituals into its tenets to enrich its religious experiences and Tibetanize the Indian religion. After the demise of Indian Buddhism in India around c. 1200 CE, Tibet became a secured homeland for the Vajrayana where its arts and architecture continued to flourish; in Tibet, Mahayana arts are often found alongside with those of the Vajrayana though not as ubiquitous as the latter. In the case of Tibetan sculptures, their materials are mostly gilt bronze, stucco, and polychrome clay; stone sculptures have been carved but these are rare and often found on rocky surfaces {Pal 1969: 31-43}. The Tibetans must have begun sculpting Buddhist images since the seventh century CE; the gilt statues of Jobo Sakyamuni (possibly clay) and Aksobhyavajra (bronze) reputedly brought to Tibet by Song-tsen-gampo's two wives probably marked the first official introduction of Buddhist sculptures into the country. The Jokhang Temple (c. 638-639 CE) in Lhasa founded by Song-tsen-gampo also contains some of the original timber columns and carvings. These columns show obvious resemblance to those in Ajanta Cave 1, 19 **[5.10, 5.12]** as the carved reliefs on their brackets depicting flying figures and slender women in swaying hips exhibit definite Indian and possibly Nepalese workmanship. This temple, which was originally built to house the Aksobhyavajra statue brought by the Nepalese princess Bhrkuti, and the surviving specimens inside are in the Indo-Nepalese style;

it was almost certainly constructed by Nepalese craftsmen {Vitali 1990: 74-77, pl. 35-37}. The next stylistic phase in Tibetan arts might be ascribed to Khotan and the Mogao caves in Dunhuang; Khotanese monks reportedly took refuge in Tibet in the early eighth century CE during which Kachu Monastery (c. 728-739 CE) was constructed for them. According to Vitali, the monastery alongwith the Sakyamuni and *bodhisattva* statues were probably the oldest ones sculpted by the Tibetans, possibly with foreign assistance {Vitali 1990: 11-15, 19-24, pl. 1-15}. The column capitals inside Kachu again show obvious dependency on Indian prototypes, particularly Ajanta Cave 17 (see {Fergusson and Burgess 1969: pl. XXXIV-XXXV}). Many Mogao caves were also constructed during the period of the Tibetan occupation likely with the participation of Tibetan craftsmen; the murals in these caves display a style akin to Tibet. Between the eleventh-twelfth centuries CE Tibet, like contemporary Bagan in Myanmar, was under heavy influences from Pala India and also Kashmir. Thanks to the great efforts of Rinchen-sangpo and Atisa, Pala arts began to flow into Tibet where it was greatly welcomed and enthusiastically embraced for centuries to come. Numerous Pala-inspired sculptures and murals were commissioned in the monasteries like Yemar and Drathang in central Tibet {Vitali 1990: 37-61, pl. 16-34, fg. 7-15} as well as the Tibetanized regions of Ladakh, Zanskar, Spiti, and Guge. The iconography during this phase was characteristically late Mahayana about Sakyamuni and Mahayana *bodhisattva*s like Avalokitesvara, Manjusri, and Vajrapani alongwith early Vajrayana deities like the Five Jina Buddhas; often these sculptures wore elaborate tiaras on their heads as typical of Pala sculptures. Multi-limbed deities were also common from the twelfth century CE on as indicative of the latest Vajrayana manifestation; an overwhelming majority of the sculptures during this phase was gilt bronze with a few rare cases in stone and wood dated between the twelfth-thirteenth centuries CE {Huntington and Huntington 1990: pl. 127-132}. The latest manifestation of the Tibetan Vajrayana was between the twelfth-fifteenth centuries CE with the emergence of the multi-limbed macabre and wrathful deities in the twelfth century CE; they often appeared in *yaganaddha* (Tibetan *yab-yum*) with their female *prajna*s {Pal 1990: S21/208-210, S23/211-213}{Linrothe 1999: fg. 195, 213-214}. These purely Tantric deities, whether in peaceful or wrathful mien, can be divided into two categories, namely the *dharmapala* (Tibetan *chos-skyong* or protecting deities) and *istadevata* (Tibetan *yi-dam* or deities associating with highest Vajrayana teachings and consecratory rituals) {Ricca and Lo Bue 1993: 74-75}. The *chos-skyong* deities include Mahakala while the *yi-dam* deities often appear in *yab-yum* with their *prajna*s like Heruka, Hevajra, Kalacakra, Samvara, Cakrasamvara, and Vajrabhaivara. Tibetan sculptures followed the same course of iconographical development as in the other countries, from deities in the peaceful mien having single limbs (Theravada and early Mahayana), peaceful mien and multiple limbs (late Mahayana and transitional Vajrayana), wrathful mien and single limbs (early Vajrayana), wrathful mien and multiple limbs (middle Vajrayana), and wrathful mien with single or multiple limbs in *yab-yum* (late Vajrayana).

Tibetan paintings also share similar stylistic affinities and artistic sources as their sculptural counterparts; they are generally divided into the categories of murals, illuminated manuscripts, and *thangka*s. The latter is a type of painting on cloth, which is the equivalent and derivative of the Indian *pata* and the Nepalese *paubha*, and different from the Chinese paintings, which are generally painted on silk or paper in the long vertical or horizontal scrolls. According to Vitali, the oldest paintings in Tibet are the murals inside the Jokhang Temple and one of its murals shows an unidentified six-armed deity in the swaying posture dated in the mid seventh century CE {Vitali 1990: 77-78, 81-82, pl. 45}. Some of the oldest Tibetan paintings can also been found outside Tibet in the Mogao caves executed during the Tibetan occupation of Dunhuang between 781-847 CE. These are long vertical banners recalling the Chinese vertical scrolls but the style and iconography, which consist of mostly *bodhisattva*s with a few accompanied annotations in Tibetan, suggest Indian influences {Kossak and Singer 1998: 4-5}{Vitali 1990: fg. 5-6}. During the Tibetan occupation, there were about forty-four caves completed in Mogao and among these Cave 112, 158-159 are the most important. Their murals depict Tibetan emperors and administrators (Cave 158-159) with a penchant for the Tibetan warm color palette of deep reddish-brown and white; Cave 158 also has a colossal 51'2" long *Parinirvana* Buddha statue, the biggest of its kind in Mogao. It is undeniably that these caves were essentially Chinese in inspiration but Tibetan artists and craftsmen certainly involved in their decorations. The next phase in Tibetan paintings (c. 1000-1249 CE), or Kadampa Style according to Pal, received influences from the international Pala Style as also manifested in the Bagan murals of Myanmar, Nepal, and Ladakh {Pal 1984: 29-45}{Kossak and Singer 1998: 32-40}{Vitali 1990: 37-61, pl. 29-34, 38-44, 46, 50}. Among the best extant Pala-Styled murals in central Tibet have been painted in the monasteries of Drathang and Shalu as well as in the Jokhang Temple; an important iconographical innovation during this phase was the lineage paintings of

Buddhist *lama*s unique to Tibet and Ladakh. The *lama* is generally depicted occupying the center of the composition and surrounded by smaller figures of other *lama*s, deities, Buddhas, and *bodhisattva*s; he is also provided with a halo and aureole, which are typically reserved for Buddhas and *bodhisattva*s in Indian and Gandhara paintings, as in the Central Asian and Chinese convention. Some of the oldest Tibetan *mandala*s had also been painted during this period; beginning about c. 1200 CE and after there appeared a class of wrathful and *yab-yum* deities reflecting a parallel development in Tibetan sculptures. During the Sakyapa's rise to power between c. 1249-1400 CE, Nepalese influences were strong in Tibet especially after the arrival and contributions of gifted Nepalese artists like Arniko to Sakya Monastery and the Mongol Yuan court in China between 1261-1263 CE {Pal 1984: 60-73}{Kossak and Singer 1998: 40-45}{Vitali 1990: 89-112}. Nepalese-influenced paintings display familiar characteristics like the oval face, deep subdue coloration especially red, and the precise and exquisite rendering of details particularly the floral scrolls and *caitya* thrones behind the deities. Some of the most beautiful Nepalese-styled Sakyapa murals can be found in the monasteries of Shalu, Gyang, and Nor and the murals in the Palkhor Tsuglagkhang and Kumbum **[6.40-6.41]** in Gyantse Monastery dated in the fifteenth century CE. The murals of the Eighty-four Siddhas in the Palkhor Tsuglagkhang are the great achievement in the history of Tibetan paintings {Schroeder 2006}. Similar murals have already been painted earlier in the Sumtsek of Alchi in Ladakh (c. 1200 CE) and in the Mustang caves in the Nepal Himalaya (fourteenth-fifteenth centuries CE) suggesting its widespread popularity; the theme likely originated in Pala India. The Kumbum murals are perhaps the most elegant and technically accomplished of all Tibetan paintings in which they employed gilt plaster in slight reliefs for the figures in combination with paintings to create a three-dimensional effect known as the pastiglia; the source of this ingenious technique might be traced back to Mogao and Alchi {Ricca and Lo Bue 1993: 102, pl. 87-88}{Goepper 1996: 273, 275}{Whitfield 2000: 75}. The late phase in Tibetan paintings, which began in the fifteenth century CE, was increasingly under the influences from the Chinese tradition, particularly in the depictions of the Chinese *lohan*s and the inclusion of landscape elements in the background {Pal 1984: 121-132}{Kossak and Singer 1998: 45-47}. On the stylistic evolution, the central figure previously dominant in the center of the composition, would progressively be reduced in scale as the background were now crowded with numerous distracting elements including human figures, rocks, trees, mountains, clouds, Chinese-styled architecture, etc.; these have greatly diminished the grandeur of the central image and the elegance of the paintings. Late Tibetan paintings also paid inordinate attention in depicting sumptuous flowing garments, which was a sure sign of Chinese influences, gaudier color scheme, and the peony flower motif.

Tibetan Buddhist architecture primarily encompasses the categories of monastery (*gompa*) and *chorten* or the Tibetan form of the Indian *stupa*. Though a few isolated image temples had been constructed as early as the seventh century CE such as the Jokhang and Ramoche, they did not appear to be widespread and were often incorporated into the monastic plans as image chapels as early as the eighth century CE as in the Kachu Monastery. Traditional Tibetan architecture, whether secular of religious, can generally be divided into two classes based on the roof forms, namely the flat roof and pitched hipped roof; the former is characteristic of the indigenous Tibetan architecture whereas the latter is definitely of a foreign origin. Tibetan flat-roofed architecture is typically constructed in sun-dried mud bricks and a post-and-beam structure with planks spaced perpendicular to the beams; the facing material is usually adobe, which is a mixture of mud reinforced with vegetal matters, and the building is typically whitewashed with lime. The parapeted rooftops in Tibetan monasteries are often accessible and also serve as outdoor terraces. The flat-roofed adobe architecture is certainly more suitable for the dry and high-altitude region like Tibet where timber is a scarce commodity; the building heights range from single to multiple stories like the fortress-like Potala Palace in Lhasa. Early Tibetan monasteries were constructed on the flat ground like Samye but subsequently perched on the hilltops commanding sweeping views of the surroundings, a feature which was also common in Gandhara **[4.2]** and Tibetanized monasteries in the Himalaya. Samye was a great monastery constructed in the first Buddhist transmission as a Buddhist academy after the Indian *mahavihara* model of Odantapura in Bihar; its original building was reconstructed in the thirteenth century CE and it too burnt down in the 1810 CE fire. Nain Singh described its ruins, likely of the thirteenth century CE building, during his visit in 1866 CE {Handa 2001: 269-274}:

> The monastery, which contains a large temple, four large colleges, and several other buildings, is enclosed by a lofty wall about a mile and a half in circumference, with gates facing the cardinal points, and along the top of the wall are many votive brick chaityas numbered 1,030, and they seemed to be

covered with inscriptions in ancient Indian characters. In the center of the enclosure stands the assembly hall, with radiating cloisters leading to four chapels, facing at equal distance the four sides of the larger temple.

In the case of Kachu Monastery, its flat-roofed *dukhang* has a central image chapel in the back that is flanked on both sides by clay images, a convention also common in Gandhara, Afghanistan, Turkistan, and Chinese Buddhist caves like Mogao [5.22-5.23] where the Tibetans probably came into contacts as early as the seventh century CE. The second Buddhist transmission, which was led by the Guge kings between the late tenth-eleventh centuries CE (Chapter 4), ushered in a new era of monastery construction in central Tibet. Due to the rivalries and recurring conflicts between competing monasteries probably starting in the thirteenth century CE alongwith the threat of foreign invasions, Tibetan monasteries gradually assumed a fortress-like massive appearance for defensive purposes while flaunting their power and wealth. Another important development in Tibetan architecture is the pitched roof which is covered in gilt sheet metal or tiles roof and certainly of foreign origins. The oldest Buddhist temple in Tibet, the multi-storied Jokhang (c. 638-639 CE), might have been constructed or assisted by Nepalese craftsmen; it likely had a pitched hipped roof of gilt metal. Its plan consists of cell-like chapels arranged around a centrally colonnaded courtyard, which is clearly in the quadrangular *vihara* tradition of Gandhara [4.2] and India [4.4]. Another temple constructed in Re-pa-chen's reign was reportedly a nine-storied structure of bricks in the lower six stories and timber-and-leather in the upper three stories and it had gilt pitched roofs hung with numerous bells {Vitali 1990: 19}; the description recalled similar architecture in Licchavi Nepal and the *dega*. The tile roof in the Chinese manner was no doubt a later development, as in Shalu Monastery (1027 CE), and uncommon in Tibet

Chorten or *mchod.rten* is the Tibetan form of the Indian *stupa*; the first known account of the *chorten* construction in Tibet was the gLing-mKhas.pa Chorten in Byang (791 CE) erected by Minister Pa.tshab-sTong.'bar-sdom.'dzam in the reign of Tri-song-detsen {Vitali 1990: 16-17}. Tibetan *chorten*s are often Commemorative, Symbolic, and Relic types; the latter might have a hollow chamber in the interior wherein a *tsha-tsha*, precious stones, herb, grains, written *mantra*s, etc. could be deposited, a practice no doubt originated in India {Misra 1998 Volume III: 259}. A *tsha-tsha* is typically a miniature *chorten* model made of clay samples collected from the

6.39. Chorten of Enlightenment

construction site that is mixed with powders of precious materials or ashes of the deceased *lama*s {Dorjee 1996: 30, 41, 131}. Tibetan Buddhist literature lists eight types of *chorten*s commemorating the Eight Events in Sakyamuni's life and the locations where these events originally occurred {Dorjee 1996: 11-18, 49-71}{Gutschow 1997: 302-303}:

(1) Nativity or Heaped Lotuses (Lumbini)
(2) Enlightenment (Bodhgaya) **[6.39]**
(3) First Sermon or Multiple Auspicious Doors (Sarnath) **[6.40-6.41]**
(4) Decease or Nirvana (Kushinagar)
(5) Descent from Trayastrimsa Heaven (Sankasya)
(6) Great Miracle (Sravasti)
(7) Reconciliation of Dissent (Rajagriha)
(8) Victory (Vaishali)

The typology of these eight *chorten*s is based on the shapes of the dome and the presence, absence, or types of steps; Type (4) is the only one with a bell-shaped dome and without steps while all others have vase-shaped domes and steps in which Type (1) has lotus steps, Type (3) has multiple-door steps, Type (5) has triple-staircase steps, Type (7) has octagonal steps, and Type (8) has three circular steps. The most common type is Type (2) or *Chorten* of Enlightenment **[6.39]** which is a tripartite structure having a plinth, a body with four steps and a dome, and a crown consisting of a solid *harmika, yasti-chattra*, umbrella, crescent and sun symbols, and finial. The crescent and sun are commonly found in the Bamiyan murals and earlier coins of Gandhara and Central Asia, which were likely of Sassanian origin. According to Klimburg-Salter, the sun-moon pair represented the divine kingship and when crowning consecrated *stupa*s they symbolized the coronation of the future Sakyamuni Buddha upon his completion of the ten *bhumi*s {Klimburg-Salter 1989: 109}; however, they likely represented *upaya* and *prajna* respectively in the esoteric Vajrayana tradition, which symbolized the highest enlightened state of *Vajra*. The painted eyes on Nepalese and Tibetan *hamika*s further reinforce the idea that the *chorten* is the embodiment of the consecrated Buddha. Some of the earliest depictions of these eight *chorten* types can be found among the murals of Shalu Monastery (1333-1335 CE) {Vitali 1990: 111, pl. 74} and Kumbum {Ricca and Lo Bue 1993: 287}. Numerous *stupa*s as the forerunners of the Tibetan *chorten*s have also been depicted in the murals of Bamiyan (Afghanistan), Kizil (Turkistan), and Alchi (Ladakh) {Snellgrove and Skorupski 1977-1980 Volume II: fg. 82}. The vase-shaped domes can also be found among the Bagan *zedi*s in Myanmar dated in the eleventh century CE, though the connection with the Tibetan *chorten* seems unlikely. The materials for the plinth and body in these *chorten*s are usually bricks faced over with plaster while the *yasti-chattra* has either stone or gilt metal discs attached to a timber shaft; the umbrella, crescent and sun symbols, and finial are typically gilt metal while the dome is occasionally provided with a single decorative niche. There are rules dictating the color scheme and proportional relationships between the various parts of a *chorten* {Dorjee 1996: 135,143-150, 160-172}; however the Tibetans apparently do not follow these rules literally. The color scheme for a *chorten*, which also corresponds to its symbolisms, has been explicitly specified in Desid's 'Proportional Manual of the Stupa Architecture:'

> The spherical pinnacle is yellow, the sun is red, the moon and the cover of the umbrella are white, and the umbrella is blue…The plaits of compassion is red, while the Formula of Compassion itself and the male-wheels are yellow, and the female-wheels and the axle-pole are red. The stupa is white, the Supporting-umbrella is blue, the Base of Ten Virtues is yellow, and the foundation is green. The Three Staircases starting from down upward are red, blue and green, respectively. The Lion Throne is white, the cornice is blue, the small edge is red, and the big edge is green in color.

In spite of these strict rules, a *chorten* is generally whitewashed for if the aforesaid rules are carried out literally the colors will appear incongruous, gaudy, and highly distracting visually. To Tibetan Buddhists, a *chorten* is also considered as a 'receptacle of offerings' and embodies *Dharmakaya* or the Body of Buddha's *Dharma* {Dorjee 1996: 121, 160}. The plinth presumably symbolizes Buddha's Lion Throne, the first step the Four Close Mindfulness, the second step the Two Perfect Abandonments, the third step the Four Stages of Miraculous Powers, the fourth step the Five Moral Faculties, the vase-base the Five Moral Powers, the dome the Seven Factors of Enlightenment, the *harmika* the Noble Eightfold Paths, the axle-pole the Ten Knowledges, the thirteen discs the Thirteen Accomplishments of Spiritual Power, the umbrella as Buddha A Leader of Sentient Beings, the moon Buddha's Brightness of Unsurpassed Wisdom, and the tiara-flag Buddha's Unsurpassed Perfectly Accomplished Enlightenment {Dorjee 1996: 121-126}. Clearly each country has developed its unique architectural forms and symbolisms for the Buddhist *stupa*. The forms, and certainly symbolisms, of the eight *chorten* types already had antecedents in India **[5.3-5.5, 5.7, 5.9-5.10]** and Gandhara **[6.15]**; their final forms likely crystallized in Central Asia (Afghanistan, Turkistan), Kashmir, and Ladakh between the eighth-eleventh centuries CE, or possibly as early as the sixth century CE among the Bamiyan and Kizil murals {Tarzi 1977 Volume II: 158-161} {Giuseppe 1988: 73-79, 101-102, pl. VII-XIV, XXXVII-XXXVIII} {Dorjee 1996: 110-113} {Pal 1969: fg. 50} {Pal 1990: 193, S3, pl. 36}. These, however, do not rule out the possibility that the Tibetans might have developed their own *chorten* forms in Tibet based on foreign models.

The famed Kumbum Chorten **[6.40-6.41]** in Gyantse Monastery is an advanced form of the Chorten of Multiple Auspicious Doors in a much bigger scale; Kumbum means 'Chorten of 100,000 Images' due a vast number of sculptures and murals inside. Gyantse has been best remembered in an international incident when Tibet was invaded by the British in 1904 CE; the attack was led

Part II. Architecture   Stupa . 231

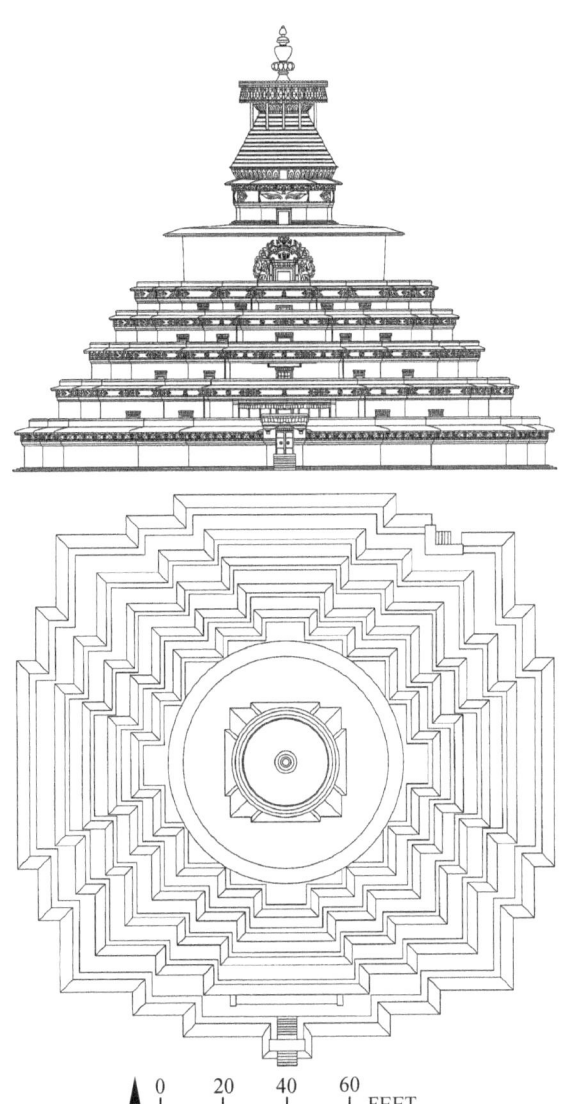

6.41. Kumbum
1427-1439, 1472-1474 CE
Gyantse, Tibet
Xizang- China

6.40. Kumbum eleveation and top view
1427-1439, 1472-1474 CE
Gyantse- Tibet
Xizang- China

by Major Francis Younghusband who shelled the town mercilessly and many Tibetans died but somehow its monastery and Kumbum miraculously survived. Gyantse again escaped destructions under the Chinese during the Cultural Revolution in the late 1960s CE. The Palkhor Tsuglagkhang next to the giant *chorten* is an image hall completed between 1418-1425 CE and its interior, as in the Kumbum, also contains precious murals especially those depicting the Eighty-four Siddhas {Schroeder 2006}. Kumbum was completed slightly later between 1427-1439 CE with the final installments of a Vajradhara and two acolyte images alongwith the gilding of the *chattravali* between 1472-1474 CE; both Palkhor Tsuglagkhang and Kumbum were reportedly constructed by Prince Rab-brtan-kun-bzang (c. 1389-1442 CE) {Ricca and Lo Bue 1993}. The plan of Kumbum is about 170' east-west and 166' north-south with the main entrance in the south; there are no known relics or *tsha-tsha*s interred in this *chorten*. It has eight stories: (4) in the diminishing terraces with the bottom terrace serving as an elevated parapeted *pradaksina* path and a stereobate for the superstructure, (1) in the slightly slanted drum-shaped dome (*bum-pa*), (1) in the *harmika*, (1) in the upturning lotus above the *harmika*, and (1) inside the gilt conical *chattravali*. The *chorten* is crowned with an umbrella and terminates in a gilt *gujar* finial; it is about 136' high having a total of seventy-five temples and chapels on the eight floors. There are four two-storied high temples in the four cardinal points on the first and third stories and these are accompanied by smaller one-storied chapels. The fenestration is in the form of clerestory windows to bring light into the temples while door openings enable pilgrims to perform *pradaksina* from the outside on the parapet and allow them to ascend to the upper floors via the chapels. The solid core, floors, and staircases of Kumbum are constructed of green bricks, with the exception of the staircases above the *bum-pa* which are a combination of bricks and timber or all timber. The structural system of the terraces conforms to the traditional Tibetan flat-roofed adobe construction as in the monasteries {Ricca and Lo Bue 1993: 39-46}. The wooden brackets on the *bum-pa* supporting the gilt metal roof above clearly borrowed from Chinese timber architecture while the *yin-yang* decorative symbols on the parapet bands also originated in China. The bulged and gilt *chattravali* on a lotus base, the gilt *gujar* finial and umbrella, and the painted eyes on the *harmika* are evidently of Nepalese origins [6.37-6.38]; nonetheless the design of Kumbum essentially conforms to the principles of a Tibetan *chorten*. Some of the most treasured artifacts in Tibet can be found inside this *chorten* including numerous sculptures and murals, which have mostly been painted by the Tibetans and perhaps Nepalese artists as well. Most statues are polychrome clay, with the exception of Vairocana in the *bum-pa* and Vajradhara in the *chattravali* in gilt metal. The murals have been painted on a prepared layer of chalk and plaster, which over the green bricks, and stylistically they exhibit characteristics of a native Tibetan style with a strong influence from the earlier Nepalese-Sakyapa idiom of the Sakyapa Period; there are indications of the Chinese tradition gaining momentum in the Gyantse murals {Ricca and Lo Bue 1993: 52-110}. The iconographies of Kumbum sculptures and murals are distributed progressively from the lower *tantra*s in the bottom floors to the highest *anuttarayoga-tantra* in the topmost floors. The first and second floors contain deities of the *kriya-tantra* and *carya-tantra* comparable to the Theravada and Mahayana traditions including Sakyamuni, Dipankara, Amitayus, Avalokitesvara, Manjursi, Samantabhadra, and Vajrapani. The third and fourth floors alongwith the *bum-pa* are devoted to the *yoga-tantra* deities of the early Vajrayana like Vajrasattva, Prajnaparamita, and the Five Jina Buddhas; the staircase vestibule on the third floor contains murals of the eight *chorten* types. The fourth floor depicts lineages of the Indian and Tibetan masters, kings, and scholars who were instrumental in the propagation of Buddhism into Tibet starting from the seventh century CE. The *harmika* contains demiurgic *yidam* deities of the highest *anuttarayoga-tantra* class and many are shown in *yab-yum* with their *prajna*s including Cakrasamvara, Hevajra, Heruka, Kalacakra, Ratnadaka, and Avalokitapadmamajala. On the topmost floor in the *chattravali* is the statue of Adi-Buddha, Vajradhara, or Vajrasattva who is the primordial Buddha from whom all Jina Buddhas are emanated from {Ricca and Lo Bue 1993: 47-51}; as already noted, Swayambhunath is also an architectural embodiment of Adi-Buddha. Kumbum also symbolically represents Buddha's *Dharmakaya* that guides pilgrims along the path to enlightenment; in fact, it is a type of Chorten of Multiple Auspicious Doors commemorating Buddha's first sermon at Sarnath and therefore personifies the body of his teachings (*Dharma*) or *Dharmakaya*. Kumbum, like Swayambhunath, is also an architectural *mandala*, a device, and a medium that aid Tantric initiates in the process of attaining enlightenment by the means of physically ascending the floors while visualizing the deities and their *mandala*s from the base to the topmost floor.

There were earlier multi-terraced pyramidal *chorten*s and predecessors of Kumbum in Tibet like Jonang (1330-1354 CE) and Gyang (1400-1415 CE), both unfortunately now in ruins {Vitali 1990: 123-133}; a slightly later descendant of Kumbum was Riwoche (1449-1456 CE) which is still in better conditions than Jonang and Gyang. Terraced *chorten*s having multiple openings like Kumbum can also be found in Ladakh like Changspa (thirteenth-fourteenth centuries CE) and Tisseru (c. 1400-1440 CE) {Dorjee 1996: 99-103}{Tucci 1988: 51, 75-76, pl. IV, X, Xia}{Snellgrove and Skorupski 1977-1980 Volume I: 82-83}. In principle, the diminishing multi-terraced design of Kumbum belongs to a similar architectural lineage as Kesariya [6.12], Borobudur [6.28-6.29], and Shwezigon [6.33-6.34]; the Kumbum galleries, unlike Borobudur, are roofed to shelter its priceless arts from the elements. Kumbum essentially exemplifies the Vajrayana concept of gradual spiritual consecration from lower to higher levels of enlightenment by literally ascending the different floors of the *chorten*, which are essentially the manifestations of different *mandala*s. Its artistic and architectural programs not only embody complex Tantric symbolisms but also function as religious instruments complementing Vajrayana consecratory rituals; in fact the Kumbum itself is an architectural *mandala* like Swayambhunath [6.37-6.38]. These quintessentially Vajrayana concepts had already been developed in the Indian Deccan caves of Elora and Orissa *stupa*s and subsequently transmitted to the western Himalaya centers like Tabo in Spiti and Alchi in Ladakh [4.14-4.15]. Kumbum is architecturally a hybrid temple-*chorten* type, or one that combines a temple and a *stupa*, comparable to the central *stupa*-temple of Somapura [4.8] and the Bagan temple-*zedi*s in Myanmar. The gilt *chattravali* set on a lotus base, the painted eyes on the *harmika*, the gilt *gujar* and umbrella are also known Nepalese conventions; lastly, there are indications of Chinese penetration in Kumbum such as the tiered bracketing system on the *bum-pa* and the *yin-yang* symbol.

Chapter 7. Temple

The Buddhist temple is not a sepulchral monument like the *stupa*, which typically inters relics or objects and in most cases can not be entered; it generally houses and displays cult objects and icons including Buddha's aniconic symbols, relics, and most commonly images where devotees can enter in the interior to worship and carry out religious ceremonies. The temple is a product of the religious ideals, nature of worship, and complex iconographical programs of the different Buddhist schools; its forms are therefore functions of the philosophical evolution of the Buddhist religion. There are several important types of Buddhist temples:

(a) Early Indian Buddhist temples [7.1-7.7] up to the third century CE were generally of an isolated type constructed for the worship of relics or aniconic symbols of Buddhas.

(b) The appearance of the anthropomorphic Buddha image in the first century CE eventually replaced all aniconic symbols of Buddha inside the sanctum sanctorum of the Buddhist temple. No where in the Buddhist world was this change more obvious than in the Mahabodhi Temple where a later Iconic temple (*pratimagriha*) housing a Buddha image [7.9-7.11] replaced an earlier Aniconic temple [7.6-7.7] that originally housed a *vajrasana* throne and the *bodhi*-tree. Aniconic worship had exclusively been practiced in India with a few cases in Sri Lanka and Gandhara; in virtually all other Asian Buddhist countries iconic worship, for which the *pratimagriha* had been created, was the only form of worship they had ever known. The *pratimagriha* typically housed a main Buddha image in the center and might be flanked by additional Buddhist acolytes like the *bodhisattva*s; the type emerged as soon as the first Buddha images had been created in the first century CE and it can be of isolated constructions [7.9-7.11] or integral parts of the monastic plan [4.4 (# 3, 12-14)].

(c) In the subsequent centuries a new type of temple appeared or the *stupa*-temple hybrid that combined the forms and functions of the *stupa* and the *pratimagriha*; this type might contain Buddha images and inter or display relics. It could be erected as an isolated structure, as in the cases of the Chinese pagodas [6.20-6.21] and many Bagan temples in Myanmar [7.14-7.15], or integral parts of a monastery like the central *stupa*-temple of Somapura [4.8].

(d) The latest and certainly the most important development of the Buddhist temple was the terraced mountain temple which was generally constructed on a grand scale; these gigantic temples are commonly found in Southeast Asia like Candi Sewu [7.12-7.13] in Java and Bayon of Angkor Thom [7.16-7.17] in Kampuchea.

Most early Buddhist temples were constructed of timber, adobe, or wattle-and-daub [7.1-7.7] and gradually switched to brick while stone was the latest material to be employed in temple construction; the temples were often covered in plaster or stucco finishes and surface embellishments such as moldings and murals. The forms of the Buddhist temple have been shaped by indigenous and foreign elements as much as the religious, particularly Buddhism, and secular ones; thus the East Asian timber pagoda [6.20-6.21] was obviously conceptualized as a Buddhist edifice and modeled entirely after secular Chinese architecture. The Javanese Buddhist *candi*s [7.12-7.13] combined features from the South Indian Dravida Hindu *ratha* and Indian Buddhist temples while Bagan Buddhist temples in Myanmar [7.14-7.15] also fused many elements from the North Indian Nagara Hindu *sikhara* into their designs; the Khmer Buddhist temple [7.16-7.17] also contained features from both the South Indian *ratha* and the North Indian *sikhara*. These cases are not unanticipated since many of these Southeast Asian countries began as Hindu countries or populated largely by Hindus and many have not been converted to Buddhism until at a very late stage; hence syncretism, whether in religion, arts, and architecture, had not been deemed as sacrilegious in these countries. Architecturally, the most uniquely Buddhist designs are the cruciform and quincunxial (*pancayatana*) designs as in Caityas 3, 12 at Nalanda [4.4 (# 3, 12)] and the central temples of Sarnath [8.5], Candi Sewu, Ananda Temple [7.14-7.15], and Bayon of Angkor Thom, alongwith the straight-edged pyramidal tower as in the Mahabodhi Temple [7.10-7.11]. These types already had earlier antecedents in the Buddhist Kushan and Gandhara architecture [6.14, 6.17-6.18, 7.9], which subsequently became very influential in India and Southeast Asia.

1. Early Indian Buddhist Temples (third century BCE-seventh centuries CE) - India, Pakistan, Sri Lanka

It is often true in Buddhist architecture that its monasteries, rock-hewn caves, and *stupa*s are better known and widely documented than its temples and when studied by scholars there were barely enough details and frequently treated as if an offshoot of Hindu architecture. But make no mistakes, the Buddhist temple has developed its own independent architectural language since the earliest days and profoundly influenced the forms of many early Hindu temples; moreover, the oldest extant Buddhist temples and foundations also predate any Hindu examples. Even great pioneering architect-scholar like James Fergusson also made some hasty conclusions {Agrawala 1968: 2-3}:

> The Buddhists very early adopting the mode of excavating their temples in the living rock their remains are imperishably preserved to us, while it is only too probably that those of the Hindu, being in less durable forms, have disappeared.

It is undeniable that early temples, whether Buddhist or Hindu, had been constructed in timber but it makes no sense to presume that the Buddhists were busy constructing their temples in brick and stone while the Hindus were building theirs in timber; Fergusson also apparently did not even distinguish between the rock-hewn caves and structural temples. The abundance in extant remains of early Buddhist monuments compared to the virtual absence of Hindu examples can be explained due to the facts that Buddhism historically received immense patronage from the population and the royalty since Asoka's time; in any case, further discussions about the Hindu temple and its relations with the Buddhist temple are not the main concern of this book. The fact is that early Indian architecture, whether secular or religious and Buddhist, Hindu, or Jain, was essentially identical in forms and it was probably not until Asoka's time that it began to develop architectural sectarianism. As already stated, during the Vedic Period the Indians adhered to a form of primitive Hinduism, which was a fusion of foreign (Aryan) and native elements; the former was based on the worship of natural gods like Surya, Agni, Indra, etc. while the latter belonged to shamanistic and animistic cults of local deities and spirits like the *yaksa*, *yaksi*, *deva*, *devata*, *naga*, *linga*, etc. Simple timber shrines were no doubt constructed for these deities and probably their effigies but no extant examples have been documented due to the perishability of timber. On the other hand, the Buddhists have been credited for the introduction of new forms of worship and their associative architecture as distinct from other Indian indigenous cults and religions. Even during Buddha's lifetime he had already been considered not simply as a charismatic founder of a famed religion but also as a superhuman worthy of worship with all due reverence equal that of a god; the places intimately associated with his life (Chapter 8) became holy shrines where devotees came to worship and certainly seek favorable boons. Other important and sacred items personally linked with Buddha's life such as his begging bowl, corporal relics, the *vajrasana* (Seat of Enlightenment or Diamond Throne), *bodhi*-tree, etc. also became the objects of veneration and shrines and temples would be constructed for them; these constituted the aniconic worship and their associative Aniconic architecture. They would be phased out by the third century CE and replaced with the iconic worship of Buddha and *bodhisattva* images and their associative architecture, which certainly appeared as early as the first century CE. The type of Buddhist temples dedicated to both aniconic and iconic worships was commonly referred to as a *caitya* (a holy shrine), a definition also encompassing the *stupa* and the *pratimagriha*. In India, the Buddhist temples are usually found in a monastic complex alongside with the other building types as in Nalanda [4.4 (#3, 12-14)].

Construction materials in early Indian architecture were mostly timber in combination with wattle-and-daub. By Asoka's time in the third century BCE a mixture of brick and timber construction, which would often be covered in several thick layers of plaster, gradually replaced timber construction; the temples at Bairat [7.1] and Ter [7.2-7.3] as well as the multi-storied towers [7.4-7.5] are the best examples of this type of construction. Stone was also employed in construction, often without the plaster coatings, probably as early as brick from the numerous rock-hewn *caityagriha*s in Bihar [5.1-5.2] and the Deccan [5.3]; the oldest extant freestanding stone Buddhist temples dated in the Gupta Dynasty in the fifth century CE like Sanchi Temple 17. Brick-and-plaster construction frequently occurred in Buddhist monuments from the first century CE on as in the Mahabodhi Temple [7.9-7.11] and Nalanda *caitya*s [4.4 (#3, 12-14)]; the interiors of Indian Buddhist temples were usually embellished with beautiful murals but none survives to this day. From the available data, it can be deduced that the dome [7.1], apsidal [4.1] and barrel vaults [7.2-7.3] were the common technologies in Indian architecture certainly dated as early as the Vedic Period upto the Kushan Dynasty; the most ubiquitous architectural element in early Indian Buddhist architecture was the *caitya*-arch [5.8]. These gradually phased out and to be replaced with the flat roof in early Gupta temples [7.2-7.3], although the *caitya*-arch continued to occur in rock-hewn caves until the end of the Gupta Dynasty. Among the most influential features developed during this second phase of the Buddhist temple are the quincunxial (*pancayatana*) and cruciform designs alongwith the straight-edged pyramidal tower [4.4

(#3, 12), 8.5 (main temple)]. The arch-and-vault, particularly the pointed arch, would be increasingly employed in many temples to bear heavier loads, especially in the Bagan temples of Myanmar, as the dome disappeared altogether from Buddhist architecture.

There are three main sources for the study and classification of early Buddhist temples including the archaeological remains, sculptural reliefs on early Indian *stupa*s, and rock-hewn caves. Their typologies are grouped according to the forms of worship and chronological sequences.

(a) Temples Based on Aniconic Worship (sixth century BCE-third centuries CE)

This type was generally constructed for the worship of Buddha's aniconic symbols like the *vajrasana*, *bodhi*-tree, *stupa*, *Buddhapada*, *dharmacakra*, flaming pillar, etc.; these temples are exclusively found in India with a few rare cases in Gandhara and Sri Lanka.

1. *Bodhigriha*

   The *bodhi*-tree is easily the most recognizable Buddhist symbol associated with Buddha and it is also intimately linked with the *vajrasana* or the seat under this very tree where he sat on the eve of his enlightenment in Bodhgaya. Ananda Coomaraswamy simply termed the worship of the holy *bodhi*-tree as 'tree-worship' and he did not specify the origin of this practice {Coomaraswamy 1992: 19-21}; in my view, it could have been originated in the religious practices of the Harappans as depicted on their seals. Already in Buddha's time, branches of the famed *bodhi*-tree in Bodhgaya had been planted throughout Bihar; an enclosure or *vedika* would typically be constructed around it to protect its sanctity and consequently transformed it into a *bodhigriha* (a *bodhi*-tree house or shrine). In the subsequent centuries, foreign pilgrims would often come to Bodhgaya to obtain its saplings to be planted in their country. The first Buddhist missionary to Sri Lanka in the third century BCE reputedly brought a sapling of the *bodhi*-tree to the island where a *bodhigriha* was built for it; many *bodhigriha*s continued to be erected in Sri Lanka as late as the eighth century CE as the one in the central precinct of Vijayarama [4.9]. The Indian Emperor Asoka probably constructed the first permanent galleried *bodhigriha* in Bodhgaya, which would later be transformed into the Mahabodhi Temple [7.9-7.11], but none of this original edifice remains {Coomaraswamy 1992: 19-21}. The first known depiction of the *bodhigriha* in Bodhgaya [7.6-7.7] was on a Bharhut relief showing a simple colonnaded building encircling the *bodhi*-tree and the *vajrasana*; the structure might have been enclosed by a wooden *vedika* but only its stone replacement survives [7.8].

2. *Caityagriha*

   As already studied in Chapter 6, the *stupa* was a type of monument originally built to inter the corporal remains of Buddha and his disciples. With the development of the temple, a *stupa* would also be incorporated into the plan and consequently transformed it into an aniconic symbol representing Buddha's invisible holy presence and his *Parinirvana* that reminded devotees of the impermanence of life. This type of edifice is called a *caityagriha* (a *caitya*-house); there are two basic types: rock-hewn [5.3-5.5, 5.7-5.11] and freestanding *caityagriha*s [7.1] and apsidal variant [7.2-7.3]. In all these cases, there is a symbolic *stupa* in the back of the apsidal end or in the center of the circular plan as the main cult object and a continuous *pradaksina* path on the aisles would be provided for ritualized circumambulation. Freestanding circular temples had been constructed as far as Sri Lanka like Thuparama [6.26-6.27] while the freestanding apsidal temples were more widespread and dated as early as the circular type. Freestanding apsidal *caityagriha*s are only found in India and Gandhara including the oldest example like Sanchi Temple 40 (third century BCE) and the latest Nagarjunakonda (third century CE) in India with the largest at Sirkap (c. 30 BCE-50 CE) in Taxila. The forms of the circular and apsidal *caityagriha*s had likely been derived from early Indian timber models [4.1, 5.1] but the first prototypes were probably not developed until the third century BCE when the *stupa* cult was given a tremendous boost by Emperor Asoka.

3. Tower Temples

   Among the carvings on early Indian Buddhist *stupa*s are depictions of tall towers [7.4-7.5] likely of timber-and-plaster construction dated between the first century BCE-first centuries CE but unfortunately no extant examples have survived {Agrawala 1968: 11}; these have octagonal and square plans possibly built to display relics or holy objects as shown on the top floor in [7.4]. India certainly constructed multi-storied buildings as evident from the depictions of secular multi-storied structures on early Indian *stupa*s [6.5].

(b) Temples Based on Iconic Worship (first century CE)

The invention of the anthropomorphic Buddha and *bodhisattva* images in the first century CE ushered in a new era in the religious worship with icons gradually replacing aniconic symbols as the main cult objects in the temple sanctum sanctorums; the *pratimagriha* began to supplant the *bodhigriha* and *caityagriha* throughout the Buddhist world. In India, the *pratimagriha* are commonly found in major Buddhist centers like the *caitya*s of Nalanda [4.4 (#3, 12-14)], Lumbini, Bodhgaya, Sarnath, and Kushinagar (Chapter 8); in the regions like East and Southeast Asia, due to the late arrival of Buddhism only the iconic worship and the *pratimagriha*s were constructed. In the case of the Mahabodhi Temple, a new *pratimagriha* [7.9] had been built around the second century CE to house a Buddha image in its sanctum and replaced the obsolete *bodhigriha* [7.6-7.7] and aniconic worship. The oldest extant freestanding Buddhist *pratimagriha* in India is Sanchi Temple 17 (c. 400-425 CE) which predates any Hindu temples {Deva 1995 Volume I-II: 13, pl. 5}.

* * *

Bairat [7.1] is among the earliest freestanding circular Buddhist *caityagriha*s in India from the fact that an Asoka edict has been found nearby; however only the outline of its brick foundation remains. The temple, which is enclosed in a 20'3" x 28'7" rectangular wall, has an outer diameter of 17'5", inner diameter of 11'5", and a *stupa* of about 5' diameter in the center. Its concentric plan creates two *pradaksina* paths that are higher than the ground floor on the outside for worshipers to perform ritualized circumambulation around the *stupa*. The temple has a brick foundation with its walls and dome likely originally constructed of wattle-and-daub; the inner wall, which encircles the *stupa* in the center, is a colonnade of brick piers alternated with octagonal timber columns. The original 6' high *stupa* was evidently stone since broken pieces of its *yasti-chattra* bearing a 'typical Mauryan polish' have been found among the debris {Sarkar 1966: 25-26}; its form was certainly similar to the *caityagriha stupa*s in the Deccan caves as in Kondivte [5.3]. The restored elevation of Bairat is about 19' high and it probably has two tiers with the main quadrantal-vaulted lower one surmounted by a dome that terminates in a finial; originally its might be embellished with murals. The form of Bairat most likely resembles similar shrines as depicted on the Bharhut reliefs {Coomaraswamy 1992: 108, fg. 6}; note that Percy Brown's reconstruction {Brown 1965: pl. VI} is slightly different from the Bharhut reliefs and my own reconstruction. The source of this circular temple has been suggested as originated from the Greek peripteral temples {Sarkar 1966: 27}{Fletcher 1975: 202, fg. 203 E-F}; however, ancient circular timber huts certainly existed in India long before the Indian contacts with the Greeks and likely the prototype for Bairat {Sarkar 1966: 27-28}{Coomaraswamy 1992: 106-107}. Almost con-

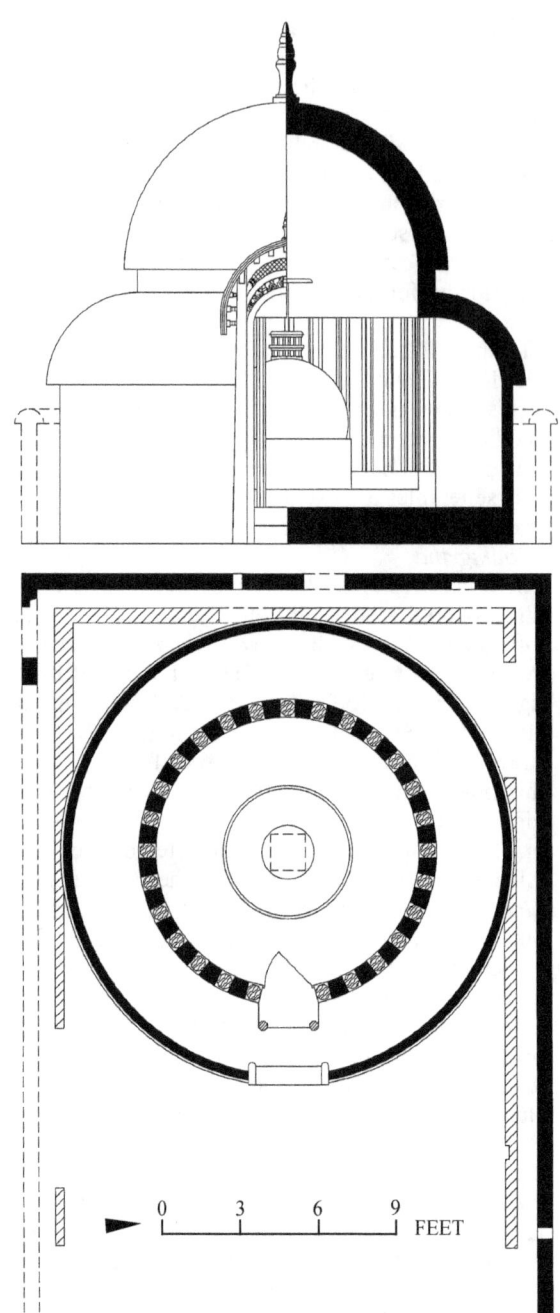

7.1. Bairat Temple plan and elevation-section (restored)
c. 250-200 BCE
Bairat- India

temporary or slightly later than Bairat were similar circular rock-hewn *caityagriha*s in Junnar-Tuljalena 3 and Guntupalli. Structural circular *caityagriha*s like Bairat were not widespread in India or foreign countries; a few rare examples were constructed in Sri Lanka like Thuparama [6.26-6.27] and Miran in Tukistan, which were no doubt derived from the Indian prototypes like Bairat.

* * *

Rock-hewn and freestanding apsidal *caityagriha*s were the most common type of Buddhist temples in India and Gandhara before the Gupta Dynasty; the popularity of the apsidal design may certainly be attributed to its pre-eminence in Indian timber architecture [4.1]. A typical example of the freestanding type is Ter Temple [7.2-7.3] originally only included the apsidal structure in the back; the flat-roofed *mandapa* (hall) and exterior pilasters and moldings were probably added in the sixth century CE after its conversion into a Hindu temple, during which the original Buddhist *stupa* in the back was removed {Agrawala 1968: 59-60}. The main 18'5" x 29'5" apsidal and barrel-vaulted sanctuary in the back of about 35' high is preceded by a 31'2" square and columned *mandapa* of about 17'4" high having a lantern ceiling of a Central Asian origin in the center; continuous moldings define the roof and base. The facade of the apsidal end is a large *caitya*-arch derived from rock-hewn *caityagriha*s [5.8] having an image niche in the center; with the exception of the now vanished *stupa*, which was undoubtedly originally constructed in stone, the building was constructed of brick and finished in plaster. No surface ornamentation has been detected in this temple unlike the similar Chezarla Temple, which has elaborate decorations. As stated earlier, among the earliest freestanding apsidal temples in India is Sanchi Temple 40 (third century BCE) and such apsidal structures were common in earlier Indian architecture like Jivakavanarama [4.1]. The apsidal end of the Ter Temple was probably contemporary with the huge apsidal temple at Sirkap (c. 30 BCE-50 CE) in Taxila. The apsidal design had also been imitated many early Hindu temples at Aihole and Mamallapuram, both dated in the seventh century CE {Agrawala 1968: 61}{Deva 1995: pl. 304A}.

* * *

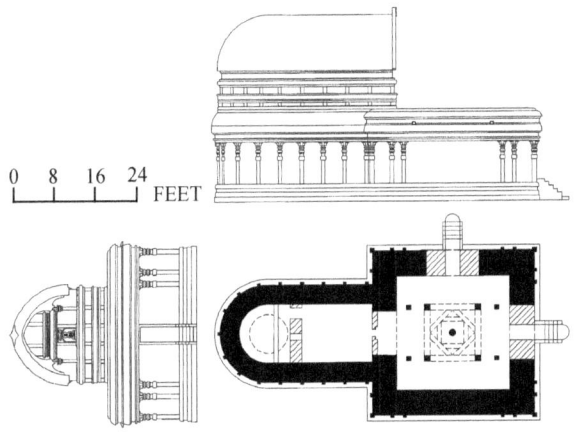

7.2. Front/side elevations and plan
First century BCE-sixth centuries CE
Ter- India

7.3. Ter Temple
First century BCE-sixth centuries CE
Ter- India

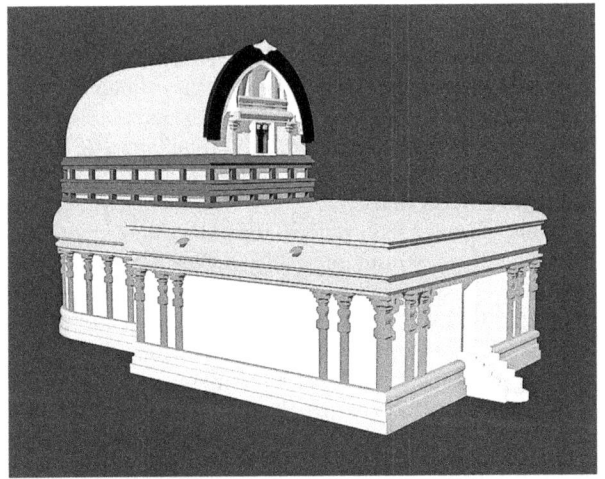

Among the fragments of sculpted reliefs recovered from several Buddhist sites show multi-storied or multi-tiered structural temples [7.4-7.5], which likely existed as early as the first century BCE {Coomaraswamy 1992: 116-118}. The sacred relic container is clearly shown in the center of the top story in [7.4] with celestial figures hovering above its roof (not shown in the drawing) as typical in the depictions of holy shrines; the interior and its stories are clearly accessible from the depiction. These two multi-storied towers have octagonal plans or square bases that turn octagonal in the upper levels and there are projecting balconies on the upper floors supported by columns alongwith *caitya*-arched dormers and grille-like windows; they have ribbed roofs that terminate in finials. My estimate of their heights is between 40'-60' and I have no doubt that these towers were common in contemporary architecture, religious or secular. They were likely constructed of timber and wattle-and-daub for the walls and roofs with brick or stone foundations;

7.4. Relief of a multi-storied temple (*left*)
First century BCE
Ghantasala Stupa, Ghantasala- India
Musee Guimet, Paris- France

7.5. Relief of a multi-storied tower (*right*)
Late first century CE
Mathura- India
Mathura Musuem, Mathura- India

sculptural reliefs, wood carvings, and complex bracketing systems were probably standard in these towers as shown in [7.5]. It is unfortunate that none of these early elegant towers survive but their marked emphasis on the verticality might have been absorbed by Gandhara architecture in its tower *stupa*s [6.18] and the Mahabodhi Temple in India [7.9-7.11]. The Chinese masonry pagodas [6.24-6.25] also inherited a few elements from these Indian towers such as the octagonal plan; however, early secular Chinese architecture already developed towering pavilions of its own [6.19] that dated as early as these Indian counterparts.

2. Mahabodhi Temple (c. 260 BCE-1450 CE) - India

The magnificent Mahabodhi Temple [7.6-7.11, 8.3-8.4] is situated about seven miles south of Gaya and undoubtedly the most eminent and holiest of all Indian Buddhist monuments as it was here that Prince Siddhartha Gautama attained the great Enlightenment under the *bodhi*-tree in c. 532 BCE and became a Buddha. The site has been known for a long time as Bodhgaya or Buddha-Gaya denoting Buddha's hermitage near the village of Urel (ancient Uruvela) on the west bank of the Phalgu River, a tributary of the Nilajana River (ancient Neranjara), all have been well documented in ancient Buddhist scriptures. An Asoka inscription mentioned a visit and conversion of Emperor Asoka to Buddhism in c. 260 BCE at *Sambodhi* (Perfect Enlightenment) and during this occasion he ordered the construction of the first *caitya* here; when Hsuan-tsang visited the temple in the seventh century CE it was known as *Mahabodhi* (Great Enlightenment) {Cunningham 1961: 2-3}{Ahir 1994: 10-13}. From Buddha's time to Asoka's, Bodhgaya was practically unknown to the outside world until the emperor's conversion to Buddhism, which instantly elevated the site as an internationally preeminent one. Thereafter, its fame continued to spread and a constant stream of Buddhists from all over India and Asia continued to arrive at the temple and Bodhgaya over the centuries where they built many monasteries, *stupa*s, temples, etc. (Chapter 8). In the past famous Buddhist pandits and pilgrims including famed Indians and foreigners like Fa-hsien, Hsuan-tsang, I-tsing, Atisa, and Dharmasvamin had studied and prostrated in the temple in reverence to Buddha's Enlightenment and for the accruement of religious merits. The site, due to its distinction among Buddhist monuments, has also attracted jealousy from rival faiths and foreign invaders who from time to time would cause numerous desecrations to it. The first incidence is believed to have been instigated by Asoka's second Queen Tishyaraksita who was jealous of the emperor's devotion to the *bodhi*-tree and cut it down in a rage; but it was later miraculously restored. Taranatha stated that the site had been destroyed by a western King Hunimanta in the first century CE; Cunningham, however, believed that this king might have been the great Buddhist persecutor Miharakula (r. 515-533 CE). The *bodhi*-tree was surely deracinated by the local Hindu Raja Sasanka in the early seventh century CE as this incidence was mentioned by Hsuan-tsang; fortunately, the temple was reportedly spared from this destruction. The sacred tree, or its sapling, was again replanted by King Purnavarman (c. 600-620 CE) shortly after and he also constructed a 24' high wall to deter future desecration {Cunningham 1961: 2-3, 30-31}{Ahir 1994: 63-64}. A series of destructive Muslim invasions around c. 1200 CE destroyed virtually all Buddhist monasteries in northern India and famed sites like Bodhgaya would probably suffer the same fate. However, eyewitness accounts by Dharmasvamin (in India c. 1234-1236 CE) stated that the Mahabodhi Temple had been walled up to deceive the Muslims that it had already been abandoned; after the menace was over the Buddhists returned to reopen the temple {Ahir 1994: 70}. Thus it might have been spared from the worst of the destructions under the Muslims' hands though the site, and

Indian Buddhism, drastically declined afterward and eventually withered away; the last renovation of the temple was recorded between c. 1302-1331 CE about the paving of granite slabs. A final record on the temple was the visit of its abbot Sakyasri Sariputra to Gyantse Monastery in Tibet in 1414 CE who had been previously invited by the Chinese Ming Emperor Yongle to his court a year before {Ricca and Lo Bue 1993: 19, 25}{Schroeder 2006: 192}; then a long silence afterward as the site was totally abandoned and left to ruin. Thus in reality the disappearance of Buddhism in India actually was around the mid fifteenth century CE while pockets of Buddhist communities lingered longer in South India until the sixteenth-seventeenth centuries CE as in Nagapattinam likely thanks to their proximity to the Buddhist country of Sri Lanka {Kim 1997: 219-221}. The remaining chapter in the history of the temple was intertwined with the struggle for the revival of Buddhism in the land of its birth and the awakening of the Indian consciousness on the Buddhist contributions to its heritage. By the sixteenth century CE, the temple had apparently been deserted for a long time when a Hindu Sivaite Mahant named Gosain Ghamandi Giri stumbled upon the peaceful ruins in 1590 CE where he decided to settle down. The site subsequently became the Mahants' possession until 1949 CE; they certainly knew the history of this great Buddhist site but they were determined to transform it into a Hindu one. On the other hand, the evidences suggesting the Mahants' willful sacrilege of this holy Buddhist site might have been overly exaggerated by some scholars; Buddha had already been declared as the ninth avatar of Visnu and the *bodhi*-tree was also devoutly worshipped by Hindus when Francis Buchanan Hamilton visited it in 1811 CE. It was not until some times after he left that the Mahants finally decided to convert it into a Siva temple; they replaced the original Pala Buddha image, which was then still sitting inside the sanctum sanctorum, with a *linga* which, according to Rajendralal Mitra, was actually a 'big votive *stupa*' {Ahir 1994: 75-77}. In fact had the Mahants not occupied the temple, it would probably have ended up as a local quarry for the villagers to collect available building materials for their various construction projects; the Ter [7.2-7.3] and Chezarla temples have been appropriated by Hindus and are still standing today while unattended *stupa*s like Bharhut, Amaravati, and Dharmarajika at Sarnath have utterly been ripped apart for building materials. Moreover, fortunately the Buddhist devouts in the neighboring Myanmar also did not entirely forget their Mahabodhi Temple for it was they who were mostly responsible for the major restorations between the eleventh-fourteenth centuries CE; after a long hiatus they again made contacts with their beloved temple in the nineteenth century CE. Initially Myanmar sent several missions for minor repairs of the temple between 1810-1823 CE and after a long negotiation with the Mahants the Myanmaris, who were sent by King Mindon-Min of Bagan, finally sought for a full restoration in 1877 CE; the work, however, suffered a complete halt in 1878 CE when the king died {Ahir 1994: 83-87}. Previously there were already limited excavations at the site by Major Meade in 1861 CE but obviously he did not focus on restoration. When the father of Indian archaeology Alexander Cunningham arrived, first in 1861 CE and later in 1879 CE, the temple had already suffered serious decays with the front pavilions, four corner turrets, and finial had already collapsed while parts of the central tower were also seriously damaged. The Myanmaris' 1877-1878 CE missions did not complete their restorative works and Cunningham, after recognizing this important gem in the architectural and cultural history of India, recommended the continuation of its full restoration. In 1880 CE, J. D. Beglar was appointed as the project restorer and construction superintendent who was probably responsible for all on-site supervisions and decisions; Cunningham was probably the project manager than directly involved in any actual works at the site. The momentous task was completed in the 1880s CE and what we see of the impeccable temple today has been the result of this skillful restoration; the missing Pala Buddha image was also recovered from the Mahants' compound and again reinstalled in its original place while the *linga* had also been covered up. The immaculate restoration instantly revived the Buddhist spirit in the Mahabodhi Temple and it also inaugurated the next phase in its history, which was the struggle for its return to the Buddhist control. The costly and beautifully restored temple immediately became a fresh property in the Mahants' hands and the British colonial government; nevertheless, this was an important first step in loosening the Mahants' grip on the temple {Ahir 1994: 89-94}. Edwin Arnold, who wrote a moving eulogy to Buddha in his acclaimed 'The Light of Asia,' visited and paid homage to the site in 1885 CE; from then on until 1893 CE he campaigned unsuccessfully for the return of the site to the Buddhists. His spirited plea inspired new generations of devout Buddhists to take up the cause and one of them was a determined Sri Lankan lay Buddhist named Anagarika Dharmapala, who was later ordained as a monk. His heroic and peaceful struggle, often in adverse conditions facing physical violence and death from Hindu extremists, lasted between c. 1891-1933 CE. Though he did not succeed in dislodging the Mahants but many Buddhist sites like

Sarnath was eventually won and turned over to the Buddhists' supervision; the construction of the Mulagandhakuti Vihara still standing at Sarnath was originally inaugurated by Dharmapala in 1931 CE. After India regained its independence a legislation, the Bodhgaya Temple Act, was passed in 1949 CE which decreed that the control of the temple was to be managed by a government-appointed committee of nine Indians including a Hindu chairman and district magistrate of Gaya, four Hindus including the Mahants, and four Buddhists; the status remains to this day. The conversion of B. R. Ambedkar and half a million of his Indian followers to Buddhism also attracted much attention and greatly boosted the Buddhist revival movement in India {Ahir 1994: 95-143}.

Before going into the discussions on the architecture, I will give a brief survey on the sculptures and inscriptions at the site; other architectural remains around and outside the main temple compound will be covered in Chapter 8. The oldest sculpture is certainly the polished sandstone *vajrasana* (c. 250-233 BCE) that contain carvings of pecking geese and honeysuckles as also observed on the Asoka pillars [3.5]. Since the *vajrasana* has carvings on all sides, the original Asoka *bodhigriha* must have been open on all sides as depicted in the Bharhut relief [7.6-7.7]; architecturally the structure was a *hammiya*. Originally the *vajrasana* was found inside the temple hidden beneath the pedestal of the current Buddha statue; it was subsequently moved outdoor to the back of the temple when the latter was converted from a *bodhigriha* to a *pratimagriha*, which was around the second century CE but certainly before Hsuan-tsang's visit in c. 637 CE when he saw it in the current location {Cunningham 1961: iii, 1, 4-5}. The oldest extant image at Bodhgaya is a Buddha statue dated in 384 CE alongwith a few Gupta sculptures dated no later than the seventh century CE; most of the remaining sculptures were carved in the Pala Dynasty (c. 750-1199 CE). The iconography of these later images consists of Buddhas and *bodhisattva*s of mostly Avalokitesvara, Manjusri, and Tara; the current Sakyamuni statue inside the main chamber in the *bhumisparsa-mudra*, the most common type of Pala Buddha images, has been dated in the late tenth century CE. Vajrayana sculptures of Yamari, Trailokavijaya, etc. had also been carved in increasing numbers at Bodhgaya from the ninth century CE on reflecting the rise of this Tantric school in eastern India {Leoshko 1988: 30-59}. There are about thirty-six inscriptions and mason marks found at the site mainly around the temple and *stupa* court; the oldest inscriptions in Brahmi are on the stone *vedika* with some from a local royal family. Of all inscriptions, there is (1) from Sri Lanka mentioning the donation of a *suchi* dated in the first century BCE, (5) belonging to Chinese pilgrims in the eleventh century CE, and (3) from Myanmar in the eleventh century CE; the remainings are Indian inscriptions dated between the first century BCE-thirteenth centuries CE {Cunningham 1961: 15-16, 56-79}{Barua 1975 Volume II: 65-76}{Leoshko 1988: 107}{Ahir 1994: 72}.

The Mahabodhi Temple complex in Bodhgaya encompasses two main areas: (a) The central one consisting of the temple [7.6-7.7, 7.9-7.11], stone *vedika* [7.8], *bodhi*-tree, and *vajrasana* and (b) the peripheral area [8.3-8.4] (Chapter 8); their original positions and designs have changed considerably over the centuries reflecting the continuing evolution in Buddhism and its architecture. In order to verify precisely the construction phases and architectural modifications of the Mahabodhi Temple over the centuries alongwith the authenticity of J. D. Beglar's restoration, it is crucial to analyze the archaeological evidences, site reports, and surveys by British archaeologists as well as travelogues from early Buddhist pilgrims like Fa-Hsien and Hsuan-tsang. As already mentioned, Emperor Asoka reputedly constructed the first temple at Bodhgaya in c. 260 BCE after his Buddhist conversion. The polished sandstone *vajrasana* slab dated in Asoka's time was originally found on top a stone throne hidden behind a larger second throne of the Early Kushan Dynasty; the latter would in turn be covered by yet another bigger third throne of the medieval period or possibly Pala Dynasty. Behind the original Asoka *vajrasana* must have once stood the *bodhi*-tree and Asoka's temple was likely a *bodhigriha* similar to the one shown in the Bharhut relief [7.6]; a Brahmi inscription on this relief clearly identifies it as the temple at Bodhgaya. Cunningham believed the depicted building in this Bharhut relief was the original Asoka temple and his hypothesis was based on the findings of pot-shaped column bases near the first throne that he dated in Asoka's time {Cunningham 1961: 4-7}. However, stylistically these pot columns likely dated in the first century BCE due to their similarity with those in the Karla caves [5.7, 5.9]. The remaining row of similar pot column bases can still be seen in the Buddha's Walk on the north side of the current temple, which also have mason marks paleographically dated in the first century BCE {Barua 1975: 66, 75-76}; the presence of remaining column bases suggests that this walkway was originally covered with a timber roof, which is further corroborated with the depiction on the Bharhut relief {Cunningham 1961: pl. V}. This *bodhigriha* in the Bharhut relief [7.6-7.7] was a Shunga building of a circular plan probably about 40' x 40' and it might originally have been enclosed by a 57' x 73' *vedika*. Cunningham's re-

Part II. Architecture   Temple . 241

7.6. Relief of Mahabodhi Temple
c. 125-100 BCE
Bharhut Stupa, Bharhut- India
Kolkata Museum, Kolkata- India

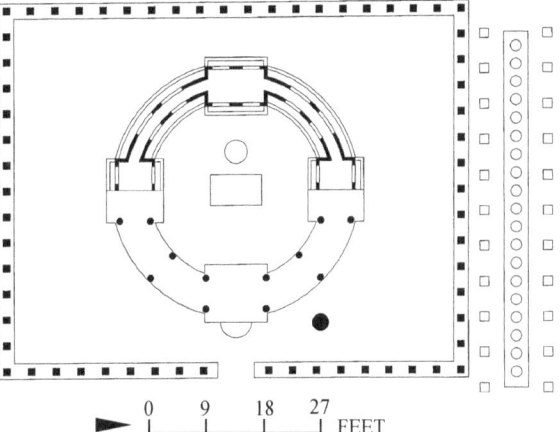

7.7. Mahabodhi Temple plan after [7.6]
c. 125-100 BCE
Bodhgaya- India

7.8. Ground *vedika*
c. 60 BCE
Mahabodhi Temple, Bodhgaya- India

stored plan of this temple, however, showed a cruciform plan that apparently did not match the circular building shown on the relief; my conjecturally restored plan combines Coomaraswamy's slightly modified circular plan with Cunningham's enclosure {Cunningham 1961: pl II} {Coomaraswamy 1992: fg. 37}. The relief depicts worshipers paying homage to the *vajrasana* and *bodhi*-tree, which is clearly enclosed inside a two-storied building; the ground floor is an open colonnaded circular hall while the upper story consists of projecting balconied modules in the center that divide that plan into quadrants, all having *caitya*-arched dormers and openings. The columns on the ground floor were likely stone while the upper story was probably timber and wattle-and-daub construction; the module in the center has a rounded chamfered mansard-typed roof while the side wings have vaulted roofs. From the relief, the *vajrasana* appears to be positioned in the center of the hypaethral *bodhigriha* and the *bodhi*-tree can clearly be seen rising behind the *vajrasana* above the roof; whistling *deva*s and hovering *kinnara*s worship the *vajrasana* and *bodhi*-tree from above with garlands in their hands. The Asoka pillar of an elephant crown in the relief is no longer traceable; the current Asoka pillar at the Lotus Tank to the south of the temple was removed from Gaya in 1956 CE {Ahir 1994: 137}. Thus the original Asoka temple first constructed by Asoka in c. 260 BCE, which was likely of a timber and wattle-and-daub building, is probably architecturally not the one depicted in the Bharhut relief; the latter temple, if it existed at all, was probably of stone and timber that replaced the original Asoka temple and certainly dated contemporary with Bharhut (c. 125-100 BCE). In the first century BCE, another renovation was initiated in which the Buddha's Walk was roofed over and supported by a stone colonnade whilst the original wooden *vedika* was replaced with a stone one **[7.8]** {Cunningham 1961: 8-10, 11-14}. This *vedika* has carvings of lotus medallions and half-medallions, figures, *jataka*s, etc. and is stylistically and chronologically between the Sanchi *torana*s **[6.4]** and Bharhut **[6.7]**. Mason marks, pot column bases, and *vedika* all have been dated in the first century BCE or c. 60 BCE {Barua 1975: 66, 75-76} {Marshall 1983 Volume I: 263-281}; the form of the original Asoka temple or the *bodhigriha* on the Bharhut relief remained unchanged during this renovation.

There is evidence that in the second century CE the earlier *bodhigriha* had been replaced by a truncated pyramidal *pratimagriha* **[7.9]** in the form of a tower as familiar in the later Mahabodhi Temple **[7.10-7.11]**. The construction of this new temple mirrored the changes in Buddhism, from the worship of aniconic symbols to the worship of tangible Buddha images. This might have been influenced by a new architectural direction introduced from Gandhara that would gradually replace the Indian tradition of the *caitya*-arched, apsidal, barrel-vaulted, and domed construction. Though none of the original vestiges of this new building remains, there are a few archaeological evidences strongly corroborating its existence and also giving clues to its original form. Cunningham's excavations discovered a relic deposit in the second plastered throne, which was hidden under the current medieval throne inside the main chamber; it contained a gold coin of King Huvishka (c. 151-185 CE), the successor of King Kanishka, and punch-marked coins contemporary with the Huvishka coin. Moreover a Kushan inscription on the *vedika* also names the temple as 'the Vajrasana Great Gandhakuti Temple' which Cunningham believed to have been inscribed when the new temple was constructed {Cunningham 1961: ii, 4-5, 20-21, 58}. Above all, another important piece of evidence

7.9. Plaque of Mahabodhi Temple
c. 150-200 CE
Kumrahar- India
Patna Museum, Patna- India

strongly suggesting the construction of a new temple is the well-known terracotta plaque from Kumrahar **[7.9]**, which B. M. Barua labeled as a 'spurious, bogus' sample; it was found alongwith a Huvishka coin nearby {Barua 1975: 45-47} {Coomaraswamy and Meister 1992: 105}. The plaque, which has a Buddhist inscription in the Kharosthi script of Gandhara dated in the second century CE, clearly shows a six-tiered straight-edged and truncated pyramidal tower in the center of an enclosed *vedika* that is crowned with *stupa* finial on the summit; repeating rows of small *caitya*-arched niches alternated with colonnette pilasters can be seen on the upper diminishing tiers as in the current Mahabodhi Temple **[7.10-7.11]**. Buddha images can be seen inside the huge arched chamber in the base and on both sides of the tower in which the positions of the latter standing images apparently matched those of the now covered-up twin temples shown on Cunningham's plan. The plaque also has a main gateway on one side as numerous votive *stupa*s and small buildings cluster around the temple and outside the enclosure just like the current plan of the compound [8.3]. A pillar of the Asoka type with an elephant capital to the right of the main entry also matches exactly the pillar in the Bharhut relief [7.6-7.7]; flying *deva*s can be seen paying homage to the temple from above which further confirms its sanctity. Percy Brown's well-known reconstruction of the temple in this plaque incorrectly included a low plinth with stairs on both sides of the entrance but this clearly does not show on the plaque {Brown 1965: pl. XL}. About its materials, I would guess that the *vedika* was stone while the temple itself was likely brick-and-plaster construction as prevalent in contemporary Gandhara architecture. The great arch-and-vault in the temple base and arcaded niches repeated in the upper tiers were also common in Indian [4.1, 5.8] and Gandhara architecture [6.16]. The semicircular arch originated in Assyria and later in Roman architecture {Fletcher 1975: 59-67, 82-84, 261-272}{Rowland 1977: 163-164}{Trachtenberg and Hyman 1986: fg. 206}. The pointed arch, however, originated in India as in the Sitamarhi cave (c. 214-206 BCE) and was employed in structural load-bearing in Gandhara at least in the second century CE as in Takht-i-bahi {ASIAR 1908-1909: 5-16}; it would later be reintroduced back to India as in the Bhirtagaon Temple (c. 450 CE) and possibly also the Mahabodhi Temple. Islamic architecture apparently began to employ the pointed arch at a later time in the eighth century CE while European Gothic architecture first used it in the eleventh century CE. The arch-and-vault system and dome were certainly known in India from at a very early time [4.1, 7.1] but its use was generally limited to non-load bearing functions; its employment in structural supports and load distributions had probably first been introduced in Gandhara. The inspirations for the towering design in the plaque probably originated from both Gandhara [6.18] and early Indian examples [7.4-7.5]. Had it been constructed, its plan would probably be between 30'-50' square and 100'-120' high based on the dimensions of the present temple. Why was the Mahabodhi Temple rebuilt at this time? The Tibetan monk-scholar Taranatha reportedly stated that the site had been destroyed by a western King Hunimanta in the first century CE, which instigated the construction of a new temple {Cunningham 1961: 31}. Notice the roofed Buddha's Walk did not show on the Kumrahar plaque as it was probably also in ruins at this time and never rebuilt; it was already in ruins before Hsuan-tsang arrived in c. 637 CE. As already mentioned, when this new Kushan temple was constructed a newly second plaster throne was installed and covered the first one; the *bodhi*-tree and Asoka *vajrasana* would accordingly be moved outdoor and most likely to the back of this new temple {Leoshko 1988: 17}. This temple might be of a similar size as its immediate predecessor but certainly smaller than the present temple in order to fit inside the *vedika*; probably no new Kushan railings were added to the old Shunga *vedika* at this stage.

The next modifications of the Mahabodhi Temple, unlike the earlier ones, are harder to decipher; for reliable information on the construction activities around the site between the fifth-tenth centuries CE one has to rely on pilgrim accounts and cross-reference these with archaeological data. The earliest and fairly credible account of Bodhgaya was told by the Chinese pilgrim Fa-Hsien who visited the site around c. 409 CE {Ahir 1994: 36}:

> Pagodas [*stupa*s] have also been raised at the following places: where Buddha, then a Bodhisattva, after having attained Buddhaship, contemplated the Bo tree for seven days [Mahabodhi Temple]…where Buddha paced east and west beneath the Bo tree for seven days [Buddha's Walk]…

From Fa-Hsien's brief description it is clear that *stupa*s or temples were present in or around the Mahabodhi Temple though he did not give any specific clues on the forms of these structures; probably they were towers since he apparently called them 'pagodas.' The next Chinese pilgrim Hsuan-tsang gave a more detailed account when he visited the site in c. 637 CE {Ahir 1994: 37-39}:

> In the middle of the enclosure surrounding the Bodhi tree is the diamond throne [*vajrasana*]…In circuit it [the enclosed *vedika*?] is 100 paces or so [250']…The Bodhi tree above [behind?] the diamond throne…To the east of the Bodhi tree there is a *vihara* [Mahabodhi Temple] about 160' or 170' high. Its lower foundation-wall is twenty or more paces [50'] in its face. The building (pile) is of blue tiles (brick) covered with chunam (burnt stone lime); all the niches in different stories hold golden figures. The four sides of the building are covered with wonderful ornamental work; in one place figures of pearls (garlands), in another figures of heavenly Rishis. The whole is surmounted by a gilded copper *Amalaka* fruit. The eastern face adjoins a storied pavilion, the projecting eaves of which rise one over the other to the height of three distinct chambers; its projecting eaves, its pillars, beams, and doors, and windows are decorated with gold and silver ornamental work, with pearls and gems let in to fill up interstices. Its somber chambers and mysterious halls have doors in each of the three stories. To the right and left of the outside

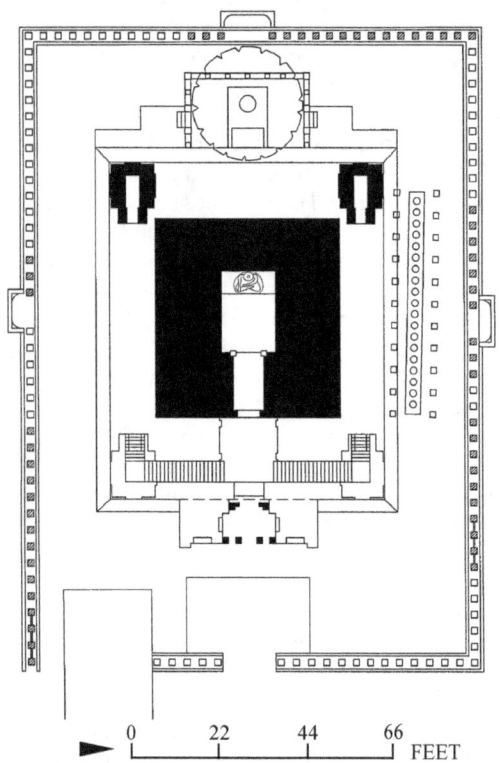

7.10. Elevation and plan (*left*)
c. 150-800 CE (final form)
Bodhgaya- India

7.11. Exterior view (*above*)
c. 150-800 CE (final form)
Bodhgaya- India

gate are niches like chambers; in the left is a figure of Avalokitesvara Bodhisattva, and in the right a figure of Maitreya Bodhisattva. They are made in white silver, and are about 10' high…The figure [Buddha statue inside the chamber] still exists in its perfect state…To the north of the Bodhi tree is a spot where Buddha walked up and down [Buddha's Walk]…He walked there east and west for a distance of ten paces or so [25']. Miraculous flowers sprang up under his foot-traces to the number of eighteen. Afterwards this space was covered in by a brick wall about 3' high.

Hsuan-tsang also stated that Asoka built the first temple then afterward, of an unspecified timeframe but certainly before his visit, a Brahmin-turned-Buddhist reconstructed it on a larger scale while his younger brother dug a tank to the south of the temple, probably the Buddhapokhar {Cunningham 1961: 21}. Hsuan-tsang's description of a multi-tiered temple, 170' high x 50' wide plan with an adjoined pavilion in the east and other details, indeed agrees with the dimensions of the current temple [7.10-7.11] but only to a certain extent; here are some inconsistencies:

- Hsuan-tsang's 50' wide face of the lower foundation-wall, which might or might not include the plinth but most likely it might not, only roughly matches the dimension of the current base of the central tower (solid shade on the plan [7.10]); the dimension of the current temple plinth is about 75'10" x 88'2", which is clearly larger than Hsuan-tsang's description. Here is Cunningham's misleading declaration stating that "the dimensions of the two temples [Hsuan-tsang's and the current temple] are exactly the same, the present building being 48' square at its base..." {Cunningham 1961: 18}. Every writer afterward wrongly quoted this incorrect dimension from his authority; the dimensions of the base of the central tower and the plinth are obviously different with the latter is the larger of the two.
- Hsuan-tsang unfortunately gave the 250' circuit as the dimension of an unspecified edifice; is it the circuit of the stone *vedika* or the plinth of the tower? Currently the base circuit of the tower (solid shade on the plan [7.10]) is about 188', the plinth 328', the circuit dimension of the outer face of the stone *vedika* 544'; clearly there are no matches between Hsuan-tsang's and any of these dimensions. If Hsuan-tsang's 250' circuit really referred to the dimension of the old Shunga *vedika* before its enlargement [7.8], as agreed by Cunningham {Cunningham 1961: 11}, then how could his 50' wide temple and its projecting pavilion possibly be fitted inside a 250' circuit *vedika*? It clearly would not fit and Hsuan-tsang's statement remains highly inconsistent. In any case, Hsuan-tsang's building apparently had a tower with a projecting multi-tiered pavilion in the east and he did not mention any walked-out roof terraces or corner turrets as he had seen at Nalanda. His descriptions of the Mahabodhi Temple, however contradictory, also closely resemble the Hindu Bhirtagaon Temple (c. 450 CE) {ASIAR 1908-1909: 5-16} and the main temple at Sarnath [8.5].

If taken Hsuan-tsang's descriptions of the temple at face value, a 170' high tower and 50' wide plan with a projecting multi-tiered pavilion in the east, his temple was evidently smaller than the current 170' high and 75'10" x 88'2" oblong plan; thus Cunningham's confident assertion that both buildings were 'the same building' does not stand up to the facts. Hsuan-tsang also commented that the Mahabodhi Temple resembled a Nalanda *caitya*, or possibly Caitya 12 [4.4 (#12)] reputedly built by King Baladitya (mid sixth century CE). Hsuan-tsang's temple was clearly higher and bigger than the Kushan temple depicted in the Kumrahar plaque [7.9] and it also had a multi-tiered pavilion in its main eastern facade. The Kushan temple might have been destroyed during Miharakula's raids of North India in the early sixth century CE and rebuilt afterward; this new temple or additions can conservatively be dated between c. 550-600 CE. The *vedika* was again reorganized and enlarged to accommodate the dimensions of the new temple; the task was probably carried out by King Purnavarman around c. 600 CE as agreed by some scholars {Barua 1975: 12-19, 79-82}{Leoshko 1988: 19}. This king reportedly erected a 20' high wall around the *bodhi*-tree, which had been uprooted by the Hindu King Sasanka earlier, to prevent future desecrations. New granite members would be added to the old sandstone Shunga *vedika* with outlet openings in the center of each side and its height remained at 10' high. The *bodhi*-tree and Asoka *vajrasana*, the latter of which was now placed over a late sixth century CE Gupta pedestal, were again moved further west as a result of the enlargement of the temple {Leoshko 1988: 14, 19}. The *vajrasana* should probably have been positioned east of the *bodhi*-tree during this renovation; the construction a huge solid plinth (c. 650-700 CE) would again cause the relocation of the *vajrasana* and *bodhi*-tree further west. When the back (west) face was restored in the 1880s CE, a sapling of the then dying *bodhi*-tree was replanted in its current position behind (west) the *vajrasana*. The Mahabodhi Temple was modified probably for the last time to its present form [7.10-7.11] some times after Hsuan-tsang left India; the new additions probably involved the remaining features of the temple including the plinth, four corner turrets, and entry portico. Cunningham noticed that the plan of the portico with its side image niches of Avalokitesvara and Maitreya and the style of its four columns were similar to the *torana* outside the main temple enclosure further east and those at Nalanda. This *torana* has been dated between c. 650-800 CE according to some authorities and therefore this latest renovation and the present form of the Mahabodhi Temple probably also dated in this period {Cunningham 1961: 26}{Leoshko 1988: 21}. This latest temple, which probably corresponded to the form of the current Mahabodhi Temple, also had a 75'10" x 88'2" plan, a nearly 25' high plinth with a multi-tiered pavilion, and a narrow projecting portico crowned with miniature *stupa*s in the eastern side; its interior was completely vaulted. The brick-and-plaster tower retained its previous 170' height and had a new quincunxial (*pancayatana*) design consisting of a seven-tiered tower that was crowned with an *amalaka*, a *stupa* finial, and four small corner turrets.

So far I have not discussed the numerous accumulated additions to the back (west face) of the temple, all of which have been removed by Cunningham during the 1880s CE restoration {Cunningham 1961: 1, 24-29}; there are controversies regarding their construction sequences relative to the various renovations of the temple:

(a) A Buddha statue in the center of the west facade on top of the *vajrasana* (V2). Relics were discovered here which Cunningham dated between c. 300-400 CE for the first relic and seventh-eighth centuries CE for the second relic.
(b) Two solid piers (H) were subsequently built on both sides of (V2). Dated 'shortly preceding Raja Purnavarman' or c. 600 CE.
(c) A wall (N) was then built in front of (V2) and completely covered it up. This addition dated between c. 600-620 CE.
(d) Two more piers (E) were again built on both sides of (N) and in front of (H) dated between the tenth-eleventh centuries CE or by the Myanmari restorations in 1035 CE and between 1079-1086 CE.
(e) Two more buttresses (F) were constructed on both sides of (H) and (E) dated in the twelfth century CE.

Cunningham called all these additions 'buttresses' since their purpose was to buttress the back facade in place as the tremendous force of the growing roots of the *bodhi*-tree threatened to topple the entire back (west) facade. The position of this *bodhi*-tree, as shown on Cunningham's plan, was then in the center and immediately behind the west facade, which appears to have been added after the already standing tree. Could this west facade be the 20' high wall seen by Hsuan-tsang that would subsequently, say between c. 650-700 CE, be converted into a 25' high plinth? Probably yes. Scholars also agreed that the *vajrasana* (V2) was probably moved outside of the inner chamber in the late sixth century CE {Leoshko 1988: 14, 19} and thus the c. 300-400 CE date that Cunningham gave for Addition (a) is not acceptable. Moreover, it is impossible to prove the style of this Buddha image as belonging in this early period; Cunningham mentioned its pedestal as having a design of '*vajra*s or thunderbolts' which was clearly a Vajrayana symbol that appeared from the seventh century CE on. It is highly probable that the statue and its pedestal could have been brought from somewhere else and affixed to the west facade. Finally, if Addition (a) dated between c. 300-400 CE then the plinth behind the Buddha statue must have been even earlier or in the Kushan Dynasty, which is an untenable hypothesis since this large plinth would not fit inside the small *vedika*. My theory is that the Buddha statue and pedestal, which had been brought from somewhere else and contained the first relic dated between c. 300-400 CE, was rededicated alongwith the second relic between the seventh-eighth centuries CE; the latter date should be ascribed to Addition (a) and slightly later than the west facade. Another controversy was the Myanmari restorations in 1035 CE and between 1079-1086 CE, the latter of which was an extensive and long restoration mostly credited to King Kyanzittha (r. 1084-1113 CE). Cunningham attributed the new stucco finish, rebuilding of the pinnacle, and the two piers (E) to this second restoration, all had been supervised by the Myanmaris and presumably executed by the local Indians {Cunningham 1961: 27-29} {Leoshko 1988: 107-108} {Ahir 1994: 72}. This lengthy and over seven-year restoration has led many to conclude that either the temple had suffered extensive damages or the restoration also encompassed many other monuments around the site. Many scholars have long suspected that the new additions, in particular the four corner turrets, pointed arch, and vaulted interior, were introduced by the Myanmaris during this restoration. First of all as already mentioned, the four corner turrets were integral components of the *pancayatana* design that already occurred in the Nalanda *vihara*s and *caitya*s [4.4 (#3, 12)], which Hsuan-tsang also saw while studying in this monastery. Secondly, pre-restoration photographs in the 1880s CE showed the eastern facade having a structural system of pointed arches stacking one on top of another in the eastern pavilion; this constitutes the relieving arch, which was commonly employed in the Bagan temples of Myanmar. It originates in Roman architecture but differs from Bagan examples in that the latter has multiple tiers of pointed arches with hollow interstices in between while Roman relieving arches are typically semicircular without the interstices. Now the important question is: could the relieving and pointed arch in the Mahabodhi Temple have existed before the Myanmari restorations? Certainly it could since it had already been employed in the Hindu Bhirtagaon Temple (c. 450 CE) {ASIAR 1908-1909: 5-16}. Moreover, it would be difficult for the Myanmari architects to introduce them when the tower was still standing without completely rebuilding the temple. My view is that the Myanmaris most likely learnt this technology, namely the pointed and relieving arch, from India and subsequently employed it in their buildings; future research is needed to resolve this contentious matter.

Another important issue is whether J. D. Beglar's 1880s CE restoration had wholeheartedly been based on existing conditions and faithfully replicated to the existing form of the temple; to answer this question one has to read Cunningham's archaeological reports on the conditions of the ruined temple before the commencement of the restoration {Cunningham 1961: i-ii, 6, 8, 24-26, 30-31, pl. XII-XV, XXI}{Barua 1975: 12-19}{Leoshko 1988: 5, 12, 22-26, 86}:

- Almost the entire eastern facade, portico, and upper pavilion had collapsed; the south and west facades were partially ruined while the north facade was leaning outward.
- Some pillars and pilasters of the east portico still remained.
- Chunks of the tower and its crowning finial were missing; the twin stairs leading up to the plinth (roof) terrace were roofless but fragments and traces of the four corner turrets on the plinth still remained.
- The *vajrasana* and buttresses on the back (west) facade still remained.
- Only the column bases of the roofed Buddha's Walk and its elevated walkway remained.
- Only half of the original *vedika* remained. Many pieces were later removed to the museums in India and Britain to be replaced with replicas.
- No trace of the Asoka pillar of an elephant capital remained.
- The *bodhi*-tree embedded in and immediately behind the center of the west facade fell down in 1876 CE and its sapling was replanted in the current position.

It is clear that all the major features that had existed since the last restoration (c. 650-800 CE) were present in Cunningham's reports. The highly successful restoration in the 1880s CE completed by J. D. Beglar, which was mainly based on a small eleventh century CE model of the Mahabodhi Temple recovered from the site, apparently did not deviate from the early medieval form of the temple. In summary, there are numerous phases in the architectural evolution of the Mahabodhi Temple; this does not take into account the repeated additions of the buttresses in the west facade as well as numerous minor repairs and stucco refinishes over the centuries to maintain its elegant appearance.

- Phase I (c. 260 BCE): The first timber temple, likely a *bodhigriha*, Buddha's Walk, and a wooden *vedika* were originally constructed by Asoka alongwith a stone *vajarasana*; the Asoka pillar of an elephant capital was probably erected in front of this temple but it is no longer extant.
- Phase II (c. 125-100 BCE): A two-storied Shunga *bodhigriha* [7.6-7.7], which probably replaced the original Asoka temple was constructed having stone columns on an open ground floor and a timber upper story; the Buddha's Walk was also covered with a timber roof supported by stone colonnades.
- Phase III (c. 60 BCE): A sandstone *vedika* [7.8] replaced the wooden *vedika*; it is distinguished from the granite members added in Phase V.
- Phase IV (c. 150-200 CE): A new Kushan brick-and-plaster temple [7.9] replaced Phase II temple; the *bodhi*-tree and Asoka *vajrasana* would accordingly be moved outside during this phase, or probably in Phase V.
- Phase V (c. 550-600 CE): Hsuan-tsang described the temple as a multi-tiered building with an adjoined pavilion in the east face that was larger than Phase IV temple but smaller than Phase VI temple. New granite *vedika stambha*s were added due to the enlargement of the temple; the *bodhi*-tree and *vajrasana* were again moved further west with the latter now placed over a Gupta pedestal,
- Phase VI (c. 650-800 CE): The plinth and four corner turrets were added between c. 650-700 CE while the entry portico was probably added between c. 700-800 CE, which completed the final form of the current temple [7.10-7.11].
- Phase VII (1035 CE, 1079-1086 CE): The temple was extensively restored by the Myanmaris; the final form of the temple already existed in Phase VI likely remained unaltered during this restoration.
- Phase VIII (c. 1302-1331 CE): Granite pavement was installed around the temple and this was the last reported renovation.
- Phase IX (1880-1890 CE): The ruined temple was again restored by J. D. Beglar with all the features of the Phase VI temple; the accumulated buttresses were also removed from the west facade and the *bodhi*-tree relocated to its current position. The four corner turrets were improperly restored as they all had a slight curvature resembling the Hindu *sikhara*s that do not match the straight-edged profile of the central tower.

No other Buddhist temples can better demonstrate the changes in the nature of Buddhist worships than the Mahabodhi Temple; when Asoka constructed the temple, Buddhism was still adhering to the ancient tradition of aniconic worship as the *bodhi*-tree and *vajrasana* symbolically represented Buddha's invisible presence and the ultimate emblems of Buddhism. The rise of the Mahayana and *bhakti* (devotion) movement in the first century CE led to the creation of the anthropomorphic Buddha and *bodhisattva* images and also replaced the *bodhi*-tree and *vajrasana* in the Mahabodhi Temple and effectively transformed it from a *bodhigriha* to a *pratimagriha*. A Buddha image was accordingly installed in the sanctum sanctorum whilst the *bodhi*-tree and *vajrasana* became sidelined and repeatedly moved further west every time the temple was expanded. The Mahabodhi Temple is also crucial in the study of the architectural evolution in India; a definite break with the ancient Indian tradition occurred in the second century CE when its longevous *caitya*-arched, vaulted, and wattle-and-daub *bodhigriha* was replaced with a brick pyramidal tower of a Gandhara origin. Another important phase in the temple architecture was the development of the *pancayatana* design which can be traced to the four-cornered bastioned plans in Ai-khanum in Afghanistan, the Kushan city of Sirsukh in Taxila, several other Gandhara monuments [6.14, 6.18]. The oldest *pancayatana* temples in India are the main temple at Sarnath (Phase II dated in the fourth century CE) [8.5] and Nalanda *caitya*s [4.4 (#3, 12)]; the Mahabodhi Temple was also a *pancayatana* design but probably about a century later than Nalanda Caitya 12. This influential design was certainly a Buddhist creation alongside the straight-edged pyramidal tower; the latter is essentially different from the curvilinear North Indian Hindu Nagara *sikhara* and the distinctly demarcated tiers of the South Indian Dravida *ratha*, both dated in the seventh century CE. The *pancayatana* temple is relatively common in Southeast Asia in Java, Kampuchea, and Myanmar; the central temple of Candi Sewu [7.12-7.13] has a central tower flanked by four smaller ones in the four cardinal points as also in the Bayon of Angkor Thom [7.16-7.17] while in the Ananda Temple [7.14-7.15] small *stupa*s can be seen on the upper tiers surrounding a central *sikhara*. The Mahabodhi Temple is a revered emblem of Buddhist architecture and the center of the Buddhist world and there are many distinguished and faithful copies of it around the world. The most well-known imitation was the Mahabodhi Temple (c. 1200 CE) in Bagan in Myanmar, Wat Chet Yot (c. 1455-1470 CE) in Chiang Mai in Thailand, the Mahabauddha Temple (c. 1564-1610 CE) in Patan in Nepal, and the Biyun Pagoda (1748 CE) in Beijing in China. Though these are essentially reproductions, they are nevertheless genuine local interpretations which vary considerably in details compared to their original Indian prototype.

3. Candi Sewu (c. 792-817 CE) - Indonesia

The tradition of constructing *candi*s (temples) in Indonesia began soon after the arrival of Hinduism and Buddhism from India in the first century CE. The oldest groups of *candi*s in Indonesia are a few brick remains of isolated Hindu *candi*s at Cibuaya (seventh-eighth centuries CE) and Buddhist *candi*s at Batujaya (sixth-eleventh centuries CE) near Jakarta alongwith the oldest extant stone *candi*s on the Dieng Plateau in central Java. The Buddhist *stupa*s in Indonesia have already been discussed in Chapter 6 and this section will focus on the Buddhist *candi*s. A brief note about the Buddhist temple architecture in Indonesia and other Southeast Asian countries is that its forms were very much influenced by Indian Buddhist and Hindu architecture, in particular the North Indian Hindu Nagara *sikhara*s and the South Indian Hindu Dravida *ratha*s; thus a mixture of elements from both religions are often observed in Indonesian *candi*s. In Indonesia, the Buddhist *candi*s are far more numerous than the *stupa*s suggesting the popularity of tangible images over relics; by the late eighth century CE, a Buddhist renaissance was already in full swing in central Java as the scale of the Buddhist *candi*s also increased dramatically. In this stage the Buddhists, thanks to the tremendous patronage from the Sailendras, were no longer simply content with constructing small isolated *candi*s as they now attempted the construction of huge temple complexes, each of which was elevated on multiple low terraces with a centrally large *candi* that is surrounded by numerous smaller *candi*s surrounding. One of such immense temple complexes is Candi Sewu [7.12-7.13], which was then the earliest and biggest temple of its kind in Indonesia and Southeast Asia; it became a profoundly influential model for later and equally large Javanese *candi*s like the Hindu Candi Loro Jonggrang and the huge multi-terraced mountain temples in Kampuchea [7.16-7.17]. Candi Sewu had been discovered earlier than Borobudur and among the earliest Europeans to have visited the site was the German Carl Friedrich Reimer in the late eighteenth century CE; in 1807 CE it was again visited by H. C. Cornelius, the same surveyor who made pioneering investigations of Borobudur. The *candi* would frequently be studied over the years when much of it was still in ruins; at last a golden opportunity would be conceived between 1981-1986 CE when a major restoration was completed. During this restoration, a small clay model of a *vina* (Indian harp) was uncovered, which evidently had no relationship with the Buddhist *candi* and might have been left there by chance. In 1985 CE during the course of dismantling and reconstructing the main temple, an 18'5" wide x 28'11" high cube was discovered underneath it that was determined to be the original foundation of Candi Sewu; its top nineteen layers were stone whereas the bottom nineteen layers were brick. Scattered remains of brick foundations have also reportedly been found below Candi Mendut and Borobudur; this brick foundation of Candi Sewu was probably contemporary with that of Candi Bhima in the Dieng group, which dated in the seventh century CE. In 1960 CE, an Old Malay inscription dated in 792 CE was discovered in Candi Sewu mentioning the expansion of a Manjusrigrha temple, which was undoubtedly the original name of Candi Sewu when it was dedicated to Manjusri. Scholars believed that Candi Sewu, a seemingly modern name meaning 'Thousand Temples,' referred to the required numbers of temples as prescribed for a Vajrayana *mandala* {Bosch 1961: 130}; the name might also allude to the original thousand timber temples before their conversion to stone.

The completely stone Candi Sewu complex [7.12-7.13] consists of 249 temples distributed over two low terraces along two axes that intersect in the center of the main temple with the main one running east-west forming a slightly rectangular plan. The 1'6" high large main terrace measures about 561' (east-west) x 607' (north-south) and on which stand rows of ancillary temples; the 1'6" high and small terrace, which is elevated on the large terrace, measures roughly 136' east-west x 139' north-south and on which stands the cruciform temple in the center. The auxiliary temples on the larger terrace are arrayed in five rows with the first row having eighty-eight temples, the second eighty temples, the third eight temples, the fourth forty-four temples, and the fifth twenty-eight temples; architecturally, these temples are grouped into three distinct types. Only the plinths of five of the eight temples of the biggest Type I in the third row still remain and their destroyed superstructures were likely crowned with mini-*stupa*s surrounding a large central one as in the extant examples; the first and fifth rows constitute Type II and the second and fourth rows Type III. Type I plan is 35'4" x 30'11" and its elevation is approximately 52'8" high, Type II 19'8" x 22'8" plan and 32'4" high, and Type III 21' x 23'6" plan and 36'1" high. Typically the superstructure of each *candi* is elevated on a low plinth with a body crowned with a large *stupa* above the central cella; Type II crown terminates in *ratna* and *stupa* finials and its porch has a curvilinear half-hip roof whereas Type III crown terminates in *stupa* finials and its porch has a curvy pedimented roof. Each of these temples has thirteen reliefs of standing *bodhisattva*s in the late or post-Gupta Style; at one time its interior likely housed a single Buddha or *bodhisattva* image certainly of Manjusri. The massive central temple of a cruciform plan is surrounded by four smaller annexed temples in the four cardinal points. According to Jacques Dumarcay, these four temples had originally been detached from the central temple but were later joined with the latter during the 792 CE renovation; thus it was originally conceived as a *pancayatana* plan {Dumarcay 1986: 21-25}{Dumarcay 1991: 49-51}. The result of this transformation was a cruciform plan of 96' x 97'2" dimension with the central temple rising to an amazing height of 101'9"; this change in Candi Sewu plan was apparently modeled after the increasingly widespread cruciform plan throughout the Buddhist world as in the nearby Candi Kalsasan (778 CE) and the main temple at Sarnath in India [8.5]. This renovation also created a *pradaksina* path, which was originally completely hypaethral but now partially covered, around the main cella. The central temple has only one entry in the east, which is also the main orientation of the complex; like the ancillary temples, it too has reliefs of *bodhisattva* figures standing in niches on the exterior. Its central cella has a raised dais that once probably housed a gilded bronze Buddha image or a group of Buddhas and *bodhisattva*s like Candi Mendut; it also has forty-one niches probably once contained gilded bronze images. Unfortunately none of Candi Sewu original icons remain and since it was once a Manjusrigrha its pantheon would certainly include Mahayana images of Buddhas and *bodhisattva*s, and certainly Manjusri, as in Borobudur and Candi Mendut. Candi Sewu is also guarded by a pair of robust and demonic-looking *yaksa*s or *raksasa*s of about 8'2" high in each entry as in the Indian tradition.

Candi Sewu was the first and largest of the highly organized temple complexes in Southeast Asia; its relative obscurity among scholars, in contrast to the celebrated status of Borobudur, has resulted in the scarcity of theories on its religious symbolisms. The most well-known theory was propagated by F. D. K. Bosch suggesting Candi Sewu as a Vajrayana *mandala*, specifically the Vajradhatu Mandala {Bosch 1961: 111-130}. Its theoretical foundations have already been discussed in <u>Chapter 2</u>; this *mandala* already appeared in East Asia by the early ninth century CE. Bosch's methodology was to assign the images, all of which have been lost, in the 'right' niches of Candi Sewu central temple to match their positions as prescribed in the Vajradhatu Mandala. Thus he placed Vairocana Buddha in the central cella and the remaining four Jina Buddhas in the four cellas surrounding the central cella; each of these Buddhas would in turn be surrounded by other lesser deities. Only three of the four Vajrabodhisattvas were assigned in the three cardinal points of the central cella exterior wall because, as Bosch said, the east was an entrance and therefore the fourth image was not required. Jacques Dumarcay

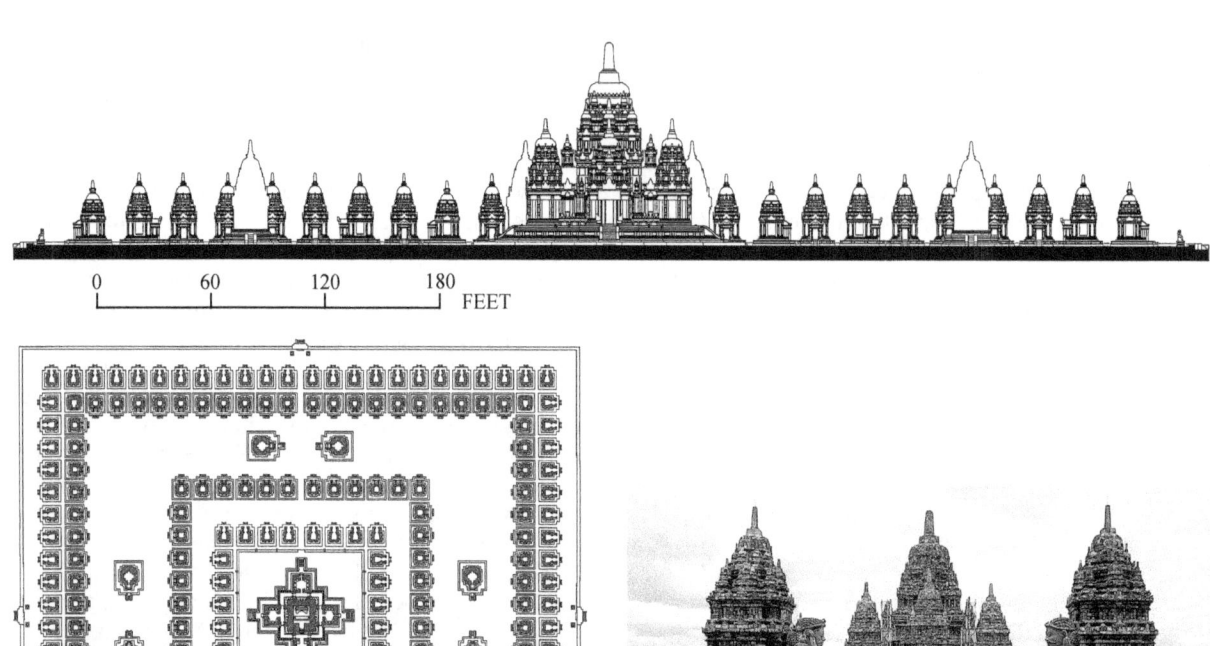

7.12. Elevation (restored) and plan
c. 792-817 CE
Yogyakarta- Indonesia

7.13. View of remaining temples
c. 792-817 CE
Yogyakarta- Indonesia

thought that Bosch's *mandala* theory was convincing as it also tallied with his and that the enlargement of Candi Sewu was to replicate a Vajrayana *mandala* reflecting a newly religious movement in central Java that was emanated from eastern India {Dumarcay 1986: 23}. However upon further reflection, there are several problems with Bosch's association of Candi Sewu with the Vajradhatu Mandala; first, the positions of the deities are inconsistent with the Vajradhatu Mandala. For examples, in the east cella Bosch grouped the four *prajna*s of Vairocana and a Vajrabodhisattva together with Aksobhya whilst the remaining three Vajrabodhisattvas were assigned to the outside wall of the central cella; the four Sacrificing Taras and four Commanding Taras in the outermost circle of this *mandala* were entirely omitted from his scheme.

Second, architecturally the squarish plan of Candi Sewu apparently does not resemble the square-and-circle Vajradhatu Mandala, as Borobudur does [6.28-6.29]. Third, the allegedly Vajrayana iconography in Candi Sewu is completely unknown since none of its original sculptures survives and so Bosch's theory was purely speculative; most likely its images were similar to the contemporary Candi Mendut and Borobudur consisting of Buddhas and *bodhisattva*s without the Tantric deities of the Vajrayana. A well-known set of small statuettes depicting deities of the Vajrayana *mandala* from Ngandjuk in eastern Java dated in the Kediri Dynasty (1050-1221 CE), or about two centuries later than Candi Sewu and Borobudur. Had the Vajrayana been predominant in central Java during the Sailendras, its Tantric deities would have already appeared in contemporary monuments like Candi Mendut and Borobudur. On the other hand, if Candi Sewu was a Vajradhatu Mandala and Borobudur as a Garbhadhatu Mandala as hypothesized then both monuments might symbolize *Nirvana* and *Samsara* respectively, or two aspects of the same non-dual reality which is Enlightenment or *Sunya*. The construction and consecration of these great monuments, conceivably two *mandala*s, would protect and bless the Sailendras' kingdom as also suggested for the early Japanese *mandala*s. In summary, the construction of Candi Sewu might have been completed in three main phases:

- Phase I (c. 600-732 CE): Its brick foundation and timber superstructure were constructed probably contemporary with the foundations of other Buddhist and Hindu monuments in central Java; it is not possible to verify the original forms or numbers of its temples but most likely each would have a body and crown elevated on a low plinth.
- Phase II (c. 732-792 CE). A large stone temple in the center of the complex was constructed and further surrounded by four smaller detached temples in the four cardinal points, which formed a *pancayatana* plan; this phase probably happened before Candi Kalasan (778 CE), which had the first integrated cruciform plan.
- Phase III (c. 792-817 CE): The four detached temples were annexed and integrated into the central temple as the hypaethral gaps between them would be partially roofed over and new doors were also installed between the connecting passages. This effectively converted the central temple from a *pancayatana* to cruciform plan {Dumarcay 1986: 21-25}{Dumarcay 1991: 49-51}; meanwhile the surrounding 248 ancillary temples were also constructed. The highly structured plan and uniformed architecture of Candi Sewu strongly suggested that it had likely been constructed and completed in a decade or so before Borobudur.

Candi Sewu was undoubtedly the first Javanese monuments that had successfully leaped beyond the old concept of an isolated temple by essentially unifying hundreds of temples into a gigantic religious complex; it possibly originally had an integrated iconographical program. Scholars suggested that Candi Sewu plan had been derived from Somapura [4.8] in Bangladesh {Rowland 1977: 448}; this is only partially true since the quincunxial and cruciform designs already had earlier precursors in Gandhara [6.14, 6.17-6.18], Nalanda *caitya*s [4.4 (#3, 12)], the Mahabodhi Temple [7.10-7.11], and the Sarnath main temple in India [8.5], and the *pancayatana parivena* monasteries in Sri Lanka {Bandaranayake 1974: 33-133}.

However, the cruciform plan of Candi Sewu could be traced back to its immediate Javanese predecessor Candi Kalasan while architecturally its temples fused the South Indian Hindu Dravida *ratha*s and early Javanese *candi*s. Above all, Candi Sewu plan with its myriad temples strongly recalls Turkistani *stupa*s like Karakhoja Stupa P and Yarkhoto (Chinese Jiaohe) dated in the sixth century CE; the latter is certainly the closest precursor of Candi Sewu {Yamamoto 1990: 206-207}{TNM 1991: 34}. The plan of Vijayarama [4.9], which composes of several precincts elevated on low terraces and surrounded by twelve small cells, is distantly akin to Candi Sewu plan. Nearly half a century after Candi Sewu another equally famous and grand central Javanese temple, the Hindu Candi Loro Jongrang, was completed in 856 CE with a design obviously modeled after Candi Sewu. About three centuries later in Kampuchea, the concept of vastly organized temple complexes first pioneered in Candi Sewu would be taken into a new height in the gigantic mountain temples like Angkor Wat and Bayon of Angkor Thom [7.16-7.17]. In these monuments, the Khmers ingeniously fused the multi-terraced pyramidal design of Borobudur and the myriad temples plan of Candi Sewu with their own galleried design to create the uniquely galleried and multi-terraced pyramidal mountain temple.

4. Ananda Temple (1105 CE) - Myanmar

A brief history on the arts and architecture of Myanmar, in particular its *zedi*s, have already been discussed in Chapter 6; this section will focus on its temples. As already mentioned, the oldest extant temples in Myanmar were erected by the Pyus at Sriksetra including Bebe, Lemyethna, and East Zegu all tentatively dated between the fifth-seventh centuries CE {Chihara 1996: 63-64}. Their oblong plans typically have a central cella attached to a projecting entry hall that is preceded by a porch with the elevation consisting of a body crowned with a diminishing terraced roof or a *sikhara* tower. Lemyethna is unique in having a cruciform plan with median entrances in the four cardinal points and a vaulted corridor in the interior. The next phase in the evolution of Myanmari temples would be inaugurated in Bagan where most of its extant temples generally dated not earlier than the eleventh century CE; these temples reached their grandest dimensions between the twelfth-thirteenth centuries CE in colossal temples like That-byin-nyu {Pichard 1992-2001: #1597}. Some of the most important early Bagan temples, counting Hindu and Buddhist, are Manuha (Pichard #1240), Kyaukku Onhmin (Pichard #154), Nan-Paya (Pichard #1239), and Nat-hlaung-gyaung (Pichard

#1600); the construction technologies in these temples typically combine the pointed arch and vault as in the *zedi*s. The followings give a brief overview of the plan and elevation types as well as the architectural elements in Bagan temples:

(a) Plans

Bagan temples are generally divided into four main plans:
1. Oblong and one-entranced (Early Bagan). This asymmetrical plan typically has an entry projection on the one end and without or with an interior corridor surrounding a solid or hollow core as in Nagayon (Pichard #1192); this plan already occurred in Sriksetra temples like Bebe and East Zegu.
2. Cruciform and four-entranced (Mid Bagan). This symmetrical and equal-sided plan has four entrances and identical porches on the four sides of a centrally square cube; it may have none or one to two interior corridors surrounding a solid core **[7.14]** (Pichard #2171). The cruciform plan, which originated in Gandhara **[6.17]** and Indian temples like the Sarnath main temple **[8.5]**, already appeared in Sriksetra temples like Lemyethna; the latter had three entrances, which was rare but also occurred in Bagan temples.
3. A combination of oblong and cruciform (Late Bagan). Like Type (1), it has an entry projection on one side alongwith smaller secondary entrances on the remaining sides (Pichard #1605); this plan had a tendency to eliminate the wall separating the porch and the central cella, which in effect created a large open plan (Pichard #43).
4. Multi-faces (Late or Post-Bagan). There are numerous examples of this type, of which the pentagonal and octagonal plans are the most common (Pichard #51, 67, 99, 1504).

(b) Elevations

Bagan temples are generally one to four stories in height with the multi-storied type generally occurring between the mid to late Bagan Period (c. 1150-1287 CE); the elevation composes of a large body to be crowned with several diminishing terraces and an imposing tower of several different profiles:
1. *Stupa*. Bagan temples are often crowned with *stupa*s (Pichard #1493) and also the curvilinear North Indian Hindu Nagara *sikhara* which architecturally blurs the distinction between its *zedi*s and temples.
2. *Stupa* having a *ratna* or ribbed dome. This type is rare (Pichard #1605) but already occurred in Javanese *candi*s like Candi Loro Jonggrang, Mamallapuram in South India, and early Mathura temples **[7.4-7.5]**.
3. Curvilinear *sikhara*. This is the most common superstructure to have crowned many Bagan temples **[7.14-7.15]** but never its *zedi*s; it is obviously derived from the North Indian Hindu Nagara *sikhara*. The summits of some Bagan temples also terminate in the Indian-styled *amalaka* as in Hindu temples (Pichard #1686, #1694) or the *stupa amalaka* (Pichard #37, #43) as in the Mahabodhi Temple **[7.10-7.11]**.
4. Pyramidal. This type is also rare (Pichard #143, #1670) and obviously imitated the Mahabodhi Temple **[7.10-7.11]** in India.

(c) Architectural Elements

Artistic and architectural elements have also been incorporated into Bagan temples, which not only complement the architecture but also infuse the sacred and mysterious religious experiences in the visitors. Windows and clerestories are carefully designed to permit more illumination into the dim interiors of Bagan temples thanks to the daring employment of the arch-and-vault technology; the subtle interplay of light and shadow in Bagan temples also greatly amplifies their forms. Among the most conspicuous features in Bagan temples is the floral and flame-shaped pediment, or the *clec*, often found above windows and entrances; early examples were typically curvy and graceful (Pichard #1239) but gradually assumed the characteristically dull and straight profile in the later temples (Pichard #771). The *clec* was undoubtedly the Myanmaris' reinterpretation and transformation of the floral and *kala-makara* pediments often observed in Indian architecture and the Indianized temples of Java and Kampuchea. The interiors of Bagan temples are usually covered in exquisite murals and many still survive today; stylistically and iconographically, these murals fall into the categories of late Mahayana and early Vajrayana; the latter category is exemplified in the murals of the Abeyadana Temple. Bagan builders also employed terracotta plaques to decorate their temples and illustrate Buddhist stories, a practice probably copied from Bengal. In his book 'Old Burma-Early Bagan' Gorden Luce, a well-known scholar on Myanmari arts and architecture, repeatedly designated many Bagan temples as 'Mon' without providing evidences to substantiate his claim {Luce 1969: 299-302}. According to him, these temples were considered 'Mon' because the inscriptions found in them were in the Mon language, Mon temples were constructed in Plan Type (1), the dimly lit interiors of Bagan temples fitted the 'romantic and poetic temperament of Old Mons,' and the *clec* was a Mon word and hence its occurrence in Mon architecture. These, however, are essentially speculative assertions, save the

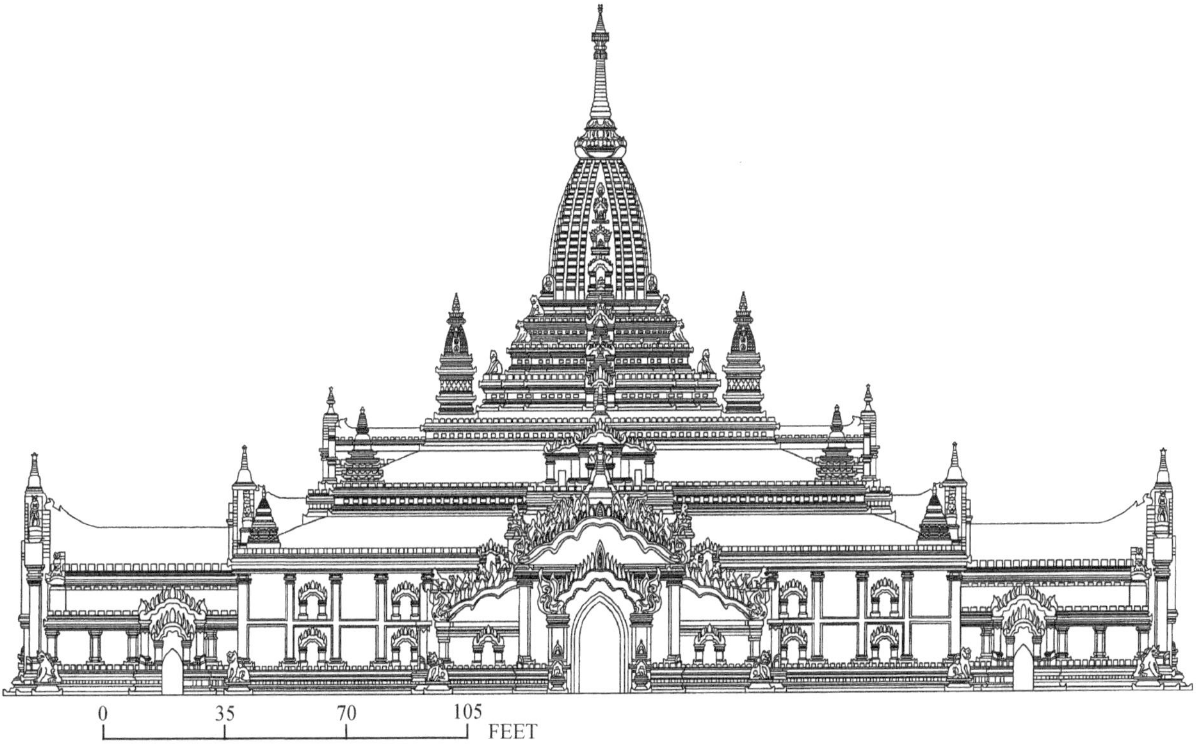

Part II. Architecture   Temple . 253

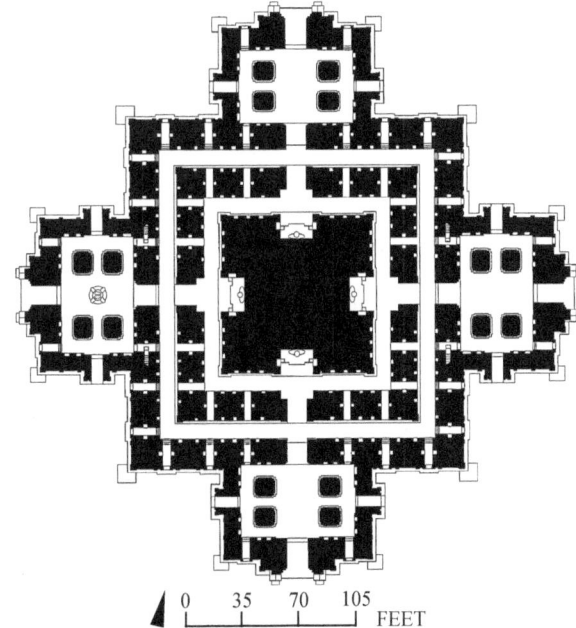

7.14. Elevation and plan
1105 CE
Bagan- Myanmar

7.15. Ananda Temple
1105 CE
Bagan- Myanmar

Mon inscriptions, since there is virtually no extant Mon architecture in Myanmar that can be dated before the pre-Bagan Period; great Bagan *zedi*s like Shwezigon indeed contain Mon inscriptions but this does not automatically qualify the monument as a Mon one. On the other hand the Pyus, unlike the Mons, were well-known early builders who constructed the oldest monuments in Myanmar at Sriksetra and Pyu architecture is undeniably the direct predecessor of Bagan architecture. Even Luce himself admitted that 'Mon' was 'a convenient label for a style quite distinctive,' an unwarranted label that evidently gave undue credits to the Mons who have yet to prove their paramount contributions to Bagan and Myanmari architecture.

One of the most elegantly designed and well-preserved of all Bagan temples is Ananda Temple **[7.14-7.15]**. Charles Duroiselle and Gordon Luce believed its original name was the corruption of 'Nanda' referring to Nandamula which was a sacred cave in the Himalaya {Luce 1969: 357-358}. However Ananda is also Buddha's famous cousin and attendant while the architecture and decorative schemes of the temple also do not resemble that of a cave. Its perfectly cruciform plan measures 345' wide having four porches projecting from a centrally solid square block; the west porch is likely the main entrance where gilded wooden statues of King Kyanzittha and Mahathera Arahan still stand. The interior of the central mass has two parallel *pradaksina* corridors running its entire length; windows and clerestories are opened on the exterior and interior walls at regular intervals to bring light as far inside as possible. The 195' elegant elevation of Ananda shows a one-storied temple with four *clec*-pedimented porches projecting out of the central block; it is essentially a tripartite design consisting of a body, two diminishing roof terraces with small *stupa*s and *sikhara*s in the four corners, and a curvilinear Hindu *sikhara* tower terminating in a *stupa*-typed finial. Henry Yule's 1858 CE elevation did not show the small *stupa*s in the lowest roof terrace which could be an oversight, or these might have been added at a more recent restoration. The temple structure is a combination of the pier-arch-vault system and a massive solid core bearing the loads of the heavy superstructure above; the material, like other Bagan buildings, is brick coated with several layers of plaster. There are other decorative elements complementing the architecture including gilded sculptures, green-glazed terracotta plaques, and murals, which have unfortunately been whitewashed over. The decorative plaques are distributed on the exterior in the continuous band in the base, roof terraces, and entry porches as well as the corridors, cross-passages, and central solid block in the interior {Luce 1969: 357-373}; a brief survey of the sculptures and decorative plaques in Ananda Temple reveals:

(a) Sculptures

There are a total of 1,535 sculptures in the interior niches and these are stone and gilded steles that are manifestly in the Indian Pala Style.

- Those in the porches depict important scenes from Sakyamuni's life such as Nativity, Enlightenment, First Sermon, *Parinirvana*, etc.
- Those in the outer (left) wall of the outer corridor depict eighty scenes from Sakyamuni's life from the beginning in Tushita Heaven up to Enlightenment; the sequence is slightly different from the relief panels of Borobudur, which were based on the Lalitavistara, wherein the depictions of Sakyamuni's life end in the First Sermon.
- Those in the inner (right) wall of the outer corridor and the inner corridor walls depict additional devotional scenes from Sakyamuni's life after Enlightenment.
- Those in the cross-passages depict additional scenes about Sakyamuni's life and a few *jataka*s; Luce believed these sculptures were rejects due to their poor conditions.
- The four standing Buddhas in the four cardinal niches of the central block presumably depict four Manusi Buddhas, namely Krakuchandra, Konakamuni, Kasyapa, and Sakyamuni; these colossal gilded statues are over 30' tall.
- Miscellaneous wooden statues are also found in the west porch depicting, according to Luce, King Kyanzittha and Mahathera Arahan.

(b) Green-glazed Terracotta Plaques

There are a total of 1,464 plaques in the niches on the roof terraces depicting the *jataka*s with accompanied Pali glosses identifying their canonical number and name. Another 552 plaques in the niches of the temple base depict scenes from Sakyamuni's life mainly about Mara's assault and defeat; these also contain Mon glosses on the bottom of the plaques. All these illustrated Buddhist stories and the *jataka*s centering on Sakyamuni's life clearly follow the Theravada tradition. The sculptures in the porches, corridors, and base were meant to lead visitors into a visual pilgrimage where stories about Sakyamuni's life and the *jataka*s would be vividly retold progressively from a worldly prince on the exterior to Enlightenment and Buddhahood in the center of the temple.

The cruciform plan of Ananda was originally developed in Gandhara **[6.17-6.18]** and subsequently reappeared in the central temples of Sarnath in India **[8.5]**,

Somapura in Bangladesh [4.8], and Candi Sewu in Java [7.12-7.13]; such plan also occurred in earlier Myanmari temples like Lemyethna at Sriksetra. Ananda Temple also incorporated a unique structural system in the porches in the form of arcades, an advanced design virtually non-existent in the architecture of other Asian countries that had naturally evolved from the earlier Nanpaya Temple (Pichard #1239); the corridor galleried plan with carved plaques in the niches of both walls suggests influences from Borobudur [6.28-6.29]. The elevation of Ananda exhibits a mature development of Sriksetra temples like Bebe and Lemyethna and it has also repeated certain features in the earlier Ptitakat-taik Library (Pichard #1587) such as the multi-tiered curvilinear roof of an Indian origin. The curvilinear *sikhara* tower of Ananda was obviously modeled after the North Indian Hindu Nagara *sikhara*; however, its crown and finial are essentially Buddhist resembling a *chattravali*. Despite its fusion of Hindu and Buddhist architecture, its decorative schemes of sculptures and murals are purely Buddhist.

5. Bayon Temple in Angkor Thom (c. 1181-1218 CE) - Kampuchea

Kampuchea (Cambodia) was among the oldest Indianized states in Southeast Asia; throughout its history, which began in the first century CE if Funan counting as the earliest documented part of its history, it remained steadfastly a Hindu state until converted to the Theravada in the late twelfth century CE. Kampuchea, like other Southeast Asian states, already had a well-developed Neolithic and Bronze Age cultures, as in the sites like Samrong Sen and Kandal, before the appearance of the Indianized state of Funan between the first-second centuries CE {Coedes 1968: 7-10}{ Jessup and Zephir 1997: 6-9}. The knowledge about Funan mainly came from archaeological data and Chinese sources; Chinese annals stated that Funan's capital was Vyadhapura about 500 li (155 miles) from the sea where archaeologists tentatively placed it near Ba Phnom in Prei Veng Province of Kampuchea. Funan is a Chinese transliteration of the Khmer word *bnam* or *phnom* meaning 'mountain,' which could designate the title of its kings or the probable location of its capital near a mountain. The Chinese also spoke of a legend on the founding of Funan about a *brahmin* named Kaundinya, undoubtedly an Indian, sailing to Funan where he married a local naked queen called Liuye; a Cham inscription also told a similar story about the founding of Funan, which evidently marked the beginning of Indianization in the country and the Indochinese peninsula. According to George Coedes, Funan at its apogee must have encompassed the territory south of ancient Champa now in southern Vietnam and the Menam (Chao Praya) valley in the west including a large area of Thailand and the Malay peninsula; the actual extent of Funan, however, remains unresolved {Coedes 1968: 36-37}. The historical site of Oc-eo near Ha Tien in Vietnam and close to the Gulf of Thailand is undisputedly the earliest Funanese site. Among the findings discovered here are objects of diverse origins (Roman, Chinese, Indian, Gandhara, Iran) and an architecture consisting of stone bases and timber superstructures; there is also a system of crisscrossing canals for agricultural cultivation. Brahmi and Sanskrit inscriptions have also been found alongwith statuettes of Siva, Visnu, Buddha, etc. indicating an early presence of Indian settlers and religions in the area; all these findings have been dated between the second-seventh centuries CE. These suggest a civilized community based on agriculture and trade with a solid political structure and a religious system based loosely on foreign (Indian) and indigenous elements. An important piece of evidence linking Oc-eo with Funan came from a Chinese description stating that the Funanese were experienced seafarers who constructed large ships capable of crossing the great sea and Oc-eo could easily fit the picture of a busy trading center. One of Funan's most valiant kings was Fan Man or Fan Shih-man who, according to the Chinese, built large seafaring vessels and sailed across the sea to conquer more than ten kingdoms, possibly in Malaysia and Indonesia; he died while leading an expedition against Chin-lin or the Gold Frontier, which Coedes identified with ancient Suvarnabhumi (Land of Gold) now in lower Myanmar. According to Coedes, this Fan Shih-man is the same Sri Mara mentioned in the Vocanh Sanskrit inscription in Champa dated in the third century CE; however, the ascription is still controversial and possibly Champa at the time was a vassal of Funan as suggested by Louis Finot. Between 225-287 CE, Funan reportedly sent several embassies to China and the North Indian kingdom of Marunda in the Ganga River then a suzerainty of the Kushans. China and India in return also sent their embassies and gifts to Funan; K'ang T'ai of the Chinese delegation in the third century CE once remarked that:

> There are walled villages, palaces, and dwellings. The men are all ugly and black, their hair frizzy; they go about naked and barefoot…They devoted themselves to agriculture…Moreover, they like to engrave ornaments and to chisel. Many of their eating utensils are silver. Taxes are paid in gold, silver, pearls, perfumes. There are books and depositories

of archives and other things. Their characters for writing resemble those of the Hu [a Central Asian people whose script was probably Kharosthi].

The Indianization of Funan continued to accelerate and would largely be crystallized by the fourth century CE and the process certainly continued until the collapse of Funan around c. 600 CE; the main cultural source in this phase for Funan was emanated from southern India with the introduction of Sanskrit, the Saka Era, Hinduism, and a host of other Indian practices. Coedes characterized this period of Indianization as a peaceful cultural migration, which had greatly been facilitated by trade, missionaries, and intermarriages, rather than a military colonization. It involved race (intermarriages between the Indians and indigenous population), language (Sanskrit and Indian literature), monarchal institution (divinized kingship), and religion (Hinduism and Buddhism); like other Southeast Asian countries, the Funanese and later Khmer kings all had *'varman'* suffixes for their names. In the early sixth century CE another Indianized country called Chenla, a name in the Chinese annals for Kampuchea throughout its medieval history, rose up from the Cham territory in a region situated around the border of modern Laos and Kampuchea; Chenla eventually absorbed Funan by the mid seventh century CE. According to a legend the lineage of the Chenla kings descended from the union of the hermit Kambu Svayambhuva, an ancestor-ruler of the Kambujas (hence the Kampucheans), and the celestial nymph Mera; the Kambu-Mera union produced the Khmers, the Kampucheans also prefer to called themselves. The Chenla King Bhavavarman I (c. 550-600 CE) was the grandson of the Funanese King Rudravarman and who also married the Funanese Princess Kambujarajalakshmi; this special relationship enabled Chenla to gradually achieve independence from Funan and eventually absorbed the latter's territory. According to Coedes, Bhavavarman I's capital at Bhavapura situated about nineteen miles northwest of Kompong Thom; King Isanavarman (r. 616-635 CE), son of Bhavavarman I's cousin King Mahendravarman, founded his capital at Isanapura a few miles northeast of Kompong Thom. Isanavarman constructed a well-known group of brick temples at Sambor Prei Kuk near his capital, which was one of the earliest sites in Southeast Asia consists of the oldest extant structures in Kampuchea. Between c. 706-802 CE Chenla was broken into two regions with Land Chenla encompassing the land north of Tonle Sap and Water Chenla or the land from Tonle Sap all the way to the sea. It was the task of Jayavarman II (r. 802-850 CE) to reunite the divided country after freeing Kampuchea from the Javanese domination; an eleventh century CE inscription at Sdok Kak Thom clearly stated that Jayavarman II returned from Java. He then crowned himself as a *cakravartin* in accordance to the Hindu consecratory rites through the intermediacy of *brahmin* priests; thus he was the first initiator of the *devaraja* cult of divinized kings that would become the hallmark of the Angkor Period. Jayavarman II founded several capitals at Indrapura (Kompong Cham or Angkor) and Mahendraparvata (Phnom Kulen) but finally decided to settle at Hariharalaya (Roluos). In 893 CE, Yasovarman I (r. 889-900 CE) moved his capital to Angkor and named it Yasodharapura where it remained Kampuchea's preeminent capital until 1431 CE when Phnom Penh became the new capital; there was a brief interlude when the capital was briefly moved from Angkor to Koh Ker during the reign of Jayavarman IV (r. 921-941 CE). The Angkor Period was the apogee of the Khmer Empire during which its arts and architecture reached their zenith with the construction of gigantic mountain temples like Angkor Wat under Suryavarman II (r. 1113-1150 CE) and Bayon of Angkor Thom [7.16-7.18] by the great Buddhist King Jayavarman VII (r. 1181-1218 CE). The Khmer Empire achieved its greatest expansion in the latter's reign encompassing Champa, much of Thailand to the Myanmari border, to Vientiane in Laos, and the Malay peninsula. The decline of the Khmer Empire after Jayavarman VII has been attributed to several factors, most likely due to the incessant costly wars with its neighbors throughout its history particularly with the Chams and the Vietnamese, the countless huge and extravagant construction projects, the collapse of its infrastructure and irrigation systems due to exhaustive coffers, etc. After Jayavarman VII's death, the Thais began to exert their independence and carved out their own territory from the disintegrated Khmer Empire; they then laid waste to Angkor several times so that the once glorious capital finally had to be abandon in 1431 CE. Angkor was briefly reoccupied and repaired in the late sixteenth century CE by King Ang Chan; some of Angkor Wat's walls, which had remained blank since the twelfth century CE, were carved during this time. The first Europeans reportedly visited Angkor were the Portuguese and Spaniards who wrote about their trips between 1583-1593 CE. Angkor was virtually forgotten afterward until 1850 CE when Frenchman Charles Bouillevaux visited it for the first time after a long silence; the French presence also corresponded to France's colonization of Indochina in the late nineteenth century CE. The next famed visitor to Angkor was Henri Mouhot between 1858-1861 CE and he later died of malaria in Luang Prabang, Laos in 1861 CE where he was buried. The pioneering archaeological efforts by the French like Louis Delaporte, Aymonier, George Groslier, Louis Finot, Henri Parmentier, Henri Marchal, Philippe Stern, Gilbert de Coral-Remusat, Jean Boisselier, Maurice Glaize, George Coedes, Madeleine Giteau and the EFEO team between the late nineteenth-early twentieth centuries CE have greatly restored the arts and architecture of Kampuchea, especially Angkor, to its former glory {Groslier and Arthaud 1966: 199}{Coedes 1968: 17, 38, 40-42, 46-47, 55-56, 65-70, 85, 97-103, 114-115, 159-163, 169-177, 180-181, 236-237}{Chihara 1996: 73-75}{Jessup and Zephir 1997: 10}{Jacques and Freeman 1997: 295-298}.

Earlier Indian settlers brought the Indian language, particularly Sanskrit, to Kampuchea where it would be employed in official inscriptions; the earliest appearance of Sanskrit was at the Funanese site of Oc-eo dated in the second century CE. In all the Khmers had issued about 1,200 inscriptions in both Sanskrit and Khmer; the next Sanskrit inscriptions, after those of Oc-eo, dated in the second half of the fifth century CE during the reign of King Jayavarman (r. 480-514 CE) by his Queen Kulaprabhavati and son Gunavarman, which have been found in Takeo (Kampuchea) and Thap-muoi (Vietnam). The first appearance of the Khmer script, which was paleographically derived from Sanskrit, was in a 612 CE inscription. The first inscription in Pali, the language of the Theravada, on a Buddha statue dated in the seventh century CE; there was another Pali inscription dated in 1309 CE marking perhaps the final triumph of the Theravada over Hinduism in Kampuchea. The last known Sanskrit and Khmer inscriptions were in Angkor Wat and Bayon of Angkor Thom dated in 1327 CE mentioning King Jayavarmadiparamesvara {Coedes 1968: 17, 40, 43, 59-60, 228}{ Jessup and Zephir 1997: 10, 150} {Jacques and Freeman 1997: 17}. Certainly by the first century CE, preeminent Indian religions like Hinduism and Buddhism had already been brought to Kampuchea across the Indian Ocean by Indian traders and missionaries; the site of Oc-eo contains many artifacts of Hindu and Buddhist origins. Funan was reportedly intermittently ruled by Indian settlers, of whom the first known ones were the Indian Chan-t'an (c. 357 CE) and Chiao Chen-ju or Kaundinya (c. 400-425 CE). The latter king, like the former, was a *brahmin* who molded all laws and political structure in the country in accordance to the Indian system and probably Hinduism was also firmly established in Funan thenceforth. Sivaism was predominant in Funan and Visnuism was also popular among the population up to the twelfth century CE. There were many temples dedicated to these Hindu sects and the earliest ones were the two Visnu temples constructed by Queen Kulaprabhavati during the reign of King Jayavarman (r. 480-514 CE). The oldest extant temples in Kampuchea, which were dedicated to Siva, are the Sambor Prei Kuk group constructed by King Isanavarman. Chinese annals also mentioned that during the aforesaid Jayavarman's reign, the Funanese worshiped Siva and "the god continually descends on Mount Mo-tan" into the *linga*. The relationship between the cult of the Siva *linga* and the pyramidal mountain temples in the later Angkor Period can thus be traced to these Funanese Hindu practices. The cult of the Siva *linga* on the mountain top was apparently different in principle from the *devaraja* cult of the Angkor Period, which was first inaugurated by Jayavarman II in 802 CE; as if he was not satisfied with simply worshiping the Siva *linga*, the king now willfully and openly identified himself with it and in effect deified himself in the process. It was on Mount Mahendra, which embodied the symbolic and mythological Mount Meru and the abode of Siva, where Jayavarman II was consecrated as a *cakravartin* by the *brahmin* priest Hiranyadama who properly prepared the rites and recited the four sacred Hindu texts Vinasikha, Nayottara, Sammoha, and Siraccheda. This complex ritual transferred the king's 'subtle essence' into the *linga* and thus effectively rendered himself as the living representative of Siva on earth; the *linga* was aptly given the name that combined the suffix '*esvara*' (as Siva is also known as Mahesvara) and the king's name, for example 'Rajendra' and '*esvara*' equals 'Rajendresvara' as the name for the king's *linga*. One inscription specifically designated the *linga* as "the god who is the royalty," meaning the king was Siva and a god-king (*devaraja*) after the completion of the ritualized consecration; this crucial religious rite ensured the security and prosperity of the kingdom even after the king's death as his essence continued to reside, or remained alive, in the *linga* and his temple became a living mausoleum. Moreover only the lineage of *brahmin* priests, evidently a priest caste, would be allowed to perform this ritual. This *devaraja* cult clearly elucidates the reasons and religious mechanisms behind the construction of numerous pyramidal mountain temples during the Angkor Period. The *devaraja* cult seems to have originated in Champa as its Cham King Bhadravarman (c. 350-400 CE) reportedly was the first to erect a temple at Mi-Son with a Siva *linga* named Bradresvara; probably this cult was subsequently embraced by the Khmer royalty {Coedes 1968: 46-47, 56, 58-61, 99-101, 114-115}{Chihara 1996: 75}.

As already mentioned, Oc-eo has yielded many Buddhist objects suggesting the contemporaneous arrival of Buddhism and Hinduism in Funan; during Jayavarman's reign (r. 480-514 CE) in 484 CE, the Funanese king sent three Buddhist monks to China and one of them was Nagasena. A Sanskrit inscription during Rudravarman's reign (r. 514-545 CE) mentioned the construction of a Buddhist structure, the first historical record of such edifice in Funan. Rudravarman also sent the Indian monk Paramartha or Gunaratna, originally from the Indian city of Ujjayini who was residing in Funan, to China alongwith Buddhist *sutra*s in 546 CE where he stayed and translated these into Chinese. There was a sudden appearance of several Buddhist sculptures mostly in the late Gupta Style dated between the late sixth-eighth centuries CE, most of which have been found in Angkor Borei as well as Battambang and Siem Riep. The iconography of these early Buddhist sculptures was mainly Buddha suggesting the Theravada presence but subsequently expanded to include Maitreya and Avalokitesvara common in the Mahayana pantheon. The presence of these Buddhist sculptures in Funan might be due to the influence from the neighboring Buddhist Mon kingdom of Dvaravati (sixth-thirteenth centuries CE) in the lower Menam River valley. A 791 CE inscription from Siem Riep also recorded the dedication of Lokesvara (a manifestation of Avalokitesvara) in the temple Prasat Ta Keam; Lokesvara would subsequently be elevated to the principal cult of the Khmer Buddhists during the Angkor Period, especially during Jayavarman VII's reign. Very few early Khmer kings actually paid attention to Buddhism as almost all of them were Hindu but notable kings like Yasovarman I (r. 889-900 CE), Rajendravarman (r. 944-968), Suryavarman I (r. 1010-1050), and Jayavarman VI (r. 1080-1107 CE) reportedly patronized Buddhism but only on a very limited scale with the construction of a few temples. The first Buddhist king to have crowned Kampuchea was Dharanindravarman II (r. 1150-1160); unfortunately, there are no Buddhist monuments that can positively be linked to him. The next and certainly most famous Buddhist king of Kampuchea was Jayavarman VII (r. 1181-1218 CE), the son of Dharanindravarman II. He was best remembered for the radical and abrupt transformation of the Khmer society into a Buddhist one, perhaps following the example of the Indian Buddhist Emperor Asoka. Like Asoka before him, Jayavarman VII deeply expressed his concerns for the welfares and sufferings of his subjects in his inscriptions; he also constructed numerous Buddhist monuments, the biggest of them all was the Bayon Temple in the center of his immense city of Angkor Thom, alongwith 121 resthouses along the highways and 102 hospitals throughout his vast empire. According to Coedes, Jayavarman VII intended to replace the previous Hindu *devaraja* cult with a Buddhist equivalent, the *Buddharaja* cult:

Instead of the Devaraja of the preceding reigns represented by a gold *linga*, however, the central sanctuary sheltered an enormous stone statue of Buddharaja. This statue was not only a Buddhist substitute for the Sivaite Devaraja but also a statue of apotheosis of the founder king…

The similarities between the cults of *devaraja* and *Buddharaja* are apparent and perhaps Jayavarman VII had been consecrated as a *Buddharaja* in the same way as his father Dharanindravarman II. The latter king was posthumously deified as Lokesvara under the name Jayavarmesvara in Preah Khan while his Queen Jayarajachudamani was also deified as Prajnaparamita in the monastery of Ta Prohm. The concept of a deified king in the disguised form of a statue was certainly nothing new as it had already been institutionalized in Java and Champa and the practice likely originated in India and Gandhara centuries before such as the royal temples and statues of King Kanishka at Surkh Kotal and Mathura. The Lokesvara cult was also very popular in Champa between the eighth-tenth centuries CE {Chutiwongs 2002: 289-313}; the well-known Buddhist Cham King Indrapura II (r. 875-898 CE) took the title 'Indralokesvara' when he founded Indrapura Monastery and dedicated a Lokesvara statue in its sanctuary. Thus the cult of a divinized Buddhist king as a representative of Buddha or *bodhisattva* on earth in the form of the royal statue or a *Buddharaja* was certainly not limited to or originated in Kampuchea as it was also widely practiced throughout Southeast Asia. The highest class of Vajrayana rituals, which involved the ritualized consecration of an initiate to speed up enlightenment, might have been employed to consecrate Jayavarman VII's *Buddharaja*. However despite the abundant availability of Tantric materials and sculptures during Jayavarman VII's reign, there was no evidence of Tantric rituals ever been practiced or specifically favored by him since he was a known worshiper of Lokesvara, a Mahayana *bodhisattva*. After his death, there was a brief period of Buddhist vandalisms or perhaps persecutions due to the revival of Hinduism under Jayavarman VIII (r. 1243-1295); but even this Hindu king could not hold back the tide of the Theravada that gradually attained its predominant status in Kampuchea that lasts to this day {Coedes 1968: 58, 60, 73-74, 94, 96, 113, 116-118, 135, 137, 153, 163, 173-177, 212-214}{Chihara 1996: 66-72, 75}{Jessup and Zephir 1997: 146-160}.

The Khmers already mastered the craft of manufacturing terracotta potteries and bronze objects such as urns and bells during the Neolithic and Bronze Age (c. 3000-0 BCE) before the advent of Indianization as found at the sites like Kandal and Samrong Sen {Jessup and Zephir 1997: 6-9}. Indian settlers brought with them arts and architecture, the earliest of which are Hindu statuettes of Siva, Visnu, Uma, Ganesa, etc. from Oc-eo dated at least in the second century CE {Chihara 1996: 75}; Hinduism remained a predominant religion in Kampuchea up to the twelfth century CE. There are twelve main styles or periods of Hindu sculptures {Giteau 1965: 37-101}{Groslier and Arthaud 1966: 203-215}{Chihara 1996: 80, 151} {Jessup and Zephir 1997: 142-145, 160-233, 236-241, 246-267, 275-277}:

- Phnom Da (c. 500-700 CE)
- Sambor Prei Kuk (c. 600-650 CE)
- Prei Khmeng (c. 650-700 CE)
- Prasat Andet (c. 675-700 CE)
- Kompong Preah (c. 700-750 CE)
- Kulen (c. 800-850 CE)
- Roluos (c. 879-893 CE)
- Bakheng (c. 893-925 CE)
- Koh Ker (c. 925-950 CE)
- Banteay Srei (c. 950-975 CE)
- Khleng (c. 975-1050 CE)
- Baphuon (c. 1050-1100 CE)
- Angkor Wat (c. 1100-1150 CE)

The iconography of the oldest group in the Phnom Da Style is Visnuite variously dated between late Funan to early Chenla Period. The styles of Phnom Da and Sambor Prei Kuk show definite influences from the Indian Gupta Style in their characteristic slight *tribhanga*, the fleshy and smooth modeling of the figures or even the earlier Mathura Style in the incised lines on the garments. The Sambor Prei Kuk lintel, which is a segmental arch carved with medallions and pearl strands issued from two *makara* mouths, recalls the architraves of the Indian *torana*s [6.7] and the stucco medallions on Amaravati dome [6.9]. The Prei Khmeng and Prasat Andet are transitional styles with the disappearance of the *makara*s to be replaced with floral or figural carvings. The figures gradually became more stylized and less voluptuous reflecting the localization and fusion of Indian and Khmer ideals that paved the way to the eventual emergence of a distinctive Khmer style in the subsequent centuries. Another highlight of Hindu sculptures is the Angkor Wat Style, which is typically carved in a very precise style and displays an exuberant movement and energy seemingly imbued with great religious spirits and symbolisms; it recalls the Indian Buddhist Andhra sculptures of Amaravati and Nagarjunakonda between the second-fourth centuries CE. A general observation on the Khmer sculptures is that the male and female figures typically have fleshy bodies, thick sensuous lips, split chins, and nude above the waist as in the Indian convention; their characteristic masculine square faces began to appear in the ninth century CE. The Khmers' excessive love for the flora and foliage can be seen in the abundance of ebullient floral and foliate embellishments painstakingly carved on their brick and stone monuments reaching its acme in Banteay Srei.

The majority of Khmer monuments bequeathed to us were dedicated to Hindu gods and mostly Sivaite. The two earliest recorded Hindu and Visnu temples constructed by Queen Kulaprabhavati in the reign of the Funanese King Jayavarman (r. 480-514 CE) most likely had timber superstructures elevated on brick foundations as common in early architecture. The oldest extant Khmer temples in the Sambor Prei Kuk group do not date earlier than the seventh century CE; among the last stone monuments of the Angkor Period was Prasat Suor Prat constructed by Indravarman II (?-1243 CE) and the additions to Angkor Wat galleries, Preah Pithu, and other minor structures by Jayavarman VIII (r. 1243-1295) {Coedes 1968: 60} {Jacques and Freeman 1997: 56, 278-287}. There are three basic types of Khmer temples:

(a) Isolated temples
    The oldest extant Khmer temples constitute a group of Sivaite structures at Sambor Prei Kuk constructed in the first half of the seventh century CE and contained inscriptions of King Isanavarman (r. 616-635 CE). These brick towers, with stone employed for structural members like door frames and lintels, have corbel-vaulted cellas housing Siva *linga*s and projecting porches on the one side; N 17 is a stone structure having arabesque carvings like typical Indian Gupta works {Dumarcay 2001: 39-44}.

(b) A group of isolated temples elevated on a same plinth or several plinths
    The Sambor Prei Kuk groups have enclosed walls around the main sanctuaries with Group N, Z perhaps having the most influential design {Dumarcay 2001: 41, 44}; their towers in the center, which are elevated on several low plinths, have quincunxial plans and four cardinal stairs recalling the plans of Nalanda Caityas 3, 12 in India [4.4 (# 3, 12)]. In the early Angkor Period there was another variant of this type, the triple-tower plan, consisting of three to five isolated and contiguous towers in a row(s) as in Preh Koh (879 CE) at Roluos; this design has undoubtedly been influenced by Java like Candi Loro Jonggrang and the Sri Lankan *pasada*.

(c) Pyramidal mountain temple on diminishing terraces
    Whereas Type (a) and (b) were generally dedicated to the worship of Siva *linga*s, the multi-terraced pyramidal mountain temple, which was the most

famous and biggest in Khmer architecture, was devoted to the cult of the *devaraja*. According to the Khmer tradition, as the king's reign commenced he immediately erected his *devaraja* temple and subsequently every new king would also construct yet another completely new *devaraja* temple, each grander and more domineering than the last as if each king was trying to surpass his predecessors; these huge temples were overwhelmingly constructed during the prosperous Angkor Period. The earliest temple of this type was the brick Prasat Ak Yom (c. 800 CE) having its five quincunxial towers erected on top of three diminishing terraces {Dumarcay 2001: pl. XXII-XXIII, 46}. Gradually the moat, as in Bakong (881 CE), and the roofed galleries, as in Ta Keo (1010-1050 CE), would be incorporated into the plan that culminated in the flawless Visnu temple of Angkor Wat (1113-1150 CE), the biggest Hindu temple in Asia. Baphuon (1050-1066 CE) was the last great Siva temple and also the last true pyramidal mountain temple, which has unfortunately collapsed under the massive loads of its solid stone terraces and crowning towers {Dumarcay 2001: 77}. Angkor Wat apparently corrected this flaw by lightening the load of the central terrace wherein the spaces between the towers would be left empty instead of solidly filled in as in Baphuon. The last and certainly the most intriguing of the greatest Khmer pyramidal mountain temples was the Buddhist Bayon in the center of Angkor Thom.

Between the eighth-ninth centuries CE Khmer architecture was perhaps more receptive to foreign ideas, especially from Java and Champa. Besides the terraced mountain temples and *stupa*s first pioneered in Java, other notable Javanese elements in the Khmer temples are the false doorways on the upper tiers of the temple, the continuous scroll patterns on the pilasters, and the jeweled motifs. The earliest Cham influences on Khmer arts are evident in the Prei Khmeng Style with some of its elements possibly derived from the Mi-Son E1 Style; the Prasat Damrei Krap temple (c. 800 CE) in Angkor was reputedly constructed by Cham architects {Coedes 1964: 82} {Giteau 1965: 56} {Dumarcay 2001: pl. XX-XXI, 28, 45}. The architecture of the Khmer *prasat* (tower) with its distinct division of plinth, body, crown terminating in the *amalaka*s and finials evolved considerably over the centuries. The earlier form of the *prasat* had been modeled after the South Indian *ratha* in the visibly demarcated and diminishing tiers of the crown, as in the Cham *kalan* and the Javanese *candi*. The crown of the *prasat*, however, generally has three or more tiers as the emphasis on the body is reduced and this gives the *prasat* its stunted proportion. For the first time in Angkor Wat, the Khmers also introduced a curvilinear profile for the crown of its *prasat*s while still keeping its distinct tiers, which now increased to five tiers having three *amalaka*s; these new features were mainly influenced by the North Indian Hindu Nagara *sikhara*, which was then at its architectural peak in India. The next radical phase in the Khmer *prasat* was inaugurated by Jayavarman VII as in Bayon in which its crown would be transformed into giant sculptured faces reflecting his idiosyncratic Buddhist devotion. The roofs of the galleries in Khmer architecture are mostly hooped consisting of carved stone blocks imitating tile roofs; all Khmer buildings employed the corbelled vault as the principal structural technology. On the construction materials, early Khmer temples up to the eighth century CE were mostly constructed of brick; gradually bricks would be employed for the towers and stone for the foundations until the tenth century CE as in Preah Koh (879 CE). The earliest multi-terraced stone temples was Bakong (881 CE) and all Khmer buildings were constructed in stone between the eleventh-thirteenth centuries CE. To maintain structural integrity and longevity for their buildings, the Khmers employed metal cramps and stone wedges to secure the stone blocks in place; these technologies reportedly originated in Sri Lanka {Dumarcay 2001: 16-17}. In the following period after the collapse of the Khmer Empire after Jayavarman VII's death, the Khmers reverted to timber construction due to the lack of resources to build huge stone buildings. There are evidences that the interiors of many Khmer temples might have been painted with sumptuous murals as a few remaining specimens have been detected in the Hindu temples of Preah Koh (879 CE) and Prasat Neang Khmau (c. 900-921 CE); however these were probably the exception rather than the rule {Jacques and Freeman 1997: 87} {Jessup and Zephir 1997: 90}.

It is now the moment to depart Hindu for Buddhist arts and architecture, which for the most parts did not become ubiquitous until the late twelfth century CE after Jayavarman VII's conversion to Buddhism. The oldest Buddhist images are a few bronze Buddha statuettes from the Funanese site of Oc-eo, probably dated between the fourth-early fifth centuries CE {Giteau 1965: 38}. The next phase in Buddhist sculptures occurred between the sixth-eighth centuries CE mostly in Funan; these were manufactured in stone, bronze, and wood with some gilded ones. The images show diverse styles and influences from Andhra to the Gupta-Sarnath Style in India and Dvaravati in Thailand as well as the local Khmer styles of Phnom Da and Prasat Andet; the iconography includes

Buddhas, Avalokitesvara, Lokesvara, and Maitreya with the latter typically having four arms. The next phase in Buddhist sculptures was between c. 900-1181 CE with most of the examples produced between c. 1050-1150 CE; the most popular type during this phase was Muchilinda Buddha in the Baphuon Style and Angkor Wat Style. The last and most important phase in Khmer Buddhist sculptures was the Bayon Style mainly during the illustrious reign of the Buddhist King Jayavarman VII (r. 1181-1218 CE). The Muchilinda Buddha remained popular and there also appeared for the first time in Khmer Buddhist arts narrative stories about Buddha's life in architectural reliefs; numerous meditative Buddha images were also produced alongwith Jayavarman's own sculptural portraits. Lokesvara achieved preeminence during Jayavarman's reign as he would be transformed into ubiquitously giant sculptures crowning many towers as in the Bayon. Vajrayana sculptures were also introduced during Jayavarman's reign like the multi-limbed images of Lokesvara, Prajnaparamita, and Hevajra. Sculptural production declined rapidly after Jayavarman's reign with a few Buddha images sculpted between the thirteenth-fourteenth centuries CE in the neo-Bayon Style; Theravada iconography of mainly Buddha images soon supplanted Mahayana and Vajrayana sculptures. A few Buddhist sculptures, which were probably produced between the fifteenth-sixteenth centuries CE during a brief reoccupation of Angkor, are all in wood and show obvious stylistic indebtedness to Thailand {Giteau 1965: 39-40, 42-46, 101-114, 117-133, 140-157, 173-174, 177-194}{Jessup and Zephir 1997: 146-160, 244-246, 268-274, 296-324, 334-339, 342-345}.

Exant examples of Buddhist architecture before Jayavarman VII are very scanty compared to Buddhist sculptures; the earliest Buddhist structures were no doubt constructed of perishable materials like timber and these have not survived. An inscription from Bati Province mentioned the construction of an unspecified Buddhist structure in the reign of the last known Funanese King Rudravarman (r. 514-550 CE); this was among the earliest reference of Buddhist architecture in Kampuchea. A 791 CE inscription from Siem Riep Province mentioned the dedication of a Lokesvara image in the Prasat Ta Keam; an inscribed stele recorded the construction of a Buddhist Saugatasrama (monastic residence) during the reign of Yasovarman I (r. 889-900 CE). The Buddhist royal architect Kavindrarimathana working under Rajendravarman (r. 944-968) reportedly erected the triple brick towers of Bat Chum (953 CE) that were surrounded by a moat. His Sanskrit inscriptions recorded its dedication for the images of Buddha, Vajrapani, and Prajnaparamita; it evidently was a Mahayana or early Vajrayana temple and the oldest extant Buddhist temple in Kampuchea. Suryavarman I (r. 1010-1050), who earned a posthumous Buddhist name Nirvanapada, probably constructed many Buddhist establishments in Lopburi, Thailand. The next king to have reportedly patronized Buddhism was Jayavarman VI (r. 1080-1107 CE) with a simple Buddhist monument associated with him or Phimai Temple in Thailand. According to Coedes, the university and temple of Preah Khan were for the most parts constructed or founded by Dharanindravarman II (r. 1150-1160), the first known Buddhist king in Kampuchea. An overwhelming majority of the Buddhist monuments in the Angkor Period had been constructed in a feverish haste during the reign of the fervent Buddhist King Jayavarman VII, who was the last of the greatest Angkor monarchs and an ardent Lokesvara devotee. He initiated the construction of numerous Buddhist monuments and public projects throughout his empire including 121 resthouses and 102 hospitals; the latter would be under the auspicious protection of Bhaishajyaguru (Medicine Buddha). Among Jayavarman VII's most important projects were the monasteries of Ta Prohm (1186 CE) and Preah Khan (1191 CE), the temples of Banteay Kdei (1181-1191 CE), Neah Pean (1191 CE), Ta Som (1191-1200 CE), Banteay Chmar, and the immense city of Angkor Thom with its enigmatic Bayon in the center. It is impossible for visitors to miss and forget the unforgettable and domineering yet gentle faces of Lokesvara crowning the gateways of Angkor Thom as well as on the myriad towers of the Bayon, Ta Prohm, Banteay Chmar, and Banteay Kdei; these are the most recognizable of all Jayavarman VII's monuments and certainly the most unconventional of all Buddhist temples. The Buddhist *stupa* (Khmer *chedei*) is another rare class of Khmer Buddhist monuments and only a few have been discovered in Kampuchea dated in the pre-Angkor and Angkor Period; even Jayavarman VII the great Buddhist monarch apparently did not erect a single *stupa* as if he had no knowledge of it or he probably preferred temples over *stupa*s in accordance to the deep-rooted Khmer tradition. There are several stone boundary pillars (c. 975-1000 CE), which were typically erected to mark the corners of a Buddhist establishment, with heights between 4'3"-7'6" and each is carved with Buddhist figures on the four faces; these resemble monolithic votive *stupa*s and strongly evoked the Licchavi *caitya*s in Nepal. There are two small authentic *stupa*s in Preah Khan complete with plinths, drums, *harmika*s, and *yasti-chattra*s; the first (fifteenth-sixteenth centuries CE) is a purely Sri Lankan *dagaba* while the second (seventeenth century CE) is in the Thai style of Ayuthaya {Gi-

262 . Part II. Architecture   Temple

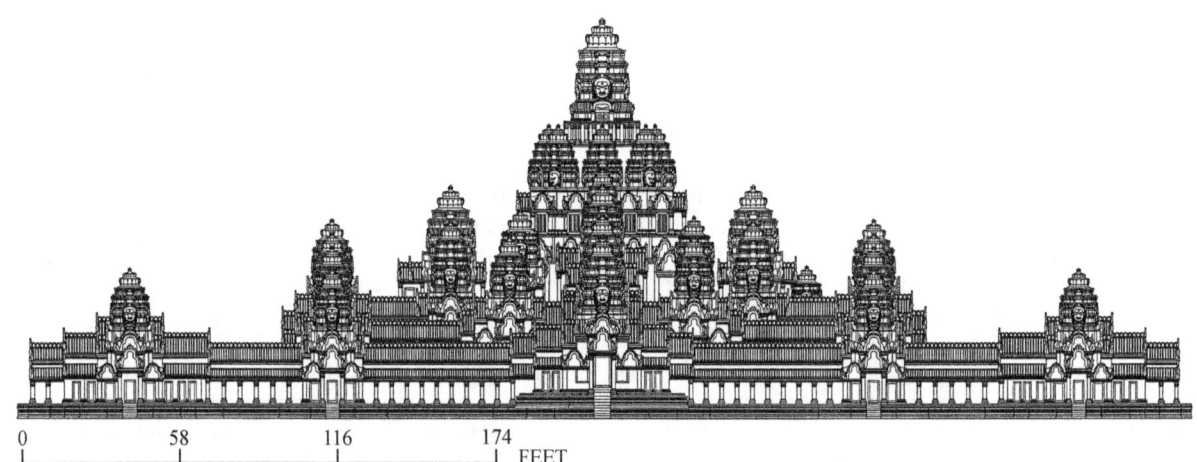

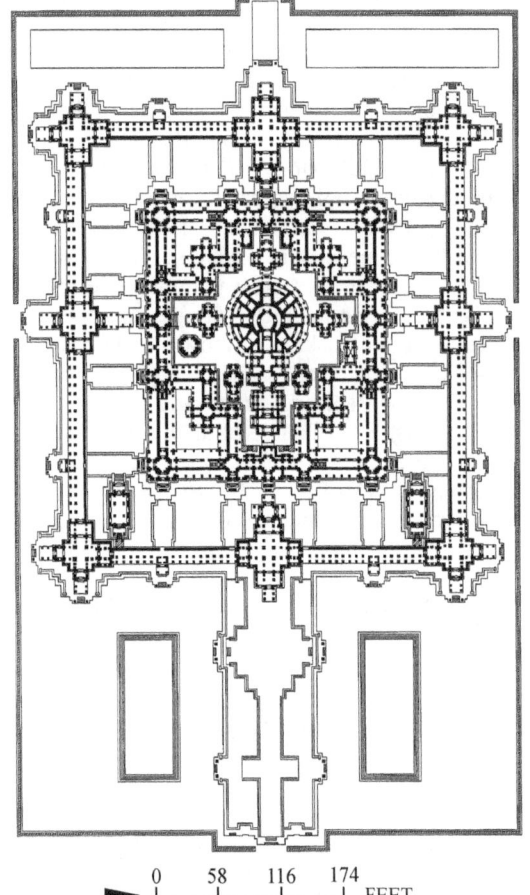

7.16. Bayon Temple elevation (restored) and plan
c. 1191-1218 CE
Angkor Thom, Siem Riep- Kampuchea

7.17. Bayon Temple
c. 1191-1218 CE
Angkor Thom, Siem Riep- Kampuchea

7.18. Bayon Temple relief on the outer gallery
c. 1191-1218 CE
Angkor Thom, Siem Riep- Kampuchea

teau 1965: 138}{Coedes 1968: 60, 94, 96, 113, 116-117, 135, 137, 153, 163, 173-177}{Chihara 1996: 147-151} {Jacques and Freeman 1997: 95-97, 126, 149-151, 224} {Jessup and Zephir 1997: 21, 242-244}.

The last of the greatest and most uniquely Khmer and Buddhist temples is no other than the enigmatic Bayon Temple [7.16-7.18] constructed by Jayavarman VII in the center of his new city Angkor Thom, which has four gateways in the four cardinal points with the main entrance facing east. The temple is about 437' x 460' for the outer rectangle and 241' x 266' for the inner rectangle plan with a height of about 140' from the ground level to the summit of the highest central tower; it is slightly smaller than its Hindu predecessor Angkor Wat. The temple is elevated on two main terraces as the third one forms the base of the cruciform gallery that skirts the terrace of the central circular temple and barely perceptible on the plan. There are three outward-facing galleries enclosing the central mass: (first) the cruciform gallery immediately below the main terrace of the central mass, (second) the corner galleries forming the inner second rectangle, and (third) the outer rectangular gallery; there are flights of stairs connecting these galleries in the four cardinal points or where there are changes in the floor levels. The walls of these galleries and interior walls of some of the towers contain narrative relief panels with some incomplete or blank; the quality of these carvings degenerated considerably compared to those of Angkor Wat half a century earlier. The outer third gallery contains non-religious themes of contemporary life and most importantly the battles between the Khmers and the Chams [7.18] which are the dominant theme in this gallery. The Chams are depicted wearing protective armors and distinctly wig-like caps on the right side while the Khmers on the left are nude in the upper bodies and do not have headgears; the two sides are clearly engaging in ferocious battles from the assortment of weapons and fighting gestures of the men and their animals. The uniformly shallow depth of the reliefs and the apparent lack of roundness in the forms suggest a decline in quality compared to the precise impeccability in earlier Angkor Wat reliefs. Scholars agreed that the inner first and second galleries, which contain narrative panels depicting Hindu scenes, might have been carved at a later time possibly during the reign of Jayavarman VIII (r. 1243-1295) who was a bigoted Hindu king to have reputedly converted the Bayon into a Hindu temple and also damaged many other Buddhist buildings {Roveda 1998: 131-150}. It is rather surprising that a monumental Buddhist temple like the Bayon is virtually devoid of Buddhist scenes while narrative scenes about Buddha's life are numerously found in some of Jayavarman VII's other famous temples like Ta Prohm. In the northeast and southeast corners of the Bayon main courtyard are two libraries; there are also traces of the foundational outlines of the twelve chapels or connecting halls that had been intentionally demolished during or after the construction. In the center is the main circular temple of about 78' diameter having radiating chapels and entrances in the cardinal and intermediate directions. There are additional halls and antechambers projecting on the eastern side of the circular mass and surrounding the latter are several buildings of various functions, which might have been constructed as an after thought than as parts of the original plan. At the heart of the central temple is a circular chapel that might once house a Muchilinda Buddha image, which was found broken in the pit below this chapel and probably damaged by Jayavarman VIII. This image alongwith a Lokesvara image and pedestal, which were discovered by Henry Parmentier in 1924 CE, prove beyond a doubt that the Bayon was originally a Buddhist temple and most likely a Mahayana one {Coedes 1963: 58}{Jacques and Freeman 1997: 256}. The most ubiquitous features of the Bayon are the fifty-five or so towers, each in the form of a giant four-faced sculpture looking out to the infinite space beyond; these mysterious gentle faces most likely depicted Lokesvara. Scholars' opinions differ considerably on the construction of the Bayon, which certainly had several phases as observed from the obvious anomalies on the plan compared to the flawless execution of its Hindu predecessor Angkor Wat {Dumarcay 2001: 92-93}{Jacques and Freeman 1997: 248-263}:

- Phase I (c. 1191-1198 CE): The temple was first founded by Jayavarman VII after he built his city Angkor Thom; the original plan was conceived as a cruciform temple in the center and enclosed by an inward-facing cruciform (first) gallery; the sculpted Lokesvara faces were probably incorporated into the towers from the start.
- Phase II (c. 1198-1205 CE): The four corner (second) galleries were constructed with their stepped-down roofs linking with the cruciform (first) galleries and together they form the inner rectangular gallery; the level of the main courtyard was accordingly raised to form a terrace. Next, the twelve chapels or connecting halls were constructed on this terrace to link with the cruciform (first) and corner (second) gallery.
- Phase III (c. 1205-1212 CE): The level of the central temple was raised higher than the cruciform (first) gallery to form a terrace that served as a new plinth for the massive circular temple in the center; the intermediate chapels were then added to the original cruciform plan and transformed it into a circu-

lar temple. The long projection on the eastern side of this circular mass was also constructed about the same time and the cruciform (first) gallery itself was also converted from inward-facing to an outward-facing one; the construction of this massive upper terrace resulted in parts of this gallery to be buried below the terrace.

- Phase IV (c. 1212-1218 CE): It was then decided that the twelve chapels would be demolished during the construction of the outer (third) gallery as their outlines could be seen positioning below the latter and the two libraries; this suggests that they had been built before the outer gallery while the two libraries were only added after this gallery had already been constructed. The constructions of these two libraries and various buildings around the circular temple on the upper terrace were probably executed at the same time. The next stage involved the construction of the long platform in the east entrance and the twin pools outside of the outer (third) gallery.

Some of the relief panels were originally left unfinished or blank probably due to the halt in the construction activities after Jayavarman VII's death; however, by this time the final form of the temple itself had probably already been completed just as we see it today. The Hindu reliefs and the low wall enclosing the temple had most likely been the works of the bigoted Hindu King Jayavarman VIII who intended to convert the Bayon into a Hindu temple. The Bayon and most of Jayavarman VII's buildings were design-build projects in which their frantic pace of construction, as observed from the numerous and likely continual modifications of the designs, reflected his burning ambitions to outdo his predecessors with what little remaining time left of his advanced age since he was already fifty-six years old when he was crowned king. It is certain that the Bayon, like all Khmer temples, was not a palace since the site of which is located to the north of the temple having its own separate gateway; moreover, there are also many theories regarding the various meanings and symbolisms of the Bayon:

- The Bayon as an architectural *mandala* symbolizing Jayavarman VII's kingdom {Coedes 1963: 65}{Coedes 1968: 175-176}{Dumarcay 2001: 25}

  This theory proposes that the changes in the Bayon design, for examples from a cruciform to rectangular plan, the additional galleries, and the four-faced towers, reflect and symbolize the spatial division of Jayavarman VII's kingdom and its gradual expansion into an empire. The temple is the embodiment of his temporal power radiating throughout his kingdom while the chapels, which reputedly housed images of the provincial guardian deities, and the towers represent the provinces of his kingdom. It is of course impossible to validate this hypothesis since some of the changes were in conformity to past Khmer, particularly Hindu, and Buddhist architectural traditions as well as due to structural requirements. The galleried architecture was the hallmark of Khmer architecture while the circular plan of the central mass with its radiating chapels had also been adopted from the Buddhist *stupa* [6.12]; the solidification and addition of the upper terrace structurally served as a strong foundation for its massive circular temple. Moreover, the supposedly geo-political *mandala* of Jayavarman VII's kingdom in this case clearly has nothing to do with the religious Vajrayana *mandala*.

- The Bayon as the body of the god and embodiment of the religious cosmo {Coedes 1963: 47-48}{Jessup and Zephir 1997: 117-121}{Dumarcay 2001: 93}

  Figuratively, the central mass appears to represent the main body of the god while the four-faced towers are his manifestations. Another variation of this theory states that Angkor Thom symbolizes Indra's capital and his Heaven of the Thiry Three Gods who were also identified as Jayavarman VII's princes and provincial governors; the Bayon is, according to this theory, Indra's palace. So far neither the iconography nor existing evidences suggest any links with Indra; the sculptures founded in the temple and the giant faces on towers clearly depict Buddha and Lokesvara not Indra; the Bayon was originally dedicated to the worship of Jayavarman VII's *Buddharaja* and Lokesvara and certainly not Indra's temple.

- The Bayon as the representation of the cosmic Mount Meru (Hindu) or Mount Sumeru (Buddhist) {Coedes 1963: 40-46}{Rowland 1977: 141-142}

  According to this theory, the Bayon central temple symbolizes the main summit of Mount Meru and the numerous towers its lesser peaks; the moat represents the cosmic ocean surrounding the sacred mountain. Unfortunately this Meru-Sumeru theory has often been a convenient cliche overused by almost every Oriental scholar to associate with virtually all religious (Hindu and Buddhist) buildings, most of which are simply fanciful speculations. It must be reminded that the architecture of the Bayon perpetuated the Khmer tradition of constructing multi-terraced pyramidal mountain temple and its closest predecessor was the massive temple of Angkor Wat as well as foreign ones like the huge Javanese *candi*s like Borobudur [6.28-6.29] and Candi Sewu [7.12-

7.13]; the moat was also common in religious architecture throughout India and the Buddhist world [4.9].
- The Bayon as an architectural expression of Vajrayana (Tantric) practices {Clark 2008}
  This recent theory suggested that the faces on the towers represented Vajrasattva, the supreme deity in the Vajrayana *anuttarayoga-tantra* class. The great flaw of this theory is that, first of all, Jayavarman VII was a known worshiper of Lokesvara, a Mahayana *bodhisattva*, and there was no evidence suggesting he ever embraced the Vajrayana. Secondly, the gentle faces on the towers with their third eyes on the forehead exhibit iconographical traits of Lokesvara and lastly all the discovered images in the Bayon, including a Muchilinda Buddha and Lokesvara, are obviously not Vajrayana.
- The Bayon as a monument for the *Buddharaja* cult {Coedes 1963: 97-100} {Coedes 1968: 175-176}
  Instead of the *devaraja* cult of the previous Hindu kings, who had been deified in the form of a royal Siva *linga*, Jayavarman VII was deified as a *Buddharaja*, that is a 'Buddha king' or a living representative of Buddha on earth and the Buddhist equivalent of the Hindu *devaraja* cult in the form of a Buddha statue installed in the central cella of the Bayon. George Coedes has cited numerous evidences for his theory. First, the relatives and members of Jayavarman VII's royal families had also been deified and their *Buddharaja* images installed in temples. Dharanindravarman II, Jayavarman VII's father, was deified in the disguised form of a Lokesvara image named Jayavarmesvara while Queen Jayarajachudamani, Jayavarman VII's mother, was deified as Prajnaparamita; Prince Srindrakumara, Jayavarman VII's son, and his body guards were also deified and their images installed in the Bayon. Second, a stele in Preah Khan recorded the dedication of twenty-three statues named Jayabuddhamahanatha (Victory-Buddha-Great Saviour), a name perhaps recalling Jayavarman VII's victory over the Chams and his rescue of the kingdom from utter ruins. An inscription on the Bayon mentioned two of these statues while another one was also found in Banteay Chmar with the 'Jayabuddhamahanatha' inscription on it; the broken Muchilinda Buddha image discovered in the bottom of the pit beneath the central tower is perhaps one of his Jayabuddhamahanatha. Thus this theory is the most convincing since it demonstrated the perpetuation of the traditional Khmer cult of deified kings and the transition from the Hindu *devaraja* cult to the Buddhist *Buddharaja*. The Bayon initially represented Jayavarman VII's kingdom where images of Buddhas, *bodhisattva*s, and provincial guardian deities were housed in the central cella and the twelve chapels; the temple was subsequently modified to reflect the worship of the *Buddharaja* and Lokesvara. The four-faced towers above all symbolize the omnipresence of the temporal and spiritual power and compassion of the king, and certainly of Buddha and Lokesvara, emanating outward to the four corners of the Khmer Empire. They proclaim to the world Jayavarman VII's conversion to Buddhism and his desire to spread Buddha's *Dharma* throughout his kingdom to ease sufferings of his people; this was in the same Buddhist tradition as Asoka when he constructed the pillars with the four addorsed lion capitals [3.3, 3.6] to spread Buddha's *Dharma* to the four corners of India and the world.

Over half a century after Jayavarman VII's death, a Chinese ambassadorial mission led by Zhou Daquan was sent by the Mongol Yuan Dynasty to Kampuchea between 1296-1297 CE; he later wrote a brief and interesting account on his visit about the contemporary life of the Khmers in Angkor {Harris 2007: 47-50}:

The walls of the city [Angkor Thom] are about twenty li [over six miles] in circumference. There are five gateways, each of them with two gates, one in front of the other. There are two gateways facing east [one for the palace and the other for the Bayon], and one gateway facing in each of the other directions. Around the outside of the city walls there is a very large moat. This is spanned by big bridges carrying large roads into the city. On either side of every bridge there are fifty-four stone deities. They look like stone generals, huge and fierce-looking... Above the gateways in the city wall there are five stone Buddha heads. Four of them face toward the four cardinal points, and one of them is placed in the middle. It is decorated with gold. On either side of the gates the stones are carved into the shape of elephants. The [city] walls are all made of piled-stones, and are about twenty-one feet high...The city walls form an exact square, with a stone tower on each of its four sides. In the center of the capital is a gold tower [the Bayon was then probably painted gold or gilt], flanked by twenty or so stone towers and a 100 or so stone chambers. To the east of it is a golden bridge [the long platform] flanked by two gold lions...Eight gold Buddhas are laid out in a row at the lowest level of stone chambers...The royal palace, officials' residences, and great houses all face east. The palace lies to the north of the gold tower [north of Bayon] with the gold bridge, near the northern gateway...

It is clear that the Bayon and Angkor Thom as seen by Zhou Daquan in the late thirteenth century CE remain essentially unchanged to this day.

In conclusion, the Bayon perpetuated the Khmer architectural tradition of building grand multi-terraced pyramidal mountain temples first inaugurated in the ninth century CE; its immediate predecessor is no other than the great Hindu temple of Angkor Wat. Jayavarman VII was the first Khmer king who broke with the tradition by constructing the first great Buddhist and also the last of the mountain temples; in doing so he was accruing religious merits and also following the exemplary deeds of the great Indian Buddhist Emperor Asoka before him. Architecturally, the Bayon is certainly the grandest and most unique Buddhist temple in the world with its serene and enigmatic four-faced towers looking down to the world in compassion; its design synthesized and drew inspirations from diverse sources of indigenous and foreign origins. The hallmarks of Khmer architecture such as the gallery, the diminishing terraces, the moat, the quincunxial and cruciform plan, and the multitude of towers are of foreign inspirations. The gallery originated in the colonnaded verandah common in the Buddhist monasteries of Gandhara [4.2] and India [4.4] while the diminishing multi-terraced design were also common in India [6.12] and Java [6.28-6.29]. The moat can also be found in Sri Lankan monasteries [4.9] while the quincunxial and cruciform plan could be traced back to Gandhara [6.17-6.18] and India [4.4 (#12), 7.10-7.11]. The sudden appearances of numerous pyramidal mountain temples in Kampuchea after Jayavarman II's return from Java were not incidental at all. The design of the Bayon, with its myriad towers on diminishing terraces clustering around a main temple alongwith its endless narrative reliefs, is essentially an architectural amalgamation of Borobudur [6.28-6.33] and Candi Sewu [7.12-7.13] in Java and hallmark Khmer features such as the moat and gallery. Above all, the genius of the Khmers was in their ability to synthesize and harmonize these diverse elements to create unique monuments of great grandeur and beauty of their own. Daigoro Chihara also suggested the similarity between the four-faced towers of the Bayon with the four pairs of eyes on the *harmika* of Swayambhunath in Nepal [6.37-6.38] {Chihara 1996: 162}; however, the giant gentle stone faces in the Bayon certainly left a deeper impression on the visitors' psyche than the painted eyes of Swayambhunath. Hindu elements are also present in the Bayon such as the curvy profile of its towers, which has obviously been influenced by the North Indian Hindu Nagara *sikhara*. The central chapel of the Bayon was the first Khmer design to have a uniquely circular plan with radiating cellas that no doubt originated in India [6.12]; however its upper tier, which has eight lesser towers surrounding a principal one that towers above them all, and the long projecting arm on the east side suggest the North Indian Hindu Nagara *sikhara* plan and elevation as in the Khajuraho temples.

Chapter 8. Four Holiest Sites

In the last days before Buddha's *Parinirvana*, he recommended his followers to visit the four holiest pilgrimage sites connected with his life: Nativity in Lumbini, Enlightenment in Bodhgaya, First Sermon in Sarnath, and Decease in Kushinagar; with the exception of Lumbini, which is located inside Nepal, all other sites are in India. As his death was impending Ananda questioned Buddha how his disciples could possibly pay homage to him when he no longer physically remained by their side, he then gave an important instruction to his disciples {Walshe 1995: 263-264}:

> Ananda, there are four places the sight of which should arouse emotion in the faithful. Which are they? "Here the Tathagata was born" is the first. "Here the Tathagata attained supreme enlightenment" is the second. "Here the Tathagata set in motion the Wheel of Dhamma" is the third. "Here the Tathagata attained the Nibbana-element without remainder" is the fourth. And Ananda, the faithful monks and nuns, male and female lay-followers will visit those places. And any who die while making the pilgimmage to these shrines with a devout heart will, at the breaking-up of the body after death, be reborn in a heavenly world.

Lumbini, Bodhgaya, and Sarnath obviously did not develop into preeminent pilgrimage centers until after Buddha preached the first sermon and founded Buddhism in c. 532 BCE while Kushinagar only became the fourth holiest site after his death in c. 487 BCE. As early as the Gupta Dynasty (c. 320-647 CE) another four secondary sites, which only ranked below the aforesaid four principal ones and all in India, had also been added to the list of the eminent pilgrimage sites including Buddha's Descent from the Trayastrimsa Heaven in Sankisa, Miracle of Sravasti in Sravasti, Offering of the Monkey in Vaishali, and Taming the Nalagiri Elephant in Rajagriha {Sahni 1914: 187-190}. These four minor sites seemed to have already existed in Asoka's time in the third century BCE as one of his pillars was found at Sankisa. The development of new pilgrimage sites was undoubtedly an attempt to accommodate the rise in new followers, sects, and different modes of worship in Buddhism. Moreover the pilgrimage sites did not exclusively belong to the historical Sakyamuni Buddha as in the centuries after his death there would appear many sites to the Buddhas in the past, present, and future, many of whom were obviously non-historical. Asoka himself went on a pilgrimage in the Nepalese Terai where he erected a pillar recording his visit and enlargement of Konakamuni Buddha Stupa at Nigali Sagar. In spite of the competition from the other Buddhas, Sakyamuni was still the historical founder of Buddhism and hence the sites associated with his life, particularly the four holiest sites, remained the most important ones and they continued to be worshiped by devotees of all Buddhist schools above all other sites. As typical in all Buddhist sites, these four holiest sites consist of monasteries, temples, *stupa*s, etc. of various sizes clustering densely around a principle edifice, usually a temple or a *stupa* that is associated with a particular event in Buddha's life. Since the lifespan of these sites lasted over 1,700 years between the sixth century BCE-twelfth centuries CE, there are numerous construction strata where new constructions would frequently be built upon existing foundations. Another common method of enlarging an existing edifice was to encase it inside a larger one and this was typical for the *stupa*s; apparently this was deemed a proper solution since it would be considered a religious sacrilege to destroy existing *stupa*s, which usually contained earlier sacred relics. If the destruction of old edifices was unavoidable when constructing new ones then old materials would generally be collected and the relics redeposited into the new monuments.

1. Lumbini, Nepal: Nativity (sixth century BCE-thirteenth centuries CE)

It was in Lumbini **[8.1-8.2]** that Prince Siddhartha Gautama was born in c. 567 BCE; the territory once belonged to India or the North Indian politico-cultural sphere but now a part of Nepal from the fact that an Asoka pillar was erected here in c. 249 BCE and another two Asoka pillars also of the same date near Taulihawa at Nigali Sagar and Gotihawa. The site is about 13 7/10 miles southwest of Bhairawa in a tranquil rural setting; it was then a favorite garden and frequent halting place for caravans traveling from Sakya, with its capital in Kapilavastu or possibly modern Tilaurakot about 17 2/5 miles west of Lumbini, to Koliya, with its capital in Devadaha about 23 3/5 miles east of Lumbini and Ramagrama as another large Koliya city further east of Devadaha. The ancient hamlet of Lumbini, as mentioned in the inscription on the Asoka pillar, has been discovered about 438 yards southwest of the Mayadevi Temple. Lumbini was named after Lumbini Devi (Queen Lumbini) of Koliya which later became

Lummindei or modern Rummindei {Rijal 1996: 8-9}{Bidari 2002: 3-4, 7}. Like the other Buddhist sites, Lumbini received a major boost in status when Asoka reportedly pilgrimaged to the place immediately after his conversion to Buddhism in c. 260 BCE. He again revisited the place in c. 249 BCE and this time he erected a stone pillar to commemorate the event; this pillar, now standing half-broken behind the Mayadevi Temple, still has an extant inscription that clearly recorded the date of Asoka's visit to Buddha's birthplace. The site continued to expand especially from the Kushan Dynasty on; the two most well-known pilgrims to have visited Lumbini were Fa-hsien (c. 409 CE) and Hsuan-tsang (c. 636 CE) who wrote detailed accounts about their sojourns. It appears that Lumbini, due to its relatively obscure location away from the North Indian heartland, did not suffer the Muslim destructions in c. 1200 CE unlike the Indian sites. The last known visitor was Ripumalla (late thirteenth-early fourteenth centuries CE), a Malla prince then wielded considerable sways in western Nepal, who engraved a few words on top of the pillar that are still extant; after his visit Lumbini sank into oblivion for nearly six centuries. In 1896 CE, three Asoka pillars were discovered by Khadga Shumsher and A. Fuhrer in Lumbini, Gotihawa, and Nigali Sagar, which finally ended any lingering doubts about the historical location Buddha's nativity and ancient Sakya; however the actual site of Kapilavastu, the capital of Sakya, remains a disputed question (Chapter 6). P. C. Mukherji made preliminary surveys of Lumbini and the Nepalese Terai in 1899 CE and wrote about his accounts in 1901 CE; he also discovered the old foundation of the Mayadevi Temple. The task of exposing this historic temple and the surrounding monuments would be left to Kesher Shumsher who excavated the area between 1933-1939 CE; the stepped pool as seen today was enlarged by him from a smaller one believed to be the original pool bathed by Queen Mayadevi before delivering the baby Siddhartha. Debala Mitra from the ASI also performed some excavations between 1957-1962 CE. The ancient village of Lumbini was finally discovered during the 1970-1971 CE excavations by B. K. Rijal; he later exposed the monasteries south of the Mayadevi Temple between 1975-1983 CE. Minor excavations had also been carried out between 1984-1997 CE most notably by the team from the Japanese Buddhist Federation. With Lumbini increasingly becoming a major international pilgrimage site, a master plan was drafted by the Japanese architect Kenzo Tange in 1978 CE for a more systematic development of the site {Rijal 1996: 3-5}{Bidari 2002: 85-97}.

The paucity of the sculptures and murals from the site, unlike the other holiest Buddhist sites in India,

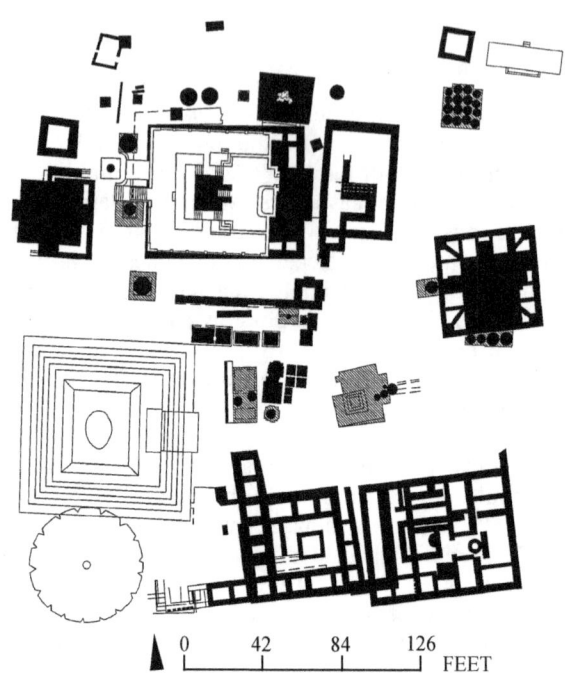

8.1. Site plan
c. 260 BCE-1300 CE
Lumbini- Nepal

8.2. Mayadevi Temple and Asoka pillar
c. 260 BCE-1300 CE
Lumbini- Nepal

clearly demonstrates that Lumbini, despite being the birthplace of Buddha, was not particularly popular to the Buddhists and this was most likely due to its isolated location; the most eminent sites, from the abundance of remains and recovered artifacts, are Bodhgaya and Sarnath.

The architectural remains at Lumbini, which spread over an area of 293' x 314', can be divided into five categories: the Asoka pillar, the sacred pool, temples, *stupa*s, and monasteries.

(a) Asoka Pillar

This pillar now reduced to a stump immediately behind (west) of the Mayadevi Temple was originally erected by Emperor Asoka during his pilgrimage tour of the Nepalese Terai; the material and form of this 2'7" diameter pillar are identical as the other Asoka pillars (Chapter 3), which is sandstone with a highly polished surface and a slight taper toward the top. Its capital was originally crowned with a horse which was reportedly seen by Hsuan-tsang lying on the ground but no longer extant; it is estimated to have once stood at about 31' above the ground. P. C. Mukherji described its capital as having 'the usual festoons in the face of the big cyma' {Rijal 1996: 117-118}{Bidari 2002: 63-64}. Most importantly, it still has an Asoka inscription stating {Hultzsch 1969: 164-165}{Bidari 2002: 60-62}:

> When King Devanampriya Priyadarsin [Asoka] had been anointed twenty years [c. 249 BCE], he came himself and worshipped [at this spot], because the Buddha Sakyamuni was born here. [He] both caused to be made a stone bearing a horse [also interpreted as a brick wall decorated with stone or a stone railing] and caused a stone pillar to be set up, [to mark the spot] that the Blessed One was born here. [He] made the village of Lumbini free of taxes, and paying [only] an eighth [1/8] share [of the produce].

A brick wall has been found about 5'6" below the ground level having large-sized bricks, a sure indication of ancient remains, which was probably the original wall and possibly contemporary with the enclosed wall of the Asoka pillar {Rijal 1996: 117-118}. Near the top of the broken pillar is another inscription and prayer by Ripumalla (late thirteenth-early fourteenth centuries CE) praying "Om mani padme hum. May Prince Ripu Malla be long victorious!" {Bidari 2002: 80}. Ripumalla was a known ruler of the Malla Dynasty in western Nepal and who was likely a follower of Tibetan Buddhism; his territory certainly once shared a common border with the western Tibetan kingdom of Guge at the time.

(b) Sacred Pool

It lies immediately southwest of the Mayadevi Temple; it was here that Queen Mayadevi bathed and afterward walked northward to the current temple where she felt an intense labor pain and, while grasping the branch of the *asoka* or *sala* tree, delivered the baby Siddhartha.

It was originally a small pond but recently widened to a large pool with descending steps faced with brick and plaster during Kesher Shumsher's excavation between 1933-1939 CE {Rijal 1996: 4}{Bidari 2002: 110-111}.

(c) Temples

There are several temples at the site, of which the most important and biggest one is the Mayadevi Temple of about 69' x 84' with its current form dated between 1998-2003 CE; below it are foundations of earlier temples with the lowest one dated back to Asoka's time. Though scholars' opinions vary considerably over its construction phases, this temple overall appears to have been constructed in six main phases {Rijal 1996: 4-7, 12, 118-119, pl. XIX-XXIV}{Bidari 2002: 73-75, 87, 91-97}:

- Phase I (third century BCE-first centuries CE): Asoka probably constructed the first temple at Lumbini in c. 260 BCE during his pilgrimage to the Buddhist sites in the Nepalese Terai; it might have been constructed before his next return and erection of a pillar in c. 249 BCE. This edifice was likely a hypaethral shrine having fifteen brick chambers and a marker stone slab inside the back central chamber to mark the exact spot where Buddha was born; these chambers were enclosed by a perimeter wall creating a *pradaksina* path in between. Notice its descriptions seemingly resemble a *bodhigriha* [7.6-7.7] which was consistent with the aniconic worship in that period.

- Phase II (second-third centuries CE): The earlier hypaethral shrine was possibly converted into a flat-roofed structure, most likely of brick and plaster. The defaced Nativity sculpture of Mayadevi delivering the baby Siddhartha in the Mathura Style found by P. C. Mukherji in the main chamber has been dated between the second-third centuries CE and probably also the construction date for this new temple.

- Phase III (seventh-eighth centuries CE): The temple was again redesigned into a classic Indian *sikhara* with a main chamber in the back to be crowned by a straight-edged pyramidal tower as in the Mahabodhi Temple [7.10-7.11]; the main chamber would be preceded with a flat-roofed anteroom or *mandapa*. Probably many Indian Buddhist temples in this period had a straight-edged pyramidal tower over the sanctum sanctorum; hence it must also be the case for the *sikhara* of the Mayadevi Temple in this phase, which was not the curvilinear North Indian Hindu Nagara *sikhara* as P. C. Mukherji believed. The excavated plinth of this phase had decorations of beautiful cyma moldings, lotus petals, and floral

motifs characteristic of Gupta or late Gupta designs.
- Phase IV (1890-1900 CE): When P. C. Mukherji visited the temple in 1899 CE he saw a modern whitewash square structure erected over the ruined temple. The local Hindus worshiped the Nativity sculpture in the main chamber, which they believed to be the Hindu goddess Rupadevi or Beautiful Queen and had no clue that this temple was the famous birthplace of Buddha.
- Phase V (1933-1939 CE): Kesher Shumsher essentially reinforced the flat roof of the temple with concrete and also erected a square *sikhara* above the roof terrace toward the back (west) end and directly above the main chamber below; this structure was at best a modern imitation of its Indian *sikhara* predecessor. Doors were also added in the northern and southern walls while stairs were added to the eastern and western walls.
- Phase VI (1998-2003 CE). When I visited Lumbini in October 2003 CE the square *sikhara* above the roof terrace had been replaced with a small Nepalese *caitya* like Swayambhunath [6.37-6.38]; the stairs were relocated to the northern and southern walls.

(d) *Stupa*s

The oldest extant remain at the site, which was believed to predate even the Asoka pillar, was a rectangular structure about 33' from the northwest corner of the Mayadevi Temple; it has been dated between the fifth-third centuries BCE and was partially covered in its northeast corner by a small late Maurya or Asoka square *stupa* {Rijal 1996: 9}. Most *stupa*s in Lumbini cluster around the Mayadevi Temple on all sides dated between the third century BCE-ninth centuries CE {Bidari 2002: 103-106}. The earliest group lies north of the Mayadevi Temple and possibly also the two *stupa*s on both sides of the Asoka pillar; these *stupa*s dated in Asoka's time in the third century BCE from its plainness and relatively small sizes. A relic casket containing human bones has been recovered from the square *stupa* near the northwest corner of the Mayadevi Temple; sixteen terracotta seals were found inside the large cruciform *stupa* about 70' east-southeast of the Mayadevi Temple with a foundation dated in Asoka's time {Rijal 1996: 9}{Bidari 2002: 106}. The *stupa* about 60' southeast of the Mayadevi Temple also has an Asoka or late Maurya foundation; the group immediately south of the Mayadevi Temple dated between the second century BCE-eighth centuries CE. The large *stupa* west of the Mayadevi Temple undoubtedly has an early foundation, possibly dated in Asoka's time but judging from its cruciform plan it does not appear to date any earlier than the fourth century CE; only the foundations of all these *stupa*s remain while their superstructures have all disappeared. The virtual absence of *stupa*s and sculptures from the Pala Dynasty (c. 750-1199 CE) in Lumbini, which are numerously found in Bodhgaya and Sarnath, is evident that the site had already been in serious decline from the ninth century CE on.

(e) Monasteries

There are remains of three large monasteries south and southeast of the Sacred Pool and the foundations certainly continue westward to the present pipal tree; these have been dated between the third century BCE-fourth centuries CE {Bidari 2002: 108-110}. Strictly speaking, only the surface foundations may be dated between the first-fourth centuries CE since they are very similar to the quadrangular monasteries of Gandhara [4.2] and do not have projecting porticos or colonnaded verandahs in the interiors as in later monasteries like Nalanda [4.4]. The presumedly rectangular assembly hall serving the monasteries east of the Mayadevi Temple might be contemporary with the southern monasteries and dated between the first-fourth centuries CE.

There were three celebrated Chinese pilgrims to have visited and wrote detailed descriptions on Lumbini, namely Seng-tsai, Fa-hsien, and Hsuan-tsang {Bidari 2002: 76-79}; Seng-tsai wrote a brief and earliest foreign account of the site when he reportedly visited it between c. 350-375 CE {Deeg 2003: 57}:

> The marvelous tree, which the excellent queen grasped when the Buddha was being born, is called *xuhe* [*asoka*]. King Asoka made out of lapis lazuli a statue of the queen in the act of grasping [the tree] and giving birth to the prince...The outlines of the marks of where the prince walked seven steps are also still preserved today. King Asoka enclosed the marks with lapis lazuli on both sides, and again had them covered over with a long slab of lapis lazuli... One still sees clearly the outlines of the seven foot prints...When the king was born, the [two] kings of the *naga*s [serpents or elephants] came to the prince and, one to the left and the other to the right, spewed water and bathed him. The one *naga* was seen to spew cold water, and the other warm water; [the water] produced two pools.

The next account was given by Fa-hsien who arrived in Lumbini about c. 409 CE {Deeg 2003: 47-48}:

> Fifty li [15 1/2 miles] to the east of the city [Kapilavastu] there is a royal park. The park is called Lumbini. [There] the wife [Mayadevi] took a bath

in a pond, left the pond from the north side, took twenty steps [paces or 50'] forward, grasped a tree with her hand and, [turning] to the east, delivered the prince. The prince came down to the earth and took seven steps. The two *naga* kings bathed the prince. On the spot where [his] body was washed a well was built...Five *yojana*s [forty-five miles] to the east of the Buddha's birthplace there is a country called Ramagrama.

The most detailed account was given by Hsuan-tsang who sojourned in Lumbini around c. 636 CE {Rijal 1996: 139-140}{Deeg 2003: 54-55}:

Going eighty or ninety li [24 9/10 to twenty-eight miles] northeast of the Arrow Spring [this spot was thirty li or 9 3/10 miles southeast of Kapilavastu], one comes to Lumbini. There is bathing pond of the Sakya clan...Twenty-four or twenty-five steps [paces or 60'-62.5'] to the north [of the pond] there is an Asoka flower tree...This is the place where the sacred birth of the bodhisattva took place...Farther to the east are two *stupa*s which were built by King Asoka, [and these] are the places where the two *naga*s bathed the prince. After the bodhisattva was born he took seven steps in each of the four cardinal directions without being supported and said: "In heaven and on earth I alone am the venerable. From now on my rebirths have come to an end"...The two *naga*s leapt out [of the earth] and rested in the air. Each of them spewed water to wash the prince - one cold, one warm. East of the *stupa* which [marks] the place where the prince was bathed, are two pure springs, and beside them two *stupa*s were built. This is the place where the two *naga*s leapt out from the earth... To the south [of the place where Mayadevi and the two *naga*s bathed the bodhisattva] there is a *stupa* [which marks] the place where the ruler of the gods, Sakra [Indra], received the bodhisattva...Nearby there are four *stupa*s; this is the place where the four heavenly kings [*lokapalas*] took the bodhisattva in their arms...The bodhisattva was born from the right thigh [of his mother]...Beside the *stupa*s of the four heavenly kings...Not far away, there is a big stone pillar, on top of it [they] have made a horse statue; it was erected by King Asoka. Later an evil naga's ferocious thunder-clap split this pillar in the middle down to the earth [the Asoka pillar could have been hit and broken by lightning before Hsuan-tsang's arrival]. At its side there is a small river flowing southeast [which] is called by the local tradition 'Oil River' [this river is about 547 yards east of the Mayadevi Temple which still retains its ancient name and called by the locals as the Telar or Oil River; it has changed course since Hsuan-tsang's visit]... Its flowing [water] is usually pinguid...From there [Lumbini] going eastward about 500 li [155 miles] in [passing] devastated fields and wild forests, [one] reaches the country of Ramagrama.

Like the other holiest sites, Buddhists from all over the world have come and constructed their national monasteries in Lumbini east of the main site; these, however, are all modern ones.

2. Bodhgaya, India: Enlightenment (sixth century BCE-mid fifteenth centuries CE)

Bodhgaya [8.3-8.4] about 7 1/2 miles south of Gaya in Bihar was the place where Buddha attained Enlightenment under the *bodhi*-tree at the age of thirty-five in c. 532 BCE; it is unquestionably the holiest pilgrimage site for Buddhists. It was initially known only to the local Indians and worshiped by the Buddhists during Buddha's ministry; it apparently did not become a preeminent international site until the visit and conversion of Emperor Asoka in c. 260 BCE where he reputedly erected a pillar of an elephant capital as depicted on the Bharhut relief [7.6], which is no longer extant, to commemorate his visit. The site encompasses three distinct zones:

- Zone A [7.6-7.11] includes the Mahabodhi Temple erected over the spot where Buddha became enlightened, *bodhi*-tree, *vajrasana*, and Buddha's Walk, all are enclosed within a 10' high sandstone *vedika*.
- Zone B [8.3-8.4] is the spacious courtyard surrounding Zone A containing mostly votive *stupa*s and smaller temples; it is also enclosed within double circuit walls creating a *pradaksina* path in between.
- Zone C is the periphery zone beyond Zone A and Zone B where foreign and Indian monasteries have been constructed over the centuries alongwith the various sites associated with Buddha's life.

The 377' x 392' Zone B [8.3-8.4] contains numerous monuments in of various sizes and materials clustering around the main temple; the most conspicuous of these are temples and votive *stupa*s constructed by Indian and foreign pilgrims over the centuries as tokens of their devotion, to earn religious merits and commemorate their visits. Cunningham reported about five strata of monuments in this zone, of which about 200 belong to the lower stratum still in good conditions; there are three types of objects found here including votive *stupa*s, temples,

272 . Part II. Architecture

8.3. Mahabodhi Temple site plan (*above*)
c. 260 BCE-1450 CE
Bodhgaya- India

8.4. Mahabodhi Temple and *bodhi*-tree (*below*)
c. 260 BCE-1450 CE
Bodhgaya- India

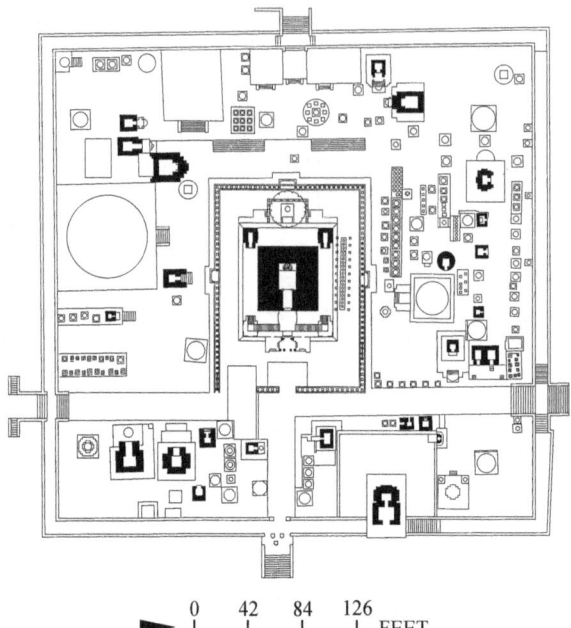

plaques, and sealings {Cunningham 1961: 34-38, 46-52}{Leoshko 1988: 62-72}. The temples typically have open interiors in which Buddhist images are displayed and where pilgrims can enter to worship. Votive *stupa*s, which are of similar materials like the temples, are constructed of stone, stone-and-brick, and clay in which the most common type is the monolithic *stupa*s numbering in the thousands and ranging in sizes between 2"-2' diameter; there are also hundreds of thousands miniature clay *stupa*s between 2"-3" or smaller. The most important and largest of all votive *stupa*s typically have five distinct tiers: the plinth, base, drum, *harmika*, and *yasti-chattra*; they also have one or four image niches in the four faces of the drum. Their architectural emphasis on the verticality, the plinth, and the elongated drum are obviously modeled after Gandhara *stupa*s **[6.15]**; from their architectural styles, inscriptions, and pilgrims' accounts one can reconstruct their approximate chronologies. The biggest votive monument in the courtyard, as also described by Hsuan-tsang, is the Asoka Stupa south of the temple but its current form is likely of a later date. The monolithic stone *stupa*s are certainly the oldest in the courtyard; one example provided by Cunningham closely resembles the *caityagriha stupa* in Bhaja Cave 12 **[5.4-5.5]** {Cunningham 1961: pl. XXIII, type A}; most of the existing votive monuments in the courtyard today were erected during the illustrious Pala Dynasty. The third category of votive objects, or the plaques and sealings, are terracotta which typically have sculptural reliefs of Buddhas and *bodhisattva*s with Buddhist creeds inscribed on them; portable terracotta plaques were very popular in Southeast Asia as in Myanmar.

The international status of Bodhgaya has been well attested from numerous famed foreign pilgrims visited the site and who wrote detailed travelogues about their sojourns; many also built commemorative monuments and left their inscriptions throughout the site. Probably the earliest foreign Buddhists visiting and settling in Bodhgaya were the Sri Lankans who were recorded as among the donors of the sandstone *vedika* **[7.8]**. They continued to expand their presence in Bodhgaya over the centuries as evident from the numerous monuments that they had dedicated throughout the site. Among these

were the Mahabodhi Sangharama by King Meghavana (r. 362-389 CE) now a huge ruin outside and north of Zone B, a temple (c. 433-459 CE) by the celebrated author Mahanama I of the Sri Lankan chronicles on the north side of the temple, and another temple (589 CE) by Mahanama II near Mahanama I's {Ahir 1994: 26-31}. The Gandharans, or the Kushans, were the next group to have their presence at the site; the Kumrahar plaque **[7.9]** likely depicted the contemporary Mahabodhi Temple which might have been constructed by them. The numerous *stupa*s and temples shown on the plaque are proofs that the site had already been crowded with monuments by the second century CE and many were certainly erected by Gandhara pilgrims; the most obvious sign of the Gandharans' presence was some Kharosthi inscriptions found at the site {Cunningham 1961: 22-23}{Leoshko 1988: 17}. The Nepalese also dedicated a few monuments from the recovered coins of the Nepalese King Pasupati which Cunningham dated between c. 300-400 CE {Cunningham 1961: 24, 34}; in my view, a fifth-sixth centuries CE date would be more acceptable. Many well-known Chinese pilgrims like Fa-hsien and Hsuan-tsang sojourned at the Mahabodhi Temple for some times and wrote lengthy accounts on the site. The famed Chinese pilgrim Fa-hsien, who visited the site around c. 409 CE, described the monuments in the courtyard {Ahir 1994: 36}:

> Pagodas [*stupa*s] have also been raised at the following places…Where the devas caused to appear a chamber built from the seven preciosities and there made offerings to Buddha for seven days; where Buddha sat facing the east on a square rock under a fig-tree when Brahma came and begged him to expound the Faith; where four heavenly kings offered to Buddha their alms-bowls...

The most detailed description of the monuments in the courtyard was given by Hsuan-tsang in c. 637 CE {Ahir 1994: 5, 39-41, 43-44}:

> [Buddha spent Week One under the *bodhi*-tree, Week Two walking back and forth at Buddha's Walk]… On the left side of the road, to the north of the place where Buddha walked is a large stone, on top of which, as it stands in a great *vihara*, is a figure of Buddha with his eyes raised and looking up. Here in former times Buddha sat for seven days contemplating the *bodhi*-tree [Week Three].
> Not far to the west of the *bodhi*-tree is a large *vihara* in which is a figure of Buddha made of brass…He stands with his face to the east…This is the place where Buddha sat on a seven-gemmed throne made by Sakra Devaraja when Brahma Raja built a hall for him of seven precious substances, after he had arrived at complete enlightenment. Whilst he thus sat for seven days in reflection of the mysterious glory [Week Four].
> Not far to the south of the *bodhi*-tree is a *stupa* about 100' high, which was built by Asoka-raja…[A *stupa* constructed] where Sakra-raja, under the guise of a grass-cutter, offered Buddha a grass bundle which he sat on under the *bodhi*-tree.
> Not far to the north of this spot is a *stupa* where Bodhisattva saw a flock of blue birds rising up as a good omen indicating his holiness and impending enlightenment.
> To the east of the *bodhi*-tree, on the left and right of the great road, there are two *stupa*s. This is the place where Mara-raja tempted Bodhisattva.
> To the northwest of the *bodhi*-tree in a *vihara* is the image of Kasyapa Buddha. To the northwest of Kasyapa statue there are two brick chambers, each containing a figure of an Earth goddess who became witnesses to Buddha's greatness when he was challenged by Mara-raja.
> To the northwest of the wall of the *bodhi*-tree is a *stupa* about 40' high; it was built by a merchant chief of Tsaukuta.
> At the southeast angle of the wall of the *bodhi*-tree is a *stupa* by the side of Nyagrodha tree. Beside it, there is a *vihara* in which is a sitting figure of Buddha. This is the spot where the great Brahmadeva exhorted Buddha, when he had first acquired enlightenment, to turn the wheel of the excellent law.
> By the side of the eastern gate of the wall of the *bodhi*-tree is a *stupa* where Mara-raja's demon army was subdued Buddha when they failed to frighten him. Not far from this are two *stupa*s built by Sakra and Brahma.

Some of the structures reported by Hsuan-tsang had already been seen earlier by Fa-hsien; these spots and their commemorative monuments were subsequently identified by Cunningham in the late nineteenth century CE {Cunningham 1961: 34-36}. In the eleventh century CE, there was another surge of Chinese pilgrims visiting the site and this time they dedicated votive structures in the courtyard complete with Chinese inscriptions {Cunningham 1961: 67-74}. The Myanmaris were the last important group of foreign Buddhists to have built a permanent settlement in Bodhgaya; their familiar presence lasted between c. 1035-1306 CE as recorded in their inscriptions at the site {Cunningham 1961: 75-77}{Ahir 1994: 72-74}. They were the first foreign Buddhists to make contacts with the site and repair the ruined Mahabodhi Temple in 1810 CE after it had been deserted for nearly five centuries; their works ultimately stirred up the Buddhist sentiments in India and abroad in an effort to reclaim the site from the Hindu Mahants.

Zone C also has numerous monuments associated with the important events in Buddha's life; this is also the area where monasteries have been constructed by Indians and foreign Buddhists from the earliest times to this day. The oldest record of a monastery at Bodhgaya was in an inscription (second century CE) mentioning the dedication of a Buddha statue in the Vajrasana Gandhakuti and Vihara; Cunningham attributed this inscription to the construction of the new Mahabodhi Temple {Cunningham 1961: 22-23, 58} that was probably concurrent with the issuance of the Kumrahar plaque. The next inscription (384 CE) mentioned the dedication of a Buddha image in a temple and monastery named Amatya-dhura Vihara {Barua 1975: 70}. Another great monastery was the Mahabodhi Sangharama, now a huge ruin north of the Mahabodhi Temple, constructed by the Sri Lankan King Meghavana with the permission from the Indian Gupta King Samudragupta (r. 330-380 CE). This monastery, which has four corner round bastions reminiscent of Gandhara design **[6.18]**, was probably one of the three monasteries mentioned by Fa-hsien in c. 409 CE and certainly seen by Hsuan-tsang in c. 637 CE; the celebrated Tibetan pilgrim Dharmasvamin and Nalanda student stayed in this monastery in 1234 CE {Ahir 1994: 26-31}. There was no record of any Chinese presence in Bodhgaya in the early days; however, I-tsing (683-727 CE) mentioned a Chinese Buddhist community and monastery about 250-300 miles east of Nalanda as early as the third century CE {Mookerji 1947: 11}. The Myanmaris certainly built their monasteries around the Mahabodhi Temple but they left no records of these; their inscriptions were all about the various repairs and offerings to this temple. Below are brief summaries of Fa-hsien's and Hsuan-tsang's descriptions of the monuments in Zone C; the first was Fa-hsien's account as witnessed in c. 409 CE {Ahir 1994: 36}:

> Where Buddha attained to Buddhaship, there are three monasteries, each with resident priests…The strictness with which…the holy brotherhood observed their vows and disciplinary regulations, and the gravity of their deportment when sitting, rising, or entering an assembly, persist down to the present day [probably Sri Lankan Theravada monks] Pagodas [*stupas*] have also been raised at the following places…where the blind dragon [*naga*], Muchilinda, coiled around Buddha for seven days to shelter him [Week Six]…where the 500 traders gave him boiled grain and honey; and where he converted the brothers Kasyapa with their disciples to the number of 1,000 souls.

A more detailed account was given by Hsuan-tsang in c. 637 CE {Ahir 1994: 41-43}:

> To the southwest of the *bodhi*-tree, outside the walls, there is a *stupa*; this is where the old house of the two shepherd girls stood who offered the ricemilk to Buddha. By the side of it is another stupa where the girls boiled the rice; by the side of the *stupa* Tathagata received the rice [Week 5].
> Outside the south gate of the *bodhi*-tree is a great tank about 700 paces [1750'] round…Still to the south there is a tank; formerly when Tathagata had just acquired perfect enlightenment, he wished to bathe; then Sakra…caused a pond [Ghosal Chak] to appear as a phantom. On the west is a great stone, which was brought from the Himalaya by Sakra [Indra], where Buddha washed his robes and dried them. By the side of this is a *stupa* where Buddha put on the old garments…Still to the south in a wood is a *stupa* where an old woman gave the old garments to Tathagata.
> To the east of the pond which Sakra caused to appear, in the midst of a wood, is the lake of the Naga king Muchalinda [west of Urel]…On the west bank is a small *vihara* in which is a figure of Buddha. Formerly, when Tathagata acquired complete enlightenment, he sat on this spot for seven days dwelt in ecstatic contemplation [Week Six]. Then Muchalinda kept guard over Tathagata; with his folds seven times round the body of Buddha, he caused many heads to appear, which overshadowed him as a parasol; therefore to the east of this lake is the dwelling of the Naga. To the east of the tank of Muchalinda is a *vihara* standing in a wood is a figure of Emaciated Buddha. At the side of this is the place where Buddha walked up and down, about seventy paces or so long [175'], and on each side of it is a Pippala tree [south of Urel]. By the side of the Pippala tree which denoted the place of Buddha's fast is a *stupa*; this is where the five Ajnata Kaundinya brothers [bodyguards sent by his father King Suddhodana and who later became Buddha's first disciples when

they heard his first sermon at Sarnath] resided and practiced austerities with Buddha.

To the southwest [should be the southeast] of the above spot is a *stupa* where Bodhisattva entered the Nairanjana to bathe [southeast of Urel or Tika Bigha]. By the side of the river, not far off, is the place where Bodhisattva received rice-milk. By the side of this is a *stupa* where the merchant-prince(s) [Tapassu and Bhallika from Utkala, Orissa] offered him the wheat and honey [Week Seven]. Not far from this spot is a *stupa* where his mother Maya descended from heaven to hear Buddha preached. By the side of this spot is a dry pool, on the border of which is a *stupa* where in former days Tathagata displayed various spiritual changes to convert those who were capable of it. By the side of this spot is a *stupa* where Tathagata converted three Kasyapa brothers of Uruvila [Urel] and 1,000 of their followers. To the northwest of the spot where the Kasyapa brothers were converted is the place Buddha overcame the fiery Naga to which Kasyapa sacrificed. To the south of Muchalinda tank is a *stupa* where Kasyapa went to save Buddha during an inundation and saw the water split between Buddha's feet which created a dry ground that he can walk on.

Outside the northern gate of the wall of the *Bodhi* tree is the Mahabodhi Sangharama built by a former king of Sinhala [Sri Lanka]. The edifice has six halls, with towers of observations of three stories; it is surrounded by a wall of defense 30'-40' high…The *stupa*s are high and large in proportion and beautifully ornamented; they contain relics of Buddha…The priests in this convent are more than 1,000 men; they studies the Great Vehicle [Mahayana] and belong to the Sthavira school [probably Theravada monks with Mahayana inclination].

The monuments surrounding Zone A, as meticulously documented by Hsuan-tsang, have already been identified by Cunningham with a great deal of certainty {Cunningham 1961: 37-41}; these, like the Mahabodhi Temple, had also been abandoned for nearly five centuries. In 1875 CE, the Myanmaris constructed a rest house for their use during the restoration of the temple and it was the first modern building constructed by a foreign Buddhist country since the abandonment of the site; gradually Buddhists from all over the world also began to come back and dedicated more monuments around the site, a process that continues to the present day.

3. Sarnath, India: First Sermon (sixth century BCE-twelfth centuries CE)

Soon after Buddha attained *Sambodhi* in Bodhgaya, he set out to Sarnath **[8.5-8.6]** about five miles north of Varanasi in Uttar Pradesh where he preached the first sermon to the five ascetic-companions who had abandoned him earlier. They became his first disciples and together they formed the Buddhist *Sangha*; this event was in c. 532 BCE and therefore the official commencement of Buddhism. Buddha spent the first rainy season here where he exhorted the newly ordained monks to go on missionaries to spread his teachings to the four corners of India. Sarnath is well-known in Buddhist scriptures as Isipatana or Rishipatana (the Place Where the Sages Fell) and Mrigadava (Deer Park) {Bhattacharya 1924: 17-31}{Sahni 1933: 1-2}. Rishipatana got its name from the legend about the 500 Pratyeka (Private) Buddhas who died, that is attained *Parinirvana*, and their ashes fell from the sky at Sarnath after they heard the news of Sakyamuni's Enlightenment. Mrigadava was the setting for a Buddhist *jataka* in which the Deer King (Buddha) was willing to sacrifice his life to save a pregnant doe from being slaughtered by the predatory king of Benares; the king, feeling ashamed and remorseful about the Deer King's selfless compassion, then set aside a tract of land for the deer herd, the Mrigadava, and banned deer hunting in the area. Sarnath, however, is a modern name and derived from the word 'Saranganatha' meaning 'Lord of the Deer,' obviously referring to Buddha; according to scholars, this name originated in the twelfth century CE. It officially became a holy site for Buddhists after Buddha's first sermon but it was not until Emperor Asoka's visit around c. 260 BCE that the place began a new epoch in arts and architecture. Asoka erected a glistening pillar **[3.3, 3.6]** engraved with his edict on the occasion and which stump still stands today in the back of the main temple; the Dharmarajika Stupa south of this temple was also likely constructed by him. The site continued to expand under the Shungas and Kushans; the Sarvastivadins, an orthodox Theravada sect, probably populated Sarnath between the first-third centuries CE but was later replaced by another Theravada sect, the Sammitiya, in the fourth century CE. Fa-hsien and Hsuan-tsang both visited Sarnath in c. 405 CE and c. 636 CE respectively when the site and Indian Buddhism were at its glorious peak; Hsuan-tsang saw about 1,500 Sammitiya monks who still held a prominent position at Sarnath since the fourth century CE {Bhattacharya 1924: 167-169}{Sahni 1933: 4-5}. Already in the early sixth century CE, Sarnath and other North Indian sites had been devastated by a series of Hephthalite invasions from the northwest, most notably by the wicked Buddhist persecutor Miharakula. Sarnath again suffered from several Muslim invasions in the early eleventh century CE, the first by Mahmud of Ghazni in 1018 CE and the second by Ahmad Nialatigin in 1033 CE; it regained some of its former glories with the restorations in 1026 CE during the Pala Dynasty and between 1114-1154 CE in the Gaharwala Dynasty. The final demise of Sarnath was in 1193 CE when it was destroyed during the Muslim invasions led by Muhammad Ghori; Sarnath was deserted afterward and faded from memories for the next six centuries {Bhattacharya 1924: 45, 66-76}{Sahni 1933: 5-6}. The reawakening of Sarnath began in 1794 CE when Jagat Singh, a local *raja* of Varanasi, completely pulled down the Dharmarajika Stupa to collect materials for the construction his new bazaar Jagatganj Mahalla. He found two relic vessels, the smaller one of marble inside a larger one of stone, with the contents of the inner one including bones, pearls, gold pots, and corals; all were scattered into the Ganga River. The Commissioner of Benares Jonathan Duncan wrote an account on the discovery of this *stupa* and obtained the two vessels, the bigger one of which was subsequently lost, which he sent to the ASB. The site began to attract archaeologists when Colonel C. Mackenzie did some preliminary explorations in 1815 CE and Alexander Cunningham also excavated the site between 1834-1836 CE. Unfortunately some forty of the fine sculptures had been left behind by Cunningham and fifty to sixty cartloads of stone were also used by the locals in the construction of the Duncan bridges over the Barna River. Major Markham Kittoe was the next person to excavate the site between 1851-1852 CE; however he carelessly used many stone blocks readily available at the site to construct the Queen's College in Varanasi. The most important excavations were carried out by F. O. Oertel between 1904-1906 CE when he discovered the main temple alongwith the Asoka pillar and its capital as well as numerous other important structures and sculptures; it was then that the identity of Sarnath as the place where Buddha originally preached the first sermon no longer remained a mystery. John Marshall with the assistance of Sten Konow also spent two seasons digging the site between 1907-1908 CE where additional artifacts and structural foundations were further exposed; next was Hargreaves' excavations between 1914-1915 CE and finally D. R. Sahni between 1917-1922 CE {Bhattacharya 1924: 79-97}{Sahni 1933: 6-9}.

The main ruins of Sarnath [8.6], the biggest of the four holiest sites, are spread over a vast area of about 794' x 965' and beyond its boundary in the north is the famed Deer Park. The octagonal Chaukhandi tower is another important monument about half a mile south of the main

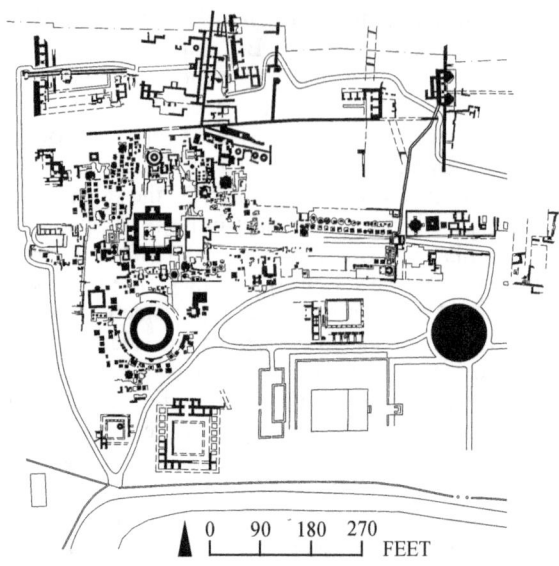

8.5. Site plan
c. 260 BCE-1200 CE
Sarnath- India

8.6. Dhamekh Stupa
c. 550-600 CE
Sarnath- India

site constructed by the Muslim Mughal Emperor Akbar in 1588 CE over a Buddhist *stupa* that commemorated the spot where Buddha first met his five disciples before giving them his first sermon, as described by Hsuan-tsang. There are thousands of sculptural specimens recovered from the site excluding hundreds that have already been taken from the site for the various construction projects in the nearby towns. The main site is grouped into two zones in which the Monastery Zone lies mainly in the north and the Worship Zone in the south also having a few monasteries; both have their own gateways and a boundary wall between them. The Worship Zone contains countless ruins including an Asoka pillar, *stupa*s most importantly Dharmarajika Stupa and Dhamekh Stupa **[8.6]**, and temples; the cruciform-planned main temple in the center west of the site is clearly the most important edifice with a wide approach avenue leading to the main entrance in the east. Close examination of the remains and recovered artifacts reveals several categories: sculptures, an Asoka pillar, *vedika*s, temples, *stupa*s, and monasteries; due to the vast amount materials here I only highlight the most notable examples {Sahni 1914}{Bhattacharya 1924: 98-145}{Sahni 1933: 9-12, 39-49}.

(a) Sculptures {Sahni 1914: 28-163, 183-216, 229-313}

Sarnath was a great sculptural center as evident from the numerous findings dated between the third century BCE-twelfth centuries CE that literally spanned the entire history of Indian Buddhist arts. The iconography varies from the Aniconic/Theravada, to the Mahayana, and lastly the Vajrayana when Sarnath and other Indian sites were under the influences of Tantricism. The most famous and oldest piece is the Asoka pillar **[3.3]** and its glistening capital **[3.6]** behind (west) the main temple, which had probably been knocked down during one of the many foreign invasions. Most importantly, the *dharmacakra* wheel on this capital was adopted by the Indian government on 22nd July 1947 as a supreme symbol on its national flag and the four-addorsed lions as the official emblem of India. Another important sculpture was the sandstone Buddha-Bodhisattva image dated in the third regnal year of the Kushan King Kanishka (c. 131 CE); this sculpture, evidently manufactured in Mathura, is one of the oldest dated anthropomorphic depictions of Buddha in India and there is another similar sculpture from Sravasti of an identical date, workmanship, and donor. During the Gupta renaissance, Sarnath was the most important sculptural center in India as it was here that the profoundly influential and refined sculptures in the Gupta-Sarnath Style had been produced; the lyrical originality and idealism of this school would subsequently be transmitted throughout the Buddhist world. The famous seated Buddha sculpture in the Gupta-Sarnath Style unearthed at Sarnath is unquestionably the most iconic of all Indian and Buddhist sculptures; it was indeed a superb product of the great artistic sensibility, technical proficiency, and religious idealism in Gupta India. The influences of the Vajrayana and Tantric elements would be felt throughout North India during the Pala Dynasty and there was no exception at Sarnath where many Vajrayana sculptures had been carved.

(b) Asoka Pillar

After his conversion to Buddhism, Asoka went on his pilgrimage tours of the Buddhist sites associated with Buddha's life throughout India and the Nepalese Terai in c. 260 BCE and during which occasions he erected many commemorative monuments or *caitya*s. The Asoka pillar **[3.3]** erected behind the main temple with its majestic capital now in the nearby Sarnath Museum **[3.6]** bore his inscription but without a specific date for its erection. Stylistically this capital, compared to the other pillars, might be dated between c. 241-233 BCE or toward the end of Asoka's reign; its stump still stands in situ about 17' high with a 2'6" bottom diameter and an estimated original height around 50' {Sahni 1933: 24-26}. The content of the inscription on this pillar or Schism Edict is similar to the one on the Asoka pillar in front of Sanchi Stupa I **[6.3]** {Hultzsch 1969: 162-164}:

> Deva[nampriya]…Pata[liputra]…The *Sangha* [can not] be divided by any one. But indeed that monk or nun who shall break up the *Sangha*, should be caused to put on white robes and to reside in a non-residence [expel from the *Sangha*]. Thus this edict must be submitted both to the *Sangha* of monks and to the *Sangha* of nuns. Thus speaks Devanampriya:
>> Let one copy of this [edict] remain with you [the *Sangha*] deposited in [your] office; and deposit ye another copy of this very [edict] with the lay-worshippers. These lay-worshippers may come on every fast-day in order to be inspired with confidence in this very edict; and invariably on every fast-day, every *Mahamatra* [high government officers, ministers] [will] come to the fast-day in order to be inspired with confidence in this very edict and to understand [it]. And as far as your district [extends], dispatch ye [an officer] everywhere according to the letter of this [edict]. In the same way cause [your subordinates] to dispatch [an officer] according to the letter of this [edict] in all the territories [surrounding] forts.

There are two other inscriptions on this pillar with the first one mentioning King Asvaghosa dated in the fortieth year of an unknown *samvat* (era), either of Saka (c. 118 CE) or Kanishka Era (c. 168 CE); the second inscription dated in the mid fourth century CE recording the presence of the Sammitiya sect {Bhattacharya 1924: 161-162, 168}.

(c) *Vedika*s

There are two important stone *vedika*s recovered from the site, one below the southern chapel of the main temple and the other northeast of the latter standing in the open at Temple 50 {Sahni 1914: 208-210} {Sahni 1933: 4, 9-10, 20, 27}. The first *vedika*, which Sahni suggested as belonging to the original *harmika vedika* of Dharmarajika Stupa that had been thrown down, is plain and similar to the ground and *harmika vedika*s of Sanchi; it can be dated between late Asoka's reign to early Shunga Dynasty between c. 240-175 BCE. The second *vedika* has medallion and half-medallion designs very similar to the *vedika*s of Sanchi Stupa II; it probably dated in c. 125 BCE.

(d) Temples

The two oldest temples at Sarnath, which only their foundations remain, are the main temple about 25' east of the Asoka pillar and the Apsidal Temple about 83' west of the latter. The plan of the Aspsidal Temple, which was constructed of very large-sized bricks dated in the third century BCE and likely contemporary with Sanchi Temple 40, is about 39' x 63' {Sahni 1933: 26}. The holiest temple at Sarnath must be the main temple where Buddha preached the first sermon and converted his five former ascetic-companions evidently from the presence of an Asoka pillar behind it; it had been constructed in several phases with the earliest one certainly commenced by Asoka in the third century BCE. This original Asoka temple could be a *bodhigriha* like the Shunga Mahabodhi Temple [7.6-7.7] as evident from the Shunga *vedika* unearthed below the southern chapel of this temple. The next two phases of this temple can be inferred from D. R. Sahni's description of the remains {Sahni 1933: 19-21}:

> The temple consisted originally of a single hall 45'6" square internally, the walls being 10' thick. From the north, west and south sides project rectangular chapels which are only entered from the outside. There was no chapel on the east side, its place being taken, of necessity, by a portico in front of the entrance. The walls of this building are now nowhere standing to a greater height than 18'. The inside walls appear to be quite plain, but externally the Main Shrine was decorated with a variety of mouldings consisting of full and half torus patterns, circular niches containing pilasters with vase-shaped bases and bracket capitals and other motifs, all reminiscent of good Gupta work…The enormous thickness of the walls suggests a lofty superstructure, which might have been a high pyramidal spire like that of the principal temple at Bodh Gaya…At a later date, which it is difficult to determine with certainty, the roof of the temple began to show signs of weakness and the addition of the massive wall 11' in thickness which now runs round three sides of the interior would appear to have been provided to prevent its collapse. The cella was thus reduced to a square chamber of 23'6" along each side. It was presumably at this time that the large rectangular platform at the back of the shrine was constructed to support the image that was worshipped in it…In the chapel on the south side was found a headless standing statue of Buddha in the posture of granting security and in Gupta style… The original floor level inside the building would appear to have been approximately the same as that of the base of the Asoka railing [probably the *harmika vedika* of Dharmarajika Stupa or the ground *vedika* of the main temple] in the southern chapel.

Sahni first described the outer shell as having 'good Gupta work,' which might conservatively be dated in the sixth century CE, and followed by the addition of the interior walls on the three sides; he also believed that the superstructure of the temple was similar to the straight-edged pyramidal tower of the Mahabodhi Temple [7.10-7.11] which I also agree. However, he seemed to have wrongly attributed the addition of the interior walls to a date later than those on the exterior shell; the reverse would be more accurate since the Mahabodhi Temple also had similar phases of construction. Overall I believe there were about main construction phases:

- Phase I (c. 260 BCE-400 CE): The earliest temple was probably a *bodhigriha* similar to the Shunga Mahabodhi Temple [7.6-7.7] and both temples had originally been commenced by Asoka.
- Phase II (c. 400-450 CE): The *bodhigriha* was converted into a straight-edge pyramidal tower as in the Kumrahar plaque [7.9] alongwith the addition of the interior walls as described by Sahni; its plan probably only had a projecting portico on the east side like the Hindu Bhirtagaon Temple (c. 450 CE). The date for its construction can be deduced from several clues that its interior floor had originally been at the same level as the base of the 4'9" high 'Asoka' *vedika*, which was now buried at least 5' below the

floor of the southern chapel. This *vedika* also had an inscription of the Sarvastivada, which obliterated an earlier inscription, dated at the latest in the fourth century CE {Sahni 1933: 4-5, 20}.

- Phase III (c. 550-600 CE): An envelope or plinth was added to increase the stability of the main tower; this was probably contemporary with Nalanda Caitya 12 **[4.4 (#12)]** and the Mahabodhi Temple Phase V. Sahni's description of its exterior decorations as 'good Gupta work' further corroborates the hypothesis that this phase was commenced when Gupta influences were still strong. Hsuan-tsang described the main temple in c. 636 CE as 'towers' suggesting that it might have had corner turrets like the Mahabodhi Temple.
- Phase IV (c. 600-700 CE): The side chapels were constructed and its roofs might have had pyramidal turrets or multi-tiered pavilions similar to the eastern facade of the Mahabodhi Temple; this converted the temple into a cruciform plan. Sahni found a Gupta statue in the southern chapel and carved door frames on all three chapels dated in the seventh century CE, which was probably the date for the erection of these chapels or possibly earlier. The temple was still standing in the eleventh century CE as evident from the inscribed blocks in the southwest corner that were added during a restoration {Sahni 1933: 19, 21}; it was most likely destroyed by the Muslims in the late twelfth century CE.

There are a few derivatives of the cruciform plan of the Sarnath main temple in Southeast Asia, most notably the central temples of Somapura in Bangladesh **[4.8]** and Candi Sewu in Java **[7.12]**, and the Ananda Temple in Myanmar **[7.14]**; this plan could be traced to Gandhara *stupa*s **[6.17-6.18]**. There is a so-called subterranean temple in the Monastery Zone about 250' to the northwest of the main temple; it is a 7'6" x 183' long passage with a chapel midway constructed of brick sizes similar to Monastery I in its eastern side and therefore likely dated between c. 1114-1154 CE {Sahni 1933: 30-31}. It peculiar design seemingly combined an escape tunnel and a shrine considering the constant threats of the Muslim invasions lurking at the Indian border during this time.

(e) *Stupa*s

There are three groups of *stupa*s at Sarnath: Dharmarajika Stupa about 50' south of the main temple, Dhamekh Stupa **[8.6]** about 450' east of the former, and the numerous votive *stupa*s clustering around these structures. As mentioned earlier the brick Dharmarajika Stupa, or what remain of its ruins, was unfortunately demolished by Jagat Singh in 1794 CE and the relics emptied into the Ganga River; it has a 100' diameter plan (latest phase) and a 13' wide elevated *pradaksina* path with stairs in the four cardinal points. Its plan is not much different than Dharmarajika in Taxila **[6.13]**, which had also reputedly been erected by Asoka; it has about seven phases of construction and restorations {Sahni 1933: 17-19}:

- Phase I (c. 241-233 BCE): Asoka reputedly constructed 84,000 *caitya*s (holy shrines) and *dharmarajika stupa*s all over his empire after his conversion to Buddhism; the former commemorated the events associated with Buddha's life and the latter specifically interred Buddha's relics. The Buddha's relics in these *stupa*s had allegedly been obtained from the original eight *stupa*s and this particular Dharmarajika at Sarnath, alongwith Dharmarajika in Taxila and Sanchi Stupa I **[6.3]**, could be one of Asoka's *dharmarajika stupa*s; evidently this Sarnath Dharmarajika had not been constructed to commemorate the event of Buddha's First Sermon as some believed since this honor would be for the main temple. Hsuan-tsang reportedly saw an Asoka pillar in front of this *stupa* but not a trace of it has been found; it was unlikely that this pillar could have been moved to the back of the main temple where the stump of an Asoka pillar still stands.
- Phase II (second-third centuries CE): This *stupa* was likely enlarged during the Kushan Dynasty.
- Phase III (fifth-sixth centuries CE): A 4'5" high circular wall was constructed around the *stupa* to form a 15'-16' wide *pradaksina* path with doors provided in the four cardinal points.
- Phase IV (seventh century CE): The *pradaksina* path was filled in to be converted into an elevated one and access would also be provided by the four flights of stairs in the four cardinal points; the form of the *stupa* in this phase probably resembled Dharmarajika Phase V **[6.13]**.
- Phase V (1026 CE). The *stupa* was restored by the two brothers Sthirapala and Vasantapala; their inscription on a Buddha's image stated "Sthirapala and Vasantapala repaired the Dharmarajika [Stupa] and the Dharmacakra [Jinavihara or Monastery I?] including the accessories, as well as the Gandhakuti [the main temple], made of stone, belonging to eight places" {Bhattacharya 1924: iv-v}.
- Phase VI (c. 1114-1154 CE). An inscription of Kumaradevi, the Buddhist Queen of King Govindachandra (r. 1114-1154 CE), found near the Dhamekh Stupa recorded the construction a monastery alongwith numerous other repairs and restorations, which most likely also included Dharmarajika.

Dhamekh Stupa [8.6] is a huge 104' high cylindrical *stupa* in the southeastern corner of the site and the most visible remain at Sarnath; its name is derived from the word *dharmeksha* meaning 'The Pondering of the Law.' It is believed to be the spot where Buddha delivered the second sermon, the Anattalakhana-sutra or the theory of Non-*atman*, to his newly ordained five disciples a few days after the first one {Singh 2003: 140}. The lower extant body is about 99' diameter and 37' high above the ground having eight image niches in the cardinal and intermediate points that might have once contained images of Eight Manusi Buddhas {Williams 1982: 169}. It is faced with carved stone blocks of refined Gupta floral designs that are structurally tied together with iron cramps while the upper smaller section is brick and was probably faced with stone at one time. The original foundation might have been founded between the third-second centuries BCE from its large-sized bricks; the *stupa* would subsequently be reconstructed several times in which the first reconstruction probably occurred between the second-third centuries CE as evident from contemporary bricks found in its lower foundation. The now visible massive cylindrical superstructure likely dated in the sixth century CE based on a discovered inscription and the exquisite Gupta-Styled floral scrolls {Bhattacharya 1924: 184}{Sahni 1933: 35-37}.

The most numerous architectural remains at the site are the small *stupa*s that have been raised by pilgrims over the centuries; these are monolithic (carved in a single stone block) or structural types (parts joined together and usually stone-and-brick combination) and most have image niches on the four sides. The majority of these are votive *stupa*s but many also contain relics particularly ashes of deceased monks; most dated in the Pala Dynasty (c. 750-1199 CE) and some in the Gupta Dynasty (c. 320-647 CE) {Sahni 1914: 217-228}{Sahni 1933: 22, 24}.

(f) Monasteries

The remains of seven monasteries at Sarnath are situated in the northernmost and southernmost areas; they were all constructed between the second-twelfth centuries CE. These are brick quadrangular *vihara*s of several stories high with the uppermost strata dated in the Pala Dynasty like the Nalanda *vihara*s [4.4], which are significantly larger than these Sarnath *vihara*s {Sahni 1933: 14-17, 28-30, 32-35, 37}. Monastery VI-VII south of Dharmarajika Stupa dated between the second-ninth centuries CE while Monastery II-IV in the northern zone beyond the demarcating wall and Monastery V to the west of the Dhamekh Stupa all dated between the fourth-twelfth centuries CE. Monastery I between Monastery II-III is presumably the Dharmacakra Jinavihara monastery mentioned in Queen Kumaradevi's inscription dated between c. 1114-1154 CE; it had probably been constructed over an older fourth century CE foundation much like the foundations of the other monasteries on the same row. Like the main temple, these monasteries face east as evident in the two huge gateways (*gopura*) in the eastern side.

The accounts the Chinese pilgrims Fa-hsien in c. 405 CE and Hsuan-tsang in c. 636 CE left vivid pictures about the state of Buddhism in contemporary Sarnath which greatly facilitate the identification of the numerous monuments around the site; below was Fa-hsien's description of Sarnath {Beal 1869: 134-137}{Bhattacharya 1924: 43-45}:

Following the course of the river Heng [Ganga] toward the west...he came to the town of Pholonai [Benares], in the kingdom of Kashi. To the northeast of the town, at the distance of ten li [three miles], you come to the temple [the main temple] situated in the Deer-park of the Immortal [Mrigadava-Rishipatana]...Since the Honourable of the Age [Buddha] accomplished the law, men of subsequent times have erected a Chapel [the main temple] in this place. Foe [Buddha] being desirous of converting Adjnata Kaundinya (Keonlin) amongst the five men, these men said amongst themselves, "...Today, when he shall come, let us be careful not to speak to him." Foe having approached the five men rose and worshipped him. At the distance of sixty paces [150'] to the north of this place [north of Dharmarajika Stupa?], Foe, looking towards the east, sat down and began to turn the wheel of law [preach the first sermon]...Twenty paces [50'] to the north is the place where Foe rehearsed his history to *Mile* [Maitreya]. Fifty paces [125'] south, is the place where the dragon [*naga*] Elapatra asked Foe, "After how long a time shall I be delivered from this dragon's body?" In all those places they have erected towers, amongst which there are two *Seng kia lan* [*vihara*s or monasteries] inhabited by ecclesiastics.

The next detailed description of Sarnath was given by Hsuan-tsang {Beal 1906 Volumne II: 44-55}{Bhattacharya 1924: 48-52, i-ii}:

To the northeast of the river Varuna [Yamuna] about ten li or so [three miles], we come to the Sangharama of Lu-ye [Mrigadava or Deer Park]. Its precincts are divided into eight portions [the eight *vihara*s?] connected by a surrounding wall. The storeyed towers with projecting eaves and the balconies are of very superior work. There are 1,500 priests in this convent who study the Little Vehicle [Hinayana or Theravada] according to the Sammatiya school. In the great enclosure is a *Vihara* [the main temple] about 200' high; above the roof is a golden-covered figure of the Amra fruit [*amalaka*]. The foundations of the building are of stone, and the stairs also, but the towers and niches are of brick. The niches are arranged on the four sides in a hundred successive lines, and in each niche is a golden figure of Buddha. In the middle of the *Vihara* is a figure of Buddha made of native copper; it is the size of life, and he is represented as turning the wheel of the law. To the southwest of the *Vihara* [the main temple] is a stone *stupa* [Dharmarajika Stupa] built by Asokaraja. Although the foundations have given way, there are still 100' or more of the wall remaining. In front of the building is a stone pillar about 70' high. The stone is altogether as bright as jade. It is glistening, and sparkles like light [could this Asoka pillar be the one behind the main temple?]...It was here that Tathagata having arrived at enlightenment [Bodhgaya], began to turn the wheel of the law [preach the first sermon]. By the side of this building and not far from it is a *stupa* [Dhamekh Stupa?]. This is the spot where Ajnata Kaudinya and the rest [Buddha's five former ascetic-companions], seeing Bodhisattva giving up his austerities, no longer kept his company, but coming to this place, gave themselves up to meditation. By the side of this is a *stupa* where five hundred Pratyeka Buddha Buddhas entered at the same time into Nirvana. There are, moreover, three *stupas* where there are traces of the sitting and walking of the three former Buddhas. By the side of this last place is a *stupa*. This is the spot where Maitreya Bodhisattva received assurance of his becoming a Buddha...To the west of this place there is a *stupa*. This is the spot where Sakya Bodhisattva received an assurance... Not for to the south of this spot are traces where the four Buddhas of a bygone age walked for exercise. The length [of the promenade] is about fifty paces [125'] and the height of the steps about 7'. It is composed of blue stones piled together. Above it is a figure of Tathagata in the attitude of walking...Within the precincts of the enclosure there are many sacred vestiges with *viharas* and *stupas* several hundred in number...

To the west of the Sangharama enclosure is a clear lake of water about 200 paces [500'] in circuit; here Tathagata occasionally bathed himself. To the west of this is a great tank about 180 paces [450'] round; here Tathagata used to wash his begging bowl. To the north of this is a lake about 150 paces [375'] round. Here Tathagata used to wash his robes...By the side of the pool where Tathagata washed his garments is a great square on which are yet to be seen the trace marks of his *Kashaya* robe. By the side of the lake, and not far off, is a *stupa*. This is where Bodhisattva, during his preparatory life, was born as a king of elephants, provided with six tusks [Shaddanta Jataka]. Not far from this, in a great forest, is a *stupa*. It was here that Devadatta and Bodhisattva in years gone by were kings of deer and settled a certain matter. Leaving this place, and going two or three li [3/5-9/10 mile] to the southwest of the Sangharama, there is a *stupa* [Chaukhandi Stupa?] about 300' high. The foundations are broad and the building high, and adorned with all sorts of carved work and with precious substances. There are no successive stages with niches; and though there is a standing pole [*yasti-chattra*] erected above the cupola, yet it has no encircling bells. By the side of it is a little *stupa*. This is the spot where Ajnata Kaundinya and the other men, five in number, declined to rise to salute Buddha.

Like the other holiest sites, Sarnath has attracted numerous modern Buddhist monasteries from all over Asia and these can be found in the periphery areas mainly in the south and east of the main site. Besides these, the Sri Lankan Mulagandhakuti Vihara east of the Dhamekh Stupa is a well-known modern structure which was inaugurated by Anagarika Dharmapala in 1931CE; it was the first symbolic success for Indian Buddhism thanks to the persistent effort of a Buddhist champion who for decades had been struggling to reclaim the Mahabodhi Temple and other Buddhist sites in India from the Hindus' control.

4. Kushinagar, India: Decease (fifth century BCE-twelfth centuries CE)

After forty-five years of restless missionary activities Buddha, severely stricken with an illness, finally managed to reach Kushinagar **[8.7-8.10]** where he ordained the last disciple Subhadda, bade farewell to his teary followers, uttered his last instructional words to the *Sangha*, and then passed into *Parinirvana*; he died in c. 487 BCE when he was eighty years old. His body was duly honored for seven days before cremated and his ashes equally divided into eight portions where *stupas* would subsequently be built for them (Chapter 6). Kushinagar is now situated about two miles southwest of Kasia in Uttar Pradesh, the village which name likely survives from the 'Kushin' of Kushinagar {Patil 1981: 13}. Asoka reportedly visited Kushinagar in c. 260 BCE where he constructed *caitya*s, *stupa*s, and pillars to honor the place of Buddha's *Parinirvana*; it was only then that the pre-eminent status of Kushinagar, like the other holiest sites, became known throughout India and beyond. Kushinagar, like Lumbini, was apparently undeveloped during the Shunga Dynasty (184-72 BCE) as evident from the total absence of the *vedika*s that were characteristic of Shunga architecture; this might have been due to its lesser popularity as a pilgrimage site and remote location compared with the eminence of Bodhgaya and Sarnath. Probably not until the Early Kushan Dynasty (c. 50-241 CE) that the site experienced a steady period of growth with the foundings of new monasteries at the site. Kushinagar next witnessed a golden phase during the Gupta Dynasty (c. 320-647 CE) when the Nirvana Stupa was greatly enlarged and the Nirvana Temple reconstructed alongwith the dedication of its huge reclining Buddha statue. It was during this time that celebrated Chinese pilgrims like Fa-hsien, Hsuan-tsang, and I-tsing visited this passing place of Buddha in c. 409 CE, c. 637 CE, and late seventh century CE respectively; they left vivid accounts on the conditions of the site and contemporary Buddhism. Kushinagar continued to be occupied until c. 1200 CE when it was abandoned as Buddhist monks were fleeing North India, which was then being overrun by ferocious Muslim invasions. The site was virtually forgotten for over five centuries until the early nineteenth century CE when Francis Buchanan Hamilton visited the site during his survey; he, however, failed to identify it as Kushinagar. Horace H. Wilson was the first to casually suggest the connection between Kasia and Kushinagar; it was the task of Alexander Cunningham who finally confirmed this fact when he visited and carefully examined the site between 1861-1862 CE. The first serious archaeological diggings were completed by A. C. L. Carlleyle between 1876-1877 CE when he successfully exposed the Nirvana Stupa and Temple alongwith the acclaimed *Parinirvana* Buddha statue. It took further excavations by J. P. Vogel between 1904-1907 CE and Hirananda Sastri between 1910-1912 CE in combination with archaeological data to finally confirm the true identity of Kushinagar. Numerous monuments surrounding the Nirvana Stupa and Temple had also been exposed including inscriptions bearing the legends 'Sri Mahaparinirvana Mahavihariyarya Bhikshu-sanghasya' (The Community of Reverend Monks Belonging to the Great Monastery of the Blessed Great Decease) and 'Parinirvana Caitya'

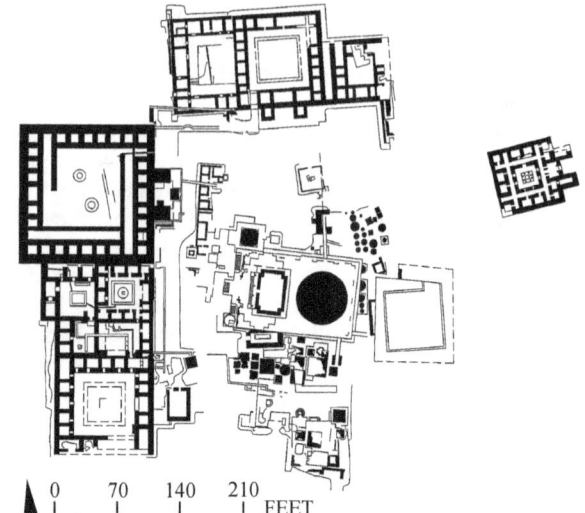

8.7. Site plan
c. 260 BCE-1200 CE
Kasia- India

8.8. Nirvana Temple and Stupa
c. 260 BCE-1200 CE
Kasia- India

(Parinirvana Stupa). The ASI subsequently undertook major efforts to restore the site first in 1927 CE and later between 1955-1956 CE with the financial contributions from foreign Buddhists, especially the Myanmaris {Patil 1981: 9-15, 19, 22}.

Greater Kushinagar composes largely of the main site **[8.7-8.9]** and Kalachuri (Mathakuar) Monastery about 656' southwest of the Nirvana Stupa, all were orig-

Part II. Architecture   Four Holiest Sites . 283

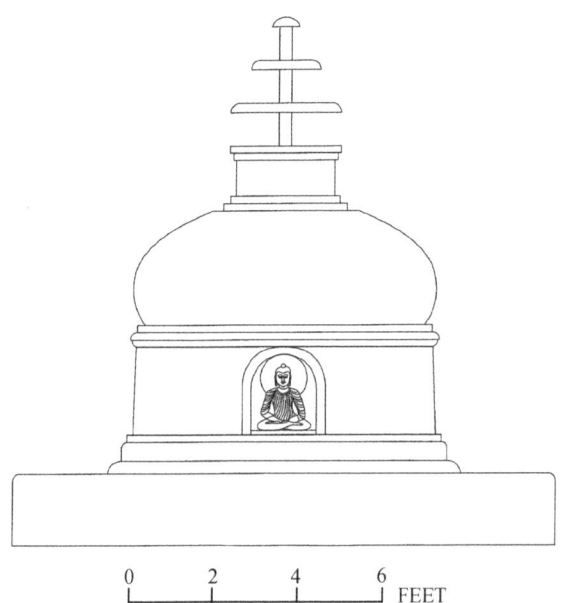

8.9. Small *stupa* inside current Nirvana Stupa
Early fifth centuries CE
Kasia- India

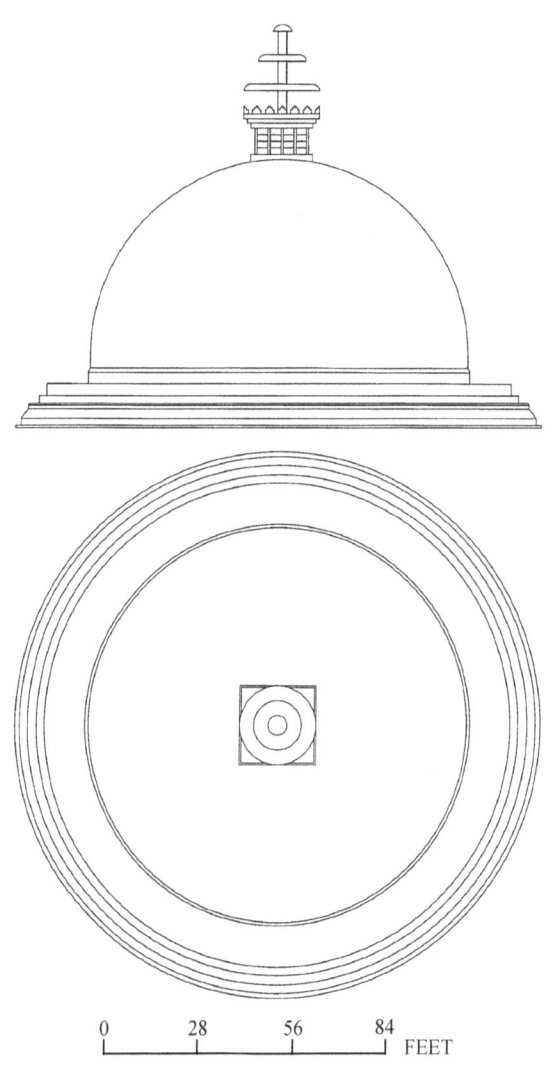

8.10. Cremation Stupa (restored) *(right)*
Fourth-twelfth centuries CE
Kasia- India

inally enclosed by the now ruined 1,250' square brick wall having a 11'10" wide entrance in the south; the Makutabandhana (Cremation) Stupa **[8.10]** is situated about a mile east of Kalachuri Monastery {Patil 1981: 30-31}. The main site of Kushinagar occupies an area about 528' x 622' in which all the remains, including Kalachuri Monastery and Makutabandhana Stupa, dated between third century BCE-eleventh centuries CE. Inventory of archaeological remains and artifacts reveals four major categories: sculptures, *stupa*s, temples, and monasteries {ASIAR 1910-1911: 63-77}{Patil 1981: 16-32}.

(a) Sculptures and Other Miscellaneous Items
Hsuan-tsang reported as having seen two Asoka pillars, one in front of the Nirvana Stupa and the other at the spot where the division of Buddha's relics occurred. Many Bharhut reliefs also depicted the Nirvana Stupa with Asoka pillars having capitals of four addorsed lions; unfortunately none can be traced today and possibly they might still be buried beneath the current plinth. The oldest sculpture is the 1'9" terracotta Buddha image inside the niche of the small *stupa* **[8.9]** now encased inside the larger Nirvana Stupa; its style shows a mixture of Gandhara and early Gupta features possibly dated in the early fifth century CE. The most important sculpture at the site is the 20' long dying Buddha statue reclining on a pedestal inside the Nirvana Temple; Hsuan-tsang saw this statue when he visited Kushinagar in c. 637 CE. It has a Gupta inscription (c. 435-455 CE) by Haribala

the donor and who was also the restorer of the Nirvana Temple and Stupa; it records, "This is the meritorious gift of Haribala, the master of the Great Vihara, and this image was fashioned by Dine…Sura." {Cunningham 1961: 59}. There is another huge 10' high Buddha statue in the *bhumisparsa-mudra* inside the Kalachuri Monastery that was dedicated between the eleventh-twelfth centuries CE judging from its Pala Style and inscription. There are also numerous terracotta figures recovered from the site dated between first-fourth centuries CE alongwith clay seals, sealings, and tablets between the fourth-eleventh centuries CE; coins have also been found and mostly dated between the first-fifth centuries CE.

(b) *Stupa*s

The holiest *stupa*s at Kushinagar are the Nirvana Stupa [8.7, 8.9] and Makutabandhana Stupa [8.10]; the former was originally constructed by the Mallas over the very spot where Buddha died and interred the eighth portion of their share of Buddha's relics while the latter was erected at the spot where Buddha's body was creamated and hence its name Cremation Stupa. However, Hsuan-tsang stated that it was at the Nirvana Temple where Buddha died while the Nirvana Stupa behind it alongwith its Asoka pillar had been constructed by Asoka; unfortunately no trace of such pillar can be found anywhere today. The current Nirvana Stupa has a 57' diameter which has been reshaped several times over the centuries; its construction can be divided into five main phases:

- Phase I (c. 487 BCE): A small *stupa* of a primitive form was constructed over Buddha's cremation spot and interred his relics; no trace of this original *stupa* was detected.
- Phase II (c. 260 BCE): Asoka reportedly visited Kushinagar after his conversion to Buddhism and probably erected pillars, *stupa*s, and commemorative *caitya*s here; since the two most important *stupa*s, the Nirvana Stupa and Makutabandhana Stupa, presumably already existed so Asoka could only renovate or possibly enlarge them.
- Phase III (early fifth century CE): During the excavation by Hirananda Sastri, a small *stupa* [8.9] of a brick-and-plaster construction was discovered inside the larger Phase IV *stupa*. It is about 12'10" square in plan and over 12' high including the *yasti-chattra*; it has a niche containing a seated terracotta Buddha figure in the *dhyana-mudra* facing west, which was also the direction Buddha faced when he died. A small earthen pot found inside this small *stupa* contained "earth and pieces of charcoal, evidently taken from the funeral pyre of some Buddhist," according to the archaeologist; however, it is impossible to ascertain the origin of these relics. The inscription and coins found inside the Phase IV *stupa* dated between c. 450-475 CE and therefore this small *stupa* must predate it; this is also corroborated by its architectural form and the style of the terracotta Buddha figure.
- Phase IV (c. 450-475 CE): The Nirvana Stupa was again enlarged and completely enveloped the aforesaid small *stupa*; this newly bigger *stupa* probably had a cylindrical form much like the slightly later Dhamekh Stupa at Sarnath [8.6]. The excavation of this *stupa* has yielded significant relics, coins, and an inscription including a Jayagupta coin and a copper vessel containing six coins of Kumaragupta I (r. 415-455 CE), a mixture of sand, charcoal, ashes, cowries, precious stones, pearls, emerald, and small copper as well as silver gold tubes; the recorded copper-plate inscription ends in a dedicatory statement stating "This is the pious gift of Haribala, the superintendent of many *vihara*s. Whatever religious merit there is herein, let it tend to the acquisition of the sublime knowledge by all creatures. The Sakya *bhiksu* Dharmananda rejoices everywhere. This copper-plate is [deposited] in the [Pari]nirvana *chaitya*." This Haribala was undoubtedly the same donor who also dedicated the reclining Buddha statue inside the Nirvana Temple, which was probably rebuilt about the same time as the Nirvana Stupa.
- Phase V (1927 CE): The *stupa* was completely restored to its current whitewashed form with a dome above the drum and to be crowned with a solid *harmika* and *yasti-chattra*; the project was financed by the Myanmari Buddhists U Po Kyu and U Po Hlaing.

The restored brick Makutabandhana or Cremation Stupa, also known as Ramabhar Stupa after the nearby Ramabhar Lake, has a 155' diameter and a huge dome crowned with a *harmika* and *yasti-chattra*; its height is estimated over 100'. Hsuan-tsang also reportedly saw an Asoka pillar with an inscription near the Cremation Stupa but it has not been possible to archaeologically confirm his account. Due to the paucity of dated materials, it is difficult to determine its construction phases but with scanty data it is still possible to establish several conjectural phases:

- Phase I (c. 487 BCE): After Buddha's cremation, the Mallas of Kushinagar reportedly erected a *stupa* over his cremation spot; no data is available to reconstruct its original appearance.
- Phase II (c. 260 BCE): Asoka might have renovated or enlarged the original *stupa* when he first visited the site in c. 260 BCE or in the later years of his reign. The large square bricks of the ruined *stupa*,

which were typically employed in the earlier periods, has been attributed by scholars to Asoka's time; however, this is still conjectural as the *stupa* might have also been enlarged in the Shunga Dynasty (184-72 BCE).
- Phase III (fourth-fifth centuries CE): There was virtually no archaeological data to precisely determine its form in this phase so that circumstantial evidences would have to be included in the analyses. First of all, there were the well-known Haribala's restorations of the Nirvana Temple and Stupa in the fifth century CE suggesting that some reconstructions might have also been performed on the Makutabandhana Stupa. Secondly, the restored drawing of this *stupa* based on its remains shows architectural similarities with Dharmarajika Stupa in Taxila [6.13] such as the low plinth, the large dome, and the complete absence of the ground *vedika*; thus the date for the *stupa* in this phase is more or less contemporary with the latest phase of Dharmarajika.
- Phase IV (eighth-twelfth centuries CE): From the findings of numerous ornamental face bricks and hundreds of clay tablets near the *stupa* dated in the Pala Dynasty, it appears that the *stupa* underwent at least some forms of restorations during this time.

There are dozens of votive *stupa*s clustering in the south, east, and northeast of the Nirvana Temple and Stupa; many others have been buried under the plinth when it was enlarged probably between the late fifth-twelfth centuries CE. The earliest structure in this group was the small square building (H) in the northeastern corner of the Nirvana Stupa; it has been dated in the Maurya or Asoka's time based on its large bricks. Many of these votive *stupa*s probably once belonged to the group surrounding the small *stupa* [8.9] and contemporaneous in date. From the oblique angles and positions of the northern and eastern groups and the large platform (C) east of the Nirvana Stupa alongwith the rectangular hall (F) south of the latter relative to the orientation of the plinth of the Nirvana Temple and Stupa, these can therefore be dated between the third century BCE-fifth centuries CE before the c. 450-475 CE restoration; the circular plans of the votive *stupa*s also suggest their early age possibly pre-Kushan. The group south of the Nirvana Temple and Stupa probably dated later in the Pala Dynasty (c. 750-1199 CE).

(c) Temples

The Nirvana Temple [8.7-8.8] and Nirvana Stupa behind it are both elevated on a 9' high plinth which probably dated about or after the c. 450-475 CE restoration; it appears that the Nirvana Temple might have been erected no earlier than the first century CE when the cult of images and the construction of temples were introduced. From available data, the construction of the Nirvana Temple can be divided into five main phases:
- Phase I (second-third centuries CE): It has already been determined that the earlier forms of the Mayadevi Temple in Lumbini [8.1-8.2], the Mahabodhi Temple in Bodhgaya [7.6-7.7], and the main temple at Sarnath [8.5] were *bodhigriha*s dedicated to some forms of aniconic worship and probably so too was the first Nirvana Temple. It is probable that a temple housing a Buddha image, most likely a *Parinirvana* one, could have been constructed in the Early Kushan Dynasty when the image worship became popular; this temple would likely have been built in front of the Nirvana Stupa as today.
- Phase II (c. 450-475 CE): As mentioned earlier, Haribala restored the Nirvana Temple and Stupa in the late fifth century CE and installed a new Gupta-Styled *Parinirvana* Buddha image in the main chamber of the temple. The form and plan of this brick-and-plaster temple could be a barrel-vaulted structure with a main chamber housing the giant sculpture and preceded by an antechamber in the western side; this temple, which would later be altered in Phase V, had been reported by A. C. L. Carlleyle during the 1876-1877 CE excavations. It is well-known that freestanding vaulted temples existed at least in the third century BCE like Sanchi Temple 40; thus it is possible that this vaulted Nirvana Temple might even have an earlier foundation dating back to Asoka's time but there is no way to verify its existence since its earlier foundations have long been buried below the plinth.
- Phase III (eighth-twelfth centuries CE): There was a surge in the construction activities during the Pala Dynasty and probably the Nirvana Temple was once again restored.
- Phase IV (1876 CE): During his 1876-1877 CE excavations, A. C. L. Carlleyle described a vaulted temple, as evident from its curved bricks recovered from the ruins, with an antechamber in the western side. The wall of the main chamber containing the image was about 10' thick obviously to bear the heavy loads of the roof and this left a narrow 2' wide space in front of the *Parinirvana* Buddha statue; based on the data, Carlleyle then proceeded to reconstruct the Nirvana Temple superstructure.
- Phase V (1955-1956 CE): The Nirvana Temple, which had earlier been restored by A. C. L. Carlleyle, was once again altered with the wall thickness

of the main chamber reduced in order to widen the interior space to accommodate more worshipers; the solid wall of the antechamber was converted into an open portico. Fortunately, this restoration still retained the vaulted roof of the temple in accordance to its ancient form.

(d) Monasteries

There are about twelve monasteries exposed at the site and most are found around the Nirvana Temple and Stupa including Monastery D-E, I-J, L-Q, Q'; the exception is Kalachuri Monastery about 656' southwest of the main site. These are all quadrangular *vihara*s with the latest Monastery D-E, I, and Kalachuri having projecting porticos on one side; the biggest is Monastery D of about 150' square and several stories in height judging from its massive 9'9" thick walls. From available archaeological data, the chronology of these monasteries can be deduced with Monastery L-O (first-sixth centuries CE), Monastery Q-Q' (first-ninth centuries CE), Kalachuri Monastery (third-twelfth centuries CE), Monastery I, P (ninth-tenth centuries CE), Monastery D (ninth-twelfth centuries CE), and Monastery E (tenth-eleventh centuries CE).

Among the pilgrims who have set foot in Kushinagar, Fa-hsien and Hsuan-tsang are the most well-known as they have left valuable information about the monuments and contemporary conditions at the site; their accounts, in conjunction with the archaeological remains, would complete the historical picture of Kushinagar. Below is Fa-hsien's account of his visit in c. 409 CE {Beal 1869: 93-94}:

> Again advancing twelve *yojana*s [108 miles] to the eastward we arrive at the town of Kushinagar. To the north of this town, on the place where world-honoured Buddha, lying by the side of the Hiranyavati River [Little Gandak], with his head to the North, and a Sal [*sala*] tree on either side of him, entered Nirvana. Also the place where Subhadra was converted, the very last of all disciples. Also where, for seven days, they paid reverence to the world-honoured Buddha, lying in his golden coffin. Also where Vajrapani threw down his golden mace, where the eight kings divided the relics; in each of the above places towers have been raised and Sangharama built, which still exist. In this city there are but few inhabitants; such families as there are connected with the resident congregation of priests.

The most detailed description was given by Hsuan-tsang during his sojourn at Kushinagar about c. 637 CE {Beal 1906 Volume II: 31-41}:

The capital of this country is in ruins, and its towns and villages waste and desolate…At the northeast angle of the city gate is a stupa which was built by Asokaraja. This is the old house of Chunda [who offered Buddha the last repast]…To the northwest of the city three or four li [9/10-1 1/5 mile], crossing the Ajiavati River [Hiranyavati or Little Gandak], on the western bank, not far, we come to a grove of sala trees…In this wood are four trees of an unsual height, which indicate the place where Tathagata died. This is a great brick *vihara* [Nirvana Temple], in which is figure of the *Nirvana* of Tathagata. He is lying with his head to the north as if asleep. By the side of this *vihara* is a *stupa* [Nirvana Stupa] built by Asokaraja; although in a ruinous state, yet it is some 200' in height. Before it is a stone pillar to record the *Nirvana* of Tathagata; although there is an inscription on it, yet there is no date as to year or month… By the side of the *vihara* [Nirvana Temple], and not far from it, is a *stupa*. This denotes the place where Bodhisattva, when practising a religious life, was born as a king of a flock of pheasants, and caused a fire to be put out…By the side of this, not far off, is a *stupa*. On this spot Bodhisattva, when practicing a religious life, being at that time a deer, saved living creatures…To the west of this place, not far off, is a *stupa*. This is where Subhadra died…Beside [the *stupa* of] Subhadra's *Nirvana* is a *stupa*; this is the place where the Vajrapani fell fainting on the earth… By the side [of the Nirvana Temple] where the diamond [of Vajrapani] fell to the earth is a *stupa*. This is the place where for seven days after Buddha died they [the Mallas and Buddha's disciples] offered religious offerings…By the side of the place where the coffin was detained is a *stupa*; this is where queen Mahamaya wept for Buddha…

To the north of the city, after crossing the river [Hiranyavati or Little Gandak River], and going 300 paces or so [750'], there is a *stupa* [Cremation Stupa]. This is the place where they burnt the body of Tathagata….By the side of the place of cremation is a *stupa*; here Tathagata, for Kasyapa's sake, revealed his feet…By the side of the place where he showed his feet is a *stupa* built by Asokaraja. This is the place where the eight kings shared the relics. In front is built a stone [Asoka?] pillar on which is written an account of this event.

Glossary

abhaya-mudra. A hand gesture of reassurance and fearlessness.
Abhidharma. See *Tripitaka*s.
abhiseka. A consecratory ritual for kings, monks, and Tantric initiates.
acarya. A pandit, scholar, and learned teacher.
addhyayoga. A house with turned-up eaves like that of a *garuda* bird.
adimukha. A projecting platform in the base of a Sri Lankan *dagaba* and equivalent to the *ayaka* in South Indian *stupa*s.
agnisala (Pali *aggisala*). A 'fire house' or a refectory and kitchen.
agni-stambha. A flaming pillar and an aniconic symbol of Buddha occurring exclusively in South Indian Buddhist arts.
Alayavijnana. Pure or Store Consciousness, a philosophical concept of the Yogacara sect.
amalaka. A truncated elliptical and fluted crown in Hindu and Buddhist *sikhara*s resembling an *amalaka* fruit.
anda. 'Egg' or the hemispherical dome in Indian Buddhist *stupa*s.
ang. A lever arm of the bracket system in Chinese and East Asian timber architecture.
Anicca. The doctrine of Impermanence.
anuttarayoga-tantra. See *Tantra*.
apsara. A class of celestial female dancers ruled by Virudhaka, the *lokapala* of the South.
arama. A permanent shelter erected during a *vassavasa* or a *sangharama*.
arhat (Pali *arahant*). Buddha's disciples and Theravada saints.
Arupadhatu. See *Tridhatu*.
asura. A class of celestial noble gods or titans in Vedic mythology with Varuna as their chief god.
atman (Pali *atta*). An essence, being, soul, self, ego, or personality in all individuals; a fundamental concept in Indian philosophy.
avadana. A category of Buddhist texts emphasizing Buddha's heroic deeds and moral courage in the past and present.
avana. A park or garden.
avasa. A temporary shelter erected during a *vassavasa*.
ayaka. A projecting platform in the base of South Indian *stupa*s.
ayaka stambha. Freestanding pillars, typically five, on the *ayaka*s of South Indian *stupa*s.

bahal. A Nepalese monastery for married Buddhist monks and their families.
bahil. A Nepalese monastery for celibate monks.
Bhagavan or *Bhagavat.* 'Blessed One,' a reverential appellation for great religious leaders like Buddha.
bhakti. Devotion.
bhiksu (Pali *bhikkhu*). Buddhist monks.
bhiksuni (Pali *bhikkhuni*). Buddhist nuns.
bhojanasala. A bath house.
bhumi. A spiritual stage, level, or floor.
bhumisparsa-mudra. A hand gesture of Earth-touching and Enlightenment.
Bodhi. Enlightenment.
bodhi-tree. A pipal tree or Tree of Enlightenment under which Buddha became enlightened; also an aniconic symbol of Buddha.
bodhigriha. A structure that encloses the sacred *bodhi*-tree, usually hypaethral in the center.
Bodhicitta. Seed of Enlightenment; a Vajrayana concept.
bodhisattva. One whose essence (*sattva*) is enlightenment (*bodhi*) typically denoting a Mahayana saint, who is often a non-historical and divine being practicing high virtues and countless sacrifices for fellow beings in the past and present lives before ultimately becoming a Buddha. Conceptually he is the Mahayana equivalent to the Theravada *arhat* and different from the Bodhisattva, or Buddha before Enlightenment and an epithet for his past births in the *jataka*s as a compassionate being.
Bon or *Bonpo.* The native and pre-Buddhist animistic and shamanistic cult of Tibet.
Brahman. The *Brahman* is a Hindu concept of a metaphysical absolute or a Supreme and Cosmic Being behind all world phenomena whilst the *Atman* is the absolute reality within a person.
Brahmana. An orthodox religious school in the late Vedic and early Epic Period recognizing the authority of Brahmin priests and the Vedas; a predecessor of later Hinduism.
brahmin. Hindu priests comprising the highest caste in Hinduism.
Buddhapada. Buddha's footprints and his aniconic symbol.
Buddharaja. The Khmer cult of a divinized Buddhist king consecrated in the form of his lifelike statue as the representative of Buddha and his *Dharma* on earth.
bum-pa. The dome in a Tibetan *chorten*.

caitya (Pali *cetiya*). Any sanctified religious entity, shrine, or structure including temples and *stupa*s. Also a Nepalese *stupa*.

caitya-arch. A great horseshoe-shaped arch on the facade of an Indian rock-hewn cave *caityagriha*.

caityagriha. 'Caitya house,' a type of Indian rock-hewn cave or freestanding structure containing a symbolic *stupa* in the center of a circular plan or at the apsidal end.

cakra. 'Wheel,' an Indian symbol of imperial righteousness. Also *dharmacakra*.

cakravartin. A 'wheel-turning king' and a universal righteous monarch.

candi. Generally denoting religious architecture in Indonesia, specifically a temple but less commonly a *stupa*.

cankamanasala. An area for walking meditation.

carya-tantra. See *Tantra*.

chandrasila. A moonstone slab generally of a semicircular shape on the entrance or landing of a stair.

chattra. 'Parasol, umbrella,' typically occurring above aniconic symbols of Buddha representing his invisible presence.

chattravali. A solidly molded and tapering spire in Sri Lankan and Southeast Asian *stupa*s.

chedei. The *stupa* as known in Kampuchea and derived from *caitya*.

chedi. The *stupa* as known in Thailand and Laos and derived from *caitya*.

chedi-tong. A type of Thai cylindrical *stupa*.

chorten. The *stupa* as known in Tibet and Tibetanized countries.

chos-skyong. The Tibetan equivalent of a *dharmapala*.

chunam. Burnt stone lime.

clec. The floral and flame-shaped pediment above windows and entrances of Bagan temples.

dagaba. A *stupa* as known in Sri Lanka and derived from *dhatu* (relics) and *garbha* (womb, chamber, receptacle, house).

dega. A Nepalese timber-and-brick temple resembling a pagoda.

deva. A class of celestial male guardian angels and gods who are the antithesis of the *asura*s with Indra (Sakra) as the chief god.

devapala. A class of celestial angelic guardians and gods.

devaraja. The Khmer cult of the god-king (*devaraja*) in the Angkor Period who is the manifestion of the Hindu god Siva in the form of a *linga* and his divine incarnation on earth in the human form; a counterpart of the Buddhist *Buddharaja*.

devata. A class of celestial female guardian angels and gods; also a terrestrial dryad.

devi. A goddess, queen.

dharani. A long *mantra* generally from a sentence to several pages.

dharma (Pali *dhamma*). Elements, morality, duty, and law (*dharma*); in Buddhism specifically referring to Buddha's teachings (*Dharma*).

dharmacakra. 'Wheel of Morality' and/or 'Wheel of *Dharma*,' a symbol representing Buddha's *Dharma*; also an aniconic symbol of Buddha.

dharmacakrapravatana-mudra. The hand gesture of Preaching associated with Buddha's First Sermon.

dharmacakravartin. A universal and religious *Dharma* 'monarch' who turns the Wheel of Truths, that is Buddha.

Dharmakaya. See *Trikaya*.

Dharma Mahamatra. Ministry of Morality created during Asoka's reign to oversee religious affairs and proper moral conducts.

dharmapala. Guardians of Buddha's *Dharma* and protecting deities.

dharmaraja. 'King of *Dharma* or *dharma*' or a virtuous and pious king usually a Buddhist one who upholds Buddha's *Dharma* like Asoka; also referring to Buddha.

dharmarajika. Monuments of religious piety encompassing *caitya*s and *stupa*s constructed by Emperor Asoka to commemorate the places associated with Buddha's life or inter Buddha's relics, respectively.

dharmavijaya. 'Conquest of Morality' originally propounded by Emperor Asoka.

dhatu. Generally as religious 'relics' but less commonly as 'world.'

dhoti. An Indian skirt and undercloth.

dhyana-mudra. A hand gesture of meditation.

dukhang. An assembly hall and principal chapel in a Tibetan monastery, which typically display Buddhist images and where important religious ceremonies are conducted.

Dukkha. 'Suffering,' the First Noble Truth in Buddha's first sermon.

durbar. A Nepalese royal palace.

dvarapala. A door or gate guardian of a *caitya*.

esvara. 'Lord,' a suffix often appended to the names of Hindu temples and Siva *linga*s.

gandharva. A class of celestial male musicians and together with the *apsara*s they are ruled by Virudhaka, the *lokapala* of the South.

garbha. 'Womb, chamber, receptacle, house,' generally

the most sacred quarter in a religious structure, a sanctum sanctorum.

garuda. A winged bird-human and vehicle of Visnu; also as a class of protectors of Buddha's *Dharma*.

ghanta. A bell, which in the Vajrayana represents the female, *prajna*, and the moon; the equivalent of *padma* and opposite of the *vajra*.

gompa. A Tibetan monastery.

gonkhang. A room reserved for the guardian deities in a Tibetan monastery.

gopura. A formal and large pavilion gateway.

griha (Pali *ghara*). A house.

guha. A natural or a man-made rock-hewn cave.

gujar. A gilt metal finial crowning a Nepalese structure; also occurring in Tibetan architecture.

gyalpo. A tribal chief in the Indian Himalaya.

halapau. The triangular shield above the *harmika* in a Nepalese *caitya*.

hammiya. A structure having a open pillared first story and a roofed second story; a pillared pavilion.

harmika. A square balustrade resembling a *vedika* or solid box crowning the dome of the Buddhist *stupa*.

hti. An umbrella crowning the Myanmari *zedi*.

istadevata. Deities associating with Tantric initiation ceremonies, consecratory rituals, and the highest Vajrayana teachings who are often depicted in *yuganaddha*.

jantagriha. A hot-bath house.

jataka. Buddhist moral folklores recounting past existences of Buddha typically as gods, humans, or animals where he is refered to as Bodhisattva and the central character in the story. The goals are to inculcate morality to the listeners, glorify Buddha as a perfect and compassionate teacher, and expound the theory of *karma*.

kala-makara. 'Monster mask' in Javanese arts and architecture and equivalent to the Indian *kurti-mukha*.

kalan. A Cham religious building or temple.

kalapustaka. A picture book.

kalpa. An eon, often referring to the past, present, and future.

Kamadhatu. See *Tridhatu*.

kami. The spirits in the Japanese indigenous Shinto cult.

kappiyakuti. A structure to store drugs in a Buddhist monastery.

karma (Pali *kamma*). 'Action, deed,' popularly as a system of rewards-punishments or moral consequences incurred by one's actions upon the surrounding environment in the past, present, and future; a good *karma* will result in a higher rebirth and a bad *karma* will result in a lower rebirth. A characteristic of all Indian religious systems and a pan-Asian concept.

kathina. A ceremony involves the distribution or offering of robes for monks and nuns.

kharuin. An administrative center in old Myanmar.

kinnara. Commonly a half-human and half-bird creature, also a half-human and half-horse creature.

kirti-mukha. 'Demon face,' a decorative element in Indian arts and architecture; the Indian counterpart of the Indonesian *kala-makara*.

kotthana. A storage and closet.

kriya-tantra. See *Tantra*.

ksatrapa. An independent domain controlled by non-Indian princes or kings.

ksatriya. The second Hindu caste of warriors, rulers, and adminstrators.

kut. The Cham ancestral cult in the form of steles venerated as the living manifestations of the deceased relatives.

kuti. A small freestanding cell-like structure.

lama. A Tibetan Buddhist monk.

lena. A rock-hewn cave residence for Buddhist monks; also known as a *vihara*.

linga. A phallus and aniconic symbol of Siva in Hinduism. *Yoni* is its female counterpart symbolizing Siva's *sakti*.

lohan. A Chinese word for an *arhat*.

lokapala. Heavenly guardians of the four corners of the world, namely Dhrtarastra the *lokapala* of the East, Virupaksa the *lokapala* of the West, Vaisravana the *lokapala* of the North, and Virudhaka the *lokapala* of the South.

mahamatra. High government officers and ministers. Also *Dharma Mahamatra*.

Mahasukha. 'Great Bliss,' the highest religious experience in the Vajrayana.

mahavihara. 'Great *vihara*,' commonly a monastic university.

mahoraga. A class of supernatural beings and protectors of Buddha's *Dharma*.

makara. A fish-bodied crocodile.

mandala. 'Circle' representing spheres or fields of individual or groups of divinities like Buddhas, *bodhisattvas*, and other Tantric deities; a religious device and medium in Vajrayana rituals to assist Tantric initiates in the process of attaining enlightenment.

mandapa. A hall, often pillared and flat-roofed, preceeding a central sanctuary in Indian architecture.

mandir. An Indian Hindu temple, usually stone.

mantra. An incantation invoking and propitiating a particular deity.

matapa. A type of rock-hewn caves having benches running along the back walls, most likely for pilgrims and the laity but also a service quarter like the refectory and kitchen.

math. A Hindu priest house.

medhi. A base or berm of the Indian *stupa*.

meru. A multi-tiered tower temple in Bali, Indonesia resembling a pagoda.

mithuna. A male-female pair or an amorous couple.

Moksa. The highest religious goal for Hindus signifying the union with the *Brahman* and attainment of spiritual release from the cumulative effects of *karma*s and *Samsara*.

mudra. A hand gesture; in Tantricism it carries additional esoteric meanings.

naga. A class of terrestrial serpent spirits ruled by Virupaksa, the *lokapala* of the West; commonly denoting a serpent but infrequently as an elephant.

nagani or *nagi.* A female *naga*.

nat. The native Myanmari cult of the spirits.

Nirmanakaya. See *Trikaya*.

Nirvana. 'Blowing out, extinction' or Enlightenment; the ultimate liberation for all sentient beings and the most important religious goal for Buddhists.

Non-*atman* (*Anatman*, Non-*atta* or *Anatta*). The Theravada theory of Non-Soul or Non-Self.

Pabbata Vihara. 'Mountain Monastery,' a type of Sri Lankan monasteries.

Padhanagriha Parivena. 'Double-platform and Meditation-house Monastic College,' a type of Sri Lankan monasteries.

padma. A lotus. In the Vajrayana it represents the female, *prajna*, and the moon; the equivalent of *ghanta* and opposite of *vajra*.

padmasana. A lotus throne or a sitting posture with two legs crossed as in meditation.

pancayatana. A quincunxial design.

Pancayatana Parivena. 'Quincunxial Monastic College,' a type of Sri Lankan monasteries.

paramita. 'Perfection,' virtues a *bodhisattva* must perfect before becoming a Buddha.

paribhagika caitya. A structure that houses or inters religious articles and objects.

Parinirvana. 'Beyond or Final *Nirvana*,' the great decease and dissolution of Buddha's earthly body.

parivena. Individual and private monastic cells within a *vihara* for monks and nuns.

pasada. A mansion having two or more stories.

pata. A type of Indian painting on cloth.

Paticca Samuppada. The theory of Dependent Origination or Causality Law consisting of twelve factors in the causal chain that perpetually traps sentient beings in *Samsara* and prevents them from becoming enlightened.

pattimokkha. Monastic rules.

paubha. A type of Newari or Nepalese religious paintings on cloth.

pavarana. A religious ceremony involving confessional observances.

Pitaka. See *Tripitaka*s.

podhi. A water cistern.

pradaksina path. A religious processional path around the base of a *caitya* for worship, which is performed by moving in the clockwise direction.

prajna (Pali *panna*). 'Wisdom;' in the Vajrayana it denotes the enlightened aspect of the female sides of Buddhas and *anuttarayoga-tantra* deities; it conceptually symbolizes the female, the moon, and the opposite of *upaya*.

prasat. A tower in Khmer temple architecture.

pratimagriha. 'Image house,' a temple housing Buddhist images.

pripih. A fabricated object or dummy in which the gods would be animated and manifested during religious occasions; often deposited below the central sanctuary of an Indonesian Hindu temple.

pura. A town or city.

purnaghata. A floral vase or Vase of Plenty; also known as *purnakalasa*.

raja. A king.

raksasa. A demon.

ratha. Pallava temple architecture as at Mamallapuram in South India consisting of isolated buildings in different forms; South Indian temples are also known as the *sikhara* in the form of a straight and multi-tiered pyramidal tower over the central cella and that is preceded by a *mandapa*.

ratna. A jewel.

Rupadhatu. See *Tridhatu*.

sakti. The female energy and consort of the male deity in Hinduism; in the Vajrayana it represents the female side of the deities below Buddha's rank.

Sakyacarya. A caste of married Nepalese (Newari) Buddhist monks; they traditionally belong to the caste of goldsmiths.

salabhanjika. 'She who plucks the *sala* flowers,' a class of dryad *yaksi*s or *devata*s.

Sambhogakaya. See *Trikaya.*

Sambodhi. Perfect Enlightenment.

Samsara. The cycle of birth and rebirth, the cycle of existence, and the world of unenlightened beings.

samvat. A year, an era.

Sangha. The community of Buddhist monks and nuns, the Buddhist order.

sangharama. A permanent monastery.

sanghati. A monk's robe.

sarika caitya. A structure that houses or inters religious relics encompassing the *stupa.*

sastra. Treatises or commentaries on Buddhist philosophy by Buddhist philosophers; these are the cornerstones of Mahayana philosophy.

siddha. 'The Perfected,' generally a non-celibate Vajrayana spiritual adept, guru, and monk already attained Enlightenment who also provides the spiritual guidance to the neophytes and uninitiated.

sikhara. Commonly a North Indian Hindu Nagara temple having a curvilinear spire towering above a central cella and preceded by a *mandapa.*

skandha. The Five Aggregates (Form, Sensation, Perception, Mental Formations, Consciousness) that make up a composite individual in Buddhist philosophy.

smasana. The Vedic Hindu fire-altar tumulus, possibly a precursor of the Buddhist *stupa.*

sopana. A flight of stair.

Sramana (Pali *Samana*). A religious heterodox movement and opponents of the *Brahmana* in the late Vedic and early Epic Period led by unorthodox (non-Hindu) leaders like Buddha; also generally referring to Buddhist monks and nuns in Buddhist literature.

srikoil. A type of Hindu temples in Kerala having a conical roof.

stambha. A freestanding pillar and also a vertical member of a *vedika.*

stupa (Pali *thupa*). A type of *caitya* and Buddhist structure typically interring Buddhist relics and also holy objects.

suchi. A horizontal bar of a *vedika.*

sudra. The fourth Hindu caste of workers and servants.

Sunya. 'Empty,' a hallmark Mahayana philosophical concept of the Madhyamika sect and also the Vajrayana symbolizing Enlightenment.

sutra (Pali *sutta*). Religious discourses or sermons in the Theravada and Mahayana (*sutra*); the *Sutra* portion of the *Tripitaka*s is considered Buddha's original words.

t'a. A Chinese word for a pagoda likely derived from *thupa.*

tantra. The foremost canonized literature of the Vajrayana which is divided into four categories in ascending order, namely *kriya-tantra* (Action *Tantra*s), *carya-tantra* (Performance *Tantra*s), *yoga-tantra* (Yoga *Tantra*s), and *anuttarayoga-tantra* (Supreme Yoga *Tantra*s). Also see *yogini-tantra*s.

t'ap. A Korean word for a pagoda likely derived from *thupa.*

thangka. A Tibetan religious painting on cloth.

tháp. A Vietnamese word for a pagoda likely derived from *thupa.*

that. A Lao word for a *stupa* probably derived from *dhatu* or *thupa.*

thera. 'Elder,' a Theravada monk.

theri. 'Elder,' a Theravada nun.

thupa. A Pali word for a Sri Lankan *stupa* and an equivalent to a *dagaba.* Also *stupa.*

thupaghara. A Sri Lankan '*thupa*-house' equivalent to a *vatadage* and the Indian circular *caityagriha.*

to. A Japanese word for a pagoda likely derived from *thupa.*

torana. An entry gateway in an Indian *stupa.*

tribhanga (tri-*bhanga*). A thrice-bent stance in the head, waist, and feet.

Tridhatu or *Triloka* (Tri-*dhatu* or Tri-*loka*). Three worlds or realms of existence, namely *Arupadhatu* or *Arupaloka* (World of Formlessness or Highest Existence), *Kamadhatu* or *Kamaloka* (World of Desire), and *Rupadhatu* or *Rupaloka* (World of Ordinary Forms and Physical Manifestations).

Trikaya (Tri-*kaya*). A Mahayana concept of the three manifested bodies of Buddha, namely *Nirmanakaya* (Physical Body), *Dharmakaya* (Absolute or Doctrinal Body), and *Sambhogakaya* (Glorified Body).

Tripitaka (Tri-*Pitaka*). Three Baskets (*pitaka*) or the canonical literature of the Theravada, namely *Sutra* (Buddha's *Dharma* in discourses and sermons), *Vinaya* (Monastic Rules), and *Abhidharma* (Scholastic Commentaries).

Triratna (Tri-*ratna*). Three Jewels of Buddhism, namely Buddha, *Dharma*, and *Sanghatsha-tsha.* Typically a miniature *chorten* model which is made up of clay samples collected from the construction site and mixed with powders of precious materials or ashes of the deceased *lama*s; it is deposited inside a *chorten* usually with precious stones, herbs, grains, written *mantra*s, etc.

tulku. A reincarnated *lama.*

udapanasala. A well-house.
uddesika caitya. A memorial shrine.
upasampada. A ceremony for ordination of a *bhiksu* or *bhiksuni.*
upatthanasala. An assembly hall.
upaya. 'Skillful Means,' which in the Vajrayana denotes the enlightened aspect of the male sides of Buddhas and *anuttarayoga-tantra* deities; it conceptually symbolizes the male, *karuna*, and the sun; the opposite of *prajna.*
uposatha. A ceremony for the recital of the *pattimokkha.*
uposathagriha. A hall for performing the *uposatha.*
urna. A turf of hairs resembling a dot between Buddha's eyebrows; one of Buddha's thirty-two major *laksana*s.
usnisa. A cranial protuberance on Buddha's head probably originated from the turban knot worn by the Indian royalty and nobility; one of Buddha's thirty-two major *laksana*s. Also a cope of a *vedika.*

vahana. A vehicle or mount of the god.
vahalkada. A frontispiece or projection in the base of a Sri Lankan *dagaba*, usually as an image chapel.
vaisya. The third Hindu caste of merchants and bankers.
Vajra. Vajra is the ultimate state of Enlightenment in the Vajrayana and equivalent of the non-dual and empty state of *Sunya*; it symbolizes the union of the male and female principles and *upaya* and *prajna*. In the Vajrayana the *vajra* (thunderbolt, diamond, unbreakable) represents the male, *karuna*, and the sun; the opposite of *ghanta* and *padma.*
Vajracarya. The highest caste of married Nepalese (Newari) Buddhist monks above the Sakyacarya; they exclusively belong to the caste of priests.
vajrasana. 'Diamond Throne' or Seat of Enlightenment where Buddha sat on the eve of his Enlightenment. Also an aniconic symbol of Buddha.
varada-mudra. A hand gesture of charity and boon-granting.
varman. A common suffix appended to the names of Indian and Southeast Asian monarchs.
vassavasa. A rain retreat where Buddhist monks and nuns congregate during the rainy season.
vatadage. A Sri Lankan circular relic house derived from *vatta* (round), *dhatu* (relic), and *griha* (house) and equivalent to the *thupagriha*; it originated in the Indian circular *caityagriha.*
vedika. A railing and protecting barrier, typically stone, enclosing the base of a *caitya* and *stupa* which physically and symbolically demarcates the sacred and the mundane. Also a balustrade on the *medhi* and *harmika.*
vidya. Science or knowledge.

vihara. A private dwelling for monks and nuns; popularly interchangeably used with *sangharama* for a Buddhist monastery.
viharapura. A monastic city centering on a *mahavihara.*
vina. An Indian harp.
Vinaya. See *Tripitaka.*

weiza. A magician-immortal in Myanmari mythology.

yab-yum. A Tibetan word equivalent of *yuganaddha.*
yaksa (Pali *yakkha*). A class of male terrestrial spirits ruled by Vaisravana, the *lokapala* of the North.
yaksi or *yaksini* (Pali *yakkhi*). A class of female terrestrial spirits and the female counterpart of the *yaksa*; also a female dryad like a *devata.*
yasti. A shaft or pole.
yasti-chattra. A shaft attached with several tiers of disc-like parasols crowing the *stupa.*
Yavana or *Yona*. A foreigner of non-Indian origin including an Asiatic or Bactrian Greek; probably derived from 'Ionia.'
yi-dam. A Tibetan word equivalent of *istadevata.*
yin-yang. 'Negative-positive, passive-active, female-male,' a Chinese Daoist symbol and concept representing the principle of duality.
yoga. A method of physical discipline and breathing control practiced by Hindu religious seekers to purify the mind and seek the eternal union with the *Brahman.*
yoga-tantra. See *Tantra.*
yogin or *yogi*. A male practitioner of yoga; also a Tantric Buddhist (Vajrayana) guru and adept.
yogini. A female *yogi* and a *siddha*'s consort; sometimes used interchangeably with *dakini.*
yogini-tantra. A class of *anuttarayoga-tantra*s involving *yuganaddha* and emphasizing females.
yojana. An ancient Indian unit of measurement approximating nine miles.
Yona. See *Yavana*
yuganaddha. In the Vajrayana it represents a religious sexual union between the male and female symbolizing the union of *upaya* and *prajna* and *Vajra* and/or *Sunya.*
yupa. An octagonal post, often a Vedic sacrificial post.
yupa-yasti. An octagonal post crowning South Indian *stupa*s; likely the forerunner of the *chattravali.*

zedi. A word denoting a *stupa* in Myanmari architecture derived from *cetiya.*
zimchung. A room for the head abbot in a Tibetan monastery.

Chronology

India (North and South)
Vedic Period (c. 1200-600 BCE)
Epic Period (c. 600 BCE-200 CE)
Sisunaga Dynasty (684-424 BCE)
Nanda Dynasty (424-323 BCE)
Maurya Dynasty (323-184 BCE)
Shunga Dynasty (184-72 BCE)
Early Kushan Dynasty (c. 50-241 CE)
Gupta Dynasty (320-647 CE)
Sasanka Dynasty (early seventh century CE)
Pala Dynasty (c. 750-1199 CE)
Varman Dynasty (1035-1150 CE)
Sena Dynasty (1096-1230 CE)

Andhra or Satavahana Dynasty (c. 228 BCE-225 CE)
Iksvaku Dynasty (225-325 CE)
Abhira Dynasty (248-416 CE)
Vakataka Dynasty (250-505 CE)
Asmaka Dynasty (sixth-seventh centuries CE)
Chalukya Dynasty (c. 543-735 CE)
Pallava Dynasty (c. 571-750 CE)
Rashtrakuta Dynasty (c. 735-982 CE)
Chola Dynasty (848-1279 CE)
Western Chalukya Dynasty (c. 973-1189 CE)
Kakatiya Dynasty (c. 1083-1343 CE)
Yavada Dynasty (c. 1173-1334 CE)
Hoysala Dynasty (c. 1187-1343 CE)
Pandya Dynasty (c. 1216-1336 CE)
Vijayanagar Dynasty (1336-1565 CE)

Bangladesh
Maurya Dynasty (323-184 BCE)
Shunga Dynasty (184-72 BCE)
Early Kushan Dynasty (c. 50-241 CE)
Pushkarna (third-fourth centuries CE)
Gupta Dynasty (320-647 CE)
Khadga Dynasty (c. 625-705 CE)
Deva Dynasty (c. 705-900 CE)
Chandra Dynasty (c. 900-1035 CE)
Varman Dynasty (1035-1150 CE)
Sena Dynasty (1096-1230 CE)

Pakistan
Indus Civilization (c. 3500-1500 BCE)
Achaemenid Persian Dynasty (c. 558-326 BCE)
Early Greek Period (c. 326-317 BCE)
Maurya Dynasty (c. 317-189 BCE)
Later Greek Period (c. 189-90 BCE)
Saka Period (c. 90 BCE-25 CE)
Parthian Period (c. 25-50 CE)
Early Kushan Dynasty (c. 50-241 CE)
Iranian-Sassanian Interlude (c. 241-390 CE)
Later or Kidara Kushan Dynasty (c. 390-454 CE)
White Huns or Hephthalites (c. 454-552 CE)
Turki-Shahi Dynasty (552-744 CE)
Hindu-Shahi Dynasty (744-1000 CE)

Afghanistan
Proto-historic Period (c. 4000-558 BCE)
Achaemenid Persian Dynasty (c. 558-326 BCE)
Early Greek Period (c. 326-317 BCE)
Maurya Dynasty (c. 317-189 BCE)
Later or Bactrian Greek Period (c. 317-90 BCE)
Saka Period (c. 90 BCE-25 CE)
Parthian Period (c. 25-50 BCE)
Early Kushan Dynasty (c. 50-241 CE)
Iranian-Sassanian Interlude (c. 241-390 CE)
Later or Kidara Kushan Dynasty (c. 390-454 CE)
White Huns or Hephthalites Dynasty (c. 454-552 CE)
Turki-Shahi Dynasty (552-744 CE)
Chinese Vassal (659-737 CE)
Hindu-Shahi Dynasty (744-1000 CE)

Central Asia
Proto-historic Period (c. 5000-558 BCE)
Achaemenid Persian Dynasty (c. 558-326 BCE)
Early Greek Period (c. 326-317 BCE)
Later or Bactrian Greek Period (c. 317-90 BCE)
Saka Period (c. 90 BCE-50 CE)
Early Kushan Dynasty (c. 50-241 CE)
Iranian-Sassanian Interlude (c. 241-454 CE)
White Huns or Hephthalites Dynasty (c. 454-552 CE)
Turki-Shahi Dynasty (552-744 CE)
Chinese Vassal (659-737 CE)

Turkistan
Kushan or Yueh-chi Period (third-second centuries BCE)
Vassals under Xiongnu (Hun) and Chinese (second century BCE-first centuries CE)
Lou-lan (third-second centuries BCE)
Chinese Rule (c. 73-300 CE)
Chinese Vassal (c. 300-435 CE)
Chinese Rule (435-552 CE)
Turki-Shahi Dynasty (552-650 CE)
Chinese Vassal (650-737 CE)
Tibetan Vassal (670-690 CE, 781-847 CE)

Uygur Dynasty (c. 745-1000 CE)
Kara-Khanid Dynasty (c. 1000-1211 CE)
Kara-Khitan Dynasty (1211-1218 CE)
Mongol Rule (1218-1368 CE)
Semi-independence, Independence (1368-1759 CE)
Chinese Qing Dynasty (1759-1911 CE)

China
Xia Dynasty (c. 2100-1600 BCE)
Shang Dynasty (c. 1600-1100 BCE)
Zhou Dynasty (c. 1100-256 BCE)
Spring and Autumn Period (770-476 BCE)
Warring States Period (476-221 BCE)
Qin Dynasty (221-206 BCE)
Han Dynasty (206 BCE-220 CE)
Three Kingdoms of Wei, Shu, Wu (220-265 CE)
Western Jin Dynasty (265-317 CE)
Northern and Southern Dynasties (317-589 CE)
Sui Dynasty (581-618 CE)
Tang Dynasty (618-907 CE)
Five Dynasties Interlude (907-960 CE)
Liao Dynasty (907-1125 CE)
Song Dynasty (960-1297 CE)
Xi Xia Dynasty (1036-1227 CE)
Jin Dynasty (1115-1234 CE)
Yuan Dynasty (1279 CE-1368 CE)
Ming Dynasty (1368-1644 CE)
Qing Dynasty (1644-1911 CE)

Korea
Proto-historic Period (third millennium-third century BCE)
Choson (c. 200-108 BCE)
Lo-lang and Tai-fang (108 BCE-313 CE)
Four Kingdoms of
Koguryo (37 BCE-668 CE)
Paekche (18 BCE-660 CE)
Silla (57 BCE-668 CE)
Karak or Kaya (42-562 CE)
Unified Silla Dynasty (668-935 CE)
Koryo Dynasty (935-1392 CE)
Yi Dynasty (1392-1910 CE)

Japan
Jomon Period (c. 10500-300 BCE)
Yayoi Period (c. 300 BCE-300 CE)
Kofun Period (c. 300-552 CE)
Asuka Period (552-645 CE)
Hakuho Period (645-710 CE)
Nara Period (710-784 CE)
Heian Period (784-1186 CE)

Kamakura Period (1186-1336 CE)
Nanbokucho Interlude (1336-1392 CE)
Muromachi Period (1392-1573 CE)
Momoyama Period (1573-1615 CE)
Edo Period (1615-1868 CE)
Meiji Period (1868 CE-current)

Vietnam
Proto-historic Van Lang (c. 2897-257 BCE)
Thuc Dynasty (257-207 BCE)
Chinese Rule (207 BCE-938 CE)
Ngo Dynasty (938-968 CE)
Dinh Dynasty (968-980 CE)
Early Le Dynasty (980-1010 CE)
Ly Dynasty (1010-1225 CE)
Tran Dynasty (1225-1400 CE)
Ho Dynasty (1400-1407 CE)
Later Le Dynasty (1428-1788 CE)
Nguyen Dynasty (1802-1945 CE)

Sri Lanka
Anuradhapura Period (fourth century BCE-tenth centuries CE)
Polonnaruva Period (eleventh-thirteenth centuries CE)

Myanmar
Mon Period (c. 0-1057 CE)
Pyu Period (c. 0-1057 CE)
Bagan Period (849-1287 CE)
Eva Dynasty (1287-1531 CE)
Pegu Dynasty (1287-1531 CE)
Toungoo Dynasty (1531-1753)
Konbaung Dynasty (1753-1824 CE)
Mandalay Dynasty (1824-1885 CE)

Indonesia
Bronze Age (third-first centuries BCE)
Proto-historic Period (first-fourth centuries CE)
Turama (fifth-seven centuries CE)
Srivijaya (c. 600-1250 CE)
First Maratam or Sanjaya Dynasty (c. 600-775 CE)
Sailendra Dynasty (c. 775-856 CE)
Second Maratam Dynasty (c. 856-928 CE)
Kediri Dynasty (1050-1221 CE)
Singosari Dynasty (1221-1293 CE)
Majapahit Dynasty (1293-1530 CE)

Kampuchea
Neolithic and Bronze Age (c. 3000 BCE-0 CE)
Funan (c. 0-600 CE)
Chenla (c. 600-802 CE)

Angkor Period (802-1431 CE)
Phnom Penh Period (1431-1945 CE)

Champa
Lin-yi (192-758 CE)
Huan-wang (758-860 CE)
Champa (808-1697 CE)

Thailand
Dvaravati Period (sixth-tenth centuries CE)
Khmer Rule (tenth-thirteenth centuries CE)
Sukhothai Period (thirteenth-fourteenth centuries CE)
Ayuthaya Period (1350-1757 CE)
Bangkok Period (1757-current)

Laos
Lan Xang Period (1353-1520 CE)
Vientiane Period (1520-1945 CE)

Nepal
Kirata Period (c. 600 BCE-100 CE)
Licchavi Period (c. 100-880 CE)
Thakuri Period (c. 880-1200 CE)
Malla Period (c. 1200-1769 CE)
Shah Dynasty (1769-2008 CE)

Indian Himalaya
Partly under Kushan Rule (second-third centuries CE)
Sen Dynasty (sixth-seventh centuries CE)
Tibetan Period (seventh-ninth centuries CE)
Guge Period (tenth-sixteenth centuries CE)
Namgyal Dynasty (1500-1842 CE)

Tibet
Yarlung Dynasty (c. 607-842 CE)
Sakyapa Period (c. 1249-1400 CE)
Gelugpa and Dalai Lama Period (c. 1400-1720 CE)

Bhutan
Tibetan Period (c. 600-900 CE)
Foundation Period (c. 900-1616 CE)
Namgyal Dynasty (1616-1728 CE)
Unification Period (1728-1907 CE)
Wangchuk Dynasty (1907-2008 CE)

Mongolia
Xiongnu or Hun Period (third century BCE-third centuries CE)
Rouran or Tartar Period (c. 300-555 CE)
Gorturk Period (555-745 CE)
Uygur Period (745-907 CE)

Vassals under Liao Dynasty (907-1125 CE) and Jin Dynasty (1115-1234 CE)
Mongol Empire (1206-1368 CE)
Post-Mongol Period (1368-1691 CE)
Vassal under Chinese Qing Dynasty (1691-1911 CE)

Map 1. Buddhist Sites in South Asia

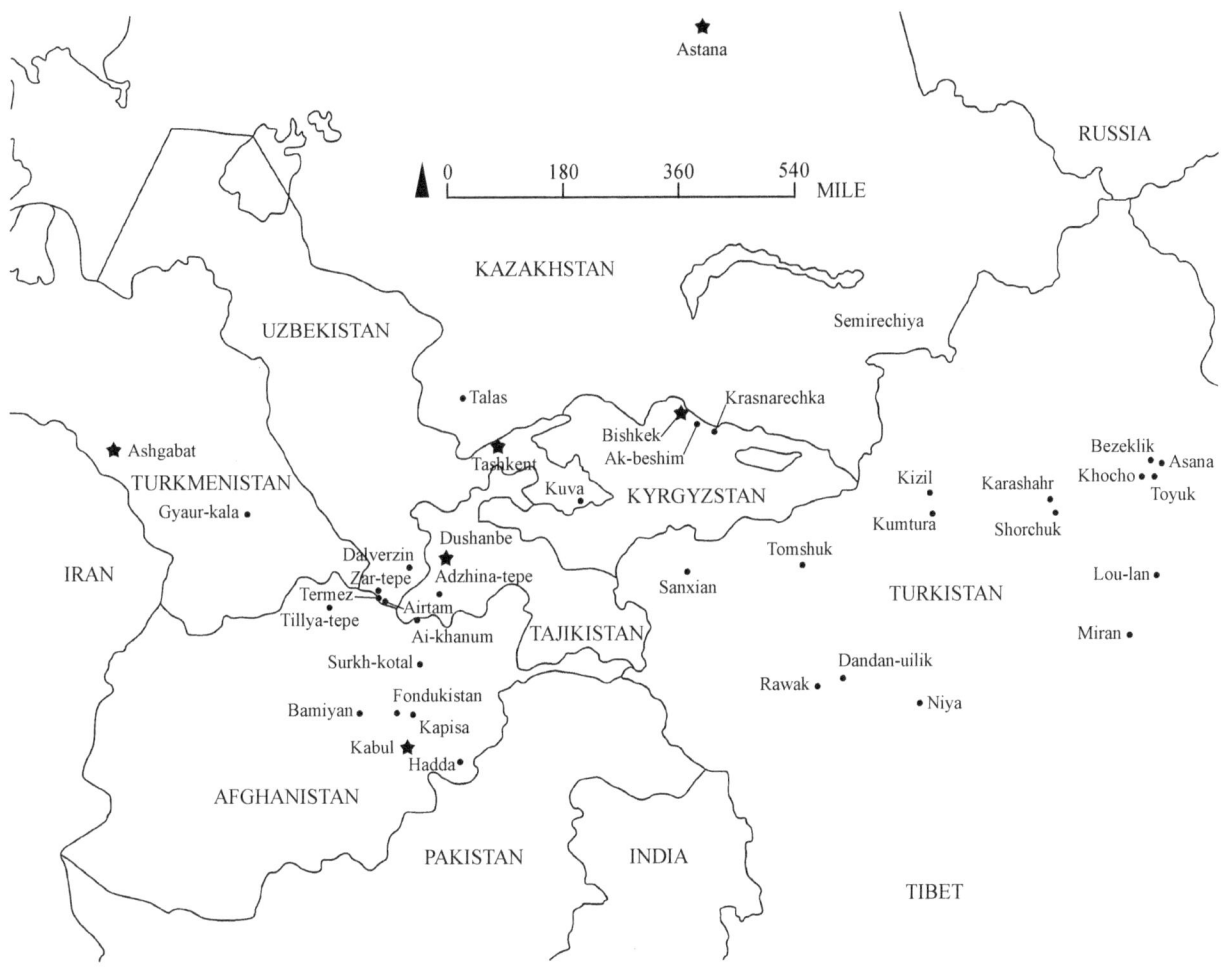

Map 2. Buddhist Sites in Central Asia

Map 3. Buddhist Sites in East Asia

Maps . 299

Map 4. Buddhist Sites in Southeast Asia

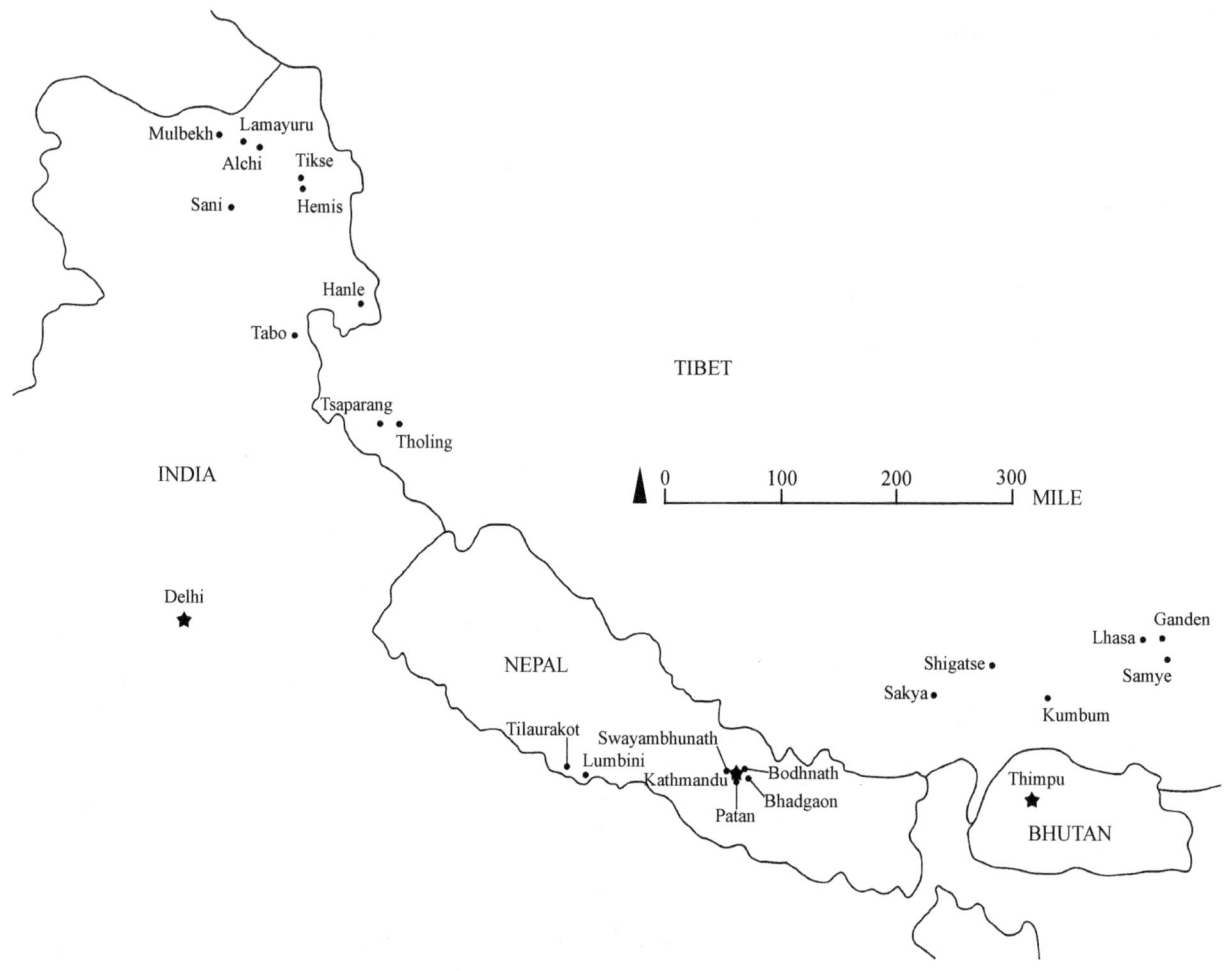

Map 5. Buddhist Sites in the Himalaya Countries

Illustrations and Credits

All maps and architectural drawings are completed by the author.

Front Cover. Mahabodhi Temple
c. 150-800 CE (final form)
Bodhgaya- India

Back Cover. Honeysuckle Motif and Dharmacakra
c. 100-75 BCE
Bharhut Stupa, Bharhut- India

Coomaraswamy, Ananda K. 1935: **7.6**, **7.8**
Dunhuang Mogao Ku 1982 Volume I: **5.23**, **5.25**
Frederic, Louis 1994: **6.32**
Jain, Jyotindra 1998: **6.6**
James Harle 1994: **5.1**
Knox, Robert 1992: **6.10**
Leoshko, Janice 1988: **7.9**
Marshall, John and Foucher, Alfred 1940 Volume II: **6.5**
Miksic, John 1990: **6.31**
Mun, Myong-dae 2000: **5.27**
Oki, Morihiro and Ito, Shoji 1991: **6.8**
Snellgrove, David and Others 1978: **6.11**
Wei, Ran 2000: **6.25**
Yazdani, Ghulam 1930-1955 Part IV: **5.11**, **5.13**

Front Cover. See **7.10**
Back Cover. Redrawn
1.1-1.2. Redrawn
4.1-4.2. Redrawn
4.3. Compiled
4.4. Redrawn
4.5. Redrawn (plan) and compiled (elevation-section)
4.8-4.9. Redrawn
4.10. Redrawn (plan) and compiled (elevation)
4.11. Redrawn
4.12. Compiled
4.13. Redrawn
4.14. Compiled
5.1. Redrawn
5.3-5.4. Redrawn
5.6-5.8. Redrawn
5.10. Redrawn
5.12. Redrawn
5.14-5.16. Redrawn
5.18. Redrawn (plan) and compiled (section)
5.20. Redrawn
5.22. Redrawn
5.24. Redrawn

6.1. Redrawn (plan) and compiled (elevation)
6.3. Redrawn
6.6. Compiled
6.9. Compiled
6.12-6.14. Redrawn (plan) and compiled (elevation)
6.17. Redrawn (plan) and compiled (elevation)
6.18. Redrawn (plan)
6.20. Redrawn
6.23. Redrawn
6.24. Compiled (plan) and redrawn (elevation)
6.26. Redrawn
6.28. Redrawn (plan) and compiled (elevation)
6.33. Redrawn
6.35. Redrawn
6.37. Redrawn
6.39. Compiled
6.40. Redrawn
7.1-7.2. Redrawn (plan) and compiled (elevation)
7.4-7.5. Redrawn
7.7. Compiled
7.10. Redrawn (plan) and compiled (elevation)
7.12. Redrawn (plan) and compiled (elevation)
7.14. Redrawn
7.16. Redrawn (plan) and compiled (elevation)
8.1. Redrawn
8.3. Redrawn
8.5. Redrawn
8.7. Redrawn
8.9. Redrawn
8.10. Redrawn (plan) and compiled (elevation)

Bibliography

Abbreviations

1'1"	One foot and one inch
1'-2'	One foot to two feet
1' x 1'	One foot by one foot
AAA	Archives of Asian Art
AACA	Archaeology and Art of Central Asia
AAK	Arts et Archeologie Khmers
AIC	Art Institute of Chicago
AIIS	American Institute of Indian Studies
AS	Asiatic Society
ASB	Asiatic Society of Bengal
ASC	Archaeological Survey of Ceylon
ASIAR	Archaeological Survey of India Annual Report
ASSI	Archaeological Survey of Southern India
ASWA	Archaeological Survey of Western India
BKB	Bharat Kala Bhavan
BL	British Library
BM	British Museum
BMFA	Boston Museum of Fine Arts
CAAM	Central Asia Antiquities Museum
CGMAG	Chandigarh Government Museum and Art Gallery
CJS	Centre of Japanese Studies
CMA	Cleveland Museum of Art
CTFRJFJYSWHJH	Cai Tuan Fa Ren Juefeng Fo Jiao Yi Shu Wen Hua Ji Hui
CTTP	China Travel and Tourism Press
CYYTPW	Choson Yujok Yumul Togam P'yonch'an Wiwonhoe
DICR	Dunhuang Institute for Cultural Relics
DM	Dacca Museum
DWWYJS	Dunhuang Wen Wu Yan Jiu Suo
EFEO	Ecole Francaise d' Extreme-Orient
EW	East and West
FSTC	Foundation for Science Technology and Civilization
GCI	Getty Conservation Institute
GLGGBWY	Guo Li Gu Gong Bo Wu Yuan
GLLSBWG	Guo Li Li Shi Bo Wu Guan
GRMCBC	Gansu Ren Min Chu Ban She
GRMMSCBC	Gansu Ren Min Mei Shu Chu Ban She
HMPH	Han'guk Munhwajae Poho Hyophoe
HSAD	Hyderabad State Archaeological Department
HZSJ	Hua Zheng Shu Ju
IA	Indian Archaeology
IATS	International Association for Tibetan Studies
ICSBA	International Centre for Study of Bengal Art
IGNCA	Indira Gandhi National Centre for the Arts
IIAO	Istituto Italiano per l'Africa e l'Oriente
IMC	Indian Museum of Calcutta
IsMEO	Istituto Italiano per il Medio ed Estremo Oriente

Bibliography . 303

IUO	Istituto Universitario Orientale
JAS	Journal of Asiatic Society
JASB	Journal of Asiatic Society Bengal
JFFJYSWHJJH	Jue Feng Fo Jiao Yi Shu Wen Hua Ji Jin Hui
JISRS	Journal of the Institute of Silk Road Studies
JKK	Jimbun Kagaku Kenkyusho
JNGS	Journal of the National Geographic Society
JRAS	Journal of Royal Asiatic Society
JRASCB	Journal of Royal Asiatic Society Ceylon Branch
JXSNGSWHJJH	Jia Xin Shui Ni Gong Si Wen Hua Ji Jin Hui
KXCBS	Ke Xue Chu Ban She
LAMA	Los Angeles Museum of Art
LDC	Lumbini Development Committee
LIRI	Lumbini International Research Institute
LPM	Lucknow Provincial Museum
MAAG	Musee des Arts Asiatiques-Guimet
MAM	Mathura Archaeological Museum
MASC	Memoirs of Archaeological Survey of Ceylon
MASI	Memoirs of Archaeological Survey of India
MDAFA	Memoires de la Delegation Archaeologique Francaise en Afghanistan
MG	Musee Guimet
MGM	Mathura Government Museum
MIK	Museum fur Indische Kunst
MIT	Massachusetts Institute of Technology
MMA	Metropolitan Museum of Art
MPP	Mission Pelliot Paul
MV	Museum fur Volkerkunde
NALWL	New American Library of World Literature
NGA	National Gallery of Art
NHSK	Nippon Hoso Shuppan Kyokai
NMI	National Museum of India
NNM	Nava Nalanda Mahavihara
NYSUP	New York State University Press
OI	Oriental Institute
PMI	Patna Museum (India)
PMP	Peshawar Museum (Pakistan)
RAS	Royal Asiatic Society
RIPCS	Royal India, Pakistan, and Ceylon Society
ROM	Royal Ontario Museum
SAA	South Asian Archaeology
SBKK	Seiiki Bunka Kunkyu Kai
SCBGS	Shanghai Chu Ban Gong Si
SDEA	Societe Des d' Extreme-Asie
SDLC	Shimla Department of Language and Culture
SGDWXCBS	Shanghai Gu Dian Wen Xue Chu Ban She
SQCBS	Shu Quan Chu Ban She
SRMCBS	Shanghai Ren Min Chu Ban She
SRMMSCBS	Shanghai Ren Min Mei Shu Chu Ban She
SSDCBS	Shanghai Shu Dian Chu Ban She
SWYCBS	Shanghai Wen Yi Chu Ban She

TH	Tibet House
TNM	Tokyo National Museum
UCP	University of Chicago Press
UIMA	University of Iowa Museum of Art
UHP	University of Hawaii Press
UMMAA	University of Missouri Museum of Art and Archaeology
UPSM	Uttar Pradesh State Museum
VIO	Verlag Inigo von Oppersdorff
WHJSHWHSYGLJ	Wen Hua Ji She Hui Wen Hua Shi Ye Guan Li Ju
WWCBS	Wen Wu Chu Ban She
XMSSYCBS	Xinjiang Mei Shu She Ying Chu Ban She
XSTSGS	Xiong Shi Tu Shu Gong Si
ZCSBSWYH	Zhonghua Cong Shu Bian Shen Wei Yuan Hui
ZCSWYH	Zhonghua Cong Shu Wei Yuan Hui
ZFJWHG	Zhonghua Fo Jiao Wen Hua Guan
ZGDYSCBS	Zhongguo Gu Dian Yi Shu Ban She
ZMTS	Zhonghua Min'guo Taibei Shi

General

Ghirshman, Roman. *Persian Art: The Parthian and Sassanian Dynasties 249 B.C. – A.D. 651*. New York, New York: Golden Press Inc. 1962.

_____. *Persia from the Origins to Alexander the Great*. Paris, France: Thames and Hudson. 1964.

Frankfort, Henri. *The Art and Architecture of the Ancient Orient*. New Haven, Connecticut: Yale University Press. 1970.

Fletcher, Banister. *A History of Architecture*. New York, New York: Charles Scribner's Sons. 1975.

Norwich, John Julius and Others. *Great Architecture of the World*. London, Britain: Mitchell Beazley Publishers. 1975.

Trachtenberg, Marvin and Hyman, Isabelle. *Architecture from Prehistory to Post-Modernism: The Western Tradition*. Englewood Cliffs, New Jersey: Prentice-Hall Inc. and New York, New York: Harry N. Abrams Inc. 1986.

Curl, James Stevens. *Dictionary of Architecture*. London, Britain: Magpie Books. 2005.

India

Mookerji, Radhakumud. *The Gupta Empire*. Bombay, India: Hind Kitabs Ltd. Publishers. 1947.

Majumdar, Ramesh Chandra. *The Vakataka-Gupta Age, circa 200-550 A. D.* Delhi, India: Motilal Banarsidass. 1967.

Fleet, John Faithful. *Inscriptions of the Early Gupta Kings and Their Successors*. Varanasi, India: Indological Book House. 1970.

Mishra, Ram Swaroop. *Inscriptions of the Early Gupta Kings and Their Successors: Supplement to Fleet's Corpus Insciptionum Indicarum, Vol. III (1888)*. Varanasi, India: Banaras Hindu University. 1971.

Gupta, Parmeshwari Lal. *The Imperial Guptas. Volume I-II*. Varanasi, India: Vishwavidyalaya Prakashan. 1974-1979.

Chhabra, Bahadurchand and Others. *Inscriptions of the Early Gupta Kings*. New Delhi, India: ASI. 1981.

Chatterjee, Rama. *Religion in Bengal during the Pala and Sena Times; Mainly on the Basis of Epigraphic and Archaeological Sources*. Calcutta, India: Punthi Pustak. 1985.

Bagchi, Jhunu. *The History and Culture of the Palas of Bengal and Bihar, cir. 750-cir. 1200 A.D.* New Delhi, India: Abhinav Publications. 1993.

Buhler, Georg. *A Legend of the Jaina Stupa at Mathura*. Wien, Germany: C. Gerold's Sohn. 1898.

Smith, Vincent Arthur. *The Jain Stupa and Other Antiquities of Mathura*. Allahabad, India: Uttar Pradesh Government Press. 1901.

Grunwedel, Albert. *Buddhist Art in India: Translated from the 'Handbuch' by Albert Grunwedel by Agnes C. Gibson; Rev. and Enl. By Jas. Burgess*. London, Britain: B. Quaritch. 1901.

_____. *Grunwedels Buddhistische Kunst in Indien*. Berlin, Germany: Wurfel Verlag. 1932.

Fergusson, James and Others. *History of Indian and Eastern Architecture, Volume 1-2*. London, England: John Murray. 1910.

Foucher, Alfred. *The Beginnings of Buddhist Art*. London, Britain: Humphrey Milford. 1917.

Hallade, Madeleine. *Etudes d'Art Indien; la Composi-*

tion Plastique dans les Reliefs de l'Inde; Art Ancien, Art Bouddhique Gupta et Postgupta. Paris, France: Adrien-Maisonneuve. 1942.

Zimmer, Henrich. *The Art of Indian Asia: Its Mythology and Transformations*. New York, New York: Pantheon Books. 1960.

Seckel, Dietrich. *The Art of Buddhism*. New York, New York: Crown Publishers. 1964.

Brown, Percy. *Indian Architecture: Buddhist and Hindu Periods*. Bombay, India: D. B. Taraporevala Sons and Co. Private Ltd. 1965.

Volwahsen, Andreas. *Living Architecture: Indian*. New York, New York: Grosset and Dunlap. 1969.

Mitra, Debala. *Buddhist Monuments*. Calcutta, India: Sahitya Samsa. 1971.

Gajjar, Irene N. *Ancient Indian Art and the West*. Bombay, India: D. B. Taraporevala Sons and Co Private Ltd. 1971.

Aiyar, Shankar Arjun. *Historical Index to the Study of Indian Temple Architecture*. Bombay, India: Chandra Print Press. 1972.

Rowland, Benjamin. *The Art and Architecture of India: Buddhist, Hindu, Jain*. Baltimore, Maryland: Penguin Books. 1977.

Sivaramamurti, Calambur. *The Art of India*. New York, New York: Harry N. Abrams. 1977.

Huntington, Susan L. and Huntington, John C. *Art of Ancient India: Buddhist, Hindu, Jain*. New York, New York: Weatherhill. 1985.

Doshi, Saryu and Others. *India and Greece: Connections and Parallels*. Mumbai, India: Marg Publications. 1985.

Pal, Pratapaditya and Others. *American Collectors of Asian Arts*. Mumbai, India: Marg Publications. 1986.

_____. *A Pot-Pourri of Early Indian Art*. Mumbai, India: Marg Publications. 1986.

_____. *On The Path to Void: Buddhist Art of the Tibetan Realm*. Mumbai, India: Marg Publications. 1996.

_____. *Sindh: Past Glory, Present Nostalgia*. Mumbai, India: Marg Publications. 2008.

_____. *Buddhist Art: Form and Meaning*. Mumbai, India: Marg Publications. 2007.

_____. *Asian Art at the Norton Simon Museum Volume 1: Art from the Indian Subcontinent*. New Haven, Connecticut: Yale University Press. 2004.

_____. *Asian Art at the Norton Simon Museum Volume 2: Art from the Himalayas and China*. New Haven, Connecticut: Yale University Press. 2004.

_____. *Asian Art at the Norton Simon Museum Volume 3: Art from Sri Lanka and Southeast Asia*. New Haven, Connecticut: Yale University Press. 2004.

Deshpande, Madhusudan Narhar. *The Caves of Panhale-Kaji (Ancient Pranakala): An Art Historical Study of Trasition from Hinayana, Tantric Vajrayana to Nath Sampradaya (Third to Fourteenth Century A. D.). MASI no. 84*. New Delhi, India: ASI. 1986.

Dehejia, Vidya. *Yogini, Cult and Temples: A Tantric Tradition*. New Delhi, India: NMI. 1986.

_____. *Indian Art*. London, Britain: Phaidon. 1997.

Michell, George. *The Hindu Temple: An Introduction to Its Meaning and Forms*. Chicago, Illinois: University of Chicago Press. 1988.

Yamamoto, Chikyo. *Introduction to Buddhist Art*. New Delhi, India: Aditya Prakashan. 1990.

Tadgell, Christopher. *History of Architecture in India: From the Dawn of Civilization to the End of the Raj*. London, Britain: Architecture Design and Technology Press. 1990.

Murthy, Krishna K. *Glimpses of Art, Architecture and Buddhist Literature in Ancient India*. New Delhi, India: Abhinav Publications. 1991.

Kossak, Steven M. and Lerner, Martin. *The Lotus Transcendent: Indian and Southeast Asian Sculpture from the Samuel Eilenberg Collection*. New Haven, Connecticut: Yale University Press. 1991.

_____ and Watts, Edith W. *The Art of South and Southeast Asia: A Resource for Educators*. New Haven, Connecticut: Yale University Press. 2004.

Fisher, Robert E. *Buddhist Art and Architecture*. New York, New York: Thames and Hudson. 1993.

Carter, Martha L. and Others. *A Treasury of Indian Coins*. Mumbai, India: Marg Publications. 1994.

Harle, James. *The Art and Architecture of the Indian Subcontinent*. New Haven, Connecticut: Yale University Press. 1994.

Bandyopadhyay, Sudipa. *Architectural Motifs in Early Medieval Art of Eastern India (Pala-Sena Period)*. Kolkata, India: R. N. Bhattacharya. 2002.

Tripathi, Aruna. *The Buddhist Art of Kausambi: (from 300 BC to AD 550)*. New Delhi, India: D. K. Printworld. 2003.

Grover, Satish. *Buddhist and Hindu Architecture in India*. New Delhi, India: CBS Publishers. 2003.

Asher, Frederick M. *Art of India: Perhistory to the Present*. London, Britain: Encyclopaedia Britannica. 2003.

Chicarelli, Charles F. *Buddhist Art: An Illustrated Introduction*. Chiang Mai, Thailand: Silkworm Books. 2004.

Sharma, Arvind. *Goddesses and Women in the Indic Religious Tradition*. Leiden, Netherlands: Brill. 2005.

Ray, Himanshu Prabha. *Coins in India: Power and Communication.* Mumbai, India: Marg Publications. 2006.

Bronkhorst, Johannes. *Greater Magadha: Studies in the Culture of Early India.* Leiden, Netherlands: Brill. 2007.

Kashmir

Ganhar, J. N. and Ganhar, P. N. *Buddhism in Kashmir and Ladakh.* New Delhi, India: P. N. Ganhar. 1956.

Goetz, Hermann. *Studies in the History and Art of Kashmir and the Indian Himalaya.* Wiesbaden, Germany: Harrassowitz. 1969.

Kaul, Manohar. *Kashmir: Hindu, Buddhist, and Muslim Architecture.* New Delhi, India: Sagar Publications. 1971.

Pal, Pratapaditya. *Bronzes of Kashmir.* Graz, Austria: Akademische Druck–u. Verlagsanstalt. 1975.

_____. *Art and Architecture of Ancient Kashmir.* Bombay, India: Marg Publications. 1989.

Kak, Ram Chandra. *Ancient Monuments of Kashmir.* Lahore, Pakistan: Verinag Publishers. 1991.

Sharma, Suresh K. and Sharma, Usha. *Kashmir Through the Ages.* Delhi, India: Deep and Deep Publications. 1998.

ASI. *Inventory of Monuments and Sites of National Importance.* New Delhi, India: ASI. 1998.

Eastern India, Bengal, Bangladesh

Chanda, R. P. *Explorations in Orissa. MASI Volume 94.* Calcutta, India: ASI. 1930.

Dani, Ahmad Hasan. *Buddhist Sculpture in East Pakistan.* Karachi, Pakistan: Pakistan Department of Archaeology. 1959.

Choudhary, Radhakrishna. *The University of Vikramasila.* Patna, India: Bihar Research Society. 1975.

Kuraishi, Mohammad Hamid. *Ancient Monuments in Bihar and Orissa.* New Delhi, India: Government of India. 1990.

Mitra, Debala. *Ratnagiri, 1958-61. MASI No. 88, Volumes I-II. 1981.* New Delhi, India: ASI. 1981.

_____. *Bronzes from Bangladesh: A Study of Buddhist Images from District Chittagong.* Delhi, India: Agam. 1982.

Shamsul Alam, A. K. M. *An Album of Archaeological Relics in Bangladesh.* Dhaka, Bangladesh: Directorate of Archaeology and Museums. 1984.

_____. *Sculptural Art of Bangladesh: Pre-Muslim Period.* Dhaka, Bangladesh: Department of Archaeology and Museums. 1985.

Hock, Nancy. *Buddhist Ideology and the Sculpture of Ratnagiri: Seventh to Thirteenth Centuries.* Berkeley, Californina: University of Californina. 1987.

Sengupta, Anasua. *Buddhist Art of Bengal, from the 3rd Century B. C. to the 13th Century A. D.* Delhi, India: Rahul Publishing House. 1993.

Haque, Enamul and Pal, Pratapaditya. *Bengal, Sites and Sights.* Mumbai, India: Marg Publications. 2003.

_____. *The Art Heritage of Bangladesh.* Dhaka, Bangladesh: ICSBA. 2007.

Bandyobadhyay, Bimal. *Buddhist Centres of Orissa: Lalitagiri, Ratnagiri, Udayagiri.* New Delhi, India: Sundeep Prakashan. 2004.

Sri Lanka

Paranavitana, Senarat. *Art and Architecture of Ceylon: Polonnaruva Period.* Colombo, Ceylon: Arts Council of Ceylon. 1954.

_____. *Inscriptions of Ceylon, Volume I.* Colombo, Ceylon: Ceylon Department of Archaeology. 1970.

_____. *Art of the Ancient Sinhalese.* Colombo, Ceylon: Lake House Investments Ltd. Publishers. 1971.

Harischandra, Brahmachari. *The Sacred City of Anuradhapura.* Delhi, India: Asian Educational Services. 1985.

Schroeder, Ulrich von. *Buddhist Sculptures of Sri Lanka.* Hong Kong, Hong Kong: Visual Dharma Publications Ltd. 1990.

Smither, James. *Archaeological Remains, Anuradhapura, Sri Lanka: Comprising the Dagabas and Certain other Ancient Ruined Structures.* Polgasovita, Sri Lanka: Academy of Sri Lankan Culture. 1993.

Berkwitz, Stephen C. *Buddhist History in the Vernacular: The Power of the Past in Late Medieval Sri Lanka.* Leiden, Netherlands: Brill. 2004.

Southeast Asia

Coral-Remusat, Gilbert de. *Les Arts de L'Indochine.* Paris, France: G. van Oest. 1938.

Parmentier, Henri. *L' Art Architectural Hindou dans L' Inde et en Extreme-Orient.* Paris, France: G. van Oest. 1948.

Grousset, Rene. *De l'Inde au Cambodge et a Java.* Monaco, France: Documents d'Art. 1950.

Groslier, Bernard Philippe. *The Art of Indochina including Thailand, Vietnam, Laos, and Cambodia.* New York, New York: Crown Publishers Inc. 1962.

Forman, Werner. *Indian Sculpture: Masterpieces of Indian, Khmer, and Cham Art.* London, Britain: Spring Books. 1962.

Swaan, Wim. *Lost Cities of Asia: Ceylon, Pagan, and*

Angkor. New York, New York: Putnam. 1966.

Rawson, Philip S. *The Art of Southeast Asia; Cambodia, Vietnam, Thailand, Laos, Burma, Java, Bali*. London, Britain: Thames and Hudson. 1990.

Moorthy, K. K. *That Lord Siva to Be Adored: A Minicompendium of 300 Shrines, Inclusive of Dwadasa Jyotirlinga Kshetras, Panchabhutasthalas, Pancharamas plus Those Situated in Nepal, Sri Lanka, Vietnam, and Indonesia*. Tirupati, India: Message Publications. 1995.

Chihara, Daigoro. *Hindu-Buddhist Architecture in Southeast Asia*. Leiden, Netherlands: E. J. Brill. 1996.

Dumarcay, Jacques. *Construction Techniques in South and Southeast Asia*. Leiden, Netherlands: Brill. 2005.

Myanmar

Strachan, Paul. *Pagan: Art and Architecture of Old Burma*. Whiting Bay, Scotland: Kiscadale. 1989.

Stadtner, Donald M. and Others. *The Art of Burma, New Studies*. Mumbai, India: Marg Publications. 1999.

Cooler, Richard M. *The Art and Culture of Burma*. Chicago, Illinois: Northern Illinois University. 2000.

Gutman, Pamela. *Burma's Lost Kingdoms: Splendours of Arakan*. Hong Kong, China: Orchid Press. 2001.

Sylvia Fraser-Lu. *Splendour in Wood: The Buddhist Monasteries of Burma*. Hong Kong, China: Orchid Press. 2001.

Bautze-Picron, Claudine. *The Buddhist Murals of Pagan*. New York, New York: Weatherhill. 2003.

Indonesia

Kempers, Bernet August Johan. *Cultural Relations between India and Java*. Calcutta, India: University of Calcutta. 1937.

_____. *Ancient Indonesian Art*. Amsterdam, Netherlands: C. P. J. Van Der Peet. 1959.

Gangoly, Ordhendra Coomar. *The Art of Java*. Calcutta, India: A. N. Gangoly. 1967.

Fontein, Jan. *The Sculpture of Indonesia*. Washington D. C., USA: National Gallery of Art. 1990.

Kinney, Ann R. *Worshiping Siva and Buddha: The Temple Art of East Java*. Honolulu, Hawaii: University of Hawaii Press. 2003.

Reichle, Natasha. *Violence and Serenity: Late Buddhist Sculpture from Indonesia*. Honolulu, Hawaii: University of Hawaii Press. 2007.

Kampuchea

Delaporte, Louis. *Voyage au Cambodge*. Paris, France: C. Delagrave. 1880.

_____. *Les Monuments du Cambodge, Etude d'Architecture Khmere. Volume I-II*. Paris, France: C. Delagrave. 1914-1924.

Lunet de Lajonquiere, Etienne Edmond. *Monuments du Cambodge. Volume I-III*. Paris, France: E. Leroux. 1902-1911.

AAK. *Arts et Archeologie Khmers. Volume I-II*. Paris, France: A. Challamel. 1921-1922.

Groslier, George. *Recherches sur les Cambodgiens s' Apres les Textes les Monuments Depuis Premiers Siecles de Notre ere*. Paris, France: Challamel. 1921.

_____. *Angkor*. Paris, France: H. Laurens. 1924.

_____. *La Sculpture Khmere Ancienne*. Paris, France. 1925.

_____. *Les Collections Khmeres du Musee Albert Sarrant a Phnom-Penh*. Paris, France: G. van Oest. 1931.

Coedes, George. *Bronzes Khmers (Ars Asiatica Volume 5)*. Paris, France: G. van Oest. 1923.

_____. *Les Collections Archeologiques du Musee National de Bangkok (Ars Asiatica Volume 12)*. Paris, France: G. van Oest. 1928.

_____. *Angkor: An Introduction*. London, Britain: Oxford University Press. 1963.

_____. *The Making of Southeast Asia*. London, Britain: Routledge and K. Paul. 1966.

_____. *The Indianized States of Southeast Asia*. Honolulu, Hawaii: East-West Center Press. 1968.

Finot, Louis and Others. *Le Temple d'Icvarapura*. Paris, France: G. van Oest. 1926.

_____. *Le Temple d'Angkor Vat*. Paris, France: G. van Oest. 1929-1932.

Candee, Helen Churchill Hungerford. *Angkor the Magnificent, the Wonder City of Ancient Cambodia*. New York, New York: Frederick A. Stokes Co. 1924.

Parmentier, Henri. *L'Art Khmer Primitif. Volume I-II*. Paris, France: G. van Oest. 1927.

_____. *History of Khmer Architecture. Eastern Art Volume III*. Paris, France: G. van Oest. 1931.

_____. *L'Art Khmer Classique*. Paris, France: G. van Oest. 1939.

_____. *Henri Parmentier's Guide to Angkor*. Saigon, Vietnam: A. Portail. 1950s.

Stern, Philippe. *Le Bayon d'Angkor et l'Evolution de l'Art Khmer*. Paris, France: P. Geuthner. 1927.

_____. *Les Monuments Khmers du Style du Bayon et Jayavarman VII*. Paris, France: Presses Universitaires de France. 1965.

Marchal, Henri. *Guide Archeologique aux Temples d' Angkor; Angkor Vat, Angkor Thom et les Monuments du petit et du Grand Circuit*. Paris, France: G. van Oest. 1928.

_____. *Guide to Angkor: Angkor Vat – Angkor Thom and Monuments of "Great Circuit" and Little Circuit"*. Saigon, Vietnam: SDEA. 1930.

_____. *L' Architecture compare dans l' Inde et l' Extreme-Orient*. Paris, France: Les Editions d'Art et d'Histoire. 1944.

_____. *Les Temples d' Angkor*. Paris, France: A. Guillot. 1955.

Casey, Robert Joseph. *Four Faces of Siva*. London, Britain: G. G. Harrap and Co. 1929.

Wales, Horace Geoffrey Quaritch. *Towards Angkor in the Footsteps of the Indian Invaders*. London, Britain: G. G. Harrap and Co. 1937.

Dickason, Deane H. *Wondrous Angkor*. Shanghai, China: Kelly and Walsh. 1939.

Coral-Remusat, Gilbert de. *L' Art Khmer, les Grandes Etapes de son Evolution*. Paris, France: G. van Oest. 1951.

Boisselier, Jean. *La Statuaire Khmere et son Evolution. Volume I-II*. Saigon, Vietnam: EFEO. 1955.

Dupont, Pierre. *La Statuaire Preangkorienne*. Ascona, Switzerland: Artibus Asiae. 1955.

MacDonald, Malcolm. *Angkor*. London, Britain: Cape. 1958.

Giteau, Madeleine. *Khmer Sculpture and the Angkor Civilization*. London, Britain: Thames and Hudson. 1965.

_____. *Histoire d' Angkor*. Paris, France Presses: Universitaires de France. 1974.

_____. *Iconographic du Cambodge Post-Angkorien*. Paris, France: EFEO. 1975.

Groslier, Bernard Philippe and Arthaud, Jacques. *Angkor: Art and Civilization*. New York, New York: Frederick A. Praeger Publishers. 1966.

Pym, Christopher. *The Ancient Civilization of Angkor*. New York, New York: New American Library. 1968.

Lee, Sherman E. *Ancient Cambodian Sculpture*. New York, New York: AS. 1969.

Cohen, Joan L. and Kalman, Bela. *Angkor: Monuments of the God-Kings*. New York, New York: Harry N. Abrams Inc. 1975.

Kulke, Hermann. *The Devaraja Cult*. Ithaca, New York: Cornell University. 1978.

Chakravarti, Adhir. *The Sdok Kak Thom Inscription*. Calcutta, India: Sanskrit College. 1978-1980.

Srivastava, Krishna Murari. *Angkor Wat and Cultural Ties with India*. New Dehli, India: Books and Books. 1987.

_____. *Apsarases at Angkor Wat, in Indian Context*. New Dehli, India: Angkor Publishers. 1994.

Freeman, Michael and Warner, Roger. *Angkor: The Hidden Glories*. Boston, Massachusetts: Houghton Mifflin. 1990.

_____. *A Guide to Khmer Temples in Thailand and Laos*. New York, New York: Weatherhill. 1998.

Glaize, Maurice. *Les Monuments du Groupe d' Angkor*. Paris, France: J. Maisonneuve. 1993.

Narasimhaiah, Barkur. *Angkor Vat, India's Contribution in Conservation (MASI no. 91)*. New Delhi, India: ASI. 1994.

Rooney, Dawn and Freeman, Michael. *Angkor: An Introduction to the Temples*. Hong Kong, Hong Kong: Odyssey. 1994.

Bonheur, Albert le and Poncar, Jaroslav. *Of Gods, Kings, and Men: Bas-reliefs of Angkor Wat and Bayon*. London, Britain: Serindia Publications. 1995.

Jessup, Helen I. and Others. *Sculpture of Angkor and Ancient Cambodia: Millennium of Glory*. Washington, USA: NGA. 1997.

Jacques, Claude and Freeman, Michael. *Angkor: Cities and Temples*. Bangkok, Thailand: River Books. 1997.

Roveda, Vittorio. *Khmer Mythology: Secrets of Angkor*. New York, New York: Weatherhill. 1998.

Dumarcay, Jacques. *Documents Graphiques de la Conservation d' Angkor: 1963-1973*. Paris, France: EFEO. 1988.

_____ and Royere, Pascal. *Cambodian Architecture, Eighth to Thirteenth Centuries*. Leiden, Netherlands: Brill. 2001.

Weng, Wei-ch'uan. *Angkor: The Khmers in Ancient Chinese Annals*. New York, New York: Oxford University Press. 2000.

Dalsheimer, Nadine. *Les Collections du Musee National de Phnom Penh*. Paris, France: Magellan and Cie. 2001.

Higham, Charles. *The Civilization of Angkor*. London, Britain: Weidenfeld and Nicolson. 2001.

Kar, Amina Ahmed. *The Angkorian Records*. New Delhi, India: Bhaskar Bhavan Administration and Trust. 2002.

Khoo, James C. M. and Others. *Art and Archaeology of Fu Nan: Pre-Khmer Kingdom of the Lower Mekong Valley*. Hong Kong, China: Orchid Press. 2003.

Coe, Michael D. *Angkor and the Khmer Civilization*. New York, New York: Thames and Hudson. 2003.

Benisti, Mireile. *Stylistics of Early Khmer Art. Volume I-II*. New Delhi, India: IGNCA. 2003.

Snellgrove, David L. *Angkor-Before and After: A Cultural History of the Khmers*. Hong Kong, China: Orchid Press. 2004.

Jessup, Helen Ibbitson. *Art and Architecture of Cambo-*

dia. London, Britain: Thames and Hudson. 2004.

_____. *Masterpieces of the National Museum of Cambodia: An Introduction to the Collection*. Norfolk, Connecticut: Friends of Khmer Culture. 2006.

Zhou, Daquan. *A Record of Cambodia: The Land and Its People (Translated by Peter Harris)*. Chiang Mai, Thailand: Silkworm Books. 2007.

Clark, Joyce and Others. *Bayon: New Perspectives*. Bangkok, Thailand: River Books. 2008.

Champa

Parmentier, Henri. *Inventaire Descriptif des Monuments Cams de l'Annam. Volume I-II*. Paris, France: EFEO. 1909.

_____. *Les Sculptures Chames au Musee de Tourane*. Paris, France: G. van Oest. 1922.

Finot, Louis and Goloubew, Victor. *Fouilles de Dai-Hu'u (Quang-Binh, Annam). Volume XXV*. Paris, France: EFEO. 1925.

Maspero, Georges. *Le Royaume de Champa*. Paris, France: G. van Oest. 1928.

Stern, Philippe. *L'Art du Champa (Ancient Annam) et son Evolution*. Paris, France: Adrien-Maisonneuve. 1942.

Boisselier, Jean. *La Statuaire du Champa*. Paris, France: EFEO. 1963.

Mus, Paul. *India Seen from the East: Indian and Indigenous Cults in Champa*. Victoria, Australia: Centre of Southeast Asian Studies-Monash University. 1975.

Cao, Xuan Pho. *Cham Sculpture: Album*. Hanoi, Vietnam: Social Sciences Publishing House. 1988.

Sharma, J. C. *Hindu Temples in Vietnam*. New Delhi, India: The Offsetters. 1997.

Guillon, Emmanuel. *Hindu-Buddhist Art of Vietnam: Treasures from Champa*. Trumbull, Connecticut: Weatherhill. 1997.

_____. *Cham Art: Treasures from the Danang Museum, Vietnam*. Bangkok, Thailand: River Books. 2007.

Hubert, Jean-Francois. *The Art of Champa*. New York, New York: Parkstone Press. 2005.

Ngo, Van Doanh. *Champa: Ancient Towers*. Hanoi, Vietnam: The Gioi Publishers. 2006.

Huynh, Thi Duoc. *Cham Sculpture and Indian Mythology*. Danang, Vietnam: Danang Publishing House. 2007.

Hardy, Andrew and Others. *Champa and the Archaeology of My Son (Vietnam)*. Honolulu, Hawaii: University of Hawaii Press. 2009.

Thailand

Brown, Robert L. *The Dvāravatī Wheels of the Law and the Indianization of South East Asia*. Leiden, Netherlands: Brill. 1995.

Gosling, Betty. *Chronology of Religious Architecture at Sukhothai: Late Thirteen to Early Fifteenth Century*. Chiang Mai, Thailand: Silkworm. 1996.

Aasen, Clarence. *Architecture of Siam: A Cultural History Interpretation*. New York, New York: Oxford University Press. 1998.

Brown, Robert L. *Art from Thailand*. Mumbai, India: Marg Publications. 1999.

Doehring, Karl. *Buddhist Stupa (Phra Chedi) Architecture of Thailand*. Bangkok, Thailand: White Lotus Co Ltd. 2000.

Stratton, Carol. *Buddhist Sculpture of Northern Thailand*. Chicago, Illinois: Serindia Publications. 2004.

Woodward, Hiram. *The Art and Architecture of Thailand: From Prehistoric Times through the Thirteenth Century*. Leiden, Netherlands: Brill. 2005.

Pakistan

Stein, Aurel. *Archaeology Reconnaissances in Northwestern India and Southeastern Iran*. London, Britain: Macmillan. 1937.

Marshall, John Hubert. *Taxila. Volume I-III*. London, Britain: Cambridge University Press. 1951.

Konow, Sten. *Kharosthi Inscriptions with the Exceptions of Those of Asoka*. Varanasi, India: Indological Book House. 1969.

Bernard, Paul and Others. *Fouilles d'Ai Khanoum. Volume I-II*. Paris, France: Klincksieck. 1973.

Wilson, Horace H. *Ariana Antiqua*. Delhi, India: Oriental Publishers. 1971.

Goswami, Jaya. *Cultural History of Ancient India: A Socio-econolic and Religio-cultural Survey of Kapisa and Gandhara*. Delhi, India: Agam Kala Prakashan. 1979.

Jettmar, Karl and Thewalt, Volker. *Between Gandhara and the Silk Roads: Rock-carvings along the Karakorum Highway: Discovered by German-Pakistani Expeditions, 1979-1984*. Mainz am Rhein, Germany: Von Zabern. 1987.

Khan, Muhammad Ashraf. *Buddhist Shrines in Swat*. Saidu Sharif, Pakistan: Swat Archaeological Museum. 1993.

Khan, Ahmad Nabi. *An Illustrated Guide, Gandhara the Enchanting Land of Buddhist Art and Culture in Pakistan, with One Hundred and Forty Photographic and Line Drawing Illustrations*. Karachi, Pakistan: Government of Pakistan. 1994.

Bhatti, Muhammad Ilyas. *Taxila, an Ancient Metrpolis*

of Gandhara: Pakistan's Glorious Heritage. Sialkot, Pakistan: Munazza IIyas. 2000.

Nadiem, Ihsan H. *Buddhist Gandhara: History, Art, and Architecture*. Lahore, Pakistan: Sang-E-Meel Publications. 2003.

_____. *Taxila in Buddhist Gandhara*. Lahore, Pakistan: Sang-E-Meel Publications. 2008.

Behrendt, Kurt A. *The Buddhist Architecture of Gandhara*. Boston, Massachusetts: Brill Academic Publishers. 2004.

Brancaccio, Pia and Others. *Gandharan Buddhism: Archaeology, Art, Texts*. Vancouver, Canada: UBC Press. 2006.

Dar, Saifurrahman. *Historical Routes through Gandhara, Pakistan: 200 B.C–200 A.D.* Lahore, Pakistan: National College of Arts. 2006.

Afghanistan

Godard, Andre and Others. *Les Antiquites Bouddhiques de Bamiyan. MDAFA II*. Paris, France: G. van Oest. 1928.

Hackin, Joseph and Others. *Nouvelles Recherches Archeologiques a Bamiyan*. Paris, France: G. van Oest. 1933.

_____. *Recherches Archeologiques au col de Khair Khaneh pres de Kabul*. Paris, France: Les Editions d'Art et d'Histoire. 1936.

_____. *Recherches Archeologiques en Asie Centrale (1931)*. Paris, France: Les Editions d'Art et d'Histoire. 1936.

_____. *Recherches Archeologiques a Begram*. Paris, France: Les Editions d'Art et d'Histoire. 1939.

_____. *Nouvelles Recherches Archeologiques a Begram, Ancienne Kapici, 1939-1940. MDAFA Volume 11*. Paris, France: Imperiale Nationale. 1954.

_____. *Diverses Recherches Archeologiques en Afghanistan. MDAFA Volume 8*. Paris, France: MDAFA. 1959.

Mizuno, Seiichi and Others. *Ancient Art of Afghanistan*. Tokyo, Japan: The Nihon Keizai Shimbun. 1964.

Fussman, Gerard and Le Berre, Marc. *Monuments Bouddhiques de la Region de Caboul. MDAFA Volume 22*. Paris, France: Diffusion de Boccard. 1976.

Narain, R. B. *Buddhist Remains in Afghanistan*. Varanasi, India: Kala Prakashan. 1991.

Pichiki'a'n, Igor' Rubenovich. *Kul'tura Baktrii: akhemenidskii I ellinisticheskii periody*. Moskva, Russia: "Nauka," Glav.red. vostochnoi lit-ry. 1991.

Tissot, Francine. *Catalogue of the National Museum of Afghanistan*. Paris, France: UNESCO Publishing. 2006.

MAAG. *Afghanistan les Tre'sors Retrouves: Collections du Musee National de Kaboul*. Paris, France: MAAG. 2006.

Krieken-Pieters, Juliette van and Others. *Art and Archaeology of Afghanistan: Its Fall and Survival. A Multidisciplinary Approach*. Leiden, Netherlands: Brill. 2006.

Ball, Warwick. *The Monuments of Afghanistan: History, Archaeology and Architecture*. London, Britain: I. B. Tauris. 2008.

Central Asia

Rice, Tamara Talbot. *Ancient Arts of Central Asia*. New York, New York: Praeger. 1965.

Litvinskii, Boris A. *Outline History of Buddhism in Central Asia*. Dushanbe, Tajikistan: International Conference on the History, Archaeology, and Culture of Central Asia in the Kushan Period. 1968.

_____ and Zeymal, I. T. *Adzhina Tepe: Architecture, Painting, Sculpture*. Moskva, Soviet Union: Iskusstvo. 1971.

Frumkin, Gregoire. *Archaeology in Soviet Central Asia*. Leiden, Netherlands: E. J. Brill. 1970.

_____. *Severnai'a' Baktrii'a'-Tokahistan: Ocheki istorii Kul'tury: drevnost'i: srednevekov'e*. Tashkent, Uzbekistan: Izd-vo "FAN". 1990.

Pugachenkova, Galina Anatol'evna. *Skul'ptura Khalchai'a'na*. Moskva, Soviet Union: Izdatel'stvo "Iskusstvo". 1971.

Rowland, Benjamin. *The Art of Central Asia*. New York, New York: Crown Publishers Inc. 1974.

Gaulier, Simone and Others. *Buddhism in Afghanistan and Central Asia. Part I-II*. Leiden, Netherlands: E. J. Brill. 1976.

MMA. *Along the Ancient Silk Routes: Central Asian Art from the West Berlin State Museums*. New York, New York: MMA. 1982.

TNM. *Central Asian Art from the Museum of Indian Art, Berlin, SMPK*. Tokyo, Japan: TNM. 1991.

Masson, V. M. and Others. *History of Civilizations of Central Asia*. Paris, France: UNESCO. 1992-2005.

Sharma, Govardhan Raj. *Kusana Studies: Papers Presented to the International Conference on the Archaeology, History and Arts of the Peopple of Central Asia in the Kusana Period, Dushambe (Tajikistan) U.S.S.R., September 25-October 4, 1968*. Allahabad, India: University of Allahabad. 1998.

Berzin, Alexander. *The Historical Interaction between the Buddhist and Islamic Cultures before the Mongol Empire*. The Berzin Archives (www.berzinarchives.

com). 2003.

Turkistan

Hedin, Sven Anders. *Central Asia and Tibet*. London, Britain: Hurst and Blackett. 1903.

Stein, Aurel. *Sand-buried Ruins of Khotan. Personal Narrative of a Journey of Archaeological and Geographical Exploration in Chinese Turkestan; with Map*. London, Britain: Hurst. 1904.

_____. *Ancient Khotan: Detailed Report of Archaeological Explorations in Chinese Turkestan*. Oxford, Britain: Clarendon Press. 1907.

_____. *Ruins of Desert Cathay: Personal Narrative of Explorations in Central Asia and Westernmost China. Volume I-II*. London, Britain: Macmillan. 1912.

_____. *Serindia: Detailed Report of Explorations in Central Asia and Westernmost China. Volume I-V*. Oxford, Britain: Clarendon Press. 1921.

_____. *Innermost Asia: Detailed Report of Explorations in Central Asia, Kansu, and Iran. Volumes I-V*. Oxford, Britain: Clarendon Press. 1928.

Le Coq, Albert von. *Chotscho*. Berlin, Germany: D. Reimer. 1913.

_____ and Waldschmidt, Ernst. *Die Buddhistische Spatantike in Mittelasien. Volumes 1-7*. Berlin, Germany: D. Reimer. 1922-1933.

_____. *Bilderatlas zur und Kulturgeschichte Mittelasiens*. Berlin, Germany: D. Reimer. 1925.

_____. *Von Land und Leuten in Ostturkistan; Berichte und Abenteuer der 4. Deutchen Turfanexpedition*. Leipzig, Germany: J. C. Hinrichs. 1928.

_____. *Buried Treasures of Chinese Turkestan*. New York, New York: Longmans, Green and Co. 1929.

Grunwedel, Albert. *Alt-Kutscha*. Berlin, Germany: O. Elsner Verlagsgesellschaft m. b. h. 1920.

Waldschmidt, Ernst. *Gandhara, Kutscha, Turfan*. Leipzig, Germany: Klinkhardt Biermann. 1925.

MV. *Turfan and Gandhara: Fruhmittelalterliche Kunst Zentralasiens*. Berlin, Germany: MV. 1957.

MPP. *Mission Paul Pelliot: Documents Archaeologique Publies Sous Les Auspices De L'Academie Des Inscriptions Et Belles-Lettres. Volumes I-XV*. Paris, France: MPP Librairie Adrien-Maisonneuve. 1961-1976.

Hatani, R. *The Ancient Buddhist Art of Central Asia and Tun-Huang. Monumenta Serindica Volume 5*. Kyoto, Japan: Monumenta Serindica. 1962.

Franz, Heinrich Gerhard. *Von Gandhara bis Pagan: Kultbauten des Buddhismus u. Hinduismus in Sud- und Zentralasien*. Graz, Germany: Akadem (Druck- u. Verlagsanst). 1979.

Yaldiz, Mariana. *Archäologie und Kunstgeschichte Chinesisch-Zentralasiens (Xinjiang)*. Leiden, Netherlands: Brill. 1987.

China

Tokiwa, Daijo. *Buddhist Monuments in China*. Tokyo, Japan: Bukkyo Shiseki Kenkyukai. 1925.

Soper, Alexander. *Literary Evidence for Early Buddhist Art in China*. Ascona, Switzerland: Artibus Asiae Publishers. 1959.

Sickman, Laurence and Soper, Alexander. *The Art and Architecture of China*. New Haven, Connecticut: Yale University Press. 1968.

Oort, H. A. van. *The Iconography of Chinese Buddhism in Traditional China, Part 1 Han to Liao, Part 2 Sung to Ch'ing*. Leiden, Netherlands: Brill. 1986.

Pirazzoli-t'Serstevens, Michele and Stierlin, Henri. *Architecture of the World: China*. Koln, Germany: Benedikt Taschen Verlag GmbH. 1994.

Steinhardt, Nancy Shatzman. *Liao Architecture*. Honolulu, Hawaii: University of Hawaii Press. 1997.

Baker, Janet and Others. *The Flowering of a Foreign Faith: New Studies in Chinese Buddhist Art*. Mumbai, India: Marg Publications. 1998.

Watson, William. *The Arts of China to A.D. 900*. New Haven, Connecticut: Yale University Press. 2000.

_____. *The Arts of China 900–1620*. New Haven, Connecticut: Yale University Press. 2003.

Karetzky, Patricia Eichenbaum. *Chinese Buddhist Art*. New York, New York: Oxford University Press. 2003.

Howard, Angela Falco and Others. *Chinese Sculpture*. New Haven, Connecticut: Yale University Press. 2006.

Wong, Dorothy C. *Chinese Steles: Pre-Buddhist and Buddhist Use of a Symbolic Form*. Honolulu, Hawaii: University of Hawaii Press. 2004.

Bao, Yuheng and Others. *Buddhist Art and Architecture of China*. Lewiston, New York: Edwin Mellen Press. 2005.

Zürcher, E. *The Buddhist Conquest of China: The Spread and Adaptation of Buddhism in Early Medieval China*. Leiden, Netherlands: Brill. 2007.

Korea

Eckardt, Andreas. *History of Korean Art*. Leipzig, Germany: Karl W. Hiersemann. 1929.

McCune, Evelyn. *The Arts of Korea: An Illustrated History*. Tokyo, Japan: Charles E. Turtle Co. 1962.

Kim, Chewon and Lee, Lena Kim. *Arts of Korea*. New York, New York: Kodansha International Ltd. 1974.

Ch'oe, Sun-u. *5000 Years of Korean Art*. Seoul, South Korea: Hyonam Publishing Co. 1979.

HMPH. *Cultural Treasures of Korea*. Soul, South Korea: Taehaktang. 1986-1989.
Sorensen, H. H. *The Iconography of Korean Buddhist Painting*. Leiden, Netherlands: Brill. 1989.
Chang, Kyong-ho. *Paekche Sach'al Konch'uk*. Soul, South Korea: Yegyong Sanopsa. 1991.
Ch'on, Kyong-hwa P'yon. *Han'guk Munhwajae Ch'onhsoi: Kukpo Pomul Chungsim*. Soul, South Korea: Paeksan Ch'ulp'ansa. 1993.
Chung, Yang-mo and Others. *Arts of Korea*. New York, New York: MMA. 1998.
Smith, Judith E. and Others. *Arts of Korea*. New Haven, Connecticut: Yale University Press. 1998.
CYYTPW and Others. *Cultural Assets and Sites in North Korea*. Soul, South Korea: Soul Taehakkyo Ch'ulp'anbu. 2000.
Washizuka, Horimitsu and Others. *Transmitting the Forms of Divinity: Early Buddhist Art from Korea and Japan*. New York, New York: Japan Society Inc. 2003.
Whitfield, Roderick and Others. *Dictionary of Korean Art and Archaeology*. Seoul, South Korea: Hollym International Corp. 2004.
Pangmulgwan, Kungnip. *National Museum of Korea*. Seoul, South Korea: Sol Publishing. 2005.
Kim, Sung-woo. *Buddhist Architecture of Korea*. Elizabeth, New Jersey: Hollym International Corporation. 2007.
Byington, Mark E. *Early Korea: Reconsidering Early Korean History through Archaeology*. Honolulu, Hawaii: University of Hawaii Press. 2008.
Lee, Soyoung and Others. *Art of the Korean Renaissance, 1400-1600*. New Haven, Connecticut: Yale University Press. 2009.

Japan
Noma, Seiroku. *The Arts of Japan*. Tokyo, Japan: Kodansha International. 1966.
Masuda, Tomoya. *Living Architecture: Japanese*. New York, New York: Grosset and Dunlap Inc. 1970.
_____ and Stierlin, Henri. *Architecture of the World: Japan*. Koln, Germany: Benedikt Taschen Verlag GmbH. 1994.
Paine, Robert Treat and Soper, Alexander. *The Art and Architecture of Japan*. New Haven, Connecticut: Yale University Press. 1981.
Nishi, Kazuo and Hozumi, Kazuo. *What is Japanese Architecture?* New York, New York: Kodansha International Ltd. 1985.
Elisseeff, Danielle and Elisseeff, Vadime. *Art of Japan*. New York, New York: Harry N. Abrams. 1985.
Kidder Jr., Edward J. *The Art of Japan*. New York, New York: Park Lane. 1985.
Mason, Penelope. *History of Japanese Art*. New York, New York: Harry N. Abrams. 1993.
Rosenfield, John. *Chōgen, the Holy One, and the Restoration of Japanese Buddhist Art*. Leiden, Netherlands: Brill. 2008.
McCallum, Donald F. *The Four Great Temples: Buddhist Art, Archaeology, and Icons of Seventh-Century Japan*. Honolulu, Hawaii: University of Hawaii Press. 2008.

Vietnam
Tran, Trong Kim. *Viet-Nam Su Luoc (History of Vietnam)*. Vietnam: Ministry of Education.
Tingley, Nancy. *Arts of Ancient Viet Nam: From River Plain to Open Sea*. New Haven, Connecticut: Yale University Press. 2009.

Nepal
Pal, Pratapaditya. *The Arts of Nepal, Part I: Sculpture*. Leiden, Netherlands: E. J. Brill. 1974.
_____. *The Arts of Nepal, Part II: Painting*. Leiden, Netherlands: E. J. Brill. 1978.
_____ and Others. *Nepal: Old Images New Insights*. Mumbai, India: Marg Publications. 2004.
Korn, Wolfgang. *The Traditional Architecture of the Kathmandu Valley*. Kathmandu, Nepal: Ratna Pustak Bhandar. 1976.
Wiesner, Ulrich. *Nepalese Temple Architecture: Its Characteristics and Its Relations to Indian Development*. Leiden, Netherlands: E. J. Brill. 1978.
Banerjee, Nil. Ratan. *Nepalese Architecture*. Delhi, India: Agam Kala Prakashan. 1980.
Bangdel, Lain S. *Early Sculptures of Nepal*. New Delhi, India: Vikas. 1982.
Gail, Adalbert J. *Tempel in Nepal. Volume I-II*. Graz, Austria: Akademische Druck u. Verlagsanstalt. 1984.
Locke, John Kerr. *Buddhist Monasteries of Nepal: A Survey of the Bahas and Bahis of the Kathmandu Valley*. Kathmandu, Nepal: Orchid Press. 2008.
Shakya, Min Bahadur. *The Iconography of Nepalese Buddhism*. Kathmandu, Nepal: Handicraft Association of Nepal. 1994.
_____. *Sacred Art of Nepal*. Kathmandu, Nepal: Handicraft Association of Nepal. 2000.
Trisuli, Dharmaratna Sakya. *Kwabaha: Hiranyavarna Mahavihara=The Golden Temple*. Lalitpur, Nepal: Hiranyavarna Mahavihara Vihara Sudhar Samiti. 1996.
Kreijger, Hugo E. *Kathmandu Valley Painting: The Jucker Collection*. Chicago, Illinois: Serindia Publications. 1999.
Powell, Robert. *Earth Door Sky Door: Paintings of Mus-*

tang. Chicago, Illinois: Serindia Publications. 2000.
Sakya, Minabahadura. *Hiranyavarna Mahavihara: A Unique Newar Buddhist Monastery*. Patan, Nepal: Nagarjuna Publication. 2004.
Bajracarya, Yadiratna. *The Gunakar Mahavihar=Chhusya Baha*. Kathmandu, Nepal: Gunakar Mahavihar Conservation Committee. 2004.
Thapa, Shanker. *Ratnakar Mahavihara: A Vajrayana Buddhist Monastery of Patan*. Delhi, India: Akhil Book Distributors. 2005.
Gutschow, Niels and Theophile, Erich. *The Sulima Pagoda: East Meets West in the Restoration of a Napalese Temple*. Hong Kong, China: Orchid Press. 2008.

Indian Himalaya, Western Tibet
Goetz, Herman. *Early Wooden Temples of Chamba*. Leiden, Netherlands: E. J. Brill. 1955.
Ohri, Vishwa Chander and Others. *Arts of Himachal*. Simla, India: SDLC. 1975.
Choudhury, Roy Pranab Chandra. *Temples and Legends of Himachal Pradesh*. Bombay, India: Bharatiya Vidya Bhavan. 1981.
Singh, Mian Goverdhan. *Art and Architecure of Himachal Pradesh*. New Delhi, India: B. R. Publishing Corp. 1983.
_____. *Wooden Temples of Himachal Pradesh*. New Delhi, India: Indus Publishing Co. 1999.
Postel, M. *Antiquities of Himachal*. Bombay, India: Franco-Indian Pharmaceuticals. 1985.
Handa, Omacanda. *Buddhist Monasteries in Himachal Pradesh*. London, Britain: Sangam Books. 1988.
_____. *Buddhist Art and Antiquities of Himachal Pradesh: Up to 8th Century A. D*. New Delhi, India: Indus Publishing Co. 1994.
_____. *Tabo Monastery and Buddhism in the Trans-Himalaya: Thousand Years of Existence of the Tabo Chos-khor*. New Delhi, India: Indus Publishing Co. 1994.
_____. *Temple Architecture of the Western Himalaya: Wooden Temples*. New Delhi, India: Indus Publishing Co. 2001.
_____. *Buddhist Western Himalaya: A Politico-Religious History*. New Delhi, India: Indus Publishing Co. 2001.
Nagar, Shanti Lal. *The Temples of Himachal Pradesh*. New Delhi, India: Aditya Prakashan. 1990.
Thakur, Laxman S. *The Architectural Heritage of Himachal Pradesh: Origin and Development of Temple Styles*. New Delhi, India: Munshiram Manoharlal Publishers. 1996.

Singh, Madanjeet. *Himalayan Art: Wall-Painting and Sculpture in Ladakh, Lahaul, and Spiti, the Siwalik Ranges, Nepal, Sikkim, Bhutan*. Greenwich, Conneticut: New York Graphic Society. 1968.
Khosla, Romi. *Buddhist Monasteries in the Western Himalaya*. Kathmandu, Nepal: Ratna Pustak Bhandar. 1979.
Klimburg-Salter, Deborah. *The Silk Route and the Diamond Path: Esoteric Buddhist Art Along the Trans-Himalayan Trade Routes*. Los Angeles, California: UCLA Art Council. 1982.
Gerner, Manfred. *Architekturen im Himalaja*. Stuttgart, Germany: Deutsche Verlags-Anstalt GmbH. 1987.
Tucci, Giuseppe. *Indo-Tibetica. Volume II (Rin-Chen-Bzan-po and the Renaissance of Buddhism in Tibet around the Millennium), Volume III (The Temples of Western Tibet and Their Artistic Symbolism. Part I-II)*. New Delhi, India: Aditya Prakashan. 1988.
Bernier, Ronald M. *Himalayan Architecture*. London, Britain: Associated Press. 1997.
Powell, Robert. *Himalayan Drawings*. Zurich, Switzerland: Volkerkundemuseum de Universitat Zurich. 2001.
Pal, Pratapaditya. *Himalayas: An Aesthetic Adventure*. Chicago, Illinois: AIC. 2003.
Pruscha, Carl and Others. *Himalayan Vernacular: Carl Pruscha*. Frankfurt, Germany: Walther Konig. 2005.
IATS. *Discoveries in Western Tibet and the Western Himalayas: Essays on History, Literature, Archaeology, and Art*. Leiden, Netherlands: E. J. Brill. 2007.

Francke, August Hermann. *Antiquities of Indian Tibet. Volume I-II*. Calcutta, India: Superintendent Government Printing. 1914-1926.
_____. *A History of Ladakh (Critical Introduction and Annotations by S. S. Gergan and F. M. Hassnain)*. New Delhi, India: Sterling Publishers. 1977.
Snellgrove, David L. and Skorupski, Tadeusz. *The Cultural Heritage of Ladakh*. Warminster, England: Aris and Phillips Ltd. 1977-1980.
Thub-bstan-dpal-idan, Dge-slori. *A Brief Guide to the Buddhist Monasteries and Royal Castles of Ladakh*. Leh, Ladakh: Thupstan Paldan. 1982.
Jina, Prem Singh. *Phyang Monastery of Ladakh*. New Delhi, India: Indus Publishing Co. 1995.
_____. *Lamayuru Monastery of Ladakh Himalaya*. Faridabad, India: Om Publications. 1999.
_____. *Thiksey Monastery of Ladakh Himalaya*. Delhi, India: Sri Satguru Publications. 2007.
Binczik, Angelika. *Hidden Treasures from Ladakh*.

Munchen, Germany: Otter Verlag. 2002.
Sharma, Janhwij. *Architectural Heritage: Ladakh.* New Delhi, India: Har-Anand-Publications. 2003.

SDLC. *Tabo Bauddha Vihara Sahasrabdi, 996-1996.* Shimla, India: SDLC. 1996.
Klimburg-Salter, Deborah E. *Tabo: A Lamp for the Kingdom: Early Indo-Tibetan Buddhist Art in the Western Himalaya.* New York, New York: Thames and Hudson. 1998.
Petech, Luciano and Others. *Inscriptions from the Tabo main temple: Texts and Translation.* Rome, Italy: IIAO. 1999.
Scherrer-Schaub, C. A. and Others. *Tabo Studies II: Manuscripts, Texts, Inscriptions, and the Arts.* Rome, Italy: IIAO. 1999.
Thakur, Laxman S. *Buddhism in the Western Himalaya: A Study of the Tabo Monastery.* New York, New York: Oxford University Press. 2001.
Luczanits, Christian. *Buddhist Sculpture in Clay: Early Western Himalayan Art, Late 10th early 13th Centuries.* Chicago, Illinois: Serindia Publications. 2004.
Linrothe, Robert and Watt, Jeff. *Demonic Divine: Himalayan Art and Beyond.* Chicago, Illinois: Serindia Publications. 2004.

Ham, Peter van. *The Forgotten Gods of Tibet: Early Buddhist Art in the Western Himalayas.* Paris, France: Menges. 1997.
Vitali, Roberto. *Records of Tholing: A Literary and Visual Reconstruction of the "Mother" Monastery in Guge.* New Delhi, India: High Asia. 1999.
Heller, Amy and Others. *Proceedings of the Tenth Seminar of the IATS, 2003, Volume 8 Discoveries in Western Tibet and the Western Himalayas: Essays on History, Literature, Archaeology and Art.* Leiden, Netherlands: Brill. 2007.

Tibet

Gordon, Antoinette K. *The Iconography of Tibetan Lamaism.* New York, New York: Paragon Book Reprint Corp. 1967.
Pal, Pratapaditya. *The Art of Tibet.* New York, New York: AS. 1969.
_____. *Tibetan Paintings: A Study of Tibetan Thankas Eleventh to Nineteenth Centuries.* Basel, Switzerland: Ravi Kumar and Sotheby Publications. 1984.
_____. *Art of Tibet.* Los Angeles, California: LAMA. 1990.
_____ and Others. *On The Path to Void: Buddhist Art of the Tibetan Realm.* Mumbai, India: Marg Publications. 1996.
Lauf, Detelf Ingo. *Tibetan Sacred Art: The Heritage of Tantra.* Hong Kong, China: Orchid Press. 1979.
Li, Jicheng. *The Realm of Tibetan Buddhism.* New Delhi, India: UBS Publisher's Distributors. 1986.
Liu, Lizhong. *Buddhist Art of the Tibetan Plateau.* San Francisco, California: China Books and Periodicals. 1988.
Raghu, Vira and Chandra, Lokesh. *Tibetan Mandalas: Vajravali and Tantra-Samuccaya.* New Delhi, India: Aditya Prakashan. 1995.
Kvaerne, Per. *The Bon Religion of Tibet: The Iconography of a Living Tradition.* Boston, Massachusetts: Shambhala. 1996.
Kossak, Steven M. and Singer, Jane C. *Sacred Visions: Early Paintings from Central Tibet.* New York, New York: MMA. 1998.
Kreijger, Hugo E. *Tibetan Painting: The Jucker Collection.* Chicago, Illinois: Serindia Publications. 2001.
Baumer, Christoph. *Tibet's Ancient Religion Bön.* Hong Kong, China: Orchid Press. 2002.
Dinwiddie, Donald and Others. *Portraits of the Masters: Bronze Sculptures of the Tibetan Buddhist Lineages.* Chicago, Illinois: Serindia Publications. 2003.
Schroeder, Ulrich von. *Empowered Masters: Tibetan Wall Paintings of Mahasiddhas at Gyantse.* Chicago, Illinois: Serindia Publications. 2006.
_____. *108 Buddhist Statues in Tibet: Evolution of Tibetan Sculptures.* Chicago, Illinois: Serindia Publications. 2008.
Linrothe, Robert. *Holy Madness: Portraits of Tantric Siddhas.* Chicago, Illinois: Serindia Publications. 2006.
Walter, Michael L. *Buddhism and Empire: The Political and Religious Culture of Early Tibet.* Leiden, Netherlands: Brill. 2009.

Part I: Background

Chapter 1. Indus Civilization

Marshall, John and Others. *Mohenjo-daro and the Indus Civilization, Volume 1-3.* London, England: Arthur Probsthain. 1931.
Wheeler, Mortimer. *Civilizations of the Indus Valley and Beyond.* London, England: Thames and Hudson. 1966.
_____. *The Indus Civilization: Supplementary Volume to the Cambridge History of India.* London, England: Cambridge University Press. 1968.
Possehl, Gregory and Others. *Ancient Cities of the Indus.* New Delhi, India: Vikas Publishing House Pvt Ltd.

1979.

———. *Harappan Civilization: A Recent Perspective*. New Delhi, India: Oxford, IBH Publishing Co Pvt Ltd, and AIIS. 1993.

———. *Indus Age: The Writing System*. Philadelphia, Pennsylvania: University of Pennsylvania Press. 1996.

Parpola, Asko and Others. *Corpus of Indus Seals and Inscriptions. Volume I-II*. Helsinki, Finland: Suomalainen Tiedeakatemia. 1987-1991.

Fairservis Jr., Walter A. *The Harappan Civilization and its Writing: A Model for the Decipherment of the Indus Script*. Leiden, Netherlands: Brill. 1992.

NMI. *Harappan Seals, Sealings, and Copper Tablets*. New Delhi, India: NMI. 2000.

McKay, Ernest. *Further Excavations at Mohenjo-daro, Volume 1-2*. New Delhi, India: Manager of Publications. 2000.

Chakrabarti, Dilip K. *Indus Civilization in India: New Discoveries*. Mumbai, India: Marg Publications. 2004.

Eltsov, Piotr Andreevich. *From Harappa to Hastinapura: A Study of the Earliest South Asian City and Civilization*. Leiden, Netherlands: Brill. 2008.

Chapter 2. Foundation of Buddhism

Robinson, Richard H. and Johnson, Willard L. *The Buddhist Religion: A Historical Introduction*. Belmont, California: Wadsworth Inc. 1982.

Radhakrishnan, Sarvepalli. *Indian Philosophy. Volume 1-2*. Oxford University Press Inc: New Delhi, India. 1989.

Buddha and His Teachings

Rahula, Walpola. *What the Buddha Taught*. New York, New York: Grove Weidenfeld. 1974.

Schumann, Hans Wolfgang. *The Historical Buddha: The Times, Life and Teachings of the Founder of Buddhismn*. London, England: The Penguin Group. 1989.

Walshe, Maurice. *The Long Discourses of the Buddha: A Translation of the Digha Nikaya*. Boston, Massachusetts: Wisdom Publications. 1995.

Theravada School

Nalinaksha, Dutt. *Buddhist Sects in India*. Calcutta, India: Firma K. L. Mukhopadhyay. 1970.

Barua, Sumangal. *Buddhist Councils and Development of Buddhism*. Calcutta, India: Atisha Memorial Publishing Society. 1997.

Mahayana School

Nalinaksha, Dutt. *Mahayana Buddhism*. Calcutta, India: Firma K. L. Mukhopadhyay. 1973.

Vajrayana School

Wayman, Alex. *The Buddhist Tantras; Light on Indo-Tibetan Esotericism*. New York, New York: S. Weiser. 1973.

Abhayadatta. *Masters of Mahamudra: Songs and Histories of the Eighty-Four Buddhist Siddhas (Translation and Commentary by Keith Dowman)*. New York, New York: NYSUP. 1985.

Snellgrove, David. *Indo-Tibetan Buddhism. Volume I-II*. Boston, Massachusetts: Shambhala Publications Inc. 1987.

Shaw, Miranda Eberle. *Passionate Enlightenment: Women in Tantric Buddhism*. Princeton, New Jersey: Princeton University Press. 1994.

Bhattacharyya, Narendra Nath. *History of the Tantric Religion: A Historical, Ritualistic, and Philosophical Study*. New Delhi, India: Manohar Publishers. 1999.

Ramachandra Rao, Saligrama Krishna. *Yoga and Tantra in India and Tibet: Yoga-Tantra-Sampradaya. Volume I-II*. Bangalore, India: Kalpatharu Research Academy. 1999-2000.

Davidson, Ronald M. *Indian Esoteric Buddhism: A Social History of the Tantric Movement*. New York, New York: Columbia University Press. 2002.

Part II: Architecture

Chapter 3. Asoka Pillar

Asoka and His Edicts

Barua, Beni Madhab. *Asoka and His Inscriptions, Volume 1-2*. Calcutta, India: New Age Publishers Private Ltd. 1968.

Hultzsch, Eugen. *Inscriptions of Asoka*. Varanasi, India: Indological Book House. 1969.

Strong, John. *The Legends of King Asoka: A Study and Translation of the Asokavadana*. Princeton, New Jersey: Princeton University Press. 1983.

Mukherjee, Bradtindra Nath. *Studies in the Aramaic Edicts of Asoka*. Calcutta, India: Indian Museum. 1984.

Chaudhury, Hemendu Bikash and Others. *Asoka 2300: Jagajjyoti, Asoka Commemoration Volume 1997 A.D./2541 B.E.* Calcutta, India: Bauddha Dharmankur Sabha. 1997.

Asoka Pillar

Ray, Niharranjan. *Maurya and Post-Maurya Art: A Study in Social and Formal Contrasts*. New Delhi, India: In-

dian Council of Historical Research. 1975.
Gupta, Swarajya Prakash. *The Roots of Indian Art: A Detailed Study of the Formative Period of Indian Art and Architecture–Third and Second Centuries B.C.–Mauryan and Late Mauryan.* Delhi, India: B.R. Publishing Corporation. 1980.
Pandey, C. B. *Mauryan Art.* Delhi, India: Bharatiya Vidya Prakashan. 1982.
Nagar, Shanti Lal. *Indian Monoliths.* New Delhi, India: Intellectual Publishing House. 1992.
Verardi, Giovanni. *Excavations at Gotihawa and a Territorial Survey in Kapilavastu District of Nepal: A Preliminary Report.* Lumbini, Nepal: LIRI. 2002.
Falk, Harry. *Asokan Sites and Artifacts.* Mainz am Rhein, Germany: Verlag Philipp von Zabern. 2006.

Chapter 4. Monastery

Jivakavanarama - India
IA. *Indian Archaeology-A Review 1954-55: 16-17 and 1958-1959: 13.* New Delhi, India: Government of India. 1954-1959.
Dutt, Sukumar. *Buddhist Monks and Monasteries of India: Their History and Their Contribution to Indian Culture.* London, Britain: George Allen and Unwin Ltd. 1962.
Sarkar, H. *Studies in Early Buddhist Architecture of India.* Delhi, India: Munshiram Manoharlal. 1966.
Chaudhury, Binayendra Nath. *Buddhist Centres in Ancient India.* Calcutta, India: Sanskrit College. 1969.
Barua, Dipak Kumar. *Viharas in Ancient India: A Survey of Buddhist Monasteries.* Calcutta, India: Indian Publications. 1969.
Schumann, Hans Wolfgang. *The Historical Buddha: The Times, Life and Teachings of the Founder of Buddhismn.* London, England: The Penguin Group. 1989.

Takht-i-Bahi - Pakistan
Cunningham, Alexander. *ASIAR 1872-1873, Volume V: 23-36.* Calcutta, India: Superintendent of Government Printing. 1875.
ASI. *ASIAR 1910-1911: 33-39.* Calcutta, India: Superintendent of Government Printing. 1914.
Marshall, John Hubert. *Taxila. Volume I-III.* London, Britain: Cambridge University Press. 1951.
_____. *Excavations at Taxila: The Stupas and Monasteries at Jaulian.* New Delhi, India: Indological Book Corp. 1979.
Konow, Sten. *Kharosthi Inscriptions with the Exceptions of Those of Asoka.* Varanasi, India: Indological Book House. 1969.

Sehrai, Fidaullah. *A Guide to Takht-i-Bahi.* Peshawar, Pakistan: Fidaullah Sehrai. 1982.
Behrendt, Kurt A. *The Buddhist Architecture of Gandhara.* Boston, Massachusetts: Brill Academic Publishers. 2004.

Nalanda - India
Kempers, Bernet August Johan. *The Bronzes of Nalanda and Hindu-Javanese Art.* Leiden, Netherlands: E. J. Brill. 1933.
Ghosh, Amalananda. *A Guide to Nalanda.* Delhi, India: Manager of Publications. 1939.
Dutt, Sukumar. *Buddhist Monks and Monasteries of India: Their History and Their Contribution to Indian Culture.* London, Britain: George Allen and Unwin Ltd. 1962.
Sankalia, Hasmukhlal Dhirajlal. *The University of Nalanda.* Delhi, India: Oriental Publishers. 1972.
NNM. *Nalanda, Past and Present: Silver Jubilee Souvenir.* Nalanda, India: Nava Nalanda Mahavihara. 1977.
Nath, Birendra. *Nalanda Murals.* New Delhi, India: Cosmo Publications. 1983.
Sastri, Hiranand. *Nalanda and Its Epigraphic Material.* Delhi, India: Sri Satguru Publications. 1986.
Kumar, Brajmohan. *Archaeology of Pataliputra and Nalanda.* Delhi, India: Ramanand Vidya Bhawan. 1987.
Stewart, Mary L. *Nalanda Mahavihara: A Study of an Indian Pala Period Buddhist Site and British Historical Archaeology, 1861-1939.* Oxford, Britain: BAR International Series 529. 1989.
Mullick, C. C. *Nalanda Sculptures: Their Bearing on Indonesian Sculptures.* Delhi, India: Pratibha Prakashan. 1991.
Thakur, Upendra. *Buddhist Cities in Early India: Buddha-Gaya, Rajagrha, Nalanda.* Delhi, India: Sundeep Prakashan. 1995.
Paul, Debjani. *The Art of Nalanda: Development of Buddhist Sculpture, AD 600-1200.* New Delhi, India: Munshiram Manohalal Publishers. 1995.
Misra, Bhaskaranatha N. *Nalanda. Volumes I-III.* Delhi, India: B. R. Publishing Corp. 1998.
Chauley, G. C. *Art and Architecture of Nalanda.* Delhi, India: Sandeep Prakashan. 2002.

Horyuji - Japan
Prip-Moller, Johannes. *Chinese Buddhist Monasteries.* London, Britain: Oxford University Press. 1937.
_____. *Chinese Buddhist Monasteries: Their Plan and Its Function as a Setting for Buddhist Monastic Life.* Hong Kong, China: Hong Kong University Press. 1967.

Soper, Alexander. *Evolution of Buddhist Architecture in Japan.* Princeton, New Jersey: Princeton University Press. 1942.

_____ and Paine, Robert. *The Art and Architecture of Japan.* New Haven, Connecticut: Yale University Press. 1981.

Naito Toichiro. *Wall Paintings of Horyuji.* Baltimore, Maryland: Waverly Press Inc. 1943.

Masuda, Tomoya. *Living Architecture: Japanese.* New York, New York: Grosset and Dunlap Inc. 1970.

Ooka, Minoru. *Temples of Nara and Their Art.* New York, New York: Weatherhill and Tokyo, Japan: Heibonsha. 1973.

Mizuno, Seiichi. *Asuka Buddhist Art: Horyu-ji.* New York, New York: John Weatherhill Inc. 1974.

Suzuki, Kakichi. *Early Buddhist Architecture in Japan.* Tokyo, Japan: Kodansha. 1980.

Somapura - Bangladesh

Dikshit, Kashinath Narayan. *Excavations of Paharpur, Bengal. MASI No. 55. 1938.* Delhi, India: Manager of Publications. 1938.

Gupta, Charu Chandra Das. *Paharpur and Its Monuments.* Calcutta, India Firma: K. L. Mukhopadhyay. 1961.

Saraswati, Sarasi Kumar. *Early Sculpture of Bengal.* Calcutta, India: Sambodhi Publications. 1962.

Dutt, Sukumar. *Buddhist Monks and Monasteries of India: Their History and Their Contribution to Indian Culture.* London, Britain: George Allen and Unwin Ltd. 1962.

Qadir, M. A. A. *A Guide to Paharpur.* Karachi, Pakistan: Department of Archaeology. 1963.

Shamsul Alam, A. K. M. *An Album of Archaeological Relics in Bangladesh.* Dhaka, Bangladesh: Directorate of Archaeology and Museums. 1984.

_____. *Sculptural Art of Bangladesh: Pre-Muslim Period.* Dhaka, Bangladesh: Department of Archaeology and Museums. 1985.

Hossain, Mosharraf and Alam, Shafiqul. *Paharpur: The World Cultural Heritage.* Dhaka, Bangladesh: Department of Archaeology. 2004.

Haque, Enamul. *The Art Heritage of Bangladesh.* Dhaka, Bangladesh: ICSBA. 2007.

Vijayarama - Sri Lanka

ASC. *Archaeological Survey of Anuradhapura, Annual Report: 1890-1891. Fifth Progress Report: April to June, 1891.* Colombo, Sri Lanka: H. C. Cottle. 1907.

Bandaranayake, Senake. *Sinhalese Monastic Architecture: the Viharas of Anuradhapura.* Leiden, Netherlands: E. J. Brill. 1974.

Basnayake, H. T. *Sri Lankan Monastic Architecture.* Delhi, India: Sri Satguru Publications. 1986.

Seneviratna, Anuradha and Polk, Benjamin. *Buddhist Monastic Architecture in Sri Lanka.* New Delhi, India: Abhinav Publications. 1997.

Indrapura - Champa

Parmentier, Henri. *Inventaire Descriptif des Monuments Cams de l' Annam. Volume I-II.* Paris, France: EFEO. 1909.

Groslier, Bernard Philippe. *The Art of Indochina including Thailand, Vietnam, Laos, and Cambodia.* New York, New York: Crown Publishers Inc. 1962.

Cao, Xuan Pho. *Cham Sculpture: Album.* Hanoi, Vietnam: Social Sciences Publishing House. 1988.

Rawson, Philip S. *The Art of Southeast Asia; Cambodia, Vietnam, Thailand, Laos, Burma, Java, Bali.* London, Britain: Thames and Hudson. 1990.

Chihara, Daigoro. *Hindu-Buddhist Architecture in Southeast Asia.* Leiden, Netherlands: E. J. Brill. 1996.

Ngô, Van Doanh. *Champa: Ancient Towers.* Hanoi, Vietnam: The Gioi Publishers. 2006.

Alchi - Ladakh

Khosla, Romi. *Buddhist Monasteries in the Western Himalaya.* Kathmandu, Nepal: Ratna Pustak Bhandar. 1979.

Pal, Pratapaditya. *Marvels of Buddhist Art: Alchi-Ladakh.* New York, New York: Ravi Kumar. 1988.

Goepper, Roger. *The 'Great Stupa' at Alchi.* Ascona, Switzerland: Artibus Asiae 53, 1/2: 111-143. 1993a.

_____. *Alchi: Ladakh's Hidden Buddhist Sanctuary: The Sumtsek.* Boston, Massachusetts: Shambhala Publications Inc. 1996.

Chapter 5. Rock-hewn Cave

India

Cunningham, Alexander. *Archaeological Reports 1861-65, Volume VI, p. 40-53. Barabar.* Simla, India: Government Central Press. 1871.

Burgess, James. *Notes on the Bauddha Rock-temples of Ajanta: Their Paintings and Sculptures, and on the Paintings of Bagh Caves, Modern Bauddha Mythology, and c. ASWA no. 9.* Bombay, India: Government Central Press. 1879.

_____. *Report on the Buddhist Cave Temples and Their Inscriptions. 1876-1879.* Varanasi, India: Indological Book House. 1964.

_____ and Fergusson, James. *The Cave Tem-*

ples of India. Delhi, India: Oriental Books Reprint Corporation. 1969.

_____ and Indraji, Bhagwanlal. *Inscriptions from Cave-Temples of Western India*. Delhi, India: Indian India. 1976.

Buhler, G. *Indian Antiquity, Journal of Oriental Research, Volume 20, 1891, p. 361-365. The Barabar and Nagarjuni Cave Inscriptions of Asoka and Dasaratha*. Bombay, India: Education Society's Press. 1891.

Marshall, John and Others. *The Bagh Caves in the Gwarlior State*. London, Britain: The India Society. 1927.

Vakil, Kanaiyalal Hardevram. *Rock-cut Temples around Bombay at Elephanta and Jogeshwari, Mandapeshwar and Kanheri*. Bombay, India: D. B. Taraporevala and Co. 1932.

Mitra, Debala. *Ajanta*. Delhi, India: The Manager of Publications. 1956.

Gupte, Ramesh Shankar. *Ajanta, Ellora and Aurangabad Caves*. Bombay, India: D. B. Taraporevala. 1962.

Spink, Walter M. *Ajanta to Ellora*. Bombay, India: Marg Publications. 1967.

_____. *Ajanta: History and Development. Volume 1-5*. Leiden, Netherlands: Brill. 2005-2008.

Hultzsch, Eugen. *Inscriptions of Asoka*. Varanasi, India: Indological Book House. 1969.

Dehejia, Vidya. *Early Buddhist Rock Temples: A Chronological Study*. London, Britain: Thames and Hudson. 1972.

Stern, Philippe. *Colonnes Indiennes d'Ajanta et d'Ellora*. Paris, France Presses: Universitaires de France. 1972.

Gupta, Swarajya Prakash. *The Roots of Indian Art: A Detailed Study of the Formative Period of Indian Art and Architecture–Third and Second Centuries B.C.–Mauryan and Late Mauryan*. Delhi, India: B.R. Publishing Corporation. 1980.

Nagaraju, Seshabhatta. *Buddhist Architecture of Western India (C. 250 B.C.-C. A.D. 300)*. Delhi, India: Agam Kala Prakashan. 1981.

Berkson, Carmel. *The Caves of Aurangabad: Early Buddhist Tantric Art in India*. New York, New York: Mapin International Inc. 1986.

Qureshi, Dulari. *Art and Vision of Aurangabad Caves*. Delhi, India: Bharatiya Kala Prakashan. 1998.

Jamkhedkar, A. P. *Ajanta*. New York, New York: Oxford University Press. 2009.

Afghanistan, Central Asia, Turkistan

Godard, Andre and Others. *Les Antiquites Bouddhiques de Bamiyan. MDAFA II*. Paris, France: G. van Oest. 1928.

Hackin, Joseph and Others. *Nouvelles Recherches Archeoloques a Bamiyan. MDAFA III*. Paris, France: G. van Oest. 1933.

_____ and J. R. *Le Site Archeologique de Bamiyan: Guide du Visiteur*. Paris, France: G. van Oest. 1934.

_____. *Diverses Recherches Archeologiques en Afghanistan. MDAFA Volume 8*. Paris, France: MDAFA. 1959.

Mizuno, Seiichi. *Haibak and Kashmir-Smast: Buddhist Cave Temples in Afghanistan and Pakistan, Surveyed in 1960*. Kyoto, Japan: Kyoto University. 1960.

Dupree, Nancy Hatch. *Bamiyan*. Kabul, Afghanistan: The Afghan Tourist Organization. 1967.

Tarzi, Zemaryalai. *L'Architecture et le Décor Rupestre des Grottes de Bamiyan. Volumes I-II*. Paris, France: Imprimerie Nationale. 1977.

Higuchi, Takayasu and Others. *Bamiyan: Art and Archaeological Researches on the Buddhist Cave Temples in Afghanistan 1970-1978. Volumes I-IV*. Kyoto, Japan: Dohosha. 1983.

Klimburg-Salter, Deborah. *The Kingdom of Bamiyan: Buddhist Art and Culture of the Hindu Kush*. Naples, Italy: IUO and Rome, Italy: IsMEO. 1989.

Warikoo, K. and Others. *Bamiyan: Challenge to the World Heritage*. New Delhi, India: Bhavana Books and Prints. 2002.

Grunwedel, Albert. *Alt-Kutscha. Volume I-II*. Berlin, Germany: O. Elsner Verlagsgesellschaft m. b. h. 1920.

Le Coq, Albert von. *Buried Treasures of Chinese Turkestan*. New York, New York: Longmans, Green and Co. 1929.

Nobuo, Kamagai. *Seiiki no Bijutsu (The Art of Chinese Turkestan). Monumenta Serindica Volume 5*. Kyoto, Japan: Monumenta Serindica. 1962.

WWCBS and Heibonsha. *Kijiru Sekkutsu (The Caves of Kizil). Volume 1-3*. Beijing, China: WWCBS and Tokyo, Japan: Heibonsha. 1983-1985.

_____. *Xinjiang Shi Ku Bi Hua*. Beijing, China: WWCBS. 1989

_____. *Kezi'er Shi Ku. Volume 1-3*. Beijing, China: WWCBS. 1989-1997.

_____. *Xinjiang Kezi'er Shi Ku Kao Gu Bao Gao*. Beijing, China: WWCBS. 1997.

Yao, Shihong. *Kezi'er Shi Ku Tan Mi*. Wulumuqi, China: XMSSYCBS. 1996.

XMSSYCBS. *Kezier Shi Ku Nei Rong Zong Lu*. Wulumuqi, China: XMSSYCBS. 2000.

Ghose, Rajeshwari and Others. *Kizil on the Silk Road: Crossroads of Commerce and Meeting of Minds*. Mumbai, India: Marg Publications. 2008.

China

Pelliot, Paul. *Les Grottes de Touen-houang. Volumes 1-6*. Paris, France: Librairie Paul Geuthner. 1914-1924.

Stein, Aurel. *The Thousand Buddhas: Ancient Buddhist Paintings from the Cave Temples of Tun-huang on the Western Frontier of China. Volume 1-3*. London, Britain: B. Quaritch Ltd. 1921.

Nagahiro, Toshio and Seiichi, Mizuno. *Unko Sekkutsu: Yun-kang, The Buddhist Cave Temples of the Fifth Century in North China. Volumes 1-16*. Kyoto, Japan: JKK. 1951-1956.

WHJSHWHSYGLJ. *Bingling Si Shi Ku*. Beijing, China: WHJSHWHSYGLJ. 1953.

Akiyama, Terukazu and Matsubara, Saburo. *Arts of China: Buddhist Cave Temples New Researches. Volume II*. Tokyo, Japan: Kodansha International Ltd. 1969.

WWCBS and Heibonsha. *Tonko Makkokutsu (The Mogao Caves, Dunhuang)*. Beijing, China: WWCBS and Tokyo, Japan: Heibonsha. 1979-1982.

_____. *Bingling Si Shi Ku*. Beijing, China: WWCBS. 1982.

_____. *Dunhuang Mogao Ku. Volume 1-5*. Beijing, China: WWCBS. 1982-1987.

DICR. *The Art Treasures of Dunhuang*. Hong Kong, China: Joint Publishing Co. 1981.

Heibonsha. *Cave Temples of Mokaoku, Tun-huang. Volume 1-5*. Tokyo, Japan: Heibonsha. 1982.

ZMTS. *Zhonghua Wu Qian Nian Wen Wu Ji Kan: Dunhuang Pian. Part 1-3*. Beijing, China: ZMTS. 1986.

Caswell, James O. *Written and Unwritten: A New History of the Buddhist Caves at Yungang*. Vancouver, Canada: University of British Columbia Press. 1988.

Rhie, Marylin Martin. *Interrelationwhips between the Buddhist Art of China and the Art of India and Central Asia from 618-755 A.D*. Napoli, Italy: IUO. 1988.

Tan, Chung and Others. *Dunhuang Art through the Eyes of Duan Wenjie*. New Delhi, India: IGNCA. 1994.

Whitfield, Roderick. *Dunhuang: Caves of the Singing Sands, Buddhist Art from the Silk Road. Volume I-II*. London, Britain: Textile and Art Publications. 1995.

Su, Bai. *Zhongguo Shi Ku Si Yan Jiu–Studies on the Caves Temples of China*. Beijing, China: WWCBS. 1996.

Ma, Shichang. *Essays on the Buddhist Cave Temples of China*. Xinzhu Shi, China: JFFJYSWHJJH. 2001.

Howard, Angela Falco. *Summit of Treasures: Buddhist Cave Art of Dazu, China*. Hong Kong, China: Orchid Press. 2001.

Li, Chongfeng. *Indian and Chinese Buddhist Chetiyagharas: A Comparative Study*. Xinzhu Shi, China: CTFRJFJYSWHJH. 2002.

KXCBS. *Xi Ri Bingling Si*. Beijing, China: KXCBS. 2004.

Korea

Eckardt, Andreas. *History of Korean Art*. Leipzig, Germany: Karl W. Hiersemann. 1929.

McCune, Evelyn. *The Arts of Korea: An Illustrated History*. Tokyo, Japan: Charles E. Turtle Co. 1962.

Kim, Wongyon. *Art and Archaeology of Ancient Korea*. Seoul, South Korea: Taekwang Publishing Co. 1986.

Mun, Myong-dae. *Seokguram: The Cave Temple of Toham-san*. Seoul, South Korea: KPI Publishing Co. 2000.

Kang, Woobang. *Korean Buddhist Sculpture: Art and Truth*. Chicago, Illinois: Art Media Resources Inc. 2005.

Chapter 6. Stupa

Combaz, Gisbert. *L'Evolution du Stupa en Asie*. Brussels, Belgium: Louvain. 1933-37.

Agrawala, Prithvi Kumar. *Mathura Railing Pillars*. Varanasi, India: Prithivi Prakashan. 1966.

Dallapiccola, Anna and Others. *The Stupa: Its Religious, Historical, and Architectural Significance*. Steiner, Germany: Wiesbaden. 1980.

Benisti, Mireille. *Contribution a l'Etude du Stupa Bouddhique Indien: les Stupa Mineurs de Bodh-Gaya et de Ratnagiri*. Paris, France: EFEO. 1981.

_____. *Stylistics of Buddhist Art in India. Volume 1-2*. New Delhi, India: IGNCA. 2003.

Snodgras, Adrian. *The Symbolism of the Stupa*. Ithaca, New York: Cornell University Southeast Asia Program. 1985.

Kottkamp, Heino. *Der Stupa als Repräsentation des Buddhisteschen Heilweges: Untersuchungen zur Entstehung und Entwicklung Architektonischer Symbolik*. Wiesbaden, Germany: O. Harrassowitz. 1992.

Das, D. Jithendra. *The Buddhist Architecture in Andhra*. Lucknow, India: Books and Books. 1993.

Bentor, Yael. *Consecration of Images and Stupas in Indo-Tibetan Tantric Buddhism*. Leiden, Netherlands: Brill. 1996.

Willis, Michael D. *Buddhist Reliquaries from Ancient India*. London, Britain: British Museum Press. 2000.

Shimada, Akira. *Buddhist Stupas in South Asia: Recent Archaeological, Art-Historical, and Historical Perspectives*. New York, New York: Oxford University Press. 2009.

Stupa - India

Piprahwa Stupa

Sinha, Bindeshwari and Roy, Sita. *Vaisali Excavations: 1958-1962*. Patna, India: Directorate of Archaeology and Museums. 1969.

Mishra, Tara Nanda. *The Location of Kapilavastu and Archaeological Excavations, 1967-1972*. Kathmandu, Nepal: LDC. 1978.

Pradhana, Bhuvana Lala. *Lumbini, Kapilawastu, Dewadaha*. Kathmandu, Nepal: Tribhuvan University. 1979.

Srivastava, Krishna. *Discovery of Kapilavastu*. New Delhi, India: Books and Books. 1986.

Rijal, Babu Krishna. *100 Years of Archaeological Research in Lumbini, Kapilavastu and Devadaha*. Kathmandu, Nepal: S. K. International Publishing House. 1996.

Verardi, Giovanni. *Excavations at Gotihawa and a Territorial Survey in Kapilavastu District of Nepal: A Preliminary Report*. Lumbini, Nepal: LIRI. 2002.

Deeg, Max. *The Places Where Siddhartha Trod: Lumbini and Kapilavastu*. Bhairahawa, Nepal: Lumbini International Research Institute. 2003.

Sanchi Stupa I

Cunningham, Alexander. *The Bhilsa Topes; or, Buddhist Monuments of Central India*. London, Britain: Smith Elder and Co. 1854.

Maisey, Fredrick. *Sanchi and Its Remains*. London, Britain: K. Paul Trench Trubner. 1892.

Marshall, John. *A Guide to Sanchi*. Calcutta, India: Superintendent Government Printing. 1918.

Mitra, Debala. *Sanchi*. New Delhi, India: ASI. 1965.

Marshall, John and Foucher, Alfred. *The Monuments of Sanchi, Volume 1-3*. Delhi, India: Swati Publications. 1983.

Srivastava, A. L. *Life in Sanchi Sculptures*. New Delhi, India: Abhinav Publications. 1983.

Dehejia, Vidya and Others. *Unseen Presence: The Buddha and Sanchi*. Bombay, India: Marg Publications. 1996.

Ghosal, Susheila. *Sanchi Rediscovered: A Journey Through Time, Bipin Ghosal 1875-1930*. New Delhi, India: Magnum Books. 2006.

Bharhut Stupa

Coomaraswamy, Ananda K. *La Sculpture de Bharhut*. Paris, France: Vanoest. 1956.

Cunningham, Alexander. *Stupa of Bharhut*. Varanasi, India: IndologicaL Book House. 1962.

Luders, Heinrich and Others. *Bharhut Inscriptions*. Ootacamund, Germany: Government Epigraphist for India. 1963.

Ghosh, Arabinda. *Remains of the Bharhut Stupa in the Indian Museum*. Calcutta, India: Indian Museum. 1978.

Barua, Beni Madhab. *Barhut*. Patna, India: Indological Book Corporation. 1979.

Rhys Davids, Caroline A.F. *Stories of the Buddha*. New York, New York: Dover Publications. 1989.

Oki, Morihiro and Ito, Shoji. *Ancient Buddhist Sites of Sanchi and Barhut*. Tokyo, Japan: Yuzankaku. 1991.

Sharma, Ramesh Chandra. *Bharhut Sculptures*. New Delhi, India: Abhinav Publications. 1994.

Amaravati Stupa

Fergusson, James. *Description of Amravati Tope, on the Banks of the Kristnah, in the Gantur Zilla: Communicated to the Royal Asiatic Society on the 17th of June, 1867*. Hertford, England: Stephen Austin. 1867.

Sewell, Robert. *Report on the Amaravati Tope and Excavations on Its Site in 1877*. London, Britain: George Edward Eyre and William Spottiswoode. 1880.

Burgess, James. *The Buddhist Stupas of Amaravati and Jaggayyapeta in the Krishna District, Madras Presidency, Surveyed in 1882*. London, Britain: Trubner and Co. 1887.

_____. *Notes on Amaravati Stupa*. Varanasi, India: Prithivi Prakashan. 1972.

Rea, Alexander. *South Indian Buddhist Antiquities*. Madras, India: Superintendent Government Press. 1894.

Barrett, Douglas. *Sculptures from Amaravati in the British Museum*. London, Britain: Trustees of the Bristish Museum. 1954.

Sivaramamurti, Calambur. *Amaravati Sculptures in the Madras Government Museum*. Madras, India: Thompson and Company Private Ltd. 1956.

Ramachandra Rao, P. R. *The Art of Nagarjunakonda*. Madras, India: Rachana. 1956.

_____. *Amaravati*. Hyderabad, India: Government of Andhra Pradesh. 2002.

Ramaswami, N. S. *Amaravati, the Art and History of the Stupa and the Temple*. Hyderabad, India: Government of Andhra Pradesh. 1975.

Knox, Robert. *Amaravati: Buddhist Sculpture from the Great Stupa*. London, Britain: British Museum Press. 1992.

Roy, Anamika. *Amaravati Stupa: A Critical Comparison of Epigraphic, Architectural and Sculptural Evidence. Volume I-II*. Delhi, India: Agam Kala Prakashan. 1994.

Longhurst, Albert Henry. *The Buddhist Antiquities of Nagarjunakonda: Madras Presidency*. MASI no. 54.

Delhi, India: Manager of Publications. 1938.
Krishna Murthy, K. *Nagarjunakonda: A Cultural Study*. Delhi, India: Concept Publishing Co. 1977.
Subramanian, K. R. *Buddhist Remains in South India and Early Andhra History, 225 A. D. to 610 A. D.* New Delhi, India: Cosmo Publications. 1981.
Stone, Elizabeth Rosen. *The Buddhist Art of Nagarjunakonda*. Delhi, India: Motilal Banarsidass Publishers Private Ltd. 1994.
Rama, K. *The Buddhist Art of Nagarjunakonda*. Delhi, India: Sundeep Prakashan. 1995.

Kesariya Stupa
Cunningham, Alexander. *Archaeological Reports 1861-65, Volume VI, p. 64-67. Kesariya*. Simla, India: Government Central Press. 1871.
Muhammad, K. K. *Kesariya: the Tallest Stupa*. Delhi, India: India Perspectives. February 2002.
Mani, Buddha Rashmi and Saran, S.C. *Purabharati: Studies in Early Archaeology and Buddhism: Commemoration in Respect of Prof. B.P. Sinha*. Delhi, India: Sharada Publishing House. 2006.
Bunce, Frederick W. *Monuments of India and Indianized States: the Plans of Major and Notable Temples, Tombs, Palaces, an Pavilions of Bangladesh, Sri Lanka, Java, the Khmer, Pagan, Thailand, Vietnam, and Malaysia, from 3rd c. BCE to CE 1854*. New Delhi, India: D. K. Printworld Ltd. 2007.

Stupa - Pakistan, Central Asia, Turkistan
Cunningham, Alexander. *ASIAR 1872-1873, Volume V.* Calcutta, India: Superintendent of Government Printing. 1875.
ASI. *ASIAR1910-1911: 25-32*. Calcutta, India: Superintendent of Government Printing. 1914.
Marshall, John Hubert. *Taxila. Volume I-III*. London, Britain: Cambridge University Press. 1951.
Wilson, Horace H. *Ariana Antiqua*. Delhi, India: Oriental Publishers. 1971.
Dobbins, Walton K. *The Stupa and Vihara of Kanishka*. Calcutta, India: AS. 1971.
Khan, Muhammad Ashraf. *Buddhist Shrines in Swat*. Saidu Sharif, Pakistan: Swat Archaeological Museum. 1993.
Faccenna. Domenico. *Saidu Sharif I (Swat, Pakistan), 2. The Buddhist Sacred Area, the Stupa Terrace. Volume I-II*. Rome, Italy: IsMEO. 1995.
Nadiem, Ihsan H. *Buddhist Gandhara: History, Art, and Architecture*. Lahore, Pakistan :Sang-E-Meel Publications. 2003.
Behrendt, Kurt A. *The Buddhist Architecture of Gandhara*. Boston, Massachusetts: Brill Academic Publishers. 2004.

T'a, T'ap, Tháp, To - China, Korea, Vietnam, Japan
Franz, Heinrich Gerhard. *Pagode, Turmtempel, Stupa: Studien zum Kultbau des Buddhismus in Indien u. Ostasien*. Akadem. Graz, Germany: Druck-u.Verlagsanst. 1978.
Liang, Ssu Cheng. *Pictorial History of Chinese Architecture*. Cambridge, Massachusetts: The MIT Press. 1984.
Wei, Ran. *Buddhist Buildings: Ancient Chinese Architecture*. New York, New York: Springer-Verlag Wien. 2000.
Steinhardt, Nancy and Others. *Chinese Architecture*. New Haven, Connecticut: Yale University Press. 2002.

Dagaba - Sri Lanka
Vacissara, Thera. *The Chronicle of the Thupa and the Thupavamsa, Translated by N. A. Jayawickrama*. London, Britain: Luzac and Company Ltd. 1971.
Paranavitana, Senarat. *Art of the Ancient Sinhalese*. Colombo, Ceylon: Lake House Investments Ltd. Publishers. 1971.
_____. *Memoirs of the Archaeological Survey of Ceylon, Volume V: The Stupa in Ceylon*. Colombo, Ceylon: ASC. 1946.
_____. *Art and Architecture of Ceylon: Polonnaruva Period*. Colombo, Ceylon: Arts Council of Ceylon. 1954.
_____. *Inscriptions of Ceylon, Volume I*. Colombo, Ceylon: Ceylon Department of Archaeology. 1970.
Harischandra, Brahmachari. *The Sacred City of Anuradhapura*. Delhi, India: Asian Educational Services. 1985.
Schroeder, Ulrich von. *Buddhist Sculptures of Sri Lanka*. Hong Kong, China: Visual Dharma Publications Ltd. 1990.
Smither, James. *Archaeological Remains, Anuradhapura, Sri Lanka: Comprising the Dagabas and Certain other Ancient Ruined Structures*. Polgasovita, Sri Lanka: Academy of Sri Lankan Culture. 1993.

Candi - Indonesia
Krom, Nicolaas Johannes. *Barabudur: Archaeological Description*. The Hague, Netherlands: Martinus Nijhoff. 1927.
_____. *Hindoe-Javaansche Kunst. Volume I-III*. The Hague, Netherlands: Martinus Nijhoff. 1923.
_____. *The Life of Buddha on the*

Stupa of Barabudur according to the Lalitavistara Text. Delhi, India: Bhartiya Publishing House. 1974.
Miksic, John. *Borobudur: Golden Tales of the Buddhas*. Boston, Massachusetts: Shambhala. 1990.
Dumarcay, Jacques. *Borobudur*. New York, New York: Oxford University Press. 1991.
Frederic, Louis. *Borobudur*. New York, New York: Abbeville Press Inc. 1996.

Zedi, Chedi, Chedei, That - Mayanmar, Thailand, Kampuchea, Laos
Lu Pe Win, U. *Pictorial Guide to Pagan*. Rangoo, Burma: Government of the Union of Burma. 1955.
Luce, Gordon H. *Old Burma-Early Pagan. Volume 1-3*. Locust Valley, New York: Artibus Asiae. 1969.
Pichard, Pierre. *Inventory of Monuments at Pagan*. Paris, France: UNESCO. 1992-2001.
Tun Aung Chain and Thein Hlaing. *Shwedagon*. Yangon, Myanmar: The Universities Press. 1996.
Moore, Elizabeth and Others. *Shwedagon: Golden Pagoda of Myanmar*. New York, New York: Thames and Hudson. 1999.

Caitya - Nepal
Kolver, Bernhard. *Rebuilding a Stupa: Architectural Drawings of the Svayambhunath*. Bonn, Germany: VGH Wissenschaftsverlag. 1992.
Gutschow, Niels. *The Nepalese Caitya: 1,500 Years of Buddhist Votive Architecture in the Kathmandu Valley*. Stuttgart, Germany and London, Britain: Edition Axel Menges. 1997.
Shakya, Hem Raj. *Sri Svayambhu Mahacaitya*. Kathmandu, Nepal: Svayambhu Vikash Mandal. 2004.

Chorten - Tibet, Indian Himalaya, Bhutan, Mongolia
Tucci, Giuseppe. *Indo-Tibetica. Volume I (Stupa: Art, Architectonics and Symbolism)*. New Delhi, India: Aditya Prakashan. 1988.
_____. *Indo-Tibetica. Volume IV (Gyantse and Its Monasteries. Part I-III)*. New Delhi, India: Aditya Prakashan. 1988.
Vitali, Roberto. *Early Temples of Central Tibet*. London, Britain: Serindia Publications. 1990.
Ricca, Franco and Lo Bue, Erberto. *The Great Stupa of Gyantse: A Complete Tibetan Pantheon of the Fifthteenth Century*. London, Britain: Serindia Publications. 1993.
Dorjee, Pema. *Stupa and Its Technology: A Tibeto-Buddhist Perspective*. Delhi, India: IGNCA. 1996.
Larsen, Knud and Sinding-Larsen, Amund. *The Lhasa Atlas: Traditional Tibetan Architecture and Townscape*. Chicago, Illinois: Serindia Publications. 2001.
Alexander, Andre. *The Temples of Lhasa: Tibetan Buddhist Architecture from the 7th to the 21st Centuries*. Chicago, Illinois: Serindia Publications. 2005.
Schroeder, Ulrich von. *Empowered Masters: Tibetan Wall Paintings of Mahasiddhas at Gyantse*. Chicago, Illinois: Serindia Publications. 2006.

Chapter 7. Temple

Early Indian Buddhist Temples - India, Pakistan, Sri Lanka
ASIAR. *ASIAR 1902-1903: Ter-Tagara*. Calcutta, India: Superintendent Government Printing. 1904.
Sahni, Daya Ram. *Archaeological Remains and Excavations of Bairat*. Jaipur, India: Jaipur State. 1923-1949.
Sarkar, H. *Studies in Early Buddhist Architecture of India*. Delhi, India: Munshiram Manoharlal. 1966.
Agrawala, Prithvi Kumar. *Gupta Temple Architecture*. Varanasi, India: Prithivi Prakasan. 1968.
Meister, Michael W and Others. *Encyclopedia of Indian Temple Architecture*. Philadelphia, Pennsylvania: University of Pennsylvania Press. 1983-2001.
Coomaraswamy, Ananda Kentish and Meister, Michael. *Essays in Early Indian Architecture*. New Delhi, India: IGNCA. 1992.
Deva, Krishna. *Temples of India. Volume I-II*. New Delhi, India: Aryan Books International. 1995.
Saoud, Rabah. *The Arch That Never Sleeps*. Manchester, United Kingdom: FSTC. 2002.

Mahabodhi Temple - India
Cunningham, Alexander. *Archaeological Reports 1861-65: Buddha Gaya, Volume I, p. 4-12*. Simla, India: Government Central Press. 1871.
_____. *Mahabodhi, or the Great Buddhist Temple under the Bodhi tree at Buddha-Gaya*. Varanasi, India: Indological Book House. 1961.
ASIAR. *ASIAR 1908-1909: Notes on Bodh-Gaya, p. 139-158*. Calcutta, India: Superintendent Government Printing. 1912.
Coomaraswamy, Ananda Kentish. *La Sculpture de Bodhgaya*. Paris, France: Les Editions d'Art et d'Histoire. 1935.
Mitra, Rajendralala. *Buddha Gaya: The Great Buddhist Temple, the Hermitage of Sakya Muni*. Varanasi, India: Indological Book House. 1972.
Barua, Beni Madhab. *Gaya and Buddha-Gaya: Early History of the Holy Land, Volume I-II*. Varanasi, India Bhartiya: Publishing House. 1975.
Benisti, Mireille. *Contribution a l'Etude du Stupa Boud-*

dhique Indien: les Stupa Mineurs de Bodh-Gaya et de Ratnagiri. Paris, France: EFEO. 1981.
Leoshko, Janice. *Bodhgaya, the Site of Enlightenment.* Bombay, India: Marg Publications. 1988.
Ahir, D. C. *Buddha Gaya through the Ages.* Delhi, India: Sri Satguru Publications. 1994.

Candi Sewu - Indonesia
Schnitger, Friedrich Martin. *The Archaeology of Hindoo Sumatra.* Leiden, Netherlands: E. J. Brill. 1937.
Bosch, F. D. K. *Selected Studies in Indonesian Archaeology.* The Hague, Netherlands: Martinus Nijhoff. 1961.
Dumarcay, Jacques. *Candi Sewu: Et L'Architecture Bouddhique du Centre de Java.* Paris, France: EFEO. 1981.
_____. *Temples of Java.* New York, New York: Oxford University Press. 1986.
_____ and Smithies, Michael. *Cultural Sites of Malaysia, Singapore, and Indonesia.* New York, New York: Oxford University Press. 1998.
Soekmono, R. *The Javanese Candi: Function and Meaning.* Leiden, Netherlands: E. J. Brill. 1995.

Ananda Temple - Myanmar
Yule, Henry. *A Narrative of the Mission Sent by the Governor-General of India to the Court of Ava in 1855.* London, Britain: Smither Elder and Co. 1858.
Duroiselle, Charles. *The Ananda Temple at Pagan (ASI no. 56).* Delhi, India: ASI. 1937.

Bayon Temple of Angkor Thom - Kampuchea
Stern, Philippe. *Le Bayon d'Angkor et l'Evolution de l'Art Khmer.* Paris, France: P. Geuthner. 1927.
_____. *Les Monuments Khmers du Style du Bayon et Jayavarman VII.* Paris, France: Presses Universitaires de France. 1965.
Marchal, Henri. *Guide Archeologique aux Temples d'Angkor; Angkor Vat, Angkor Thom et les Monuments du petit et du Grand Circuit.* Paris, France: G. van Oest. 1928.
_____. *Guide to Angkor: Angkor Vat–Angkor Thom and Monuments of "Great Circuit" and Little Circuit."* Saigon, Vietnam: SDEA. 1930.
Coedes, George. *The Indianized States of Southeast Asia.* Honolulu, Hawaii: East-West Center Press. 1968.
Cohen, Joan L. and Kalman, Bela. *Angkor: Monuments of the God-Kings.* New York, New York: Harry N. Abrams Inc. 1975.
Glaize, Maurice. *Les Monuments du Groupe d'Angkor.* Paris, France: J. Maisonneuve. 1993.
Bonheur, Albert le and Poncar, Jaroslav. *Of Gods, Kings, and Men: Bas-reliefs of Angkor Wat and Bayon.* London, Britain: Serindia Publications. 1995.
Jacques, Claude and Freeman, Michael. *Angkor: Cities and Temples.* Bangkok, Thailand: River Books. 1997.
Roveda, Vittorio. *Khmer Mythology: Secrets of Angkor.* New York, New York: Weatherhill Inc. 1998.
Dumarcay, Jacques. *Cambodian Architecture, Eighth to Thirteenth Centuries.* Leiden, Netherlands: Brill. 2001.
Zhou, Daquan. *A Record of Cambodia: The Land and Its People (Translated by Peter Harris).* Chiang Mai, Thailand: Silkworm Books. 2007.
Clark, Joyce and Others. *Bayon: New Perspectives.* Bangkok, Thailand: River Books. 2008.

Chapter 8. Four Holiest Sites
Faxian. *Travels of Fah-Hian and Sung-Yun, Buddhist Pilgims, from China to India (400 A. D. and 518 A. D.) (Translated from Chinese by Samuel Beal).* London, Britain: Trubner. 1869.
_____. *A Record of Buddhistic Kingdoms; Being an Account by the Chinese Monk Fa-Hsien of His Travels in India and Ceylon, A. D. 399-414, in Search of the Buddhist Books of Discipline (Translated and Annotated with A Corean Recension of the Chinese Text by James Legge).* Oxford, Britain: Clarendon Press. 1886.
_____. *The Pilgrimage of Fa Hian (from the French edition of the Foe Koue Ki of MM. Remusat, Klaproth, and Landresse).* Calcutta, India: The Bangabasi Office. 1912.
_____. *The Travels of Fa-Hsien (399-414 A. D.).* London, England: Cambridge University Press. 1923.
Grousset, Rene. *In the Footsteps of the Buddha.* London, Britain: G. Routledge and Sons, Ltd. 1932.
Yijing. *Record of the Buddhist Religion as Practised in India and the Malay Archipelago (A. D. 671-695). (Translated by J. Takakusu.)* Oxford, Britain: Clarendon Press. 1896.
_____. *Chinese Monks in India: Biography of Eminent Monks Who Went to the Western World in Search of the Law during the Great T'ang Dynasty. (Translated by Latika Lahiri.)* Delhi, India: Motilal Banarsidass. 1986.
Watters, Thomas. *On Yuan Chwang's Travels in India, 629-645 A. D. Volume I-II.* London, Britain: RAS. 1904-1905.
Xuanzang. *Si-yu-ki. Buddhist Records of the Western World. (Translated from the Chinese of Hiuen Tsiang (A. D. 629) by Samuel Beal. Volume I-II.)* London, Britain: Trubner and Co. 1906.
Biruni, Muhammad ibn Ahmad. *Alberruni's India. An*

Account of the Religion, Philosophy, Literature, Geography, Chronology, Astronomy, Customs, Laws and Astrology of India about A. D. 1030. Volume I-II. London, Britain: K. Paul, Trench, Trubner and Co. Ltd. 1910.

Huili. *The Life of Hiuen-Tsiang, by the Shaman Hwui Li. (With an introduction containing an account of the works of I-tsing by Samuel Beal.)* London, Britain: Trubner. 1914.

Chag Lo-tsa-ba. *Biography of Dharmasvamin (Chag lo tsa-ba Chos-rje-dpal), a Tibetan Monk Pilgrim. (Translated by George Roerich.)* Patna, India: K. P. Jayaswal Research Institute. 1959.

Raven-Hart, Rowland. *Where the Buddha Trod: A Buddhist Pilgrimage*. Colombo, Sri Lanka: Lakehouse Investments. 1966.

Chaudhury, Binayendra Nath. *Buddhist Centres in Ancient India*. Calcutta, India: Sanskrit College. 1969.

Tarthang Tulku. *Holy Places of the Buddha*. Berkeley, California: Dharma Publishing. 1994.

Bernstein, Richard. *Ultimate Journey: Retracing the Path of an Ancient Buddhist Monk Who Crossed Asia in Search of Enlightenment*. New York, New York: A. A. Knopf. 2001.

Singh, Rana P. B. *Where the Buddha Walked: A Companion to the Buddhist Places of India*. Varanasi, India: Indica Books. 2003.

Dwivedi, Sunita. *Buddhist Heritage Sites of India*. New Delhi, India: Rupa and Co. 2006.

Lumbini - Nepal

Pradhana, Bhuvana Lala. *Lumbini, Kapilawastu, Dewadaha*. Kathmandu, Nepal: Tribhuvan University. 1979.

Rijal, Babu Krishna. *100 Years of Archaeological Research in Lumbini, Kapilavastu and Devadaha*. Kathmandu, Nepal: S. K. International Publishing House. 1996.

_____. *Archaeological Remains of Kapilavastu, Lumbini and Devadaha*. Kathmandu, Nepal: Educational Enterprises Pvt. Ltd. 1979.

Deeg, Max. *The Places Where Siddhartha Trod: Lumbini and Kapilavastu*. Bhairahawa, Nepal: Lumbini International Research Institute. 2003.

Bidari, Basanta. *Lumbini: A Heaven of Sacred Refuge*. Kathmandu, Nepal: Basanta Bidari. 2002.

Bodhgaya - India

Mitra, Rajendralala. *Buddha Gaya: The Great Buddhist Temple, the Hermitage of Sakya Muni*. Varanasi, India: Indological Book House. 1972.

Barua, Beni Madhab. *Gaya and Buddha-Gaya: Early History of the Holy Land, Volume I-II*. Varanasi, India: Bhartiya Publishing House. 1975.

ASIAR. *ASIAR 1908-1909: Notes on Bodh-Gaya, p. 139-158*. Calcutta, India: Superintendent Government Printing. 1912.

Benisti, Mireille. *Contribution a l'Etude du Stupa Bouddhique Indien: les Stupa Mineurs de Bodh-Gaya et de Ratnagiri*. Paris, France: EFEO. 1981.

Leoshko, Janice. *Bodhgaya, the Site of Enlightenment*. Bombay, India: Marg Publications. 1988.

Ahir, D. C. *Buddha Gaya Through the Ages*. Delhi, India: Sri Satguru Publications. 1994.

Asher, Frederick M. *Bodh Gaya*. New York, New York: Oxford University Press. 2008.

Sarnath - India

Sahni, Daya Ram. *Catalogue of the Museum of Archaeology at Sarnath*. Calcutta, India: Superintendent Government Printing. 1914.

_____. *Guide to the Buddhist Ruins of Sarnath*. Delhi, India: Manager of Publications. 1933.

Bhattacharya, Brindevan Chandra. *The History of Sarnath, or, the Cradle of Buddhism from the Earliest Times to the Muhammedan Conquest, including an Archaeological Guide to the Monuments and the Museum*. Benares, India: Tara Printing Works. 1924.

Agrawala, Vasudeva Sharana. *The Wheel Flag of India. Chakra-Dhvaja. Being a History and Exposition of the Meaning of the Dharma-Chakra and the Sarnath Lion Capital*. Varanasi, India: Prithivi Prakashan. 1964.

Caturvedi, Sitarama. *The Capital of Buddhism, Sarnath; Including Places of Buddhistic Pilgrimage*. Varanasi, India: Orient Publishers. 1968.

Kushinagar - India

Carlleye, A. C. L. *ASIAR Volume 18: Report of a Tour in the Gorakhpur District in 1875-76 and 1876-1877*. Varanasi, India: Indological Book House. 1969.

ASI. *ASIAR 1910-1911: 63-77*. Calcutta, India: Superintendent of Government Printing. 1914.

Patil, D. R. *Kusinara*. New Delhi, India: ASI. 1981.

Index

Pages are in roman and figures are in bold; also see Glossary for *italic* headings.

abhaya-mudra, 25, 199, 209
Abhidharma, 19-21
abhiseka, 24
acarya, 61
addhyayoga, 48
adimukha, 190
Ado, 136
Afghanistan; Balkh, 115-116; Begram ivories, 96; Buddhism, 20, 33-34, 115-116, 125; Fullol, 116; Hindu Kush, 50, 116, 120, 123; Kabul, 116; Kandahar, 34, 50, 115-116; Kapisa (Begram), 51, 116; Mundigak, 116; Shortugai, 7. Also Bactria
Afghanistan, Buddhist sites; Fondukistan, 120; Ghazni, 116, 276; Guldara Stupa, 177, 179; Hadda, 115-116, 124; Kabul, 116; Kapisa, 116; Paitava, 116, 124-125; Parvan, 116; Shotorak, 116, 124-125; Tope-i-rustam Stupa, 179. Also Bactria, Buddhist sites
Afghanistan, dynasties and periods; Achaemenid Persia/Parthian/Sassanian, 35, 50, 116; Early/Later Greek, 50-51, 115-116; Hindu-Shahi, 115-116; Later/Kidara Kushan, 116-117; Maurya, 30; Saka, 51; Turki-Shahi, 115-116, 124-125; White Huns/Hephthalites, 115-116. Also Chronology
Afghanistan, Hindu sites, 116
Afghanistan, rock-hewn caves, 120. Also Bamiyan
agnisala, 48
agni-stambha/flaming pillar, 167, 235
Ahmad Nialatigin, 276
Ai-khanum, 44, 115-116, 155, 179, 248
Ajanta caves, **5.10-5.13**, 62, 66, 76, 94, 96, 98-100, 106, 108, 110-114, 121, 128, 168, 187, 226-227; Cave #1, 114, 226; Cave #19, 112-114, 187, 226
Ajivika, 30, 32, 35, 98, 102-104; and Jainism, 32, 102; and Maurya emperors, 102; founder Makkhali Gosala, 32, 102
Akbar, Emperor, 39, 277
Alara Kalama, 170
Alayavijnana, 22
Al-Biruni, 4, 115
Alchi, **4.13-4.15**, 26, 46, 87-96; Sumtsek, 26, 92-96, 121, 228. Also Alchi Style; Indo-Kashmiri Style
Alchi Style, 96
Alexander, the Great, 30, 35, 44, 50, 115
Alexander, James E., 110
Allakappa, 143
Altin-tepe, 7

amalaka, 85, 112, 189, 195, 222, 243, 246, 252, 260, 281
Amaravati Stupa, **6.9-6.11**, 76, 96, 99, 109, 141-142, 149-150, 152, 161-169, 173, 176, 187, 189-191, 192, 204, 206, 222, 239, 259; and Gandhara *stupa*s, 163-165, 173, 176; and North Indian *stupa*s, 163-165; symbolisms, 165-166. Also Andhra and South Indian *stupa*s
Amaravati Style, 82, 169, 194. Also Andhra Style
Ambedkar, B. R., 240
American, 118, 130
Amitabha Buddha, 21-22, 25, 95, 135, 199, 220-221; Amitayus, 25, 96; Western Paradise, 21-22, 182
Amu Darya River, 7, 116
Ananda Temple, **7.14-7.15**, 28, 74, 179, 213, 233, 248, 251-255, 279
anda, 53, 141-143, 147-148, 150, 152, 156, 163-167, 173-174
Andher Stupa I-III, 20, 147-148
Andhra(s), 98, 108, 162, 169; arts, 96, 101, 166-167, 169, 206, 259-260; Empire, 162
Andhra Pradesh, 30, 81, 83, 99-100, 161-162, 167
Andhra and South Indian *stupa*s, 53, 121, 142, 162, 165, 167, 174, 189-190, 206; characteristics, 162, 165. Also Amaravati Stupa
Andhra Style, 76, 82, 162, 167; Nagarjunakonda, 167-169. Also Amaravati Style
ang, 185
Angkor Thom, 82, 258, 260-261, 263-266; Zhou Daquan's account, 265-266. Also Bayon Temple
An-hsuan, 118
Anicca, 17
Aniconic; arts and architecture, Phase, School, 4, 97-102, 104, 106, 108, 110, 112, 114, 140, 149-150, 152-153, 156, 160, 165-167, 169, 221-222; symbols, 25, 99, 149, 152-153, 160, 162, 165-167, 169, 221-222, 233-242, 249, 269, 277, 285
An-shih-kao, 118
Aparantaka, 20, 115
apsara, 96, 134
Arab(s), 116-117
Arabian Peninsula, 7
Aramaic, 33-34, 50, 53, 115
architecture, Buddhist designs and types, 28; cruciform, 62, 71-72, 74, 121, 171-172, 176, 178-180, 185-186, 189, 192, 205, 233-234, 240, 249, 251-252, 254, 263-264, 266, 270, 277, 279; multi-terraced, 74, 84, 116, 119, 141, 171, 189, 195, 201, 204-205, 208, 210, 212,

218, 232, 248, 255, 260, 264, 266; quincunxial/*pancayatana*, 4, 64, 66, 76-77, 119, 172, 174, 176, 192, 233-234, 246, 248-249, 251, 259-260, 266; straight-edged pyramidal tower, 208, 233-234, 242, 247-248, 269, 278
architecture, technologies; arcade, 207; arch, 11, 13, 55, 57, 109, 102, 119-121, 207, 235, 243, 246, 252; dome, 53, 64-65, 73, 103-104, 112, 119-121, 125-127, 137-142, 144, 148-150, 152, 156, 158, 162-163, 165, 171-177, 179, 187, 189-192, 196, 200-201, 207-210, 219, 221-224, 229-231, 234-236, 243, 252, 259, 284-285; vault, 49, 53, 55, 57, 70, 84, 97, 100-103, 104-106, 108-109, 113, 120-122, 127, 137, 147, 207-208, 234-235, 237, 242-243, 246, 252, 254, 260, 278, 285; origin and influence, 4, 55, 208, 243, 246. Also *caitya*-arch
arhat, 18-22, 25, 134, 138-139, 143, 155, 182
Arnold, Edwin, 239
Arthasastra, 41
Arupadhatu: see *Tridhatu*
Aryan, 9, 30, 50, 116, 160, 234
ASB, 102, 276
Asher, Frederick, 74
ASI, 59, 72, 122, 268, 282
Asia, 46-47, 50-51, 54-55, 75; Central, 9, 20, 26, 51, 53-54, 58, 97, 114-118, 121; cultural spheres, 27, 46, 193; South, 6, 45; Southeast, 21, 27, 81-82, 97, 140, 142, 162, 190, 192-194, 205-207, 233, 236, 248-249, 255-256, 258, 272, 279; West, 7-8, 50-51, 55, 57
Asia Minor, 44
Asoka, boulder and tablet edicts, 33-35, 41-42, 50, 115, 236
Asoka, Buddhist edicts, 34-35, 238; Allahabad-Kausambi, 35, 39; Nigali Sagar, 31, 35, 38, 267; Rummindei (Lumbini), 31, 33-34, 38-39, 41, 214, 267, 269; Sanchi, 35, 152, 155; Sarnath, 31, 35, 39, 42, 277
Asoka, edicts and inscriptions, 31, 34-36, 38-39, 50, 102, 115; and Achaemenid Persia, 35-36. Also Aramaic; Brahmi; Greek; Kharosthi
Asoka, Emperor, 34, 50; Asokavadana, 31-32, 173; and Buddhism, 19-20, 30-35, 146-147, 238, 268, 275, 282; daughter Sanghamitra, 20, 31, 75-76, 147; daughter Carumati, 219; Queen Kaluvati, 35; Queen Tishyaraksita, 219, 238; son Kunala, 50; son Mahendra, 20, 31, 75-76, 147, 190; younger brother Tissakumara, 20. Also Asoka, Buddhist edicts
Asoka, non-Buddhist edicts, 34-35, 102-103; Allahabad-Kausambi, 34-35; Queen Edict, 35; Sudama, 35, 102-103; Visvakarma, 35, 102-103
Asoka pillars, 4, 28, 31, 33, 35-45, 145-147, 150, 152, 154, 160-161, 165-166, 169-171, 214, 242-243, 247, 267-269, 271, 276-279, 283-284; Allahabad-Kausambi, 36, 39-40, 42, 44-45, 155; and Chinese pillars, 45; and cave pillars, 108-109; and Indian emblem, 44, 277; and Vedic *yupa*, 43-44; Bodhgaya, 40-41, 242-243, 247; Delhi-Mirath, 36, 38; Delhi-Topra, 31, 36, 38, 41; Gotihawa, 36, 38-41, 145-146, 213, 267-268; Jetavana, 39-40; Kausambi, 36, 39-42; Kesariya, 40, 42, 170-171; Kushinagar, 40-41, 282-284, 286; Lauriya Araraj, 38; Lauriya Nandangarh, **3.2**, 36, 39-40, 42; Nigali Sagar, 31, 38-42, 145-146, 213-214, 267-268; Patna, 40, 42-43; Rampurva #1, 36, 39-40; Rampurva #2, **3.5**, 36, 39, 41-44; Rummindei (Lumbini), 31, 38-42, 145, 213, 267-269, 271; Sanchi, **6.3**, 36, 39, 41-43, 147, 150, 152, 155 , 277; Sankisa, 36, 39-42, 44, 267; Sarnath, **3.3, 3.6**, 33, 36, 39-44, 108, 152, 155, 275-279, 281; sources, 43-45, 116, 154; symbolisms, 41-44; Taxila, 50, 115; Udaigiri-Vidisa, 38, 40, 42; Vaishali, **3.1, 3.4**, 28, 36, 39-42, 44
Asoka pillar edicts, 28, 30-36, 38-39, 41-44, 50, 115, 152, 155, 275, 277, 279; Schism Edict, 39, 152, 155, 277
Assyria(n), arts and architecture, 40, 55, 243
asura, 138-139
atman, 15-18
Aurangzeb, Emperor, 122
Avalokitesvara, 22-23, 25-26, 58, 66, 76, 82-84, 87, 95, 134-135, 138-139, 194, 200, 206, 215-216, 222, 227, 232, 240, 244-245, 258, 261; Lokesvara, 26, 82, 85-86, 95, 258, 261, 263-265; Padmapani, 26, 73
avasa, 47-48
ayaka, 162-163, 165-166, 190, 207
ayaka stambha, 76, 162-166; symbolism, 165-166, 176
Aymonier, 257

Bactria, 20, 44, 115-118; Dilberjin, 116; Fullol, 116; Surkh Kotal, 116, 258. Also Ai-khanum
Bactria, Buddhist sites, 116
Bagan, arts, 206, 227, 252, 254
Bagan, architecture, 28, 73, 120, 205-210, 212-213, 230, 232-233, 235, 246, 248, 251-255, and world architecture, 207-208; structural system, 207-208, 252; types of temples, 252; types of *zedi*s, 208. Also Ananda Temple; Shwedagon; Shwezigon; *zedi*
bahal, 217
bahil, 217
Bairat Temple, **7.1**, 55, 100, 140, 192, 207, 234, 236-237
Bakhtiyar Khalji, 60, 71
Bamiyan caves, **5.14-5.17**, 46, 52, 96, 115-117, 120-129, 131-132, 134-135, 139, 218, 230; Cave #733 (XV), 125-127, 132; construction technique, 122-123; East Buddha, 117, 122-125, 127; East Buddha Cave (#155), 117, 122-124, 126; features, 121-122; *Parinirvana* Buddha, 123-125; pilgrim accounts, 123; sources, 121,

125; types, 120-121; West Buddha, 122-126; West Buddha Cave (#620), 122-123, 126
Bandaranayake, Senake, 76-77, 192
Banerjee, R. D., 72
Bangladesh, 4, 46, 60, 70-73, 87, 98, 216, 251, 255, 279; Buddhism, 70-71. Also Bengal
Bangladesh, dynasties and periods, 70-71. Also Chronology
Bangladesh, monasteries, 70-74. Also Somapura
Barabar caves, 29-30, 32, 35, 40, 42, 44-45, 49, 102-105; inscriptions, 35, 102. Also Lomas Risi
Barrett, Douglas, 163, 166-167
Barua, B. M., 33, 142-143, 156-161, 242
Bayon Temple, **7.16-7.18**, 73-74, 87, 119, 176, 179, 233, 248, 251, 255-266; symbolisms, 264-265; Zhou Daquan's account, 265-266. Also Angkor Thom
Beglar, J. D., 239-240, 247
Bela, Szechenyi, 130
Bellew, H. W., 56
Bena ka Garh, Raja, 170
Bengal, 26, 28, 30, 59-60, 70-71, 74, 217, 223; Buddhism, 60, 70-71; West Bengal, 70
Bengal, monasteries, 70-72, 74; Varaha, 70, 103
Benisti, Mireile, 142, 166
Bhagavan, 16, 22
Bhaja caves, **5.4-5.6**, 46, 58, 99-101, 104, 105-108, 114, 125, 152, 176, 272; Cave #12, 105-107, 272; Cave #22, 106-108
bhakti, 248
Bhalloka, Rajaharsa, 223
Bhamala Stupa, **6.17**, 54, 57, 74, 178-180, 185, 205
Bhandarkar, D. R., 72
Bharhut Stupa, **6.6-6.8, 7.6, Backcover**, 29, 49, 75-76, 98, 103, 105, 107-108, 128, 141, 144, 147, 149-169, 173-175, 199, 205; symbolisms, 158-159
bhojanasala, 77
Bhrkuti, Princess, 214, 224, 226
bhumi, 140, 202
bhumisparsa-mudra, 25-26, 139, 171, 199-200, 206, 240, 284
Bhutan, 89-90, 193, 224; Buddhism, 89, 193, 224
Bhutan, dynasties and periods: see Chronology
Bihar, 16, 19, 26, 28, 32, 36, 47, 55, 59-60, 63, 70-72, 97-99, 102-105, 161-162, 228, 234-235, 271; Arrow Spring, 271, 145-146; Barabar hills, 30, 32, 35, 40, 42, 44-45, 49, 102; Gaya, 40, 98, 102-103, 238, 240, 242, 271; Nagarjuni hills, 49, 102; Nalanda, 59, 61-62; Pataliputra (Patna), 19, 30, 41-42, 44, 242; Piprahwa-Ganwaria, 143-146, 150; Rajagriha (Rajir), 19, 40, 47-49, 59, 98, 102, 143, 146, 168, 229, 267; Vaishali, 19, 28, 36, 46, 48, 143-144, 170, 213, 229, 267. Also Bodhgaya

Bihar, rock-hewn caves, 98, 102. Also Barabar, Nagajuni, Rajir caves
Bodhgaya, **7.6-7.11, 8.3-8.4, Frontcover**, 16, 31, 40-41, 75, 139-140, 210, 229, 235-236, 238, 267-268, 270-275, 281-282, 285; pilgrims' accounts, 273-275; zones, 240, 271. Also Mahabodhi Temple
Bodhi, 16, 139. Also Enlightenment
Bodhicitta, 24
bodhigriha, 76-77, 80, 235-236, 240-242, 247-248, 269, 278
bodhi-tree, 16, 64, 75-77, 80, 152, 160, 166-167, 189, 233-235, 238-248, 271, 272-275
bodhisattva, 21-26, 76, 95, 101, 114, 140-141, 155-156, 160, 178, 180, 187, 200, 202, 215-216, 222, 227, 234-235, 248-249, 258-259, 265
bodhisattva(s), Mahayana, 25-26, 129, 134-135, 138-141, 200, 216, 222, 227, 258, 265; Manjusri (Monju), 25, 73, 94-96, 134, 138-139, 186, 194, 200, 216, 220, 222, 227, 240, 249; Samantabhadra, 25, 138, 199-200, 203, 232; Vajrapani, 25, 62, 114, 194, 216, 222, 227, 232, 261, 286; Vimalakirti (Yuima), 138, 186. Also Avalokitesvara
bodhisattva(s), pensive, 137
bodhisattva(s), Vajra, 25
Boisselier, Jean, 257
Bon (Bonpo), 22, 224-226
Borobudur, **6.28-6.32**, 74, 140-141, 171-179, 193, 195-205, 210, 212-213, 222, 224, 232, 248-251, 254-255, 264, 266; architectural peculiarities, 204; construction theories, 201; symbolisms, 201-203
Bosch, F. D. K., 249-250
Bouillevaux, Charles, 256
Brahman, 15-18
Brahmanism, 26, 32-33
Brahmana, 15, 62
Brahmi, 70, 75-76, 88, 112, 144-145, 148, 155, 157, 159, 161, 169, 240, 255; Asoka edicts, 31, 34-36, 41, 152, 162, 166
brahmin, 14, 73, 128, 143, 153-154, 245, 255-257
Britain, 52, 130, 148, 159, 247; Stonehenge, 159
British (Brit), 36, 52, 59, 110, 118-119, 147-148, 162, 196, 206, 210, 230, 239-240
Broadley, A. M., 59, 64
Brown, Percy, 4, 57, 163-164, 236, 243
Buddha, aniconic symbols, 105, 152-153, 160, 162, 165-167, 221-222, 233, 235; *Buddhapada*, 152, 160, 167, 235; *bodhi*-tree, 152, 160, 166-167, 234-235; *dharma-cakra*, 39-40, 42-43, 105, 108, 152, 160, 166-167, 235, 174, 277; flaming pillar, 167, 235; *stupa*, 152, 160, 165-166, 235; *swastika*, 162; *triratna*, 105, 149, 152-

153, 160, 167; *vajrasana*, 152, 160, 233-235, 241-242
Buddha, founder of Buddhism, 4, 14-26, 28, 31-35, 39, 41-43, 46-48, 50, 54, 57, 59-61, 70, 73, 75, 102, 140, 142-148, 150, 153, 155, 160, 168-170, 173, 213, 215, 235, 238-240; Bodhisattva, 159; Siddhartha Gautama, 144, 199, 238; Sakyamuni, 16, 34, 39, 132, 140, 210, 213; Tathagata, 16. Also Four Holiest Pilgrimage Sites
Buddha, Life Scenes, 57, 62, 83, 87, 95-96, 167, 203, 210
Buddha, Future: see Maitreya
Buddha's begging bowl, 75, 140, 170, 234
Buddha's disciples; Ananda, 19, 267; Angulimala, 50; Ajnata-Kaundinya (Annata-Kondanna), 16, 48, 143, 274, 281; Devadatta, 48, 168; Dhaniya, 48; Mahakassapa (Kasyapa), 19, 274-275, 286; Maudgalyayana (Moggallana), 42, 48, 59 , 143, 147-148, 155; Sariputra (Sariputta), 42, 48, 59, 143, 147-148, 155; Subhadda, 181; Upali, 19, 59
Buddha's lay devotees; Anathapindika, 47; King Bimbisara, 47-48, 50; Chunda, 286; Ghosita, 47; Jivaka, 47-48, 50; King Prasenajit (Pasenadi), 50; Pavarika, 59
Buddha's teachings, 16-18, 280; Dharmacakrapravartana-sutra (first sermon), 14, 16, 18, 43, 46, 267, 275-278, 280-281
Buddhas, Mahayana, 22; Bhaishajyaguru (Medicine Buddha), 261; Dipankara, 123, 232; Jayabuddhamahanatha, 265; Prabhutaratna, 131, 134. Also Amitabha Buddha
Buddhas, Theravada; Emaciated, 274; Jobo Sakyamuni, 224-226; Muchilinda, 261, 263, 265, 274; *Parinirvana*, 123-125, 131, 282, 285; Pratyeka (Pacceka), 143, 275, 285. Also Buddha, founder of Buddhism; Eight Manusi Buddhas; Maitreya, Future Buddha
Buddhas, Vajrayana, 25-26; Aksobhyavajra, 224-226; Amoghasiddhi, 25, 95, 199, 220-222; Adi-Buddha, 25-26, 203, 220, 222-223, 232; Aksobhya, 25-26, 95, 199-200, 203, 220-222, 250; Jina/Dhyani Buddhas, 165-166, 203, 219-224, 227, 232; Mahavairocana, 25-26, 203; Ratnasambhava, 25, 95, 199, 220-222; Vairocana, 24-245, 67, 94-96, 124, 200, 203, 220-223, 232. Also Vajrayana, arts and iconography
Buddhabhadra, 65, 242
Buddhapada: see Buddha, aniconic symbols
Buddharaja, 82-83, 258, 264-265
Buddhism, 4, 14-27; and Hinduism, 14-16, 32-33; schism, 19-20; councils, 18-20, 31, 51, 53, 59, 75, 115, 140, 147-148, 205, Also Asoka pillar edicts, Schism Edict; Buddha's teachings, Theravada School, Mahayana School, Vajrayana School; Tantric; *Triratna*
Buddhist architecture, criteria, 28-29
Buddhist missionaries, 20, 47, 51, 59, 66, 75-76, 81, 88-89, 136, 148, 205, 212, 215, 235, 281

Buddhist pilgrims; Dharmasvamin, 59, 61, 65-66, 238, 274; Fa-hsien, 36, 40, 50-51, 54, 56, 59-60, 70, 75, 117-118, 120, 125, 130, 145-146, 169, 172, 179, 181, 194, 215, 238, 240, 243, 268, 270, 273-275, 280, 282, 286; Hsuan-tsang, 36, 39-40, 50, 54, 56, 59-61, 63-65, 70, 88, 90, 110, 112, 115, 117-118, 120, 122-126, 130, 140, 145-146, 170, 172, 238, 240, 243-247, 268-275, 277, 279-280, 282-284, 286; Hui-chao, 115, 123-125; I-tsing, 57, 59-61, 63-65, 70, 82, 100, 112, 194, 238, 274, 282; Ou-khong, 88; Seng-tsai, 270; Sung-yun, 56, 118, 125, 172, 179-180
Bulandibagh, 40, 44
Bulayas, 143
Burma: see Myanmar
Buston, 214, 226
Butkara I, 53-54, 173-174
bum-pa, 231-232
Burgess, James, 162

caitya, 64, 66, 142, 173, 194, 208, 218, 234, 279; types, 140
caitya, Nepalese, 215, 218-219, 270. Also Swayambhunath
caitya-arch, 84, 101, 103, 106, 109-110, 113, 234, 237
caityagriha, 4, 29, 55, 58, 97, 100-101, 104, 108-109, 112, 114, 127-128, 131, 135, 139, 176, 187, 235-236
cakravartin, 43-44, 143, 256-257
Cambodia: see Kampuchea
candi, 84, 87, 140, 194-196, 248, 252, 260; and *stupa*s, 196; construction, 196; symbolisms, 196; types, 195
Candi Sewu, **7.12-7.13**, 74, 81, 87, 119, 176,179, 193, 195-196, 204-205, 233, 248-251, 255, 264, 266, 279; symbolisms, 249-251
cankamanasala, 48
Cao Yijin, 129, 134
Cao Yuanzhong, 134
Carlleyle, A. C. L., 282, 285
Central Asia, arts and architecture, 97, 117, 121, 135, 137, 230; Buddhism, 4, 26, 115-117
Central Asia, dynasties and periods, 115, 117-118, 224. Also Chronology
Central Asian Style, Buddhist paintings, 133-134
Central Asia Style, non-Buddhist paintings: see Sogdian School
Chai Jung, 69, 183-184
Champa, 46, 73, 80-87, 169, 181, 192, 194-195, 206-207, 215, 255-258, 260; and India, 80-82; arts and architecture, 83-85, 207; Buddhism, 82-83. Also Indrapura Monastery; *kalan*
Champa, Buddhist sites, 85. Also Indrapura Monastery
Champa, dynasties and periods, 81-82. Also Chronology

Champa, Hindu sites, 83-85; Mi-Son, 81-83, 85, 87, 196, 257, 260. Also *kalan*
Champa, kings, 81-87, 255, 257
Chandra, G. C., 59, 72
Chandra, Lokesh, 124
chandrasila, 101
chattravali, 73, 142, 188-190, 192, 198, 200, 208, 210, 218-219, 222, 231-232, 255
chedei, 194, 205, 208, 261
chedi, 140, 194, 208
chedi-tong, 196
Chihara, Daigoro, 201-202, 204, 266
China, 4, 20, 46, 51, 69, 94, 97, 117-121, 126-137, 139, 172, 181-183, 185-188, 194, 205, 208, 215, 217, 220, 224-228, 231-232, 248, 255, 258; arts and architecture, 182-189; Buddhism, 4, 129-130, 181-182, 258; 'Record of the Three Kingdoms,' 183; Silk Road, 97, 115, 118-120, 126, 129, 181, 193; Xinjiang: see Turkistan; Xizang: see Tibet. Also Mogao caves; Songyue
China, Buddhist paintings: see Chinese Style
China, dynasties and periods, 45, 66-67, 118, 129-131, 135-136, 181-183, 185-186, 194, 239; Han, 117, 121, 129, 135-137, 181, 183-187; Northern Wei, 66, 69, 118, 129, 131, 134-135, 137, 181-182, 186-187; Tang, 66, 69, 118, 129-131, 134-137, 139, 181, 183, 185-186, 218, 225; Yuan, 129, 217, 228, 265. Also Chronology
China, emperors; Empress Wu, 130; Kubilai Khan: see Mongolia, kings; Mingdi, 181; Qin-shih-huang, 182; Wudi, 129, 135; Xuanzong, 183; Yongle, 239
China, Han pottery models, **6.19**, 183-184; and timber pagoda, 185-186
China, monasteries, 69, 181-183, 187
China and East Asia, pagoda, 28, 66-70, 80, 87, 121, 131, 137, 139-141, 171, 179-181, 183-189, 208, 213, 217-218, 233, 238; and cave, votive pagodas **6.22-6.23**, 128, 131, 135, 187; and Cham *stupa*s, 87; and Gandhara *stupa*s, 141, 180, 183, 186-187, 189; and Han pottery models, 185-186; and Indian *sikhara*, 188-189; and Nepalese *dega*, 217-218; timber, 183-186; masonry, 186-189; Great Wild Goose, 69; Jiangsu, 69, 183; Sakya, 185; Yongningsi, 187. Also Horyuji, Songyue pagodas
China, rock-hewn caves, 128-135, 182; Binglingsi, 97, 128, 182; Longmen, 128, 139; Maijishan, 128, 182; Yungang, 69, 124-125, 127-128, 135, 182, 186-187. Also Mogao
China, tombs; Gao Yi, 187; Han, 121, 183; Mawangdui, 136, 182; Xiao Jing, 45
Chinese Style, Buddhist paintings, 69, 131, 133-134, 136
chorten, 96, 140-141, 208, 219, 222, 224, 228-230; types, 229-230. Also Kumbum

chos-skyong, 25, 227
Christianity, 4, 117-118, 121, 176, 193
Christian churches, 4, 55, 117-118, 121, 208, 243; and Buddhist architecture, 4, 55, 121, 208, 243
chunam, 243
Chunar, 38, 174
clec, 252, 254
Coedes, George, 255-258, 261, 265
coins, 51, 53, 60, 64, 70, 145-146, 155, 167, 172, 176-178, 230, 242, 273, 284
Cole, Major, 148, 150, 153
Confucianism, 21, 181-182
Coomaraswamy, Ananda K., 235, 241
Coral-Remusat, Gilbert de, 257
Cornelius, H. C., 196, 248
Cousens, Henry, 108
Crompton, Lieutenant, 56
Cunningham, Alexander, 52, 56-57, 59, 72, 147-148, 156, 158-161, 169, 238-242, 245-247, 271-276, 282
Cyrene (Libya), 20

dagaba, 73, 75-76, 140, 183, 189-190. Also Sri Lanka, *dagaba*s; Thuparama
Dales, George, 9
Daoism, 21, 130, 134, 181-182; gods, 134
De Cadpari, 201
Deccan, 25, 29-30, 45, 53, 97-99, 101-102, 149, 162, 169, 203, 232, 234, 236
Deccan, Buddhist rock-hewn caves, 29-30, 45, 53, 97-99, 102-104, 149, 162, 169, 234, 236; Bedsa, 99, 101, 108; Jivadan-Virar, 99, 104; Kanheri, 99, 101, 104, 108-109, 121; Kondane, 99, 108; Junnar-Tuljalena, 99-100, 104, 237; Nasik, 98-99, 101, 108, 162; Pitalkhora, 99-101, 103, 108. Also Ajanta, Bhaja, Elora, Karla, Kondivte caves; rock-hewn caves, Indian Buddhist
dega, 217-218, 229, and pagoda, 217-218; and *meru*, 218
Delaporte, Louis, 257
Desid, 230
deva, 138, 234
devapala, 209, 221
devaraja cult, 202, 256-258, 260, 265
devata, 234
devi(s), Goddesses of Offering, 25
Dhamaraksa, 129
dharani, 23
Dharma. Also Buddha's teachings
dharmacakra, 39-40, 42-43, 108, 174, 277; and Indian Flag, 44, 277; symbolisms, 43-44, 174. Also Buddha, aniconic symbols
dharmacakrapravatana-mudra, 25, 199-200
dharmacakravartin, 174

Dharmagupta, 130
Dharmakirti, 162
Dharmaksema, 130
Dharmamitra, 130
Dharma Man Tuladhar, Lama, 224
Dharmananda, 224, 284
dharmapala, 25, 95, 138, 227
Dharmapala, Anagarika, 239-240, 281
dharmaraja, 196
dharmarajika, 173, 279
Dharmarajika Stupa, India: see India, Buddhist *stupa*s
Dharmarajika Stupa, Pakistan, **6.13**, 46, 53-54, 57, 74, 77, 133, 165, 173-174, 178, 223, 279, 285
Dharmaratna, 181
dharmavijaya, 31, 36, 44
dhyana-mudra, 25, 76, 199, 206, 284
Dikshit, K. N., 72
Dongyang, Prince, 134
Dong-duong Monastery: see Indrapura Monastery
Drona, Brahmin, 128, 143, 153-154
Dubreuil, Jouveau, 163, 165-166
Dumarcay, Jacques, 201, 204, 249
Duncan, Jonathan, 176
dukhang, 91, 95, 229
durbar, 214, 217
Duroiselle, Charles, 254
dvarapala, 69, 83, 86-87, 106, 131, 135, 167, 203
Dvaravati, 84, 176, 205, 258, 260

East Asia, 27, 51, 58, 67, 70, 97, 140, 167, 171-172, 181, 187, 193, 224
East Turkistan: see Turkistan
Eckardt, Andreas, 137
Egypt, 6-8, 20, 44
Eight Manusi Buddhas, 134, 153, 159, 165-166, 209-211, 254, 280; Kasyapa, 165, 209-210, 254, 273; Konakamuni, 35, 38, 157, 254, 267; Krakucchanda, 39, 145-146, 165; Vipasyin, 220. Also Buddha, founder of Buddhism; Maitreya
Eight Secondary Pilgrimage Sites, 267; Rajagriha: see Bihar, Rajagriha; Sankisa: see Asoka pillars; Sravasti: see Uttar Pradesh; Vaishali: see Asoka pillars, Bihar. Also Four Holiest Pilgrimage Sites
Eight Events, 229; Descent from the Trayastrimsa Heaven, 267; Miracle of Sravasti, 267; Offering of the Monkey, 267; Taming the Nalagiri Elephant, 87, 168, 267. Also Four Events
Elam, 7
Elamite, 7
Elliot, Walter, 162
Elora, 95-101, 139, 203, 224, 232

Ephthalites: see Hephthalites
Epirus, 20
Era; Azes, 58; Common, 53, 58, 101, 115, 117; Kanishka, 278; Nepal/Newar, 214; Saka, 214, 256
Erp, Thadedus van, 197
Esoteric Buddhism: see Vajrayana School
esvara, 215, 257
European, 56, 59, 118-119, 130, 183, 200, 248, 256

Faccenna, Domenico, 52, 174, 176
Fairservis, Walter, 7
Fell, Captain, 147
Ferghana, 118
Fergusson, James, 4, 101, 104, 107, 165, 234
Finot, Louis, 255, 257
Fisher, Robert E., 4
five sciences, 61
Foucher, Alfred, 43, 52, 149, 161
Four Events, Life Scenes, 43, 57, 62, 83, 87, 95-96, 149, 153, 167, 203, 210. Also Eight Events
Four Holiest Pilgrimage Sites, 267. Also Lumbini, Bodhgaya, Sarnath, Kushinagar; Eight Secondary Pilgrimage Sites
Four Signs of Suffering, 16, 199
France, 52, 84, 130, 238, 256; EFEO, 257; Napoleon III, Emperor, 148
Fraser, Major, 211
Frederic, Louis, 199, 201-202
French, 52, 56, 85, 119, 122, 148, 256-257
Funan, 81, 255-261; architecture, 257, 259, 261; K'ang T'ai's account, 255-256; Oc-eo, 255, 257, 259-260; Princess Kambujarajalakshmi, 256; Queen Kulaprabhavati, 257, 259
Funan, kings; Chan-t'an, 257; Kaundinya (Chiao Chen-ju), 257; Kaundinya, Brahmin, 255; Fan Man (Fan Shih-man), 255; Gunavarman, 257; Jayavarman, 257, 259; Rudravarman, 256, 258, 261
Fuhrer, A., 268
Furuzawa, Y., 197

Gandhara, 20, 33, 48, 50-52, 99, 116-117, 161; architecture, 4, 46-55, 57-59, 66, 69-70, 72-74, 77, 109, 117, 120, 124, 140-142, 162, 165, 171-181, 192, 222, 235, 242-243, 248; arts, 25, 51-52, 55, 57-58, 115-117, 137, 166-167, 229-230; Gandhara Style, 51-52, 54, 122, 216; Buddhism, 4, 20, 34, 50-55, 59, 115, 125, 162, 273. Also Pakistan
gandharva, 138
Ganga (Ganges) Civilization, 13; River, 16, 30, 70, 142, 255, 276, 279-280
garuda, 38, 48, 138, 216, 221

Germans, 119, 126, 137, 248
ghanta, 23, 25-26, 222
Ghosh, Amalananda, 59, 64
Gijjhakuta (Vulture Peak), 47-48, 139
Giteau, Madeleine, 257
Glaize, Maurice, 257
gompa, 90, 228
gopura, 86-87, 280
Gosain Ghamandi Giri, 239
Gottsche, 137
Grantha script, 193
Greco-Roman, 52-53, 57-58, 115-116, 167, 172, 175-178
Greece, 44
Greek(s), 20, 30, 35, 40-41, 44-45, 50-53, 94, 99, 108, 115-117, 154-155, 236; language: Asoka edicts, 34, 50, 115. Also *Yavana*
Greek, arts and architecture, 40, 44-45, 50-52, 154-155; and Indian arts and architecture, 40, 44, 50, 52-53, 94, 115-116, 154-155, 236; Corinthian, 44, 51, 57, 172, 174-178; Doric, 44; Ionic, 44, 51-53, 94, 96, 172, 176. Also Ai-khanum
Greek(s), Asian/Bactrian, 50-53, 108, 116, 154-155; Hermaeus, 51; Menander (Milinda), 51
Groslier, George, 257
Grunwedel, Albert, 118, 127
Guge, 25, 88-91, 97, 99, 225, 227, 229, 269; second transmission, 88-89, 225, 229
Guge, kings; Tashi-gon, 88; Yeshe-O (Khor-re), 25, 88-89, 91, 225
Guge, monasteries; Tholing, 88-89, 91
guha, 48, 100
gujar, 217, 222, 224, 231-232
Gunabhadra, 130
Gunaratna, 258
Gupta kings, 60, 63-64; Baladitya, 60, 63-64, 245; Bhanugupta, 125; Jayagupta, 284; Kumaragupta I, 60, 63-64, 284; Sakraditya, 60, 63-65; Samudragupta, 62, 274
Gupta Style, sculptures, 73, 76, 168-169, 194, 216, 249, 258-259, 280; Gupta-Mathura, 125; Gupta-Sarnath, 62, 71, 84, 113, 260, 277; *Parinirvana* Buddha, 282, 285
Gupta, S. P., 41
Gutschow, Niels, 218-219, 223
gyalpo, 88
Gyantse Monastery, 228, 239. Also Kumbum

Hadda, 115-116, 124
halapau, 219, 222, 224
Hamilton, Francis Buchanan, 59, 72, 239, 282
hammiya, 48, 240
Harappa(n), 6-13, 34, 44, 55, 75, 235. Also Indus Civilization
Hargreaves, H., 57, 276
Haribala, 283-285
Harle, James, 4
harmika, 53, 64, 73, 104, 106, 141-142, 144, 147, 149-150, 152, 156, 158, 163, 166, 171-175, 177, 186, 189-190, 200, 207-208, 210, 212-213, 218-219, 221-224, 230-232, 266, 272, 278, 284
Harrer, Heinrich, 225
Harvard University, 130
Hedin, Sven, 118
Hephthalites, 54, 56, 63, 115, 124, 275
Hephthalites, kings; Miharakula, 54, 125, 238, 245, 276; Toramana, 125
Himalaya, 20, 27, 30, 87-96, 145, 193, 213, 224, 228, 232, 254, 274; Buddhism, 20, 27, 88-89, 193, 224. Also Alchi; Ladakh; Zanskar; Lahaul; Spiti; Kinnaur
Himalaya, arts and architecture, 88-97, 145, 228, 232; and Tibetan architecture, 90, 228, 230, 232. Also Ladakh; Alchi
Himavanta, 20, 88
Hinayana, 21, 123, 281. Also Theravada School
Hindu; dynasties, 52, 70-71, 115-116; Mahant, 239-240, 274
Hindu, arts and architecture, 4, 28, 49, 61-62, 73, 81, 83-84, 87, 98-99, 104, 118-119, 134, 138, 160, 162, 167, 176, 180, 189, 192-196, 201-202, 206-208, 214, 216-217, 233-234, 236-237, 245-248, 251-252, 254-255, 257, 259-260, 263-266, 269, 278. Also *sikhara*
Hindu, gods, 51, 134, 138, 160, 195-196, 215, 270; Agni, 14, 73, 158, 234; Brahma, 14, 82, 134, 138, 160, 195, 273; Durga, 189, 215; Ganesh, 73, 134, 167; Indra (Sakra), 14, 98, 107, 128, 134, 138, 199, 271, 273-274; Katyayani, 102; Krishna, 73, 102; Kumara, 134; Lakshmi/Goja-Lakshmi, 149, 161, 169; Mahadeva, 73; Mahesvara, 216, 257; Nandi, Siva's vehicle, 73; Narayana, 215; Parvati, 116, 216; Rama, 160, 213; Rupadevi, 270; Sita, 160, 213; Siva, 38, 62, 73, 81-82, 84-85, 87, 116, 118, 134, 195, 216, 218, 239, 255, 257, 259-260, 265; Surya, 14-15, 70, 107, 134, 234; Uma, 216, 259; Varuna, 14; Visnu, 14-15, 38, 60, 70, 73, 82-83, 134, 167, 195, 206, 215-216, 226, 239, 255, 257, 259-260; Yama, 14
Hinduism, 8, 13-14, 23, 26, 38, 43, 51, 58, 60, 70, 73, 81-83, 98, 116-118, 142, 193-194, 201, 206, 210, 214-215, 234, 248, 256-259; caste, 14-15, 26, 33, 215, 257; Sankhya, 61; Sivaism, 82, 215, 257; Vedic, 14, 23, 26, 43, 142, 234; Visnuism, 215, 257. Also Tantric, Hinduism
Hiranyadama, priest, 257
Hoenig, A., 201

Hongbian, 130
Horyuji, monastery, **4.5-4.7**, 46, 66-70, 80, 185-186
Horyuji, pagoda, **6.20-6.21**, 179, 184-186
Hungarian, 118
Huns, 117-118, 129; King Hunimanta, 238, 243; White: see Hephthalites
Huntington, Susan, 4, 61

Iconic, arts and architecture, Phase, 4, 97-101, 104, 108, 110, 112, 233-236, 242-266
Ievers, 77
Ijzerman, J. W., 196
India, 4, 7-9, 14-16, 19-22, 28, 30-31, 35-36, 40, 44-45, 50-51, 58-60, 63-64, 70-71, 90, 97-99, 102, 108, 110, 115-116, 143-148, 161-163, 167, 170-171, 238-240, 267-268, 272-277, 281-282; Buddhism, 4, 15-27, 30-48, 58-61, 98-100, 108-112, 140-141, 143, 146-148, 150, 153, 155-156, 161-163, 168-170, 235, 238-240, 267-268, 271-277, 281-284; Aihole, 189, 237; Gujarat, 6-7, 20, 51, 57, 115, 200; Haryana, 6; Himachal Pradesh, 88, 90, 217; Jambudvipa, 92, 108, 179, 202; Karnataka, 20, 217; Kerala, 192, 217; Madhya Pradesh, 36; Maharashtra, 20, 97-98, 111; Mid-India/Middle India, 63-64, 70; Mughal, 90, 217, 277; Punjab, 6; Rajasthan, 6, 51; Vedisa, 147, 151, 154-155. Also Hinduism; Jainism; Buddhist pilgrims; Uttar Pradesh
India, architecture, types, 48
India, Buddhist paintings/murals, 46, 62, 71, 76, 96-99, 100, 112-114, 118, 128, 206, 216, 227-228
India, Buddhist monasteries; Ghositarama, 47, 49; Jagaddala, 59, 71; Jetavanarama, 47-49; Lalitagiri, 59, 71; Odantapura, 59-60, 71, 228; Pavarikambavanarama, 59; Pubbarama, 47; Ratnagiri, 59, 71, 83, 119, 207; types, 46; Udayagiri, 59, 71, 83, 99; Valabhi, 59; Vikramasila, 59-60, 71-72, 89, 119, 215, 225. Also Jivakavanarama; Nalanda; Veluvanarama
India, Buddhist *stupa*s; and Asian *stupa*s, 75, 140-142, 144, 172-173, 176, 207-208, 210, 212-213, 223-224, 230, 234; Andher, 20, 147-148; Bhattiprolu, 162; Bhojur, 147; components, 141-142; Cremation/Makutabandhana, **8.10**, 283-286; Devnimori, 57, 200; Dharmarajika, 140, 275-281, 285; Dhamekh, **8.6**, 207-208, 224, 276-277, 279-281, 284; Ghantasala, 238; Jaggayyapeta, 162; Konakamuni, 35, 38, 157, 267; Krakucchanda, 145-146; Lauriya-Nandangargh, 158; Mathura, 109, 149-150, 165, 171, 176, 200; Nagarjunakonda, 53, 70, 96, 121, 162, 165, 167-169, 174, 259; Nirvana, **8.8-8.9**, 282-286; Old School, 169; origins, 142; reliefs of, 156, 163, 171, 176; Satdhara, 147; Sonari, 20, 147-148; theories of symbolisms, 158-159; *vedika*s, 149-150. Also Amaravati, Bharhut, Kesariya, Piprahwa, Sanchi; *stupa*; *stupa*, earliest; *stupa*, types
India, Buddhist temples, 4, 46, 189, 195, 207, 233-248; Chezarla, 237, 239; Mayadevi Temple, 267-270, 285; Nagarjunakonda, 70, 235; Nirvana, **8.8**, 185, 282-286; reliefs of temples, **7.4-7.6, 7.9**; Sanchi Temple 17, 234, 236; Sanchi Temple 40, 147, 235, 237, 278, 285; Sarnath, 74, 234, 245, 248, 251-252, 276-281, 285; types, 233, 235-236. Also Bairat; *caitya*; Mahabodhi Temple; *stupa*-temple; Ter Temple
India, Buddhist temples, Aniconic, 233-242. Also Aniconic; *bodhigriha*; *caityagriha*
India, Buddhist temples, Iconic, 242-248. Also *caitya*; Iconic; *pratimagriha*
India, dynasties and periods, 14-15, 30-31, 51, 58, 60, 63-64, 70-71, 90, 98, 108, 110, 112, 145-146, 162, 167, 238-240, 267-268, 276-277, 282; Epic, 14-15, 142; Gupta, 38, 40, 60, 63-64, 70, 150, 155, 168, 274; Maurya, 9, 19, 30, 35-36, 41, 50, 70, 98, 102-103; Mughal, 90, 217, 277; Pala, 28, 59-60, 62, 64, 71, 74, 98, 194, 206, 227, 270, 276, 280; Pallava, 80, 84, 194-195, 206; Sasanka, 70, 238, 245; Shunga, 51, 98, 150, 157, 282; Vakataka, 76, 98, 110, 112, 169; Vedic, 14, 30, 142, 145-146, 234. Also Chronology
India, early republics and tribes; Anga, 70; Buliya, 143; Koliya, 16, 143, 213, 267, 271; Kosala, 15, 50, 145-146; Licchavi, 143, 146, 170, 213-219, 221-222, 229, 261; Magadha, 15, 30, 47-48, 50, 70, 98, 143, 145; Malla, 143, 153-154, 213, 215; Moriya, 143, 213; Sakya, 15-16, 39, 144-146, 213, 267-268, 271; Vajji Federation, 213-214
India, Hindu caves, 98-99
India, Hindu temples, 61, 162, 189, 192-193, 195, 207, 234, 236-237, 252; Aihole, 189, 237; Bhirtagaon, 84, 195, 207, 243, 245-246, 278; Deogarh, 83-84; Dravida, 233, 248, 251; Durga, 189, 215; Irinnalakuda, 192; Kailasha Temple, 98; Khajuraho, 266; Mamallapuram, 49, 80, 84, 87, 98, 195, 208, 237, 252; Nagara, 189, 233, 248, 252, 255, 260, 266, 269; Temple 2, 61-62. Also *ratha*; *sikhara*; *srikoil*
India, Jain architecture, 4, 28, 32, 61, 73-74, 98, 104, 150, 234; *stupa*s, 150
India, kings; Ajatasatru, 143, 146; Akbar, 39, 277; Asvaghosa, 278; Bimbisara, 47, 48, 50; Bindusara, 30; Chandragupta, 30, 41; Chagalaraja, 60; Dalhanemi, 43; Dasaratha, 98-99, 102, 104; Dhanabhuti, 157, 161; Govindachandra, 279; Harisena, 110; Harshavardhana (Harsha), 63-64, 70; Janak, 213; Kalasoka, 19; Prasenajit, 50; Purnavarman, 63, 193, 238, 245-246; Pushyamitra, 98; Sasanka, 238, 245; Simhavarman, 169; Sultan Feroz Shah, 38; Vasisthiputra Pulumavi, 108; Virudhaka, 145-146; Yasodharman, 63, 125. Also

Asoka, Emperor; Kushan, Gupta, Pala kings
Indochina, 81, 256
Indo-Kashmiri Style, 92, 94, 96
Indo-Mughal, 217
Indonesia, 4, 81, 83-85, 140-142, 169, 171, 176, 179, 181, 192-205, 208, 215, 218, 224, 248-251; architecture, 140-142, 176, 194-205, 218, 248-251; arts, 194, 203, 250; Buddhism, 64, 194-195, 248
Indonesia, Buddhist *candi*s, 193-195, 201, 204, 233, 248; Banyjunibo, 195; Batujaya, 193-196; Kalasan, 195-196, 204, 251; Mendut, 195-196, 201, 249-251; Ngawen, 195; Pawon, 195, 201; Plaosan, 87, 193, 195-196; Sajiwan, 195; Sari, 87, 195. Also *candi*; Candi Sewu
Indonesia, *candi*s, 195-196; and Asian temples, 195-196, 248. Also *candi*
Indonesia, dynasties and periods, 192-194; Central Javanese, 193-196, 198; East Javanese, 81, 84, 193-196, 201; Kediri, 193, 203, 250; Majapahit, 81, 194; Sailendra, 81, 83, 85, 193, 195, 198, 204; Second Maratam, 81, 193, 195. Also Chronology
Indonesia, Hindu *candi*s, 193-195, 248-249; Loro Jonggrang, 193, 195, 208, 248, 252, 259. Also *candi*
Indonesia, kings; Balaputradeva, 64, 194; Mulavarman, 193; Pikatan, 193; Purnavarman 193
Indonesia, monasteries, 196
Indonesia, *stupa-candi*s, 196; Maligai, 196; Sunberawan, 196. Also Borobudur
Indra (Sakra); and Pancasika, 128; Heaven (Abode) of the Thiry Three Gods, 264; Mount Meru Paradise, 153; Trayastrimsa (Tavatimsa), 229, 267
Indrapura Monastery, **4.11-4.12**, 46, 73, 80-87, 258
Indus Civilization, 4, 6-14, 36, 45, 50, 58, 110, 116, 155; and Near East, 7-8; and Hinduism, 13-14; architecture, 11-13; reasons for decline, 9; script, 6-7, 75; urban planning, 9-11. Also Harappa Civilization
Indus Civilization, sites, 6-8. Also Harappa; Mohenjodaro
Iran, 7, 51, 116, 119-121, 125, 255; God Rustam, 118; Iranian, 51, 54, 115-116, 118, 121, 123, 125; Parthia, 118; Parthian; 52, 58, 118; Sassanian, 51, 115-116, 121, 125, 230. Also Manichaeanism; Persia; Zoroastrianism
Iran, arts and architecture; Firuzabad Palace, 121; aivan, 117; Sassanian Style, painting, 116, 124; Yahya-tepe, 7
Iran, dynasties and periods; Achaemenid, 35, 50; Parthian, 52; Sassanid, 51, 54. Also Persia
Iran, kings; Artaxerxes, 44; Darius, 35-36, 44; Gondophares, 58; Shapur I, 51; Shapur II, 51
Islam, 4, 26, 52, 55, 71, 89, 115-119, 122, 130, 176, 194, 217, 223, 243; Muslim, 4, 50, 52, 60, 71, 115, 119, 122, 124, 128, 238, 268, 276-277, 279, 282
Islam, architecture; and Buddhist architecture, 4, 55, 176, 243; mosque, 4, 90, 176; Taj Mahal, 176
istadevata, 25, 227
Italians, 52, 54, 174, 214
Iwamoto, Y., 201

Jagatganj Mahalla, 276
Jain, 3, 28, 32, 59, 61-62, 73-74, 98, 104, 150, 234. Also India, Jain architecture
Jainism, 15, 51, 70, 102; founder Nigantha Nataputtra or Mahavira, 32, 102
Jammu-and-Kashmir, 90
jantagriha, 48
Japan, 46, 66-69, 75, 94, 118, 120-122, 130, 136-137, 145, 183, 179, 181, 184-186, 198, 203, 217, 251, 268; arts and architecture, 65-66; Buddhism, 66-69; Nara, 7, 66, 69, 184; Shinto, 66
Japan, dynasties and periods, 66, 69. Also Chronology
Japan, kings; Shomu, 67
Japan, monasteries, 67-69; and continental monastery, 69. Also Horyuji, monastery
Japan, pagoda, 69, 183, 185-186, 217; and continental pagoda, 69. Also Horyuji, pagoda; *to*
JASB, 59, 64
jataka, 21, 31, 57, 62, 66, 107, 128, 141, 149-150, 153, 155, 159-161, 167, 178, 199, 203, 206, 210, 242, 254, 275; Chaddanta, 153; Dipankara, 62; Five Hundred Bandits, 134; Horse-headed Fairy, 153; Kalingabodhi, 140; Mahakapi, 153, 199; Mahasattva, 182; Miga/Ruru, 159, 199; Rishyasringa, 153; Shaddanta, 281; Sibi, 199; Syama, 153; Visvantara, 153, 199
Jaulian Stupa A11, **6.18**, 179-180
Jaulian Stupa A16, **6.16**, 177-178
Jigten Gonpo, 93-94
Jivakavanarama, **4.1**, 46-50, 53, 55, 58, 102, 105, 207, 237
Johnson, Captain, 147

Kalama, 170
kala-makara, 114, 194, 252
kalan, 84-85, 87, 195, 260; and Asian temples, 83-85, 195-196, 207, 260. Also Indrapura Monastery
kalapustaka, 217
kalpa, 165
Kamadhatu: see *Tridhatu*
Kamalavati, 170
Kampuchea, 73-74, 81-85, 87, 119, 151, 169, 176, 181, 193-195, 201-202, 205-207, 215, 233, 248, 251-252, 255-266; Angkor, 81-83, 85, 195, 255-257, 260-261, 265; Angkor Thom, 73-74, 82, 233, 248, 251, 255-261,

263-266; architecture, 73-74, 85, 87, 119, 151, 176, 194-195, 201-202, 205, 207-208, 215, 233, 248, 251-252, 259-266; arts, 83-84, 169, 255, 258-261; Buddhism, 193, 206, 255-258, 260-261; Kandal, 255, 259; K'ang T'ai's account, 255-256; Khmer Empire, 82, 256, 260, 265; Koh Ker, 256; Sambor, 81; Samrong Sen, 255, 259; Vyadhapura, 255; Yasodharapura, 256; Zhou Daquan's account, 265-266. Also *Buddharaja*, *devaraja* cults; Mount Mahendra

Kampuchea, dynasties and periods, 255-257; Angkor, 256-261; Chenla, 81, 256, 259. Also Chronology; Funan, kings

Kampuchea, Buddhist architecture and sites, 251, 261-266; Banteay Chmar, 261, 265; Banteay Kdei, 261; Bat Chum, 261; Neah Pean, 261; Prasat Ta Keam, 258, 261; Preah Khan, 258, 261, 265; Saugatasrama, 261; Ta Prohm, 258, 261, 263; Ta Som, 261. Also Bayon; Funan, architecture

Kampuchea, *chedei*: see *chedei*

Kampuchea, Hindu architecture and sites, 201-202, 205, 215, 248, 251, 259-260; Angkor Wat, 196, 251, 256-257, 259-261, 263-264, 266; Bakong, 201, 205, 260; Baphuon, 259-261; Koh Ker, 256, 259; Phnom Bakheng, 201; Phnom Kulen, 256; Prasat Ak Yom, 260; Prasat Damrei Krap, 83, 260; Prasat Neang Khmau, 260; Prasat Suor Prat, 259; Preah Pithu, 259; Preh Koh, 259; Sambor Prei Kuk, 84, 256-257, 259; Takeo, 257. Also Funan, architecture; Thailand, temples

Kampuchea, kings, 256, 258, 266; Ang Chan, 256; Bhavavarman I, 256; Dharanindravarman II, 258, 261, 265; Indravarman II, 259; Isanavarman, 81, 256-257, 259; Jayarajachudamani, Queen, 258, 265; Jayavarmadiparamesvara, 257; Jayavarman II, 256-257, 266; Jayavarman IV, 256; Jayavarman VI, 258, 261; Jayavarman VII, 82, 85, 256, 258, 260-261, 263-266; Jayavarman VIII, 258-259, 263-264; Mahendravarman, 256; Rajendravarman, 81, 258, 261; Suryavarman I, 258, 261; Suryavarman II, 81, 256-257; Yasovarman I, 256, 258, 261

Kang Senghui, 181

Kanishka (Shah-ji-ki-dheri) Stupa, **6.18**, 51, 53, 55, 140, 172, 178-181

Kapilavastu, 15-16, 143, 145-147, 199, 213, 215, 267-268, 270-271; and Piprahwa-Ganwaria, 145-146; and Tilaurakot, 146-147

kappiyakuti, 48

Karla caves, **5.7-5.9**, 98-100, 108-110, 113-114, 162, 176, 240

karma, 15-16, 18

Kashmir, 19-20, 30, 49-53, 60, 74, 88-90, 95-96; King Lalitaditya, 73. Also Jammu-and-Kashmir

Kashmir, sites, 74

Kashmiri Style: see Indo-Kashmiri Style

Kashmir-Smast, 120

Kasyapa Matanga, 181

kathina, 47-49

Kavindrarimathana, architect, 261

Kazakhstan, 114, 117; Buddhism: see Central Asia, Buddhism

Kazakhstan, Buddhist sites, 117

Kesariya Stupa, **6.12**, 169-171

Kharosthi, 34, 50-51, 58, 88, 115, 161, 174, 242, 256, 273; Asoka edicts, 34, 50, 115

kharuin, 205

Kim Taesong, Prime Minister, 137

kinnara, 138

Kinnaur, 88, 90; Kinnar, 88; Kirata, 88

Kinnaur, kings; Detsu-gon, 88

kirti-mukha, 113, 194

Kittoe, Markham, 40, 59, 102, 171, 276

Kizil caves, **5.18-5.19**, 46, 115, 117, 119-120, 122, 125-129, 131-132, 134-135, 139, 230

Klimburg-Salter, Deborah, 124-125, 230

Knox, Robert, 163

Kondivte caves, **5.3**, 99, 104-106, 108, 114, 176, 236

Konow, Sten, 276

Korea, 66, 69, 97, 115, 121, 123, 126, 128, 135-138, 139, 181, 183, 186; Buddhism, 66, 136-137; architecture, 136-139; arts, 136-137

Korea, dynasties and periods, 135-136; Koguryo, 69, 121, 135-137, 139; Paekche, 66, 69, 135-136, 185; Silla, 69, 136. Also Chronology

Korea, kings; Kyongkok, 137

Korea, pagoda, 69, 183, 185-186; Kumgangsa (Paekche), 69, 185

Korea, monasteries, 69; Hungnyunsa, 136; Hwangnyongsa, 69; Kumgangsa (Koguryo), 69; Kumgangsa (Paekche), 69, 185; Pulguksa, 137; Sumunsa, 136

Korea, rock-hewn caves: see Seokguram

Korea, tombs, 121, 128, 136-137, 139

Korn, Wolfgang, 217

kotthana, 47

Kreitner, Gustav, 130

Ksatrapa Nahapana, 98

ksatriya, 14

Ksetri, Devapala, 219

Krom, N. J., 197

Kumaradevi, Queen, 279-280

Kumarajiva, 118, 129

Kumbum, **6.40-6.41**, 26, 89, 95-96, 141, 205, 208, 222, 224, 228, 230-232

Kumrahar; Hall, 36, 39, 44; plaque, **7.9**, 178, 242-243,

245, 273-274, 278
Kuraishi, M., 59
Kushan(s), 20, 70, 88, 115, 117, 129, 155, 176, 178, 180, 187, 233, 242-243, 245, 247-248, 277, 285; Dynasty, 10, 51, 53, 115-116, 120, 146, 150, 155, 177, 234, 246, 268, 279, 285; Early, 88, 116, 240, 2812; Empire, 51; Later/Kidara, 51, 54, 116-117, 124-125, 176. Also Yueh-chi
Kushan, kings; Huvishka, 176-177, 242; Kanishka (I), 20, 51, 53-55, 88, 116-117, 162, 174, 177, 179-180, 182, 242, 258, 277-278; Kanishka II, 180; Vasudeva I, 54, 176-178
Kushinagar, **8.7-8.10**, 16, 40-41, 128, 140, 143, 153-154, 170, 229, 236, 267, 281-286; pilgrims' accounts, 286
kut, 82
Kyrgyzstan, 114, 117; Buddhism: see Central Asia, Buddhism
Kyrgyzstan, Buddhist sites, 117

Ladakh, 26, 46, 87-94, 97, 121, 126, 206, 213, 227-228, 230, 232; Buddhism: see Himalaya, Buddhism; Dard, 88
Ladakh, *chorten*s; Changspa, 213, 232; Tisseru, 232. Also *chorten*
Ladakh, dynasties and periods, 87-90. Also Chronology
Ladakh, kings; Pelgyi-gon, 88; Sengge Namgyal, 90; Tashi Namgyal, 93
Ladakh, monasteries, 46, 89-92, 94. Also Alchi
Lahaul, 87-88, 90-91; Kirata, 88; Mon, 88
Lahaul, kings; Detsu-gon, 88
Lahaul, monasteries; Gandhola/Guru Ghantal, 91; Keylang, 90-91
Lake Anavatpa, 202
Lake Manasarovar, 202
lama, 89, 225-226, 228
Lamaism, 22, 224. Also Tibet, Buddhism
lantern ceiling, 120-121, 125-127, 131-133, 135, 137, 237
Laos, 194, 205, 208, 213, 256
Laos, *that*, 194, 205, 208; That Laung, 208
Laos, dynasties and periods: see Chronology
Le Coq, Albert von, 118-119, 127
Leitner, Dr., 56
lena, 97, 100-101, 107, 112, 114
Li Junxiu, 130
linga, 62, 81-82, 84-85, 195, 234, 239, 257-258, 265
Litvinsky, Boris, 117
Loczy, Lajos, 130
lohan, 228. Also *arhat*
lokapala, 69, 131, 134-135, 153, 160, 271
Lomas Risi cave, **5.1-5.2**, 29, 45, 49, 98, 101-105, 109, 154, 159; and Deccan *caityagriha*s, 103-104
Loriyan Tangai Stupa, **6.15**, 176-177, 180
Luce, Gordon H., 208, 252, 254
Lumbini, **8.1-8.2**, 15, 33-35, 38-39, 41-43, 140, 145-146, 213-214, 221, 229, 236, 267-271, 285; pilgrims' accounts, 270-271
Lumsden, Lieutenant, 56

Mackenzie, Colonel, 162, 276
Maclagan, General, 56
Mahabodhi Temple, **7.6-7.11**, **8.3-8.4**, **Frontcover**, 28, 31, 64, 66, 73-74, 140, 149-150, 153, 176, 178, 180, 194, 207-208, 217, 233-236, 238-248, 251-252, 269, 285; Bodhgaya Temple Act, 240; controversies, 245; pilgrims' accounts, 243-244. Also Kumrahar plaque
mahamatra, 41, 277
Mahanama I, 273
Mahanama II, 273
Maharattha, 20
Mahasukha, 24
Mahathera Arahan, 254
mahavihara, 46, 59-60, 71, 74, 228
Mahayana, philosophers; Asanga, 21; Dinnaga, 61; Nagarjuna, 21, 162, 221; Vasubhanhu, 21
Mahayana School and sects, 20-27, 31-32, 46, 53-54, 58-62, 64, 66, 70-71, 73, 76, 80, 82-83, 85, 95-97, 99-105, 108, 110, 112-114, 118, 123-126, 130-131, 134-136, 138-141, 160, 162, 178, 193-194, 199-200, 202-203, 206, 210, 215-216, 222, 224, 226-227, 232, 248-249, 252, 258, 261, 263, 265, 275, 277; Madhyamika, 22; Pure Land, 21, 69; Yogacara, 22, 61; Zen, 67. Also Northern Buddhism
Mahindravarman, Prince, 85
Mahisamandala, 20
Mahmud of Ghazni, 276
mahoraga, 138
Maisey, Frederick, 147
Maitreya; Bodhisattva, 21, 25, 58, 95, 114, 194, 200, 206, 216, 244-245, 258, 261, 280-281; Future Buddha, 21, 124, 131, 165, 211; Miroku, 186; pensive, 137
Maitricandra, 223
Majumdar, N. G., 149-150, 155, 157
makara, 83, 113-114, 135, 167, 190, 194, 196, 210, 252, 259
Malaysia, 81, 193, 255-256; Kedah, 193
mandala, 20, 24-26, 28, 62, 94-96, 99, 140-141, 203, 217, 223-224, 228, 232, 249-251, 264; Dharmadhatu, 220-222; Garbhadhatu, 203, 251; symbolisms, 24; types, 24; Vajradhatu, 25, 203, 249-251; Vairocana, 24-25, 94-96
mandala, architectural, 95, 140-141, 166, 203, 223-224,

232, 264; Orissa *stupa*s, 166, 203, 232. Also Alchi; Borobudur; Elora; Kumbum; Swayambhunath
mandapa, 189, 237, 269
mandir, 217
Manichaeanism, 115, 117-118
mantra, 23-24, 222, 229
maps, 296-300
Marananda, 136
Marchal, Henri, 257
Marshall, Captain, 59
Marshall, John, 8, 10-11, 39, 52-55, 58, 116, 125, 148, 150-152, 156, 172-174, 178, 276
matapa, 101, 105
math, 217
Mathura temples, **7.5**, 187, 208, 252, 258, 237-238
Maukhari Anantavarman, Prince, 102
Maurya, arts and architecture, 36, 40-41, 44-45, 49, 99, 101-105, 145, 154, 157, 166, 236, 270, 285. Also Asoka pillars; Bihar caves; Kumrahar, Hall
Mayadevi (Queen Maya), 16, 43, 149, 161, 167, 268-271, 275
mchod.rten: see *chorten*
Meade, Major, 239
medhi, 141-142, 144, 147-150, 152, 155-156, 158, 160, 163-167, 172-174
Megasthenes, 30, 41
meru, 218
Mesopotamia, 6-8, 44; and Indus Civilization, 7-8; King Sargon, 7; Meluhha, 7
Miran, 51, 115, 119-120, 129, 172, 237; architecture, 119-120, 172, 237
Misra, Bhaskaranatha, 61-63
Mitra, Debala, 4, 268
Mitra, Rajendralal, 239
mithuna, 106, 110, 114, 153, 156, 160, 167
Mogao caves, **5.20-5.23**, 46, 69, 90, 94, 96-97, 115, 120-121, 127-135, 139, 182-183, 185, 225, 227-229; Library Cave #17, 130; Cave #285, 121, 127-128, 131-135; Cave #427, 128, 131, 133-135, 139; 'Mogaoku Ji,' 130; 'Shachou Ti Chih,' 130
Mohenjo-daro, **1.1-1.3**, 6-13, 50, 55, 58, 66, 70, 74, 100-101, 172, 208
Moksa, 15, 18; and *Nirvana*, 18
monastery, types, 46
Mongolia, 27, 90, 193, 224; Buddhism, 27, 224; Mongol, 82, 90, 122, 130, 136, 206, 217, 225-226, 228, 265
Mongolia, dynasties and periods: see Chronology
Mongolia, kings; Altan Khan, 226; Genghis Khan, 122; Kubilai Khan, 217
Monism, 14-15
Mother Goddess, 8

motifs; Greek anthemion and palmette, 40, 44; honeysuckles, 36, 39, 161; swastika, 29, 102-103, 159, 162
Mouhot, Henri, 256
Mount Kailash, 88, 202
Mount Mahendra/Mahendraparvata, 256-257
Mount Meru, 153, 202, 257, 264
Mount Sumeru, 202, 264
mudra, 23, 25, 199-200
Muhammad Ghori, 276
Muhammad, K. K., 169
Mukherji, P.C., 145-146, 268-270
Mus, Paul, 82
museums; Art Institute of Chicago, 176; British, 147-148, 162; Chennai, 162-163, 168; Fogg Art, 130; Gansu, 187; Indian Museum Kolkata, 57, 158-159, 177, 222; Lahore, 56; Musee Guimet, 238; National Museum Delhi, 37; New York Metropolitan, 176; Patna, 44, 242; Sarnath, 37, 277; Shandong, 183; Swat, 175; Taxila, 178, 180; Victoria-Albert, 148
Myanmar, 19-20, 73-74, 81, 120, 141-142, 171, 194, 201, 205-213, 218, 233, 235, 239, 246, 248, 251-255; architecture, 28, 73-74, 120, 141-142, 194, 201, 205-213, 218, 221, 227, 230, 232, 246, 248, 251-255; arts, 206, 227; Bagan, 28, 73, 120, 205-210, 212-213, 227, 230, 232-233, 235, 239, 246, 248, 251-254; Buddhism, 19-20, 205-206, 210; Mon, 205-206, 209-210, 212, 252, 254, 258; Mranmar, 205, 210; Pyu, 205-207, 212, 254
Myanmar, Buddhist temples, 251-254; Abeyadana, 206, 210, 252; Bebe, 207, 251-252, 255; East Zegu, 207, 251-252; Kyaukku Onhmin, 251; Lemyethna, 207, 251-252, 255; Mahabodhi Temple, 248; Manuha, 206, 251; Ma-nu-ha-hpaya, 207; Nagayon, 252; Nat-hlaung-gyaung, 206-207, 251; Pitakat-taik Library, 206; Thatbyin-nyu, 207, 209, 251. Also Ananda Temple; Bagan, architecture
Myanmar, dynasties and periods, 205-207, 209, 212. Also Chronology
Myanmar, Hindu temples; Hlaung-gyaung, 251; Nanpaya, 206, 255. Also Bagan, architecture
Myanmar, kings and queens; Aniriddha, 205, 208-209, 212; Bhayinnaung, 209; Bodawpaya, 209; Byinnya U, 212; Byinnyakyan, 212; Byinnyawaru, 212; Byinnyayan, 212; Caw Rahan, 208; Dhammaceti, 210, 212; Duttabaung, 212; Hsinbyushin, 212; Klon-phlu-man, 208; Kyanzittha, 206, 208-209, 246, 254; Mindon-Min, 239; Mohnyin, 207; Narapathisithu, 209; Okkalapa, 210; Queen Abeyadana, 206; Queen Saw Mi Phwa, 209; Queen Shin Saw Bu, 212
Myanmar, temples, 28, 120, 206-208, 232, 246, 248, 251-255. Also Bagan, architecture
Myanmar, *zedi*s, 141-142, 194, 201, 205-213, 230, 232;

and Indian *stupa*s, 207; Bawbawgyi, 207-208; Beikthano, 207; types, 208; Hpet-leik, 210; Payagyi, 207; Payama, 207; Shwemawdaw, 213; Shwesandaw, 205, 209-210, 213. Also Bagan, architecture; Shwedagon; Shwezigon; *zedi*

naga, 80, 114, 128, 138, 190, 234, 270-271, 274-275, 280; Elapatra, 280
Nagabodhi, 162
Nagarjuni caves, 49, 102; Gopika, 49, 102, 105; Vadathi, 102; Vapiya, 102
Nagaraju, Seshabhatta, 99, 104, 107
Nagari script, 169
Nagasena, 51, 2578
Nalanda, **4.4**, 28, 46-47, 57-66, 70-74, 89, 145, 176, 181, 194, 207, 224, 233-234, 236, 245-246, 248, 251, 259, 270, 274, 279-280; *caitya*s, 64, 176, 234, 236, 245, 248, 251; Caitya #2, 73; Caitya #3, 181, 233, 248, 259; Caitya #12, 77, 233, 245, 248, 259, 279; pilgrims' accounts, 63-66; *stupa*s, 64-65; *vihara*s, 28, 62-64, 72, 145, 246, 280; Vihara #1, 194
Napoleon III, Emperor: see France
nat, 206
Nazim, N., 59
Near East, 8, 30, 36, 44-45, 155, 160-161; arts and architecture, 36, 44-45, 155, 160-161
Nepal, 15, 31, 34-35, 62, 140, 145-146, 174, 206, 213-221, 224-228, 248, 261, 266-271; architecture, 140, 174, 217-224, 228, 248, 261, 266; Arniko, 214, 217, 226, 228; arts, 62, 206, 213, 215-217, 227; Buddhism, 213-217, 219, 221, 224; Licchavis, 214, 216-219, 221-222, 229, 261; Kiratas, 213-214; Mallas, 214, 216, 268-269; Mustang, 90, 228; Newars, 213-216, 220; traveler's account, 218; Thakuris, 214, 219, 221. Also Asoka pillars; India, early republics and tribes, Licchavi, Sakya; Kapilavastu; Lumbini; Tilaurakot
Nepal, Buddhist monasteries, 214, 216-217; Ananda Kuti Vihara, 221; Cabahil, 217, 219, 223; Kimdol, 221; Swayambhunath, 214; Thuparama, 216; types, 217
Nepal, Buddhist rock-hewn caves, 228
Nepal, Buddhist temples, 217, 221, 248; Mahabauddha, 248; Matsyendranath, 217
Nepal, *caitya*s, 140, 174, 218-224, 261, 266; types, 219. Also Swayambhunath
Nepal, dynasties and periods, 213-215; Licchavi, 214, 216-219, 221; Malla, 214, 216-217, 221; Shah, 213, 216, 221; Thakuri, 214, 216, 219, 221. Also Chronology
Nepal, Hindu temples, 217-218; Changu Narayan, 214, 218; Guhyesvari, 221; Pasupatinath, 218, 221
Nepal, kings; Amsuvarman, 214, 218; Anandamalla, 213; Anantamalla, 214; Dharmakara, 221; Gunakamadeva, 213; Jayabhimadeva, 214; Jayapratapamalla, 221, 224; Jayadeva II, 214, 218, 221; Laksmikamadeva I, 214; Manadeva I, 214, 216, 218; Narendradeva, 214; Pasupati, 273; Pratapamalla, 221; Prthivi Narayan Shah, 213; Prithvimalla, 214; Punyamalla, 214; Ripumalla, 214, 268-269; Sankaradeva, 214, 221, 223; Sivadeva II, 214; Sivasimhamalla, 224; Sthitirajamalla/ Jayasthitimalla, 214-215; Vrsadeva, 213-214, 221, 223; Yaksamalla, 214
Nhuche Raj, 221
Nhuche Tej, 221
Nigrodha, 32
Nikator, Seluecus, 30
Nirmanakaya: see *Trikaya*
Nirvana, 17-18, 21-25, 123, 182, 208, 212, 229, 251, 281, 286; and Hindu *Moksa*, 18
North Africa, 30
North Asia, 193
Northern Buddhism, 27. Also Mahayana School

Oertel, F. O., 276
Oldenburg, Sergei, 130
Old Malay language, 193, 249
Orientalists, 130
Orissa, 25-26, 30, 59-60, 70-71, 83, 166, 203, 206, 232, 275; Kalinga, 30-32, 70
Otani Kozui, Count, 119
Oxus River: see Amu Darya

pabbata vihara, 76-77
padhanagriha parivena, 76-77, 79
padma, 23, 222
padmasana, 219
Page, J. A., 59
pagoda: see China and East Asia, pagoda
Paisaci, 169
Pakistan, 4, 6-10, 12, 20, 31, 33-34, 50-54, 56-57, 89, 115-116, 140, 162, 171, 173-175, 177-180, 225, 233. Also Gandhara; Indus and Harappa Civilization
Pakistan, dynasties and periods; Achaemenid Persia/ Parthian/Sassanian, 50-53, 58, 115-116; Early Greek, 44, 50; Early Kushan, 20, 51-53, 70, 88, 91, 115-116, 176-177, 180, 248; Hindu-Shahi, 115; Indus Civilization, 6, 8; Later Greek, 50-51; Later/Kadara Kushan, 51, 54, 176; Maurya, 50; Saka, 51, 53; White Huns/Hephthalites, 51, 54, 56, 115, 124-125. Also Chronology
Pakistan, kings: see Kushan, Hephthalites kings
Pakistan, monasteries, 54-55. Dharmarajika, Khader Mohra-Akhauri, Chir Tope A-C, D1-D2, Jandial A-B, Kalawan, Giri, Kunala-Ghai, Pippala, Mohra Moradu,

Jaulian, Lalchak, Bhamala, Jamalgarhi, Sahri Bahlol, Butkara, Saidu Sharif. Also Takht-i-bahi
Pakistan, *stupa*s, 57, 140, 171-181; Ali Masjid, 178; Butkara I, 53-54, 173-174; Chakpat, 173; characteristics, 172; Manikyala, 53, 173; Mirpurkhas, 57; Sahri Bahlol, 54, 179; Takht-i-bahi, **4.3**, 46, 74; types, 173-181. Also Kanishka; Loriyan Tangai; Saidu Sharif Stupa I; Taxila, *stupa*s
Pal, Pratapaditya, 216, 227
Pala, 25, 28, 59-62, 64-65, 71-74, 76, 83-84, 87, 89-90, 96, 98, 119, 194, 206, 214, 216, 222, 227-228, 239-240, 254, 270, 272, 276-277, 280, 284-285
Pala, kings; Devapala, 62, 64, 71, 74, 194; Dharmapala, 64, 71, 73-74; Gopala I, 71; Mahipala I, 74; Ramapala, 71
Pala Style, 62, 76, 96, 194, 206, 216, 227, 254, 284
Pali, 17, 19, 21, 31, 140, 160, 183, 189, 218, 254, 257
Pallavas, 80, 84, 194-195, 206
pancayatana, 233-234, 246, 247-249, 251
pancayatana parivena, 76-77, 251
Paramartha, 258
paramita, 202
Paranavitana, Senarat, 191-192
paribhagika caitya, 140
Parinirvana, 18-19, 87, 105, 123-125, 131, 140, 178, 186, 227, 235, 254, 267, 275, 281-282, 285
parivena, 48
Parmentier, Henri, 85, 201, 257, 263
pasada, 48, 77, 259
pastiglia technique, 96, 228
pata, 227
Paticca Samuppada, 17
Pa.tshab-sTong.'bar-sdom.'dzam, Minister, 229
pattimokkha, 47
paubha, 216-217, 227
pavarana, 47-49
Pelliot, Paul, 119, 130, 134
Persia, 7, 30, 35-36, 44, 50, 115-117; Persepolis, 44
Philippines, 193
Pichard, Pierre, 207-210, 251-252, 255
Pippalavana, 143
Piprahwa Stupa, **6.1-6.2**, 44, 139, 142-146, 149, 157, 160, 175, 191, 218
Piprahwa-Ganwaria, 144-145. Also Kapilavastu; Tilaurakot
Pitaka: see *Tripitaka*
podhi, 100
Portugese, 182
pradaksina path, 38, 61, 72, 99, 105, 118, 120-121, 126, 130, 134, 136, 140-143, 149, 155, 158, 162-163, 170, 172, 174, 177, 184, 197, 201, 203, 207, 209-211, 230, 235-236, 249, 254, 269, 271, 279
prajna, 17, 23-26, 221-224, 230
prajna(s) of Buddhas, 25, 221-222; Mamaki, 25, 220, 222; Pandara, 25, 220, 222; Prajnaparamita, 25-26, 94-95, 194, 222, 232, 258, 261, 265; Locana, 25, 220, 222; Tara, 25, 62, 66, 73-74, 80, 83, 87, 194, 216, 220, 222, 240; Vajradhatvisvari, 25, 222
Prakrit, 112, 155, 169
prasat, 84, 260
pratimagriha, 54-55, 58, 77, 80, 100, 119, 173-174, 233-234, 236, 240, 242, 248
Prejevalsky, Nikolai, 118, 130
Princep, James, 31
pripih, 196, 215
Pugachenkova, Galina, 117
Purang, 88, 214
Purang, kings; Early Mallas, 214; Tashi-gon, 88
Pure Land: see Mahayana School and sects
purnaghata, 76, 80, 137, 160, 190, 195

Rab-brtan-kun-bzang, Prince, 231
Raffles, Thomas Stamford, 196
Rahula, 16
Rajir caves, 98, 102; Sitamarhi, 55, 102, 243; Son Bhandar, 45, 102, 105
raksasa, 249
Ramayana, 142-143, 160, 213
Rangchung Dorje, 225
RAS, 110
ratha, 84, 87, 233, 248, 260
Ray, Niharranjan, 33, 35
Rea, Alexander, 162
Regel, Albert, 118
Reimer, Carl Friedrich, 248
relics and reliquaries, Buddhist, 48, 64-65, 68, 75, 171, 179-180, 237, 242, 246, 270, 276
Rijal, B. K., 268
Rinchen-sangpo, 89, 91, 96, 227
Robertson, 162
rock-hewn caves, characteristics, 97
rock-hewn caves, Hindu, 98-99, 103; Aihole, 98-99; Badami, 98-99; Udayagiri, 99. Also Elora, Hindu caves
rock-hewn caves, Indian Buddhist, 97-114; characteristics, 101; construction method, 101; Guntupalli, 100, 192, 237; types, 97, 100-101. Also Deccan, Buddhist rock-hewn caves
rock-hewn caves, Jain, 98, 103; Elora, 98
Rome, 50
Roman(s), arts and architecture, 4, 13, 52-53, 55, 57-58, 115-116, 121, 167, 172, 175-178, 243, 246, 255
Rowland, Benjamin, 4, 41, 74, 83, 124

Roy, Anamika, 166
Rupadhatu: see *Tridhatu*
Russian, 117, 130

Sabari dBanphyug, 162
Sahni, D. R., 276, 278-279
Saidu Sharif I Stupa, **6.14**
Saka(s), 51, 53, 116-117, 214, 256, 278; Scythians, 51
Saka, kings; Azes II, 53
sakti, 24-26, 99
Sakyacarya, 215, 217
Sakyamuni: see Buddha, founder of Buddhism
Sakya Pandita, 226
Sakyasri Sariputra, 239
salabhanjika, 150
Sambhogakaya: see *Trikaya*
Sambodhi, 238, 275
Samsara, 15-18, 21-22, 24, 251
Samudra, 32
samvat: see Glossary. Also Era
Sanchi, 20, 35-36, 39, 41-43, 46, 50, 53-54, 75-77, 97-98, 100, 105-108, 125, 140, 143, 147-158, 160-163, 165-167, 169, 171, 173, 176, 199, 205; Stupa II, 20, 108, 147-149, 278; Stupa III, 147, 149
Sanchi Stupa I, **6.3-6.5**, 42, 75, 147-156
Sangha, 16, 18-21, 26, 31-32, 35, 46-49, 58, 66, 75, 86, 98, 101, 121, 136, 147, 152, 161, 182, 217, 225-226, 275, 277, 281
sangharama, 32, 47-49, 53-54
sanghati, 122, 124, 167
Sanskrit, 14, 22, 81, 112, 118, 155, 169, 183, 189, 193, 214, 218, 221, 223, 255-258, 261
Santikaracarya, 223
sarika caitya, 140
Sarnath, **8.5-8.6**, 4, 16, 18, 31, 33, 35-37, 39-44, 46, 62, 71, 74, 84, 87, 108, 113, 140, 152, 155, 179, 200, 207, 216, 224, 229, 232-233, 236, 239-240, 245, 248-249, 251-252, 254, 260, 267-268, 270, 275-286; pilgrims' accounts, 280-281
sastra, 22
Sastri, Hirananda, 59, 282, 284
Satavahana(s): see Andhra
Schumann, Hans, 146
Scythians: see Sakas
Seckel, Dietrich, 4
Seokguram cave, **5.24-5.25**, 97, 135-139
Serindia, 117. Also Turkistan
Sewell, Robert, 162
sexual symbolisms, in arts and architecture, 25, 222
Shah-ji-ki-dheri Stupa: see Kanishka Stupa
Shakya, Hem Raj, 220-222

Shams-ud-din, Sultan, 217, 223
Shotoku, Prince, 66-67, 186
Shumsher, Khadga, 268-270
Shundao, 136
Shwedagon, **6.35-6.36**, 141, 171, 206, 210-213, 221
Shwezigon, **6.33.6.34**, 74, 201, 205-206, 208-210, 212-213, 232
siddha, 23; Eighty-four Siddhas, 95, 228, 231
Sikh, 90. Also Singh
sikhara, 28, 53, 61, 119, 188-189, 207-208, 251-252, 254-255, 269-270
sikhara, Buddhist: see India, Buddhist temples
sikhara, Hindu, 28, 53, 61, 119, 208, 233, 248, 252, 255, 260, 266, 269-270; and Buddhist *sikhara*, 189; and Chinese pagoda, 188-189; Dravida, 233, 248, 251; Nagara, 189, 233, 248, 252, 255, 260, 266, 269; origin, 189. Also India, Hindu temples; *ratha*
Silabhadhra, 60
Simharasmi, 61
Singh; Gulab, 90; Jagat, 276, 279; Nain, 228; Ranjit, 56; Zorawar, 90
Sivaramamurti, Calambur, 163-164, 166-167, 169
sKal-ldan-shes-rab, 92
skandha, 16-18, 26
smasana, 142-144
Smith, John, 110
Smith, Vincent, 43, 146
Snellgrove, David, 24
Sogdiana (Sogdia), 117-118
Sogdian School, paintings, 117, 125
Somapura, **4.8**, 28, 46, 58-59, 61, 66, 70-74, 87, 119, 141, 179, 195, 205, 208, 210, 232-233, 251, 255, 279
Songyue, **6.24-6.25**, 171, 180, 182, 187-189
Soparaka, 108
Soper, Alexander, 69, 188
Southern Buddhism, 27. Also Theravada School
Soviet Union, 117
Spaniards, 256
Spiti, 26, 87-91, 96, 227, 232; Kirata, 88
Spiti, kings; Detsu-gon, 88
Spiti, monasteries; Lha-lun, 89, 91; Tabo, 26, 89, 91, 95-96, 232
Spooner, D. B., 57, 59
Sramana, 15-16
srikoil, 192
Sri Lanka, 20-21, 27, 31, 46, 70, 74-81, 87, 97, 140, 142, 146-147, 162-163, 165, 169, 176, 183, 189-192, 194-195, 204-206, 209, 216, 221-222, 224, 233, 235, 237, 239-240, 251, 259-261, 266, 272-275, 281; arts and architecture, 46, 73, 75-81, 87, 97, 140, 162-163, 165, 169, 176, 183, 189-192, 194, 204-205, 207-208, 221-

222, 224, 233, 234, 237, 251, 259-261, 266, 281; Buddhism, 20-21, 27, 31, 60, 75-76, 115, 146-147, 194-195, 205-206, 209, 216, 233, 235, 240
Sri Lanka, rock-hewn caves, 97
Sri Lanka, *dagaba*s, 46, 73, 75-76, 140, 142, 165, 176, 183, 189-192, 195, 204-205, 208, 222, 224, 235, 237, 261; Ambasthala, 75, 190; Abhayagiri, 75-76, 189-190, 192; Attanagalla, 190; Jetavana, 39-40, 75-77, 189-190, 204; Ruvenvali, 46, 176, 189-190, 192; types, 189-190. Also *dagaba*; Thuparama; Vijayarama
Sri Lanka, dynasties and periods, 74-75; Anuradhapura, 74-75, 77, 190; Polonnaruva, 75, 80, 190, 192. Also Chronology
Sri Lanka, kings; Aggabodhi VI, 192; Devanampiya Tissa, 74-75, 190; Dutthagamani, 75, 189; Mahasena, 75, 77; Meghavana, 273-274; Pandukabhaya, 74; Parakramabahu I, 192; Vasabha, 192; Vattagamani, 75; Vijayabahu I, 75
Sri Lanka, monasteries, 76-81, 189, 221, 240, 251, 266, 281; Abhayagirivihara, 75, 77, 189; Jetavanavihara, 77, 189; Mahavihara, 75-76, 189; Mahameghavana, 75-76; Mihintale, 75-76; Mulagandhakuti Vihara, 240, 281; *parivena*s, 76-77, 79, 251; types, 76-77. Also Vijayarama
Srindrakumara, Prince, 265
Srivastava, Krishna, 146
stambha, 141, 149-150, 152, 156, 158-159, 161-164, 166-167, 176
Stein, Aurel, 52, 118, 130
Stern, Philippe, 85, 257
Stewart, Mary, 59
Stokes, Lieutenants, 56
Stutterheim, 197
stupa, 4, 10, 20, 28, 30-32, 35, 38, 41-42, 45-46, 48, 50-55, 57, 64-66, 69-76, 87-88, 97-98, 100-101, 104-110, 112-113, 119, 121-124, 127, 129, 131, 133, 139-166, 171-180, 183, 186-187, 189-190, 192, 196-198; 200-205, 207-208, 210, 212-213, 218, 222-224, 228-230, 232-240, 242-243, 246, 248-249, 251-252, 254, 260-261, 264, 267, 269-277, 279-286. Also India, Buddhist *stupa*s
stupa-pillar, 127
stupa-temple, 119
stupa, earliest, 48, 141, 143, 208, 232-233; Ajnata-Kaundinya, 48, 143; Maudgalyayana, 48, 143; Rajagriha, 143, 146; Ramagrama, 143, 146; Sariputra, 48, 143; Vaishali, 143-144. Also Four Holiest Sites; Kapilavastu
stupa, types, 140; Commemorative, 55, 140, 218, 229; Object, 140, 143; Relic, 28, 55, 100, 140, 229; Symbolic, 100, 105, 113, 140, 203, 218, 222, 229; Votive, 53, 55, 57, 64, 66, 73, 140, 148, 166, 171, 177-178,

189, 196, 217-218, 221-222, 228, 239, 242, 261, 271-272, 279-280, 284
Suddhodana, King, 15, 274
Sudhana, 199-200, 202
sudra, 14
Sunya, 22, 24-26, 203, 222, 251
Supurjaya, 61
Sutra: see *Tripitaka*
*sutra*s, 26, 68, 91, 94, 100, 118, 129-130, 181, 215-216; Anattalakhana-sutra, 280; Bhadracari, 200; Cakkavatti-sihanada-sutra, 43; Dharmacakrapravartana-sutra, 16; Gandavyuha, 199-200, 202-203; Lalitavistara, 199, 254; Lotus, 139; Mahakarmavibhanga, 198; Mahaparinirvana-sutra, 141-143, 153, 170; Pancaraksa-sutra, 216; Prajnaparamita-sutra, 216
Svennam Simha, Lama, 221
Swayambhunath, **6.37-6.38**, 140-141, 174, 213-224, 232, 266, 270; symbolisms, 222-224
Swedish, 118
Syria(n), 4, 20, 115, 117

t'a, 139, 183
Tachibana Zuicho, 130
Tajikistan, 114, 117; Pandjikent, 117
Tajikistan, Buddhist sites; Adzhina-tepe, 117; Budhism: see Central Asia, Buddhism
Takht-i-bahi, **4.2-4.3**, 46, 50-59, 66, 74, 132, 207, 243
Talibans, 52, 121-122
Tamil Nadu, 98; Chennai, 162-163, 168; Madras, 110; Nagapattinam, 169, 240; Tamil, 183
Tapassa and Bhallika, brothers, 210
Tange, Kenzo, 268
Tanguts, 129
tantra, 23-26, 89, 96, 203, 223, 232, 265. Also Vajrayana, literature
Tantric, 4, 22-26, 46, 60, 84, 89, 91, 94-97, 99, 118, 124, 194, 206, 216, 219, 222, 224, 227, 232, 240, 250, 258, 265, 277; Buddhism, 4, 22-26, 46, 60, 84, 89, 91, 94-97, 118, 124, 194, 206, 216, 219, 222, 224, 227, 232, 250, 277; Hinduism, 22-23, 99. Also Vajrayana School
Taoism: see Daoism
t'ap, 181, 183
Taranatha, 74, 162, 226, 238, 243
Tarzi, Zemaryalai, 122
Taxila, 33-34, 48, 50-54, 56, 70, 115-116, 119, 165, 173, 178-180, 235, 237, 248, 279, 285; Bhir Mound, 50, 52; Sirkap, 51-53, 174, 176, 178, 235, 237; Sirsukh, 51-52, 179, 248; Takshasila, 50
Taxila, Buddhist temples; Sirkap Apsidal Temple, 53, 70, 237
Taxila, Greek temples; Jandial, 52, 116, 119, 189; Mohra

Maliaran, 53
Taxila, *stupa*s; Jamalgahri, 174; Sirkap Block E' Stupa, 53, 165, 174; Sirkap Block F Stupa, 53; Sirkap Block G Stupa, 53, 176. Also Bhamala; Dharmarajika, Pakistan; Jaulian Stupa A11, A16
Taylor, General, 147
Telugu, 169
temple, types, 233
temple-*chorten*, 232
Ter Temple, **7.2-7.3**, 28, 49, 237
Thailand, 84, 176, 194, 205, 208, 248, 255-256, 258, 260-261. Also Dvaravati
Thailand, *chedi*; Chedi Phra Paton, 176. Also *chedi*
Thailand, dynasties and periods: see Chronology
Thailand, kings; Chulalongkorn, 197
Thailand, temples; Lopburi, 261; Phimai, 261; Wat Chet Yot, 248
Thailand, *stupa*s, 196. Also *chedi-tong*
thangka, 216, 225, 227
tháp, 181, 183
that: see Laos, *that*
thera, 21, 129, 136
Theravada, philosophers; Buddhaghosa, 75; Nagasena, 51
Theravada School and sects, 18-27, 31-32, 46, 51, 53, 57-59, 61, 70, 75-76, 80, 82, 97, 99-101, 104, 106, 108, 110, 112, 114, 117-118, 123-124, 126, 130, 134, 139-141, 154, 169, 193-194, 203, 205-206, 210, 215-216, 223-224, 227, 232, 254-255, 258, 261, 274-275, 277, 281; Caityaka, 169; Dharmottariya, 108-109; Lokottaravada, 124; Mahasanghika, 19-22, 109, 117; Mulasarvastivada, 82; Sammitya, 59; Sarvastivada, 20-22, 53, 82, 117, 126, 279; Sravaka, 223; Theravada Sect, 20-21; Vibhajjavada, 21. Also Southern Buddhism
Theravada, saints and monks, 19-20, 31, 75-76, 112, 147-148, 190, 205, 212; Mahendra (Mihinda), 20, 31, 75-76, 147, 190; Moggaliputa Tissa, 20, 31-32, 148; Sanghamitra, 20, 31, 75-76, 147; Sona, 20, 205, 212; Uttara, 20, 205, 212
Thonmi Sambhota, 224
Three Worlds: see *Tridhathu*
thupa, 140, 183, 189-190, 208. Also *dagaba*; *stupa*
thupaghara, 192; and Indian circular *caityagriha*, 192
Thuparama Dagaba, **6.26-6.27**, 75, 190-192, 216, 235, 237
Tibet, 11, 22, 25-27, 46, 58, 60, 72, 74, 87-96, 118, 120, 129-130, 140-141, 162, 172, 193, 202, 205-206, 208, 214-217, 221-232, 239, 243, 269, 274; architecture, 11, 26, 46, 58, 72, 74, 88-92, 96, 140-141, 172, 193, 205, 208, 214-215, 222, 225, 228-232, 239; arts, 88, 90, 96, 206, 216-217, 226-228; Buddhism, 22, 25-27, 60, 89-90, 93, 95, 215, 224-226, 239, 269, 274; Drigungpa, 89, 94, 225; Drugpa, 89; Gelugpa, 89-90, 94, 226; Kadampa, 89, 225; Kagyupa, 89, 225; Karmapa, 89, 225-226; Nyingmapa, 89, 225; Sakyapa, 89, 225-226, 228, 232. Also Bon (Bonpo); Guge; Purang
Tibet, *chorten*s, 26, 89, 96, 140-141, 172, 205, 208, 222, 229-232; eight *chorten* types, **6.39**, 229-230; gLing-mKhas.pa, 229; Gyang, 232; Jonang, 232; Riwoche, 232; symbolisms, 230, 232. Also Kumbum
Tibet, dynasties and periods, 224-226; Gelugpa and Dalai Lama, 226; Sakyapa, 226, 232; Yarlung, 88, 224-225. Also Chronology
Tibet, kings; Dalai Lama, 89, 215, 226; dGe.'dun.grub, 226; Khri-lde-gtsug-rtsan, 225; Lang-darma, 88, 225; Lopsang-gyatso, 226; Namri-tsong-tsen, 224; Nyima-gon, 88; Queen Kong-co, 225; Re-pa-chen, 225, 229; Sonam-gyatso, 226; Song-tsen-gampo, 88, 214, 224, 226; Tri-song-detsen, 225, 229
Tibet, monasteries, 46, 58, 72, 74, 89-91, 214-215, 217, 222, 225-229, 239; Kachu, 91, 225, 227-229; Potala, 226, 228; Sakya, 217, 225, 228; Samye, 91, 215, 225, 228; Shalu, 214, 222, 225-230. Also Guge, monasteries; Gyantse
Tibet, temples, 229; Jokhang, 224, 226-229; Ramoche, 224, 228
Tilaurakot, 145-146, 213, 267. Also Kapilavastu; Piprahwa-Ganwaria
Tirtha Raj Manadhar, 221
to, 183
torana, 103, 139-141, 143, 147-153, 155-161, 174
Trans-Himalaya: see Himalaya
tribhanga, 183, 216, 259
Trikaya, 22
Tripitaka, 19-21, 160, 226; Abhidharma, 19-21; Cullavagga, 46; Digha-nikaya, 43, 143; Majjhima-nikaya, 170; *Sutra*, 19, 21-22; *Vinaya*, 18-19, 21-22, 59, 76
Triratna, 74, 105, 149, 152-153, 160, 167
tsha-tsha, 229, 231
Tsong-khapa, 226
Tshul-khrims'od, 92-93, 95
Tucci, Giuseppe, 214
tulku, 225-226
T'ung Shih-hu, 124
Turks; Eastern, 118, 126; Western, 115, 117-118, 124
Turkistan, 20, 46, 51, 54, 58, 74, 87, 114-115, 117-122, 126-132, 134-136, 139, 171-172, 177, 179-182, 186-187, 189, 219, 224-225, 227, 229-230, 251; arts, 115, 118-119, 128; architecture, 46, 54, 58, 74, 87, 117, 119-122, 126-128, 132, 134-135, 139, 171-172, 177, 179-180, 183, 186-187, 189, 219, 251; Buddhism, 115, 118, 181. Also Miran; Yueh-chi

Turkistan, rock-hewn caves, 120-122, 126-128, 132, 135, 139, 230; Bezeklik, 118, 120; types, 127. Also Kizil

Turkistan, Buddhist sites, 120; Balawaste, 118, 120; Dandan-uilik, 118, 120; Karakhoja, 74, 87, 119-120, 251; Khocho, 119-120; Lou-lan, 51, 118-120, 129; Rawak, 120, 172, 179; Yarkhoto (Jiaohe), 74, 87, 119-120, 251. Also Miran; Turkistan, rock-hewn caves

Turkistan, dynasties and periods, 115, 117-118, 129, 224-225. Also Chronology

Turkistan, *stupa*s, 74, 87, 119, 171-172, 177, 179-180, 183, 186-187, 189, 219, 251; Karakhoja Stupa P, 74, 87, 119, 251; Kharakhoto, 90, 219; Khocho, 119; Miran, 51, 119, 172, 237; Rawak, 172, 179; Yarkhoto (Jiaohe), 74, 87, 119, 251

Turkmenistan, 51, 115, 117-118, 121, 126, 172, 176; Anau, 117; Buddhism, 51, 115, 117-118; Dzheytun, 117; Nisa Palace, 121

Turkmenistan, Buddhist sites; Gyaur-kala, 115, 117, 172, 176; Merv, 51

udapanasala, 48
uddesika caitya, 140
Uddiyana, 51
UNESCO, 197, 204
Upagupta, 32, 219
Upanisads, 14-15, 17-18, 26
upasampada, 47-49
upatthanasala, 48, 77
upaya, 23-24, 26, 222, 224, 230
U Po Hlaing, 284
U Po Kyu, 284
uposatha, 47-49, 76, 207
uposathagriha, 48, 76-77, 80
urna, 222
usnisa (cope), 141, 148, 156, 158, 167
usnisa (topknot), 26
Uttar Pradesh, 16, 36, 47, 51, 71, 159, 213, 215, 275, 282; Sravasti, 39-41, 47, 145, 229, 267, 277. Also Kushinagar; Sarnath
Uzbekistan, 114-115, 117; Buddhism: see Central Asia, Buddhism
Uzbekistan, Buddhist sites, 115, 117

vahalkada, 189-190
Vaishali Stupa: see Stupa, earliest
vaisya, 14
vajra, 23, 25-26, 221-222, 224
Vajra, 23-26, 222, 224, 230
Vajracarya, 215, 217
vajrasana, 152, 160, 233-235, 240-243, 245-248, 271
Vajrayana, architecture, 4, 28, 46, 85, 95-97, 99, 140-141, 166, 206, 226, 249-250, 252. Also *mandala*, architectural

Vajrayana, arts and iconography, 21, 23-26, 62, 73, 80, 95, 99-100, 118, 124, 139, 166, 194, 206, 216-217, 226-227, 232, 240, 249, 261, 262, 277; Cakrasamvara, 25-26, 227, 232; Heruka, 25-26, 62, 227, 232; Hevajra, 24-26, 227, 232, 261; Kalacakra, 25-26, 227, 232; Mahakala, 25, 94-96, 216, 227; Nairatmya, 24, 216; Samvara, 25-26, 216, 227; Vajrabhaivara, 25-26, 227; Vajradhara, 25, 222, 231-232; Vajrapani, 25, 62, 114, 194, 216, 222, 227, 232, 261, 286; Vajrasattva, 25, 95, 194, 222, 232; Yamantaka, 25, 62, 95. Also Buddhas, Vajrayana; *prajna*(s) of Buddhas; *siddha*

Vajrayana, literature; Buddhadkapala-yogini-tantra-raja, 23; Guhyasamaja-tantra, 23

Vajrayana, monasteries; Jagaddala, 59, 71; Lalitagiri, 59, 71; Odantapura, 59-60, 71, 228; Ratnagiri, 59, 71, 83, 119, 207; Udayagiri, 59, 71, 83, 99; Vikramasila, 59-60, 71-72, 89, 119, 215, 225. Also Alchi; Somapura

Vajrayana, rock-hewn caves, 25, 95-97, 99-100, 118, 130, 203, 224, 232. Also Elora

Vajrayana, saints; Amoghavajra, 60, 130, 194; Atisa, 60, 72, 89, 215, 225, 227, 238; Naropa, 60; Padmasambhava, 60, 89, 96, 215, 225; Rahulasribhadra, 60; Ratnaraksita, 215; Santaraksita, 60, 96, 215, 225; Vajrabodhi, 60, 130, 194

Vajrayana School and sects, 18, 22-27, 46, 60, 71, 89, 95-96, 118, 130, 193-194, 206, 215, 224-225, 277; and Hinduism, 18, 23, 26

Vajrayana Style, 206, 216

Vajrayana, *stupa*s: see Borobudur; Kumbum; Swayambhunath

Vakataka Style, 76, 169
Vanaratna, 162
Vanavasi, 20
varada-mudra, 25, 199
varman, 193, 256
vassavasa, 29, 47, 103
Vasu Reddi Nayudu, 162-163
vatadage, 190-192. Also Sri Lanka, *dagaba*s
Veda(s), 9, 14-15, 23, 61, 70
vedika, 53, 100-101, 104, 106, 108-109, 113, 125, 140-144, 147-152, 154-156, 158-167, 172-177, 192, 218, 235, 240, 242-243, 245-247, 271-272, 277-279, 282, 285
Veluvanarama, 47-49; Ambalatthika, 48-49
Vethadipa, 143
Vietnam, 81-82, 84-86, 181, 183, 194, 255-257
Vietnam, dynasties and periods, 82. Also Chronology
vihara, 10, 28, 48, 54-55, 57-59, 62-66, 73-74, 76-77, 79-80, 85, 87, 89, 91-92, 97, 100, 119, 122, 128, 131-133,

171, 229, 243, 273-274, 286. Also *mahavihara*
viharapura, 71-72, 74, 87, 91
Vijayarama, **4.9-4.10**, 46, 74-81, 87, 190, 192, 205, 235, 251
Vilulasrimitra, 74
Vinaya: see *Tripitaka*
Vishnugupta, Kautilya, 41
Vogel, J. P., 282

Wang Hsuan-tse, 214, 218
Wang Yuanlu, 130
Warner, Langdon, 130
Wenchen, Princess, 224
West, the, 55, 115, 167, 208
Western, 4; arts and architecture, 50-52, 155, 172; Civilization, 116; colonialism, 52, 118; exploration, 118-119, 126-127, 130; World, 50-51, 117
Western Paradise: see Amitabha Buddha
Westmacott, Vesey, 72
Wheeler, Mortimer, 7
White Huns: see Hephthalites
Whitfield, Roderick, 131
Wickremasinghe, 79
Wiesner, Ulrich, 218
Wilcher, Sergeant, 56
Wilson, Horace H., 52, 282

Xinjiang: see Turkistan
Xizang: see Tibet

yab-yum, 25, 227-228, 232. Also *yuganaddha*
yaksa, 25, 76, 80, 134, 138, 149, 152-153, 160, 166-167, 190, 206, 234, 249
yaksi (*yaksini*), 70, 76, 106, 110, 149-150, 152-153, 160, 166-167, 234; Didarganj, 45, 152, 154
Yamamoto, Chikyo, 4
Yamuna River, 30, 280
yasti-chattra, 64, 69, 73, 101, 104, 108, 112, 142, 144, 150, 156, 158, 162-163, 165-166, 169, 172, 174-177, 179-180, 183, 185-187, 189, 192, 212, 218-219, 221-224, 230, 261, 272, 281, 284
Yavana (*Yona*), 20, 99, 108, 115
yi-dam, 25, 227, 232
yin-yang, 232
yoga, 15-16, 18, 23, 25, 89; and Buddhist meditation, 18
yoga-tantra, 23-26, 89, 91, 94, 96, 203, 223, 232
yogin (*yogi*), 15
Yona: see *Yavana*
Yosadhara, Princess, 16
Yoshikawa Koichiro, 130
Younghusband, Francis, 231

Yueh-chi, 20, 51, 117-118, 129. Also Kushan(s)
yuganaddha, 23-26, 71, 216. Also *yab-yum*
Yule, Henry, 254
yupa, 43, 142, 158, 165-166; and Asoka pillars, 43; and Buddhist *yasti-chattra*, 165
yupa-yasti, 162-163, 165-166

Zanskar, 87-92, 227; Mon, 88
Zanskar, kings; Detsu-gon, 88; Yeshe-O (Khor-re), 25, 88-89, 91, 225
Zanskar, monasteries, 88-89, 91-92
zedi, 140, 194, 205, 208-213
Zhang Qian (Chan Chien), 117, 129
Zhang Yichao, 129
Zhou Daquan, 265-266
Zoroastrianism, 50-51, 53, 115-118; temples, 116; Zoroaster, 115

www.ingramcontent.com/pod-product-compliance
Lightning Source LLC
Chambersburg PA
CBHW080542230426
43663CB00015B/2677